This book is accompanied by 1 CD-ROM(s)
Check on Issue and Return

ONE WEEK LOAN

Press

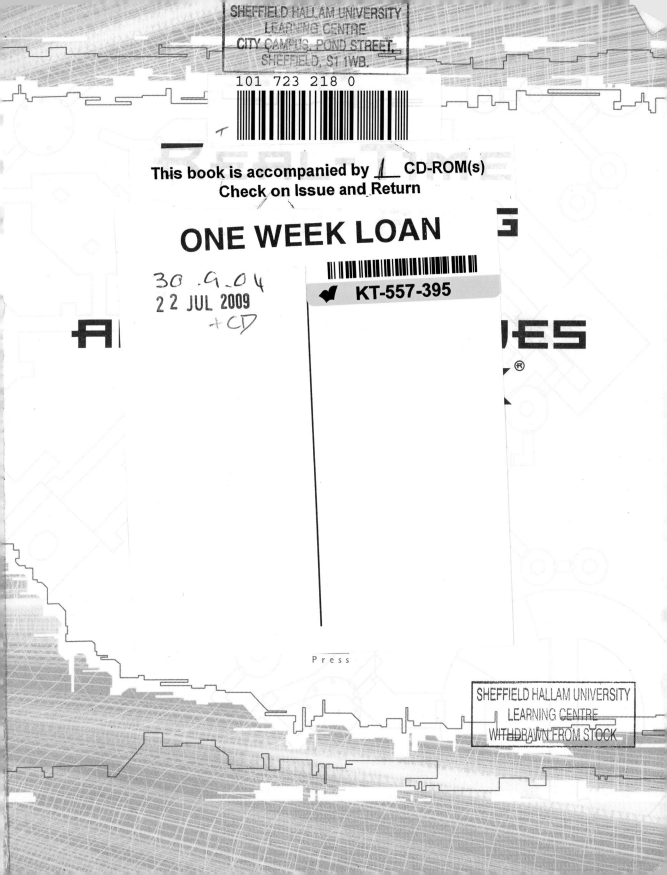

Real-Time Rendering Tricks and Techniques in DirectX®

Kelly Dempski

Premier
Press

Premier Press, Inc. is a registered trademark of Premier Press, Inc.

Publisher: Stacy L. Hiquet

Copy Editor: Kris Simmons

Marketing Manager: Heather Buzzingham

Interior Layout: Danielle Foster

Managing Editor: Sandy Doell

Cover Design: Mike Tanamachi

Acquisitions Editor: Mitzi Foster

CD-ROM Producer: Carson McGuire

Series Editor: André LaMothe

Indexer: Kelly Talbot

Senior Project Editor: Heather Talbot

Proofreader: Jenny Davidson

Technical Reviewer: André LaMothe

ISBN: 1-931841-27-6

Library of Congress Catalog Card Number: 2001097326

Printed in the United States of America

02 03 04 05 06 RI 10 9 8 7 6 5 4 3 2 1

For Rachel

Foreword

O ver the past few years, the field of real-time graphics has come into its own. Consumer-level graphics processors are now available with speed and capabilities rivaling the most expensive workstations of just a few years ago.

In addition, recent papers presented at Siggraph, the premier graphics research conference and exhibition, have been more and more focused on real-time graphics, as opposed to off-line rendering techniques.

The biggest advance in consumer real-time graphics over the past year has been the advent of programmable shading technology as found in the NVIDIA GeForce3™ and GeForce4™ Ti line of products, in addition to the Microsoft Xbox™ GPU (Graphics Processing Unit), and the Radeon™ 8500 series from ATI Technologies.

Now, instead of being tied into a fixed-function lighting model that includes diffuse and specular terms evaluated per-vertex, one can program a custom lighting solution, taking into account per-pixel bump mapping, reflection, refraction, Fresnel, and self-shadowing terms. This flexibility not only improves the capability of realistic traditional rendering, but opens the door to non-photorealistic techniques, such as cel shading, hatching, and the like.

This very flexibility does come at a cost, however, and one aspect of this cost is complexity. As developers fashion their shading models to consider more and more factors, each parameter to the shading function must be provided somehow. Initially, these will be supplied via artist-authored texture maps and geometric models. Over time, however, as graphics processors (GPUs) become even more programmable, many parameters will be filled in procedurally via pseudo-random noise generation. It will fall to the artists to merely specify a material type such as 'marble', 'oak', etc. and a few parameters, and the actual pattern of the surface will be created on the fly in real time.

Another way the complexity of programmable shading becomes expensive is via education. It's much simpler to learn the ins and outs of a 'configurable' vertex or pixel engine, like that exposed by a GPU such as the original GeForce or GeForce2. Learning not only what to do, but also what is possible is a challenge to be sure.

In one sense, it's trivial to implement an algorithm with a fully general CPU with true floating point capability, but it takes a real-time graphics programmer's talent to get last year's research paper running in real time on today's hardware, with limited floating point capability and processing time.

Lastly, the blessing of flexibility comes with the curse of the new. Due to the recent development of real-time programmable shading, the tools are only now beginning to catch up. Major 3D authoring applications are tackling this problem now, so hopefully the next major revision of your favorite 3D authoring tool will include full support for this exciting new technology.

Over time, real-time graphics languages will move from the current mix of floating-point and fixed-point assembly level, to fully general floating point throughout the pipeline. They will also shed the form of assembly languages, and look more like high-level languages, with loops, conditionals, and function calls, as well as professional IDEs (Integrated Development Environments) specifically tailored to real-time graphics needs.

Hopefully you will find *Real-Time Rendering Tricks and Techniques in DirectX* a good starting place to begin your journey into the future of real-time graphics.

D. Sim Dietrich Jr.
February 2002

Acknowledgments

I can't thank my wife Rachel enough. She has graciously put up with six frantic months of writing. Her contributions ranged anywhere from simple emotional support to helping me debug pixel shaders in the early hours of the morning. This book would not have been possible without her patience and support.

I'd like to thank all my friends and family for their support. I've had less time to spend with the people who are important to me. Thank you for your patience these past months.

Thanks to Stan Taylor, Anatole Gershman, Edy Liongosari, and everyone at Accenture Technology Labs for their support. Many thanks to Scott Kurth for proofreading, suggestions, and the occasional reality check. Also, many thanks to Mitu Singh for taking the time to help me with many of the images and equations. I have the privilege of working with a fantastic group of people.

Also, I'd like to thank all the other people who worked on this book. I really appreciate the help of Emi Smith, Mitzi Foster, Heather Talbot, Kris Simmons, and André LaMothe. Thanks to all of you for walking me through my first book.

Finally, I need to thank Philip Taylor (Microsoft), Jason Mitchell (ATI), Sim Dietrich (nVidia), and many other presenters from each of these three companies. Much of what I have learned comes from their excellent presentations and online materials. Their direct and indirect help is greatly appreciated. Also, I'd like to thank Sim Dietrich for taking the time and effort to write the foreword.

All the people mentioned above contributed in some way to the better aspects of this book. I deeply appreciate their contributions.

About the Author

Kelly Dempski has been a researcher at Accenture's Technology Labs for seven years. His research work has been in the areas of multimedia, Virtual Reality, Augmented Reality, and Interactive TV, with a strong focus on photo-realistic rendering and interactive techniques. He has authored several papers and one of his projects is part of the Smithsonian Institution's permanent collection on Information Technology.

Contents at a Glance

Introduction XXXVII

Part One
First Things First 1

Chapter 1
3D Graphics: A Historical Perspective 3

Chapter 2
A Refresher Course in Vectors 9

Chapter 3
A Refresher Course in Matrices 21

Chapter 4
A Look at Colors and Lighting 31

Chapter 5
A Look at the Graphics Pipeline 43

Part Two
Building the Sandbox 53

Chapter 6
Setting Up the Environment and
Simple Win32 App 55

Chapter 7
Creating and Managing the Direct3D Device 69

Part Three
Let the Rendering Begin!

Part Three
Let the Rendering Begin! 93

CHAPTER 8
EVERYTHING STARTS WITH THE VERTEX 95

CHAPTER 9
USING TRANSFORMATIONS 115

CHAPTER 10
FROM VERTICES TO GEOMETRY 133

CHAPTER 11
FIXED FUNCTION LIGHTING 161

CHAPTER 12
INTRODUCTION TO TEXTURES 187

CHAPTER 13
TEXTURE STAGE STATES 213

CHAPTER 14
DEPTH TESTING AND ALPHA BLENDING 237

Part Four
Shaders 257

CHAPTER 15
VERTEX SHADERS 259

CHAPTER 16
PIXEL SHADERS 289

Part Five
Vertex Shader Techniques 319

CHAPTER 17
USING SHADERS WITH MESHES 321

CHAPTER 18
SIMPLE AND COMPLEX GEOMETRIC MANIPULATION
WITH VERTEX SHADERS 337

CHAPTER 19
BILLBOARDS AND VERTEX SHADERS 353

CHAPTER 20
WORKING OUTSIDE OF CARTESIAN COORDINATES 369

CHAPTER 21
BEZIER PATCHES 385

CHAPTER 22
CHARACTER ANIMATION—
MATRIX PALETTE SKINNING 411

CHAPTER 23
SIMPLE COLOR MANIPULATION 433

CHAPTER 24
DO-IT-YOURSELF LIGHTING IN A VERTEX SHADER 447

CHAPTER 25
CARTOON SHADING 465

CHAPTER 26
REFLECTION AND REFRACTION 479

CHAPTER 27
SHADOWS PART 1—PLANAR SHADOWS 499

CHAPTER 28
SHADOWS PART 2—SHADOW VOLUMES 519

CHAPTER 29
SHADOWS PART 3—SHADOW MAPS 541

Part Six

Pixel Shader Techniques 563

CHAPTER 30
PER-PIXEL LIGHTING 565

CHAPTER 31
PER-PIXEL LIGHTING—BUMP MAPPING 587

CHAPTER 32
PER-VERTEX TECHNIQUES DONE PER PIXEL 609

Part Seven
Other Useful Techniques 631

CHAPTER 33
RENDERING TO A TEXTURE—
FULL-SCREEN MOTION BLUR 633

CHAPTER 34
2D RENDERING—JUST DROP A "D" 657

CHAPTER 35
DIRECTSHOW! USING VIDEO AS A TEXTURE 679

CHAPTER 36
IMAGE PROCESSING WITH PIXEL SHADERS 701

CHAPTER 37
A MUCH BETTER WAY TO DRAW TEXT 727

CHAPTER 38
PERFECT TIMING 749

CHAPTER 39
THE STENCIL BUFFER 759

CHAPTER 40
PICKING! A PLETHORA OF PRACTICAL
PICKING PROCEDURES 773

IN CONCLUSION 797

INDEX 799

Contents

Introduction ································· XXXVII

Part One
First Things First ································· 1

Chapter 1
3D Graphics: A Historical
Perspective ································· 3

Hardware Advances on the PC ································· 4
Hardware Advances on Gaming Consoles ································· 5
Advances in Movies ································· 6
A Brief History of DirectX ································· 6
A Word about OpenGL ································· 7

Chapter 2
A Refresher Course in Vectors ······· 9

What Is a Vector? ································· 10
Normalizing Vectors ································· 11
Vector Arithmetic ································· 11
Vector Dot Product ································· 13
Vector Cross Product ································· 15
Quaternions ································· 16
Vectors in D3DX ································· 17
In Conclusion… ································· 19

CHAPTER 3
A REFRESHER COURSE IN MATRICES 21

What Is a Matrix? 22

The Identity Matrix 24

The Translation Matrix 24

The Scaling Matrix 25

The Rotation Matrix 25

Matrix Concatenation 26

Matrices and D3DX 27

In Conclusion… 28

CHAPTER 4
A LOOK AT COLORS AND LIGHTING 31

What Is Color? 32

Ambient and Emissive Lighting 34

Diffuse Lighting 35

Specular Lighting 36

Other Light Types 38

Putting It All Together with Direct3D 39

Shading Types 39

In Conclusion… 41

CHAPTER 5
A LOOK AT THE GRAPHICS PIPELINE 43

The Direct3D Pipeline 44

Vertex Data and Higher-Order Surfaces 45

The Fixed-Function Transform and Lighting Stage 46

Vertex Shaders 47

The Clipper 48

Multitexturing 48

Pixel Shaders 49

Fog 49

Depth, Stencil, and Alpha Tests 50

The Frame Buffer 50

Performance Considerations 50

In Conclusion… 51

Part Two
Building the Sandbox 53

CHAPTER 6
SETTING UP THE ENVIRONMENT
AND SIMPLE WIN32 APP 55

A Look at the SDK 56

Setting Up the Environment 58

A Simple Win32 Application 59

   Checking Out Executable.h 59

   Checking Out Application.h 60

   Checking Out Executable.cpp 61

   Checking Out Application.cpp 63

Compiling and Running the Simple Application 65

In Review: Why Did We Do It That Way? 67

In Conclusion… 67

CHAPTER 7
CREATING AND MANAGING
THE DIRECT3D DEVICE 69

What Is the Direct3D Device? 70
Step 1: Creating the Direct3D Object 71
Step 2: Learning More about the Hardware 72
Step 3: Creating the Direct3D Device 73
Step 4: Resetting a Lost Device 76
Step 5: Destroying a Device 77
Rendering with the Direct3D Device 77
Clearing the Device 78
Application.h Revisited 79
Application.cpp Revisited 82
In Conclusion… 91

Part Three
Let the Rendering Begin!........................... 93

CHAPTER 8
EVERYTHING STARTS WITH THE VERTEX ... 95

What Is a Vertex? 96
No Really, What Is a Vertex? 97
Creating Vertices 98
Destroying the Vertex Buffer 101
Setting and Changing Vertex Data 101
Rendering Vertices 103
Performance Considerations 105

Finally, Something on the Screen! 106

In Conclusion… 112

CHAPTER 9
USING TRANSFORMATIONS 115

What Do You Mean by Transformations? 116

The World Transformation 117

The View Transformation 117

Building World and View Transformations 118

The Projection Transformation 120

Transformations and the D3D Device 122

Using Matrix Stacks 123

The Viewport 124

Putting It All Together 125

Suggested Exercises 131

Performance Considerations 132

In Conclusion… 132

CHAPTER 10
FROM VERTICES TO GEOMETRY 133

Turning Vertices into Surfaces 134

Rendering Surfaces 135

Rendering with Triangle Lists 136

Rendering with Triangle Fans 137

Rendering with Triangle Strips 137

Rendering with Indexed Primitives 139

Loading and Rendering .X Files 141

Performance Considerations 143

The Code 144

In Conclusion… 159

CHAPTER 11
FIXED FUNCTION LIGHTING ■■■■■■■■■■■■■■■■■ 161

The D3DLIGHT8 Structure 162

Directional Lights.. 163

Point Lights 163

Spot Lights 165

Setting Up the Device for Lighting 167

The Application 168

The Code 170

In Conclusion… 184

CHAPTER 12
INTRODUCTION TO TEXTURES ■■■■■■■■■■■■■ 187

Textures—The Inside Story 188

Surfaces and Memory 189

Width, Height, and the Powers of Two 190

Surface Levels and Mip Maps 190

Creating Textures 191

Textures and Vertices 194

Textures and the Device 197

Performance Considerations 198

Advanced Topics 198

Textures and Color 198

The Texture Matrix 199

Multitexturing 199

The Application 199

In Conclusion… 211

CHAPTER 13
TEXTURE STAGE STATES 213

Setting the Texture Stage State 214

Blending and Multitexturing 215

D3DTSS_COLOROP and D3DTSS_ALPHAOP 216

D3DTSS_COLORARG1, D3DTSS_COLORARG2,
D3DTSS_ALPHAARG1, and D3DTSS_ALPHAARG2 217

Triadic Operations (D3DTSS_COLORARG0 and
D3DTSS_ALPHAARG0) 218

D3DTSS_RESULTARG 218

Checking the Device Caps 218

Bump Mapping 218

Texture Coordinate States 219

D3DTSS_TEXCOORDINDEX 219

D3DTSS_ADDRESSU, D3DTSS_ADDRESSV,
and D3DTSS_ADDRESSW 220

D3DTSS_BORDERCOLOR 221

D3DTSS_TEXTURETRANSFORMFLAGS 221

Checking the Device Caps 222

Texture Filtering and Mip Maps 222

D3DTSS_MAGFILTER 222

D3DTSS_MINFILTER 224

D3DTSS_MIPFILTER 224

D3DTSS_MIPMAPLODBIAS 224

D3DTSS_MAXMIPLEVEL 224

D3DTSS_MAXANISOTROPY 224

Checking the Device Caps 225

Texture Stage States and Shaders 225
The Code 225
In Conclusion… 234

CHAPTER 14
DEPTH TESTING AND ALPHA BLENDING ... 237

Depth Testing 238
    W Buffering 240
    Z Bias 241
    Clearing the Depth Buffer 241
Alpha Blending 241
    Alpha in 32-Bit File Formats 242
    Alpha in the DirectX Texture Tool 242
    Alpha from ColorKey 242
    Enabling Alpha Blending 243
Alpha Test 244
Performance Considerations 245
The Code 245
In Conclusion… 255

Part Four
Shaders 257

CHAPTER 15
VERTEX SHADERS 259

What Is a Vertex Shader? 261
    Vertex Data Registers 262
    Constant Registers 263

The Address Register 263

The Temporary Registers 263

Vertex Output 263

The Shader Code **264**

Swizzling and Write Masks **267**

Shader Implementation **268**

Shaders and the Device 268

Creating the Declaration 269

Assembling the Shader 271

Creating the Shader 273

Using the Shader 273

Destroying the Shader 274

Using Shaders with Computed Geometry **274**

Using Shaders with Meshes **275**

The Basic Shader **275**

Transformations in the Basic Shader 275

Setting Other Vertex Data 277

Performance Issues **277**

The Code **277**

In Conclusion… **286**

CHAPTER 16

PIXEL SHADERS 289

What Is a Pixel Shader? **290**

Pixel Shader Versions **291**

The Inputs, Outputs, and Operation of a Pixel Shader **292**

Color Registers 292

Temporary and Output Registers 293

Constant Registers 293

Texture Registers 293

Dependent Texture Reads **293**

Pixel Shader Instructions **294**

Instruction Pairing.. 298

Texture Addressing Instructions 298

Pixel Shader Modifiers..**303**

Pixel Shader Limitations and Caveats **304**

Determining Pixel Shader Support **306**

Assembling, Creating, and Using Pixel Shaders **306**

A Very Simple Pixel Shader Application **307**

Simple Lighting in a Vertex Shader **308**

Simple Blending in a Pixel Shader **309**

Simple Pixel Shader Application **311**

In Conclusion… **316**

Part Five
Vertex Shader Techniques 319

CHAPTER 17
USING SHADERS WITH MESHES 321

The Basic Idea 322

From Materials to Vertex Colors..323

From Vertex Colors to Vertex Data 325

Performance Considerations 325

The Implementation 326

In Conclusion… 335

Chapter 18
Simple and Complex Geometric
Manipulation with Vertex Shaders ... 337

Expanding Vertices along Their Normals 338
Warping Vertices with a Sine Wave 341
The Implementation 345
Ideas for Extensions to the Sample 350
In Conclusion… 351

Chapter 19
Billboards and Vertex Shaders 353

The Basic Idea behind Billboards 354
The Billboard Shader 355
The Implementation 359
Other Billboard Ideas 366
In Conclusion… 367

Chapter 20
Working Outside of Cartesian
Coordinates 369

Cartesian and Other Coordinate Systems 370
Mapping between Coordinate Systems in a Vertex Shader 372
The Application Code 375
Applications of This Technique 383
In Conclusion… 383

CHAPTER 21
BEZIER PATCHES ··················· 385

Lines and Curves and Patches, Oh… 386

Deriving Surface Normals with "Calculus" 390

Computing the Patch Values in a Shader 393

The Bezier Application 396

Uses and Advantages of Bezier Patches 407

Connecting Curves and Patches 408

In Conclusion… 408

CHAPTER 22
CHARACTER ANIMATION—
MATRIX PALETTE SKINNING ·········· 411

Character Animation Techniques 412

The Address Register 416

Matrix Palette Skinning in a Shader 416

The Application 419

Other Uses for Palettes 430

In Conclusion… 430

CHAPTER 23
SIMPLE COLOR MANIPULATION ········· 433

Encoding Depth into the Vertex Color 434

The Depth Shader 435

The Depth Encoding Application 438

The X-Ray Shader 439

The X-Ray Application 442

In Conclusion… 446

CHAPTER 24
DO-IT-YOURSELF LIGHTING
IN A VERTEX SHADER 447

Converting Light Vectors to Object Space 448
The Directional Light Shader 452
The Point Light Shader 454
The Spot Light Shader 456
The Application Code 459
Multiple Lights in One Shader 462
In Conclusion… 462

CHAPTER 25
CARTOON SHADING 465

Shaders, Textures, and Complex Functions 466
Applying the Approach to the Toon Shader (Part 1) 468
Applying the Approach to the Toon Shader (Part 2) 469
Putting It All Together in a Shader 471
The Toon Shading Application 473
Ideas for Texture Changes 475
Ideas for Shader Changes 476
In Conclusion… 476

CHAPTER 26
REFLECTION AND REFRACTION 479

Environmental Mapping and Cube Maps 480
Changing Cube Maps Dynamically 481
Computing Reflection Vectors 482
Computing Approximate Refraction Vectors 485

The Reflection/Refraction Vertex Shader 487

The Application Code 489

Other Uses for Cube Maps 496

In Conclusion… 497

Chapter 27
Shadows Part 1—Planar Shadows ... 499

Casting Shadows on a Plane 500

The Plane Equation 501

The Shadow Matrix 503

The Stencil Buffer and Shadows 504

The Planar Shadow Application 506

Limitations and Areas for Improvement 515

In Conclusion… 517

Chapter 28
Shadows Part 2—Shadow Volumes ... 519

Shadow Volumes Explained 520

The Shadow Volume Shader 526

The Shadow Volume Application 528

Advantages and Disadvantages of Shadow Volumes 536

In Conclusion… 538

Chapter 29
Shadows Part 3—Shadow Maps 541

The Shadow Map Concept 542

Rendering the Light Viewpoint to a Texture 545

Texture Mapping the World 546

The Depth Comparison Vertex Shader 549

The Shadow Mapping Pixel Shader 550

The Shadow Map Application 551

Limitations and Improvements 560

In Conclusion… 561

Part Six
Pixel Shader Techniques 563

CHAPTER 30
PER-PIXEL LIGHTING ■■■■■■■■■■■■■■■■■■■ 565

Simple Light Maps 566

Per-Pixel Lighting with Pixel Shaders 567

Per-Pixel Spot Lights 569

Per-Pixel Spot Light Vertex Shader 572

Per-Pixel Spot Light Pixel Shader 574

Per-Pixel Spot Light Application 575

Per-Pixel Point Lights.. 578

Per-Pixel Point-Light Vertex Shader 579

Per-Pixel Point-Light Pixel Shader 580

Per-Pixel Point-Light Application 581

Limitations... 583

In Conclusion… 584

CHAPTER 31
PER-PIXEL LIGHTING—BUMP MAPPING ■■■ 587

Bump Mapping Concepts 588

Creating and Using Normal Maps.. 590

Creating Texture Space Basis Vectors 592

Bump Mapping Vertex Shader 594

Bump Mapping without a Pixel Shader 596

Bump Mapping Pixel Shader 603

Limitations and Areas for Improvement 605

In Conclusion… 606

CHAPTER 32
PER-VERTEX TECHNIQUES
DONE PER PIXEL •••••••••••••••••••••••• 609

Per-Pixel Reflection 610

Using texm3x3pad 611

The Reflective Bump Mapping Vertex Shader 613

The Reflective Bump Mapping Pixel Shader 616

Reflective Bump Mapping Application 617

Per-Pixel Toon Shading 622

Per-Pixel Toon Vertex Shader 623

Per-Pixel Toon Pixel Shader 624

Per-Pixel Toon Application 628

In Conclusion… 629

Part Seven
Other Useful Techniques 631

CHAPTER 33
RENDERING TO A TEXTURE—FULL-SCREEN
MOTION BLUR •••••••••••••••••••••••••••• 633

Creating a Texture as a Render Target.. 634

Obtaining Surfaces from Texture Render Targets 636

Rendering to a Texture Render Target 637

Rendering to a Dynamic Cube Map 638

Motion Blur 640

Motion Blur as a Post-Processing Technique 642

The Motion-Blur Application 643

Performance Implications 654

In Conclusion… 654

Chapter 34
2D Rendering—Just Drop a "D" 657

Alas, Poor DirectDraw. I Knew It… 658

Step 1: Lose a "D" 659

Sprites—Image Is Everything 663

Using Vertices in 2D 664

A Very Simple 2D Application 666

Performance Implications 671

Possible Extensions 675

In Conclusion… 675

Chapter 35
DirectShow:
Using Video as a Texture 679

DirectShow in a Nutshell 680

I Want My MP3 682

The Operation of the Video-to-Texture Filter 683

Preparing to Build the Texture Class 685

The Texture Filter Class 686

The Video Texture Application 696

In Conclusion… 698

CHAPTER 36
IMAGE PROCESSING WITH
PIXEL SHADERS 701

The Advantage of Post Processing 702

Full-Screen Color Manipulations with Pixel Shaders 703

    A Black-and-White Filter 703

    Adjusting Brightness 704

    Inverting the Scene 707

    Solarizing an Image 707

    Adjusting Contrast 709

    Sepia-Toning an Image 712

Using Color Curves to Manipulate Color 713

Image Processing with Convolution Kernels 719

Performance Considerations 724

In Conclusion... 725

CHAPTER 37
A MUCH BETTER WAY TO DRAW TEXT ... 727

The Basic Idea 728

The Implementation 730

In Conclusion... 747

CHAPTER 38
PERFECT TIMING 749

Low-Resolution Timing 750

High-Resolution Timing 751

Some General Words about Animation 752

The Implementation 754

In Conclusion... 757

Chapter 39

The Stencil Buffer 759

The Purpose of the Stencil Buffer and Stencil Test 760

Stencil Buffer Render States 762

Enabling the Stencil Buffer 762

Setting a Test Reference Value 762

Setting the Comparison Function 763

Setting the Update Operations 764

Stencil Masks 765

Stenciled Sniper Scope 765

In Conclusion… 771

Chapter 40

Picking: A Plethora of Practical

Picking Procedures 773

Very Simple 2D Picking 774

Ray Picking 776

Terrain Following with Ray Picking 779

A Picture Perfect Per-Pixel Picking Procedure 785

The Per-Pixel Pick Vertex Shader 785

Per-Pixel Pick Application 786

Other Uses for Per-Pixel Picking 793

Performance Issues 794

In Conclusion… 795

In Conclusion… 797

Index 799

Letter from the Series Editor

Let me start by saying, buy this book! *Real-Time Rendering Tricks and Techniques in DirectX* is simply the most advanced DirectX book on the market—period! The material in this book will be found in no other book, and that's all there is to it. I am certain that the author Kelly Dempski is an alien from another world since there's no way a human could know this much about advanced DirectX. I know since I am from another planet <SMILE>. This book covers all the topics you have always heard about, but never knew exactly how to implement in real time.

In recent times, Direct3D has become a very complex and powerful API that leverages hardware to the max. The programmers at Microsoft are not playing games with it and Direct3D is in sync with the hardware that it supports, meaning if there is hardware out there that does something, you can be sure that Direct3D can take advantage of it. In fact, Direct3D has support for operations that don't exist. Makes me wonder if Bill has a time machine. The only downfall to all this technology and functionality is that the learning curve is many months to years—and that's no joke. Try learning Direct3D on your own, and it will take you 1–2 years to master it. The days of just figuring things out are over, you need a master to teach you, and then you can advance from there.

Real-Time Rendering Tricks and Techniques in DirectX starts off making no assumptions about what you know. The first part of the book covers mathematics, matrices, and more. After that groundwork is laid, general Direct3D is covered in l, so we are all on the same page. The coverage of Direct3D alone is worth the price of the book. However, after the basic Direct3D coverage, the book starts into special effects programming using various advanced techniques like vertex shaders and pixel shaders. This stuff is completely voodoo. It's not like it's hard, but you simply would have no idea where to start if you were to read the DirectX SDK. Kelly knows where to start, where to end, and what goes in the middle.

Now, I don't want to get you too excited, but if you read this book you WILL know how to perform such operations as advanced texture blending, lighting, shadow mapping, refraction, reflection, fog, and a bazillion other cool effects such as "cartoon" shading. What I like about this book is that it really does live up to its title, and the material is extremely advanced, but at the same time very easy to understand. The author makes things like refraction seem so easy. He's like, "a dot product here, change the angle there, texture index, and output it, and whammo done!"—and you're like sitting there going "wow, it works!". The point is that something like refraction or reflection seems easy theoretically, but when you try to do it, knowing where to begin is the problem. With *Real-Time Rendering Tricks and Techniques in DirectX*, you don't have to worry about that; you will learn the best approaches to every advanced rendering technique known to humanity and be able to skip the learning and experimentation that comes with trial and error. Additionally, the book has interesting tips and asides into the insides of DirectX and why something should or should not be done in a specific way; thus, no stone is left unturned.

Well, I can't tell you how much I recommend this book; you will be a Direct3D master by the end of reading it. And if that wasn't enough, it even covers how to use DirectShow! I finally can play a damn video!

Sincerely,

André LaMothe
SERIES EDITOR

Introduction

If you're reading this book at home, good—because I have every intention of making this a book that you can use as a reference for a long time. If you're reading this at the bookstore, then bring it home (they appreciate it if you pay first) because it's terribly inconvenient to run to the bookstore each time you need to implement one of the cool techniques this book describes. When I taught a programming class, I told them, "I don't know everything, but I know *where to find* everything." Every good programmer has a couple of books that are good to refer to periodically. This is one of those books, but before we get to the good stuff, let's get some basic introductions out of the way.

Who Is This Book For?

Simply put, this book is for you! If you're reading this, you picked this book off the shelf because you have an interest in learning some of the more interesting parts of graphics programming. This book covers advanced features in a way that is easy for beginners to grasp. Beginners who start at the beginning and work their way through should have no problem learning as the techniques become more advanced. Experienced users can use this book as a reference, jumping from chapter to chapter as they need to learn or brush up on certain techniques.

How Should You Read This Book?

The goal of this book is two-fold. First, I want you to be able to read this book through and gain an understanding of all the new features available in today's graphics cards. After that, I want you to be able to use this as a reference when you begin to use those features day to day. It is a good idea to read the book cover to cover, at least skimming chapters to get a feel for what is possible. Then later, as you have specific needs, read those chapters in depth. Frequently, I answer questions from people who weren't even aware of a technique, much less how to implement it. Your initial reading will help to plant some good ideas in your head.

Also, many of the techniques in this book are implemented around one or two examples that highlight the technique. While you're reading this, it's important to view each technique as a tool that can be reapplied and combined with other techniques to solve a given problem. For each technique, I'll discuss the broader possibilities, but in many cases, you might discover a use for a technique that I never imagined. That's the best thing that can happen. If you've gotten to the point that you can easily rework and reapply the techniques to a wider range of problems, then you have a great understanding of the technology.

What Is Included?

I explain higher-level concepts in a way that is clear to all levels of readers. The text itself explains the basic techniques, as well as a step-by-step breakdown of the source code. The CD contains all the source code and media needed to run the examples. In addition, I've included some tools to help get you started in creating your own media.

Who Am I?

I am a researcher with Accenture Technology Labs. A large part of my job involves speaking to people about technology and what the future holds for businesses and consumers. Some past projects have received various awards and numerous publications. My most recent projects involved work in augmented and virtual reality, and many other projects involved gaming consoles and realistic graphics. I'm not a game programmer, but a large part of my work involves using and understanding the same technologies. I have the luxury of working with new hardware and software before it becomes readily available, and it's my job to figure it out and develop something new and interesting. Unlike many other authors of advanced books, I do not have a background in pure mathematics or computer science. My background is in engineering. From that perspective, my focus is implementing techniques and getting things done rather than providing theoretical musings. And if for some reason I don't succeed, you know where to reach me!

Kelly Dempski
Graphics_book@hotmail.com

Part One

First Things First

If you're like me, you're dying to jump headlong into the code. Slow down! These first several chapters deal with some of the basic concepts you'll need in later chapters. Advanced readers might want to skip this section entirely, although I recommend skimming through the sections just to make sure that you really know the material. For beginner readers, it's a good idea to read these chapters carefully. Different people will pick up on the concepts at different rates. These chapters move through the material quickly. If you read a chapter once and you don't fully understand it, don't worry too much. Later chapters continually explain and use the concepts. I know for me personally, I don't truly understand something until I use it. If you're like me, read the chapters, digest what you can, and wait until you start coding. Then, return to these earlier chapters to reinforce the concepts behind the code.

Here's a brief breakdown of the chapters in this section:

- Chapter 1, "3D Graphics: A Historical Perspective," is a brief look back at the last couple years of technological development in the area of 3D graphics. It's not a complete retrospective, but it should give you an idea of why this is an interesting time to be in the field.

- Chapter 2, "A Refresher Course in Vectors," runs through the definition of a vector and the ways to mathematically manipulate vectors. Because so many of the techniques are based on vector math, I highly recommend that you read this chapter.

- Chapter 3, "A Refresher Course in Matrices," briefly explains matrices and the associated math. It explains matrices from an abstract perspective, and beginners might need to get to the later chapter on transformations before they completely understand. The discontinuity is intentional. I want to keep the abstract theory separate from the implementation because the theory is reused throughout many different implementations.

- Chapter 4, "A Look at Colors and Lighting," explains the basics of color and lighting. This theory provides the basis of many shader operations in later chapters. If you've never implemented your own lighting before, reading this chapter is a must.

- Chapter 5, "A Look at the Graphics Pipeline," is the final look at "the basics." You will look at how data moves through the graphics card and where performance bottlenecks can occur. This chapter provides a basis for later performance tips.

CHAPTER I

3D Graphics: A Historical Perspective

I was in school when DOOM came out, and it worked like a charm on my state-of-the-art 486/25. At the time, 3D graphics were unheard of on a consumer PC, and even super-expensive SGI machines were not extremely powerful. A couple years later, when Quake was released, 3D hardware acceleration was not at all mainstream, and the initial version of Quake ran with a fast software renderer. However, Quake was the "killer app" that pushed 3D hardware acceleration into people's homes and offices. In July 2001, *Final Fantasy* debuted as the first "hyper-realistic," completely computer-generated feature film. Less than a month later, nVidia's booth at SIGGRAPH featured scenes from *Final Fantasy* running in real time on its current generation of hardware. It wasn't as high quality as the movie, but it was very impressive. In a few short years, there have been considerable advances in the field. How did we get here? To answer that, you have to look at the following.

- Hardware advances on the PC.
- Hardware advances on gaming consoles.
- Advances in movies.
- A brief history of DirectX.
- A word about OpenGL.

Hardware Advances on the PC

Prior to Quake, there was no killer app for accelerated graphics on consumer PCs. Once 3D games became popular, several hardware vendors began offering 3D accelerators at consumer prices. We can track the evolution of hardware by looking at the product offerings of a particular vendor over the years. If you look at nVidia, you see that one of its first hardware accelerators was the TNT, which was released shortly after Quake in 1995 and was followed a year later by the TNT2. Over the years, new products and product revisions improved at an exponential rate. In fact, nVidia claims that it advances at Moore's Law *cubed*!

It becomes difficult to accurately chart the advances because we cannot just chart processor speed. The geForce represents a discontinuity as the first graphics processing unit (GPU), capable of doing transform and lighting operations that were previously done on the CPU. The geForce2 added more features and faster memory, and the geForce3 had a significantly more advanced feature set. In addition to increasing the processing speed of the chip, the overall work done per clock cycle has increased significantly. The geForce3 was the first GPU to feature hardware-supported vertex and pixel shaders. These shaders allow developers to manipulate geometry and pixels directly on the hardware. Special effects traditionally performed on the CPU are now done by dedicated 3D hardware, and the performance increase allows for cutting-edge effects to be rendered in real time for games and other interactive media and entertainment. These shaders form the basis of many of the tricks and techniques discussed in the later chapters. In fact, one of the purposes of this book is to explore the use of shaders and how you can use this new technology as a powerful tool.

Not only has hardware dramatically increased in performance, but also the penetration of 3D acceleration hardware is rapidly approaching 100 percent. In fact, all consumer PCs shipped by major manufacturers include some form of 3D acceleration. Very powerful geForce2 cards are being sold for less than US$100, and even laptops and other mobile devices feature 3D acceleration in growing amounts. Most of this book was written on a laptop that outperforms my 1999 SGI workstation! Hardware that supports shaders is not ubiquitous yet, but game developers need to be aware of these new features because the install base is guaranteed to grow rapidly. The PC is an unpredictable platform. Some customers might have the latest and greatest hardware, and others may have old 2D cards, but if you ignore these new features, you will fall behind.

Hardware Advances on Gaming Consoles

Although nVidia claims to run at Moore's Law cubed, offering new products every six months, consoles must have a longer lifespan. In fact, for several years, the performance of gaming consoles did not increase dramatically. The Atari 2600 had a 1MHz processor in 1978, and gains were modest throughout the 80s and early 90s. In the mid 90s, consoles started to increase in power, following the curve of the PC hardware accelerators. However, starting in 2000 and into 2001, console power took a dramatic upswing with the introduction of Sony's PS2 and Microsoft's Xbox. In fact, Sony had a bit of a snag when the Japanese government claimed that the PS2 might fall under the jurisdiction of laws governing the export of supercomputing technology! The Xbox features much higher performance numbers, but fans of the PS2 support Sony religiously. In fact, comparisons between the PS2 and the Xbox are the cause of many a flame war. Regardless of which console is truly the best, or what will come next, the fact remains that tens of millions of people have extremely high-powered graphics computers sitting in their living rooms. In fact, gaming console sales are expected to outnumber VCR sales in the near future. Now that consoles are a big business, advances in technology should accelerate. One of the nice things about the Xbox is that many of the techniques you will learn here are directly applicable on the Xbox. This is an interesting departure from the usual "proprietary" aspects of console development.

Advances in Movies

One of the first movies to really blow people away with computer-generated (CG) effects was *Jurassic Park*. The first *Jurassic Park* movie featured realistic dinosaurs rendered with technology specially invented for that movie. The techniques were continually enhanced in many movies, leading up to *Star Wars Episode 1*, which was the first movie to feature an all-digital realistic character, to *Final Fantasy*, where everything was computer generated. Many of the techniques developed for those movies were too processor-intensive to do in real time, but advances in techniques and hardware are making more and more of those techniques possible to render in games. Many of the shaders used by movie houses to create realistic skin and hair are now possible to implement on the latest hardware. Also, geometry techniques such as morphing or "skinning" can now occur in real time. The first *Jurassic Park* movie featured textures that were skinned over the moving skeletons of the dinosaurs. A simplified form of skinning is now standard in 3D games. The third *Jurassic Park* movie expanded on that, creating volumetric skin and fat tissue that stretches and jiggles as the dinosaur moves, creating a more realistic effect. I bet that this type of technique will be implemented in games in the not-too-distant future.

A Brief History of DirectX

To effectively use all this new hardware, you need an effective API. Early on, the API was fragmented on Windows platforms. Many people from the 3D workstation world were using OpenGL, while others were using 3DFX's proprietary Glide API. Still others were developing their own custom software solutions. Whether you like Microsoft or not, DirectX did a good thing by homogenizing the platforms, giving hardware vendors a common API set, and then actually enforcing the specification. Now, developers have a more stable target to work toward, and instead of writing several different versions of a renderer, they can spend time writing a better game.

Despite this, early versions of Direct3D were a bit clumsy and difficult to use. An old plan file from John Carmack (the engine developer for id Software) describes all the faults of early Direct3D. Many of the points were fair at the time, and that plan is still referenced today by people who don't like Direct3D, but the fact is that as of version 8.0, the API is dramatically better and easier to use. Significant changes affected the way 3D data is rendered, and the 2D-only API DirectDraw was dropped entirely. One of the reasons for this is that hardware is increasingly tuned to draw 3D very effectively. Using the 3D hardware to draw 2D is a much better use of the hardware than traditional 2D methods. Also gone is the difference between retained mode and immediate mode. Retained mode was often criticized for being bloated and slow but much easier for beginners. Current versions of the API feature a more user-friendly immediate mode (although it's not explicitly called that anymore) and a streamlined helper library, D3DX.

D3DX is, for the most part, highly optimized and not just a modernized retained mode. It includes several subsets of functions that handle the basic but necessary tasks of setting up matrices and vectors and performing mathematical operations. Also, several "ease-of-use" functions do everything from texture loading from a variety of image formats to optimizing 3D meshes. Veterans of Direct3D programming sometimes make the mistake of equating D3DX with D3DRM (Direct3D Retained Mode), which was slow. This is not the case, and you should use D3DX whenever it makes sense to. In the next chapters, I begin to show some of the basic utility functions of D3DX.

As I mentioned earlier, one of the most exciting developments in both hardware and the DirectX API is the development of shaders. DX8.0 features a full shader API for shader-compatible hardware. For hardware that doesn't support shaders, vendors have supplied drivers that implement vertex shaders very efficiently in hardware emulation. Most of the techniques discussed in this book were not possible in earlier versions of DirectX. Others were possible but much more difficult to implement effectively. For experienced DirectX programmers, it should be clear how much more powerful the new API is. For people who are new to DirectX, the new features should help you get started.

A Word about OpenGL

The PS2-versus-Xbox religious war is a pillow fight compared to the some of the battles that are waged over DirectX versus OpenGL. It's gotten bad enough that, when someone asked about OpenGL in a DirectX newsgroup, one of the Microsoft DirectX people replied immediately and accused him of trying to start a flame war. That response, in turn, started a flame war of its own. So it is with great trepidation that I weigh in on the topic.

I'll say first that I have done more than my fair share of OpenGL programming both on SGI machines and PCs. I find it easy to use and even enjoyable, so much so that I have recommended to several new people that they get their feet wet in OpenGL before moving to DirectX. If you are trying to decide which API to use, the short answer is that you should become educated and make educated decisions. In fact, I think most of the flame wars are waged between people who are ignorant about one or the other API (or both). There are advantages and disadvantages to each. If you are developing a product, look at your target platforms and feature set and decide which API best suits your needs. If you are a hobbyist or just getting started, spend some time looking at both and decide which you're most comfortable with.

The good news is that although the code in this book is developed with and for DirectX graphics, most of the concepts are applicable to any 3D API. If you are an experienced OpenGL programmer, you can easily port the code to OpenGL with minimal pain. So let's get started!

CHAPTER 2

A Refresher Course in Vectors

If you have worked with graphics at all, you have been working with vectors, whether you knew it or not. In Tetris, for example, the falling pieces follow a vector. In a drawing program, any pixel on the screen is a position that can be represented as a vector. In this chapter, you will look at what vectors are and how you can work with them. I will discuss the following points.

- The definition of a vector.
- Normalizing a vector.
- Vector arithmetic.
- The use of the vector dot product.
- The use of the vector cross product.
- A brief explanation of quaternions.
- Using D3DX vector structures.

What Is a Vector?

A vector, in the simplest terms, is a set of numbers that describe a position or direction somewhere in a given coordinate system. In 3D graphics, that coordinate system, or "space," tends to be described in Cartesian coordinates by (X, Y, Z). In 2D graphics, the space is usually (X, Y). Figure 2.1 shows each type of vector.

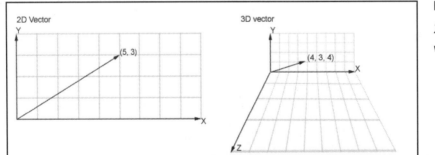

Figure 2.1

2D and 3D vectors.

Note that vectors are different from *scalars*, which are numbers that represent only a single value or magnitude. For instance, 60mph is a scalar value, but 60mph heading north can be considered a vector. Vectors are not limited to three dimensions. Physicists talk about space-time, which is at least four dimensions, and some search algorithms are based on spaces of hundreds of dimensions. But in every case, we use vectors to describe where an object is or which direction it is headed. For instance, we can say a light is at point (X, Y, Z) and its direction is (x, y, z). Because of this, vectors form the mathematical basis for almost everything done in 3D graphics. So you have to learn how to manipulate them for your own devious purposes.

Normalizing Vectors

Vectors contain both magnitude (length) and direction. However, in some cases, it's useful to separate one from the other. You might want to know just the length, or you might want to work with the direction as a *normalized unit vector*, a vector with a length of one, but the same direction. (Note that this is different from a normal vector, which I discuss later.) To compute the magnitude of a vector, simply apply the Pythagorean theorem:

$$|V| = |(X,Y,Z)| = \sqrt{(X^2 + Y^2 + Z^2)}$$

After you compute the magnitude, you can find the normalized unit vector by dividing each component by the magnitude:

$$N = \left[\frac{X}{|V|}, \frac{Y}{|V|}, \frac{Z}{|V|}\right]$$

Figure 2.2 shows an example of how you can compute the length of a vector and derive a unit vector with the same direction.

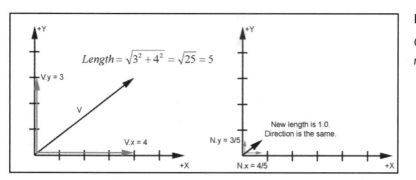

Figure 2.2

Computing a normalized unit vector.

You will see many uses for normalized vectors in the coming chapters.

Vector Arithmetic

Vectors are essentially sets of numbers, so arithmetic vector operations are different from operations between two numbers. There are a few simple rules to remember. You can add or subtract vectors only with other vectors. Furthermore, the two vectors must have the same number of dimensions. Assuming the two vectors match, addition is easy. Simply add the individual components of one vector to the individual components of the other:

$$(X_1,Y_1,Z_1) + (X_2,Y_2,Z_2) = (X_1 + X_2, Y_1 + Y_2, Z_1 + Z_2)$$

This is easy to demonstrate graphically, using the "head-to-tail" rule, as shown in Figure 2.3.

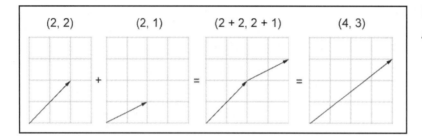

(2, 2)   (2, 1)   (2 + 2, 2 + 1)   (4, 3)

Figure 2.3

Adding two vectors.

Vector multiplication is the opposite. You can only perform simple multiplication between a vector and a scalar. This has the effect of lengthening or shortening a vector without changing its direction. In this case, the scalar is applied to each component:

$$(X,Y,Z)*A = (X*A,Y*A,Z*A)$$

This is shown in Figure 2.4. The multiplication operation scales the vector to a new length.

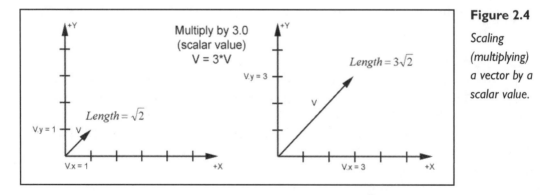

Figure 2.4

Scaling (multiplying) a vector by a scalar value.

Vector arithmetic can be useful, but it does have its limits. Vectors have interesting properties exposed by two operations that are unique to vectors, the dot product and the cross product.

Vector Dot Product

The dot product of two vectors produces a scalar value. You can use the dot product to find the angle between two vectors. This is useful in lighting calculations where you are trying to find out how closely the direction of the light matches the direction of the surface it's hitting. Figure 2.5 shows this in abstract. The two vectors point in different directions and I want to know how different those directions are. This is where the dot product is useful. Figure 2.5 will supply the parameters for the dot product equations below.

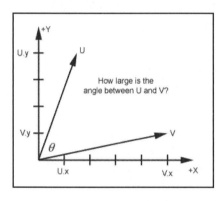

Figure 2.5

Two vectors in different directions.

There are two ways to compute the dot product. The first way involves using the components of the two vectors. Given two vectors, use the following formula:

$$U \bullet V = (X_u, Y_u, Z_u) \bullet (X_v, Y_v, Z_v) = (X_u * X_v) + (Y_u * Y_v) + (Z_u * Z_v)$$

The other method is useful if you know the magnitude of the two vectors and the angle between them:

$$U \bullet V = |U||V|\cos\theta$$

Therefore, the dot product is determined by the angle. As the angle between two vectors increases, the cosine of that angle decreases and so does the dot product. In most cases, the first formula is more useful because you'll have the vector components. However, it is useful to use both formulas together to find the angle between the two vectors. Equating the two formulas and solving for theta gives us the following formula:

$$\theta = \alpha\cos\left[\frac{(X_u * X_v) + (Y_u * Y_v) + (Z_u * Z_v)}{|U||V|}\right]$$

Figure 2.6 shows several examples of vectors and their dot products. As you can see, dot product values range from −1 to +1 depending on the relative directions of the two vectors.

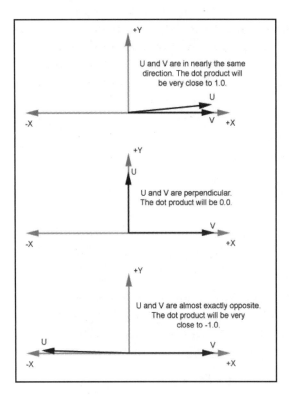

Figure 2.6

Vector combinations and their dot products.

Figure 2.6 shows that two vectors at right angles to each other have a dot product of 0. This can also be illustrated with the following equation.

U = (1,0)

V = (0,1)

U•V = (1*0) + (0*1) = 0

The dot product is one of the most useful and ubiquitous vector operations I use in this book. Finding the angles between vectors helps determine lighting, orientation, and many other 3D attributes. Also, many calculations are less concerned with the actual angle and are implemented more efficiently using the dot product itself. The dot product appears in nearly every technique in this book. It is an invaluable tool. But you're not done yet. There's one last useful vector operation.

Vector Cross Product

The cross product of two vectors is perhaps the most difficult to conceptualize. Computing the cross product of two vectors gives you a third vector that is perpendicular to both of the original vectors. To visualize this, imagine three points in space, as in Figure 2.7. Mathematically speaking, those three points define a plane for which there is only one perpendicular "up direction." Using those three points, you can get two vectors, V_{ab} and V_{ac}. The cross product of those two vectors is perpendicular to the two vectors and is therefore perpendicular to the plane.

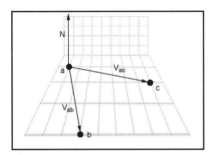

Figure 2.7

The cross product of two vectors.

Like the dot product, the cross product of two vectors can be computed in two different ways. The first way is the most useful because you will usually have the actual vector components (X, Y, Z):

$$U \times V = N = (X_n, Y_n, Z_n)$$

$$X_n = (Y_u * Z_v) - (Z_u * Y_v)$$
$$Y_n = (Z_u * X_v) - (X_u * Z_v)$$
$$Z_n = (X_u * Y_v) - (Y_u * X_v)$$

Figure 2.8 shows the simplest example of this equation. The two input vectors point straight along two of the three main axes. The resulting vector is pointing straight out of the page.

It is important to note here that the vector N is perpendicular to the two vectors, but it is not necessarily a unit vector. You might need to normalize N to obtain a unit vector. This is the easiest way to find the vector that is perpendicular to a surface, something very necessary in lighting and shading calculations. It is also important to note that the cross product is not commutative. Changing the order of operations changes the sign of the cross product:

$$U \times V = -(V \times U)$$

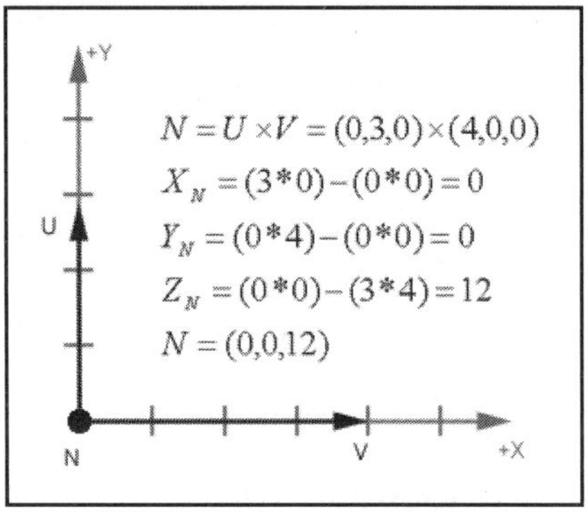

Figure 2.8

Computing a simple cross product.

The second method is useful if you already know the angle between the two vectors. You can also rearrange it so that you can solve for the angle if you know the cross product:

U×V = N*|U||V|sinθ

Remember that vectors can only be multiplied by scalar values. In the preceding formula, the normal vector N is multiplied by the magnitudes of the two vectors and the sine of the angle. If you combine the two formulas, you can solve for the angle between two vectors. This means that if you have two vectors and you want to figure out how to turn from one to the other, you can use the cross product to find the angle you need to turn and the axis you need to turn about. Now that I'm talking about angles, I'm really talking about rotation. The vectors I've been talking about so far describe positions and directions in space, but there is a different kind of vector you can use to describe rotations.

Quaternions

Mathematically, the theory behind quaternions can be quite complex. I mean that literally: Quaternions were originally developed to deal with complex numbers! The DirectX documentation describes quaternions as a four-dimensional vector describing an axis of rotation and the angle around that axis:

Q = (V,ω) = (X,Y,Z,ω)

Although that is an oversimplification in a mathematical sense, it is a good functional definition for your purposes. Using quaternions, you can specify an axis of rotation and the angle, as shown in Figure 2.9.

During an animation, quaternions make rotations much easier. Once you know the axis, you simply increment the angle ω with each frame. You can do several

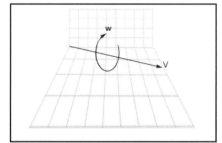

Figure 2.9

A quaternion in 3D.

mathematical operations on quaternions, and in later chapters I show some concrete examples of their usefulness. In fact, quaternions are conceptually one of the most difficult things to understand. The later chapter dealing with terrain will provide some insight into how you can effectively use quaternions. However, whether we're talking about simple vectors or quaternions, we can make our lives easier by using mathematical functions supplied in the D3DX libraries.

Vectors in D3DX

So far, I've been discussing vectors in purely mathematical terms. Although it's important to know how to do these things ourselves, we don't have to. D3DX contains many of these functions. Many people choose to recreate these functions, thinking that they can write a better cross-product function than the D3DX one. I urge you not to do this. The creators of D3DX have gone to great lengths not only to create tight code, but also to optimize that code for specialized instruction sets such as MMX and 3Dnow. It would be a lot of work to duplicate that effort.

In a few chapters, I talk more about actually using the D3DX functions in code, but for now, let's talk about the data structures and some of the functions while the theory is still fresh in your mind. To start, D3DX includes four different categories of vectors, shown in Table 2.1.

I do not list all the D3DX functions here, but Table 2.2 contains a few of the basic functions you can use to deal with vectors. Later chapters highlight specific functions, but most functions adhere to the same standard form. There are functions for each vector data type. Table 2.2 features the 3D functions, but the 2D and 4D functions are equivalent.

In general, D3DX function parameters are a pointer to the output result and pointers to the appropriate numbers of inputs. In addition to an output parameter, the functions also return the result in a return value, so functions can serve as

Table 2.1   D3DX Vector Data Types

Data Type	Comments
D3DXVECTOR2	A 2D vector (FLOAT X, FLOAT Y)
D3DXVECTOR3	A 3D vector (FLOAT X, FLOAT Y, FLOAT Z)
D3DXVECTOR4	A 4D vector (FLOAT X, FLOAT Y, FLOAT Z, FLOAT W)
D3DXQUATERNION	A 4D quaternion (FLOAT X, FLOAT Y, FLOAT Z, FLOAT w)

Table 2.2   D3DX Vector Functions

Function Name	Comments
D3DXVec3Add(D3DXVECTOR3* pOutput, D3DXVECTOR3* pVector1, D3DXVECTOR3* pVector2)	Adds two vectors
D3DXVec3Subtract(D3DXVECTOR3* pOutput, D3DXVECTOR3* pVector1, D3DXVECTOR3* pVector2)	Subtracts two vectors
D3DXVec3Cross(D3DXVECTOR3* pOutput, D3DXVECTOR3* pVector1, D3DXVECTOR3* pVector2)	Computes the cross product of two vectors
D3DXVec3Dot(D3DXVECTOR3* pOutput, D3DXVECTOR3* pVector1, D3DXVECTOR3* pVector2)	Computes the dot product of two vectors
D3DXVec3Length(D3DXVECTOR3 *pVector)	Computes the length of a vector and returns a FLOAT
D3DXVec3Normalize(D3DXVECTOR3* pOutput, D3DXVECTOR3* pVector)	Computes the normalized vector
D3DXQuaternionRotationAxis (D3DXQUATERNION*pOutput, D3DXVECTOR3* pAxis, FLOAT RotationAngle)	Creates a quaternion from an axis and angle (in radians)

parameters to other functions. Later, I explain how to use many of these functions. For now, just be assured that much of the work is done for you, and you do not need to worry about implementing your own math library.

In Conclusion...

Vectors form the basis of nearly everything you will do in the coming chapters. Many of the more advanced tricks are based heavily on vector math and understanding how vectors representing light rays, camera directions, and surface normals interact with each other. In later chapters, you will learn more about vectors, but the following points serve as a good foundation for what you will be doing:

- Vectors represent positions, orientations, and directions in multidimensional space.
- You can compute the magnitudes of vectors using the Pythagorean theorem.
- Vectors can be normalized into unit vectors describing their direction.
- You can add or subtract vectors by applying the operations to each component separately.
- Vectors can only be multiplied by scalar values.
- The vector dot product is a scalar value that describes how directionally similar two vectors are.
- The vector cross product is a normal vector that is perpendicular to both vectors.
- You can use the vector cross product to find the angle of rotation between two vectors.
- Quaternions can be used as compact representations of rotations in 3D space.
- The D3DX library contains the mathematical functions you need to do most forms of vector math.

CHAPTER 3

A Refresher Course in Matrices

You can't get far into 3D graphics before you run into matrices. In fact, most 3D APIs force you to use matrices to get anything on the screen at all. Matrices and matrix math can be confusing for the novice or casual programmer, so this chapter explains matrices in simple terms. You will look at some of the properties of matrices that make them ideal for 3D graphics and explain how they are used to affect 3D data. Once I explain all that, you will look at how D3DX comes to the rescue (again!) and shields the programmer from the intricacies of matrices. Although this chapter provides a brief abstract overview of matrices, the concepts might not truly sink in until you use them firsthand. If you are new to matrices, read this chapter, digest what you can, and then move on. Many of the concepts should become more understandable once you start using them in code in the later chapters.

What Is a Matrix?

Most people meet matrices for the first time in algebra class, where they are used as a tool for solving systems of linear equations. Matrices provide a way to boil a set of equations down to a compact set of numbers. You can then manipulate that set of numbers in special ways. For instance, here is a simple set of 3D equations and the matrix equivalent:

$$X^I = 2X + 4Y + 6Z$$
$$Y^I = 4X + 8Y + 12Z$$
$$Z^I = 8X + 16Y + 24Z$$

$$[X^I \, Y^I \, Z^I] = \begin{bmatrix} 2 & 4 & 6 \\ 4 & 8 & 12 \\ 8 & 16 & 24 \end{bmatrix} \begin{bmatrix} X \\ Y \\ Z \end{bmatrix}$$

The matrix in the above equation is useful because it allows you to store variables in a general and compact form. The following equations illustrate the general procedure for solving equations with matrices.

$$[X^I \, Y^I \, Z^I] = [X \, Y \, Z] \begin{bmatrix} M_{11} & M_{12} & M_{13} \\ M_{21} & M_{22} & M_{23} \\ M_{31} & M_{32} & M_{33} \end{bmatrix}$$

$$X^I = (X*M_{11}) + (Y*M_{21}) + (Z*M_{31})$$
$$Y^I = (X*M_{12}) + (Y*M_{22}) + (Z*M_{32})$$
$$Z^I = (X*M_{13}) + (Y*M_{23}) + (Z*M_{33})$$

Instead of dealing with arbitrary sets of arithmetic equations, we can develop software and, more importantly, hardware that is able to manipulate matrices quickly and efficiently. In fact, today's 3D hardware does just that! Although equations might be more readable to us mere mortals, the matrix representation is much easier for the computer to process.

NOTE

You may see other notations and representations for matrices in other sources. For example, many OpenGL texts describe a different matrix order. Both representations are correct in their own contexts. These matrices have been set up to match the DirectX notation.

The preceding sample shows how you can use matrices to perform multiplication. However, there are certainly cases where you will also want to perform addition. One way to do this is to perform matrix multiplication and addition separately. But ideally, you'd like to treat all operations in the same homogeneous manner. You can do this if you use the concept of *homogeneous coordinates*. Introduce a variable W that has no spatial properties. For the most part, W simply exists to make the math work out. So you can perform addition easily if you always set $W = 1$, as shown here:

$$W = 1$$
$$X^I = 3X + 5 = 3X + 5W$$

$$[X^I] = [3 \ 5] \begin{bmatrix} X \\ W \end{bmatrix} = [3 \ 5] \begin{bmatrix} X \\ 1 \end{bmatrix}$$

With the introduction of homogeneous coordinates, you can treat addition the same as multiplication, a property that's very useful in some transformations. In Chapter 9, I show practical examples of how the transformations are actually used. Until then, the following sections introduce you to the structure of 3D transformations such as the identity matrix and translation, rotation, and scaling matrices.

The Identity Matrix

The identity matrix is the simplest transformation matrix. In fact, it doesn't perform any transformations at all! It takes the form shown here. The product of any matrix M and the identity matrix is equal to the matrix M:

$$MI = M$$

$$I = \begin{bmatrix} 1 & 0 & 0 & 0 \\ 0 & 1 & 0 & 0 \\ 0 & 0 & 1 & 0 \\ 0 & 0 & 0 & 1 \end{bmatrix}$$

It is important to understand the structure of the identity matrix because it makes a good starting point for all other matrices. If you want to "clear" a matrix, or if you need a starting point for a custom-crafted matrix, the identity matrix is what you want. In fact, portions of the identity matrix are easy to see in the real transformation matrices next.

The Translation Matrix

Translation is a fancy way of saying that something is moving from one place to another. This is a simple additive process, and it takes the form shown here in equation and matrix form. Note the effect of the homogeneous coordinates:

$$X^I = X + a$$
$$Y^I = Y + b$$
$$Z^I = Z + c$$

$$[X^I \ Y^I \ Z^I \ 1] = \begin{bmatrix} 1 & 0 & 0 & a \\ 0 & 1 & 0 & b \\ 0 & 0 & 1 & c \\ 0 & 0 & 0 & 1 \end{bmatrix} \begin{bmatrix} X \\ Y \\ Z \\ 1 \end{bmatrix}$$

All translation matrices take this form (with different values in the fourth row).

The Scaling Matrix

The scaling matrix scales data by multiplying it by some factor:

$$X^| = X*a$$
$$Y^| = Y*b$$
$$Z^| = Z*c$$

$$[X^|\ Y^|\ Z^|\ |] = \begin{bmatrix} a & 0 & 0 & 0 \\ 0 & b & 0 & 0 \\ 0 & 0 & c & 0 \\ 0 & 0 & 0 & | \end{bmatrix} \begin{bmatrix} X \\ Y \\ Z \\ | \end{bmatrix}$$

Although scaling is purely multiplicative, you maintain the extra fourth dimension to make it compatible with the translation matrix. This is the advantage of the homogeneous coordinates. I talk about how to use matrices together after I explain the final transformation matrix.

The Rotation Matrix

The final type of transformation matrix is the rotation matrix. The complete rotation matrix contains the rotations about all three axes. However, to simplify the explanation, I show each rotation matrix separately, and the next section explains how they can be combined. The three rotation matrices follow:

$$\text{Rotation } \theta \text{ about the X axis} : R = \begin{bmatrix} | & 0 & 0 & 0 \\ 0 & \cos\theta & -\sin\theta & 0 \\ 0 & \sin\theta & \cos\theta & 0 \\ 0 & 0 & 0 & | \end{bmatrix}$$

$$\text{Rotation } \theta \text{ about the Y axis} : R = \begin{bmatrix} \cos\theta & 0 & -\sin\theta & 0 \\ 0 & | & 0 & 0 \\ -\sin\theta & 0 & \cos\theta & 0 \\ 0 & 0 & 0 & | \end{bmatrix}$$

$$\text{Rotation } \theta \text{ about the Z axis} : R = \begin{bmatrix} \cos\theta & -\sin\theta & 0 & 0 \\ \sin\theta & \cos\theta & 0 & 0 \\ 0 & 0 & | & 0 \\ 0 & 0 & 0 & | \end{bmatrix}$$

To demonstrate this, I have rotated a vector about the Z-axis, as shown in Figure 3.1. In the figure, a vector is rotated 90 degrees about the Z-axis. As you can see, this operation changes a vector pointing in the X direction to a vector pointing in the Y direction.

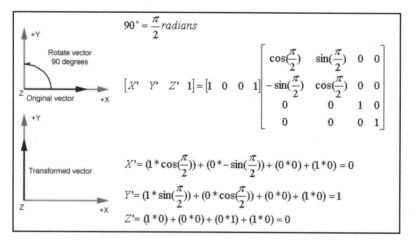

Figure 3.1

Rotating a vector with a matrix.

$$90° = \frac{\pi}{2} radians$$

$$[X' \quad Y' \quad Z' \quad 1] = [1 \quad 0 \quad 0 \quad 1] \begin{bmatrix} \cos(\frac{\pi}{2}) & \sin(\frac{\pi}{2}) & 0 & 0 \\ -\sin(\frac{\pi}{2}) & \cos(\frac{\pi}{2}) & 0 & 0 \\ 0 & 0 & 1 & 0 \\ 0 & 0 & 0 & 1 \end{bmatrix}$$

$$X' = (1 * \cos(\frac{\pi}{2})) + (0 * -\sin(\frac{\pi}{2})) + (0 * 0) + (1 * 0) = 0$$

$$Y' = (1 * \sin(\frac{\pi}{2})) + (0 * \cos(\frac{\pi}{2})) + (0 * 0) + (1 * 0) = 1$$

$$Z' = (1 * 0) + (0 * 0) + (0 * 1) + (1 * 0) = 0$$

Putting all these matrices together yields one big (and ugly) rotation matrix. To do this, you have to know how to concatenate multiple matrices.

Matrix Concatenation

To combine the effects of multiple matrices, you must concatenate the matrices together. This is another reason you deal with matrices. Once each equation is in matrix form, the matrix is simply a set of numbers that can be manipulated with matrix arithmetic. In this case, you concatenate the matrices by multiplying them together. The product of two or more matrices contains all the data necessary to apply all the transformations. One important thing to note is that the order in which the matrices are multiplied is critical. For instance, scaling and then translating is different from translating and then scaling. In the former, the scaling factor is not applied to the translation. In the latter, the translation distance is also scaled. In Chapter 9, the sample program demonstrates how you should apply transformations to move objects around in space. In matrix multiplication, the second matrix is the first operand. So if you want to translate with a matrix T and then scale with S, you use the following equation:

M = S*T

This is very important to remember: If you are ever transforming 3D objects and they are not behaving the way you are expecting, there is a good chance that you've made a mistake in the order of your matrix multiplication.

Matrices and D3DX

By now you've probably noticed that I have not gone into the actual mathematical methods for dealing with matrices. This is because D3DX contains most, if not all, of the functions you need to perform the matrix math. In addition to vector functions, D3DX contains functions that perform basic mathematical operations between matrices, as well as some higher-level functions that allow you to build new matrices based on vectors and quaternions. As with vectors, keep in mind that the D3DX functions are highly optimized, and there is probably no good reason for you to implement these functions yourself.

Before you look at the D3DX functions, it's important to understand the matrix data types shown in Table 3.1.

There are many D3DX matrix functions available. All the function names start with D3DXMatrix, and they are handled in similar ways. Rather than list every single matrix function, Table 3.2 is a representative sample of the most useful functions and functions that implement the ideas discussed earlier. I show more functions and their uses in later chapters, when I can explain them in context.

Table 3.1 D3DX Matrix Data Types

Data Type	Comments
D3DMATRIX	This is a 4×4 matrix. This structure contains 16 float values that are accessible by their row-column name. For instance, the value in the third row, second column would be _32.
D3DXMATRIX	This is the C++ version of D3DMATRIX. It features overloaded functions that allow us to more easily manipulate the matrices.

Table 3.2   D3DX Matrix Functions

Function	Comments
`D3DXMatrixIdentity(D3DXMATRIX* pOutput)`	Creates an identity matrix.
`D3DXMatrixTranslation(D3DXMATRIX* pOutput, FLOAT X, FLOAT Y, FLOAT Z)`	Creates a translation matrix.
`D3DXMatrixRotationX (D3DXMATRIX* pOutput, FLOAT Angle)` `D3DXMatrixRotationY (D3DXMATRIX* pOutput, FLOAT Angle)` `D3DXMatrixRotationZ (D3DXMATRIX* pOutput, FLOAT Angle)`	Creates a rotation matrix for axis rotations. Note that the `Angle` parameter should be in radians.
`D3DXMatrixScaling(D3DXMATRIX* pOutput, FLOAT XScale, FLOAT YScale, FLOAT ZScale)`	Creates a scaling matrix.
`D3DXMatrixMultiply(D3DXMATRIX* pOutput, D3DXMATRIX* pMatrix1, D3DXMATRIX* pMatrix2)`	Multiplies M1 * M2 and outputs the resulting matrix.

In addition to an output parameter, the output is also passed out of the function as a return value. This allows you to use functions as input to other functions. Because of the nature of many of these calls, the code can end up looking almost unreadable, so this book does not do it, but it is an option.

In Conclusion...

If this chapter has been your first exposure to matrices, I suspect you might still be a little unclear about how they are used. Starting in Part 3 and moving forward, everything you do will involve matrices in one way or another. When you get to the point of actually using matrices, I spend more time talking about the usage and the pitfalls. As you begin to actually use them, everything will become much clearer. In the meantime, here are a few simple points that are important to remember:

- Matrices are an efficient way to represent equations that affect the way you draw 3D data.

- Homogeneous coordinates allow you to encapsulate multiplicative operations and additive operations into the same matrix, rather than deal with two matrices.

- The identity matrix is an ideal starting point for building new matrices or "clearing out" old ones. Sometimes no effect is a good effect.
- The translation, scaling, and rotation matrices are the basis for all spatial transformations.
- You can combine the effects of multiple matrices by multiplying the individual matrices together, that is, concatenate them.
- In matrix multiplication, order matters!
- The D3DX libraries contain most of the useful functions needed for building and manipulating matrices.

CHAPTER 4

A Look at Colors and Lighting

V ectors and matrices determine the overall position and shape of a 3D object, but to really examine graphics, you need to take a look at color. Also, if your 3D world is going to be interesting and realistic-looking, I need to talk about lighting and shading. As with the previous chapters, this chapter provides a brief look at the abstract concepts of color and lighting. These topics are continually reinforced in the later chapters when you actually start writing code. If you don't fully understand some of the concepts here, don't worry. By the end of this book, you will understand more about the following topics than you ever wanted to know.

- Color.
- Ambient and emissive lighting.
- Diffuse lighting.
- Specular lighting.
- Attenuated lights.
- Lights in Direct3D.
- Shading types.

What Is Color?

That is a dangerous question. People with names like Newton and Einstein have written a lot about the nature of color itself. I'm not really qualified to critique their work. Instead, I spend a little time talking about colors from a computer-graphics perspective.

One of the first terms you encounter is "color space." Many different color spaces are mostly dependent on the output medium. For example, many printing processes use the CMYK (cyan, magenta, yellow, and black) color space because that's how the inks are mixed. Television and video use different variations of HSB (hue, saturation, and brightness) color spaces because of the different bandwidth requirements of the different channels. (Humans are much more sensitive to changes in brightness than to changes in color.) But you are dealing with computers, and except for specialized cases, computers use an RGB (red, green, blue) color space. Usually, the final color is eight bits per channel, yielding a total of $(2^8 * 2^8 * 2^8) = 16.7$ million colors.

Most cards offer 16-bit color modes, or even 8-bit color, but those colors are usually full RGB values before they are quantized for final output to the screen. All the samples in the book assume that you are running with 24-bit or 32-bit color. The reason is that many of the techniques rely on a higher number of bits to demonstrate the effects. Also, any card capable of running the techniques in this book will be capable of running in 32-bit, at least at lower screen resolutions. In cases where you really want to use 16 bits, try the technique first in 32-bit mode and then experiment with lower bit depths. In some cases, full 32-bit might be slightly faster because the card does not need to quantize down to a lower bit depth before the final output to the screen.

Conceptually, colors consist of different amounts of red, green, and blue. But there's one other channel that makes up the final 8 bits in a 32-bit color: the alpha channel. The alpha channel isn't really a color; it's the amount of transparency of that color, so it affects how the color blends with other colors already occupying a given pixel. For final output to the monitor, transparency doesn't really make sense, so typically people talk about RGBA during the processing of a color and RGB for the final output.

> **NOTE**
>
> Quantizing colors means confining a large range of colors to a smaller range of colors. This is usually done by creating a color palette that best approximates the colors that are actually used in the case of 32-bit colors on an 8-bit screen. Each 32-bit color is then mapped to the closest 8-bit approximation. This was quite an issue for several years, but most new cards are more than capable of displaying full 32-bit images.

For all four channels, a color depth of 32 bits means that each channel is represented by one byte with a value from 0 to 255. However, when calculating lighting, it is sometimes mathematically advantageous to think of the numbers as floating-point values ranging from 0.0 to 1.0. These values have more precision than bytes, so they are better for calculations. The floating-point values are mapped back down to the byte equivalent (0.5 becomes 128, for example) when they are rendered to the screen. For most of the color calculations in this book, assume I am using numbers in the range of 0.0 to 1.0 unless otherwise noted.

I can talk about the abstract notion of colors until I turn blue…. Let's talk about how they are actually used. All visible color is determined not only by object color, but also by lighting. For example, in a perfectly dark room, all objects appear black, regardless of the object color. In the next sections, I talk about how objects are lit and how that affects what the viewer sees. In the following examples, it is best to think of objects as made up of surfaces. Each surface has a normal vector, which is the vector perpendicular to the surface, as described in Chapter 1. When I talk about how objects are lit, I explain it in terms of how each surface on the object is lit. When I talk about lighting calculations, the final output surface color is denoted as C_F.

Ambient and Emissive Lighting

Imagine a room with one lamp on the ceiling shining down on the floor. The lamp lights the floor as expected, but some light also hits the walls, the ceiling, and any other objects in the room. This is because the rays of light strike the floor and bounce to the wall, the ceiling, and all around the room. This creates the effect that at least some of the light in the room is coming from all directions. This is why the ceiling is at least somewhat lit, even though the lamp is shining away from it. This type of lighting is called ambient lighting. The color contribution for ambient lighting is simply the product of the ambient color of the light and the ambient color of the object:

$$C_F = C_L C_A$$

That equation shows that if you set your ambient light to full white, your object will be full color. This can produce a washed-out and unreal appearance. Typically, 3D scenes have a small ambient component and rely on other lighting calculations to add depth and visual interest to the scene.

Emissive lighting is similar to ambient lighting except that it describes the amount of light emitted by the object itself. The color contribution for emissive lighting is simple:

$$C_F = C_E$$

The result is the same as if you had specified a certain amount of ambient lighting for that one object. The object shown in Figure 4.1 could either be a sphere under full ambient lighting in the scene or a sphere emitting white light with no lighting in the scene.

Figure 4.1

Ambient-lit sphere.

Although ambient lighting is a good start for lighting objects based on an overall amount of light in the scene, it doesn't produce any of the shading that adds visual cues and realism to the scene. You need lighting models that take into account the direction of the lighting.

Diffuse Lighting

Diffuse lighting models the type of lighting that occurs when rays of light strike an object and then are reflected in many different directions (thereby contributing to ambient lighting). This is ideal for dull or matte surfaces, where the surface has many variations that cause the light to scatter or diffuse when it hits the object. Because the light is reflected in all directions, the amount of lighting looks the same to all viewers, and the intensity of the light is a function of the angle between the light vector (L) and a given surface normal (N):

$$C_F = C_L C_D \cos\Theta$$

Many times, it might be easier to use the dot product than to compute the cosine. Because of the way the dot product is used, the light vector in this case is the vector from the surface to the light. If the surface normal and the light vector have been normalized, the dot product equivalent becomes the following:

$$C_F = C_L C_D (N \cdot L)$$

Figure 4.2 shows a graphical representation of the two equations.

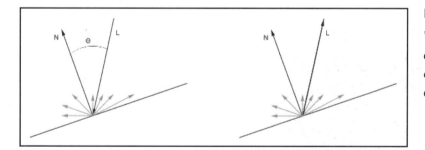

Figure 4.2

Vector diagrams for cosine and dot-product diffuse lighting equations.

Figure 4.3a shows the same sphere from Figure 4.1, only this time it is lit by an overhead light and no ambient lighting. Notice how the top of the sphere is brighter. This is because the rays from the overhead light and the surface normals on top of the sphere are nearly parallel. Only the top of the sphere is lit because the surface normals on the bottom face away from the light. Figure 4.3b shows the same scene, but with a small ambient lighting component.

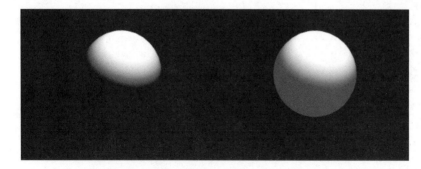

Figure 4.3

*Sphere
(a) with only diffuse
lighting and
(b) with diffuse and
ambient lighting.*

In real scenes, a couple of lights cause enough reflections to create ambient light, but in 3D graphics, lights are more idealized, so an added ambient component helps to mimic the effect of reflected ambient light. Adding a small ambient component is more efficient than adding more lights because it takes much less processing power.

Most of the shaded lighting in 3D graphics is based on diffuse lighting because most materials at least partially diffuse the light that strikes them. Diffuse lighting also supplies a relatively cheap way to calculate nice shading across an object's surface. The last important thing to remember about diffuse lighting is that because the light is evenly diffused, it appears the same for all viewers. However, real reflected light is not the same for all viewers, so you need a third lighting model.

Specular Lighting

Specular lighting models the fact that shiny surfaces reflect light in specific directions rather than diffused in all directions. Unlike diffuse lighting, specular lighting is dependent on the direction vector of the viewer (V). Specular highlights appear on surfaces where the vector of the reflected light (R) is directed toward the viewer. For different viewers, this set of surfaces might be different, so specular highlights appear in different places for different viewers. Also, the shininess of an object determines its specular power (P). Shinier objects have a higher specular power. The specular lighting equation takes the form of

$$C_F = C_L C_s (R \cdot V)^P$$
$$R = 2N(N \cdot L) - L$$

The reflection vector is computationally expensive and must be computed for every surface in the scene. It turns out that an approximation using a "halfway vector" can yield good results with fewer computations. The halfway vector is the vector that is halfway between the light vector and the view vector:

$$H = (L + V) / |L + V|$$

In addition to being easier to compute than R, it is computed less often. The halfway vector is computed only when the viewer moves or the light moves. You can use the halfway vector to approximate the specular reflection of every surface in the scene using the following revised specular equation:

$$C_F = C_L C_s (H \cdot N)^P$$

The rationale behind the halfway vector approximation is that the halfway vector represents the surface normal that would yield the most reflection to the viewer. Therefore, as the surface normal approaches the halfway vector, the amount of reflected light increases. This is the dot product in action! Figure 4.4 shows the graphical representation of the two equations.

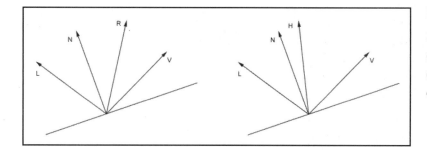

Figure 4.4

Specular lighting with (a) full method and (b) halfway vector approximation.

Figure 4.5 shows how specular highlights affect the scene. Figure 4.5a shows the diffusely lit sphere from 4.3b, 4.5b shows the same scene with added specular highlights, and 4.5c shows just the specular component of the scene.

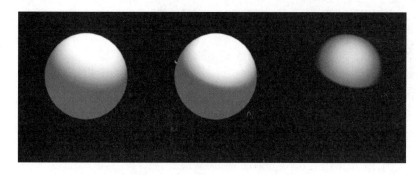

Figure 4.5

Specular lighting: (a) none, (b) added specular, (c) specular only.

Like the other lighting models, the output of the specular lighting calculations is dependent on the specular color of the object. For most objects, this is white, meaning that it reflects the color of the light as a shiny surface would. This will yield good results for most objects, although some materials may have colored specular reflections.

Other Light Types

So far, I mentioned only ambient lights and directional lights where light intensity is a function of the angle between the light and the surface. Some lights attenuate, or lose intensity, over distance. In the real world, all lights attenuate over distance, but it is sometimes convenient and computationally advantageous to ignore that. For instance, sunlight attenuates, but for most objects, their relative distance is so small compared with their distance from the sun that you can ignore the attenuation factor. For a flashlight or a torch in a dark cave, you should not ignore the attenuation factor. Consider the flashlight and torch two new types of lights. The torch can be modeled as a point light, which projects light in all directions and attenuates over distance. The flashlight can be modeled as a spot light, which projects light in a cone that attenuates over an angle. Spot light cones consist of two regions: the umbra, or inner cone where the light does not attenuate over the angle, and the penumbra, the outer ring where the light gradually falls off to zero. Figure 4.6a shows a scene lit with a point light. Notice the light intensity as a function of distance. Figure 4.6b shows the same scene lit with a spot light. The umbra is the central, fully lit region, and the penumbra is the region where the intensity falls to zero.

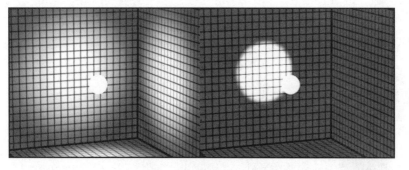

Figure 4.6

Attenuated lights.

The three types of lights I've discussed are enumerated in Direct3D as D3DLIGHTTYPE. When deciding which type to use, you balance the desired effect, the desired quality, and the computational cost. Directional lights are the easiest to compute but lack the subtleties of attenuated lighting. Point lights look a little bit better but cost a little more (and might not be the desired effect). Spot lights are the most realistic directional light but are computationally more expensive. I discuss these lights in depth in later chapters when I look at the implementation details.

Putting It All Together with Direct3D

Although I've described each lighting component separately, you usually use them together to obtain the complete look of the object, as shown in Figure 4.5b. The combined result of all three lighting models is the following equation:

$$C_F = C_E + C_{L(ambient)}C_A + \Sigma C_{L(directional)}(C_D(N \bullet L) + C_s(H \bullet N)^P)$$

This equation shows that the final output color of a given surface is the emissive color, plus the effects of ambient lighting, plus the sum of the effects of the directional lighting. Note that you could drop some components if there were no emissive color of if there were no ambient lighting in the scene. Also note that the computational cost of lighting increases as the number of lights increases. Careful placement and use of lights is important. There is also a limit to how many lights are directly supported by the hardware.

In later chapters, you will do most of your lighting in vertex shaders and pixel shaders because that will give you a lot of flexibility. However, it's important to spend a little time talking about the kinds of lights supported by the DirectX 8.0 API. In Direct3D, lights are defined by the D3DLIGHT8 structure described in Table 4.1.

I go into more detail about using the D3DLIGHT8 structure after you set up your rendering device in code. Because most of the lighting in later chapters will be implemented in your own shaders, the table provides a good reference for the types of parameters your shaders will need.

Shading Types

Earlier, I told you to think of an object as a set of surfaces, and throughout this chapter I've talked about how light and color affect a given surface. It's now time to take a look at how those individual surfaces come together to create a final shaded object. For all of the lighting calculations so far, I've described equations in terms of the surface normal because objects in computer graphics consist of a finite number of surfaces. When those surfaces are rendered together, a final object is constructed. Different types of shading determine how those surfaces appear

Table 4.1 Members of the D3DLIGHT8 Structure

Member	Data Type	Comments
Type	D3DLIGHTTYPE	Type of light used (directional, point, or spot).
Diffuse	D3DCOLORVALUE	The diffuse color emitted by the light, to be used in the lighting calculation.
Specular	D3DCOLORVALUE	The specular color emitted by the light, to be used in the lighting calculation.
Ambient	D3DCOLORVALUE	The ambient color emitted by the light, to be used in the lighting calculation.
Position	D3DVECTOR	The position of the light in space. This member is ignored if the light type is directional.
Direction	D3DVECTOR	The direction the light is pointing. This member is not used for point lights and should be nonzero for spot and directional lights.
Range	FLOAT	This is the maximum effective range for this light and is not used for directional lights. Because of the usage, this value should not exceed the square root of the maximum value of a FLOAT.
Falloff	FLOAT	This member shapes the falloff of light within the penumbra. A higher value creates a more rapid exponential falloff. A value of 1.0 creates a linear falloff and is less computationally expensive.
Attenuation0, Attenuation1, Attenuation2	FLOAT	The three attenuation members are used as inputs to a function that shapes the attenuation curve over distance. The function is $A_{total} = 1 / (A_0 + A_1 D + A_2 D^2)$. You can use this to determine how the light attenuates through space. Typically, A_0 and A_2 are zero and A_1 is some constant value.
Theta	FLOAT	Angle (in radians) of the umbra of a spot light. This must not exceed the value of Phi.
Phi	FLOAT	Angle (in radians) of the penumbra.

together. Direct3D has two usable shading modes, which are enumerated in D3DSHADEMODE. The two modes are D3DSHADE_FLAT and D3DSHADE_GOURAUD.

Flat shading, shown in Figure 4.7, is the simplest type of shading. Each surface is lit individually using its own normal vector. This creates a rough, faceted appearance that, although useful for disco balls, is unrealistic for most fashionable objects.

Figure 4.7

Sphere with flat shading.

This shading method does not take into effect that individual surfaces are actually parts of a larger object. Smooth shading types, such as Gouraud shading, take into account the continuity of a surface.

Most 3D implementations use Gouraud shading because it gives good results for minimal computational overhead. When setting up surface data for use with Gouraud shading, you assign normals on a per-vertex basis rather than a per-surface basis. The normal for each vertex is the average of the surface normals for all surfaces that use that vertex. Then, as each surface is rendered, lighting values are computed for each vertex and then interpolated over the surface. The results are the smoothly shaded objects shown in previous figures.

Gouraud shading is not the only method of smooth shading, but it is one of the easiest. In later chapters, I describe more shading methods and provide the implementation details.

In Conclusion...

In this chapter, you've taken a look at the basic ideas of color and light and how to use them to create 3D objects. These are only the most basic concepts, and later chapters delve into the actual code and implementation details of everything described here. I also describe many other types of lighting and shading, ranging from more realistic depictions of actual materials to nonrealistic cartoons. As with the other chapters in this section, these ideas are continually revisited and reinforced as the chapters go on. In the meantime, you should remember the following concepts:

- All chapters deal with 32-bit color, although the device can handle displaying lower bit depths if necessary.
- For calculations, all colors are normalized to the range of 0.0 to 1.0 unless otherwise noted.
- You can use ambient lighting in moderation to add an overall light level to the scene.
- You can use diffuse lighting to shade most materials.
- You use specular lighting for shiny materials.
- Directional lights only use angles to calculate lighting and do not attenuate.
- Point lights radiate light in all directions and attenuate over distance.
- Spot lights emit light in a cone and attenuate over both distance and angle (within the penumbra) and are computationally expensive.
- The `D3DLIGHT8` structure encapsulates many of the parameters needed for the lighting equation.
- Gouraud shading uses averaged surface normals and interpolated lighting values to produce smoothly shaded objects.

CHAPTER 5

A Look at the Graphics Pipeline

Back in the days of DOOM and Quake, almost all the steps in 3D rendering were performed by the CPU. It wasn't until the final step that pixels were actually manipulated on the video card to produce a frame of the game. Now, current hardware does almost all the rendering steps in hardware, freeing up the CPU for other tasks such as game logic and artificial intelligence. Through the years, the hardware support for the pipeline has both deepened and widened. The first 3D chips that came onto the market shortly after Quake supported the rasterization and then the texturing. Later, chips added hardware support for transformation and lighting. Starting with the geForce3, hardware functionality began to widen, adding support for vertex shaders and pixel shaders, as well as support for higher-order surfaces such as ATI's TRUFORM.

Throughout this book, the chapters stress various performance pitfalls and considerations for each of those steps. To fully understand the best way to deal with the hardware, you need to understand what the hardware is doing. This chapter will introduce the following concepts.

- The Direct3D rendering pipeline.
- Vertex data and higher-order surfaces.
- Fixed-function transform and lighting.
- Vertex shaders.
- The clipping stage.
- Multitexturing and pixel shaders for texture blending.
- The fog stage.
- Per pixel depth, alpha, and stencil tests.
- Output on the frame buffer.
- Performance considerations.

The Direct3D Pipeline

Figure 5.1 shows the different steps in the 3D pipeline.

Before 3D data moves through the pipeline, it starts in the system memory and CPU, where it is defined and (in good practice) sent to either AGP (Accelerated Graphics Port) memory or memory on the video card. Once the processing actually starts, either it is sent down the fixed transformation and lighting pipeline or it is routed through a programmable vertex shader. The output of both of these paths

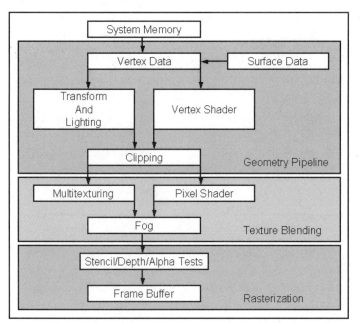

Figure 5.1

The Direct3D rendering pipeline.

leads into the clipping stage, where geometry that is not visible is discarded to save processing power by not rendering it.

Once the vertices are transformed, they move to the blending stage. Here they either move through the standard multitexturing pipeline or move through the newly supported pixel shaders. Fog (if any) is added after these stages.

Finally, the data is ready to be drawn onto the screen. Here, each fragment (usually a pixel) is tested to see whether the new data should be drawn over the old data, blended with the old data, or discarded. Once that's decided, the data becomes part of the frame buffer, which is eventually pushed to the screen.

That was a whirlwind tour of the pipeline; now I break down each section into detail.

Vertex Data and Higher-Order Surfaces

Vertices are the basic geometric unit, as I discuss in exhausting detail in later chapters. Each 3D object consists of one or more vertices. Sometimes these vertices are loaded from a file (such as a character model); other times they are generated mathematically (such as a sphere). Either way, they are usually created by some process on the CPU and placed into memory that is easily accessible to the video card.

The exception to this is the use of various forms of higher-order surfaces such as N patches in DirectX 8.0 or TRUFORM meshes on ATI hardware. These surfaces behave differently in that the hardware uses the properties of a rough mesh to produce a smoother one by creating new vertices on the hardware. These vertices do not have to be moved across the bus, enabling developers to use smoother meshes without necessarily decreasing performance. I discuss higher-order meshes in a later chapter when I go over exactly how to create them, but it's important to realize they are really the only mechanism for creating geometry in the hardware.

> ### Higher-order Surfaces
>
> A higher-order surface is a surface that is defined with mathematical functions rather than individual data points. If they are supported by the hardware, they allow the video card to create vertices on the card rather than on the CPU. This can streamline the process of moving geometry around the system. They can also be used to smooth lower resolution models. Chapter 21, "Bezier Patches," demonstrates a technique for manipulating your own higher-order surface with a vertex shader.

The Fixed-Function Transform and Lighting Stage

By now I've spent a lot of time talking about the matrices used for transformations and the mathematics of lighting. Before the advent of hardware transformation and lighting (T&L), all of that math was done on the CPU. This meant that the CPU had to juggle AI, game logic, and much of the grunt work of rendering. Hardware T&L moved the math to the card, freeing up the CPU. The purpose of the T&L stage is to apply all the matrix operations to each vertex. Once the vertex is transformed, the card can calculate the lighting with any hardware lights defined by calls to the API. This is one of the reasons that there is a limit on the number of hardware lights. This stage of the pipeline must manage them all correctly. A new alternative to the fixed-function pipeline is the idea of a hardware-supported vertex shader.

Vertex Shaders

Even though I don't look at vertex shaders in depth for several more chapters, I can't talk about the pipeline without talking about this new innovation. Vertex shaders add an incredible amount of flexibility to the pipeline. Before vertex shaders, hardware T&L could handle transforming the data according to the standard transformations, but it couldn't handle arbitrarily changing vertex data in hardware. Therefore, animations, such as moving characters with bulging muscles, had to have the geometry manipulated on the CPU and then moved to the card. Doing this for each frame of a game can be very costly. Vertex shaders allow the developer to write short programs that run and manipulate data on the hardware.

In a way, the name "shader" can be confusing. Vertex shaders can shade geometry in the lighting sense by calculating the lighting equations per vertex, but they can also manipulate all the vertex data. You can use this manipulation for everything from geometric manipulation to setting new texture coordinates. The power of a shader goes far beyond the lighting definition of shading. Figure 5.2 shows a shader that manipulates the actual geometry of an object.

Depending on the complexity of the shader, animations might still have an associated performance cost, but this is usually lessened by the fact that data does not have to move across the bus.

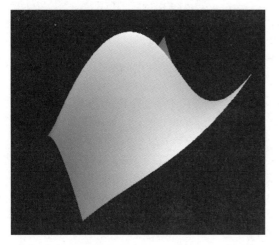

Figure 5.2

A sample vertex shader.

This raises another point. Theoretically, a very fast CPU may be able to transform vertices faster than the video card. However, it is becoming apparent that a lot of performance cost is incurred from moving data to and from the card. Unless you have the combination of a very fast CPU and an old video card, it's best to maximize the amount of processing done on the graphics card.

It's important to note that, unlike higher-order surfaces, vertex shaders cannot create or destroy vertices. Part of the reason for this is that vertex shaders were written to be capable of running in parallel. The ability to create or destroy vertices would create interdependencies between vertices, which would violate this constraint.

Also important to note is that if you use vertex shaders, they replace the fixed-function pipeline. Therefore, you must implement all lighting, transformation, and so on in the shader if your application still needs those features. For instance, if you write a shader to warp geometry, but still want diffuse lighting, you must add the diffuse-lighting calculation to the vertex shader. I explain this more when you actually start working with shaders.

The Clipper

After the vertex is transformed in either the fixed-function pipeline or a vertex shader, it is passed along to the clipper. Here the hardware makes decisions about what geometry should be carried onto the next stages. For instance, if after transformation a piece of geometry is behind the camera, there's no reason to continue processing it. You can throw away anything the viewer cannot see. This is one way a shader could destroy vertices: The vertices could be transformed in such a way to move them behind the camera. This step allows the hardware to pare away useless geometry before making the relatively costly step of texturing.

Multitexturing

The texturing stage is where geometry can move beyond the boredom of simple lit triangles to be covered with exciting textures—assuming, of course, that the developer wants it that way. In this stage, the number of textures you can apply in a single pass is a function of how many texture pipelines the chip supports. For instance, on geForce3 class cards, the developer can specify up to four different textures to use when texturing a piece of geometry. That number will only increase as the hardware gets better.

Multitexturing is important in creating realistic scenes. One of the more common uses of multitexturing is lightmapping. This technique involves using one or more textures to define the overall look of a given object and another set of textures to map different lighting effects on the object. If used effectively, this technique can create high-quality lighting effects with precomputed lighting textures. I discuss multitexturing and the associated API calls in depth in later chapters.

Pixel Shaders

Pixel shaders, like vertex shaders, are a new feature in 3D hardware. Whereas vertex shaders create the opportunity for more flexibility with geometry, pixel shaders allow for more flexibility with pixels. This flexibility allows for interesting effects in the way that individual pixels or texels (texture elements) are selected, blended, or rendered. You can use pixel shaders to perform per-pixel lighting on simple geometry, as shown in Figure 5.3.

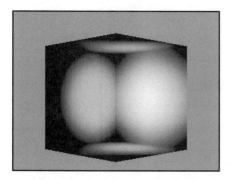

Figure 5.3

A sample pixel shader.

You can also use them to retrieve values from complex functions encoded into textures, thereby creating the look and feel of materials such as cloth and hair. I go into many more pixel-shader examples throughout the coming chapters, ranging from per-pixel lighting to image processing.

Fog

The final step in determining what a given pixel element looks like is fog. Fog can be based on distance, elevation, or anything else if you are using a vertex shader. Fogging geometry over distance can help provide depth cues to players looking into a scene. Fogging based on elevation can help produce misty bogs or cloudy mountains. In many cases, fog is used to hide the limit to how far the player can see. After a certain distance, items become foggy until they eventually fade away entirely. Once they go beyond the viewing range, the clipper can remove them entirely. Adding fog to a scene ensures that objects don't just disappear at a certain distance.

Depth, Stencil, and Alpha Tests

Each of these tests deserves a full chapter to adequately explain their power. In later chapters, I discuss these tests in depth when I have more context for them. From a pipeline perspective, these tests represent the final gauntlet a pixel must run before it gets to the screen or is thrown away. You can enable or disable each of these tests, which involves comparing a given pixel against the current contents of the frame buffer. The depth test looks at the depth of the new pixel and checks whether it is closer to the viewer than the current pixel in that place. If it is, it replaces the pixel. If not, it goes the way of the Dodo. The stencil test is a binary operation. The developer can define test parameters and data in the stencil buffer. If the new pixel doesn't pass the test, the current pixel is not changed. This is shown in Chapter 39 in Figure 39.2. Alpha tests are more flexible. In its most common usage, the alpha test defines how the new pixel blends with the old pixel to create effects such as semitransparent geometry. However, you can set the alpha blending options in many different ways to create other effects. Later chapters provide more in-depth explanations of each of these tests.

The Frame Buffer

Every pixel's goal and every vertex's dream comes down to the frame buffer. Typically, this is a back buffer, which sits in video memory waiting to be pushed to the front buffer and therefore to the screen. After every object in the scene is rendered, all the pixels are processed, and all the tests are passed, the code makes one function call to flip the buffers and happiness fills the screen (in most cases).

Sometimes the frame buffer does not get sent directly to the monitor at all. Another powerful technique is to render everything to a texture, which you can then use on a piece of geometry. One simple example is a mirror. The program can render the scene once from the viewpoint of the mirror using a texture as the render target instead of the frame buffer. Then, without showing that rendering on the screen, the program can swap the texture out of being the render target and render the scene from the viewer's viewpoint, texturing the mirror with the previously created texture. You can create many effects this way, but I'm getting ahead of myself.

Performance Considerations

One of the points of knowing all this background is to understand that the pipeline is full of bottlenecks waiting to happen. A chain is only as strong as its weakest link, and every stage in the pipeline is a potential weak link. Looking back, before 3D cards, video cards were mostly measured by their fill rate. Fill rate is basically the measure of how fast the card can paint pixels on the screen. When cards were slower than the CPU feeding them, applications were "fill rate limited." When fast 2D cards became available, the CPUs could not process the geometry fast enough, and the applications could be "geometry limited." Here are a couple things to watch out for:

- Be aware of how often you are manipulating data on the CPU. It doesn't matter how fast your CPU or GPU is if the path between them is slow to traverse. The system bus is very slow compared to the data paths through the card itself.

- Be aware of how much geometry is actually being pumped through the geometry pipeline, including geometry that you don't necessarily see. Because of clipping, you might see only a little simple geometry on the screen, but there might be a lot running through your shader.

- Be aware of your texture size. Cards are increasingly limited by their ability to move textures from memory to the screen. The processors are fast enough that the speed of the memory is actually the bottleneck! Don't use enormous textures if you don't have to.

- Be aware of what your texture blending is doing. Make sure you're not doing more than you have to.

- Be aware of which tests you have enabled. If you don't need the depth test, make sure it is disabled.

I go into these and many other performance considerations in the following chapters. The performance point to remember here is that you need to keep in mind each phase of the pipeline has its own performance characteristics and considerations. If your card says that it can render 100 million polygons, but you are only getting 10 million, you may be limited by something you're doing with textures. Knowing how the pipeline works and how hard your application hits each part will help you sort out performance problems.

In Conclusion...

Like the other chapters in this part, this chapter should provide a basis for understanding the later chapters. Understanding the pipeline will provide a basis for working with performance issues and efficiency issues that can arise with some of the more complex techniques. Many of the concepts in this chapter have been vague, pending in-depth explanations in later chapters. You can't fully explore the pipeline until you begin writing code that uses it! However, once you do get into the code, I continually refer to many of the points in this chapter. The actual code begins next chapter, but first, let's recap with some points to remember:

- Geometry data can be generated on the CPU and passed to the card or created on the card with higher-order surfaces.

- Fixed-function hardware T&L provides all the basic transform and lighting capabilities.

- Vertex shaders provide more flexibility with geometry manipulation than the fixed-function pipeline. However, once you use vertex shaders, you must implement all required features in the shader.

- You can use multitexturing to blend textures for many effects. However, you should consider hardware limitations when you need many textures.

- Pixel shaders provide more flexibility for manipulating pixels and texels.

- You can use fog to give the viewer depth cues and also hide the effects of the clipper.

- The depth, stencil, and alpha tests conspire to determine whether a given pixel gets to the monitor.

- Consider the pipeline a chain with several potential weak links. Knowing how your application affects each link will create a better understanding of how to effectively use the available hardware.

Part Two

Building the Sandbox

Okay, enough of the theory, it's time to write some code! Before you get started with actual graphics techniques, this section has a couple of chapters that implement the framework that will be the "sandbox" you'll play in. You have many excellent resources for frameworks using the DirectX API, including books, online resources, and an excellent framework in the DirectX SDK itself. These chapters outline the basics of a DirectX graphics framework and explain the theory behind the SDK framework.

Here's a breakdown of the chapters in this section:

- Chapter 6, "Setting Up the Environment and Simple Win32 App," is aimed at users who have little experience with the DirectX SDK. You will take a look at the SDK itself, set up the environment with the correct paths, and develop a simple Win32 application.

- Chapter 7, "Creating and Managing the Direct3D Device," builds on the previous one, introducing the Direct3D device that is the heart of your framework. I talk about how to create the device, use it, and destroy it. You will also extend your framework to let you easily plug in new features in later chapters.

CHAPTER 6

SETTING UP THE ENVIRONMENT AND SIMPLE WIN32 APP

If you already have experience working with the DirectX SDK, much of this chapter might be old news to you. However, it's best to be familiar with this chapter because much of the setup here carries over to all the chapters. This chapter assumes that you already have the DirectX SDK in your possession. I will introduce a simple application framework based on the following concepts:

- Dealing with the DirectX SDK.
- Setting up a build environment.
- Building a simple Win32 application.
- Compiling and running the application.

A Look at the SDK

The first thing you'll need to do is install the SDK. I deal with many SDKs, so I have a directory called c:\SDKs where I install all my SDKs. Therefore, the path for my SDK is c:\SDKs\DX8SDK. However, I'm in no position to tell you how to use your hard drive, so install it anywhere you want. Please keep in mind that if you downloaded the SDK, you might need to first unzip it and then install it. Also, for your purposes, I am only talking about the VC++ part of the SDK. If you installed other parts, such as the Visual Basic samples, your paths might be slightly different. In any case, I simply refer to the installed path as the SDK path, wherever yours may be.

After you've installed the SDK, you have the following file structure:

\bin	This folder contains precompiled binaries and tools.
\DXUtils	The most useful ones are the DXCapsViewer, which shows device capabilities, and DXTex, a texture tool that you can use to create textures in the .dds format.
\Xfiles	This folder contains the tools you'll use to convert from common 3D file formats to the .X file format used by DirectX Graphics.
\Doc	This folder contains the SDK documentation. This is an extremely valuable resource.
\DirectX8	The most useful file here is the precompiled help file for the SDK itself. Some books explain the API by simply rehashing the documentation. I've tried to give alternative explanations, so read the documentation for another viewpoint.

\DirectXEULAs	This folder includes the end user license agreements. It's probably a good idea to read and understand these documents because they might affect how you distribute your work.
\Include	This folder contains all the header files needed to compile the basic SDK examples. In the next section, I talk about how to set up your development environment to use this directory.
\Lib	These are all of the library files for DirectX. You will link with some of these when you compile. Each sample source file will include a list of the files that must be linked in by the compiler.
\Samples\Multimedia	This directory contains the sample code included with the SDK. These samples are valuable in understanding the basics of using DirectX. For your purposes, you'll be using only two of the subfolders.
\Common	This directory includes subdirectories for the header files and source files needed to use the application framework developed by the DirectX team. This framework is useful, but this book implements an alternative simple framework to better demonstrate the concepts. As you become more familiar with the concepts, you might want to look at the more advanced framework to see the added functionality. In practice, you will probably develop your own framework that best suits your particular needs.
\Direct3D	This directory contains the source code for all the Direct3D sample applications. Although this book does not discuss those samples specifically, many of the concepts are similar. These samples are an excellent resource to see how someone else did something.

Although I do not really discuss the SDK samples or framework specifically, it's worthwhile to explore the SDK and get to know the resources available to you. Frequently, people ask questions that are readily answered by the SDK. The SDK is one of the best resources available to you, so getting to know your way around it is important.

Setting Up the Environment

Once the SDK is installed, it's time to set up your development. I will explain how to get things started in Visual C++ 6.0. If you use a different IDE, follow its instructions for modifying include and library paths. We are essentially setting up the paths that the IDE uses to find files.

Open VC++, go to Tools, Options, and click on the Directories tab. Here you can choose which directories are being set. You'll start with the directories for the Include Files. Figure 6.1 shows the dialog. Add the following directory to your include path setting:

```
[Your SDK path]\Include
```

`[Your SDK path]` is the path in which you put the SDK. This will add the Include directory to the paths the compiler searches. If you plan to use the "common" framework, you could also add the following:

```
[Your SDK path]\Multimedia\Common\Include
```

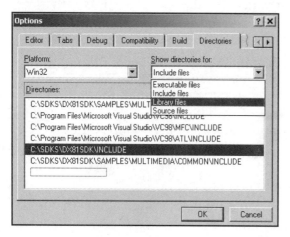

Figure 6.1

The Options dialog box for include files.

Now, select Library Files from the Show Directories For drop-down box. Here you will add the paths for the library files. Add the SDK path:

```
[Your SDK path]\Lib
```

After you set all your paths, you are ready to start coding!

A Simple Win32 Application

You're finally about to write some code. In the following code and throughout the book, the samples are in C++. This is to make full use of some of the features of D3DX as well as provide some simple encapsulation. If you are not a C++ expert, there is no need to panic. The chief focus of this book is to teach graphical concepts, not proper object-oriented programming practice. For this reason, the samples in the book are designed for readability, ease of understanding, and, in some cases, optimization from a graphics point of view. My goal is to teach the concepts and allow you to design your own real "engine" using an architecture that best suits your needs.

As mentioned earlier, the SDK contains an excellent application framework. You are building your own mostly as a learning exercise. Although the SDK framework is good, it is sometimes a little too complex for beginners. Building your own lets you have complete control over all the code. If you already have a framework and you are comfortable with DirectX, you can probably incorporate the later chapters into your own code. However, all of the samples assume this simple framework.

Because you are writing in DirectX, you are writing in Windows. All the code in this book runs on any version of Windows supporting DirectX 8.0 or higher (W9X, NT4, W2K, WinXP). Unless specifically stated, "Windows" refers to any version of Windows you're comfortable with. Almost all Windows applications consist of three basic steps: window creation, event and message handling, and window destruction. This all begins when the operating system calls a function called WinMain. The framework has a simple file that contains WinMain. When the OS calls WinMain, it creates an application object that will handle all the real functioning of the window and, eventually, the rendering. The following sections discuss the files used in the simple application. These files are located on the CD in a directory called \Code\Chapter6.

Checking Out Executable.h

Executable.h is the header file that contains the prototypes for the functions used by the OS to communicate with the application. Take a look at the important parts.

The following header file contains the definitions of all the basic windows types. It is included with most Windows applications and you also need it here:

```
#include <windows.h>
```

The following function is called by the OS to start the application. You will use it to create an application object that will handle window creation and rendering:

```
INT WINAPI WinMain(HINSTANCE hInst, HINSTANCE, LPSTR, INT);
```

The OS calls this function every time there is a message to send to the application. Messages are the mechanism for communicating events, such as mouse clicks, window resizing, or window closing.

```
LRESULT WINAPI EntryMessageHandler(HWND hWnd, UINT Message,
                WPARAM wParam, LPARAM lParam);
```

Executable.h is simple but very important because it defines the code called by the OS. In your simple framework, you are going to create a class that handles all the actual application processing. For right now, this will be a simple wrapper, but you will extend it in a later chapter.

Checking Out Application.h

Application.h contains the class definition for your simple application class. In this chapter, I'm more concerned about the basics of setting up a Windows application, so I don't talk about rendering code until the next chapter. For now, here is the simple definition from Application.h:

Again, include windows.h for the definitions of some basic Windows data types:

```
#include <windows.h>
class CHostApplication
{
```

The next two functions are the constructor and destructor. They are called when an object is first created and later when it is finally destroyed. This is typically where any initialization or cleanup occurs:

```
public:
    CHostApplication();
    virtual ~CHostApplication();
```

The following function is the same as the message handler defined in Executable.h. In fact, as the next sections show, EntryMessageHandler simply calls MessageHandler to allow the application class to decide how messages are handled:

```
    LRESULT WINAPI MessageHandler(HWND hWnd, UINT msg, WPARAM wParam,
                LPARAM lParam);
```

This function starts the actual processing:

```
void Go();
```

This is the handle to the application window. When the window is created, this is the identifier the application uses whenever it needs to change the windows or refer to it for any reason. These last three variables are marked as protected to protect them from possible misuse by other code. Only this class or subclasses of this class can directly modify them:

```
protected:
    HWND m_hWnd;
```

These are the basic window size parameters. You can modify them to change the default window size for an application.

```
    long m_WindowWidth;
    long m_WindowHeight;
};
```

This defines your application class. This class will be the basis for your applications in the coming chapters. In the next chapter, I expand the class definition a little to accommodate the actual Direct3D device, and later chapters extend the class to handle the specific needs of each technique. To see how the class is actually used, read on.

Checking Out Executable.cpp

Executable.cpp contains the actual code for WinMain and the message handler. Its primary use is to create an instance of the application object. Here is a breakdown of the code:

Include the header file I discussed earlier. This also means that all the definitions from windows.h are included:

```
#include "executable.h"
```

This adds the class definition, which is needed so that you can create the object. Note that as you extend the application class for each chapter, you will include the extended classes header here:

```
#include "application.h"
```

You also create a static global pointer to an application object. In general, it's considered bad practice to create global variables. However, this variable must be accessible to `WinMain` and `EntryMessageHandler`, so in this case, it's a reasonable exception. Note that the specific type of this pointer changes in later chapters:

```
static CHostApplication *g_pHostApplication = NULL;
```

When `WinMain` is called, it simply creates a new instance of the application object and calls the `Go` function to tell the application to actually start processing. This function does not return until the application is ready to quit. Therefore, when you return from this call, it's time to end the program:

```
INT WINAPI WinMain(HINSTANCE hInst, HINSTANCE, LPSTR, INT)
{
    g_pHostApplication = new CHostApplication();
    g_pHostApplication->Go();
```

This deletes the application object and frees up any memory associated with it. This also calls the destructor, which cleans up any internal data:

```
    delete (g_pHostApplication);
```

Finally, when you're done processing and everything is cleaned up, you exit the function, ending the program:

```
    return 0;
}
```

The following is the message-handler function that the operating system calls when it wants to pass a message to the application. This function passes the message along and lets the application object do the actual processing. The results are then returned back to the OS. In general, it's bad practice to use a pointer without checking first to see whether it's valid. However, as you have things set up, the object will always be created before messages are sent, and the application exits after the pointer is deleted, so you're probably okay. But in general, using pointers blindly could get you into trouble.

```
LRESULT WINAPI EntryMessageHandler(HWND hWnd, UINT Message,
                WPARAM wParam, LPARAM lParam)
{
    return g_pHostApplication->MessageHandler(hWnd, Message,
                wParam, lParam);
}
```

As you can see, the code in Executable.cpp is just a pass through to the application object. So let's look at Application.cpp for the final piece of the puzzle.

Checking Out Application.cpp

The following code shows how to create a basic windowed application. Currently, the application only has the most basic functionality; later you will add code to add Direct3D functionality.

Include the header files. You include Application.h because it defines the contents of this file. You include Executable.h because the application needs to know the name of `EntryMessageHandler` when it creates the window:

```
#include "Executable.h"
#include "Application.h"
```

The constructor is simple. It initializes the default size of the window. Child classes can reset these values in their constructors to override the default values:

```
CHostApplication::CHostApplication()
{
    m_WindowWidth = 640;
    m_WindowHeight = 480;
}
```

The `Go` function is where the magic unfolds. Here, the window is created, and messages are pumped through the application. When the application receives a message to quit, the function returns and everything ends:

```
void CHostApplication::Go()
{
```

The operating system uses this structure to define the type of Windows application you want to create. Note that the "class" here is different from the object-oriented definition of class. For your purposes, most of these parameters are not useful (hence the many `NULL` parameters). It is important to point out that `EntryMessageHandler` is your globally defined message handler. Adding it to the window class tells the OS what function to call to handle messages. Once this class is registered, you use it to create your window:

```
    WNDCLASSEX WindowClass = {sizeof(WNDCLASSEX), CS_CLASSDC,
                EntryMessageHandler, 0, 0,
                GetModuleHandle(NULL), NULL, NULL, NULL,
                NULL, "Host Application", NULL};
    RegisterClassEx(&WindowClass);
```

Here, you create the window. Among other things, you pass the name of your recently created window class and your default width and height. If everything goes well, you are rewarded with a window handle:

```
m_hWnd = CreateWindow("Host Application", "Host Application",
            WS_OVERLAPPEDWINDOW, 0, 0, m_WindowWidth,
            m_WindowHeight, GetDesktopWindow(), NULL,
            WindowClass.hInstance, NULL);
```

If you have successfully created the window, make it visible. If for some reason the window was not created, there is no point in going on. You might as well quit now:

```
if(m_hWnd)
    ShowWindow(m_hWnd, SW_SHOW);
else
    return;
```

This is commonly referred to as a message pump. The `while` loop continues to pull messages from the message queue until a quit message is received. The message pump ensures that messages continue to move through the system with your handler processing the messages. When the pump receives a message to quit, the `while` loop ends and the function returns:

```
MSG Message;
PeekMessage(&Message, 0, 0, 0, PM_REMOVE);
while (Message.message != WM_QUIT)
{
    TranslateMessage(&Message);
    DispatchMessage(&Message);
    PeekMessage(&Message, 0, 0, 0, PM_REMOVE);
}
}
```

The destructor makes sure that the window itself is destroyed if it exists:

```
CHostApplication::~CHostApplication()
{
    if (m_hWnd)
        DestroyWindow(m_hWnd);
}
```

The following is the actual message handler. Messages arrive here after being passed through the global message handler. The `switch` statement allows you to choose which messages you want to respond to. For now, you care only about the quit message, and all others are passed to the default message handler. The default handler handles the basic window operations, such as resizing, moving, and so on.

```
LRESULT WINAPI CHostApplication::MessageHandler(HWND hWnd,
            UINT Message, WPARAM wParam, LPARAM lParam)
{
    switch(Message)
    {
       case WM_DESTROY:
           PostQuitMessage(0);
           return 0;
    }
    return DefWindowProc(hWnd, Message, wParam, lParam);
}
```

That's all the code; now you can compile and see what it does.

Compiling and Running the Simple Application

For VC++ users, the workspace and project files are included on the CD. For others, simply compile the source files, and link with kernel32.lib and user32.lib. After compiling, run the application. The result should be similar to Figure 6.2.

Notice that the window doesn't repaint. This is not a bug. Usually, Windows applications respond to a paint message when they need to repaint themselves. Because you will eventually be "painting" with a Direct3D device, I have omitted the code that would have painted the window. In the next chapter, you'll finally add the actual Direct3D code. Figure 6.2 makes the point that your window will not paint itself in the normal Windows way. Instead, you'll paint everything with the Direct3D device.

Figure 6.3 shows how this simple application operates. Notice that there is no code for drawing anything. Yet....

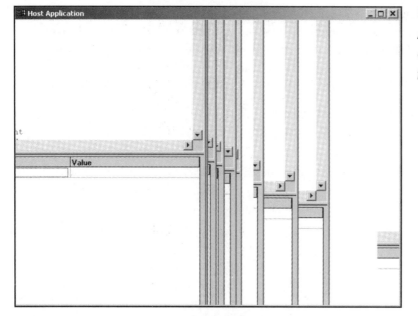

Figure 6.2

A very simple application. Note the painting issues.

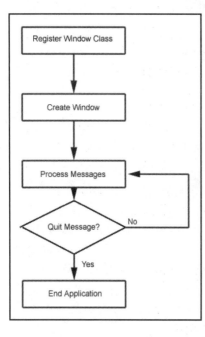

Figure 6.3

The lifespan of the simple application.

In Review: Why Did We Do It That Way?

If you were writing your own application, you'd probably do things differently. In this first chapter, you're just trying to get the basic Windows functionality out of the way. In later chapters, CHostApplication takes care of all the basics, leaving you free to concentrate on the graphics. You placed WinMain in a separate file from the application class because if it were in the same file, it would complicate things once you started subclassing CHostApplication. Keeping them separate means that you can change which class WinMain instantiates without changing the code in Application.cpp. All of these reasons are based on the fact that you are setting things up to be a framework for many different applications. If you are writing one application, you can consolidate some of these functions.

In Conclusion...

In this chapter, you have concentrated solely on setting up a simple Windows application. For experienced programmers, this chapter is purely review and an introduction to the basic framework. For others, this chapter has touched on the most basic aspects of Windows programming. In the next chapter, you will expand the CHostApplication class and add actual Direct3D code. For now, review some of the key points of this chapter:

- The SDK contains a well-organized application framework. You are creating your own framework so that I can easily explain some of the key concepts.

- The SDK also contains many samples that are helpful to the beginner.

- The operating system calls WinMain to start an application. Your framework uses WinMain to create an instance of an application class.

- CHostApplication provides basic functionality. In later chapters, you'll subclass CHostApplication to suit your needs.

- Windows applications receive input and commands via messages. Message-handling functions process those messages.

- The application in this chapter is just a precursor to the actual Direct3D-enabled application. Read on for more!

CHAPTER 7

CREATING AND MANAGING THE DIRECT3D DEVICE

The point of the previous chapter was to get the basics of your Windows application out of the way so that you could focus entirely on Direct3D in this and every other chapter. Before I can talk about vertices and polygons, I need to talk about the Direct3D device and how to deal with it properly. All the code in this chapter comes from the \Code\Chapter07 directory on the CD. Before rendering anything, I need to cover the following topics:

- Explaining the Direct3D device.
- Creating a D3D object.
- Querying device capabilities.
- Creating a Direct3D device.
- Resetting a lost device.
- Destroying a device.
- Rendering with a device.
- Clearing the device.
- Building the new concepts into the application framework.

What Is the Direct3D Device?

Every graphics API has a basic entity that maintains the overall state of the drawing functions. If you're programming with the Windows GDI, it's the device context (DC). If you're programming in Java, it's the `Graphics` object. With Direct3D, it's a Direct3D device or in API terms, `IDirect3DDevice8`. The device manages and maintains everything from allocating texture memory to transformation matrices to blending states. Many methods of `IDirect3DDevice8` handle these tasks, but I do not go through a laundry list of them here. Instead, each chapter presents these methods in context—so when I talk about textures, I talk about the texture-management methods of `IDirect3DDevice8`. In this chapter, I talk about how the device itself is created and maintained.

Table 7.1 shows the three basic types of devices.

Of the three types, the HAL device is by far the most useful because it takes advantage of hardware acceleration. The reference device is supplied to serve as a fully featured reference design for developers. This means that it emulates all possible DirectX features in software, but at a significant performance penalty. The software device can use third-party software renderers, but there are currently none available. The

Table 7.1   D3DDEVTYPE Definitions

Device Type	Comments
D3DDEVTYPE_HAL	A HAL (hardware abstraction layer) device uses hardware for rendering.
D3DDEVTYPE_REF	A REF (reference) device is implemented in software but uses specialized CPU optimizations when available.
D3DDEVTYPE_SW	A SW (software) device uses a third-party software renderer if one has been made available.

samples in this book run well with the HAL device on all DirectX 8.0 compatible cards. If you do not have a card that supports higher-level features such as pixel shaders, it might be necessary to use the reference device to see the samples in action.

In this chapter, you will add device maintenance features to the existing CHostApplication class. Note that you are not creating a subclass; you are adding more basic features to code that you started in the last chapter. By the end of this chapter, you will have a complete base class on which to base the code for the different techniques.

Step 1: Creating the Direct3D Object

The first step to creating a Direct3D Device is creating the actual Direct3D object. This object handles the most basic functions of Direct3D, namely creating the device and providing a way to query the hardware for capabilities. Creating the Direct3D object is simple: The function takes one parameter that is defined by the SDK. Here is an example:

```
LPDIRECT3D8 pD3D = Direct3DCreate8(D3D_SDK_VERSION);
```

Once this object is created, it serves as a gateway to the Direct3D functionality. If you know exactly what kind of hardware your application is running on, you can blindly create and use a device. For real-world applications, it is best to learn more about the hardware by using the Direct3D object's querying functions.

Step 2: Learning More about the Hardware

The Direct3D object includes many methods that you can use to query the capabilities of the hardware. For now, I focus on the two most frequently used functions, `GetDeviceCaps` and `EnumAdapterModes`.

You can use `GetDeviceCaps` to query the capabilities of each device type. Here is the function prototype and sample usage:

```
HRESULT IDirect3D8::GetDeviceCaps(UINT Adapter, D3DDEVTYPE DeviceType,
                D3DCAPS8 *pDeviceCaps);

D3DCAPS8 DeviceCaps;
HRESULT hr = pD3D->GetDeviceCaps(D3DADAPTER_DEFAULT, D3DDEVTYPE_HAL,
                &DeviceCaps);
```

The first parameter specifies the adapter or video card that is to be queried. I am not going to discuss multi-monitor systems specifically, so the default adapter is the only one you'll query. The second parameter is the device type that you are interested in, and the third parameter is the capabilities structure that is filled by the function. The capabilities listed in this structure cover all aspects of the hardware, ranging from the maximum number of lights to the supported vertex shader version. In each chapter, I talk about how to make sure the device supports a given technique.

If `GetDeviceCaps` queries the raw capabilities and limitations of the hardware, `EnumAdapterModes` queries the possible ways to manage the screen itself. Enumerating the available display modes helps the application determine which screen resolutions and pixel formats are available for a given device. To determine the number of available modes to enumerate, the application can call `GetAdapterModeCount`. The function prototypes follow:

```
UINT IDirect3D8::GetAdapterModeCount(UINT Adapter);
HRESULT IDirect3D8::EnumAdapterModes(UINT Adapter, UINT Mode,
                D3DDISPLAYMODE *pMode);
```

The first parameter is the same adapter identifier used with `GetDeviceCaps`. The second parameter identifies which mode is to be queried. If this value is greater than the result of `GetAdapterModeCount`, this function fails. The last parameter is a pointer to a display mode structure that is filled by the function. This structure identifies the width, height, refresh rate, and pixel format for a given mode.

When used together, `GetDeviceCaps` and `EnumAdapterModes` can help you make the most out of a given piece of hardware and help "future proof" your game. Many older games are still fun to play but are limited to 640x480, even on high-end cards. In most cases, you should design your game to allow the user to select from a set of resolutions that the card can support. This allows the card and the user to decide how to get the most out of the hardware. Once you've learned the capabilities of the hardware, you can go ahead and create a device.

Step 3: Creating the Direct3D Device

Creating the device itself involves one function call, but that function requires you to know many of the things you learned in the previous section. The function prototype is next, followed by several tables that further define the parameters:

```
HRESULT IDirect3D8::CreateDevice(UINT Adapter, D3DDEVTYPE DeviceType,
                HWND hFocusWindow, DWORD BehaviorFlags,
                D3DPRESENT_PARAMETERS *pPresentationParameters,
                IDirect3DDevice8   **pNewDevice);
```

The first four parameters can be encapsulated into a structure called `D3DDEVICE_CREATION_PARAMETERS` for easy storage. The first two parameters are the same as in the previous steps. The window handle defines the window that determines whether the device has focus. Table 7.2 describes the behavior flags, and Table 7.3 outlines the presentation parameters. Finally, the final parameter is the address of the returned pointer of the newly created device (or `NULL` if the function fails). The behavior and operation of the device are mostly defined by the data in the following tables.

One important point to remember is that you can logically OR these flags together, however you can only specify one type of vertex processing.

The presentation parameters structure is perhaps the most involved part of the creation process. Table 7.3 explains each member of the structure.

The present parameters can seem quite complicated, and in fact, they can be the cause of many failures when calling `CreateDevice`. However, in most cases, many of the parameters are zero or some other default value. The most important things to remember are the differences between windowed and full-screen applications and using valid formats. In most cases, if `CreateDevice` fails, it's because you asked for a format that your device can't support. Also, when creating a device, it is useful to save a copy of the presentation parameters. You might temporarily lose a device, and you need the presentation parameters to reset the device.

Table 7.2   Device Behavior Flags

Flag	Comments
D3DCREATE_HARDWARE_VERTEXPROCESSING	This flag specifies that all vertices must be processed by the hardware.
D3DCREATE_SOFTWARE_VERTEXPROCESSING	This flag specifies that all vertices must be processed in software. In some cases, this is more flexible than hardware, but at a performance penalty.
D3DCREATE_MIXED_VERTEXPROCESSING	Setting this flag allows the application to dynamically specify what type of vertex processing should be used.
D3DCREATE_FPU_PRESERVE	This will ensure double-precision floating-point math operations. This can degrade performance and in most cases is not needed.
D3DCREATE_MULTITHREADED	This will ensure that the device is safe to use with multiple threads but will probably degrade overall performance.
D3DCREATE_PUREDEVICE	This flag forces the device to behave in an "all or nothing" hardware mode. If hardware vertex processing is not supported, it will not emulate it in software.

Table 7.3 D3DPRESENT_PARAMETERS Structure

Member	Comments
UINT BackBufferWidth	This defines the width of the back buffer for full-screen applications. For windowed applications, the device tracks the window's width.
UINT BackBufferHeight	See the preceding comment.
D3DFORMAT BackBufferFormat	This defines the pixel format of the back buffer for full-screen applications. For windowed applications, the device uses the format of the current display mode.

Table 7.3 (continued)

Member	Comments
UNIT BackBufferCount	This is the number of back buffers (0, 1, 2, or 3). A value of zero is treated as one. Increasing the number of back buffers allows the device to continue writing to one back buffer while another is being swapped to the screen.
D3DMULTISAMPLE_TYPE MultiSampleType	This specifies the type of multisampling (antialiasing) that should be performed. Check the device caps to see what the hardware supports. Also, you can only use this value with D3DSWAPEFFECT_DISCARD.
D3DSWAPEFFECT SwapEffect	The swap effect determines whether data is preserved when it moves to the screen. D3DSWAPEFFECT_DISCARD yields the highest performance because it selects the most efficient presentation technique.
HWND hDeviceWindow	In windowed applications, this is the handle to the actual window that serves as a target for the device.
BOOL Windowed	This flag specifies whether the application is windowed or full screen.
BOOL EnableAutoDepthStencil	If this flag is set, the device handles the creation and management of the depth-stencil buffer. If this flag is TRUE, the next member must be a valid format.
D3DFORMAT AutoDepthStencilFormat	This is the format used if the preceding member is TRUE. This must be a valid depth-stencil format for the device.
DWORD Flags	Currently, the only flag (other than 0) is D3DPRESENTFLAG_LOCKABLE_BACKBUFFER. This specifies that the back buffer is lockable. In general, locking the back buffer decreases performance.
UINT FullScreen_RefreshRateInHz	For windowed applications, this value must be set to 0. For full-screen applications, this value can be one of the values returned by EnumAdapterDisplayModes. There are also two predefined values: D3DPRESENT_RATE_DEFAULT, in which the application chooses a rate, or D3DPRESENT_RATE_UNLIMITED, in which the application chooses the highest possible rate.
UINT FullScreen_PresentationInterval	This flag determines whether the application waits for a vertical retrace. For windowed applications, this value must be 0. Other flags can range from immediate (the driver does not wait) to a wait of up to four retraces.

Step 4: Resetting a Lost Device

Sometimes you might lose a device and need to reset it. One of the more common causes is when a full-screen application loses focus or a windowed application is minimized. A lost device means that data can no longer be rendered until the device is reset.

Some games try to circumvent this by disabling the Alt+Tab key combination, making it impossible to switch applications. This move is a bad idea for a couple of reasons. The first is that you can't create a situation where an instant messenger pop-up causes your game to crash. The other is that the user tends to get upset when an application tries to bend the standard rules for Windows applications. The best thing to do is to bite the bullet and learn how to reset the device.

The application can query the state of the device by calling `TestCooperativeLevel`:

```
HRESULT IDirect3DDevice8::TestCooperativeLevel();
```

If the call to `TestCooperativeLevel` fails, the device is lost and rendering is not possible. At this point, it's usually good to wait and call `TestCooperativeLevel` again. Because rendering is impossible, application processing should not process any drawing code because it would waste processor time. Instead, wait until `TestCooperativeLevel` returns `D3DERR_DEVICENOTRESET`. At this point, the application should try calling `Reset` with the saved present parameters. The prototype follows:

```
HRESULT IDirect3DDevice8::Reset(D3DPRESENT_PARAMETERS
*pPresentParameters);
```

If the call to `Reset` succeeds, the device is restored and the application can resume rendering. If not, it should wait and try again until the call does succeed or perhaps until the wait time exceeds some timeout. Following is an example of the process:

```
HRESULT Result = pD3DDevice->TestCooperativeLevel();
while(Result == D3DERR_DEVICELOST)
{
    while(Result != D3DERR_DEVICENOTRESET)
    {
        Sleep(1000);
        Result = pD3DDevice->TestCooperativeLevel();
    }
    if (FAILED(pD3DDevice->Reset(&m_PresentParameters)))
        Result = D3DERR_DEVICELOST;
}
```

I have now talked about how you manage the lifetime of the device. There is one more step. Eventually, you must destroy the device.

Step 5: Destroying a Device

Destroying the device is easy. It's simply a matter of calling `Release`:

```
HRESULT IDirect3DDevice8::Release();
```

This code releases the device, but it is generally a good idea to first release any objects that are associated with the device, such as textures and vertex buffers.

Rendering with the Direct3D Device

The whole point of the previous five steps was to create a device that you could use to render your awesome 3D scenes. I don't know about you, but I'm dying to get started! Once your device is created and you're sure it hasn't been lost, you can begin rendering your scene. You do this with the aptly named `BeginScene`:

```
HRESULT IDirect3DDevice8::BeginScene();
```

This tells the device that you are about to render a scene. The device then sets up internal structures and waits for instructions. Once you send all the instructions for a given scene, the application can call `EndScene`:

```
HRESULT IDirect3DDevice8::EndScene();
```

Note that scenes cannot be embedded; you must can `EndScene` before beginning a new scene. Also, it is usually advantageous to place as many instructions as possible into a single scene.

Once the scene is rendered, the application tells the device to put the graphics on the screen by calling `Present`:

```
HRESULT IDirect3DDevice8::Present(CONST RECT *pSourceRect,
             CONST RECT *pDestRect,
             HWND hDestinationWindow,
             CONST RGNDATA *pDirtyRegion);
```

In general, most of the time these parameters should all be NULL. (The last parameter must always be NULL.) Using all NULLs places the entire rendered scene in the default window specified in the present parameters. Changing the source and destination rectangles is possible, but it's been my experience that it's better to change the way the scene is rendered and present everything than to play with these parameters.

One final piece of the puzzle is a fairly fundamental part of rendering, and that is clearing the device.

Clearing the Device

Clearing in this context means that you are erasing the current contents of the frame buffer in preparation for a new scene. Some people try to do this by rendering a large rectangle onto the buffer. This is very poor form. Don't do it that way. The hardware is capable of performing very fast clears of the buffer when the application calls `Clear`. Following is the function prototype followed by an explanation of the parameters in Table 7.4:

```
HRESULT IDirect3DDevice::Clear(DWORD RectCount, CONST D3DRECT *pRects,
            DWORD Flags, D3DCOLOR Color, float DepthValue,
            DWORD StencilValue);
```

Table 7.4   Clear Parameters

Flag	Comments
DWORD RectCount	Specifies the number of subrectangles to clear. A value of 0 clears the entire buffer.
D3DRECT *pRects	Pointers to the subrectangles. The number of rectangles must equal RectCount. A value of NULL clears the entire buffer.
DWORD Flags	Specifies which buffers to clear. Possible values are D3DCLEAR_TARGET, D3DCLEAR_STENCIL, and D3DCLEAR_ZBUFFER. You can use these flags in any combination. Most applications are only concerned with the target frame buffer and the Z (depth) buffer.
D3DCOLOR Color	This is the color used to fill the frame buffer.
FLOAT DepthValue	This is the value used to fill the depth buffer. This value ranges from 0.0 to 1.0, and the usual clear value is 1.0.
DWORD StencilValue	This is the value used to fill the stencil buffer. Its valid range depends on the bit depth of the stencil buffer.

As with Present, it is usually best to clear the entire scene rather than deal with particular subrectangles. Clear is usually called before a scene is rendered to "clear the slate," but you can also call it mid-scene to help with stencil operations or certain depth effects.

So those are the pieces you need in place for your device to work. The source code for this chapter completes the basic framework you started in the last chapter. Before you move on to the real rendering, let's revisit the source code and see how it has changed.

Application.h Revisited

The new application class includes several data members and functions needed to maintain the device and make the new functionality accessible to subclasses. The new code for Application.h follows with explanations for the new features.

You include the Direct3D header files because you will be using Direct3D data types. Note that you no longer include windows.h because the DirectX header files also include the basic types. If, for some reason you want to keep it, including windows.h will not cause any errors:

```
#include <d3d8.h>
#include <d3dx8.h>
class CHostApplication
{
public:
    CHostApplication();
    virtual ~CHostApplication();
    LRESULT WINAPI MessageHandler(HWND hWnd, UINT msg, WPARAM wParam,
                LPARAM lParam);
    void Go();
```

The following methods are protected because they should be accessed only by this class or child classes:

```
protected:
```

The InitializeD3D function initializes the Direct3D object that you use to create the Direct3D device:

```
    HRESULT InitializeD3D();
```

This is the generalized device creation function. You can call this function directly using all the parameters, or the application can call one of the following simplified functions:

```
HRESULT CreateDevice(D3DDEVICE_CREATION_PARAMETERS *pCreateParms,
         D3DPRESENT_PARAMETERS    *pPresentParms);
```

This is a simplified utility function for creating a windowed application:

```
HRESULT EasyCreateWindowed(HWND WindowHandle,
         D3DDEVTYPE DeviceType,
         DWORD Behavior);
```

This function is a utility function to create a quick and dirty full-screen application:

```
HRESULT EasyCreateFullScreen(D3DDISPLAYMODE *pMode,
         D3DDEVTYPE DeviceType,
         DWORD Behavior);
```

This function implements the wait-and-reset procedure explained earlier:

```
HRESULT RestoreDevice();
```

The application can call this function to query the device about all available modes. The SDK framework includes a more full-featured version of this including device confirmation. For the sake of simplicity, your framework simply gives the application access to all modes:

```
long EnumerateModes(D3DDISPLAYMODE *pModes, long ModeCount);
```

This function takes care of destroying the device:

```
HRESULT DestroyDevice();
```

This function is called before rendering begins. It calls `Clear` and `BeginScene`. Other applications can override this function to do things, such as change the clear color or other clear parameters, but that new function must call `BeginScene` or rendering will fail:

```
virtual void PreRender();
```

This function is called after everything is rendered. It calls `EndScene` and `Present`. As stated earlier, applications that override this function must call `EndScene`:

```
virtual HRESULT PostRender();
```

The following eight functions are hooks provided for child classes of this class. If the child class overrides these functions, the base class calls them when it needs to notify the child class of certain events. For example, the child class can override HandleMessage and provide custom responses to input messages. It can also override PreReset to make sure that all device-dependent objects, such as textures, are cleaned up before the device is reset:

```
    virtual BOOL PreInitialize();
    virtual BOOL PostInitialize();
    virtual BOOL PreTerminate();
    virtual BOOL PostTerminate();
    virtual void Render();
    virtual BOOL PreReset();
    virtual BOOL PostReset();
    virtual BOOL HandleMessage(MSG *pMessage);
protected:
    HWND m_hWnd;
    long m_WindowWidth;
    long m_WindowHeight;
```

This is the pointer to the all-important Direct3D device:

```
    LPDIRECT3DDEVICE8 m_pD3DDevice;
```

This is the pointer to our Direct3D object:

```
    LPDIRECT3D8     m_pD3D;
```

These two member variables act as saved copies of the device-creation parameters, which will be useful in the event that the device needs to be reset or recreated:

```
    D3DPRESENT_PARAMETERS     m_PresentParameters;
    D3DDEVICE_CREATION_PARAMETERS m_CreationParameters;
```

This flag is set to TRUE by default and can be set to FALSE by this class or child classes to instruct the application to stop rendering frames.

```
    BOOL m_Continue;
};
```

The following section describes the implementation of the now-complete class and includes many of the concepts from this chapter.

Application.cpp Revisited

The following is the new application implementation, which includes the device-maintenance features of this chapter. Notice that some of the code from the last chapter has been moved around to accommodate these new features. This revision is the last for CHostApplication. Any further changes are implemented in the form of derived classes developed for each chapter.

Figure 7.1 shows the revised flow chart for this application. The overall flow is the same, but now includes the device management and rendering code.

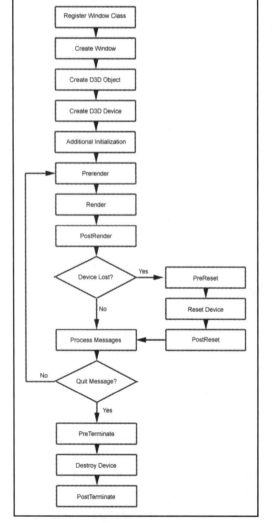

Figure 7.1

Application flow.

Because of the sheer amount of code, only the changed or added code is commented:

```
#include "Executable.h"
#include "Application.h"

CHostApplication::CHostApplication()
{
    m_WindowWidth = 640;
    m_WindowHeight = 480;
}


void CHostApplication::Go()
{
    WNDCLASSEX WindowClass = {sizeof(WNDCLASSEX),CS_CLASSDC,
                EntryMessageHandler, 0, 0,
                GetModuleHandle(NULL), NULL, NULL,
                NULL, NULL, "Host Application", NULL};
    RegisterClassEx(&WindowClass);

    m_hWnd = CreateWindow("Host Application", "Host Application",
                WS_OVERLAPPEDWINDOW, 0, 0, m_WindowWidth,
                m_WindowHeight, GetDesktopWindow(), NULL,
                WindowClass.hInstance, NULL);
    if(m_hWnd)
        ShowWindow(m_hWnd, SW_SHOW);
```

Here you initialize the Continue flag. The application continues rendering until it receives a quit message or until this flag is set to FALSE:

```
    m_Continue = TRUE;
```

This is your first call to one of the virtual functions. Child classes can implement this function if they want to initialize something before the D3D object is created. If the child class returns FALSE, the application stops:

```
    if (!PreInitialize())
        return;
```

This function simply creates the D3D object, as described earlier in this chapter. The actual function is implemented later in the code:

```
    InitializeD3D();
```

This is the one loose end with this file. In this chapter, you call `EasyCreateWindowed` so that you have something to show. In later chapters, this function call is removed, and child classes should create either a windowed or a full-screen device by overriding the `PostInitialize` function:

```
if (FAILED(EasyCreateWindowed(m_hWnd, D3DDEVTYPE_HAL,
                D3DCREATE_HARDWARE_VERTEXPROCESSING)))
    return;
```

You call this once the D3D device is created. Again, if the child class returns `FALSE`, everything grinds to a halt:

```
if (!PostInitialize())
    return;
```

Your message loop is now augmented with the rendering code. This means that the application renders frames as quickly as it can but still responds to messages in a timely fashion:

```
MSG Message;
PeekMessage(&Message, 0, 0, 0, PM_REMOVE);
while (Message.message != WM_QUIT && m_Continue)
{
```

This gives the child classes the opportunity to do whatever they may need to do before beginning the actual scene:

```
    PreRender();
```

Here is where the framework tells the child to render anything it wants to render. In later chapters, this is where most of the magic happens:

```
    Render();
```

Now you call `PostRender` to complete the rendering process. `PostRender` returns the result of `Present`, which is used here to determine whether the device has been lost. If the device has been lost, you call `PreReset` and then `RestoreDevice` to restore it. Once the device is restored, you tell the child class about it by calling `PostReset`. Here, the child class should reinitialize anything that might have been lost when the device was lost:

```
    if (D3DERR_DEVICELOST == PostRender())
    {
        PreReset();
        RestoreDevice();
```

```
            PostReset();
        }
```

If the child class processes the message and returns FALSE, you should stop rendering frames:

```
        TranslateMessage(&Message);
        DispatchMessage(&Message);
        PeekMessage(&Message, 0, 0, 0, PM_REMOVE);
        m_Continue = HandleMessage(&Message);
    }
```

If you've gotten this far, it's time to quit. Here the framework gives the child class the opportunity to clean up before the device is destroyed:

```
    PreTerminate();
```

And with this, the device is gone. You are well on the road to ending the application for good:

```
    DestroyDevice();
```

The child class now has one last chance for any final clean-up:

```
    PostTerminate();
}
```

The PreRender function handles the initial stages of rendering. It clears the buffers and calls BeginScene. If applications choose to override this function, they can change the parameters of Clear and add more initialization code, but they must be sure to call BeginScene:

```
void CHostApplication::PreRender()
{
    m_pD3DDevice->Clear(0, NULL, D3DCLEAR_TARGET | D3DCLEAR_ZBUFFER,
            D3DCOLOR_XRGB(0, 0, 0), 1.0f, 0);
    m_pD3DDevice->BeginScene();
    return;
}
```

PostRender is the last thing that's called for a given frame. Any application that overrides this function should call EndScene, and the return value of this function must be the result of Present or the framework will not handle lost devices properly:

```
HRESULT CHostApplication::PostRender()
{
```

```
    m_pD3DDevice->EndScene();
    return m_pD3DDevice->Present(NULL, NULL, NULL, NULL);
}
```

The last thing the application does is release the D3D object:

```
CHostApplication::~CHostApplication()
{
    if (m_pD3D)
        m_pD3D->Release();
    m_pD3D = NULL;
}
```

This is the default message handler for the application class. Most of the real work happens in the overrideable HandleMessage function, but this still provides a hook for the global message handler:

```
LRESULT WINAPI CHostApplication::MessageHandler(HWND hWnd,
            UINT Message, PARAM wParam, LPARAM lParam)
{
    switch(Message)
    {
      case WM_DESTROY:
          PostQuitMessage(0);
          return 0;
    }
    return DefWindowProc(hWnd, Message, wParam, lParam);
}
```

This creates the basic D3D object and initializes the device to a NULL value so that you can easily check whether it has been created:

```
HRESULT CHostApplication::InitializeD3D()
{
    m_pD3D = Direct3DCreate8(D3D_SDK_VERSION);
    m_pD3DDevice = NULL;
    return S_OK;
}


HRESULT CHostApplication::CreateDevice(
        D3DDEVICE_CREATION_PARAMETERS *pCreateParms,
        D3DPRESENT_PARAMETERS        *pPresentParms)
{
```

Keep copies of the parameters so that you can easily reset or recreate the device:

```
memcpy(&m_CreationParameters, pCreateParms,
    sizeof(D3DDEVICE_CREATION_PARAMETERS));
memcpy(&m_PresentParameters, pPresentParms,
    sizeof(D3DPRESENT_PARAMETERS));
```

This call actually creates the device. If it is successful, the device member variable will be valid and usable:

```
return m_pD3D->CreateDevice(pCreateParms->AdapterOrdinal,
             pCreateParms->DeviceType,
             pCreateParms->hFocusWindow,
             pCreateParms->BehaviorFlags,
             pPresentParms, &m_pD3DDevice);
}
```

The following function destroys the device and reinitializes the pointer to NULL. If a device has been created, you should call this function before attempting to recreate the device (if you are changing from windowed to full screen, for instance):

```
HRESULT CHostApplication::DestroyDevice()
{
    if (m_pD3DDevice)
        m_pD3DDevice->Release();
    m_pD3DDevice = NULL;
    return S_OK;
}


long CHostApplication::EnumerateModes(D3DDISPLAYMODE *pModes,
    long ModeCount)
{
```

First, get the actual number of available modes:

```
long Count = m_pD3D->GetAdapterModeCount(D3DADAPTER_DEFAULT);
```

Next, make sure that you don't ask for more than the number of modes that actually exist:

```
if (ModeCount > Count)
    ModeCount = Count;
```

Now, fill the supplied structures with the mode information and return the actual number of available modes. This way, the application could call this function with NULL parameters to obtain the count and then call the function again with a valid pointer:

```
for (long ModeIndex = 0; ModeIndex < ModeCount; ModeIndex++)
{
    m_pD3D->EnumAdapterModes(D3DADAPTER_DEFAULT, ModeIndex,
                &(pModes[ModeIndex]));
}
return Count;
}
```

This function is the actual implementation of the technique discussed earlier. The only real difference here is that this version includes a message pump so that messages are continually processed while the application is waiting for the device to be reset:

```
HRESULT CHostApplication::RestoreDevice()
{
    HRESULT Result = m_pD3DDevice->TestCooperativeLevel();
    while(Result == D3DERR_DEVICELOST)
    {
        while(Result != D3DERR_DEVICENOTRESET)
        {
            Sleep(1000);
            MSG Message;
            PeekMessage(&Message, 0, 0, 0, PM_REMOVE);
            TranslateMessage(&Message);
            DispatchMessage(&Message);

            Result = m_pD3DDevice->TestCooperativeLevel();
        }
        if (FAILED(m_pD3DDevice->Reset(&m_PresentParameters)))
            Result = D3DERR_DEVICELOST;
    }
    return S_OK;
}
```

This function provides a wrapper around CreateDevice. This is convenient when debugging on a known piece of hardware where you don't need to continually query the device capabilities. I have supplied values that work well on geForce2 and geForce3 cards. If you need to, replace the default values with ones that work well on your hardware.:

```cpp
HRESULT CHostApplication::EasyCreateWindowed(HWND WindowHandle,
                     D3DDEVTYPE DeviceType,
                     DWORD Behavior)
{
    D3DDISPLAYMODE CurrentMode;
    if (SUCCEEDED(m_pD3D->GetAdapterDisplayMode(D3DADAPTER_DEFAULT,
                     &CurrentMode)))
    {
        ZeroMemory(&m_PresentParameters,
            sizeof(D3DPRESENT_PARAMETERS));
        m_PresentParameters.Windowed = TRUE;
        m_PresentParameters.SwapEffect = D3DSWAPEFFECT_DISCARD;
        m_PresentParameters.BackBufferFormat = CurrentMode.Format;
        m_PresentParameters.EnableAutoDepthStencil = TRUE;
        m_PresentParameters.AutoDepthStencilFormat = D3DFMT_D16;

        m_CreationParameters.AdapterOrdinal = D3DADAPTER_DEFAULT;
        m_CreationParameters.DeviceType   = DeviceType;
        m_CreationParameters.hFocusWindow  = WindowHandle;
        m_CreationParameters.BehaviorFlags = Behavior;

        return CreateDevice(&m_CreationParameters,
            &m_PresentParameters);
    }
    return E_FAIL;
}
```

This is another convenience function for creating full-screen devices. Again, it is meant as a convenience for the programmer, so feel free to change the values to whatever works for you:

```cpp
HRESULT HostApplication::EasyCreateFullScreen(D3DDISPLAYMODE *pMode,
                     D3DDEVTYPE DeviceType,
                     DWORD Behavior)
{
    ZeroMemory(&m_PresentParameters, sizeof(D3DPRESENT_PARAMETERS));
    m_PresentParameters.Windowed = FALSE;
    m_PresentParameters.SwapEffect = D3DSWAPEFFECT_DISCARD;
```

```
    m_PresentParameters.BackBufferWidth = pMode->Width;
    m_PresentParameters.BackBufferHeight = pMode->Height;
    m_PresentParameters.BackBufferFormat = pMode->Format;
    m_PresentParameters.FullScreen_RefreshRateInHz =
        pMode->RefreshRate;
    m_PresentParameters.EnableAutoDepthStencil = TRUE;
    m_PresentParameters.AutoDepthStencilFormat = D3DFMT_D16;

    m_CreationParameters.AdapterOrdinal = D3DADAPTER_DEFAULT;
    m_CreationParameters.DeviceType   = DeviceType;
    m_CreationParameters.BehaviorFlags = Behavior;
    m_CreationParameters.hFocusWindow  = m_hWnd;

    return CreateDevice(&m_CreationParameters, &m_PresentParameters);
}
```

This is the basic implementation of the overrideable message handler. Child classes can override this to provide their own functionality:

```
BOOL CHostApplication::HandleMessage(MSG *pMessage)
{
    if (pMessage->message == WM_KEYDOWN &&
        pMessage->wParam == VK_ESCAPE)
        return FALSE;
    return TRUE;
}
```

These last nine functions are just placeholders for functions that may or may not be overridden by child classes. In this base class, the default behavior is to do nothing and return TRUE. In later chapters, the bulk of the work happens in functions such as PostInitialize and Render.

```
void CHostApplication::PreRender(){return;}
void CHostApplication::Render(){}
void CHostApplication::PostRender(){return;}

BOOL CHostApplication::PreInitialize(){return TRUE;}
BOOL CHostApplication::PreTerminate(){return TRUE;}
BOOL CHostApplication::PostInitialize(){return TRUE;}
BOOL CHostApplication::PostTerminate(){return TRUE;}
BOOL CHostApplication::PreReset(){return TRUE;}
BOOL CHostApplication::PostReset(){return TRUE;}
```

In Conclusion...

You now have all the pieces of your simple framework. I haven't spent a lot of energy managing modes or determining formats because the SDK framework shows how to do that in excruciating detail. The purpose of this framework is to introduce you to the basics so that you can make sense of the SDK samples and also to provide a framework that is good enough to support the really cool techniques in later chapters. If you are designing a game that must run on many different platforms, you will need to build out the mode-management features, but this should provide a strong starting base. As always, let's talk about a couple of key points:

- The Direct3D device is the entity that manages and supplies rendering capabilities.
- The reference device supplies all the capabilities, but at a stiff performance penalty. It's not good for real use, but it can be good for testing.
- Predetermined device settings are great for experimenting on your own hardware, but real applications must query the hardware before determining what parameters should be used to create a device.
- Device-creation parameters have a strong impact on the overall performance of the device.
- Devices can be lost and reset, but a good application does not eat up processor power while the device cannot render.
- Your framework now provides several functions that can be overridden by child classes. From now on, you will create child classes rather than make changes to these basic files.

Part Three

Let the Rendering Begin!

The previous sections concentrated on the boring but necessary aspects of understanding how the Direct3D device works and how to set things up for rendering. Now, you will finally begin rendering graphics. You're still not quite ready to check out cool techniques, but this section covers all the fundamentals of rendering. For experienced users, much of these next chapters might seem like review. However, whenever possible, I address some of the deeper aspects of rendering, especially in the performance discussions. There should be new material here for nearly everyone.

Here's a breakdown of the chapters in this section:

- By the end of Chapter 8, "Everything Starts with the Vertex," you'll know more than you ever wanted to know about the most primitive of primitives—the humble vertex.

- Chapter 9, "Using Transformations," takes all the theory I discussed in Chapter 3 and shows how you can use matrices to manipulate the data you're drawing on screen.

- Chapter 10, "From Vertices to Geometry," is where the rendering becomes interesting. I talk about how the vertex is really used and get into the theory and practice of drawing data as quickly as possible.

- In all of the shader techniques, you will implement your own lighting. However, Chapter 11, "Fixed Function Lighting," briefly touches on how to use the lighting features built into DirectX.

- Chapter 12, "Introduction to Textures," covers the last basic entity. I discuss how you create and load them and all the cool ways to use them.

- Now that you finally have real geometry and textures on the screen, I can begin to talk about the various states that determine how textures are applied and blended. Chapter 13, "Texture Stage States," talks about the texture stage states that determine how textures are actually applied to meshes. I will also explain how to blend textures using color operations and multiple textures.

- Pixels must pass several tests before they are actually rendered to the screen. Chapter 14, "Depth Testing and Alpha Blending," describes two of these tests. I'll explain the importance of depth testing and demonstrate the finer points of rendering semitransparent objects.

CHAPTER 8

EVERYTHING STARTS WITH THE VERTEX

The most basic geometric primitive in 3D graphics is the vertex. It is the basic building block of all the other geometric primitives. By the end of this chapter, you will understand more than you ever thought possible about the way vertices are created and used. And of course, I discuss how to wield your powers to destroy that which you've created. The code for this chapter is on the CD in \Code\Chapter08. This chapter continues to build on the previous chapters by adding the following concepts:

- Understanding vertices.
- Creating vertices and vertex buffers.
- Destroying a vertex buffer.
- Locking a vertex buffer and changing vertex data.
- Rendering the vertices.
- Understanding the performance implications.
- Building vertex rendering into the application framework.

What Is a Vertex?

Geometry class teaches that any position in space can be represented by the mathematical notion of a point. We also learn that two points in space define a line and that three points in space can define a triangle, as shown in Figure 8.1. This sounds like exactly what we need for 3D graphics! We need a basic entity that will serve as a building block for drawing points, lines, and surfaces.

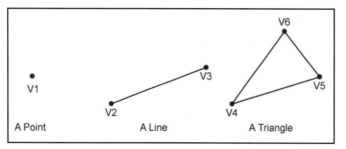

Figure 8.1

Everything starts with vertices.

The vertex is that basic entity. 3D hardware is specially designed to process vertices quickly and efficiently and to use them to draw points, lines, and surfaces (triangles). All geometry manipulation on the graphics card begins with vertex manipulation. Only after the vertices are manipulated does the card begin thinking about how to actually draw the geometry. Therefore, everything you draw in 3D begins with the vertex!

No Really, What Is a Vertex?

In concrete programming terms, a vertex is an instance of a data structure that contains the attributes of a point on your surface, line, or point in space. This data structure is passed through the pipeline, and the values are used and manipulated along the way. In DirectX, you can change the format of this data structure to fit the requirements of a specific rendering task. You can render simple geometry using a format that only contains the X,Y,Z position of the vertex. Multitextured, multicolored, lit geometry can be represented by a more comprehensive format. These formats are specified as Flexible Vertex Formats (FVFs). FVFs are defined as a combination of flags that specify the format of a given set of vertices. Table 8.1 describes these flags.

It's important to remember that you cannot use some of these flags together. For instance, it doesn't make sense to combine the D3DFVF_XYZRHW flag with the D3DFVF_NORMAL flag because pretransformed and lit vertices would not need a normal vector. Likewise, you cannot use the flags for untransformed and pretransformed vertices in the same format.

Equally important to remember is that Table 8.1 lists the flags in the order in which DirectX expects the data to appear. For instance, if a format specifies position, color, and texture coordinate information, the vertex structure must be arranged in that order. Following is a code snippet that shows some sample vertex formats and their corresponding data structures:

```
#define D3DFVF_TRANSFORMEDVERTEX (D3DFVF_XYZRHW | D3DFVF_DIFFUSE)

struct TRANSFORMED_VERTEX
{
  float x, y, z, rhw;
  DWORD color;
};

#define D3DFVF_SIMPLEVERTEX (D3DFVF_XYZ | D3DFVF_NORMAL |
    D3DFVF_DIFFUSE)

struct SIMPLE_VERTEX
{
```

```
    FLOAT x, y, z;
    FLOAT nx, ny, nz;
    DWORD d;
};
```

You can define a data type based on what attributes you want to be included in the vertex. Those attributes are defined in the FVF, and that FVF tells the device the layout of your custom vertex format. This creates a flexible way to create and use vertices in a wide variety of ways. In fact, as you'll see later, you can use the vertex format to store all sorts of things. When you get into shaders, you will abuse the FVF in many ways. Shaders allow you to redefine how vertices are processed, so there is no reason that the texture coordinate data must be valid texture coordinates. I'm getting ahead of myself, but I want to reinforce the point that these flags tell the standard pipeline what data to expect, but shaders allow you to treat these attributes as free slots for all sorts of data. I address this in Part 4. For now, back to the discussion of vertices!

Creating Vertices

At this point, I have defined what a vertex is and the data structure that defines vertices; now you just need to create them. One fairly obvious method would be to simply allocate a block of memory as you would any other data. Why not? There are DirectX functions that accept user memory pointers…but you must resist the urge! There are such functions, but 99.99 percent of the time, they are a bad choice in terms of performance. They are bad enough that I do not discuss them here. If you use them, I suppose we could still be friends, but I might talk about you behind your back, and you'll never get a good table at restaurants.

What you really want to do is create a vertex buffer. The reason a vertex buffer is preferable is that the device tries to place the buffer in video memory or at least AGP memory. This ensures that the card can get to the data as quickly as possible, which means good performance. A vertex buffer is actually created by the device with a call to `IDirect3DDevice8::CreateVertexBuffer`. As usual, the function prototype here is followed by tables of parameters:

```
HRESULT IDirect3DDevice8::CreateVertexBuffer(UINT BufferLength,
        DWORD Usage, DWORD FVF, D3DPOOL MemoryPool,
        IDirect3DvertexBuffer8 **ppVertexBuffer);
```

The buffer length parameter specifies the size of the buffer in bytes. The FVF parameter is the format of the vertices in the buffer. Assuming this function succeeds, the last parameter is set to a valid vertex buffer pointer. The `Usage`

Table 8.1 FVF Flag Definitions

Flag	Comments
D3DFVF_XYZ	This flag specifies the use of three FLOATs to represent the X,Y,Z position of the vertices. Vertices using this flag are sent through the geometry pipeline to be transformed.
D3DFVF_XYZRHW	This flag specifies the use of four FLOATs to represent the pretransformed screen position of the vertices. In addition to the X,Y,Z position, the fourth value is the reciprocal W value. The RHW value will only become important when I talk about the W buffer. Vertices defined with this flag bypass the transformation and lighting portion of the pipeline; the device assumes that the application has already done that.
D3DFVF_XYZB1 - D3DFVF_XYZB5	Certain forms of animation allow multiple matrices to be used as "bones" that drive the animation. Each vertex may be affected by each of these bones with a different weight. These flags specify how many weights are included in the format. Each weight requires one FLOAT, so D3DFVF_XYZB2 requires two FLOAT values. Although there are flags for up to five blend weights, DirectX 8.0 supports only three. I use these values when I talk about animation later.
D3DFVF_LASTBETA_UBYTE4	If this flag is specified, the last blend weight is treated as a DWORD instead of a FLOAT.
D3DFVF_NORMAL	This flag specifies that the vertex format include a vertex normal vector represented by three FLOATs (X,Y,Z). For example, if this vertex is part of a surface, the normal value would probably be the surface normal at this point.
D3DFVF_PSIZE	This flag specifies that the format include a single FLOAT value defining the point size for vertices. The effect of this flag can depend on the hardware and device capabilities.
D3DFVF_DIFFUSE	Formats that include this flag include a DWORD value that encodes a 32-bit RGBA diffuse color.
D3DFVF_SPECULAR	Same as preceding for specular color.
D3DFVF_TEX0 - D3DFVF_TEX8	These flags specify the total number of texture coordinates used in this format. In most cases, each set of texture coordinates is represented by two FLOAT values, but you can set the actual size with the next flag.
D3DFVF_TEXTUREFORMAT1- D3DFVF_TEXTUREFORMAT4	This flag specifies how many FLOAT values are used to define each set of texture coordinates. The default size is D3DFVF_TEXTUREFORMAT2.

parameter can be a combination of the flags in Table 8.2, and the `MemoryPool` parameter can be set to one of the values in Table 8.3.

The following code shows how to create a static buffer in video memory with 10 simple vertices (the FVF was defined earlier):

```
LPDirect3DVertexBuffer8 m_pVertexBuffer;
if (FAILED(m_pD3DDevice->CreateVertexBuffer(
        10 *sizeof(SIMPLE_VERTEX),
        D3DUSAGE_WRITEONLY,
        D3DFVF_SIMPLEVERTEX,
        D3DPOOL_DEFAULT,
        &m_pVertexBuffer)))
```

This call creates a vertex buffer. Now all you have to do is fill it with actual data.

Table 8.2   Vertex Buffer Usage Flags

Flag	Comments
D3DUSAGE_DONOTCLIP	This flag tells the device not to clip any of the vertices in this buffer during rendering. If you set this flag, you should disable clipping on the device before rendering this vertex buffer.
D3DUSAGE_DYNAMIC	The dynamic tells the device that the contents of this buffer may change frequently. The device places dynamic buffers in AGP memory and static buffers directly in video memory. Note that there is no explicit flag for static buffers. The absence of this flag implies static usage.
D3DUSAGE_RTPATCHES	You use this flag for vertex buffers that are used for higher-order meshes.
D3DUSAGE_NPATCHES	You use this flag when the vertex buffer will be used for N patches.
D3DUSAGE_POINTS	This flag specifies that the vertex buffer will be used to draw point sprites or point lists.
D3DUSAGE_SOFTWAREPROCESSING	If you use this flag, this buffer will be processed in software.
D3DUSAGE_WRITEONLY	If you use this flag, the vertex buffer can only be written to. Attempts to read from the buffer will fail.

Table 8.3   D3DPOOL Values

Value	Comments
D3DPOOL_DEFAULT	Resources created with this flag are usually created in either system or AGP memory. This is recommended for vertex buffers. Dynamic vertex buffers must be created with this pool parameter.
D3DPOOL_MANAGED	Resources created with this flag are managed by the device. The device keeps a copy of the data in system memory and copies it into video memory as needed. If the device is lost, DirectX uses the system copy to recreate it transparently. This saves the application the trouble of recreating the buffers.
D3DPOOL_SYSTEMMEM	Resources are created in system memory. This is typically not the best setting for vertex buffers because the memory is not directly accessible by the hardware.

Destroying the Vertex Buffer

After all that work to create the buffer, destroying the buffer is easy. Simply call:

```
HRESULT IDirect3DvertexBuffer8:Release();
```

This destroys the buffer and cleans up any resources associated with it.

Setting and Changing Vertex Data

Because vertex buffers can exist in video memory or in memory that is managed by the device, you cannot directly change the values. To access the values, the application must call IDirect3DvertexBuffer8::Lock. Lock returns a pointer to the vertices that you can use to change the values:

```
HRESULT IDirect3DvertexBuffer8::Lock(UINT StartingOffset,
        UINT BufferSize, BYTE **ppLockedBuffer, DWORD Flags);
```

The StartingOffset is the offset to where the locked data begins. The BufferSize is the number of locked bytes. The ppLockedBuffer parameter is a pointer to be set to the locked data, and the Flags are defined Table 8.4.

Table 8.4   Vertex Buffer Locking Flags

Flag	Comments
D3DLOCK_DISCARD	This flag tells the device to throw away the old data and return a new pointer. This can be good for performance because the device does not have to stall the pipeline while retrieving the old data. This only works for dynamic buffers.
D3DLOCK_NOOVERWRITE	This flag allows for optimizations while appending data to a preexisting buffer. If you are adding data to a buffer, this flag is recommended.
D3DLOCK_NOSYSLOCK	Normally, locking the vertex buffer locks system-wide resources. Long duration locks might want to include this flag so that the system can continue during the locking operation.
D3DLOCK_READONLY	You can specify this flag when the application only wants to read the buffer. You cannot use it with a write-only vertex buffer.

Once the buffer is locked, you can use the returned pointer to set the vertex values. Once the values are set, the application can call unlock to return the new data to the device:

```
HRESULT IDirect3DvertexBuffer8::Unlock();
```

Continuing with the sample, the following code sets the vertex values in your vertex buffer:

```
TRANSFORMED_VERTEX *pVertices;
m_pVertexBuffer->Lock(0, 10 * sizeof(TRANSFORMED_VERTEX),
     (BYTE **)&pVertices, D3DLOCK_DISCARD);
for (long Index = 0; Index < 10; Index++)
{
  pVertices[Index].x = SOME_VALUE;
  pVertices[Index].y = SOME_VALUE;

  pVertices[Index].z = 1.0f;
  pVertices[Index].rhw = 1.0f;

  pVertices[Index].color = 0xffffffff;
}
m_pVertexBuffer->Unlock();
```

The buffer is now filled and ready to be used. You can send the vertices through the pipeline to be rendered.

Rendering Vertices

Finally, you're about to put something on the screen. In all the previous code snippets, I've talked about pretransformed vertices because I haven't talked about transforms yet. (That's the next chapter.) I continue on that thread. Compared to all the setup you've done, the actual rendering is simple. There are three things you need to consider.

The first thing is that you need to tell the device what sorts of vertices it's dealing with. You do this with a call to `IDirect3DDevice8::SetVertexShader`. In this context, the vertex shader is actually the FVF (Flexible Vertex Format) of your vertices. Weird, I know… Using the FVF tells the device what the vertex format is and that the vertices should be processed in the standard pipeline. You only call this function when the format changes, not every time you render. The function looks like this:

```
HRESULT IDirect3DDevice8::SetVertexShader(DWORD FVF);
```

The second step is to tell the device where the vertices are coming from. You do this by passing the vertex buffer to `IDirect3DDevice::SetStreamSource`. This tells the device where the vertices are stored. Again, you only call this function if you need to specify a different vertex buffer. The function looks like this:

```
HRESULT IDirect3DDevice::SetStreamSource(UINT StreamNumber,
        IDirect3DvertexBuffer8 *pVertexBuffer,
        UINT Stride);
```

The `StreamNumber` parameter specifies which stream to associate to this vertex buffer. Until you get into vertex shaders, you will only be using stream 0. The `Stride` parameter specifies the size in bytes for each vertex. Again, until you get into vertex shaders, the stride must be the size of the vertex as specified by your FVF.

The last step tells the device to actually draw the vertices. You do this by calling `IDirect3DDevice::DrawPrimitive`. The function follows:

```
HRESULT IDirect3DDevice8::DrawPrimitive(D3DPRIMITIVETYPE Type,
        UINT StartVertex,
        UINT PrimitiveCount);
```

I discuss these parameters at length in Chapter 10 because they have the greatest impact on rendering actual geometry. Because I am only talking about single vertices for now, the type is D3DPT_POINTLIST, and the count is the number of points you want to render.

Continuing the running sample code, this is how you would render your set of vertices:

```
m_pD3DDevice->SetVertexShader(D3DFVF_SIMPLEVERTEX);
m_pD3DDevice->SetStreamSource(0, m_pVertexBuffer,
    sizeof(SIMPLE_VERTEX));
m_pD3DDevice->DrawPrimitive(D3DPT_POINTLIST, 0, NUM_VERTICES);
```

You now have all the pieces in place to actually render something to the screen. Figure 8.2 shows each of these steps. You don't need to execute these steps each frame.

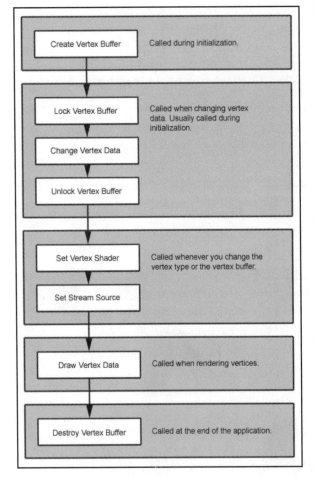

Figure 8.2

Vertex buffer operations.

But I'm still going to make you wait a little bit longer. Let's back up a little, revisit what you have learned, and look at it from the performance perspective.

Performance Considerations

Before I say anything about performance, remember that performance is ultimately a function of what exactly you're trying to do. Therefore, these are some rules of thumb, but you should always experiment to find the best approach for you. The following is a laundry list of things to consider:

- In general, locking the vertex buffer is a costly operation and should be avoided when possible. Often a lock is necessary, but I've heard horror stories of people locking, setting three vertices, rendering, and repeating. Instead, add many more vertices in a single lock.

- Be very aware of the flags used when creating and locking the vertex buffer. Different flag or flag combinations could make measurable performance differences. When in doubt, experiment until you find the best setup.

- Usually, the more vertices you can send to the card in a single call, the better. The numbers differ for different cards and different applications, but a general rule of thumb is that the number should be in the thousands, not in the tens of vertices.

- Calling `SetVertexShader` is a costly operation. It forces the device to stop and prepare for the new type of data. If you're dealing with different FVFs, group your geometry by FVF to avoid switching back and forth. Some people even go so far as to render every other frame in different orders to avoid unnecessary switches!

- Because switching formats is costly, create formats based on attributes, not on objects. Therefore, don't create one format for cars and another format for airplanes if they share the same attributes. Instead, create one format for single textured vertices, another for multitextured vertices, and so on, and use the correct format for all appropriate objects.

- Setting the stream source is also a costly operation. Again, rendering calls should be batched together to take the most advantage of a single vertex buffer before switching.

- As stated earlier, the more geometry you can process in a single call, the better. This applies to `DrawPrimitive` as well. In some cases, you might not be able to send thousands of vertices at the same time, but in general, do as much as you can.

Most of the rules of thumb can be summed up by the frequently heard rule "Batching is everything." Always maximize the amount of work you can do in a single call, and minimize the number of times you force the device to switch to a new state. In my work, I almost never lock the vertex buffer (except during initialization), and I minimize how often I reset anything. If you are frequently locking the buffer or making format changes, take a good long look and ask yourself whether you really need to do that. Chances are pretty good that you'll find many ways to optimize your code. But remember, the best way to optimize is by experimenting and finding the best approach for the given task.

Finally, Something on the Screen!

For a graphics book, you've now gone an awfully long time without anything to look at. Remember, patience is a virtue! The code included on the CD for this chapter is extremely simple, but it demonstrates all the key concepts I've discussed. I struggled with the idea of how to show graphics without talking about transformations and how to show transformations without talking about graphics. I finally decided to have this sample use pretransformed vertices and the next chapter explain transformations. Therefore, all the vertices in this sample are represented in screen coordinates.

As promised, the code for this chapter builds off your previously developed framework. I made one very small change to the CHostApplication class (disabling the call to create the device), and I changed Executable.cpp to instantiate a new class. The rest of the code is contained in the CVertexApplication class, which is derived from CHostApplication. Let's take a look at the class definition in VertexApplication.h.

You need to include the base class definition before you can build off it. This new class inherits all the basic functionality from CHostApplication and overrides several of the virtual functions you built into the framework:

```
#include "Application.h"
class CVertexApplication : public CHostApplication
{
public:
```

These three functions handle the creation, filling, and destruction of the vertex buffer. You build them as their own functions because you can call them on initialization or when the device is reset. In this sample application, the buffer is also refilled with a circle before each render:

```
BOOL CreateVertexBuffer();
BOOL FillVertexBuffer();
void DestroyVertexBuffer();
```

The constructor and destructor handle some basic initialization and clean-up, but most of the real work is done by the following functions:

```
CVertexApplication();
virtual ~CVertexApplication();
```

You call this after the D3D object is created. Here you create the actual device and the vertex buffer:

```
virtual BOOL PostInitialize();
```

This function makes sure that the vertex buffer is released before the framework destroys the device:

```
virtual BOOL PreTerminate();
```

You call these functions when the device is lost. PreReset handles releasing the vertex buffer before the device is reset, and PostReset recreates the buffer once the device has been reset:

```
virtual BOOL PreReset();
virtual BOOL PostReset();
```

This is the function you've been waiting for. This function renders your vertices onto the screen and opens up a whole new world of rendering:

```
virtual void Render();
```

This is your vertex buffer. This is the reason you are here.

```
    LPDIRECT3DVERTEXBUFFER8 m_pVertexBuffer;
};
```

As you can see, the class is pretty straightforward. You just have to make sure that the vertex buffer is created and destroyed at the appropriate times and draw it when the framework asks you to. Let's see the actual implementation in VertexApplication.cpp.

Make sure to include the class definition:

```
#include "VertexApplication.h"
```

Here you define the format and associated structure for a vertex with a pretransformed position and a simple color. You set all the vertex colors to white, but you could experiment with other colors:

```
#define D3DFVF_SIMPLEVERTEX (D3DFVF_XYZRHW | D3DFVF_DIFFUSE)

struct SIMPLE_VERTEX
{
    float x, y, z, rhw;
    DWORD color;
};
```

This sets the number of vertices to process and draw. Changing this number draws more or fewer vertices on the screen. I have picked a high number to ensure you have something to look at:

```
#define NUM_VERTICES 1000
```

This defines a simple random-number macro. This application fills the screen with randomly placed circles, so this macro simplifies the creation of random float values in the range of 0.0 to 1.0 that you can then multiply by the width and height of the device:

```
#define RANDOM_NUMBER ((float)rand() / (float)RAND_MAX)
```

The constructor initializes the vertex buffer pointer to NULL so that you aren't dealing with some random garbage pointer.

```
CVertexApplication::CVertexApplication()
{
  m_pVertexBuffer = NULL;
}
```

The destructor handles any cases where the vertex buffer has not been released. This could happen if you had some other failure in the framework:

```
CVertexApplication::~CVertexApplication()
{
  DestroyVertexBuffer();
}
```

PostInitialize tries to create a device using the convenience function you built into the framework. If this fails, you don't even try to create the vertex buffer. If it succeeds, the application tries to create the buffer:

```
BOOL CVertexApplication::PostInitialize()
{
```

```
      if (FAILED(EasyCreateWindowed(m_hWnd, D3DDEVTYPE_HAL,
            D3DCREATE_HARDWARE_VERTEXPROCESSING)))
        return FALSE;
      return CreateVertexBuffer();
}
```

Here you attempt to create a vertex buffer that will exist in video memory. The flags
have been chosen to maximize the performance for a simple point list. Also, because
the memory pool is the default, the device will not recreate the buffer if it is lost. This is
a good platform for simple experiments. Change the flags and see what happens. Also,
change the memory pool to managed and remove the code from the reset functions.
Because this is your first and most simple example, spend some time playing with it:

```
BOOL CVertexApplication::CreateVertexBuffer()
{
   if (FAILED(m_pD3DDevice->CreateVertexBuffer(
       NUM_VERTICES * sizeof(SIMPLE_VERTEX),
       D3DUSAGE_WRITEONLY | D3DUSAGE_DYNAMIC | D3DUSAGE_POINTS,
       D3DFVF_SIMPLEVERTEX, D3DPOOL_DEFAULT,
       &m_pVertexBuffer)))
      return FALSE;
```

This is a simple optimization example. For this application, you know you are never
going to use a different buffer or a different format, so you set them here and forget
about it. This is better than calling these functions every time you render a frame.
When the device gets reset, the buffer is recreated and these calls are repeated:

```
   m_pD3DDevice->SetVertexShader(D3DFVF_SIMPLEVERTEX);
   m_pD3DDevice->SetStreamSource(0, m_pVertexBuffer,
       sizeof(SIMPLE_VERTEX));
   return TRUE;
}
```

This function destroys the vertex buffer and reinitializes the pointer:

```
void CVertexApplication::DestroyVertexBuffer()
{
   if (m_pVertexBuffer)
   {
     m_pVertexBuffer->Release();
     m_pVertexBuffer = NULL;
   }
}
```

`PreReset` cleans up the buffer that was associated with the lost device. It is necessary to release this buffer before the device is reset:

```
BOOL CVertexApplication::PreReset()
{
  DestroyVertexBuffer();
  return TRUE;
}
```

`PostReset` is called after the device has been reset. It must recreate the vertex buffer that was lost when the device was lost. To verify these functions, use a full-screen device and switch applications and then switch back:

```
BOOL CVertexApplication::PostReset()
{
  return CreateVertexBuffer();
}
```

Each time you render, you refill the buffer and tell the device to draw the contents. This call draws the entire buffer:

```
void CVertexApplication::Render()
{
  FillVertexBuffer();
  m_pD3DDevice->DrawPrimitive(D3DPT_POINTLIST, 0, NUM_VERTICES);
}
```

This function is called before the device is destroyed. Under normal conditions, this is where the vertex buffer will be destroyed:

```
BOOL CVertexApplication::PreTerminate()
{
  DestroyVertexBuffer();
  return TRUE;
}
```

This function handles refilling the buffer with data. In this sample, you are using many points to approximate a circle. Please note: This is a really bad way to draw circles, but it does show off the mechanics of using vertices:

```
BOOL CVertexApplication::FillVertexBuffer()
{
  if (!m_pVertexBuffer)
```

```
    return FALSE;

SIMPLE_VERTEX *pVertices;
```

You attempt to lock the buffer as efficiently as possible. Because you are refilling the whole buffer, you can discard the old one. If for some reason something fails, you stop:

```
if (FAILED(m_pVertexBuffer->Lock(0, NUM_VERTICES *
        sizeof(SIMPLE_VERTEX),
        (BYTE **)&pVertices,
        D3DLOCK_DISCARD)))
{
  DestroyVertexBuffer();
  return FALSE;
}
float XOffset = 640.0f * RANDOM_NUMBER;
float YOffset = 480.0f * RANDOM_NUMBER;
```

Because you are dealing with pretransformed vertices, the position of the vertices is given in screen coordinates. You use these values because the default windowed device is 640x480. If you have changed the function or changed the device, you should change these values. The values of Z and RHW are set to default values of 1.0:

```
for (long Index = 0; Index < NUM_VERTICES; Index++)
{
  float Angle = (float)Index / (float)NUM_VERTICES * 2.0f * D3DX_PI;

  pVertices[Index].x = XOffset + 50.0f * cos(Angle);
  pVertices[Index].y = YOffset + 50.0f * sin(Angle);

  pVertices[Index].z = 1.0f;
  pVertices[Index].rhw = 1.0f;

  pVertices[Index].color = 0xffffffff;
}
m_pVertexBuffer->Unlock();
return TRUE;
}
```

You might notice that I just finished telling you to lock the vertex buffer as infrequently as possible, but here I am doing it every frame. Am I a hypocrite?

Maybe, but this is one example where it makes sense to lock the buffer because pretransformed vertices must be transformed by your code. In the next chapter, I talk about how to change the data on the GPU without locking. For now, the expected output appears in Figure 8.3. The window should show a circle moving randomly around the screen. Please note that this isn't the best way to draw a circle, but I wanted to put something simple on the screen.

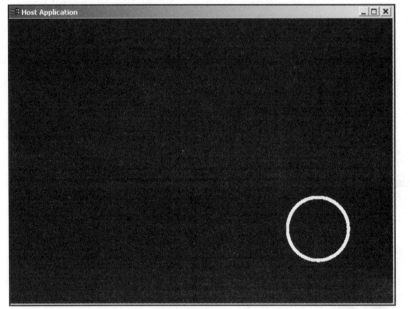

Figure 8.3

Your first real application.

You're starting simple, but things are about to get more interesting pretty quickly.

In Conclusion...

The purpose of this chapter was to explain the fundamentals of creating and managing vertices. The first sample is boring, but if you understand the code and some of the performance considerations, you have a good foundation for the next chapters. Let's recap the important bits:

- A vertex can be defined as a point in space that serves as the building block for rendering points, lines, and surfaces.
- Vertex formats define the attributes of the vertices.
- Vertices should be created in vertex buffers. We are purposely ignoring the cases where they are not.

- Vertices should be created and locked with flags that are carefully selected based on the way they are going to be used. Always optimize the way they move between system and video memory.

- There are several optimization rules of thumb, but the underlying rule is that operations and data should be batched in such a way as to minimize the amount of switching and to maximize the data passed to the device.

- The code for this chapter created nothing more than a bad TV set, but it illustrates many of the fundamentals that remain important in the coming chapters.

CHAPTER 9

USING
TRANSFORMATIONS

In Chapter 3, you took a look at matrices and saw how you could use them to produce transformations, such as translation and rotation; but without any graphics, I could only talk about them in the abstract. Now that I've discussed vertices, I can talk about how transformation matrices can affect those vertices. In this chapter, I talk about how you use these matrices with the Direct3D device. The code for this chapter is on the CD in \Code\Chapter09. This chapter covers the following concepts:

- Understanding transformations.
- The world transformation.
- The view transformation.
- Building complex transformations.
- The projection transformation.
- Using transformations with the Direct3D device.
- Using matrix stacks.
- Setting the viewport.
- Using transformations in the application.
- Understanding performance implications.

What Do You Mean by Transformations?

To best understand how you use transformations when creating 3D graphics, consider the following. Imagine you are in a theme park, taking a photograph of a merry-go-round. The merry-go-round has a shape and geometry, but it also has some position and orientation in space. You have some position in space as well (on the ground). The correlation between the position of the merry-go-round and your position and orientation determines whether it is behind you, in front of you, and so on. Also, the lens of the camera has some effect on the final outcome of the picture. A zoom lens makes the object appear closer or farther. You point and shoot, and the picture is "rendered" onto the film. The film itself also affects the contents of the photo. The format of the film determines the size and resolution of the final picture. In this example, the final image on the picture is a product of how the object's position, your position, the camera lens, and the film interact to map the three-dimensional features of the merry-go-round to the two-dimensional image on the film. Transformations in 3D graphics work exactly the same way. In 3D graphics, we have world transformations determining the position of objects in the scene, a view transformation determining the camera position, a projection transformation determining the properties of the "lens" of the camera, and a viewport, which maps the information to actual pixels. Let's take a look at each transformation and then bring them all together.

The World Transformation

As I talked about in the last chapter, you use vertices define 3D objects. These vertices each represent a position in space, and that position is relative to some origin. But when you render a 3D scene, you want to be able to move objects around the 3D world. As you saw in the last chapter, you could manipulate each vertex to a new position in the world, but a better way is to use a world-transformation matrix and allow the 3D hardware or software to process each vertex in the transformation pipeline. The most basic usage of the world matrix is to easily move a predefined object around a virtual space, but there is another side benefit. You can use it to easily draw several instances of the same object by using one vertex buffer with several different transformation matrices. Of course, the hardware must transform the vertices multiple times, but using only one set of geometry saves memory and bandwidth to the video card. Figure 9.1 shows the same geometry rendered twice in two different positions and orientations. In terms of the geometry data being sent to the video card, there is only one model.

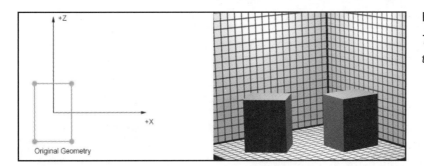

Figure 9.1

Two instances of transformed geometry.

The View Transformation

Whereas the world transformation defines the position and orientation of objects in space, the view transformation defines the position and orientation of the camera in space. Vertices converted to world coordinates after the world transformation are said to be in eye coordinates after the view transformation. Once an object is in eye coordinates, the basic geometric relationship between the object and the viewer is known. In practical terms, you can use the world transformations to build a 3D world and the view transformation to move a camera around the world. Figure 9.2 shows the objects from Figure 9.1 from two different viewpoints.

Figure 9.2

Scene from Figure 9.1 from two different viewpoints.

Building World and View Transformations

Although world and view matrices are conceptually different, they are the same mechanically, meaning that the way the transformation matrices are built is the same for both types of transforms. As I began discussing in Chapter 3, transformation matrices adhere to certain formats, and you can concatenate those matrices with multiplication. In this chapter, I can talk about how these matrices actually affect the geometry. In the following examples, I discuss how you can manipulate the world matrix to move geometry in a scene, but keep in mind that the same operations apply to moving the camera with the view matrix.

Figure 9.3a shows an overhead view of some simple geometry defined around the origin. To understand how transformations work, it's best to think about not only the geometry, but also the coordinate system of the geometry, or model coordinates. Understanding how transformations work is easier if you imagine that the transformations are affecting the coordinate system and the vertices are just along for the ride. For instance, Figure 9.3b shows the effect of applying a translation matrix. It moves not only the vertices, but also the coordinate system. Figure 9.3c shows the effect of applying a rotation matrix. Notice that the coordinate system rotates.

Understanding the effect on the coordinate system is key to understanding the effect of multiple matrices and why the order of operations is so important when building a matrix. Figure 9.4a shows the effect of translation followed by rotation. This sequence of operations moves the coordinate system and then rotates the axes about a new center. Figure 9.4b shows the effect of rotation followed by translation. Here the results are very different. First the coordinate system rotates, and then the translation occurs along the new rotated axes. If you were animating Figure 9.4, the

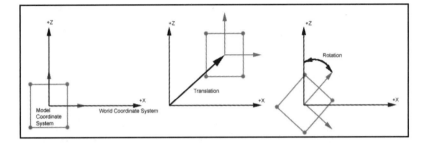

Figure 9.3

The effects of simple transformations.

first sequence would produce a simple rotation at some offset position, and the second sequence would produce more of an orbiting effect. As you can see, order definitely matters. Rotations affect not only the geometry itself, but also the coordinate system, so translations that occur after rotations might not necessarily happen in the direction you think they should.

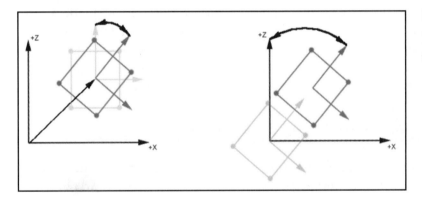

Figure 9.4

The effects of multiple transformations.

Another potential problem to recognize is the effect of geometry that is offset from the origin. This can happen if the geometry was defined in a modeling package, and the model was not centered where you think it should be. Figure 9.5 shows geometry that is not centered on the origin. This is the equivalent to a "built-in" translation matrix. Therefore, all transformations should take that into account. For instance, if a rotation matrix is applied, the result is an orbiting effect because the axes rotate, but the geometry maintains a constant distance from the axes. You could solve the problem by first translating the model to the origin. This will nullify the built-in translation, and then you can rotate. Of course, the easiest way to deal with this is to make sure your models are centered on an appropriate point. If you are building your own models, this isn't too much of an issue. However, in my experience, models you can download or buy frequently need cleaning up before you can transform them nicely.

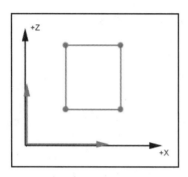

Figure 9.5

Geometry offset from the origin.

The preceding caveats also apply to scaling. If scaling is applied last in the order of operations, it scales only the geometry. If a scaling matrix is applied somewhere in the middle of the operations, it affects all the transformations that occur after it.

I can't stress enough the importance of the order of operations. The key to understanding the effects of transformations is visualizing how each step affects the coordinate system and the impact it has on later steps. These transformations affect how objects and viewers move throughout the world. Next, you will look at the projection transformation, which is still matrix based but is not based on translations and rotations.

The Projection Transformation

The projection transformation is perhaps the most complicated transformation to visualize. Unlike the world and view matrices, which encode positions and rotations, the projection matrix encodes properties of the virtual camera. These properties create a view frustum, which is the volume of space viewable by the camera. The frustum is shown in Figure 9.6.

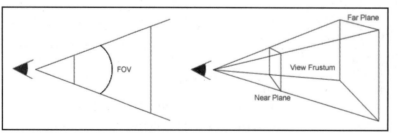

Figure 9.6

The view frustum.

The near and far planes define the distances in which objects are visible. Objects that are either too close or too far are not included in the final rendering. The field-of-view (FOV) angle defines the width and height of the view. For instance, a zoom lens has a lower field of view, meaning that a smaller part of the view occupies a larger part of the image, which makes the final zoomed object bigger.

The features of the projection matrix determine how the vertices in eye coordinates are mapped to window coordinates, in some cases applying perspective and clipping geometry outside of the frustum. This leads to one optimization point. The pipeline must process all points within the frustum. If possible, limiting the range of the far plane could limit the amount of data that must be processed. Depending on the situation, you might want to be sure that you do not overextend your planes.

Later in this chapter, you'll look at other factors that influence the way the projection matrix is used to produce the final screen output. For now, it's important to note that the projection transformation is the last of the three main transforms. It defines the lens of your virtual camera. Figure 9.7 shows the same scene rendered with two different projection matrices. The camera in the second matrix has a lower FOV, effectively a zoom lens.

Figure 9.7

Scene from Figure 9.1 with two different "lenses."

The D3DX library contains 10 different functions for creating projection matrices. There are left-handed and right-handed versions of each of five types. Handedness basically determines whether the positive Z direction is going toward or away from the viewer. Because DirectX uses a left-handed system (+Z leading away from the viewer), I concentrate on the five left-landed types, as shown in Table 9.1.

These functions provide an easy way to create projection matrices. For 3D examples, I mostly use D3DXMatrixPerspectiveFovLH because its parameters fit best with a camera analogy. 2D examples use D3DXMatrixOrthoLH to demonstrate the advantages of using a projection matrix that does not have perspective.

Now that you have taken a look at all the matrices, look at how you actually use them.

Table 9.1   D3DX Projection Matrix Functions

Function Name	Comments

`D3DXMATRIX* D3DXMatrixPerspective`
`FovLH(D3DXMATRIX *pOut, FLOAT FOV,`
`FLOAT AspectRatio, FLOAT ZNear,`
`FLOAT ZFar);`
	This function generates a projection matrix based on a field of view, the aspect ratio of the viewport, the distance of the near plane from the viewer, and the distance of the far plane from the viewer. Remember that the FOV is in radians.

`D3DXMATRIX* D3DXMatrixPerspectiveLH`
`(D3DXMATRIX *pOut, FLOAT Width,`
`FLOAT Height, FLOAT ZNear, FLOAT ZFar);`
	This function generates a projection matrix based on the distances of the near and far view planes, as well as the width and height of the viewport.

`D3DXMATRIX* D3DXMatrixPerspective`
`OffCenterLH(D3DXMATRIX *pOut,`
`FLOAT XNear, FLOAT XFar, FLOAT YNear,`
`FLOAT YFar, FLOAT ZNear, FLOAT ZFar);`
	You can use this function to generate a custom projection matrix based on properties of the view volume.

`D3DXMATRIX* D3DXMatrixOrthoLH`
`(D3DXMATRIX *pOut, FLOAT Width,`
`FLOAT Height, FLOAT ZNear, FLOAT ZFar);`
	This function generates an orthographic (perspectiveless) matrix with the origin in the center of the screen. This is extremely useful for the chapters that concentrate on 2D graphics.

`D3DXMATRIX* D3DXMatrixOrthoOffCenterLH`
`(D3DXMATRIX *pOut, FLOAT XNear,`
`FLOAT XFar, FLOAT YNear, FLOAT YFar,`
`FLOAT ZNear, FLOAT ZFar);`
	This function generates an orthographic (perspectiveless) matrix with an arbitrary origin.

Transformations and the D3D Device

Of course, all of the preceding is just more boring theory unless you can use it effectively in your DirectX application, so let's talk about how these transformations are actually used. The first thing to remember is that the device stores only one transformation at a time for each of the three types I have talked about so far. (There are more types, which I talk about later.) Therefore, once you set a given transform, that transform is applied to all objects until the transform is changed.

This is great for things that probably don't change that often, such as the projection matrix, but you should be aware that transformations you set for one piece of geometry affect subsequent ones unless you explicitly set the transform.

Once you have your transformation matrices, set the transforms by calling SetTransform:

```
HRESULT IDirect3DDevice::SetTransform(D3DTRANSFORMSTATETYPE State,
        CONST D3DMATRIX *pMatrix);
```

The first parameter specifies the transform that should be set. The following code shows how to set the three transformations I've talked about so far:

```
m_pD3DDevice->SetTransform(D3DTS_PROJECTION, &m_ProjectionMatrix);
m_pD3DDevice->SetTransform(D3DTS_VIEW, &m_ViewMatrix);
m_pD3DDevice->SetTransform(D3DTS_WORLD, &m_WorldMatrix);
```

You can set these transforms as frequently or infrequently as needed, but they affect everything that is rendered while they are set.

Using Matrix Stacks

OpenGL programmers are accustomed to the notion of a stack that manages transformation matrices. Although DirectX doesn't have a built-in notion of stacks the way OpenGL does, the D3DX library does include a helper interface called ID3DXMatrixStack. This interface contains basic stack operations such as Push and Pop, as well as several methods to help build transformations. However, unlike in OpenGL, you must explicitly pass the contents of the stack to SetTransform because the device itself does not maintain a stack. Stacks can be useful when you use them to track and manage the state of transformations while rendering a complex object. For example, consider the ship shown in Figure 9.8.

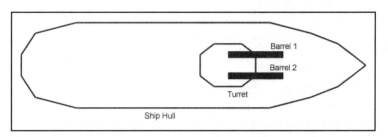

Figure 9.8

A relatively complex ship model.

Suppose you know the position and the orientation of the ship at sea, and you also know the position of the turret relative to the ship and the position of the barrels relative to the turret. Instead of computing multiple matrices for each object and then storing each matrix, you can use a stack and render the ship with the following steps:

1. Create a stack interface with `D3DXCreateMatrixStack`.
2. Compute the matrix for the ship's position and push that onto the stack.
3. Set the top of the stack as the current world transform and render the hull.
4. Push the stack and concatenate the relative transform for the turret.
5. Set the top of the stack as the current world transform and render the turret.
6. Push the stack and concatenate the relative transform for the first barrel.
7. Set the top of the stack as the current world transform and render the first barrel.
8. Pop the stack, which places the turret transform on top.
9. Push the stack and concatenate the relative transform for the second barrel.
10. Set the top of the stack as the current world transform and render the second barrel.
11. Pop the stack, which places the turret transform on top.
12. Pop the stack, which places the ship transform on top.
13. Render the other parts of the ship the same way.

Most of the examples in this book deal with simple objects, so I do not use stacks because I don't need them and to keep things simple. However, if you are rendering complex objects, keep in mind that a matrix stack can be a valuable tool to help manage multiple matrix changes.

The matrix stack is the last concept that concerns the actual transformation matrices. Whether you manage the transformations with a stack or with a set of matrices, you have now gone through the matrix-based transformations. One last transformation maps data to the actual window.

The Viewport

Viewports do not involve transformation matrices, but they do make sense to discuss at this point. Once the three transformation steps are done, the device still needs to determine how the data is finally mapped to each pixel. You help the device do this by defining a viewport. Under normal circumstances, the viewport is defined by the size of the window in a windowed application or the resolution of the screen in a full-screen application, so many times you don't need to set it explicitly. However,

DirectX also allows the programmer to specify a portion of the window as a viewport. This can be useful when rendering multiple views in the same window or using other effects such as a sniper scope. In the sample application for this chapter, you will create multiple viewports to show different transformations.

A viewport is defined with the `D3DVIEWPORT8` structure. This structure defines the rectangular position of the viewport within the window or screen, as well as the near and far Z planes. Before setting a new viewport, it's usually a good idea to save a copy of the old one with `GetViewport`:

```
HRESULT IDirect3DDevice::GetViewport(D3DVIEWPORT8 *pViewport);
```

This is a good idea because the viewport should probably be reset when you are done rendering. Like the transformations, the current viewport continually affects rendering until it is set to something else. If you don't reset the viewport, other pieces of code might make assumptions that turn out to be incorrect. Once you save a copy of the viewport, you can set a different one with `SetViewport`:

```
HRESULT IDirect3DDevice::SetViewport(D3DVIEWPORT8 *pViewport);
```

This defines a new subsection of the window, and drawing occurs in that rectangle. If the new viewport is outside of the device boundaries, `SetViewport` fails. One important thing to keep in mind is that the ratio of the dimensions of the viewport should match the aspect ratio of the projection matrix (or vice versa). If not, objects can appear squished.

Putting It All Together

I think that the best way to illustrate the concepts from this chapter is to demonstrate them in practice. The sample application for this chapter builds on the code from the previous chapter, applying transformations to your simple circle of points. Because there is so much duplicated code, I only discuss the new material, but the actual source code on the CD is complete.

This application renders four different views of the same vertex buffer. Each view applies a different world transform, demonstrating the effects of the order of operations. Before I get started discussing the code, it's important to remember that the following code is just the tip of the iceberg in terms of what you can do with transformations. I strongly encourage you to experiment with this code, changing the order of operations or adding new operations. After discussing the code, I suggest a few exercises you can try.

As always, take a look at the header file for your new class, TransformApplication.h:

```
class CTransformApplication : public CHostApplication
{
public:
```

This is your only new function. This function is called when the application starts and needs to build a new set of viewports. In the full source-code listing, you also include Render, PostReset, and so on, as well as the member variables for your old vertex buffer:

```
  void InitializeViewports();
```

These are your new transformation matrices for the three main transforms. The view matrix is set once at the very beginning of the application, and the projection and world matrices are set every frame:

```
  D3DXMATRIX m_WorldMatrix;
  D3DXMATRIX m_ViewMatrix;
  D3DXMATRIX m_ProjectionMatrix;
```

The last member variables are the new viewports. Each viewport shows the circle from Chapter 8 with a different transformation matrix applied. The transformations are rotation, scaling-rotation-translation, translation-rotation, and rotation-translation-rotation-scaling.

```
  D3DVIEWPORT8 m_RViewport;
  D3DVIEWPORT8 m_SRTViewport;
  D3DVIEWPORT8 m_TRViewport;
  D3DVIEWPORT8 m_RTRSViewport;
};
```

I go into more detail about the actual transformations in TransformApplication.cpp, shown next. Remember, I show only the new code:

Now that you are going to be using actual transforms, you use the standard FVF format for vertices and drop the RHW member from the vertex structure:

```
#define D3DFVF_SIMPLEVERTEX (D3DFVF_XYZ | D3DFVF_DIFFUSE)
struct SIMPLE_VERTEX
{
  float x, y, z;
  DWORD color;
};
```

For this application, you limit your number of vertices to a small number so that there are gaps between the points. This helps you see the rotations:

```
#define NUM_VERTICES 20
BOOL CTransformApplication::PostInitialize()
{
```

This is just another windowed application. Feel free to try the full-screen version using the full-screen creation function:

```
    if (FAILED(EasyCreateWindowed(m_hWnd, D3DDEVTYPE_HAL,
            D3DCREATE_HARDWARE_VERTEXPROCESSING)))
        return FALSE;
```

I haven't really talked about render states yet, but here you disable lighting. The reason you need to do this is that the vertices are moving through the transformation and lighting pipeline. If you don't disable lighting, everything will be black (because you don't have any lights), and there will be nothing to see!

```
    m_pD3DDevice->SetRenderState(D3DRS_LIGHTING, FALSE);
```

Here you set the view matrix to the identity matrix. This means that the viewer is sitting at the origin facing in the positive Z direction. For this example, you don't move the viewer, but I talk about how you can change that:

```
    D3DXMatrixIdentity(&m_ViewMatrix);
    m_pD3DDevice->SetTransform(D3DTS_VIEW, &m_ViewMatrix);
```

The last new thing is the initialization of the new viewports that will be used to render the different views of the vertices. All vertex buffer initialization code is the same as in the last chapter except that the new vertices do not have the RHW member:

```
    InitializeViewports();
    return CreateVertexBuffer();
}
```

The first thing you do is get the current viewport so that you know the dimensions. Each of your viewports occupies a quarter of the main viewport. The following code simply breaks the viewport into four subrectangles:

```
void CTransformApplication::InitializeViewports()
{
  D3DVIEWPORT8 MainViewport;
  m_pD3DDevice->GetViewport(&MainViewport);
```

```
m_RViewport.Width = m_SRTViewport.Width = m_TRViewport.Width =
m_RTRSViewport.Width = MainViewport.Width / 2;
m_RViewport.Height = m_SRTViewport.Height = m_TRViewport.Height =
m_RTRSViewport.Height = MainViewport.Height / 2;

m_RViewport.Y = m_SRTViewport.Y = 0;
m_RViewport.X = m_TRViewport.X = 0;

m_TRViewport.Y = m_RTRSViewport.Y = MainViewport.Height / 2;
m_SRTViewport.X = m_RTRSViewport.X = MainViewport.Width / 2;

m_RViewport.MinZ = m_SRTViewport.MinZ =
m_TRViewport.MinZ = m_RTRSViewport.MinZ = 0.0f;
m_RViewport.MaxZ = m_SRTViewport.MaxZ =
m_TRViewport.MaxZ = m_RTRSViewport.MaxZ = 1.0f;
}
```

One thing to remember is that the Z limit of each viewport ranges from 0.0 to 1.0. This is because the depth buffer is normalized to 1.0 no matter what distance you set for the far Z plane of the frustum. Each viewport can have a custom depth range, but here you set each one to have the full range. Once the viewports are set up, the application begins rendering:

```
void CTransformApplication::Render()
{
```

Because this is a windowed application, the user can resize the window to some new aspect ratio. Here you get the client rectangle of the window and use that to build a projection matrix with the proper aspect ratio. Notice also that the field of view is given in radians. This is very important because if you make the mistake of thinking in degrees, your projection matrix will produce unexpected results:

```
RECT WindowRect;
GetClientRect(m_hWnd, &WindowRect);
D3DXMatrixPerspectiveFovLH(&m_ProjectionMatrix, D3DX_PI / 4,
        (float)(WindowRect.right - WindowRect.left) /
        (float)(WindowRect.bottom - WindowRect.top),
        1.0f, 100.0f);
m_pD3DDevice->SetTransform(D3DTS_PROJECTION, &m_ProjectionMatrix);
```

Here are your four matrices that will serve as building blocks for your four transformations. You can use each of these together to produce more complex transformations:

```
D3DXMATRIX RotationMatrix1;
D3DXMATRIX RotationMatrix2;
D3DXMATRIX TranslationMatrix;
D3DXMATRIX ScalingMatrix;
```

The first thing you do is save a copy of your current viewport. This is so you can restore the viewport to its initial condition once your four viewports are rendered:

```
D3DVIEWPORT8 MainViewport;
m_pD3DDevice->GetViewport(&MainViewport);
```

Your two rotation matrices use the system timer to generate some arbitrary rotation about the Z-axis. It's not terribly important what the rotation actually is, and this is the easiest way to make up some value. You use the first matrix for simple rotations. The second matrix rotates in the opposite direction; it is used in the viewport that shows an orbiting effect. The second rotation matrix corrects for the first rotation, creating the effect of an orbit without rotating the geometry:

```
D3DXMatrixRotationZ(&RotationMatrix1, (float)GetTickCount()
  / 1000.0f);
D3DXMatrixRotationZ(&RotationMatrix2, -(float)GetTickCount()
  / 1000.0f);
```

The translation and scaling matrices are pretty simple. The translation matrix moves the coordinate system three units in the positive X direction, and the scaling matrix scales Y values by one half:

```
D3DXMatrixTranslation(&TranslationMatrix, 3.0f, 0.0f, 0.0f);
D3DXMatrixScaling(&ScalingMatrix, 1.0f, 0.5f, 1.0f);
```

This is your first and simplest viewport. It shows the effect of a simple rotation matrix. The viewport is set to the upper-left corner, the world transform is set, and the vertex buffer is rendered:

```
m_pD3DDevice->SetViewport(&m_RViewport);
m_WorldMatrix = RotationMatrix1;
m_pD3DDevice->SetTransform(D3DTS_WORLD, &m_WorldMatrix);
m_pD3DDevice->DrawPrimitive(D3DPT_POINTLIST, 0, NUM_VERTICES);
```

This is a more complex combination of transformations. This code applies a scaling matrix, followed by a rotation and translation. This creates the orbiting effect described earlier, but notice how the scaling factor scales the Y values of both the circle and the orbit. The orbit is now elliptical because the scaling factor affects the translation values. Notice that the scaling factor does not scale the magnitude of the angle of rotation, only the translation. Also, remember that the actual multiplication order is the reverse of the order in which each transformation is applied:

```
m_pD3DDevice->SetViewport(&m_SRTViewport);
m_WorldMatrix = TranslationMatrix * RotationMatrix1 * ScalingMatrix;
m_pD3DDevice->SetTransform(D3DTS_WORLD, &m_WorldMatrix);
m_pD3DDevice->DrawPrimitive(D3DPT_POINTLIST, 0, NUM_VERTICES);
```

This is another relatively simple transformation. Here, the object is translated and then rotated. Again, notice the order of multiplication:

```
m_pD3DDevice->SetViewport(&m_TRViewport);
m_WorldMatrix = RotationMatrix1 * TranslationMatrix;
m_pD3DDevice->SetTransform(D3DTS_WORLD, &m_WorldMatrix);
m_pD3DDevice->DrawPrimitive(D3DPT_POINTLIST, 0, NUM_VERTICES);
```

Here is your most complex transformation. The object is first rotated and translated, producing the orbit effect. It is then rotated in the opposite direction by the second rotation matrix, which corrects the actual rotation of the geometry. Finally, the scaling matrix squashes the geometry along the Y-axis. However, notice that, unlike the previously scaled transformation, the actual path of the orbit is circular. This is because the scaling matrix is applied at the end. It only affects the geometry, not the other transformations:

```
m_pD3DDevice->SetViewport(&m_RTRSViewport);
m_WorldMatrix = ScalingMatrix * RotationMatrix2 *
    TranslationMatrix * RotationMatrix1;
m_pD3DDevice->SetTransform(D3DTS_WORLD, &m_WorldMatrix);
m_pD3DDevice->DrawPrimitive(D3DPT_POINTLIST, 0, NUM_VERTICES);
```

The last thing you do is reset the viewport. This is especially important in your framework because you clear the viewport in the base class. If you did not reset the viewport to the entire window, Clear would clear only the last viewport you set.

```
m_pD3DDevice->SetViewport(&MainViewport);
}
```

In general, different parts of a 3D rendering application should clean up after themselves. This step becomes very important when I talk about textures and render states. Figure 9.9 shows what the application should look like.

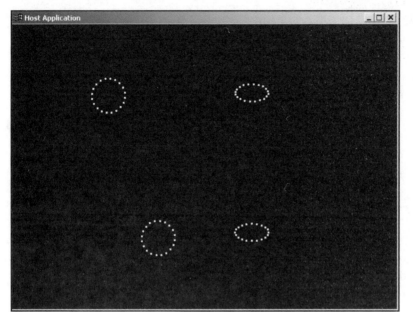

Figure 9.9

Examples of different transformations.

Suggested Exercises

The sample application for this chapter should provide a pretty good basis for understanding the effects of different transformations, but there is always more you can do. Here are a few suggested exercises you can try:

1. Set the view transform instead of the world transform. For simple rotations about the Z-axis, this should produce nearly the same results as setting the world transform, provided that you set the world transform to the identity matrix.

2. Experiment with different values for the FOV of the perspective matrix. Lower values should produce a zoom effect. Higher values will "zoom out." Beware of values that are either too large or too small. Values that are too small might zoom too much; values that are larger that 180 degrees will flip the axes. Once you understand the limits, it can be worthwhile to explore the effect of exceeding them. That way, you'll recognize the error if you ever see that as a bug in your program.

3. Try many different transforms with different orders of operation. The more familiar you can get with the effects, the less likely you'll make a mistake.

4. Add keyboard support by incrementing some value in the message handler as a response to a `WM_KEYDOWN` message. Then use that value in your rotations or translations.

5. Use the `ID3DXMatrixStack` to manage transformations. Look through the SDK documentation and rework the matrices to use the stack functions.

You can try many variations. The important thing is that you leave this chapter with a good understanding of how different transformations affect the final output on the screen.

Performance Considerations

There aren't many performance considerations to worry about when setting transforms. Of course, there is a slight cost associated with setting transforms and computing matrices, but it's minimal. In general, batching is always a good thing, but don't worry too much about the cost of `SetTransform`. In fact, a call to `SetTransform` is probably cheaper than locking the vertices and transforming them on the CPU. In most cases, it is best to take advantage of the hardware T&L and use matrices to transform data. It is much cheaper to send 16 floating-point values to the card than it is to send several thousand new vertices.

In Conclusion...

Applying transformations can be powerful, useful, and confusing. As always, review some of the more important points:

- You can use world matrices to move geometry around the virtual scene.
- You can reuse geometry by rendering a vertex buffer multiple times with different world transformations.
- The view matrix controls the position and orientation of the virtual camera.
- The projection matrix controls the lens of the virtual camera, setting perspective and field of view.
- You can build complex transformations by concatenating multiple matrices.
- Order matters when concatenating matrices.
- You can use stacks to manage complex transformations.

CHAPTER 10

FROM VERTICES TO GEOMETRY

F ace it: simple vertices are boring. This work doesn't really get interesting until you learn about surfaces, triangles, and geometry. Things are about to get interesting. In previous chapters, I tried to set things up as much as possible. I talked about vertices as a basis for geometry. I talked about transformations so that you can easily present and view the geometry. Now, you have all the necessary pieces to see how vertices are used to build something more interesting. This chapter does not talk about lines, concentrating instead on triangles. However, all the points made here also apply to lines. (There's a pun in there somewhere.) I'm not spending time on lines because once you understand triangles, the line primitives should be extremely easy to handle if you need to. One thing to remember in this chapter is that you will need to involve some concepts that you haven't yet fully explored, such as lighting. If you don't fully understand these new concepts, don't worry; you will fully explore them in later chapters. The code for this chapter is located on the CD in the \code\Chapter10 directory. This chapter introduces the following concepts.

- Using vertices to build surfaces.
- Rendering surfaces.
- Using triangle lists.
- Using triangle fans.
- Using triangle strips.
- Rendering indexed primitives.
- Loading and rendering meshes in .X files.
- Performance implications of different rendering techniques.
- Adding mesh rendering to an application.

Turning Vertices into Surfaces

I spent the last couple chapters talking about vertices because they represent positions in space. However, interesting objects occupy many positions in space, and they are most often represented in 3D graphics by their outer surfaces. These outer surfaces are usually represented by triangles. In the case of curved surfaces, you can use sets of triangles to approximate the surface to varying degrees of accuracy. Also, once I start talking about surfaces, it makes sense to talk about surface normals (vectors that are perpendicular to each surface).

If you are using smooth shading, surface normals are actually represented as vertex normals, where the normal vector for each vertex is the average of the normal vectors for all the triangles that share that vertex, as shown in Figure 10.1.

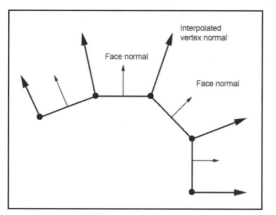

Figure 10.1

Vertex normal on a surface.

The standard DirectX lighting model lights surfaces per vertex. This means that the math for lighting is computed for each vertex. Because each triangle has three vertices, the device must interpolate the shaded values across each triangle. The combination of averaged normals as shown in Figure 10.1 and interpolated shading across each surface creates the smooth shading shown in most of the renderings in this book.

Because you want to add this new piece of information about normals to your vertices, you have to expand your vertex format. You do this by redefining your FVF with the D3DFVF_NORMAL flag as defined in Chapter 8. This, along with the position and color information, makes up the minimum format for rendering lit surfaces. Once you revise your vertex format, I can begin talking about how you actually render the triangles themselves.

Rendering Surfaces

Processing vertices can be expensive if you have too many of them, so the challenge of rendering surfaces becomes how you represent a given surface with a set of triangles and how to do it in the most efficient manner.

It turns out that it is not so easy. For instance, if you are modeling a cylinder, the sides of that cylinder must consist of a collection of flat sides. If you use too few sides, the cylinder appears blocky with visible edges. If you use too many sides, you might end up using more data than is actually visible to the eye, causing unnecessary processing. This first problem is usually one an artist must solve using a modeling program, the constraints of the given project, and a little experimentation. I'm not going to spend a lot of time talking about that. Instead, I am going to focus on a second problem. Once you know what your geometry is, how do you render that in the optimal way?

From previous chapters, you know that vertices are stored in vertex buffers. You also know that you can draw the contents of the vertex buffer by calling `DrawPrimitive`. You have been using this to draw sets of vertices, but now it's time to talk about triangles. You can draw three types of triangle primitives: the triangle list, the triangle fan, and the triangle strip. Let's look at each type individually and explore the pros and cons of each.

Rendering with Triangle Lists

The triangle list is the easiest of the triangle primitives to understand. Each triangle is represented in the vertex buffer by a set of three vertices. The first three vertices represent the first triangle, the second three vertices represent the second triangle, and so on. Figure 10.2 shows how a triangle list uses a set of vertices.

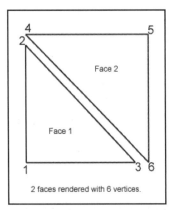

Figure 10.2

Triangles in a triangle list.

You do this with the following call to `DrawPrimitive`:

```
m_pD3DDevice->DrawPrimitive(D3DPT_TRIANGLELIST, 0, 2);
```

Note that the number of primitives specified in the third parameter is the number of triangles drawn (2), not the number of vertices used (6). This is the easiest way to represent triangles, but Figure 10.2 also demonstrates the major drawback. Many times, triangles in a continuous surface share common vertices, but in a triangle list, each common point is repeated multiple times. Imagine rendering a cube. Eight points are all you need to define a cube, but a cube rendered with a triangle list requires 12 triangles and 36 vertices. This means that a triangle list requires the hardware to process 28 more vertices than it needs to. Even in Figure 10.2, the number of required vertices increases by 50 percent. It makes more sense to reuse vertices, and in fact you can.

Rendering with Triangle Fans

One way of reusing vertices is to use triangle fans. A triangle fan uses the first vertex as a shared vertex for the rest of the vertices, as shown in Figure 10.3.

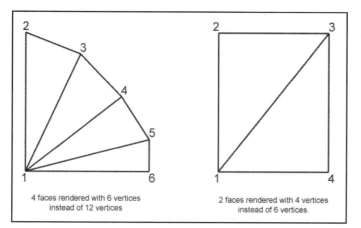

4 faces rendered with 6 vertices instead of 12 vertices

2 faces rendered with 4 vertices instead of 6 vertices.

Figure 10.3

Triangles in a triangle fan.

This is the first example of reusing vertices, and the following code draws two triangles:

```
m_pD3DDevice->DrawPrimitive(D3DPT_TRIANGLEFAN, 0, 2);
```

Notice that when drawing two triangles, you still specify two primitives even though the number of vertices used drops from six to four. However, this is not terribly useful because it only applies well to circular or fan-shaped objects. Although you can use triangle fans to produce rectangular shapes, it's usually not the easiest solution. A more general solution is a triangle strip.

Rendering with Triangle Strips

Triangle strips provide a way to reuse vertices by rendering long strips in sequences, such as the one shown in Figure 10.4.

Figure 10.4

Triangles in a triangle strip.

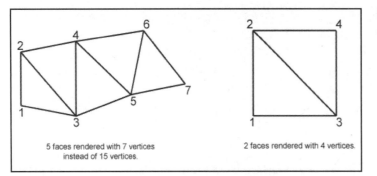

5 faces rendered with 7 vertices
instead of 15 vertices.

2 faces rendered with 4 vertices.

Because vertices are reused, this is a better way of drawing sets of triangles than the triangle list. The code to do this is the same as earlier, with the different primitive type:

```
m_pD3DDevice->DrawPrimitive(D3DPT_TRIANGLESTRIP, 0, 2);
```

The important thing to remember about strips is that the order matters. Because every new vertex is coupled with the previous two, you need to make sure that the order makes sense.

Another thing to consider with triangle strips is that sharing vertices does have some drawbacks. For instance, Figure 10.5 shows a typical hard-edged corner. As the figure shows, each side has a different surface normal. However, the shared vertex can have only one normal vector. This presents a problem because an averaged normal vector doesn't produce the correct hard edge for the lighting. One way to work around this is to create degenerate triangles. A degenerate triangle is not really visible, but provides a way to transition between vertices by smoothing the normals around the corner. For example, in Figure 10.5, the two sides of the corner have different surface normals, so instead of the two sides sharing different vertices, I insert a third thin face between them. If this face were larger and actually visible, it would show the effect of the different normals, but because it is extremely thin, you never see it. It is not meant to be visible, only to provide a transition between the faces.

One last thing to consider is that the strips are usually not easy to derive in complex models. There are utilities for breaking models into efficient strips, but they can sometimes complicate the authoring process, and the techniques are not perfect. In the sample code for this chapter, I show that it's easy to create strips for simple geometric shapes, but the task becomes harder for organic or complex objects such as characters or vehicles. So you have to look for ways to get the vertex to reuse strips and fans without the complication of authoring strips. And again, you can do that.

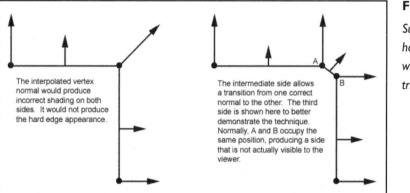

The interpolated vertex normal would produce incorrect shading on both sides. It would not produce the hard edge appearance.

The intermediate side allows a transition from one correct normal to the other. The third side is shown here to better demonstrate the technique. Normally, A and B occupy the same position, producing a side that is not actually visible to the viewer.

Rendering with Indexed Primitives

So far, all of the discussions have been based on vertex buffers where the order of the vertices affects the triangles you draw. Strips exploit that ordering by basing subsequent triangles off of previous vertices, but with certain drawbacks. What is needed is a way to render triangles independently of the order of the vertices in the vertex buffer. This is the conceptual basis of the index buffer. Index buffers store the indices of vertices in an arbitrary order. You can base multiple primitives on vertices independently of where each vertex is in the vertex buffer. Also, the index buffer can reference the same vertex more than once. This offers a performance advantage over triangle lists in that you can reuse a single vertex multiple times and an authoring advantage over strips in that the process is less complicated.

You can use index buffers to draw any of the three triangle primitives. In the past, conventional wisdom has been that indexed triangle strips are the most efficient way to render geometry. However, one presentation by Microsoft's D3DX team stated that it found little or no performance difference between rendering indexed triangle lists and indexed triangle strips, at least on the current generation of hardware. If you think about what is actually happening, this makes sense. Vertices run through the T&L part of the pipeline before they are used to actually draw the geometry. As long as vertices are not specified twice (as in nonindexed lists), the performance should be roughly the same for primitives of any type. Some pieces of hardware can further optimize strips, but the performance gains might be too small to warrant the hassle of creating strips. If you are concerned with getting the absolute best performance, you might want to experiment with indexed strips, but in most cases, indexed lists should be sufficient.

Index buffers are similar to vertex buffers, and they are represented by the `IDirect3DIndexBuffer8` interface. A device creates index buffers with calls to `CreateIndexBuffer`:

```
HRESULT IDirect3DDevice8::CreateIndexBuffer(UINT Length, DWORD Usage,
                    D3DFORMAT IndexFormat,
                    D3DPOOL MemoryPool,
                    IDirect3DIndexBuffer8 **ppIndexBuffer);
```

Most of these parameters are the same as described in Chapter 8 for vertex buffers with the obvious exception of the index buffer itself and the format. Unlike vertex buffers, the format of the indices can only be `D3DFMT_INDEX16` or `D3DFMT_INDEX32`, corresponding to 16-bit or 32-bit integers for each index. Note that because the `Length` parameter is length of the buffer in bytes, the length is dependent on the index format. A mismatch between the format and length parameters could lead to failures down the line.

Once the index buffer is created, you need to change the way you render primitives. In addition to setting the stream source to the desired vertex buffer, you must also set the index buffer with a call to `SetIndices`:

```
HRESULT IDirect3DDevice8::SetIndices(IDirect3DIndexBuffer8
                *pIndexBuffer, UINT IndexOffset);
```

This call takes a pointer to the index buffer and an index offset. The index offset is added to all indices before vertices are actually fetched. In most cases, the value of this second parameter is 0. Once the index buffer is set, you can draw indexed primitives with the aptly named `DrawIndexedPrimitive`:

```
HRESULT IDirect3DDevice8::DrawIndexedPrimitive(D3DPRIMITIVETYPE Type,
            UINT MinIndex, UINT NumVertices,
            UINT StartIndex, UINT PrimitiveCount);
```

This call draws indexed primitives based on the currently set index and vertex buffers. The new parameters `MinIndex` and `NumVertices` specify the valid range for indices used in this call. Indices that are in the index buffer but outside of this range cause this function to fail. Depending on the values for these two parameters, the device might also try to optimize vertex processing, but in most cases, you can specify the full range of vertices.

When I start explaining the code for this chapter, I go into more detail about the actual implementation, but the important thing to remember from this discussion is that there are many ways to render triangles—and usually the most optimal ways require the minimum of vertex data. In most cases, rendering the data as indexed triangle lists is a good solution, and that's the way many models are stored in DirectX's .X file format. Let's examine how to deal with .X files.

Loading and Rendering .X Files

If you are creating simple geometry in code, arranging the data in optimal ways can be easy, but most of the time, models are created in a 3D modeling package and saved as geometry in a file. Now that you know the basics of how to render geometry, let's look at how you can read data from an .X file and explore the different ways you can render the geometry.

The .X file format is a relatively robust format for storing 3D information. An increasing number of 3D modeling applications feature the ability to save files in the .X format, but some do not. If your 3D modeling program cannot save .X files, or if you have a 3D file in a different format, the SDK includes utilities, such as conv3ds.exe, to convert file formats. The following discussion assumes that the data is stored as an .X file. Once you have .X files, the D3DX library comes to the rescue once again and supplies several interfaces and functions for dealing with meshes.

The easiest way to read mesh data from an .X file is to use D3DXLoadMeshFromX. The following code shows the function prototype, and Table 10.1 describes the parameters:

```
HRESULT D3DXLoadMeshFromX(LPSTR pFileName, DWORD MeshOptions,
            LPDIRECT3DDEVICE8 pDevice,
            LPD3DXBUFFER *ppAdjacencyInfo,
            LPD3DXBUFFER *ppMaterials,
            PDWORD pNumMaterials, LPD3DXMESH *ppMesh);
```

After the .X file is read, the output is a mesh object. The ID3DXMesh interface has many members that give the user a finer grain of control over the mesh itself. Some of these functions allow direct access to the vertex and index buffers for the mesh. Others are used to optimize the mesh. When I begin talking about vertex shaders, you will need to deconstruct mesh objects to get at the raw data. And I also talk about some of the member functions of the ID3DXMesh interface. When I talk about mesh optimization, I discuss the optimization functions. For now, I concentrate on the basic approaches to rendering the mesh object once it is loaded with D3DXLoadMeshFromX.

When the mesh is loaded, D3DXLoadMeshFromX creates a mesh object and a buffer containing all the materials used by the mesh object. So far, I have only talked about vertex colors. I talk more about materials in the chapter on lighting, but the quick

Table 10.1   D3DXLoadMeshFromX Parameters

Parameter	Comments
LPSTR pFileName	This is the file name of the .X file. This must include the path and the file name.
DWORD MeshOptions	This parameter can be a combination of the D3DXMESH_ flags, which correspond to the memory pool and usage options for vertex and index buffers. The same performance and usage considerations apply here as they do for other vertex buffers.
LPDIRECT3DDEVICE8 pDevice	This is the device that will host this new resource.
LPD3DXBUFFER *ppAdjacencyInfo	This is an array that holds three DWORDs per face. These DWORDs denote the triangles that share common edges with each triangle.
LPD3DXBUFFER *ppMaterials	This is an array of D3DXMATERIAL structures. These structures contain color information for each face as well as the file name of any texture map. In this chapter's source code, I use the material structure out of necessity, and I explain the structure in greater depth in Chapter 11.
PDWORD pNumMaterials	This is a pointer to a DWORD that is filled by the function to specify the number of materials listed in the preceding structure.
LPD3DXMESH *ppMesh	This is the mesh object that contains the geometric information from the .X file.

explanation is that the device uses materials to define colors when lighting is enabled. When you get into vertex shaders, you will go back to using vertex colors because you will be creating your own lights in the vertex shaders. The D3DX functions return materials stored as an array of D3DXMATERIAL structures. This array contains all the color and texture information used in the mesh object. Simple meshes can use only one material. Others can specify a different material for every face. The connection between materials and mesh faces lies in a data member of the ID3DXMesh object called the attribute buffer. This is an array of DWORDs that specifies the material for each face. The first value in the buffer corresponds to the array index of the material for the first face, and so on. Therefore, you can think of each material as defining a subset of faces that use that material. In most simple rendering code, you draw meshes using DrawSubset:

```
HRESULT ID3DXMesh::DrawSubset(DWORD AttributeID);
```

Here, the AttributeID parameter corresponds to an index in the array of materials. For instance, drawing the subset for attribute 0 draws all the faces that use the first material in the array. This leads to a performance consideration. Unless the mesh has been optimized, the attribute buffer is not guaranteed to be sorted by attribute. If this is the case, a call to DrawSubset results in a linear search through the entire attribute buffer for all faces with a given attribute. For a large mesh with n different materials, this could result in n searches though a large array. You can definitely do better. For this reason, it is usually a good idea to either optimize the mesh using the built-in optimization functions or at least be aware of what is actually happening when you call DrawSubset.

Other than the considerations with using materials, ID3DXMesh renders models exactly the same way I described with indexed triangle lists. The performance considerations I talked about with vertex buffers and rendering primitives apply to ID3DXMesh as well. The real advantages to using the mesh interface are .X file access and the optimization functions.

Performance Considerations

I've hinted at several performance considerations throughout this chapter, but it is worthwhile to reiterate some of them here. First, as always, it's best to keep the number of vertices as low as possible. This is a matter of not only dealing with optimized 3D assets, but also rendering those assets as efficiently as possible. As I've shown, the best way to render geometry is with either indexed strips or indexed lists. Indexed lists might be slightly less efficient, but overall they are easier to work with.

Batching is always something to keep in mind. The issues with meshes and searches through the attribute buffer are not only a matter of the searches through memory. It is also a good idea to optimize the mesh to limit the number of times you set materials and textures. I have heard anecdotes about developers who render their objects differently for even and odd frames to take advantage of device states that were set on the previous frame. This is probably not an extreme you need to go to, but it shows the importance of thinking about how you use the vertices and the device.

Finally, in this chapter, you've started to use lighting and set different render states such as lighting and culling. I discuss these features in their own chapter soon, but it is sometimes easy to forget that these things are enabled, costing resources. If you are not using something like lighting, remember to turn it off. But first, remember the rule about batching. Do not turn the lighting on and off. Render all lit objects first with lighting on, and then turn it off for all the objects that do not use lighting.

The Code

In previous chapters, I've shown the source code and explained it as you walk through. Things are now starting to get complex enough where I should give a high level explanation before you start.

The code for this chapter highlights many of the basic concepts I've discussed. It renders four different basic geometry types and a mesh object. Figure 10.6 shows a screenshot from the sample application.

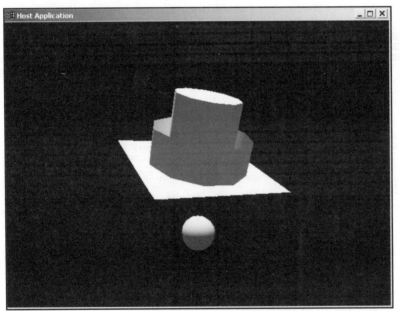

Figure 10.6

Rendering geometry and a mesh.

You create the rectangular plane using a triangle list. You create the inner cylinder with a triangle strip and the top of the cylinder with a triangle fan. You create the outermost cylinder with an indexed triangle list, reusing the vertices from the triangle trip. You resize the outer cylinder by applying a scaling transformation. Finally, the dual spheres are loaded from an .X file and rendered below the other objects. The actual application spins these objects around so that you can see the shape and the effects of lighting.

Take a look at the code, starting with GeometryApplication.h. As in the previous chapter, I am only going to highlight new code for both the header and the implementation file. The complete source code is on the CD:

```
#include "Application.h"
```

One of the first things you might notice is that you move the vertex definition out of the implementation file and into the header file. This is so you can create member functions that use the structure as a parameter. Also, you remove the color member from the structure. When dealing with lighting and materials, there's no reason to specify colors in the vertex format:

```
struct GEOMETRY_VERTEX
{
    float x, y, z;
    float nx, ny, nz;
};
class CGeometryApplication : public CHostApplication
{
public:
```

Lighting and transformation now require you to do a lot more setup on the device itself. Therefore, you use a new function to reset the device states when the device is reset. This is in addition to the previous code that recreates the vertex buffers:

```
void SetupDevice();
```

The following two functions load and draw the mesh object. They were not included with the other geometry functions because the mesh is loaded into managed memory. Therefore, it does not need to be recreated if the device is restored:

```
void RenderMesh();
BOOL LoadMesh();
```

You call the next two functions whenever the device is created or restored. They handle creating the vertex buffer and the new index buffer, as well as calling the functions that create the actual vertex data:

```
BOOL CreateGeometry();
BOOL FillVertexBuffer();
void DestroyGeometry();
```

The following functions fill the vertex and index buffers. When the index buffer is initialized, only the values of the index buffer are filled. The vertices for the indexed primitive are reused values from the triangle strip:

```
void InitializeIndexed();
void InitializeList(GEOMETRY_VERTEX *pVertices);
void InitializeStrip(GEOMETRY_VERTEX *pVertices);
void InitializeFan(GEOMETRY_VERTEX *pVertices);
```

The next function initializes the DirectX light used in the sample. In the full source code, this line is followed by the standard functions such as PostReset, Render, and so on:

```
void InitializeLights();
```

The following are the interface pointers to the buffer and mesh objects you will be rendering. These pointers are created by the device methods and the D3DX functions:

```
LPDIRECT3DVERTEXBUFFER8 m_pVertexBuffer;
LPDIRECT3DINDEXBUFFER8 m_pIndexBuffer;
LPD3DXMESH m_pMesh;
```

You have several material variables shown below. The first material is one you define and apply to the simple geometry. The material array is a list of materials defined by the mesh. You also keep track of the number of materials so you can loop through them when you draw subsets of the mesh.

```
D3DMATERIAL8 m_ShapeMaterial;
D3DMATERIAL8 *m_pMeshMaterials;
DWORD       m_NumMaterials;
```

In the full source code, you also retain the transformation matrices you defined in the last chapter. This defines the new application class for this chapter. Now, look at GeometryApplication.cpp to see how these new concepts are actually implemented:

```
#include "GeometryApplication.h"
```

You redefine your vertex format to exclude color information because you are using materials. Almost all of the shader techniques include at least one color in the format because you will be implementing your own lighting, but for now, there is no point in defining vertex colors:

```
#define D3DFVF_GEOMETRYVERTEX (D3DFVF_XYZ | D3DFVF_NORMAL)
```

The following definitions make it easy to experiment with different resolutions for the strips and fans you use to draw the cylinders. Change the number of sides and see the effects. For explanations of how the number of vertices relates to the number of sides, see the explanations later in the chapter when I talk about filling the vertex buffer:

```
#define NUM_LIST_VERTICES 6
#define NUM_FAN_SIDES    10
#define NUM_FAN_VERTICES  NUM_FAN_SIDES + 2
#define NUM_STRIP_SIDES  10
#define NUM_STRIP_VERTICES (2 * NUM_STRIP_SIDES) + 2
#define FAN_OFFSET    NUM_LIST_VERTICES
#define STRIP_OFFSET  FAN_OFFSET + NUM_FAN_VERTICES
#define NUM_VERTICES (NUM_LIST_VERTICES + NUM_FAN_VERTICES + NUM_STRIP_VERTICES)
```

As you've seen in previous chapters, it is good to initialize the pointers to NULL to ensure that you don't try to use a pointer for an object that's not really created. Also, the destructor destroys all buffers:

```
CGeometryApplication::CGeometryApplication()
{
    m_pVertexBuffer = NULL;
    m_pIndexBuffer  = NULL;
    m_pMesh       = NULL;
    m_pMeshMaterials = NULL;
    m_NumMaterials  = 0;
}
CGeometryApplication::~CGeometryApplication()
{
    DestroyGeometry();
}
```

After the device is created, the device states are set and the simple geometric shapes are created. Finally, you load the mesh file. This is the only time you need to load the mesh because the mesh exists in managed memory. Therefore, it doesn't need to be recreated if the device is lost:

```
BOOL CGeometryApplication::PostInitialize()
{
    if (FAILED(EasyCreateWindowed(m_hWnd, D3DDEVTYPE_HAL,
                D3DCREATE_HARDWARE_VERTEXPROCESSING)))
```

```
            return FALSE;

        SetupDevice();

        if (!CreateGeometry())
            return FALSE;

        return LoadMesh();
}
```

The following function sets up the device, setting a default view and projection matrix. In the previous chapter, the projection matrix was set in the render function to account for changes in the window shape. Here you set it once. You also turn off culling because triangles in strips have alternating winding orders. Finally, you set up the lights:

```
void CGeometryApplication::SetupDevice()
{
    D3DXMatrixIdentity(&m_ViewMatrix);
    m_pD3DDevice->SetTransform(D3DTS_VIEW, &m_ViewMatrix);

    RECT WindowRect;
    GetClientRect(m_hWnd, &WindowRect);
    D3DXMatrixPerspectiveFovLH(&m_ProjectionMatrix, D3DX_PI / 4,
                (float)(WindowRect.right - WindowRect.left) /
                (float)(WindowRect.bottom - WindowRect.top),
                 1.0f, 100.0f);
    m_pD3DDevice->SetTransform(D3DTS_PROJECTION, &m_ProjectionMatrix);

    m_pD3DDevice->SetRenderState(D3DRS_CULLMODE, D3DCULL_NONE);

    InitializeLights();
}
```

The PostReset function now not only recreates geometry, but also resets the device states by calling SetupDevice. This is because the reset device does not retain the device states from the previously created device:

```
BOOL CGeometryApplication::PreReset()
{
    DestroyGeometry();
    return TRUE;
```

```
}

BOOL CGeometryApplication::PostReset()
{
    SetupDevice();
    return CreateGeometry();
}
```

Now, in addition to cleaning up your vertex buffers, you must also clean up the mesh object and the array of materials:

```
BOOL CGeometryApplication::PreTerminate()
{
    DestroyGeometry();

    if (m_pMesh)
    {
        m_pMesh->Release();
        m_pMesh = NULL;
    }

    if (m_pMeshMaterials)
    {
        delete m_pMeshMaterials;
        m_pMeshMaterials = NULL;
    }

    return TRUE;
}
```

Here you create the vertex buffer as you have in previous chapters, but you also create an index buffer for your indexed primitives. You create and initialize the material that will be used for your geometry before you fill the vertex buffer:

```
BOOL CGeometryApplication::CreateGeometry()
{
    if (FAILED(m_pD3DDevice->CreateVertexBuffer(
            NUM_VERTICES * sizeof(GEOMETRY_VERTEX),
            D3DUSAGE_WRITEONLY, D3DFVF_GEOMETRYVERTEX,
            D3DPOOL_DEFAULT, &m_pVertexBuffer)))
```

```
        return FALSE;

    if (FAILED(m_pD3DDevice->CreateIndexBuffer(
            sizeof(short) * NUM_STRIP_SIDES * 2 * 3,
            D3DUSAGE_WRITEONLY, D3DFMT_INDEX16,
            D3DPOOL_DEFAULT, &m_pIndexBuffer)))
        return FALSE;

    ZeroMemory( &m_ShapeMaterial, sizeof(D3DMATERIAL8) );
    m_ShapeMaterial.Diffuse.r = m_ShapeMaterial.Ambient.r = 1.0f;
    m_ShapeMaterial.Diffuse.g = m_ShapeMaterial.Ambient.g = 1.0f;
    m_ShapeMaterial.Diffuse.b = m_ShapeMaterial.Ambient.b = 1.0f;
    m_ShapeMaterial.Diffuse.a = m_ShapeMaterial.Ambient.a = 1.0f;

    FillVertexBuffer();

    return TRUE;
}
```

First, you load the mesh itself. In this chapter, you don't care about the adjacency information because you are not going to use it for anything. You create a mesh and an array of materials.

```
BOOL CGeometryApplication::LoadMesh()
{
    LPD3DXBUFFER pD3DXMtrlBuffer;

    if(FAILED(D3DXLoadMeshFromX("..\\media\\TwoSpheres.x", D3DXMESH_MANAGED,
                m_pD3DDevice, NULL, &pD3DXMtrlBuffer,
                &m_NumMaterials, &m_pMesh)))
        return FALSE;
```

The following code repackages the array into an array of simple materials. The materials are stored in a generic D3DXBUFFER, but the data stored in the array is in the form of a D3DXMATERIAL array. Here, you recast the array so that you can use it more easily:

```
    D3DXMATERIAL* d3dxMaterials =
            (D3DXMATERIAL*)pD3DXMtrlBuffer->GetBufferPointer();
```

You allocate an array of materials that will be used when you render each subset of the mesh:

```
    m_pMeshMaterials = new D3DMATERIAL8[m_NumMaterials];
```

You loop through each material and copy it to your own array. You also set the ambient color to the diffuse color. In most realistic cases, the ambient color should be the same as the diffuse color, but in some circumstances, you might want different colors:

```
for(long MatCount = 0; MatCount < m_NumMaterials; MatCount++)
{
    m_pMeshMaterials[MatCount] = d3dxMaterials[MatCount].MatD3D;
    m_pMeshMaterials[MatCount].Ambient =
    m_pMeshMaterials[MatCount].Diffuse;
}

    pD3DXMtrlBuffer->Release();

    return TRUE;
}
```

In previous chapters, you've made sure to release the vertex buffer. Now you must do the same for the index buffer:

```
void CGeometryApplication::DestroyGeometry()
{
    if (m_pVertexBuffer)
    {
        m_pVertexBuffer->Release();
        m_pVertexBuffer = NULL;
    }

    if (m_pIndexBuffer)
    {
        m_pIndexBuffer->Release();
        m_pIndexBuffer = NULL;
    }
}
```

Before you render the mesh, you set a transform matrix to push the mesh down and away from the camera, which is at the origin. You also spin the mesh so that you can see many different views. For this example, the exact transformation is not important; you can experiment with different values to see the object from different viewpoints:

```
void CGeometryApplication::Render()
{
```

```
D3DXMATRIX Translation;
D3DXMATRIX Rotation;
D3DXMATRIX Scaling;

D3DXMatrixRotationYawPitchRoll(&Rotation,
        (float)GetTickCount() / 100.0f,
        0.0, 0.0f);
D3DXMatrixTranslation(&Translation, 0.0f, -1.0f, 5.0f);
m_WorldMatrix = Rotation * Translation;
m_pD3DDevice->SetTransform(D3DTS_WORLD, &m_WorldMatrix);

RenderMesh();
```

Here, you set up everything you need to render your own geometry. In previous chapters, you were able to set these once in the initialization functions. Now, you must reset them each time because the mesh object has set the vertex buffer and so on for its own diabolic purposes. Note that the index buffer uses STRIP_OFFSET as an offset that is added to each index. This is not the typical usage, but you are using it here so that it becomes almost trivial to set up your index buffer:

```
m_pD3DDevice->SetVertexShader(D3DFVF_GEOMETRYVERTEX);
m_pD3DDevice->SetStreamSource(0, m_pVertexBuffer,
            sizeof(GEOMETRY_VERTEX));

m_pD3DDevice->SetIndices(m_pIndexBuffer, STRIP_OFFSET);

m_pD3DDevice->SetMaterial(&m_ShapeMaterial);
```

Again, you set a transform that will apply to all of your geometry. This transform will push it away from the origin, tip it away from the viewer for a more dramatic view, and rotate the object:

```
D3DXMatrixRotationYawPitchRoll(&Rotation,
            (float)GetTickCount() / 1000.0f,
            D3DX_PI / 8.0f, 0.0f);
D3DXMatrixTranslation(&Translation, 0.0f, 0.0f, 5.0f);
m_WorldMatrix = Rotation * Translation;
m_pD3DDevice->SetTransform(D3DTS_WORLD, &m_WorldMatrix);
```

The following code draws the three basic primitives: a rectangle made from two triangles, a triangle fan for the top of a cylinder, and a triangle strip for the sides of the cylinder. Note that the number of sides for the cylinder is doubled because each side is made from two triangles:

```
m_pD3DDevice->DrawPrimitive(D3DPT_TRIANGLELIST, 0, 2);

m_pD3DDevice->DrawPrimitive(D3DPT_TRIANGLEFAN, FAN_OFFSET,
            NUM_FAN_SIDES);

m_pD3DDevice->DrawPrimitive(D3DPT_TRIANGLESTRIP, STRIP_OFFSET,
            NUM_STRIP_SIDES * 2);
```

The outer cylinder is built from an indexed triangle list that indexes into the vertices set by the triangle strip. The data itself is the same for both cylinders, but before you draw the outer cylinder, you add a scaling factor to the world transform, which affects the data and makes the outer cylinder shorter and wider:

```
D3DXMatrixScaling(&Scaling, 1.5f, 0.5f, 1.5f);
m_WorldMatrix = Scaling * m_WorldMatrix;
m_pD3DDevice->SetTransform(D3DTS_WORLD, &m_WorldMatrix);
m_pD3DDevice->DrawIndexedPrimitive(D3DPT_TRIANGLELIST,
                0, NUM_VERTICES,
                0, NUM_STRIP_SIDES * 2);
}
```

The code to render the mesh is simple. You loop through all materials, set the material, and then draw the subset related to that material. Note that the vertex data doesn't contain any color information. You could easily change the rendering of an .X file by using your own materials. For instance, instead of setting the material based on the material array, change the material to the one you created for your own geometry:

```
void CGeometryApplication::RenderMesh()
{
    for(DWORD MatCount = 0; MatCount < m_NumMaterials; MatCount++)
    {
        m_pD3DDevice->SetMaterial(&m_pMeshMaterials[MatCount]);

        m_pMesh->DrawSubset(MatCount);
    }
}
```

The following function is essentially the same as in previous samples. However, this code breaks the vertex creation into several sections for easier explanation. Note that the index buffer function doesn't need access to the vertices themselves:

```
BOOL CGeometryApplication::FillVertexBuffer()
{
    if (!m_pVertexBuffer)
        return FALSE;

    GEOMETRY_VERTEX *pVertices;
    if (FAILED(m_pVertexBuffer->Lock(0,
                  NUM_VERTICES * sizeof(GEOMETRY_VERTEX),
                  (BYTE **)&pVertices, D3DLOCK_DISCARD)))
    {
        DestroyGeometry();
        return FALSE;
    }

    InitializeList(pVertices);
    InitializeFan(pVertices);
    InitializeStrip(pVertices);
    InitializeIndexed();

    m_pVertexBuffer->Unlock();

    return TRUE;
}
```

This function creates the vertices for the fan. The rationale for the code appears in Figure 10.7.

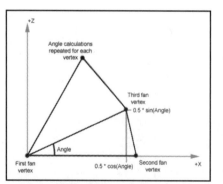

Figure 10.7

The layout of the triangle fan.

The following function first sets the center vertex and then draws each outer vertex. The last vertex is rendered separately so that rounding errors do not produce an incomplete circle. You set the last values explicitly so that the edges match up. The number of vertices used is two more than the number of sides because it takes three vertices to draw the first triangle and only one vertex to draw each subsequent triangle. Each vertex has a normal vector pointing straight up in the Y direction:

```
void CGeometryApplication::InitializeFan(GEOMETRY_VERTEX *pVertices)
{
    pVertices[FAN_OFFSET].x = pVertices[FAN_OFFSET].z = 0.0f;
    pVertices[FAN_OFFSET].y = 1.0f;
    pVertices[FAN_OFFSET].nx = pVertices[FAN_OFFSET].nz = 0.0f;
    pVertices[FAN_OFFSET].ny = 1.0f;

    for (long FanIndex = 0; FanIndex < NUM_FAN_VERTICES - 2;
        FanIndex++)
    {
        float Angle = (float)(FanIndex) * (2.0f * D3DX_PI) /
                (float)(NUM_FAN_VERTICES - 2);

        pVertices[FAN_OFFSET + FanIndex + 1].x = 0.5f * cos(Angle);
        pVertices[FAN_OFFSET + FanIndex + 1].z = 0.5f * sin(Angle);

        pVertices[FAN_OFFSET + FanIndex + 1].y = 1.0f;

        pVertices[FAN_OFFSET + FanIndex + 1].nx =
        pVertices[FAN_OFFSET + FanIndex + 1].nz = 0.0f;
        pVertices[FAN_OFFSET + FanIndex + 1].ny = 1.0f;
    }

    pVertices[FAN_OFFSET + NUM_FAN_VERTICES - 1].x = 0.5f;
    pVertices[FAN_OFFSET + NUM_FAN_VERTICES - 1].z = 0.0f;

    pVertices[FAN_OFFSET + NUM_FAN_VERTICES - 1].y = 1.0f;

    pVertices[FAN_OFFSET + NUM_FAN_VERTICES - 1].nx =
    pVertices[FAN_OFFSET + NUM_FAN_VERTICES - 1].nz = 0.0f;
    pVertices[FAN_OFFSET + NUM_FAN_VERTICES - 1].ny = 1.0f;
}
```

This code demonstrates how a triangle strip is created. Figure 10.8 shows a section of the side of the cylinder, with vertices alternating between the top and bottom of the cylinder.

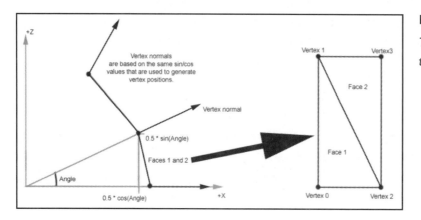

Figure 10.8

The layout of the triangle strip.

The total number of vertices used is two times the number of sides plus two. This equation is used because each rectangular side requires two triangles. Also, the reason for adding two is the same as for the fan. The first triangle requires three vertices and every other one requires one vertex. The normals for each side point in the same direction as the vector you used to define the vertex position. Using unscaled sine and cosine values produces a normalized normal vector:

```
void CGeometryApplication::InitializeStrip(GEOMETRY_VERTEX *pVertices)
{
    for (long StripIndex = 0; StripIndex < NUM_STRIP_VERTICES;
      StripIndex += 2)
    {
        float Angle = (float)(StripIndex) * (2.0f * D3DX_PI) /
              (float)(NUM_STRIP_SIDES * 2);

        pVertices[STRIP_OFFSET + StripIndex].x =
        pVertices[STRIP_OFFSET + StripIndex + 1].x = 0.5f * cos(Angle);
        pVertices[STRIP_OFFSET + StripIndex].z =
        pVertices[STRIP_OFFSET + StripIndex + 1].z = 0.5f * sin(Angle);

        pVertices[STRIP_OFFSET + StripIndex].y   = 0.0f;
```

```
        pVertices[STRIP_OFFSET + StripIndex + 1].y = 1.0f;

        pVertices[STRIP_OFFSET + StripIndex].nx =
        pVertices[STRIP_OFFSET + StripIndex + 1].nx = cos(Angle);
        pVertices[STRIP_OFFSET + StripIndex].nz =
        pVertices[STRIP_OFFSET + StripIndex + 1].nz = sin(Angle);
        pVertices[STRIP_OFFSET + StripIndex].ny =
        pVertices[STRIP_OFFSET + StripIndex + 1].ny = 0.0f;
    }
}
```

Even this simple function shows how much redundancy occurs in triangle lists. Here you are setting up only two triangles, and much of the vertex information is redundant:

```
void CGeometryApplication::InitializeList(GEOMETRY_VERTEX *pVertices)
{
    pVertices[0].x = -1.0f;
    pVertices[0].z = -1.0f;

    pVertices[1].x = pVertices[3].x = -1.0f;
    pVertices[1].z = pVertices[3].z = 1.0f;

    pVertices[2].x = pVertices[4].x = 1.0f;
    pVertices[2].z = pVertices[4].z = -1.0f;

    pVertices[5].x = 1.0f;
    pVertices[5].z = 1.0f;

    pVertices[0].y = pVertices[1].y =
    pVertices[2].y = pVertices[3].y =
    pVertices[4].y = pVertices[5].y = 0.0f;

    pVertices[0].nx = pVertices[1].nx =
    pVertices[2].nx = pVertices[3].nx =
    pVertices[4].nx = pVertices[5].nx = 0.0f;
    pVertices[0].ny = pVertices[1].ny =
    pVertices[2].ny = pVertices[3].ny =
    pVertices[4].ny = pVertices[5].ny = 1.0f;
    pVertices[0].nz = pVertices[1].nz =
```

```
    pVertices[2].nz = pVertices[3].nz =
    pVertices[4].nz = pVertices[5].nz = 0.0f;
}
```

In this code, you create an index buffer for an indexed triangle list. The number of indices used is equal to the number of sides times two triangles per side, times three vertices per triangle. Using a triangle list can bloat the number of indices, but you are not using more actual vertices than you were with the strip. Because the vertices are the entities that actually get processed in the pipeline, increasing the number of indices isn't too bad. It does use memory, but the amount of space used is small compared to the vertices themselves. Because you are reusing the strip data, creating the indices is pretty simple. For other models, the indices might not be this orderly. Notice that you can start your indices at zero because you used an offset in the call to SetIndices earlier. Alternatively, you could have added STRIP_OFFSET to each index here and used zero as the offset for SetIndices. I wanted to show the atypical way here, although in most cases, you might want to do it the other way:

```
void CGeometryApplication::InitializeIndexed()
{
    short *pIndices;
    m_pIndexBuffer->Lock(0, sizeof(short) * NUM_STRIP_SIDES * 2 * 3,
            (BYTE **)&pIndices, D3DLOCK_DISCARD);

    for (short Triangle = 0; Triangle < NUM_STRIP_SIDES * 2;
        Triangle++)
    {
        pIndices[(Triangle * 3) + 0] = Triangle;
        pIndices[(Triangle * 3) + 1] = Triangle + 1;
        pIndices[(Triangle * 3) + 2] = Triangle + 2;
    }

    m_pIndexBuffer->Unlock();
}
```

Here you initialize a light so that you can see the shaded sides of the geometry. I go into more depth about lighting in the next chapter. For now, the code creates a directional white light shining straight down. It then sets this new light and enables the light. Finally, you make sure lighting is enabled and tell the device to use a small amount of ambient light.

```
void CGeometryApplication::InitializeLights()
{
    D3DLIGHT8 Light;
    ZeroMemory(&Light, sizeof(D3DLIGHT8));
    Light.Type = D3DLIGHT_DIRECTIONAL;
    Light.Diffuse.r = Light.Diffuse.g = Light.Diffuse.b = 1.0f;
    Light.Direction = D3DXVECTOR3(0.0f, -1.0f, 0.0f);
    Light.Range     = 100.0f;

    m_pD3DDevice->SetLight(0, &Light);
    m_pD3DDevice->LightEnable(0, TRUE);

    m_pD3DDevice->SetRenderState(D3DRS_LIGHTING, TRUE);
    m_pD3DDevice->SetRenderState(D3DRS_AMBIENT, 0x00101010);
}
```

In Conclusion...

It's been a long trip, but you finally have real 3D graphics. By now, you have transformed and lit geometry, and I can begin to talk about doing interesting things with it. The final chapters of this part complete the basics, talking about lighting, textures, and more device states. After that, you will begin to change your geometry with vertex shaders. But I am getting ahead of myself again. For now, you know the drill: Let's review what you have learned:

- This part has concentrated on moving from vertices to geometry. The geometry I've talked about has been triangles, but everything I've talked about here also applies to lines.

- Vertex normals define how a surface is lit. In most cases, the vertex normal should be the average of all of the surface normals of the surfaces defined with that vertex. When you use smooth shading, the color of every point on the shape is interpolated from the colors and shading of the three vertices.

- The number-one performance consideration (for raw geometry) is the minimization of the number of vertices that are processed.

- Degenerate triangles might lie around the house and drink the last can of soda, but they can also be useful when drawing certain types of geometry.

- Indexed primitives usually make the best reuse of vertices. Indexed triangle lists are arguably the best performance/convenience tradeoff.

- The `ID3DXMesh` interface and associated D3DX functions provide a simple way to access and manipulate data stored in .X files.

- This is neither the first nor the last time I'll say this, but you should always look for opportunities to batch things such as vertex buffers, materials, and device states.

CHAPTER 11

FIXED FUNCTION LIGHTING

B ecause this book concentrates on shaders, you will concentrate on writing shaders that produce lighting effects, and you will almost never use the lighting functions of DirectX Graphics. However, it makes sense to spend a little time going over the fixed function lights. The purpose of this chapter is not really to discuss fixed function lights in great detail, but rather to give new users a basis of comparison for the lighting you will implement with vertex and pixel shaders. With that in mind, I go over DirectX lighting very quickly. If you are an experienced DirectX user, most of this is review. If you are a new user, this chapter introduces you to the concepts you need to get started. In either case, please understand that shaders can be more flexible and useful. The following concepts are only for review.

- Using the D3DLIGHT8 structure.
- Creating directional lights with D3DLIGHT8.
- Creating point lights with D3DLIGHT8.
- Creating spot lights with D3DLIGHT8.
- Setting up lighting on the D3D device.
- Building lighting into an application.
- Understanding the effect of lighting of meshes of different resolutions.

The D3DLIGHT8 Structure

I introduced the D3DLIGHT8 structure in Chapter 4 as the way that DirectX defines lights. In Chapter 4, I spent time talking about how the final color of a vertex is affected by different lighting types, but I didn't really talk about how the lights themselves work. The equations from Chapter 4 assume an intensity of light at a given point, but I didn't talk about how that intensity changes. Now you will revisit lighting from the perspective of the lights and see how the intensity of light hitting a given vertex can be a function of distance and angle. Remember that a light's intensity and color are the same, and I sometimes use the two terms interchangeably.

In this chapter, you'll create some lights using this structure and create some very simple lighting effects. In later chapters involving shaders, you can still use this structure to store the properties of your lights whenever it makes sense to. You'll do that for two reasons. First, using the D3DLIGHT8 structure makes it easier for experienced programmers to make the transition from the standard lights to lighting in shaders. Secondly, it makes it easy for you to toggle from fixed function lights to shader lights if you choose to compare the effects of each. So even though

I don't spend very much time talking about DirectX lighting, you might continue to use the DirectX structure for lights.

In the code for the previous chapter, you implemented lights so that the geometry would be shaded and easier to see. Creating the light itself was straightforward:

```
D3DLIGHT8 light;
ZeroMemory(&light, sizeof(D3DLIGHT8));
```

This snippet of code creates a light structure and then sets all the values to zero. Setting all the values to zero ensures there is no garbage data in the structure that might adversely affect your lighting. After the structure is created, you can set each member to the values you need. If you do not need certain values for certain light types (such as attenuation with directional lights), those values can remain zero. In the code for this chapter, you'll set values for several different light types. Some of this is a review of material from Chapter 4, but let's go over the way that each light type uses members of the D3DLIGHT8 structure.

Directional Lights

Directional lights are extremely simple to set up because they use the fewest number of factors in the lighting computations. To create a directional light, set the light type to directional, zero out the structure as shown earlier, and set the direction and the color:

```
ZeroMemory(&light, sizeof(D3DLIGHT8));
light.Type       = D3DLIGHT_DIRECTIONAL;
light.Diffuse.r = light.Diffuse.g = light.Diffuse.b = 1.0f;
light.Direction = D3DXVECTOR3(0.0f, -1.0f, 0.0f);
```

In this case, the light is white and points straight down, like sunlight that is directly overhead. Notice that there is no position for the light. You can think of a directional light as coming from an infinitely far distance and striking every point in space. It also has no attenuation or range, so all points are hit with the same intensity. This, of course, is unrealistic, but it makes the math computationally inexpensive. In the context of Chapter 4, the light intensity for any given vertex is simply the diffuse color of the light.

Point Lights

Directional lights have a direction and no position. Point lights are the opposite. They have a position, but light emanates in all directions. So far, I have conceptualized directional lights as sunlight. Point lights can be conceptualized as torches or flares where a light source is casting an orb of light onto surrounding objects. Here is an example of how to set up a point light:

```
ZeroMemory(&light, sizeof(D3DLIGHT8));
light.Type        = D3DLIGHT_POINT;
light.Diffuse.r   = light.Diffuse.g = light.Diffuse.b = 1.0f;
light.Position    = D3DXVECTOR3(0.0f, 1.0f, 0.0f);
light.Range       = 5.0f;
light.Attenuation0 = 0.0f;
light.Attenuation1 = 1.0f;
```

Now, the light is still white but is positioned one unit above the origin and shining in all directions. There is a maximum range for this light, and it does not light many objects beyond this range. It also attenuates (changes in intensity) over that range. As discussed, the equation for attenuation is

$$\frac{1}{D^2}$$

Figure 11.1 shows how different attenuation parameters shape the intensity curve over the range of the light. Note that point lights become more computationally expensive as you add the Attenuation1 and Attenuation2 terms.

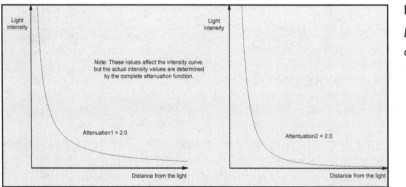

Figure 11.1

Examples of attenuation.

Point lights are more realistic than directional lights in that they more accurately model some real forms of lights, but they do come at a cost. For point lights, the light intensity at any given point is a function of its distance from that point. So if you were writing your own lighting calculations (as you will with shaders), you would first calculate the intensity using the attenuation equation and then use that intensity in your diffuse and specular lighting calculations. The angle for those calculations is the angle of the vector between the vertex position and the point light position.

Spot Lights

You are probably familiar with spot lights if you are either a movie star or an escaped convict. If the point light is a torch, then you can consider the spot light a search light. Like point lights, spot lights have a maximum range, and they attenuate over distance. Unlike point lights, spot lights shine in a specific direction, and the rays of light form a cone with two distinct regions. The *umbra*, or inner part of the cone, contains light that attenuates over distance but not over the radius of the umbra. The Phi member of the light structure defines this inner region. The *penumbra*, or outer part of the cone, is the region where light attenuates not only over distance, but also over the radius. The Theta member of the structure defines the angle of the penumbra, and Falloff represents the change in intensity. Figure 11.2 shows the spot light cone.

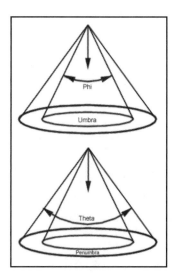

Figure 11.2

Spot light cone.

Combining the Attenuation and Falloff parameters for spot lights yields the following equation:

$$L = \text{Attenuation Term} * \text{Falloff Term} * \text{LightColor}$$

$$\text{Falloff} =$$

1.0 where the point is within the umbra
0.0 where the point is outside the penumbra

$$\left[\frac{\cos(angle) - \cos(\frac{\phi}{2})}{\cos(\frac{\theta}{2}) - \cos(\frac{\phi}{2})} \right]^{\text{Falloff}} \quad \text{Where the point is within the penumbra}$$

Figure 11.3 shows the effect of different `Falloff` values. Note that there is a performance cost associated with `Falloff` values other than 1. Although other values might create a better appearance, a value of 1 is often good enough.

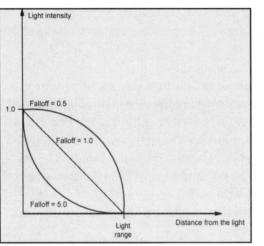

Figure 11.3

`Falloff` *values and their curves.*

Having said all that, the following code creates a spot light:

```
ZeroMemory(&light, sizeof(D3DLIGHT8));
light.Type        = D3DLIGHT_SPOT;
light.Diffuse.r   = light.Diffuse.g = light.Diffuse.b = 1.0f;
light.Direction   = D3DXVECTOR3(0.0f, -1.0f, 0.0f);
light.Position    = D3DXVECTOR3(0.0f,  5.0f, 0.0f);
light.Theta       = D3DX_PI / 4.0f;
light.Phi         = D3DX_PI / 2.0f;
light.Falloff     = 5.0f;
light.Range       = 10.0f;
```

This code creates a spot light that is five units above the origin and shines straight down. The other parameters shape the cone and the falloff between the umbra and the penumbra.

As you can see from all of the equations and parameters, a lot of computation goes into calculating the spot light intensity at any given vertex. Once the intensity is calculated, you must still enter that value into all the actual lighting calculations.

Setting Up the Device for Lighting

So far I've discussed the lights, but you must set up the device to actually use the lights. Devices have a maximum number of lights they can manage at any given time. You can find the number of lights available by asking the device:

```
D3DCAPS8 Caps;
m_pD3DDevice->GetDeviceCaps(&Caps);
DWORD NumLights = Caps.MaxActiveLights;
```

When you're setting and using lights, do not exceed this number of lights. When I start talking about vertex shaders, I show how to use an arbitrary number of lights. Once you ensure that lights are available, you must enable lighting by setting the device state:

```
m_pD3DDevice->SetRenderState(D3DRS_LIGHTING, TRUE);
```

You can also set the device to use a global ambient lighting value. Setting this value does not consume one of the available lights:

```
m_pD3DDevice->SetRenderState(D3DRS_AMBIENT, 0x00101010);
```

Setting some low ambient value is usually preferable because it simulates the real effect of stray rays of light bouncing around the environment and illuminating surfaces that the actual lights might never hit.

The next step is to tell the device which lights you actually want to enable. This can be useful if you want to use some lights for some objects and not for others. For instance, if you have several spot lights, but you have geometry that you know is well outside the range of those lights, you could disable the spot lights when drawing the geometry and then enable the spot lights when drawing the geometry you know is within range. This can help you optimize performance. The following code shows how to enable specific lights. The first parameter is the identifier of the light, and the value should not exceed the number of available lights minus one:

```
m_pD3DDevice->LightEnable(0, TRUE);
```

The last step is to actually set each light. Once a D3DLIGHT8 structure is populated, you can pass it to the device:

```
m_pD3DDevice->SetLight(0, &light);
```

Note that this structure sets the parameters for a given light, but the device does not monitor that structure for changes. For instance, if you change the position of the light by changing the structure, you must call SetLight again to inform the device of the changes.

After these steps are complete, the device lights vertices using the parameters you set and the equations from this chapter and Chapter 4. If the hardware supports hardware T&L, the computation happens on the graphics hardware; otherwise, it happens on the CPU.

The Application

The sample application is a very basic framework for experimenting with the effects of different lights. The application implements all three lights, but the spot and point lights are the most interesting. To demonstrate the effects of lighting, the application loads a single mesh file that contains five different subsets of different materials. Each subset is a simple plane, but they have different numbers of vertices.

Figure 11.4 shows the effect of the point light on four of the subsets.

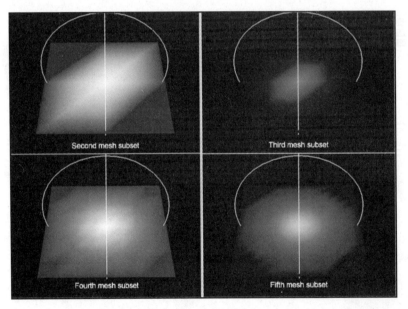

Figure 11.4

Point lights on meshes.

The simple sphere shows position and range of the point light. Vertices that fall inside the range of the sphere are lit according to the parameters of the light. Vertices that fall outside the range of the light are not lit, but the device interpolates the colors of vertices over each triangle. This demonstrates the tension between creating efficient meshes with a limited number of vertices and creating meshes with nice smooth lighting.

Figure 11.5 shows the same set of meshes lit with a spot light.

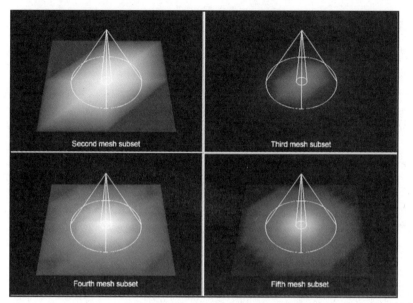

Figure 11.5

Spot lights on meshes.

Simple lines and circles help to visualize the umbra and penumbra. As with the point light, only vertices that fall within the penumbra are actually lit. One of the things to note here is that spot lights are probably not worth the expense if you are lighting small, low-resolution meshes.

Note that there is a subset that is not shown in the figures above. It is a very low-resolution mesh with vertices only on the four corners of the plane. If all four vertices are outside the range of a light, the whole plane is unlit. This is not an error; it's just the way per vertex lighting works. In later chapters, I talk about per pixel lighting, which you can use to produce better results for low-resolution meshes.

This application is a simple demonstration. The user interface consists of two keys. Press F1 to cycle through the different resolution meshes, and press F2 to cycle through the different light types. I also recommend that you experiment with the different parameters and animate the lights to see the effects. The following code demonstrates all the basic pieces. Feel free to change them to explore the ways that the lights work. To keep things as simple as possible, the light visualization code does not include the ability to rotate the graphical representations of the lights, but changing the light direction in the `D3DLIGHT8` structure changes the direction of the light. Finally, if you like, you can load a different mesh, but remember that the application code renders only one subset at a time. If you want, change the mesh rendering code to render differently. In any case, make sure you understand the code before you make any changes; otherwise, you might get some confusing results.

The Code

Continuing the trend from the previous chapters, you will be subclassing the framework application class with your new lighting code. These files appear on the CD in the \Code\Chapter11 directory. Take a look at the new LightingApplication.h:

```
#include "Application.h"

class CLightingApplication : public CHostApplication
{
public:
        CLightingApplication();
        virtual ~CLightingApplication();
```

These three functions handle the creation, rendering, and destruction of the vertex buffer you use to draw the visualizations of the lights. These lights are set up as line strips, and they behave the same way as the vertex buffers you've used in previous chapters:

```
        void RenderLightVisuals();
        void DestroyLightVisuals();
        BOOL InitializeLightVisuals();
```

These functions make sure that the device is set to use lighting and that all the lights are actually initialized. SetupDevice is a separate function so you can set up the device after a reset. If you want to change the lighting parameters, change the code in InitializeLights:

```
        void SetupDevice();
        void InitializeLights();
```

This function loads the mesh file. This particular application assumes that the mesh object contains several subsets of varying resolutions:

```
        BOOL LoadMesh();
```

These are the standard overridden functions you use to build in your own functionality. For this application, take a close look at HandleMessage to see how you handle the keyboard input that changes the lights and mesh subsets:

```
        virtual BOOL PostInitialize();
        virtual BOOL PreTerminate();
        virtual BOOL PreReset();
        virtual BOOL PostReset();
```

```
virtual void Render();
virtual BOOL HandleMessage(MSG *pMessage);
```

These are your mesh variables. Usually, you would load a mesh and then render all of the subsets on every frame. For this application, you load all the subsets but render only one of them per frame. The subset specified by m_CurrentSubset is the only one drawn each frame:

```
LPD3DXMESH      m_pMesh;
D3DMATERIAL8 *m_pMeshMaterials;
DWORD           m_NumMaterials;
DWORD           m_CurrentSubset;
```

Similar to the mesh variables, the light variables create three different light structures, and the m_CurrentLight member determines which light is used in a given frame. You can manipulate these light structures to change the lighting parameters:

```
D3DLIGHT8 m_Light[3];
DWORD m_CurrentLight;
```

This vertex buffer stores the vertices used in your light visualizations for the point light and spot light. All of the line strips are stored in this one buffer:

```
LPDIRECT3DVERTEXBUFFER8 m_pLightsBuffer;
D3DXMATRIX m_WorldMatrix;
D3DXMATRIX m_ViewMatrix;
D3DXMATRIX m_ProjectionMatrix;
};
```

As you can see, your new lighting class is fairly simple. You have a mesh object, a set of lights, and a set of functions that handle drawing the cones and spheres of lights to give you a better indication of what is actually going on. Take a look at LightingApplication.cpp to see how this all comes together:

```
#include "LightingApplication.h"
```

These definitions index into your array of lighting structures. If you choose to add more lights to this sample application, make sure you make changes here so that the application can properly loop through the lights:

```
#define SPOT_LIGHT      0
#define DIR_LIGHT       1
#define POINT_LIGHT     2
#define MAX_LIGHT       2
```

Here you define the numbers of vertices that are used to draw the lights themselves. The cone points represent two edges of the cone with three points each. There is no real point to changing this number unless you change the rendering code to draw a more complex cone. You can set the number of circle points to draw a higher- or lower-resolution circle. Higher values create smoother circles. I arbitrarily picked a value that produced a decent circle. Note that in Chapter 8 you drew a circle with many vertices, and I mentioned that really wasn't the proper way to draw a circle. Here you do it the right way. If you are planning to draw circles or curves, use this chapter as an example. I talk about this more when you actually set up and render the vertex buffer:

```
#define NUM_CIRCLE_POINTS    40
#define NUM_CONE_POINTS       6
#define NUM_VERTICES (NUM_CIRCLE_POINTS + NUM_CONE_POINTS)
```

This is your very simple vertex structure and format. Because you are only using this for simple lines, you don't need vertex normals or any other additional data:

```
struct VISUALS_VERTEX
{
       float x, y, z;
       DWORD diffuse;
};
#define D3DFVF_VISUALSVERTEX (D3DFVF_XYZ | D3DFVF_DIFFUSE)
```

As usual, you need to be sure that all of your counters and pointers are set to something valid. Sometimes it's easy to forget this, but if these variables are set to invalid numbers and you try to render a nonexistent subset, that's bad:

```
CLightingApplication::CLightingApplication()
{
       m_pMesh           = NULL;
       m_pMeshMaterials  = NULL;
       m_NumMaterials    = 0;
       m_CurrentSubset   = 0;
       m_CurrentLight    = 0;
       m_pLightsBuffer   = NULL;
}
CLightingApplication::~CLightingApplication()
{
}
```

This code is basically the same as what you've seen in previous chapters. The only difference is that you make sure to get the device properly set up, and you make sure that the light visuals and mesh are created:

```
BOOL CLightingApplication::PostInitialize()
{
        if (FAILED(EasyCreateWindowed(m_hWnd, D3DDEVTYPE_HAL,
                            D3DCREATE_HARDWARE_VERTEXPROCESSING)))
            return FALSE;

        SetupDevice();

        if (!InitializeLightVisuals())
            return FALSE;

        return LoadMesh();
}
void CLightingApplication::SetupDevice()
{
```

Earlier I promised that I would slowly sneak D3DX functions into the code of various chapters. This is the first time you've used D3DXMatrixLookAtLH. In this case, you are setting up a view matrix where the camera is placed up and back but looking down at the origin. The final parameter is the "up vector," which in this case is set to straight up. This might seem pretty obvious, but in some cases you might want to use other vectors for the up vector:

```
        D3DXMatrixLookAtLH(&m_ViewMatrix,
                        &D3DXVECTOR3(0.0f, 20.0f, -20.0f),
                        &D3DXVECTOR3(0.0f, 0.0f, 0.0f),
                        &D3DXVECTOR3(0.0f, 1.0f, 0.0f));
        m_pD3DDevice->SetTransform(D3DTS_VIEW, &m_ViewMatrix);
```

You also make sure to set the world matrix to the identity matrix and set up a projection matrix. If you want to change these settings and animate the world or the camera, you can move most of this functionality to the Render function. For many of these samples, I'm trying to keep everything simple, but please experiment. Even if you totally change the code, you can always get the original from the CD:

```
        D3DXMatrixIdentity(&m_WorldMatrix);
        m_pD3DDevice->SetTransform(D3DTS_WORLD, &m_WorldMatrix);

        RECT WindowRect;
```

```
GetClientRect(m_hWnd, &WindowRect);
D3DXMatrixPerspectiveFovLH(&m_ProjectionMatrix,
            D3DX_PI / 8,
            (float)(WindowRect.right - WindowRect.left) /
            (float)(WindowRect.bottom - WindowRect.top),
            1.0f, 500.0f);
m_pD3DDevice->SetTransform(D3DTS_PROJECTION,
&m_ProjectionMatrix);
```

Here is a snippet of code that checks the number of lights. In this sample, you don't really use that value because you are only using one light, but for more complex applications, you might want to check this value:

```
D3DCAPS8 Caps;
m_pD3DDevice->GetDeviceCaps(&Caps);
DWORD NumLights = Caps.MaxActiveLights;
```

In this last set of calls, you enable lighting, enable the first light itself, and set a small amount of ambient light in the scene before calling the function that actually sets up the light structures:

```
m_pD3DDevice->SetRenderState(D3DRS_LIGHTING, TRUE);
m_pD3DDevice->LightEnable(0, TRUE);
m_pD3DDevice->SetRenderState(D3DRS_AMBIENT, 0x00101010);


InitializeLights();
}
```

As in the previous chapter, your mesh object lives in managed memory. Therefore, when the device is reset, you only need to worry about your homemade vertex buffer. The device takes care of the mesh object:

```
BOOL CLightingApplication::PreReset()
{
    DestroyLightVisuals();
    return TRUE;
}
```

Once the device is reset, make sure that all the device states are set, and then re-create the vertex buffer and the data:

```
BOOL CLightingApplication::PostReset()
{
    SetupDevice();
```

```
        return InitializeLightVisuals();
}
```

This is the same thing you've seen in the last few chapters. As always, clean up after yourself:

```
BOOL CLightingApplication::PreTerminate()
{
        DestroyLightVisuals();
        if (m_pMesh)
        {
                m_pMesh->Release();
                m_pMesh = NULL;
        }
        if (m_pMeshMaterials)
        {
                delete m_pMeshMaterials;
                m_pMeshMaterials = NULL;
        }
        return TRUE;
}
```

Here you use the F1 key to cycle through the different meshes. On faster machines, you might actually receive this message more than once if you hold down the key. Basically, you just increment the subset identifier until you get too high. Then you set it back to the beginning:

```
BOOL CLightingApplication::HandleMessage(MSG *pMessage)
{
        if (pMessage->message == WM_KEYDOWN &&
            pMessage->wParam== VK_F1)
        {
                if (++m_CurrentSubset > m_NumMaterials - 1)
                        m_CurrentSubset = 0;
        }
```

You use the F2 key in the same way, only to cycle through the available lights. If you add more lights to the sample, this code should still work, assuming that you make sure to set the value of MAX_LIGHT properly:

```
        if (pMessage->message == WM_KEYDOWN &&
            pMessage->wParam
```

```
                == VK_F2)
            {
                    if (++m_CurrentLight > MAX_LIGHT)
                            m_CurrentLight = 0;
            }
```

It's important to pass the message back to the base class before continuing. This ensures that basic messages are handled properly:

```
        return CHostApplication::HandleMessage(pMessage);
}
```

This mesh-loading code is identical to the code from the previous chapter—but there is a minor semantic difference to keep in mind. This application assumes that each material corresponds to a completely separate mesh rather than subsets of a single mesh. This doesn't affect how the mesh is loaded, but if you want to change the behavior of this application, this might be an important thing to keep in mind:

```
BOOL CLightingApplication::LoadMesh()
{
        LPD3DXBUFFER pD3DXMtrlBuffer;

        if(FAILED(D3DXLoadMeshFromX("..\\media\\planes.x",
                            D3DXMESH_MANAGED,
                            m_pD3DDevice, NULL, &pD3DXMtrlBuffer,
                            &m_NumMaterials, &m_pMesh)))
         return FALSE;

        D3DXMATERIAL* d3dxMaterials;
        d3dxMaterials = (D3DXMATERIAL*)pD3DXMtrlBuffer->
        GetBufferPointer();

        m_pMeshMaterials = new D3DMATERIAL8[m_NumMaterials];

        for(long MatCount = 0; MatCount < m_NumMaterials; MatCount++)
        {
                m_pMeshMaterials[MatCount] =
                d3dxMaterials[MatCount].MatD3D;
                m_pMeshMaterials[MatCount].Ambient =
                                m_pMeshMaterials[MatCount].Diffuse;
```

```
        }

        pD3DXMtrlBuffer->Release();

        return TRUE;
}
```

Here you make sure that lighting is enabled because it gets disabled when you draw the lines and circles. You also set the light because it may have been changed with a keyboard command. If you were worried about optimization, you would probably want to place the SetLight call in the message handler so that the light is only set when necessary rather than with each frame. However, in these first samples, I am choosing clarity over performance. Also, if you animate any of the lighting parameters, you need to reset the light each frame:

```
void CLightingApplication::Render()
{
        m_pD3DDevice->SetRenderState(D3DRS_LIGHTING, TRUE);
        m_pD3DDevice->SetLight(0, &m_Light[m_CurrentLight]);
```

The material denotes the subset, which in your case denotes which resolution mesh you want to display. Set the material and then draw the individual subset. The data is now in the hands of the device. It draws the mesh and uses the lighting parameters and the vertex information (including the vertex normal) to compute the lighting for each vertex. The math I discussed is invisible to you. You get shaded geometry thanks to hardware:

```
        m_pD3DDevice->SetMaterial(&m_pMeshMaterials[m_CurrentSubset]);
        m_pMesh->DrawSubset(m_CurrentSubset);
```

Finally, you draw the lights themselves, completing this particular frame:

```
        RenderLightVisuals();
}
```

This code creates a point light that is white and positioned one-and-a-half units above the origin. Here the light has a range of five units and attenuates linearly over that range. With this or any of the following light structures, you can experiment with changing these values either here or in the Render function. For example, you might want to set up the initial values here but change the position of the light within the Render function to move the light around:

```
void CLightingApplication::InitializeLights()
{
```

```
ZeroMemory(&m_Light[POINT_LIGHT], sizeof(D3DLIGHT8));
m_Light[POINT_LIGHT].Type          = D3DLIGHT_POINT;
m_Light[POINT_LIGHT].Diffuse.r     =
            m_Light[POINT_LIGHT].Diffuse.g =
            m_Light[POINT_LIGHT].Diffuse.b = 1.0f;
m_Light[POINT_LIGHT].Position      =
            D3DXVECTOR3(0.0f, 1.5f, 0.0f);
m_Light[POINT_LIGHT].Range         = 5.0f;
m_Light[POINT_LIGHT].Attenuation0 = 0.0f;
m_Light[POINT_LIGHT].Attenuation1 = 1.0f;
```

The second light is a simple directional light. I include it here for the sake of completeness, but the previous sample application was really a better place to experiment with directional lights because of the curved surfaces. Conversely, I include a flat plane for this sample because it is much easier to see the subtle effects of attenuation on a flat surface:

```
ZeroMemory(&m_Light[DIR_LIGHT], sizeof(D3DLIGHT8));
m_Light[DIR_LIGHT].Type          = D3DLIGHT_DIRECTIONAL;
m_Light[DIR_LIGHT].Diffuse.r     =
            m_Light[DIR_LIGHT].Diffuse.g =
            m_Light[DIR_LIGHT].Diffuse.b = 1.0f;
m_Light[DIR_LIGHT].Direction     =
            D3DXVECTOR3(-1.0f, -1.0f, 1.0f);
```

The last light you set is the spot light. Notice how many more parameters it needs to define how it acts. This should give you an indication of how much math is necessary to achieve spot light effects. I also include another D3DX function here. (It's actually a macro.) D3DXToRadian converts degree values to radians. This can be useful if you are used to thinking in degrees:

```
ZeroMemory(&m_Light[SPOT_LIGHT], sizeof(D3DLIGHT8));
m_Light[SPOT_LIGHT].Type          = D3DLIGHT_SPOT;
m_Light[SPOT_LIGHT].Diffuse.r     =
            m_Light[SPOT_LIGHT].Diffuse.g =
            m_Light[SPOT_LIGHT].Diffuse.b = 1.0f;
m_Light[SPOT_LIGHT].Direction     =
            D3DXVECTOR3(0.0f, -1.0f, 0.0f);
m_Light[SPOT_LIGHT].Position      =
            D3DXVECTOR3(0.0f,  5.0f, 0.0f);
m_Light[SPOT_LIGHT].Theta         = D3DXToRadian(10.0f);
```

```
        m_Light[SPOT_LIGHT].Phi            = D3DXToRadian(60.0f);
        m_Light[SPOT_LIGHT].Falloff        = 5.0f;
        m_Light[SPOT_LIGHT].Range          = 10.0f;
}
BOOL CLightingApplication::InitializeLightVisuals()
{
        if (FAILED(m_pD3DDevice->CreateVertexBuffer(NUM_VERTICES *
                                        sizeof(VISUALS_VERTEX),
                                        D3DUSAGE_WRITEONLY,
                                        D3DFVF_VISUALSVERTEX,
                                        D3DPOOL_DEFAULT,
                                        &m_pLightsBuffer)))
                return FALSE;

        VISUALS_VERTEX *pVertices;

        if (FAILED(m_pLightsBuffer->Lock(0,
                        NUM_VERTICES * sizeof(VISUALS_VERTEX),
                        (BYTE **)&pVertices,
                        0)))
        {
                DestroyLightVisuals();
                return FALSE;
        }
```

These lines are the same set of vertex buffer functions that you have been using for the past several chapters. The only real difference is this last memset line. Here you use memset to set all the bytes in the vertex buffer to 255. This is a quick and easy way to set all the vertex colors to white. Later, you set the position data, but all the color data remains unchanged at 255, so you never have to explicitly set the color values:

```
        memset(pVertices, 0xFF, NUM_VERTICES * sizeof(VISUALS_VERTEX));
```

These first six vertices represent the sides of the spot light cone. Every dimension is set to a unit value so that you can easily size the data with a scaling matrix. You can use these same six vertices to draw umbras and penumbras of any size:

```
        pVertices[0].x = -1.0f; pVertices[0].y = -1.0f;
         pVertices[0].z = 0.0f;
        pVertices[1].x =  0.0f; pVertices[1].y =  0.0f;
         pVertices[1].z = 0.0f;
```

```
pVertices[2].x =  1.0f; pVertices[2].y = -1.0f;
 pVertices[2].z = 0.0f;

pVertices[3].x = 0.0f; pVertices[3].y = -1.0f;
 pVertices[3].z = -1.0f;
pVertices[4].x = 0.0f; pVertices[4].y =  0.0f;
 pVertices[4].z =  0.0f;
pVertices[5].x = 0.0f; pVertices[5].y = -1.0f;
 pVertices[5].z =  1.0f;
```

Here you create a circle with a radius of one. You set the last vertex separately to ensure that the circle is actually closed. You might notice that you have only one set of vertices for one circle, but you need to draw several circles (the umbra, penumbra, and the point sphere sides). You'll take a closer look at this later:

```
long Counter;
for (Counter = 0; Counter < NUM_CIRCLE_POINTS - 1; Counter++)
{
        float Angle = 2.0f * D3DX_PI /
                        (NUM_CIRCLE_POINTS- 1) * Counter;
        pVertices[Counter + NUM_CONE_POINTS].x = cos(Angle);
        pVertices[Counter + NUM_CONE_POINTS].y = sin(Angle);
        pVertices[Counter + NUM_CONE_POINTS].z = 0.0f;

}
pVertices[Counter + NUM_CONE_POINTS].x = 1.0f;
pVertices[Counter + NUM_CONE_POINTS].y = 0.0f;
pVertices[Counter + NUM_CONE_POINTS].z = 0.0f;
m_pLightsBuffer->Unlock();

        return TRUE;
}
```

As always, make your mother proud and clean up after yourself:

```
void CLightingApplication::DestroyLightVisuals()
{
        if (m_pLightsBuffer)
        {
                m_pLightsBuffer->Release();
                m_pLightsBuffer = NULL;
        }
```

```
}
void CLightingApplication::RenderLightVisuals()
{
        D3DXMATRIX Translation;
        D3DXMATRIX Rotation;
        D3DXMATRIX Scaling;
        D3DXMATRIX Transform;
```

This function looks like the typical vertex rendering function. You turn off lighting because it doesn't make sense in the context of these simple lines and then you set the FVF and the stream source:

```
m_pD3DDevice->SetRenderState(D3DRS_LIGHTING, FALSE);
m_pD3DDevice->SetVertexShader(D3DFVF_VISUALSVERTEX);
m_pD3DDevice->SetStreamSource(0, m_pLightsBuffer,
                              sizeof(VISUALS_VERTEX));
```

If you are using the spot light, create a translation matrix that will move the cone vertices to the position of the light:

```
if (m_CurrentLight == SPOT_LIGHT)
{
        D3DXMatrixTranslation(&Translation,
                              m_Light[SPOT_LIGHT].Position.x,
                              m_Light[SPOT_LIGHT].Position.y,
                              m_Light[SPOT_LIGHT].Position.z);
```

When the cone shifts to the spot light position, you need to figure out how you are going to scale the cone to show the parameters of the spot light. In this case, you assume that you want to draw the cone from the light position down to the origin. Now the length of the cone is simply the length of the position vector, which you compute by introducing another D3DX function. Once the length is computed, you can use a little trigonometry to find the width of the cone. In this first case, you figure out the width of the penumbra. Once the width and height are computed, you can create a scaling matrix that will stretch the cone in your vertex buffer to the correct shape:

```
FLOAT ConeLength =
        D3DXVec3Length(&D3DXVECTOR3
        (m_Light[SPOT_LIGHT].Position));

FLOAT ConeWidth = ConeLength *
```

```
                         tan(m_Light[SPOT_LIGHT].Phi / 2.0f);
D3DXMatrixScaling(&Scaling, ConeWidth, ConeLength,
 ConeWidth);
```

Finally, you set up your world matrix and draw the penumbra. One obvious omission here is a rotation matrix that allows you to properly draw the spot light if you change the direction to anything other than straight down. It's true that, as the code stands, the spot light visualization does not properly show a rotated spot light (although the lighting effects are displayed properly). This omission is intentional because the methods to do this are slightly more than trivial, and I want to focus on lighting. The procedure needed to properly rotate the light is discussed more in Chapter 40, which focuses more on jumping through mathematical hoops:

```
Transform = Scaling * Translation;
m_pD3DDevice->SetTransform(D3DTS_WORLD, &Transform);
m_pD3DDevice->DrawPrimitive(D3DPT_LINESTRIP, 0, 2);
m_pD3DDevice->DrawPrimitive(D3DPT_LINESTRIP, 3, 2);
```

This code draws the circular base of the penumbra cone on the flat plane. It translates the circle to the position of the light but keeps the height at ground level. The circle defined in the vertex buffer is not aligned with the ground plane, so you create a rotation matrix to correct that. You also scale the circle to the width of the penumbra. Finally, you set the world matrix and render the circle. You could make a strong argument that it is much easier to simply create several different circles in the vertex buffer rather than work so hard to reuse one circle. One reason I jump through so many hoops to reuse the circle is to drive home the point about transformations allowing you to reuse geometry. In a real application, you probably want to create more geometry and simple transforms, especially if you choose to implement code to actually rotate the spot light visuals:

```
D3DXMatrixTranslation(&Translation,
                m_Light[SPOT_LIGHT].Position.x,
                0.0f, m_Light[SPOT_LIGHT].Position.z);
D3DXMatrixRotationX(&Rotation, D3DX_PI / 2.0f);
D3DXMatrixScaling(&Scaling, ConeWidth,
                    ConeWidth,
 ConeWidth);
Transform = Rotation * Scaling * Translation;
m_pD3DDevice->SetTransform(D3DTS_WORLD, &Transform);
m_pD3DDevice->DrawPrimitive(D3DPT_LINESTRIP,
   NUM_CONE_POINTS, NUM_CIRCLE_POINTS - 1);
```

```
D3DXMatrixTranslation(&Translation,
                      m_Light[SPOT_LIGHT].Position.x,
                      m_Light[SPOT_LIGHT].Position.y,
                      m_Light[SPOT_LIGHT].Position.z);

ConeWidth = ConeLength * tan(m_Light[SPOT_LIGHT].Theta
 / 2.0f);
D3DXMatrixScaling(&Scaling, ConeWidth, ConeLength,
 ConeWidth);

Transform = Scaling * Translation;
m_pD3DDevice->SetTransform(D3DTS_WORLD, &Transform);

m_pD3DDevice->DrawPrimitive(D3DPT_LINESTRIP, 0, 2);
m_pD3DDevice->DrawPrimitive(D3DPT_LINESTRIP, 3, 2);
```

This code draws the umbra using the same procedure:

```
D3DXMatrixTranslation(&Translation,
                      m_Light[SPOT_LIGHT].Position.x,
                      0.0f, m_Light[SPOT_LIGHT].Position.z);

D3DXMatrixRotationX(&Rotation, D3DX_PI / 2.0f);
D3DXMatrixScaling(&Scaling, ConeWidth, ConeWidth,
 ConeWidth);
Transform = Rotation * Scaling * Translation;
m_pD3DDevice->SetTransform(D3DTS_WORLD, &Transform);

m_pD3DDevice->DrawPrimitive(D3DPT_LINESTRIP,
 NUM_CONE_POINTS, NUM_CIRCLE_POINTS - 1);
}
```

This code creates a simple sphere representing a point light. You translate the circle
to the light's position, scale it to the point light range, and draw the first circle. Then,
you rotate by 90 degrees and render the second circle, creating a simple sphere:

```
if (m_CurrentLight == POINT_LIGHT)
{
        D3DXMatrixTranslation(&Translation,
                      m_Light[POINT_LIGHT].Position.x,
                      m_Light[POINT_LIGHT].Position.y,
```

```
                                m_Light[POINT_LIGHT].Position.z);

        D3DXMatrixScaling(&Scaling, m_Light[POINT_LIGHT].Range,
                                    m_Light[POINT_LIGHT].Range,
                                    m_Light[POINT_LIGHT].Range);


        Transform = Scaling * Translation;
        m_pD3DDevice->SetTransform(D3DTS_WORLD, &Transform);
        m_pD3DDevice->DrawPrimitive(D3DPT_LINESTRIP,
         NUM_CONE_POINTS, NUM_CIRCLE_POINTS - 1);


        D3DXMatrixRotationY(&Rotation, D3DX_PI / 2.0f);
        Transform = Scaling * Rotation * Translation;
        m_pD3DDevice->SetTransform(D3DTS_WORLD, &Transform);
        m_pD3DDevice->DrawPrimitive(D3DPT_LINESTRIP,
         NUM_CONE_POINTS, NUM_CIRCLE_POINTS - 1);

    }
```

The last thing you do is reset the world transform to an identity matrix to make sure that your transformations do not affect how other objects are rendered.

```
        D3DXMatrixIdentity(&Transform);
        m_pD3DDevice->SetTransform(D3DTS_WORLD, &Transform);
}
```

In Conclusion...

As was stated at the beginning of this chapter, this was the first and last time you are really going to look at DirectX Graphics lights in any detail because you are going to implement most of your lighting in shaders. However, the concepts of this chapter should provide a basis for comparison between your "homegrown" lights and the lights that are natively part of the API. Before moving on, take time to experiment with animating the lights and changing the light parameters. If you don't understand specific parameters or concepts, change the parameters and experiment to get a better idea. Also keep in mind that some lights might not show up well on lower-resolution geometry. For example, it is difficult to see the subtle effects of falloff on a very simple mesh. If you are getting results that don't seem correct, make sure you are using one of the better subsets. After you get the correct results, examine the other meshes to see how a degradation in mesh resolution leads to a degradation in shading. The more you experiment here, the easier it is to grasp the implementation details of shaders.

Of course, I end the chapter with some points to remember:

- Fixed function lighting can be useful, but once you get into shaders, you will be implementing your own lighting effects. The purpose of this chapter is to provide an introduction to the different light types.

- Directional lights are the least computationally expensive lights, but they lack subtle and realistic attenuation effects. They are a good choice if you want to create lights that fill a space, such as sunlight or fluorescent lights.

- Point lights incorporate attenuation but radiate in all directions. They are good for more discrete sources of light such as torches or fireballs.

- Spot lights incorporate more attenuation and falloff effects but are much more computationally expensive than directional lights.

- Often lighting decisions involve choosing between realistic and "good enough." For instance, all light attenuates over distance, but in some environments or situations, it's just not worth the added processing time to use more expensive lights.

- Experiment with this code. Change the lights and play with their settings. Very soon, you'll be implementing these effects in your own shaders.

CHAPTER 12

INTRODUCTION TO TEXTURES

So far, all of the 3D objects you've seen consist of flat, lit surfaces built from collections of vertices. They lack the visual detail of real objects. One way to add more detail is to add more geometry, but that can become computationally expensive. Another way is to add a texture, which is basically a picture mapped onto the surfaces of the object. For instance, if an object is made of woven cloth, you can create fantastic results by modeling every thread in the cloth, but a much saner way of adding the detail is to add a texture that looks like woven cloth. Simple textures can create very good results, and the results get even better when I start talking about bump maps and per-pixel lighting.

In the following chapters and throughout the rest of the book, you will be using textures for many different uses, ranging from simple texturing to light mapping, bump mapping, and look-up tables for complex functions. The purpose of this chapter is to introduce the basics of textures and how they are used. You are going to take a look at how textures are created, stored, changed, and used. This serves as a starting point for later chapters when you get into more advanced techniques. But first I talk about the basics.

- How textures are stored in memory.
- Understanding the dimensions of a texture.
- The structure and use of mip maps.
- Creating textures.
- Mapping textures to vertices.
- Telling the device about the texture.
- Performance implications of using textures.
- A sneak peek at advanced texturing techniques.

Textures—The Inside Story

Before I talk about textures themselves, I must delve into some of the concepts that go into texturing. To fully understand how to create a texture, you'll start by looking at how they are stored in memory and how they are used. Once you look at the internals of how textures work, you'll be able to talk more about how to make them work most effectively.

Surfaces and Memory

The earlier versions of DirectX featured the DirectDraw API for rendering 2D graphics. DirectDraw stored image data in an object called a surface, which in the context of images was different from the geometric concept of a surface. DirectDraw surfaces stored bitmap data, optimally in video memory. When DirectDraw was asked to draw something, it would copy the image data from one surface to another as quickly as possible. Surfaces were better than simple blocks of system memory because the DirectDraw API could manage them effectively and optimize their usage as much as possible.

With the newer versions of DirectX, the notion of using a surface to move image data directly to the screen has largely disappeared. In most cases, it's much better to take advantage of the pipeline described in Chapter 5. However, surfaces remain the basic storage object for image data, only they are now contained within the more pipeline-friendly texture object. In the context of textures, individual elements of the image are called *texels* (texture elements).

Surface memory, whether it resides in system memory or video memory, is conceptually a rectangle with a given width and height, but it is really one linear range of bytes. It is a common misconception that the number of bytes in a surface is equal to the width multiplied by the height and the number of bytes per pixel, but as Figure 12.1 shows, this is not necessarily the case.

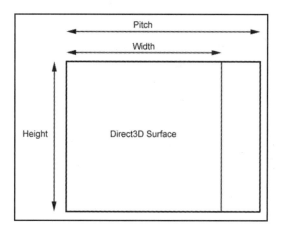

Figure 12.1

Image data in memory.

Although you might define a surface by a given width and height, it may have allocated more memory at the end of each row of data. The length of each row of data is called the pitch, and it may or may not be equal to the width of the surface. This is extremely important to remember, and you will take a look at this later in this chapter.

Width, Height, and the Powers of Two

Most graphics cards and implementations restrict texture dimensions to powers of two. This means that textures are restricted to sizes such as 1x1, 16x16, 128x128, and so on. Note that this does not mean that they need to be square. Sizes such as 128x16 are also legal. There are a couple of reasons for this restriction, but the biggest reason is that dimensions which are powers of two are easier for the device to manipulate quickly. In future versions of hardware, this requirement might be relaxed, but for the foreseeable future, you should expect that the hardware will require textures to have dimensions with powers of two.

While I'm on the subject of width and height, remember that the bigger the texture is, the more data there is to move around the pipeline. Keep your textures as small as possible.

Surface Levels and Mip Maps

In most cases, the manipulation done to the contents of surfaces was minimal for 2D graphics applications. Most of the time, surfaces contained simple sprites that were copied to various locations on the screen. In 3D graphics, textures can be applied to objects that are constantly changing their position and orientation in relation to the camera. As an object gets farther away, that object is drawn using fewer and fewer pixels on the screen. If the object is textured, that means that the texture must be scaled smaller and smaller as the object gets farther away. The device can do this, but it must process the texture, which can introduce visual artifacts. Also, it is not optimal to process a large amount of data if you are only affecting a handful of texels.

You can address both of these problems with mip maps. Mip maps are usually used to represent several different scaled versions of the same image. For example, if you have a 256x256 texture, you could create mip maps ranging from 128x128 down to 1x1. A textured object that is very close to the camera and therefore very large might be drawn with the 256x256 texture. The same object might be drawn with the 1x1 texture when it is very far away or very small. Usually the device makes decisions about which version to use.

What's a Mip Map?

The word *mip* comes from the Latin phrase *multim im parvo*, which means that there are many things in one package. A *mip map* is a texture that contains several small textures. Originally, I wanted to write this whole book it Latin, but it's easier just to say mip.

The device can create a range of mip maps when the texture is created, or an artist can create different mip map levels at design time. Creating the descending levels by hand gives the artist the opportunity to tweak the image to get the best quality with the smaller number of texels, but no rule says the levels must have the same contents. For instance, you can create a set of maps that change color as the maps get smaller. Figure 12.2 shows several levels of a mip-mapped texture. In the top row, the smaller images are resized versions of the largest texture. In the bottom row, the images are smaller, but the text has been tweaked at each level to enhance readability.

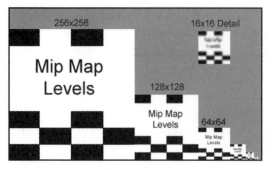

Figure 12.2

Mip map levels.

A texture object can be a set of one or more surfaces, depending on how many different levels of mip maps you need. Each one of these levels is a separate surface object managed by the texture. You can deal with each surface level independently. Throughout the rest of this chapter, you will look at how the individual levels are created, accessed, and used to render textured objects.

Creating Textures

Before you try to create a texture, it's best to find out what sorts of limitations the device may have. You can do this by calling your old friend GetDeviceCaps. As always, the D3DCAPS8 structure is chock full of information about what the hardware can and can't handle. For simple texture creation, the most important members to check are MaxTextureWidth and MaxTextureHeight. These define how big the texture can be. Current hardware supports textures of 2,048x2,048 and above, but many older cards are limited to 256x256 and possibly lower. Other members of the D3DCAPS8 structure might also be useful. The TextureCaps member is a set of flags that tells you whether the device is limited to square textures, whether it supports mip maps, and much more.

In DirectX 8.0, simple textures are represented by the IDirect3DTexture8 interface. This interface is inherited from IDirect3DBaseTexture8, which serves as a base class for simple textures as well as more complex textures, such as cube map and volume textures. In this chapter, I only talk about the simple textures. The other types warrant more in-depth discussion in later chapters. An application can create a texture object by calling IDirect3DDevice::CreateTexture:

```
HRESULT IDirect3DDevice8::CreateTexture(UINT Width, UINT Height,
        UINT Levels, DWORD Usage, D3DFORMAT Format,
        D3DPOOL Pool,
        IDirect3DTexture8 **ppTexture);
```

The Width and the Height are the requested dimensions of the texture. (Remember the powers-of-two requirement.) The Levels parameter is the number of requested mip map levels. If this parameter is 0, the device creates sublevels of the texture from the requested dimensions down to 1x1.

The Usage parameter allows the texture to be created and set up for certain specialized operations such as rendering to a texture. That can be a powerful tool, and it is prominent in some of the later chapters. If you are creating a texture that is going to be applied to an object, set this parameter to zero.

The Format parameter must be a member of the D3DFORMAT enumerated type that represents a pixel format. All the samples in this book use 32-bit textures with the format D3DFMT_A8R8G8B8 unless otherwise specified. The reason is that when you get into pixel shaders, you will need all four channels available to you. Also, current hardware easily supports 32-bit textures with little performance penalty. In fact, in some cases 32-bit textures are better because the hardware might be optimized for 32-bit operations. If for some reason you are constrained to 16-bit textures, most of the concepts in these chapters should still apply.

The Pool parameter is subject to the same constraints I discussed for vertex buffers. In most cases, you should create textures with the D3DPOOL_MANAGED setting, although some chapters demonstrate the uses of other settings.

If this function succeeds, you will have a valid and usable texture object. You can then find out more about it with some of the members of IDirect3DTexture8. The first thing you can ask is how many levels were actually created. To do so, call GetLevelCount:

```
DWORD IDirect3DTexture8::GetLevelCount();
```

This returns the number of surface levels contained within the texture object. Once you know how many levels are available, you can call GetLevelDesc to get the information about each level:

```
HRESULT IDirect3DTexture8::GetLevelDesc(UINT Level,
                        D3DSURFACE_DESC *pDescription);
```

The D3DSURFACE_DESC structure contains information about each level. You can use this to see the width and height of each level, which should tell you which mip map is there. If you decide to manipulate the data in a level, you can get the actual surface by calling GetSurfaceLevel:

```
HRESULT IDirect3DTexture8::GetSurfaceLevel(UINT Level,
                              IDirect3DSurface8 **ppSurface);
```

You now have the pointer to the surface itself. If you had some image data, you could now copy it to the surface. To do so, call LockRect on the new surface object:

```
HRESULT IDirect3DSurface8::LockRect(D3DLOCKED_RECT *pLockedRect,
                             CONST RECT *pRect,
                             DWORD Flags);
```

The application requests a rectangular subset of the surface or the entire surface if pRect was NULL. The function returns a D3DLOCKED_RECT structure containing the pitch of the surface along with the requested bits. The data is now ready to be changed. For write operations, set the Flags parameter to zero. Once the data is changed, the application can call UnlockRect and release the surface pointer:

```
HRESULT IDirect3DSurface8::UnlockRect();
```

I have just demonstrated how to create a texture object and jump through all the hoops to set the texture data, but it's a lot of work and I'm pretty lazy. Most of the time, texture data is stored in a bitmap file, and it would be nice to have an easy function that would allow you to load a file and easily create a texture object based on that file. The D3DX library comes to the rescue again.

The easiest way to load a texture from a file is to use the D3DXCreateTextureFromFile function. If it succeeds, this function creates a valid texture object from an image file. There are analogous functions for loading a texture from a file in memory and from a resource. I am only going to look at the file functions, but the other versions are similar:

```
HRESULT D3DXCreateTextureFromFile(LPDIRECT3DDEVICE8 pDevice,
    LPCSTR FileName, LPDIRECT3DTEXTURE8 pTexture);
```

You can use the D3DXCreateTextureFromFile function to easily load an image file into a texture, but sometimes it can be a little too simple. The D3DXCreateTextureFromFileEx function gives you more control over how the texture is loaded:

```
HRESULT D3DXCreateTextureFromFileEx(LPDIRECT3DDEVICE8 pDevice,
                    LPCWSTR pFileName, UINT Width, UINT Height,
                    UINT MipLevels, DWORD Usage,
                    D3DFORMAT Format, D3DPOOL Pool,
```

```
                    DWORD Filter, DWORD MipFilter,
                    D3DCOLOR ColorKey,
                    D3DXIMAGE_INFO *pImageInfo,
                    PALETTEENTRY *pPalette,
                    LPDIRECT3DTEXTURE8 *ppTexture);
```

The D3DXCreateTextureFromFileEx function exposes the parameters from CreateTexture along with some new ones. When you set the width and height, a value of D3DX_DEFAULT tells D3DX to use the size of the source image. The filter parameters describe how the image is to be filtered when it is being resized to fit the texture or to build mip maps. If a color key is specified, that color is transparent in the loaded texture. You can use the D3DXIMAGE_INFO structure to retrieve information about the source image. Finally, you can use the palette structure to set a palette. Because you are using 32-bit textures, this parameter should be set to NULL.

The D3DX texture creation functions are capable of reading several different file formats, but remember that the amount of texture memory used by the texture depends on the pixel format of the texture, not the size of the file. For instance, if you load a JPEG file as a texture, chances are that the texture will take up much more memory than the size of the JPEG file.

The D3DX functions create the new texture in managed memory. They also try to create a valid texture size for the image. For instance, if the image is 640x480, it might try to create a 1,024x512 texture to satisfy the powers-of-two requirement, or it might try to create a 256x256 texture to satisfy a size limitation of the hardware. In either case, the image is stretched to fill the created texture. This can be advantageous because you are almost guaranteed that you can load images of nearly any size, but stretching can produce artifacts or other undesirable side effects. The best way to prevent this is to size textures appropriately when you are creating the files. That way, you can get the best quality textures and use space as efficiently as possible.

Textures and Vertices

I've talked about how to create the texture, but the texture isn't really worth much if you can't use it with your vertices. So far, the rendering you have done has used simple colored triangles. This is because your vertex format has included only color information. To use textures, you need to augment the vertex format with information about how the texture will be mapped onto the geometry. You do this with texture coordinates.

Texture coordinates map a given vertex to a given location in the texture. Regardless of width and height, locations in the texture range from 0.0 to 1.0 and are typically denoted with u and v. Therefore, if you want to draw a simple rectangle displaying the entire texture, you can set the vertices with texture coordinates (0.0, 0.0), (1.0, 0.0), (0.0, 1.0), (1.0, 1.0), where the first set of coordinates is the upper-left corner of the texture and the last set is the lower-right corner. In this case, the shape of the texture on the screen depends on the vertices, not the texture dimensions. For instance, if you have a 128x128 texture, but the vertices are set up to cover an entire 1,024x768 screen, the texture is stretched to cover the entire rectangle. In the general case, textures are stretched and interpolated between the texture coordinates on the three vertices of a triangle.

Texture coordinates are not limited to the values of 0.0 or 1.0. Values less than 1 index to the corresponding location in the texture. Figure 12.3 shows how you can map a texture using different values. In these examples, every piece of data is the same except for the texture coordinates.

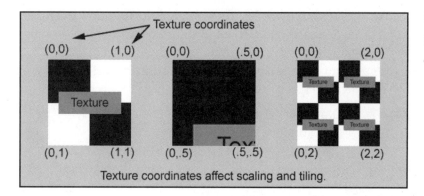

Figure 12.3

Simple texture coordinates.

Texture coordinates are not limited to the range of 0.0 to 1.0 either. In the default case, values greater than 1 result in the texture being repeated between the vertices. In the next chapter, you'll look at some ways that you can change the repeating behavior, but repeating the texture is the most common behavior. Figure 12.4 shows how you can use this to greatly reduce the size of your texture if the texture is a repeating pattern. Imagine a checkerboard fills the screen for a simple game of checkers. You can create a large texture that corresponds to the screen size, but it is better to have a small texture and let the device stretch it for you. Better yet, because of the nature of a checkerboard, you can have a very small texture that is a small portion of the board and then repeat it. By doing this, the texture is 1/16 the size of the full checkerboard pattern and a lot smaller than the image that appears on the screen. This reduces the amount of data that needs to move through the pipeline.

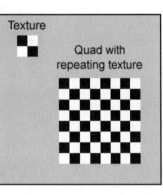

Figure 12.4

Repeating checkerboard patterns.

These are just some simple examples of how texture coordinates work, but the concepts hold true in less straightforward cases. If you create a triangle shaped like a tiny sliver and you map the texture onto that, the texture is stretched and pulled to cover the triangle. The next chapter talks a little more about how the device processes the texture when it is being stretched.

Now that you have looked at how texture coordinates work, let's look at how to add them to your vertex format. A device can use up to eight different textures (although this might be limited by the specific hardware you're using). The following FVF definition defines your vertex as having one set of texture coordinates. D3DFVF_TEX1 is used for one texture, D3DFVF_TEX2 is used for two, and so on:

```
#define D3DFVF_TEXTUREDVERTEX (D3DFVF_XYZ | D3DFVF_DIFFUSE |
                               D3DFVF_TEX1)
struct TEXTUREDVERTEX
{
    FLOAT x, y, z;
    DWORD d;
    FLOAT u, v;
};
```

So far, I've limited the discussion to 2D textures because those are the most widely used, but it is possible to have a 1D texture, which is just like any other texture, but with a height of 1. 1D textures can be useful with vertex or pixel shaders. The format for a vertex with a 1D texture coordinate follows. In this case, the D3DFVF_TEXCOORDSIZEx flag tells the device there is only one texture coordinate:

```
#define D3DFVF_TEXTUREDVERTEX (D3DFVF_XYZ | D3DFVF_DIFFUSE |
                     D3DFVF_TEX1 | D3DFVF_TEXCOORDSIZE1(0))
```

```
struct TEXTUREDVERTEX
{
    FLOAT x, y, z;
    DWORD d;
    FLOAT u;
};
```

After the format is created, you can set the texture coordinate values just as you set all the other vertex data. Lock the buffer, set the data, and unlock the buffer. So far, you have the texture and the vertex format. The last thing you need to do is tell the device to use the texture.

Textures and the Device

DirectX allows a device to use up to eight textures at a time. Each of these textures is represented by a texture stage, which can have many different settings and states, as you'll see in the next chapter. For the device to use a texture, you must set that texture to a given stage using the SetTexture function:

```
HRESULT IDirect3DDevice8::SetTexture::SetTexture(DWORD Stage,
                                   IDirect3DBaseTexture8 *pTexture);
```

For the purposes of this chapter, the texture parameter is always a pointer to an IDirect3DTexture8 interface, although in later chapters the syntax is the same for other texture types. The Stage parameter has a valid range between 0 and 7. You set the texture only for the stages you use. All other stages default to NULL. When you are done with a texture, or you want to disable texturing for a given stage, set the texture for that stage to NULL. It is good practice to make sure all texture stages are set to NULL before ending the program because SetTexture increments the reference count of the texture when it is set and decrements it when it is set to something else. If the reference count does not get decremented, you could have resource leaks. The following code demonstrates the way to do this:

```
m_pD3DDevice->SetTexture(0, m_pTexture1);
// Render some stuff
m_pD3DDevice->SetTexture(0, m_pTexture2);
// Render more stuff
m_pD3DDevice->SetTexture(0, m_NULL);
// Done?
```

Performance Considerations

Textures take up a lot of memory. That affects not only storage space, but also rendering time because all of that memory must be pushed through the pipeline as objects are rendered. As I mentioned before, if there are ways to get by with smaller textures, do so. If a texture has a lot of repetition, create a smaller version of that texture and tile it using texture coordinates greater than 1.0.

On the flipside, if you have a lot of very small textures, you might want to place them all into one medium-sized texture and use texture coordinates to index into the different regions. This is the idea behind the text-rendering functions I talk about in later chapters. The downside of this is that it does not allow you to tile the subtextures in many cases, so sometimes you just need to experiment to see what's best for your application.

You also don't want to call SetTexture any more than you have to because setting the texture is expensive. The previous code snippet demonstrates the basic usage of SetTexture, but take it with a grain of salt. You do not need to set all the textures to NULL at the end of every frame. That can be expensive, and it wouldn't really accomplish anything. Only set textures when you need to, and batch textured objects together as much as possible.

Performance, as it relates to textures, is heavily dependent on your hardware and your application. Whenever possible, I give more performance tips, but in reality you should understand some of these basic tips and then experiment to see what works best for your specific situation.

Advanced Topics

In later chapters, you will be doing some very cool things with textures, so I don't want to get too far ahead, but a couple of topics deserve a quick explanation in this chapter. These ideas are expanded in later chapters, so these sections are brief.

Textures and Color

The interaction between vertex colors and textures is discussed in the next chapter, but it does have an effect on the code from this chapter. The default mode of interaction between the vertex colors (whether set as vertex colors or computed from the lighting) is modulation or, in other words, multiplication. If you think of colors as being in the range of 0.0 to 1.0, the texel color is multiplied by the vertex color to produce the final output color at a given pixel. In the previous chapter, you took a look at how per-vertex lighting was interpolated across triangles. The output in a given pixel on the screen is the product (in the mathematical sense) of the interpolated vertex color value and the texel color value at the interpolated texture coordinate. As a shaded surface goes from light to dark, the texture is darkened accordingly. This is just the default behavior. The next chapter looks at how to change that.

The Texture Matrix

You've taken a look at how you can use the world transform to alter the position information in a vertex. The same concepts apply to the texture coordinate information. In this chapter, you will look at how you can use very simple transforms to affect the texture coordinates, but in later chapters you will look at how you can use the texture matrix to produce cool effects such as projective texturing and shadow mapping. Unlike other transformations, to enable the texture transforms you must tell the device that you will be using them.

Multitexturing

The preceding discussion focused on setting one texture, but there are up to eight texture stages, and you can apply multiple textures to the same geometry, provided the vertices have more texture coordinates and the proper texture count in the FVF. Once the vertices are set properly, you can set more texture stages and place multiple textures on the same object. In the next chapter, you'll take a look at how to do that and how to change the way multiple textures interact.

The Application

Because so many chapters use textures and related concepts, the sample application for this chapter is relatively simple. Figure 12.5 shows a screenshot.

The sample application draws four instances of the same quad, all with different textures or different texture coordinates. You might think I went a little crazy with the texture matrix. Instead of creating different rectangles with different texture coordinates, the application shows how you can use the texture matrix to scale the texture coordinates. For instance, the basic vertex data contains coordinates ranging from 0.0 to 1.0. When you create a scaling matrix that scales by 2.0, the new coordinates are in the range of 0.0 to 2.0, and so on. This is great for reuse but can obscure what's really going on. If you are not sure what is happening, change the

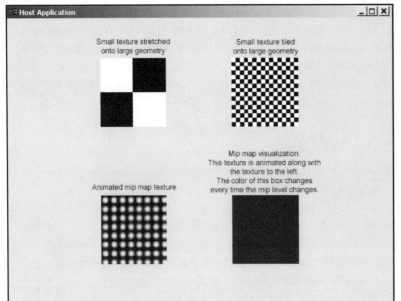

Figure 12.5

Simple textured quads in the sample app.

texture coordinates directly in the vertex data, get a feel for how the coordinates work, and then go back to the matrices. The matrices are a great way to easily show many different coordinates, but in practical terms, usually texture coordinates are fixed. All this business with the matrix is for demonstration purposes.

The top row shows how you can use very simple textures to fill large spaces. The checkerboard pattern is an extremely small 2x2 texture. The upper-left rectangle shows how you can scale that very small texture to fill a larger space. The upper-right rectangle uses the same texture, but the texture coordinates are set to repeat the texture eight times in both dimensions. You get a full chessboard with a very small texture. This effect is most useful for things such as brick walls and similar repeating patterns.

The second row demonstrates mip maps. The lower-left rectangle is textured with an image loaded from a file. As the texture matrix scales the coordinates, the rectangle is filled with more repetitions of the texture. As each single image becomes smaller, the device uses the smaller mip maps to draw the texture, but it is difficult to see the transition between the different levels. (This is a good thing.) To better demonstrate what is going on, the lower-right rectangle is textured with a very simple texture created in code. Each level of that texture is colored according to its dimensions. The largest level of 256x256 is colored RGB(255, 255, 255), which is white. The 128x128 level is colored a middle gray at RGB(128, 128, 128). As the levels get smaller, the mip maps get darker. On the lower-right rectangle, you can explicitly see when the different levels are used. So every time the gray rectangle changes color, you know that the level has changed for each of the textures in the second row. Figure 12.6 highlights the change.

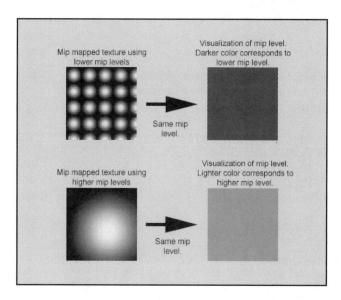

Figure 12.6

Different mip map levels.

Let's take a look at the code. TextureApplication.h is similar to the other application header files you've created:

```
#include "Application.h"

class CTextureApplication : public CHostApplication
{
public:
```

Call this function to create the custom textures. Because you are creating the textures in managed memory, you call this function only once. The device restores them automatically if need be:

```
    BOOL CreateCustomTextures();
    void SetupDevice();
    BOOL CreateGeometry();
    void DestroyGeometry();

    CTextureApplication();
```

```
virtual ~CTextureApplication();

virtual BOOL PostInitialize();
virtual BOOL PreTerminate();
virtual BOOL PreReset();
virtual BOOL PostReset();
virtual void Render();
```

This application uses a different clear color so you can easily see the textures. This is the first application in which you override the PreRender function so you can control the clear color before rendering:

```
virtual void PreRender();
LPDIRECT3DVERTEXBUFFER8 m_pVertexBuffer;
```

The following code shows your three textures. The first is created with image data loaded from a file. The last two are created using the basic creation functions, and then the contents are set in code:

```
LPDIRECT3DTEXTURE8 m_pImageTexture;
LPDIRECT3DTEXTURE8 m_pMipMapTexture;
LPDIRECT3DTEXTURE8 m_pCheckerTexture;
// These matrices are reusable transformation matrices
D3DXMATRIX m_WorldMatrix;
D3DXMATRIX m_ViewMatrix;
D3DXMATRIX m_ProjectionMatrix;
};
```

The implementation of the new class is fairly simple. You create a single triangle strip to build your rectangles and then apply your textures. Let's look at TextureApplication.cpp:

```
#include "TextureApplication.h"
```

The FVF and vertex structure now include the proper data for one set of 2D texture coordinates. Because you are not lighting anything, there is no need for vertex normals, and so on. As an exercise, you might want to add a color component and set the vertex colors to see how the color of the vertices affects the way the textured rectangles look. To do this, add color data to the FVF and the structure and set the colors when creating the vertex buffer:

```
#define D3DFVF_TEXTUREVERTEX (D3DFVF_XYZ | D3DFVF_TEX1)

struct TEXTURE_VERTEX
```

```
{
    float x, y, z;
    float u, v;
};
```

As usual, it's just good practice to initialize the pointers:

```
CTextureApplication::CTextureApplication()
{
    m_pVertexBuffer    = NULL;
    m_pCheckerTexture  = NULL;
    m_pMipMapTexture   = NULL;
    m_pImageTexture    = NULL;
}
CTextureApplication::~CTextureApplication()
{
    DestroyGeometry();
}


BOOL CTextureApplication::PostInitialize()
{
    if (FAILED(EasyCreateWindowed(m_hWnd, D3DDEVTYPE_HAL,
                        D3DCREATE_HARDWARE_VERTEXPROCESSING)))
        return FALSE;

    SetupDevice();

    if (!CreateGeometry())
        return FALSE;
```

Call the function that creates the simple textures. This is the only time this function is called:

```
    if (!CreateCustomTextures())
        return FALSE;
```

Create the last texture from a file. Here you use the more simple form of the D3DX texture creation functions because you don't need any special processing. Descending levels of mip maps are created "under the hood":

```
    if (FAILED(D3DXCreateTextureFromFile(m_pD3DDevice,
                                    "..\\media\\light.bmp",
```

```
                                                    &m_pImageTexture)))
              return FALSE;
        return TRUE;
}


void CTextureApplication::SetupDevice()
{
        D3DXMatrixIdentity(&m_ViewMatrix);
        m_pD3DDevice->SetTransform(D3DTS_VIEW, &m_ViewMatrix);

        RECT WindowRect;
        GetClientRect(m_hWnd, &WindowRect);
        D3DXMatrixPerspectiveFovLH(&m_ProjectionMatrix,
                D3DX_PI / 4,
                (float)(WindowRect.right - WindowRect.left) /
                (float)(WindowRect.bottom - WindowRect.top),
                    1.0f, 100.0f);
        m_pD3DDevice->SetTransform(D3DTS_PROJECTION,
                                &m_ProjectionMatrix);


        m_pD3DDevice->SetRenderState(D3DRS_CULLMODE, D3DCULL_NONE);
        m_pD3DDevice->SetRenderState(D3DRS_LIGHTING, FALSE);
```

The next chapter concentrates solely on texture stage states and what you can use them for. Here you are telling the device how to process the texture transformation matrix. This informs the device to process the matrix for 2D texture coordinates:

```
        m_pD3DDevice->SetTextureStageState(0,
                            D3DTSS_TEXTURETRANSFORMFLAGS,
                            D3DTTFF_COUNT2);
```

Here is another mysterious texture stage state. In this case, you are telling the device how to process mip maps. The concepts of filtering is discussed in the next chapter:

```
        m_pD3DDevice->SetTextureStageState(0, D3DTSS_MIPFILTER,
                                        D3DTEXF_POINT);
```

```
}


BOOL CTextureApplication::PreReset()
{
        DestroyGeometry();
        return TRUE;
```

```
}

BOOL CTextureApplication::PostReset()
{
      SetupDevice();
      return CreateGeometry();
}


BOOL CTextureApplication::PreTerminate()
{
      DestroyGeometry();
```

Here you are a good citizen again and make sure that the texture is not being used before you destroy it. This helps ensure that everything is happy, both this time and the next time you run a DirectX application:

```
      m_pD3DDevice->SetTexture(0, NULL);
```

Destroying the textures is straightforward. If they exist, send them the way of the dodo by calling Release. This is where the SetTexture call becomes important. If the texture is still in use by the device, calling Release only once might not fully destroy the object, creating memory leaks. That's bad:

```
      if (m_pCheckerTexture)
            m_pCheckerTexture->Release();

      if (m_pMipMapTexture)
            m_pMipMapTexture->Release();

      if (m_pImageTexture)
            m_pImageTexture->Release();
      return TRUE;
}


BOOL CTextureApplication::CreateGeometry()
{
      if (FAILED(m_pD3DDevice->CreateVertexBuffer(4 *
                              sizeof(TEXTURE_VERTEX),
                              D3DUSAGE_WRITEONLY,
                              D3DFVF_TEXTUREVERTEX,
                              D3DPOOL_DEFAULT,
                              &m_pVertexBuffer)))
```

```
            return FALSE;

    TEXTURE_VERTEX *pVertices;

    if (FAILED(m_pVertexBuffer->Lock(0, 4 * sizeof(TEXTURE_VERTEX),
                                     (BYTE **)&pVertices,
                                     0)))
    {
            DestroyGeometry();
            return FALSE;
    }
    pVertices[0].x = -1.0f; pVertices[0].y =  1.0f;
     pVertices[0].z = 10.0f;
    pVertices[1].x =  1.0f; pVertices[1].y =  1.0f;
     pVertices[1].z = 10.0f;
    pVertices[2].x = -1.0f; pVertices[2].y = -1.0f;
     pVertices[2].z = 10.0f;
    pVertices[3].x =  1.0f; pVertices[3].y = -1.0f;
     pVertices[3].z = 10.0f;
```

For this chapter, the vertex creation is essentially the same as what you've seen in previous chapters. The only difference here is that you set the vertex coordinates as shown. The coordinates are set to 1.0 because you will be scaling them with the texture matrix. If you find the texture matrix confusing, comment out the lines that use the texture matrix and change the texture coordinates directly in this part of the code. Once you are comfortable with the effects of different texture coordinates, reset these texture coordinates to 1.0 and enable the texture matrix:

```
    pVertices[0].u = 0.0f; pVertices[0].v = 0.0f;
    pVertices[1].u = 1.0f; pVertices[1].v = 0.0f;
    pVertices[2].u = 0.0f; pVertices[2].v = 1.0f;
    pVertices[3].u = 1.0f; pVertices[3].v = 1.0f;
    m_pVertexBuffer->Unlock();
```

Because you are never going to be switching sources or shaders, you can set them once here and forget about it. If the device is reset, this function is called again anyway:

```
    m_pD3DDevice->SetStreamSource(0, m_pVertexBuffer,
                                  sizeof(TEXTURE_VERTEX));
    m_pD3DDevice->SetVertexShader(D3DFVF_TEXTUREVERTEX);
    return TRUE;
```

```
      }

void CTextureApplication::DestroyGeometry()
{
      if (m_pVertexBuffer)
      {
            m_pVertexBuffer->Release();
            m_pVertexBuffer = NULL;
      }
}
```

You override the `PreRender` function so that you can use a background color that doesn't clash with your black and white textures. The one important thing to remember is that if you override the `PreRender` function, you must call `BeginScene` or nothing (good) will happen:

```
void CTextureApplication::PreRender()
{
      m_pD3DDevice->Clear(0, NULL, D3DCLEAR_TARGET |
            D3DCLEAR_ZBUFFER, D3DCOLOR_XRGB(0, 0, 255), 1.0f, 0);
      m_pD3DDevice->BeginScene();


}


void CTextureApplication::Render()
{
```

The first thing you do is create a texture matrix variable and use it to make sure that the texture transform is set to the identity matrix before you draw your first rectangle:

```
      D3DXMATRIX TextureMatrix;
      D3DXMatrixIdentity(&TextureMatrix);
      m_pD3DDevice->SetTransform(D3DTS_TEXTURE0, &TextureMatrix);
```

Here you set the checkerboard texture as your current texture. This texture affects all textured primitives until you explicitly set a new texture:

```
      m_pD3DDevice->SetTexture(0, m_pCheckerTexture);
```

The first rectangle shows the 2x2 texture as it appears in memory, except that it is stretched to fill a much larger space. This operation is very fast because the texture is tiny and the 3D card is good at simple operations such as stretching. One of the points to see here is that if you don't need a lot of detail, a very small texture can fill a very large space. There is sometimes no need for large textures:

```
D3DXMatrixTranslation(&m_WorldMatrix, -2.0f, 2.0f, 0.0f);
m_pD3DDevice->SetTransform(D3DTS_WORLD, &m_WorldMatrix);
m_pD3DDevice->DrawPrimitive(D3DPT_TRIANGLESTRIP, 0, 2);
```

This second rectangle is based on the same geometry and the same texture, only this time the texture coordinates are scaled by the texture transformation matrix. This scales the coordinates by 8.0, meaning that the texture is tiled eight times in both directions. If you are texturing a large area and you can find pattern, exploit the pattern as much as possible:

```
D3DXMatrixScaling(&TextureMatrix, 8.0f, 8.0f, 1.0f);
m_pD3DDevice->SetTransform(D3DTS_TEXTURE0, &TextureMatrix);
D3DXMatrixTranslation(&m_WorldMatrix, 2.0f, 2.0f, 0.0f);
m_pD3DDevice->SetTransform(D3DTS_WORLD, &m_WorldMatrix);
m_pD3DDevice->DrawPrimitive(D3DPT_TRIANGLESTRIP, 0, 2);
```

As in previous chapters, you create an arbitrary scale factor by getting the cosine of the tick count. Getting the tick count ensures that you get incremental values. Taking the cosine limits the range of values. You add one and multiply it to tweak the range:

```
float ScaleFactor = (cos((float)GetTickCount() / 1000.0f) +
                     1.0) * 10.0f;
```

With the new scale factor, you can create a texture matrix that continually animates the texture coordinates in a nice, orderly fashion. Once you are comfortable with all of this, create translation or rotation matrices to see their effects. As it is written here, the scaling matrix forces the texture to repeat, prompting the device to use smaller and smaller mip maps. The special mip map texture makes it easier to see that effect:

```
D3DXMatrixScaling(&TextureMatrix, ScaleFactor,
                  ScaleFactor, 1.0f);
m_pD3DDevice->SetTransform(D3DTS_TEXTURE0, &TextureMatrix);
```

Set the texture to the image loaded from the file. The individual mip map levels were created by the driver:

```
m_pD3DDevice->SetTexture(0, m_pImageTexture);
D3DXMatrixTranslation(&m_WorldMatrix, -2.0f, -2.0f, 0.0f);
m_pD3DDevice->SetTransform(D3DTS_WORLD, &m_WorldMatrix);
m_pD3DDevice->DrawPrimitive(D3DPT_TRIANGLESTRIP, 0, 2);
```

Now use the special mip map texture. Note that the texture coordinates are the same for both the image texture and this texture. As you see the shades of gray changing on the simple texture, you know that they are also changing on the image texture:

```
m_pD3DDevice->SetTexture(0, m_pMipMapTexture);
D3DXMatrixTranslation(&m_WorldMatrix, 2.0f, -2.0f, 0.0f);
m_pD3DDevice->SetTransform(D3DTS_WORLD, &m_WorldMatrix);
m_pD3DDevice->DrawPrimitive(D3DPT_TRIANGLESTRIP, 0, 2);


}


BOOL CTextureApplication::CreateCustomTextures()
{
```

These are some working variables that you can use when you lock your surface and your surface data:

```
LPDIRECT3DSURFACE8 pWorkSurface;
D3DLOCKED_RECT      WorkRect;
```

This call creates a very small 2x2 texture that will serve as the checkerboard pattern. Using 32 bits for a simple black and white texture is overkill, but in later chapters, the 32 bits are needed:

```
if (FAILED(m_pD3DDevice->CreateTexture(2, 2, 0, 0,
                                       D3DFMT_A8R8G8B8,
                                       D3DPOOL_MANAGED,
                                       &m_pCheckerTexture)))
        return FALSE;
```

First you get the surface and then lock the rectangle. Using NULL as the rectangle parameter prompts the surface to give you the full surface—in this case, a whopping 2x2 rectangle:

```
m_pCheckerTexture->GetSurfaceLevel(0, &pWorkSurface);
pWorkSurface->LockRect(&WorkRect, NULL, 0);
```

Setting the pattern is just a matter of setting the first four bytes (one pixel) to 255 (white), followed by the next four bytes set to black. Then you set the second row, making sure you take into account the pitch of the surface. In most cases, the pitch will just be 8 for this simple texture, but it's important you don't get too sloppy:

```
memset((BYTE *)WorkRect.pBits, 0xff, 4);
memset((BYTE *)WorkRect.pBits + 4, 0x00, 4);
```

```
memset((BYTE *)WorkRect.pBits + WorkRect.Pitch, 0x00, 4);
memset((BYTE *)WorkRect.pBits + WorkRect.Pitch + 4, 0xff, 4);
```

Once you're done, unlock the rectangle, which updates the surface data. Then, release the surface itself. Now the texture itself is back in control:

```
pWorkSurface->UnlockRect();
pWorkSurface->Release();
```

Here you create a 256x256 texture to match the 256x256 texture loaded from the file. The device creates the descending levels of 128x128, 64x64, and so on down to 1x1. Again, 32 bits is overkill:

```
if (FAILED(m_pD3DDevice->CreateTexture(256, 256, 0, 0,
                                       D3DFMT_A8R8G8B8,
                                       D3DPOOL_MANAGED,
                                       &m_pMipMapTexture)))
        return FALSE;
```

Here you loop through each level of the texture and get the description. The description lists width and height, among other properties, and you use the width to set the color. Because the widths of the levels range from 256 to 1, the color for each level ranges from 255 (white) to 0 (black) when you set all four channels to the color value:

```
for (long Level = 0;
     Level <           m_pMipMapTexture->GetLevelCount(); Level++)
{
        D3DSURFACE_DESC LevelDescription;
        m_pMipMapTexture->GetLevelDesc(Level,
                                       &LevelDescription);

        BYTE Color = (BYTE)LevelDescription.Width - 1;
```

This surface is handled a little differently just to show a different approach. Here you lock the rectangle directly instead of obtaining the surface and then locking the rectangle. Both approaches are valid and accomplish the same thing. The only difference here is that you do not have access to the interface of the surface itself. That's fine because you don't really need it, but in some cases you might. If that's the case, use the first approach:

```
m_pMipMapTexture->LockRect(Level, &WorkRect, NULL, 0);
```

Here you set all the bytes in each row to the color value. Again, it is possible that your pitch will be equal to the byte width of the rows themselves, but it's not an ironclad guarantee. It's better to establish good habits now:

```
for (long Row = 0; Row < LevelDescription.Height; Row++)
{
        memset((BYTE *)WorkRect.pBits +
             (Row * WorkRect.Pitch),
             Color,
             LevelDescription.Width * 4);
}
```

Finally, you unlock the rectangle. There's no surface to release:

```
        m_pMipMapTexture->UnlockRect(Level);
    }


    return TRUE;
}
```

If you were writing a real application, chances are that you'd do certain things differently, such as change the format of the textures or use four separate rectangles in the vertex buffer instead of reusing one. The point of this application was to demonstrate the simple concepts behind texturing. I encourage you to experiment with some of the settings until you get a feel for how texture mapping works. You might even want to go back to a previous chapter and apply textures to the simple geometric shapes you created earlier.

In Conclusion...

I have really just scratched the surface here, and in many cases I've had to defer topics to "later chapters." I did this to enable you to concentrate on the most basic concepts while leaving the advanced topics to later chapters. In some cases, the concepts require their own separate chapters to themselves. You should come out of this chapter with a basic understanding of what a texture is and how it is used, but you won't really have the full story until after you're done with the next chapter. Even then, things don't get really interesting until I talk about the advanced techniques themselves. In the meantime, let's go over some points to remember:

- A surface is the entity that stores image/bitmap/texel data in a way that is easily accessed by the device.

- A texture contains one or more surfaces. The surface is a holder for the data, but the device interacts with the texture when mapping the data onto geometry.

- Mip maps provide a mechanism for specifying multiresolution textures.

- You can map textures onto geometry by adding texture coordinates to the vertex format.

- Texture coordinates greater than 1.0 cause the texture to repeat (unless the texture stage is set to do something different).

- Textures can consume a lot of resources and slow down performance if used improperly. Use the smallest textures you can get away with.

- Batch textured objects together to avoid unnecessary texture switching.

CHAPTER 13

TEXTURE STAGE STATES

In the previous chapter, you looked at some of the fundamentals of textures and setting texture stages. The code had a couple of mysterious calls to `SetTextureStageState`, along with the promise that this chapter would fill in the blanks. This chapter rounds out the discussion of the basics of texturing by describing how to control texturing by setting the state of each texture stage. The state of each stage defines how the device deals with that texture and how the texture can interact with other texture stages or in some cases with the vertex data. Many books focus on creating a wide variety of effects by manipulating various stage states to influence blending and texture mapping. Because the focus of this book is shaders, this chapter concentrates less on the blending aspects of texture stage states and more on the way that the device processes the texture before each texel is handed to the pixel shader.

> **NOTE**
>
> Many of these stage states are dependent on whether the device supports them. If you are writing an application that is going to be widely distributed and you want to be absolutely sure that the device supports your settings, you should check the device capabilities with `GetDeviceCaps` and have a fallback plan in case the setting is not supported. If you try a setting from this chapter and it doesn't seem to have an effect, chances are the device does not support that setting.

Rather than present a laundry list of all the texture stage states, I cluster the individual states according to their basic functionality. With that in mind, this chapter covers the following concepts:

- Setting the texture stage states.
- Blending textures with color operations.
- Setting texture coordinate states to control mapping.
- Controlling texture filtering and mip mapping.
- Interacting with shaders.

Setting the Texture Stage State

As you saw in the last chapter, you can set textures to one or more of up to eight different stages. Each stage has a default state, and the sample code from the previous chapter worked with most of those defaults. Now you will experiment with setting different stage states. You set a texture stage state with the appropriately named `SetTextureStageState`:

```
HRESULT IDirect3DDevice8::SetTextureStageState(DWORD Stage,
                              D3DTEXTURESTAGESTATETYPE Type,
                              DWORD Value);
```

The first parameter determines the stage being set. The second parameter is one of several stage state types, which I discuss later. The final parameter is the actual setting. The state type determines the range of values for this parameter.

As you've seen with transformation matrices, textures, and other settings, the texture stage state remains true until it is set to something else. There is no reason to set the stage state unless you need to set it to a new setting. Each setting remains in effect throughout the lifetime of the device.

The following sections list each of the state types by general category. Whenever possible, I've grouped them together in a way that makes the most logical sense. In some cases (such as bump mapping), a full discussion is deferred until a later chapter when I have the chance to discuss the topic in depth.

Blending and Multitexturing

The topic of blending and multitexturing is covered extensively in other texts and examples. Also, the new pixel shader syntax supercedes much of the blending functionality. It is for these reasons that this chapter provides only a basic explanation on the topic of blending multiple textures. If you set multiple texture stages and a set of vertices has more than one set of texture coordinates, multiple textures are applied to the geometry. This is called multitexturing. Figure 13.1 shows two single-textured rectangles and one multitextured rectangle.

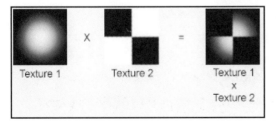

Figure 13.1

Multitextured rectangles.

The color values of the textures must be blended with some mathematical function, and you can set that function with different stage state parameters. In Figure 13.1, the top two rectangles each display a single texture. The lower-left rectangle multiplies the texture values together, but the lower-right rectangle subtracts the second texture from the first. You can use many different operations and settings together to produce interesting effects.

The texture stage state types involved with blending are described in the following sections.

D3DTSS_COLOROP and D3DTSS_ALPHAOP

The D3DTSS_COLOROP state sets the color operation used to blend the textures. The D3DTSS_ALPHAOP state sets the operation applied to the alpha channels of the textures. When you use these types, the Value parameter must be a member of the D3DTEXTUREOP enumerated type. Table 13.1 describes some of these operations.

Table 13.1   D3DTEXTUREOP Values

D3DTEXTUREOP	Comments
D3DTOP_DISABLE	This operation disables this stage and every stage after. Setting this value for stage 0 disables texturing altogether. This is the default value for every stage greater than 0.
D3DTOP_SELECTARG1	The first argument is the output for this stage. There is no computation involved.
D3DTOP_SELECTARG2	The second argument is the output for this stage.
D3DTOP_MODULATE	The two arguments are multiplied together to produce the output value. This is the default operation for stage 0.
D3DTOP_MODULATE2X	The arguments are multiplied and the results are then multiplied by two. This has the effect of brightening the output.
D3DTOP_MODULATE4X	The arguments are multiplied and then multiplied by four, brightening the result even more.
D3DTOP_ADD	The arguments are added together to produce the output value.
D3DTOP_ADDSIGNED	The arguments are added and biases result by –0.5. This creates a result in the range of –0.5 to 0.5.
D3DTOP_ADDSIGNED2X	This operation is the same as the preceding, only multiplied by two.
D3DTOP_SUBTRACT	The second argument is subtracted from the first argument.
D3DTOP_ADDSMOOTH	The product of the two arguments is subtracted from the sum.

There are many more operations available, but the table gives a flavor of what you can do. If you'd like to experiment with other operations, the SDK sample application MFCTex provides an easy way to experiment. These operations assume that one or more arguments are set.

D3DTSS_COLORARG1, D3DTSS_COLORARG2, D3DTSS_ALPHAARG1, and D3DTSS_ALPHAARG2

You set this stage state to define the arguments for the operations shown earlier. There are several possible texture argument flags, as shown in Table 13.2.

Table 13.2   Texture Argument Flags

Flag	Comments
D3DTA_TEXTURE	The texture color is the argument in the operations. This is the default setting for the first argument.
D3DTA_CURRENT	The result from the previous stage is used as the argument. This is the default setting for the second argument.
D3DTA_DIFFUSE	The diffuse color of the vertices is used as the argument.
D3DTA_SPECULAR	Once the specular color is computed, it is used as the argument.
D3DTA_TEMP	If the device supports a temporary register, you can use it as an argument for color operations. This is only really useful if the temporary register is written to in another stage.
D3DTA_TFACTOR	The texture factor is used as an argument. The texture factor is discussed more in the next chapter.
D3DTA_ALPHAREPLICATE	This is an argument modifier that you can use with the preceding arguments. This modifier replicates the alpha value to all of the color channels.
D3DTA_COMPLEMENT	This is an argument modifier that you can use with the preceding arguments. This modifier replaces each value (X) with its complement (1.0–X).

Triadic Operations (D3DTSS_COLORARG0 and D3DTSS_ALPHAARG0)

Some of the texture operations are triadic, meaning that they take three arguments. If the device supports triadic operations, you can specify these states to set the third parameter. These arguments are ignored for operations that take only two arguments.

D3DTSS_RESULTARG

The default operation of the device is to place the result of each blending argument in the current texture register (D3DTA_CURRENT). However, if the device supports it, you can place the result in a temporary register (D3DTA_TEMP). This temporary register can then be used by other stages as an input. However, the final color value that gets passed further along the pipeline is taken from D3DTA_CURRENT, so the last active stage must write to D3DTA_CURRENT.

Checking the Device Caps

The device stores texture operation capabilities in the TextureOpCaps member of the D3DCAPS8 structure. Each capability is of the form D3DTEXOPCAPS_*operation*. The capability flag for D3DTOP_ADD is D3DTEXOPCAPS_ADD. You can check the device for compatibility by ANDing the caps structure member with the flag:

```
BOOL SupportsAddSigned = Caps.TextureOpCaps & D3DTEXOPCAPS_ADDSIGNED;
```

Bump Mapping

The subject of bump mapping is fully explained in its own chapter. However, four texture stage states define a 2x2 matrix used in bump mapping calculations. These stage states are D3DTSS_BUMPENVMAT00, D3DTSS_BUMPENVMAT01, D3DTSS_BUMPENVMAT10, and D3DTSS_BUMPENVMAT11. You can set each of these states to a FLOAT, and the default value for each of these states is 0.0.

Two states affect the luminance of the bump map. These states are D3DTSS_BUMPENVLSCALE, which sets the scale for the bump map luminance, and D3DTSS_BUMPENVLOFFSET, which sets the offset for the luminance. Each of these must be set to a FLOAT. The default value for both is 0.0.

Chapter 31 explains how different values affect the bump map.

Texture Coordinate States

Several stage states affect the way the texture coordinates themselves are processed by the device. Each of these states affects the coordinates differently, and some are ignored when using vertex shaders. Here is a description of each.

D3DTSS_TEXCOORDINDEX

This state tells the stage which texture coordinates to use. The default value for each stage is the index of that stage. If you are not using a vertex shader, you can use this state to tell the device to use the texture coordinates from a different stage. If you are using a vertex shader, this state is ignored and the texture coordinates are passed into the vertex shader in the order they are declared. You can combine the value for this setting with the flags listed in Table 13.3. These flags are useful for texture-coordinate generation for an environmental map texture. If you use one of these flags, the texture coordinate index value does not determine the actual texture coordinates; it determines how the texture is wrapped based on the address state of that stage.

Table 13.3 Texture Coordinate Index Flags

Flag	Comments
D3DTSS_TCI_CAMERASPACENORMAL	The texture coordinates for this stage are contained in the normal vector, which is transformed to camera space.
D3DTSS_TCI_CAMERASPACEPOSITION	The same as the preceding flag, only this time the texture coordinates are based on the transformed vertex position.
D3DTSS_TCI_CAMERASPACEREFLECTIONVECTOR	The reflection vector is computed from the position and normal vectors, transformed to camera space, and then used as the texture coordinates.
D3DTSS_TCI_PASSTHRU	Use the basic texture coordinates. You can use this flag to disable the other flags.

D3DTSS_ADDRESSU, D3DTSS_ADDRESSV, and D3DTSS_ADDRESSW

In the previous chapter, you saw that the default mode for dealing with texture coordinates outside of the range of 0.0 to 1.0 was to repeat the texture. This tiling behavior is called wrapping, but it's not the only mode. There are actually five different ways to deal with texture coordinates outside of the 0.0 to 1.0 range. These three states set the addressing mode for the u and v coordinates, along with the w coordinate for 3D textures. Table 13.4 lists the addressing modes. Each coordinate can have its own mode in any combination.

Table 13.4 D3DTEXTUREADDRESS Modes

Mode	Comments
D3DTADDRESS_WRAP	This is the default behavior. The texture is tiled for coordinates greater than 1.0. For instance, a coordinate of 1.5 tiles the texture one and a half times. A value of 5.0 repeats the texture five times. This is shown on the first rectangle in Figure 13.2.
D3DTADDRESS_MIRROR	This is the same as the preceding mode, only this time the texture is mirrored as it is tiled. For instance, if the u address is set to this mode, the texture is flipped along the vertical axis each time it repeats. This is shown on the second rectangle in Figure 13.2.
D3DTADDRESS_CLAMP	This causes coordinates outside of the range of 0.0 to 1.0 to be clamped to either 0.0 or 1.0. This is also true for interpolated texture coordinates within the polygon. For example, if the texture coordinates along the horizontal axis in a rectangle are from 0.0 to 1.5, the texture is drawn normally until the interpolated texture coordinate reaches 1.0. From then on, the last column of texels repeats. This is shown on the third rectangle in Figure 13.2.
D3DTADDRESS_BORDER	If any texture coordinates fall outside of the 0.0 to 1.0 range, the texture is not drawn. Instead, all pixels are drawn using the border color. The fourth rectangle in Figure 13.2 shows this behavior.
D3DTADDRESS_MIRRORONCE	This mode effectively mirrors around 0.0 by taking the absolute value of the texture coordinate. Texture coordinates less than 0.0 are treated as their greater-than-0.0 equivalents.

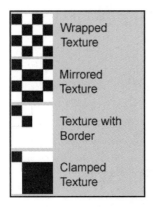

Figure 13.2

Different addressing modes applied to rectangles.

Wrapped Texture

Mirrored Texture

Texture with Border

Clamped Texture

D3DTSS_BORDERCOLOR

This stage state sets the border color used if the addressing mode is set to D3DTADDRESS_BORDER. This is a full 32-bit value. The default value is 0.

D3DTSS_TEXTURETRANSFORMFLAGS

As you saw in the last chapter, this stage state tells the device how to process the texture coordinates with a texture matrix. You must set the value of this stage to a member of the D3DTEXTURETRANSFORMFLAGS enumerated type. Table 13.5 describes the values.

Table 13.5 D3DTEXTURETRANSFORMFLAGS

Flag	Comments
D3DTTFF_DISABLE	The texture coordinates are not transformed by a texture matrix.
D3DTTFF_COUNTx	The texture coordinates are processed as x dimensional coordinates. For example, D3DTTFF_COUNT2 processes 2D coordinates. The valid values of x are 1 through 4.
D3DTTFF_PROJECTED	The coordinates are dealt with as a projected texture. You will take a close look at projected textures in a later chapter.

Checking the Device Caps

The device stores texture-addressing capabilities in the `TextureAddressCaps` member of the `D3DCAPS8` structure. Each capability is of the form `D3DPTADDRESSCAPS_`*mode*. The capability flag for `D3DTADDRESS_BORDER` is `D3DPTADDRESSCAPS_BORDER`. You can check the device for compatibility by `AND`ing the caps structure member with the flag:

```
BOOL SupportsClamp = Caps.TextureAddressCaps & D3DPTADDRESSCAPS_CLAMP;
```

Texture Filtering and Mip Maps

In the previous chapter, you saw how you can use mip maps to generate textures at lower levels of detail. You also saw how different values of texture coordinates can cause a texture to stretch or shrink across a given piece of geometry. When the device processes textures to fill different areas, it must apply certain operations to generate larger or smaller textures. This process is called filtering. Filtering is used both to generate mip maps and to resize a given level when it is actually applied to geometry. Table 13.6 describes the filtering modes followed by several states that affect filtering.

> ## Gauss—Isn't He the Magnet Guy?
>
> Carl Friedrich Gauss is responsible for many discoveries and scientific insights. He made contributions to the studies of magnetism, statistics, mathematics, and many others. He never worked in the field of computer graphics (having died in 1855). The texture filtering method carries his name because it is based on his work in how different values affect a final outcome. His theories are useful in many fields. Computer graphics is but one of them.

D3DTSS_MAGFILTER

This filtering mode controls the way that texels are mapped onto a larger area. When a texture must be magnified, the device uses this filtering mode to interpolate more pixels. Figure 13.3 shows how a texture is magnified with a linear filter.

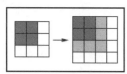

Figure 13.3

Texture magnification.

Table 13.6   **D3DTEXTUREFILTERTYPEs**

Type	Comments
D3DTEXF_NONE	When used as the mip map filter type, this setting disables mip maps entirely.
D3DTEXF_POINT	This method of filtering chooses whichever texel is nearest to the destination pixel. This is the simplest filtering mode, but it can produce jagged effects. You can use this as either a magnification or a minification filter.
D3DTEXF_LINEAR	This method computes a pixel value based on a weighted average of the four nearest texels in a 2x2 area. This method is much smoother than the nearest-point version because of the averaging effect, but this same effect has a downside. If you are encoding specific values into a texture on a per-pixel basis, this method and all the following methods can cause the data to be changed in ways that are not necessarily predictable. In most cases, this doesn't cause a problem, but it is something to be aware of. You can use this as either a magnification or a minification filter.
D3DTEXF_ANISOTROPIC	Anisotropic filtering accounts for the angle between the viewer and the surface. This method of filtering can produce good results, especially when used on surfaces that are at large angles from the view (such as a floor stretching into the distance). However, it can be computationally intensive. You can use this as either a magnification or a minification filter.
D3DTEXF_FLATCUBIC	This method of filtering is similar to D3DTEXF_LINEAR except that it uses more of the surrounding pixels during magnification. When averaging, all pixel values are averaged equally.
D3DTEXF_GAUSSIANCUBIC	This method is the same as the preceding type, only the values in this case are weighted differently.

D3DTSS_MINFILTER

This filtering mode controls the way that texels are mapped to a smaller area. As the area becomes smaller, different mip maps might be used, but a texture might still need to be minified between mip-level transitions. Figure 13.4 shows the effect of minification with a linear filter.

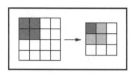

Figure 13.4

Texture minification.

D3DTSS_MIPFILTER

Similar to the preceding filtering mode, this filter determines how textures are minified during mip map generation. Setting this value to D3DTEXF_NONE disables mip map generation.

D3DTSS_MIPMAPLODBIAS

This stage state does not really affect filtering. Instead it controls which mip map is used. Adding a positive bias causes the device to use a higher mip map level than it normally would. Adding a negative bias forces the device to use a lower level. For example, setting a positive bias of +1.0 forces the device to use a higher mip map level, which means that a smaller mip map is used and less data is transferred, possibly increasing performance at the cost of quality. This value is a FLOAT value, but because the SetTextureStageState function takes a DWORD value, this value must be cast to a DWORD.

D3DTSS_MAXMIPLEVEL

This stage state sets the maximum mip map level that can be used. The default value is zero, meaning that the device has access to all mip map levels.

D3DTSS_MAXANISOTROPY

This state identifies the maximum level of anisotropy to use when anisotropic filtering is enabled. You can find the maximum value of this setting by calling GetDeviceCaps. The default value is 1, but you can disable anisotropic filtering by setting this value to 0.

Checking the Device Caps

The device stores texture filtering capabilities in the `TextureFilterCaps` member of the `D3DCAPS8` structure. Each capability is listed for the type of operation (mag, min, or mip) and the filter type. The capability flag for `D3DTEXF_LINEAR` for the magnification filter is `D3DPTFILTERCAPS_MAGFLINEAR`. You can check the device for compatibility by `AND`ing the caps structure member with the flag:

```
BOOL SupportsMipPoint = Caps.TextureFilterCaps &
                        D3DPTFILTERCAPS_MIPPOINT;
```

Texture Stage States and Shaders

Much of the texture blending functionality is now available in pixel shaders. When you get into pixel shaders and begin using them, many of the texture blending states will be ignored by the shader in favor of instructions in the shader itself. However, all of the filtering, bump mapping, and texture coordinate states remain valid because they determine which texels are actually sent to the shaders, or they are not available in the shader instruction set.

When using vertex shaders, the `D3DTSS_TEXCOORDINDEX` state is ignored. Texture coordinates are passed to the shader in the order they were declared.

The Code

Because so many resources are devoted to describing the blending aspect of texture stages, the following sample focuses on the filtering and texture coordinate aspects. If you are interested in exploring the blending aspects of `SetTextureStageState`, look at MFCTex in the SDK samples. That application lets you easily experiment with different modes and see the code used to generate them. When I begin talking about pixel shaders, much of the discussion involves the "new way" of blending. In the meantime, it's more valuable to understand the nuances of filtering and texture coordinates because these states determine how data is passed to the pixel shaders.

Figure 13.5 shows the application in action. The application displays a texture-mapped floor and wall with different addressing modes and filtering modes.

When the application starts, it checks the device capabilities and alerts the user about modes that are not supported by the device. Once the application starts, press the F1 key to cycle through addressing modes. Press F2 to cycle through filtering

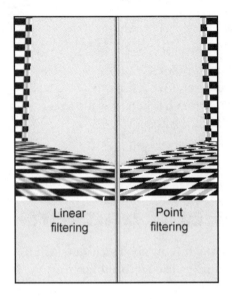

Figure 13.5

Two different filtering modes.

Linear filtering

Point filtering

modes. To simplify the application, I haven't added code to omit the unsupported modes. As you cycle through, the device just ignores each unsupported mode. Experiment with the different modes to get a feel for how they work. Also, you might notice that you are still using a checkerboard, but it is no longer a 2x2 texture. This is because the 2x2 texture leaves little information to actually filter. Also, I added an off-center red line to make it easier to see the difference between wrapped and mirrored textures.

The new class is `CTextureStateApplication`. There are few changes to the header file. The following listing is abbreviated, but the full listing is available on the CD (\Code\Chapter 13):

```
#include "Application.h"

class CTextureStateApplication : public CHostApplication
{
public:
```

This function checks the device capabilities and alerts the user if modes are not available. Once you understand the capabilities of your device, you might want to disable this function:

```
    void VerifyModes();
```

You need to change the background color again:

```
    virtual void PreRender();
```

These two member variables control which modes are in effect. These are incremented as longs, but they are cast to appropriate data types when passed to `SetTextureStageState`:

```
long m_CurrentFilterMode;
long m_CurrentAddressMode;
```

In this case, the texture is loaded from a file. It is still a simple checkerboard pattern, but it is higher resolution so there are more pixels to filter.

```
LPDIRECT3DTEXTURE8 m_pCheckerTexture;
};
```

Now take a look at TextureStateApplication.cpp:

```
#include "TextureStateApplication.h"
```

The vertex format is the same simple single-textured format you used in the last chapter:

```
#define D3DFVF_TEXTUREVERTEX (D3DFVF_XYZ | D3DFVF_TEX1)

struct TEXTURE_VERTEX
{
    float x, y, z;
    float u, v;
};
```

As usual, it's good to initialize everything. In this case, the modes are each set to 1, which should be valid modes on most hardware:

```
CTextureStateApplication::CTextureStateApplication()
{
    m_pVertexBuffer   = NULL;
    m_pCheckerTexture = NULL;

    m_CurrentFilterMode = 1;
    m_CurrentAddressMode = 1;
}
CTextureStateApplication::~CTextureStateApplication()
{
    DestroyGeometry();
}


BOOL CTextureStateApplication::PostInitialize()
```

```
{
        if (FAILED(EasyCreateWindowed(m_hWnd, D3DDEVTYPE_HAL,
                                D3DCREATE_HARDWARE_VERTEXPROCESSING)))
            return FALSE;

        SetupDevice();

        if (!CreateGeometry())
            return FALSE;
```

Here, the checkerboard pattern is loaded from a file. Open the file in an image editor to see what it really looks like. The off-center red line makes the mirrored mode more obvious. Feel free to substitute your own texture to see the effects:

```
        if (FAILED(D3DXCreateTextureFromFile(m_pD3DDevice,
                                        "Checker.bmp",
                                        &m_pCheckerTexture)))
            return FALSE;
```

The VerifyModes function lists the unsupported modes. Because you don't have any user interface yet, it uses message boxes to list each unsupported mode. Frankly, I find this annoying. If you agree, run the application once to see which modes are not supported and then comment out the line:

```
        VerifyModes();
        return TRUE;
}


void CTextureStateApplication::SetupDevice()
{
        D3DXMatrixLookAtLH(&m_ViewMatrix,
                        &D3DXVECTOR3(0.0f, 0.25f, 2.0f),
                            &D3DXVECTOR3(0.0f, 0.0f, 0.0f),
                                &D3DXVECTOR3(0.0f, 1.0f, 0.0f));
        m_pD3DDevice->SetTransform(D3DTS_VIEW, &m_ViewMatrix);

        RECT WindowRect;
        GetClientRect(m_hWnd, &WindowRect);
        D3DXMatrixPerspectiveFovLH(&m_ProjectionMatrix,
                        D3DX_PI / 4,
```

```
                         (float)(WindowRect.right - WindowRect.left) /
                         (float)(WindowRect.bottom - WindowRect.top),
                                 1.0f, 100.0f);
        m_pD3DDevice->SetTransform(D3DTS_PROJECTION,
                                   &m_ProjectionMatrix);


        m_pD3DDevice->SetRenderState(D3DRS_CULLMODE, D3DCULL_NONE);
        m_pD3DDevice->SetRenderState(D3DRS_LIGHTING, FALSE);
}


BOOL CTextureStateApplication::HandleMessage(MSG *pMessage)
{
        if (pMessage->message == WM_KEYDOWN &&
            pMessage->wParam == VK_F1)
        {
```

Here you increment the addressing mode within the valid range and then use it to set both the u and v modes. If you want to experiment with setting only one of the two modes, comment out the other line. Note that the value is cast to the D3DTEXTUREADDRESS enumerated type:

```
                if (++m_CurrentAddressMode > 5)
                        m_CurrentAddressMode = 1;

                m_pD3DDevice->SetTextureStageState(0, D3DTSS_ADDRESSU,
                        (D3DTEXTUREADDRESS)m_CurrentAddressMode);
                m_pD3DDevice->SetTextureStageState(0, D3DTSS_ADDRESSV,
                        (D3DTEXTUREADDRESS)m_CurrentAddressMode);
        }
        if (pMessage->message == WM_KEYDOWN &&
            pMessage->wParam == VK_F2)
        {
                if (++m_CurrentFilterMode > 5)
                        m_CurrentFilterMode = 1;
```

This code sets the filter mode for all three operations. In some cases, certain modes might be valid for one operation but not the others. If you'd like to experiment with different mixtures of modes, add code that changes individual operations with different keystrokes. For the most part, this should give you a good general feel for how the modes work. Many pieces of hardware might not support several of the modes. If that is the case, you can still run the application with the REF device to see the filtering in action:

```
            m_pD3DDevice->SetTextureStageState(0, D3DTSS_MIPFILTER,
                    (D3DTEXTUREFILTERTYPE)m_CurrentFilterMode);
            m_pD3DDevice->SetTextureStageState(0, D3DTSS_MINFILTER,
                    (D3DTEXTUREFILTERTYPE)m_CurrentFilterMode);
            m_pD3DDevice->SetTextureStageState(0, D3DTSS_MAGFILTER,
                    (D3DTEXTUREFILTERTYPE)m_CurrentFilterMode);
    }
    return CHostApplication::HandleMessage(pMessage);
}


BOOL CTextureStateApplication::PreReset()
{
    DestroyGeometry();
    return TRUE;
}

BOOL CTextureStateApplication::PostReset()
{
    SetupDevice();
    return CreateGeometry();
}

BOOL CTextureStateApplication::PreTerminate()
{
    DestroyGeometry();

    m_pD3DDevice->SetTexture(0, NULL);

    if (m_pCheckerTexture)
        m_pCheckerTexture->Release();

    return TRUE;
}


BOOL CTextureStateApplication::CreateGeometry()
```

```
{
    if (FAILED(m_pD3DDevice->CreateVertexBuffer(6 *
                                      sizeof(TEXTURE_VERTEX),
                                      D3DUSAGE_WRITEONLY,
                                      D3DFVF_TEXTUREVERTEX,
                                      D3DPOOL_DEFAULT,
                                      &m_pVertexBuffer)))
        return FALSE;

    TEXTURE_VERTEX *pVertices;

    if (FAILED(m_pVertexBuffer->Lock(0, 6 * sizeof(TEXTURE_VERTEX),
                                      (BYTE **)&pVertices,
                                      0)))
    {
        DestroyGeometry();
        return FALSE;
    }

    pVertices[0].x = -1.0f; pVertices[0].y = 0.0f;
     pVertices[0].z =  1.0f;
    pVertices[1].x =  1.0f; pVertices[1].y = 0.0f;
     pVertices[1].z =  1.0f;
    pVertices[2].x = -1.0f; pVertices[2].y = 0.0f;
     pVertices[2].z = -1.0f;
    pVertices[3].x =  1.0f; pVertices[3].y = 0.0f;
     pVertices[3].z = -1.0f;
    pVertices[4].x = -1.0f; pVertices[4].y = 1.0f;
     pVertices[4].z = -1.0f;
    pVertices[5].x =  1.0f; pVertices[5].y = 1.0f;
     pVertices[5].z = -1.0f;
```

This application creates a set of vertices in the usual manner. Note that unlike the last application, this sample does not use a texture matrix to change the texture coordinates. If the addressing mode is set to wrap or mirror, the texture repeats 20 times; otherwise, it behaves according to the addressing mode:

```
    pVertices[0].u = -10.0f; pVertices[0].v = -10.0f;
    pVertices[1].u =  10.0f; pVertices[1].v = -10.0f;
    pVertices[2].u = -10.0f; pVertices[2].v =  10.0f;
```

```
        pVertices[3].u =  10.0f; pVertices[3].v =  10.0f;
        pVertices[4].u = -10.0f; pVertices[4].v = -10.0f;
        pVertices[5].u =  10.0f; pVertices[5].v = -10.0f;
        m_pVertexBuffer->Unlock();

        m_pD3DDevice->SetStreamSource(0, m_pVertexBuffer,
                                  sizeof(TEXTURE_VERTEX));
        m_pD3DDevice->SetVertexShader(D3DFVF_TEXTUREVERTEX);

        return TRUE;
}


void CTextureStateApplication::DestroyGeometry()
{
        if (m_pVertexBuffer)
        {
                m_pVertexBuffer->Release();
                m_pVertexBuffer = NULL;
        }
}
```

Again you override PreRender so that you can change the clear color:

```
void CTextureStateApplication::PreRender()
{
        m_pD3DDevice->Clear(0, NULL, D3DCLEAR_TARGET |
            D3DCLEAR_ZBUFFER,
                        D3DCOLOR_XRGB(0, 0, 255), 1.0f, 0);

        m_pD3DDevice->BeginScene();
}
```

This is the usual vertex buffer rendering code. Here you render four primitives—
two for the "floor" and two for the "wall":

```
void CTextureStateApplication::Render()
{
        m_pD3DDevice->SetTexture(0, m_pCheckerTexture);
        m_pD3DDevice->DrawPrimitive(D3DPT_TRIANGLESTRIP, 0, 4);
}
void CTextureStateApplication::VerifyModes()
```

```
{
    D3DCAPS8 Caps;
    m_pD3DDevice->GetDeviceCaps(&Caps);
```

First you check the addressing modes. Most of these modes should be supported. If
the border mode is supported, the default border color is black:

```
    if (!(Caps.TextureAddressCaps & D3DPTADDRESSCAPS_BORDER))
        MessageBox(m_hWnd, "The Border Addressing mode
                is not available.", "", MB_OK);

    if (!(Caps.TextureAddressCaps & D3DPTADDRESSCAPS_CLAMP))
        MessageBox(m_hWnd, "The Clamp Addressing mode
                is not available.", "", MB_OK);

    if (!(Caps.TextureAddressCaps & D3DPTADDRESSCAPS_MIRROR))
        MessageBox(m_hWnd, "The Mirror Addressing mode
                is not available.", "", MB_OK);

    if (!(Caps.TextureAddressCaps & D3DPTADDRESSCAPS_MIRRORONCE))
        MessageBox(m_hWnd, "The Mirror Once Addressing mode
                is not available.", "", MB_OK);

    if (!(Caps.TextureAddressCaps & D3DPTADDRESSCAPS_WRAP))
        MessageBox(m_hWnd, "The Wrap Addressing mode
                is not available.", "", MB_OK);
    if (!(Caps.TextureFilterCaps & D3DPTFILTERCAPS_MAGFPOINT))
        MessageBox(m_hWnd, "The Point Filtering mode
                is not available.", "", MB_OK);

    if (!(Caps.TextureFilterCaps & D3DPTFILTERCAPS_MAGFLINEAR))
        MessageBox(m_hWnd, "The Linear Filtering mode
                is not available.", "", MB_OK);

    if (!(Caps.TextureFilterCaps & D3DPTFILTERCAPS_MAGFANISOTROPIC))
        MessageBox(m_hWnd, "The Anisotropic Filtering mode
                is not available.", "", MB_OK);

    if (!(Caps.TextureFilterCaps & D3DPTFILTERCAPS_MAGFAFLATCUBIC))
        MessageBox(m_hWnd, "The Cubic Filtering mode
```

```
                                    is not available.", "", MB_OK);

        if (!(Caps.TextureFilterCaps &
              D3DPTFILTERCAPS_MAGFGAUSSIANCUBIC))
              MessageBox(m_hWnd, "The Gaussian Cubic Filtering mode
                        is not available.", "", MB_OK);
}
```

Depending on the hardware, many of these filtering modes might not be available. Also, you are making the assumption that if they are supported for the magnification operation, they are supported for all operations. This is not necessarily a good assumption, but this function is abbreviated for simplicity. In any case, both point and linear filters should be available. Take a look at how they affect the texel data. The other filters behave similarly to the linear filter in that they average (blur) texel values. The differences lie in how much they blur the values and how much detail is retained.

In Conclusion...

Many readers might be shocked and dismayed that I have omitted blending operations from the sample. There are many reasons for this, not the least of which is the fact that MFCTex is such a good sample. My intentions with this chapter were to explain many of the settings to provide a context for using MFCTex, as well as set up the context for pixel shaders. Shaders represent the new way of blending, and as shader hardware becomes prevalent, the interesting blending operations will probably happen in shaders. The next chapter features a brief look at how blending modes are set, but after that, all blending will be done with shaders.

More importantly, I wanted to cover all the other aspects of the texture states because there seems to be relatively little available on those topics. This chapter should give you a good feel for how the other texture states are used and how textures are mapped. Let's recap the important bits:

- All texture stage states are listed in the device capabilities structure. To be completely sure a given setting is available, check the caps.

- Texture blending between states is based on a blending operation and two (in some cases, three) arguments.

- The texture coordinate index states determine whether the texture coordinates are used as-is or they are computed in hardware.

- The texture addressing modes determine how the device deals with coordinates outside the range 0.0 to 1.0. The most common setting is to wrap or repeat the texture, and some hardware might not support all settings.

- The texture transform settings determine how texture matrices affect texture coordinates. The subject of projected textures is addressed later.

- The texture filtering settings determine how the device filters textures when they are resized during texture mapping. It's possible that certain hardware does not support many of the filtering modes.

- Many texture stage states are ignored when working with vertex or pixel shaders.

- All texture stage states are persistent until they are reset. If you set a blending operation, that operation applies to all objects unless it is explicitly changed. As usual, minimize changes by batching objects (where it makes sense to).

CHAPTER 14

DEPTH TESTING AND ALPHA BLENDING

E ach chapter in this part has highlighted the steps needed to draw content to the screen. I discussed how to set up the vertices, how to transform and light them, and how to apply textures. The final step I need to discuss is what happens to the data right before it actually gets drawn to the frame buffer.

This final step is called rasterization. The transformation operations discussed in the previous chapters determine how and where geometric data is converted to pixels on the screen. The color, lighting, and texture operations determine the color of that pixel. By the end of this chapter, you will have walked through most of the fixed-function pipeline. The following concepts apply to the tests each pixel must pass before it reaches the screen:

- Depth testing and the Z buffer.
- W buffering—an alternative to Z buffering.
- Setting the Z bias.
- Clearing the depth buffer.
- Alpha blending transparent pixels.
- Creating transparent textures.
- Alpha testing for faster transparency.
- Performance considerations for per pixel tests.

Depth Testing

When you draw a 2D scene, it's usually pretty easy to determine what objects are in front of each other. Like a painter, you can draw the background, the various objects in the scene, and perhaps a set of foreground objects. As long as you are fairly careful about the order of drawing, everything works out pretty well. Graphics programmers use this technique in simple cases, referring to it as the *Painters Algorithm.*

3D rendering is usually a different story. For any given pixel, it is difficult to determine what is being shown and which object is in front of the others. As each triangle is rasterized, you must make a decision about whether the new pixel is closer to the viewer and thus should be drawn, or whether the new pixel is actually behind the previously drawn objects and should be ignored.

This problem is solved with a depth buffer and depth testing. The depth buffer is enabled by default, but you can enable or disable it by setting the render state:

```
m_pD3DDevice->SetRenderState(D3DRS_ZENABLE, TRUE);
```

As objects are drawn, the device updates a depth buffer in addition to the color buffer. The value of each pixel in the depth buffer is the distance between the viewer and that pixel. Figure 14.1 shows a rendered scene and an image of that scene's depth buffer.

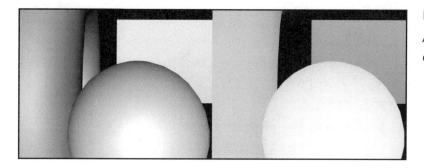

Figure 14.1

A scene and the contents of its depth buffer.

The values in the depth buffer are not stored as literal distances from the viewer. Depth values range from 0.0 to 1.0. Pixels that fall exactly on the near plane have a value of 0.0; pixels that fall exactly on the far plane have a value of 1.0. Note that the accuracy of the depth test is limited by the bit count of the depth buffer. If your near and far planes are too far apart, you might have problems with the accuracy of the depth test. For example, an 8-bit depth buffer, has only 256 different depth values. If your near and far planes are 256,000 units apart, pixels less than 1,000 units apart might not compare correctly because there just isn't enough resolution. Of course, this is a worst-case scenario, but it's important to keep this in mind when setting near and far planes or when rendering objects that are very close to each other.

As each new pixel is drawn onto the screen, the device tests its depth value against the value currently in the depth buffer. If the new pixel passes the test, the depth buffer is updated with the new value, and the color buffer is either replaced or blended with the new pixel color. This test is one of the comparison functions listed in Table 14.1.

In depth testing, the reference value is the current value of the pixel in the depth buffer. You can set the testing function with another render state setting:

```
m_pD3DDevice->SetRenderState(D3DRS_ZFUNC, D3DCMP_ALWAYS);
```

The default comparison function is D3DCMP_LESSEQUAL. Only pixels with a depth value that is less (closer to the viewer) or equal are used to update the color buffer. All others are thrown away because other objects are in front of them. This is the usual behavior, although some multipass techniques might require a different comparison function.

Table 14.1   D3DCMPFUNC Values

Value	Comments
D3DCMP_NEVER	The test never passes.
D3DCMP_LESS	The test passes if the new value is less than the reference value.
D3DCMP_EQUAL	The test passes if the new value is equal to the reference value.
D3DCMP_LESSEQUAL	The test passes if the new value is less than or equal to the reference value.
D3DCMP_GREATER	The test passes if the new value is greater than the reference value.
D3DCMP_NOTEQUAL	The test passes if the new value is not equal to the reference value.
D3DCMP_GREATEREQUAL	The test passes if the new value is greater than or equal to the reference value.
D3DCMP_ALWAYS	The test always passes.

W Buffering

As you may have noticed, all the depth test settings are named "Z enable" or Z function." The most common type of depth buffer is a Z buffer, but it has a drawback. Because of the way the Z buffer is computed, depth values are unevenly distributed. This means that near objects can be rendered correctly, but far objects might have problems testing correctly. Some people solve this by using W buffering.

W buffering, if it is supported by the hardware, uses the W component that you added to the homogeneous coordinates. The W buffer distributes

> **NOTE**
>
> W buffering can be very useful for depth testing, but it can also cause problems when you are doing some forms of cube mapping and other effects. The Z buffer is a more general depth buffering solution despite its limitations.

depth information in a more linear manner, which might help eliminate some visual artifacts, but it is still ultimately limited by the resolution of the depth buffer. Also, W buffering can be incompatible with some forms of environmental mapping. To be consistent, you will not be using W buffering in this book, but keep it in mind if you encounter a situation where Z buffers are insufficient for your specific needs. You enable the W buffer with the following render state:

```
m_pD3DDevice->SetRenderState(D3DRS_ZENABLE, D3DZB_USEW);
```

Z Bias

Sometimes two objects must be rendered at the same depth. This occurs frequently in techniques that require multiple rendering passes, such as planar shadows (discussed in a later chapter). Under normal conditions, these objects might pass or fail the depth test with unpredictable results. If this is the case, you can bias the depth test for different objects with the following render state:

```
m_pD3DDevice->SetRenderState(D3DRS_ZBIAS, 1);
```

The value of the Z bias can be any value between 0 and 16. Higher values render in front of lower values. When drawing two passes, set the bias to 0 for the first pass and render the object. Then, set the bias to 1 and render the second pass. The second pass is guaranteed to pass the depth test. Under normal conditions, it's best to set the bias back to 0.

Clearing the Depth Buffer

In previous calls to Clear, you have set the clear value of the depth buffer to 1.0. Because 1.0 is the farthest value, the depth buffer can be rewritten by any pixel that appears in the view volume. If for some reason that is not the behavior you need, you can set the clear value lower. For instance, if you set the clear value to 0.0, all new pixels fail the depth test and nothing is rendered. Most of the time, you should set this value to 1.0.

Alpha Blending

Assuming the new pixel has passed the test, it can be updated in the actual color buffer. In previous chapters, all polygons and textures were completely opaque, but transparent or semitransparent rendering is possible using the alpha channel. When you use 32-bit colors, the alpha channel consists of the final 8 bits, creating 256 different levels of transparency. An alpha value of 0.0 is completely transparent; a value of 1.0 is completely opaque. Alpha values can be part of the vertex color, or they can be part of a texture. Also, as discussed in the last chapter, they can be derived from alpha operations within the texture stage states and may be a function of the vertex color and several different textures.

Setting the alpha value of a vertex is simple. Just set the alpha channel of that color to whatever value you need. Setting the alpha value in a texture might require a bit more work.

Alpha in 32-Bit File Formats

Certain file formats such as Targa (.tga) files may contain an alpha channel if the image editor saved it properly. If this is the case, the D3DX functions load the texture properly with the alpha channel intact. If your image editor supports it, you can manipulate the colors and the alpha channel and save the texture in a .tga file—and you have a full 32-bit texture.

Alpha in the DirectX Texture Tool

If your image editor does not support these file formats, you can use the texture tool provided with the DirectX SDK. The DirectX texture tool allows you to load a bitmap, load an alpha channel, and save a .dds file that you can easily load with D3DX. To do this, start the texture tool and choose the Open option from the File menu. Open an image file, which will serve as the color portion of your texture. Now choose Open onto Alpha Channel of this Texture from the File menu and open an image file. The grayscale version of this new file serves as the alpha channel for this texture. The texture tool adjusts the colors in the displayed bitmap to give a visual representation of the 32-bit texture. Figure 14.2 shows the texture tool in action.

After the file is created, the D3DX functions can load the new texture with the alpha channel intact.

Alpha from ColorKey

As you may recall, the D3DXCreateTextureFromFileEx function has a ColorKey parameter. If this color is set, D3DX analyzes the image file and replaces every occurrence of that color with a fully transparent alpha value. This is great for producing simple transparency, but it can produce hard edges. Because the alpha values are either fully transparent or fully opaque, there is no way to produce smoother gradations of transparency the way you might be able to with an image editor.

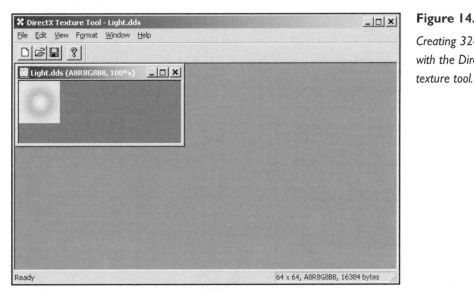

Figure 14.2

Creating 32-bit textures with the DirectX texture tool.

Enabling Alpha Blending

Once you have transparency in your textures or vertices, you still need to enable alpha blending in the device:

```
m_pD3DDevice->SetRenderState(D3DRS_ALPHABLENDENABLE, TRUE);
```

Once alpha blending is enabled, you still need to set the blending modes for both the source and the destination colors. The blending modes determine how the source color (the new pixel) and the destination color (the current pixel) each contribute to the new color. The most common modes follow:

```
m_pD3DDevice->SetRenderState(D3DRS_SRCBLEND, D3DBLEND_SRCALPHA);
m_pD3DDevice->SetRenderState(D3DRS_DESTBLEND, D3DBLEND_INVSRCALPHA);
```

This is the most common setting because it calculates basic transparency. For instance, suppose you were rendering a dirty window using an alpha value of 0.1, which is fairly transparent. These settings give you a final color using the following equation:

$$R = 0.9*D + 0.1*S$$

Most of the contribution still comes from the current color because the new object is so transparent. The documentation describes many other blending modes. These modes can be useful in some multipass rendering operations but for simple transparency, use the settings shown here.

When drawing transparent objects, keep in mind that both alpha blending and depth testing affect the output. Imagine looking through a window. If you render the interior first and then the window, everything will be correct. If you render the window and then the interior, the interior will fail the depth test and never get rendered. You'll be looking through a window at nothing. There are some ways around this, but the best way to avoid it is to pay attention to the order in which you render objects.

Alpha Test

The last test I talk about is the alpha test. The alpha test is somewhat similar to the depth test in that it allows you to set a comparison function that determines whether or not a pixel is drawn. Imagine a texture that's been loaded with a color key. There may be many pixels never rendered because they are fully transparent, yet the hardware must compute the blended color for each of those pixels. However, if the alpha value is zero, there's no need to blend; the new pixel doesn't contribute anything!

That's where the alpha test comes in. If the alpha test is enabled, the hardware compares the alpha value of each pixel to a reference value before it blends the colors. If the pixel fails the alpha test, the pixel is discarded right away and the hardware doesn't spend any time computing the new colors.

There is another benefit as well. If you create 2D sprites or billboards and you do not alpha test, the device updates the depth buffer based on the shape of the polygon. If you enable alpha testing, the depth buffer is only updated when there are visible pixels in the texture. This helps ensure a correct depth buffer. This effect is demonstrated in the sample code.

Enabling alpha testing involves three steps. You must enable testing, set a comparison function (as described in Table 14.1), and set a reference value. The following code sets up an alpha test that discards all pixels with alpha values of 0:

```
m_pD3DDevice->SetRenderState(D3DRS_ALPHATESTENABLE, TRUE);
m_pD3DDevice->SetRenderState(D3DRS_ALPHAREF, 0x00000000);
m_pD3DDevice->SetRenderState(D3DRS_ALPHAFUNC, D3DCMP_GREATER);
```

Any pixel with a pixel value of 0 is immediately discarded. In fact, in simple cases, you don't even have to enable blending at all.

Performance Considerations

Any of these tests takes time. If you are doing something extremely simple and you don't need depth testing, turn it off. If you don't have any transparency, do not enable alpha blending. Also, if you have only a few transparent objects, turn blending on for those objects but off for everything else.

The alpha test, on the other hand, can be your friend. Performing the alpha test is much cheaper than alpha blending, so the more pixels you can discard with the test, the better off you'll be. Of course, if you know that everything will pass the test because you have no transparent objects, make sure you disable the test.

The performance usage of these tests is mostly common sense. Remember that these are simple operations, but they are occurring for each and every pixel, usually several times per pixel in complex scenes. Even when running at 640x480, this can mean a couple million tests per frame. In cases where they help you, turn them on. Turn them off when they don't help you.

The Code

The sample application for this chapter demonstrates the effects of depth testing, alpha testing, and alpha blending on textured geometry. I also revisit last chapter's texture stage states and demonstrate how you can use them to modify alpha values on the fly. One thing to keep in mind about this source code is that it is another "Do as I say, not as I do" chapter. The render states and textures are set many times. In this simple application, it doesn't really matter, but in other applications it's a good idea to minimize these changes as much as possible. The tests are the focus here, not efficient rendering.

The first thing this application does is load two texture files. The first texture is stored as a .dds file with an explicit alpha channel. The second texture is stored as a bitmap, and you will use a color key to set the alpha values. Figure 14.3 shows these two textures and the alpha channel.

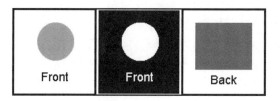

Figure 14.3

A "front" texture, its alpha channel, and a "back" texture.

Figure 14.4 shows the application in action. There are four instances of two rectangles. The rectangle labeled Back is farther from the viewer than the rectangle labeled Front.

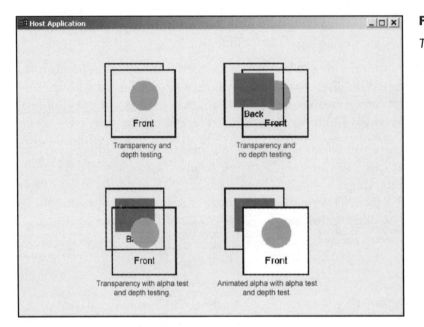

Figure 14.4

The testing application.

The upper-left instance shows the two rectangles with alpha blending enabled, depth testing enabled, and alpha testing disabled. The front rectangle correctly occludes the back rectangle. The upper-right instance shows the same two rectangles, only this time the depth test is disabled. Because the back rectangle is drawn second, it obscures the front rectangle. In most cases, this is not correct, so the depth test is re-enabled for the last two instances.

The lower-left instance shows the effect of the alpha test. Looking back at the upper left, you can see that the front rectangle is transparent; it blends with the background, but it also obscures the back rectangle. This is because the depth buffer still gets set for the front rectangle, even though the transparent regions are fully transparent. Now, in the lower left, the alpha test makes sure the transparent pixels are never drawn, so they do not set the pixels in the depth buffer. When the back rectangle is drawn, it passes the depth test everywhere the front rectangle was fully transparent. In this particular case, the effect is not perfect. Figure 14.5 shows a close-up of the lower-left instance.

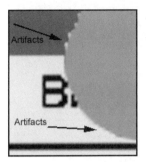

Figure 14.5

Close-up of alpha-tested region.

The alpha test passes every pixel but pixels that are fully transparent. Because of filtering, some pixels were semi-transparent. These pixels passed the alpha test and block the back rectangle, causing visual artifacts. In this case, you could tweak the alpha test reference value and tweak the filter settings to avoid these artifacts.

Take a look at the code. Because the header file is so similar to the previous examples, I'm going to skip the code listing (although it's available on the CD, of course). The only important thing to note is that you now have two texture objects for your front and back textures. Take a look at TestingApplication.cpp, from the \Code\Chapter14 directory on the CD:

```
#include "TestingApplication.h"
```

Like the previous chapters, this application continues to use simple single-textured vertices:

```
#define D3DFVF_TEXTUREVERTEX (D3DFVF_XYZ | D3DFVF_TEX1)

struct TEXTURE_VERTEX
{
      float x, y, z;
      float u, v;
};
```

Initialization and destruction remain mostly unchanged:

```
CTestingApplication::CTestingApplication()
{
      m_pVertexBuffer = NULL;
      m_pFrontTexture = NULL;
      m_pBackTexture  = NULL;
```

```
}

CTestingApplication::~CTestingApplication()
{
        DestroyGeometry();
}
BOOL CTestingApplication::PostInitialize()
{
        if (FAILED(EasyCreateWindowed(m_hWnd, D3DDEVTYPE_HAL,
                            D3DCREATE_HARDWARE_VERTEXPROCESSING)))
                return FALSE;

        SetupDevice();

        if (!CreateGeometry())
                return FALSE;
```

The only real change here is that you load two textures. The front texture is loaded from a .dds file. The more basic D3DX function uses all the default parameters.

```
        if (FAILED(D3DXCreateTextureFromFile(m_pD3DDevice,
                                "..\\media\\Front.dds",
                                &m_pFrontTexture)))
                return FALSE;
```

The back texture is loaded with the extended D3DX function. Each of the parameters used is essentially a default parameter with the exception of the color key parameter. Here, every white pixel is set to full transparency. (0xFFFFFFFF is the hex value for white.)

```
        if (FAILED(D3DXCreateTextureFromFileEx(m_pD3DDevice,
                                "..\\Media\\Back.bmp",
                                0, 0, 0, 0, D3DFMT_A8R8G8B8,
                                D3DPOOL_MANAGED, D3DX_DEFAULT,
                                D3DX_DEFAULT, 0xFFFFFFFF,
                                NULL, NULL,
                                &m_pBackTexture)))
                return FALSE;

        return TRUE;
```

```
}
void CTestingApplication::SetupDevice()
{
        D3DXMatrixIdentity(&m_ViewMatrix);
        m_pD3DDevice->SetTransform(D3DTS_VIEW, &m_ViewMatrix);

        RECT WindowRect;
        GetClientRect(m_hWnd, &WindowRect);
        D3DXMatrixPerspectiveFovLH(&m_ProjectionMatrix,
                   D3DX_PI / 4,
                   (float)(WindowRect.right - WindowRect.left) /
                   (float)(WindowRect.bottom - WindowRect.top),
                   1.0f, 100.0f);
        m_pD3DDevice->SetTransform(D3DTS_PROJECTION,
                                &m_ProjectionMatrix);
```

Here you set all the render states that are not going to change over the life of the device. Alpha blending is enabled, along with the "standard" blending modes. The reference value for the alpha test is set in the middle of the range, and the comparison function allows any alpha value that is greater to pass. I explain this effect more fully later:

```
        m_pD3DDevice->SetRenderState(D3DRS_CULLMODE, D3DCULL_NONE);
        m_pD3DDevice->SetRenderState(D3DRS_LIGHTING, FALSE);

        m_pD3DDevice->SetRenderState(D3DRS_ALPHABLENDENABLE, TRUE);
        m_pD3DDevice->SetRenderState(D3DRS_SRCBLEND,
         D3DBLEND_SRCALPHA);
        m_pD3DDevice->SetRenderState(D3DRS_DESTBLEND,
                                    D3DBLEND_INVSRCALPHA);
        m_pD3DDevice->SetRenderState(D3DRS_ALPHAREF, 0x00000088);
        m_pD3DDevice->SetRenderState(D3DRS_ALPHAFUNC, D3DCMP_GREATER);
}
BOOL CTestingApplication::PreReset()
{
        DestroyGeometry();
        return TRUE;
}


BOOL CTestingApplication::PostReset()
```

```
{
        SetupDevice();
        return CreateGeometry();
}
```

The last several lines are more of the usual. Just make sure that both textures are released:

```
BOOL CTestingApplication::PreTerminate()
{
        DestroyGeometry();

        m_pD3DDevice->SetTexture(0, NULL);

        if (m_pFrontTexture)
                m_pFrontTexture->Release();

        if (m_pBackTexture)
                m_pBackTexture->Release();

        return TRUE;
}
```

Here you create a vertex buffer big enough for two rectangles of four points each. You could be using one rectangle and just resetting the world transform more often, but in this case it's probably more efficient to use a little more memory and save the cost of setting the world matrix more often:

```
BOOL CTestingApplication::CreateGeometry()
{
        if (FAILED(m_pD3DDevice->CreateVertexBuffer(8 *
                                        sizeof(TEXTURE_VERTEX),
                                        D3DUSAGE_WRITEONLY,
                                        D3DFVF_TEXTUREVERTEX,
                                        D3DPOOL_DEFAULT,
                                        &m_pVertexBuffer)))
                return FALSE;

        TEXTURE_VERTEX *pVertices;

        if (FAILED(m_pVertexBuffer->Lock(0, 8 * sizeof(TEXTURE_VERTEX),
```

```
                                (BYTE **)&pVertices,
                                0)))
    {
         DestroyGeometry();
         return FALSE;
    }
    pVertices[0].x = -1.0f; pVertices[0].y =  1.0f;
     pVertices[0].z = 10.0f;
    pVertices[1].x =  1.0f; pVertices[1].y =  1.0f;
     pVertices[1].z = 10.0f;
    pVertices[2].x = -1.0f; pVertices[2].y = -1.0f;
     pVertices[2].z = 10.0f;
    pVertices[3].x =  1.0f; pVertices[3].y = -1.0f;
     pVertices[3].z = 10.0f;
```

The back rectangle is set up to be farther along the z axis, as well as a little up and to the left. The texture coordinates are the same for the two rectangles:

```
    pVertices[4].x = -1.5f; pVertices[4].y =  1.5f;
     pVertices[4].z = 11.0f;
    pVertices[5].x =  0.5f; pVertices[5].y =  1.5f;
     pVertices[5].z = 11.0f;
    pVertices[6].x = -1.5f; pVertices[6].y = -0.5f;
     pVertices[6].z = 11.0f;
    pVertices[7].x =  0.5f; pVertices[7].y = -0.5f;
     pVertices[7].z = 11.0f;


    pVertices[0].u = 0.0f; pVertices[0].v = 0.0f;
    pVertices[1].u = 1.0f; pVertices[1].v = 0.0f;
    pVertices[2].u = 0.0f; pVertices[2].v = 1.0f;
    pVertices[3].u = 1.0f; pVertices[3].v = 1.0f;


    pVertices[4].u = 0.0f; pVertices[4].v = 0.0f;
    pVertices[5].u = 1.0f; pVertices[5].v = 0.0f;
    pVertices[6].u = 0.0f; pVertices[6].v = 1.0f;
    pVertices[7].u = 1.0f; pVertices[7].v = 1.0f;
    m_pVertexBuffer->Unlock();

    m_pD3DDevice->SetStreamSource(0, m_pVertexBuffer,
                                  sizeof(TEXTURE_VERTEX));
```

```
        m_pD3DDevice->SetVertexShader(D3DFVF_TEXTUREVERTEX);

        return TRUE;
}

void CTestingApplication::DestroyGeometry()
{
        if (m_pVertexBuffer)
        {
                m_pVertexBuffer->Release();
                m_pVertexBuffer = NULL;
        }
}
```

Again, you set the clear color in your own PreRender. You might want to experiment with not clearing the Z buffer or clearing it to a different value just to see the effect.

```
void CTestingApplication::PreRender()
{
        m_pD3DDevice->Clear(0, NULL,
                                D3DCLEAR_TARGET |
                                D3DCLEAR_ZBUFFER,
                                D3DCOLOR_XRGB(0, 255, 255), 1.0f, 0);

        m_pD3DDevice->BeginScene();
}
```

The Render function is where all the real magic happens:

```
void CTestingApplication::Render()
{
```

This code renders the upper-left instance shown in Figure 14.4. Depth testing is enabled, but alpha testing is not. If you could see the Z buffer, you'd see the full front rectangle, although much of it is transparent. This is because the full textured rectangle is rendered, which sets the depth buffer. Then, the transparent parts of the texture are blended with the background. Because they are fully transparent, the background shows completely through, but as far as the depth buffer is concerned, those new pixels are there:

```
        m_pD3DDevice->SetRenderState(D3DRS_ZENABLE, TRUE);
        D3DXMatrixTranslation(&m_WorldMatrix, -2.0f, 2.0f, 0.0f);
```

```
m_pD3DDevice->SetTransform(D3DTS_WORLD, &m_WorldMatrix);
m_pD3DDevice->SetTexture(0, m_pFrontTexture);
m_pD3DDevice->DrawPrimitive(D3DPT_TRIANGLESTRIP, 0, 2);
m_pD3DDevice->SetTexture(0, m_pBackTexture);
m_pD3DDevice->DrawPrimitive(D3DPT_TRIANGLESTRIP, 4, 2);
```

Here you turn off depth testing. This is the upper-right instance shown in Figure 14.4. The back rectangle obscures the front rectangle because it is the last one drawn. With no depth test, it's a "last pixel wins" operation. In this simple case, you could just render the rectangles in the opposite order to get the "correct" effect, but with more complex geometry, it's not quite that easy:

```
m_pD3DDevice->SetRenderState(D3DRS_ZENABLE, FALSE);
D3DXMatrixTranslation(&m_WorldMatrix, 2.0f, 2.0f, 0.0f);
m_pD3DDevice->SetTransform(D3DTS_WORLD, &m_WorldMatrix);
m_pD3DDevice->SetTexture(0, m_pFrontTexture);
m_pD3DDevice->DrawPrimitive(D3DPT_TRIANGLESTRIP, 0, 2);
m_pD3DDevice->SetTexture(0, m_pBackTexture);
m_pD3DDevice->DrawPrimitive(D3DPT_TRIANGLESTRIP, 4, 2);
```

In this third instance (the lower left on Figure 14.4), you see the combined effect of the depth test and the alpha test. Alpha testing is enabled, and all the transparent areas of the front rectangle are never drawn. If you rendered the front rectangle and looked at the depth buffer, you'd see something similar to the color buffer. Only the opaque areas would be in the depth buffer. When the back rectangle is drawn, it fails the depth test in all the areas where the front rectangle was opaque and passes in the other areas. The overall effect is correct with the exception of the visual artifacts described earlier. This also gives you slightly better performance because the device doesn't compute the blending for the transparent front pixels.

This approach has yielded the correct effect here, but it is not a general solution for transparent objects. Many times, the front object has varying levels of transparency and the alpha test is really a binary operation. In most cases, you still might need to ensure that the front objects are rendered before the behind objects to get the desired effect of looking through the transparent object:

```
m_pD3DDevice->SetRenderState(D3DRS_ALPHATESTENABLE, TRUE);
m_pD3DDevice->SetRenderState(D3DRS_ZENABLE, TRUE);
D3DXMatrixTranslation(&m_WorldMatrix, -2.0f, -2.0f, 0.0f);
m_pD3DDevice->SetTransform(D3DTS_WORLD, &m_WorldMatrix);
m_pD3DDevice->SetTexture(0, m_pFrontTexture);
m_pD3DDevice->DrawPrimitive(D3DPT_TRIANGLESTRIP, 0, 2);
```

```
m_pD3DDevice->SetTexture(0, m_pBackTexture);
m_pD3DDevice->DrawPrimitive(D3DPT_TRIANGLESTRIP, 4, 2);
```

This last instance is really just a demonstration of how the texture blending states work and how they affect alpha blending and alpha testing. Here you create a color using the cosine of the tick count method to produce a value in the right range. You then use that new color to set the texture factor for the device. The texture factor is a variable you can change without altering values in the texture or in the vertex buffer. Setting this value is more efficient than locking a texture or a vertex buffer and changing the underlying data.

Once the texture factor is set, you change the alpha operation for the first texture stage to add, and you set the arguments to the texture factor and the texture itself. The overall effect is pretty straightforward. For the most part, texels in your two textures are either mostly opaque (255) or fully transparent (0). The nifty cosine function changes the texture factor, which gets added to the alpha values. The fully opaque values are clamped to 255 and remain fully opaque. The transparent values are incremented, becoming less transparent. As a result, the front rectangle fades in and out.

The only loose end is the alpha test. Half of the time, the back rectangle shows through because you set the reference value to the middle of the range. Half of the time, it does not. There is no middle ground. As an exercise, swap the order in which the two rectangles are rendered and disable the alpha test. The result should be that the two rectangles are nicely blended together as the front rectangle becomes more or less transparent:

```
BYTE CurrentColor = (BYTE)(127.0f *
            (cos((float)GetTickCount() / 1000.0f) + 1.0));

m_pD3DDevice->SetRenderState(D3DRS_TEXTUREFACTOR,
                D3DCOLOR_ARGB(CurrentColor, CurrentColor,
                              CurrentColor, CurrentColor));

m_pD3DDevice->SetTextureStageState(0, D3DTSS_ALPHAOP,
                                    D3DTOP_ADD);
m_pD3DDevice->SetTextureStageState(0, D3DTSS_ALPHAARG1,
                                    D3DTA_TEXTURE);
m_pD3DDevice->SetTextureStageState(0, D3DTSS_ALPHAARG2,
                                    D3DTA_TFACTOR);
D3DXMatrixTranslation(&m_WorldMatrix, 2.0f, -2.0f, 0.0f);
m_pD3DDevice->SetTransform(D3DTS_WORLD, &m_WorldMatrix);
```

```
m_pD3DDevice->SetTexture(0, m_pFrontTexture);
m_pD3DDevice->DrawPrimitive(D3DPT_TRIANGLESTRIP, 0, 2);
```

Before you draw the back rectangle, set the texture factor back to 0. Because the alpha operation is additive, this essentially disables the alpha operation, which is what you want when the first two instances on the next frame are rendered:

```
m_pD3DDevice->SetRenderState(D3DRS_TEXTUREFACTOR,
                             D3DCOLOR_ARGB(0, 0, 0, 0));
m_pD3DDevice->SetTexture(0, m_pBackTexture);
m_pD3DDevice->DrawPrimitive(D3DPT_TRIANGLESTRIP, 4, 2);
```

The last thing you did was turn off the alpha test, ensuring that the test is disabled for the first instances of the next frame. Remember that all of these settings remain active until they are explicitly changed. Sometimes your rendering will not look right and you will dig through your code trying to find out what's wrong. It could be that your first frame rendered correctly but set up things badly for every frame thereafter. It's good to think about how one frame affects another.

```
m_pD3DDevice->SetRenderState(D3DRS_ALPHATESTENABLE, FALSE);
}
```

In Conclusion...

This is the last chapter to look at the basics. You've walked down the pipeline and seen how to create vertices, how to transform and light them, texture them, turn them into pixels, and finally test those pixels to determine who stays and who goes. I'm sure there's a metaphor there, but I leave you to draw your own conclusions (or would it be render your own opinions?).

Anyway, the next part begins to delve into the wonderful and mysterious world of shaders. Before you go there, continue the proud tradition of reviewing what you have looked at:

- The depth test is enabled by default and makes sure that overlapping objects are rendered properly.
- The contents of the depth buffer are a function of the near and far plane of the projection matrix and the bit depth of the buffer itself. It is possible for the depth buffer to behave improperly if there is not enough resolution available.
- The W buffer provides an alternative depth-buffering technique that has a more linear distribution of depth values. This can be advantageous in some cases and detrimental in others.

- You can use the Z bias factor to cheat in cases where the depth buffer may otherwise produce bad results.
- When clearing the depth buffer, remember that depth buffer values range from 0.0 to 1.0 rather than a real distance value.
- Alpha blending allows you to render objects with varying degrees of transparency. This is often very fast on better graphics cards.
- The DirectX texture tool is good for creating textures with transparency information.
- The D3DX extended texture creation functions allow you to set a color key value for simple transparency.
- Alpha blending is computationally expensive enough that you should probably disable it if you know you aren't using it.
- The alpha test is a way to discard pixels that would never get seen. For more complex scenes, this can be good for performance because alpha blending is a per-pixel operation that can occur several million times per frame. The alpha test allows you to discard pixels early, saving computation time.
- Filtered textures can produce artifacts when using the alpha test, although there are ways to work around that. Either tweak the reference value or the filtering mode. In the worst case, disable the alpha test.

Part Four

Shaders

The purpose of Part 3 was to ensure that you understood the basics of 3D rendering. If you skipped it, it might be worthwhile to go back and skim. I include material that doesn't usually appear in these types of books and that might be useful for the techniques later.

The purpose of this part is to describe shaders. This part has only two chapters, but I want to make sure that you get the fundamentals down before moving on to the cool stuff. You're still laying down groundwork, but this should be newer material for a lot of people. Here's a rundown of what I discuss:

- Chapter 15, "Vertex Shaders," describes what a vertex shader is and how you use them. I don't spend a ton of time talking about applications; that's what the later chapters are for. If you've already worked with shaders, this material will mostly be review, but I recommend reading it anyway.

- Chapter 16, "Pixel Shaders," talks about how to set up pixel shaders and provides some basic examples. Pixel shaders are a little less understood than vertex shaders, but they are just as powerful, if not more powerful. This chapter lays the groundwork for the later chapters when you'll do some really interesting stuff.

CHAPTER 15

VERTEX SHADERS

Before I talk about anything, take a look back at Figure 5.1. The diagram of the pipeline shows vertex data funneling into either the fixed function transform and lighting part of the pipeline or into the mysterious vertex shader portion of the pipeline. The last several chapters have taught you a lot about transformation and lighting. It works really well. Why am I switching gears and talking about the box on the right when the box on the left has been so good to us?

SIGGRAPH '99 had a panel discussion about the future of graphics hardware. The panelists talked about where things were heading and took questions from the crowd about desired features. One of the more interesting and recurring requests was to give the programmer more control over what was actually going on inside the card. This was coupled with a recognition that some trends seemed to be moving away from the traditional lighting and rendering approaches and into more nonphotorealistic and stylistic approaches, such as cartoon rendering and other forms of lighting. The consensus seemed to be that the hardware was general enough to handle these forms of rendering if only the programmers could open the card and have a lower level of access to the hardware.

In early 2001, nVidia released the geForce3, which was the first card to offer that level of access when used with DirectX 8.0 or the appropriate OpenGL extensions. In DirectX lingo, that access was offered through vertex shaders. Microsoft and several other vendors worked closely to ensure that the drivers for other cards offered good CPU emulation if the hardware did not support shaders natively. (Although the fallback CPU emulation is very good, the explanations throughout this chapter are written with hardware shaders in mind. In most cases, the concepts apply equally well to both.) Finally, programmers had more control over how vertices were actually processed. You can use that control to implement all kinds of special effects and new rendering techniques. The rest of the book illustrates cool techniques. This chapter will concentrate on the basics.

- Why would you use a vertex shader?
- Inputs and outputs of vertex shaders.
- Vertex shader instructions.
- Device/shader interactions.
- Assembling and creating a shader.
- Using your shader.
- Destroying the shader.
- Simple transformations in a vertex shader.
- Writing your first vertex shader application.

What Is a Vertex Shader?

In the days before hardware transform and lighting, basic vertex manipulation happened on the CPU, and the resulting data was passed to the graphics card for rasterization and the rest of the pipeline. When graphics cards moved to hardware T&L, the task of vertex processing was handed to the graphics card, freeing up the CPU for other tasks. Within the fixed function portion of the pipeline, vertices are processed using programs resident in the graphics hardware. Vertices are transformed with matrices, and the hardware uses the standard lighting equations to solve the lighting equations for each vertex. Vertex shaders are alternatives to those resident programs. They offer the programmer a way to directly control how the hardware processes a set of vertices. If programmers choose to use vertex shaders, they have total control over how the vertices are transformed, lit, and otherwise manipulated.

The word "shader" can be a little confusing. Another way to think about vertex shaders is to think of them as "vertex manipulators." In OpenGL, they are called vertex programs. Shaders are short programs that take vertices and constants as inputs, do some processing, and output the resulting vertices. One thing to keep in mind is that they process each vertex independently. A vertex shader has no notion of triangles or other primitives.

Remember that the newest generations of GPUs have more transistors than most CPUs. Vertex shaders allow programmers like you and me to use all that silicon for our own diabolical purposes. I mentioned earlier that in most of my programs, I almost never lock the vertex buffers after they are initially filled. This is partly because the transformation matrices are so powerful, but also because vertex shaders can handle almost everything else when it comes to manipulating the vertices. Affecting vertex data on the card helps performance in two ways. It saves the cost of transferring new data from the CPU to the graphics card, and it also utilizes the best processor for the task. The graphics chip is extremely tuned for doing vector math. As you will see later, it can do some pretty complex calculations in one processor cycle. In most cases, this means that the graphics card is much faster at doing vertex calculations even though its clock speed might be slower than the CPU.

Figure 15.1 shows a conceptual drawing of a vertex shader. I briefly explain the components here and fill in the blanks as you move on.

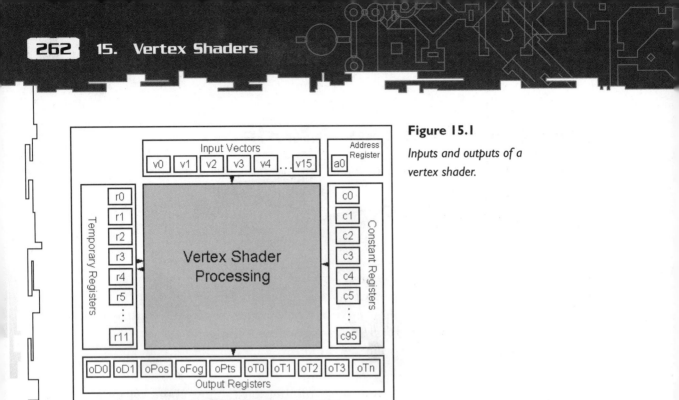

Figure 15.1

Inputs and outputs of a vertex shader.

Processing in a Shader

Shaders are more flexible due to the fact that all of the data feeds into the programmable ALU (Arithmetic Logic Unit) instead of traveling down the fixed function pipeline. The ALU is capable of doing very fast and efficient vector arithmetic. The ALU is almost always better than the CPU for vector operations.

Vertex Data Registers

The vertex shader is run once per vertex, and its principle input is a vertex. I discuss vertex formats when you get to the point of actually creating a shader, but one thing to remember is that vertex data is loosely typed. Because you have complete control over the way vertex data is processed, you can arrange vertex data however you want. For instance, when you sent vertices down the fixed function pipeline to be lit, you had to put the vertex normal and the vertex color in the right parts of the vertex. If you didn't, the hardware would process the wrong data in the wrong way and you'd get garbage. With vertex shaders, you can send vertex data in whatever format you want, as long as you know how to handle that format within the shader. Doing this just for fun is not a good idea because it makes your code very confusing, but some of the techniques use this feature to store data in otherwise unused portions of the vertices. Each vertex can input up to 16 vectors of 4 float values each.

Constant Registers

Vertex shaders have access to a set of constants that are persistent for read access across instances of the shaders. The most common usage of the constants is to set transformation matrices or other data that affects many vertices. Remember that vertex shaders are executed for every vertex. If an operation is repeated for every vertex, it is usually worthwhile to do that operation once and pass the result as a constant. For instance, don't pass several matrices and concatenate them in a shader; concatenate them once and pass the result. The maximum number of available constants is exposed in the `MaxVertexShaderConst` member of the `D3DCAPS8` structure.

The Address Register

The address register is a special entity that allows you to index into the constants. For instance, you can set several constants and then store an index in an unused portion of the vertex data. As each vertex is processed, you set the address register to the index value and the proper constant is used. The address register can be a very powerful tool, but it is perhaps the most confusing part of shaders. I hold off on a complete explanation until you work on a technique that demonstrates the address register in action.

The Temporary Registers

Shaders have a series of registers that you can use to hold data during complex calculations. For instance, a series of instructions might compute the dot product, then multiply the result by a vector, and add that to another vector. Throughout that operation, these temporary registers can hold values. These registers do not remain persistent across vertex shader instances.

Vertex Output

The output of the vertex shader is a processed vertex. Unlike the input vertex data, the output is strongly typed. For instance, the position data must be in transformed homogeneous screen coordinates, or you don't see anything on the screen. The only exception to this general rule is when you use the vertex shaders with pixel shaders. In this case, a vertex shader might set an output color that has nothing to do with the final rendered color but is instead an input to a pixel shader that will use that data for further processing. In cases where you are not using pixel shaders, the output of the vertex shader is in a format that is usable by the other stages of the pipeline. Table 15.1 lists the five different types of output.

Table 15.1   Vertex Shader Output Registers

Output Variable	Comments
oPos	The output position in transformed screen coordinates.
oD*n*	Two color outputs (oD1 and oD2). Each is a 4D vector.
oT*n*	Four texture coordinate outputs (oT0 through oT3). Each is a 4D vector.
oFog	The output fog value. It is treated as one FLOAT value.
oPts	The output point size value. It is treated as one FLOAT value.

Now that you've seen the ins and outs of vertex shaders, take a look at some of what goes into writing a shader. Many of the instructions and concepts won't make complete sense until later when you actually use them, but I lay the groundwork here.

The Shader Code

Shaders are short programs written in a language very much like assembly language. These programs are compiled on the CPU and passed to the graphics card for actual use. The shader programs must not exceed 128 instructions, which seems limited but is adequate in most cases. These instructions are listed in Table 15.2. Each instruction takes one cycle to complete—which is true even for more complex operations, such as dot product or distance calculations.

The fact that each of these instructions executes in one cycle means that the speed of the shader is directly proportional to the number of instructions used. Whenever possible, look for opportunities to reduce instruction count. Instructions such as mad can be especially useful.

There are also instruction macros defined for vertex shaders. These macros perform common tasks as sets of basic instructions. The matrix multiplication macros can be useful for common tasks. Also, they are often optimized in software if the shader falls back to software processing. The other macros might not be as useful because they concentrate on higher precision, which you do not usually need. The downside of these macros is that they could obscure the real number of instructions in the shader. For example, the m4x4 macro uses four instructions. If you decide to take advantage of the macros, remember to pay careful attention to the instruction count and remember that macros usually use more than one instruction. Table 15.3 lists the macros.

Table 15.2 Vertex Shader Instructions

Instruction	Format	Comments
mov	mov Result, Input0	Simply moves a value from one register to another. This is useful when simply passing values such as texture coordinates through the shader and when swizzling components. (Swizzling is discussed later.)
max	max Result, Input0, Input1	Finds the maximum value of each component and passes each maximum value to the result vector.
min	min Result, Input0, Input1	Finds the minimum values of each component and passes those values to the result vector.
sge	sge Result, Input0, Input1	"Set on greater than or equal." This instruction sets the component values of the result vector to 1.0 if each component of Input0 is greater than or equal to that component of Input1. Otherwise, it sets that component to 0.0.
slt	slt Result, Input0, Input1	"Set if less than." This instruction is similar to sge, except that it checks to see whether the components of Input0 are less than those of Input1.
add	add Result, Input0, Input1	Computes the sum of two vectors for each component of the two input vectors.
sub	sub Result, Input0, Input1	Computes the difference between two vectors (Input0 − Input1) on a per-component basis. The instruction sub r0, r1, r2 is the same as using add r0, r1, -r2. Negating the register is a free operation, hence the two forms are equivalent computationally, but there might be optimization opportunities there.
mul	mul Result, Input0, Input1	Computes the product of two vectors. You may remember that vectors cannot be directly multiplied. This is a component-wise multiply. For example, Result.x = Input0.x * Input1.x.

Table 15.2 (continued)

Instruction	Format	Comments
rcp	rcp Result, Input0	Computes the reciprocal of each component of a vector. You can use this for division by computing the reciprocal and then passing the result to the mul instruction.
mad	mad Result, Input0, Input1, Input2	This instruction can be very useful because it performs two operations in a single cycle. It multiplies the first two inputs and then adds the last input.
dp3	dp3 Result, Input0, Input1	Computes the dot product of two vectors using only the first three components.
dp4	dp4 Result, Input0, Input1	Computes the dot product of two vectors using all four components.
rsq	rsq Result, Input0	Computes the reciprocal square root of a scalar value. The x component of the input vector is used unless it is swizzled. The result is written to all components of the output vector.
dst	dst Result, Input0, Input1	Computes a distance value from the two inputs. Input0 is expected in the form of (NA, d*d, d*d, NA), and Input1 is expected in the form of (NA, 1/d, NA, 1/d). This instruction can be confusing, so you will look at it later when you have a real use for it.
lit	lit Result, Input0	Computes the diffuse and specular lighting factors. The dot products of the lighting vectors must be stored in the input vector. You'll take a closer look at this when you implement your own lighting in the shader.
expp	expp Result, Input0	Computes 2 to the power of Input0.w with partial precision. The result is stored in Result.x, and the other components store data useful in computing a more accurate result.
logp	logp Result, Input0	Similar to expp, this instruction computes the log base 2 of Input0.w and provides additional data in the other components.

Table 15.3   Vertex Shader Macros

Macro	Format	Comments
m3x2	m3x2 Result, Vector0, Matrix0	Multiplies the input vector by a 3x2 matrix.
m3x3	m3x3 Result, Vector0, Matrix0	Multiplies the input vector by a 3x3 matrix.
m3x4	m3x4 Result, Vector0, Matrix0	Multiplies the input vector by a 3x4 matrix.
m4x3	m4x3 Result, Vector0, Matrix0	Multiplies the input vector by a 4x3 matrix.
m4x4	m4x4 Result, Vector0, Matrix0	Multiplies the input vector by a 4x4 matrix.
exp	exp Result, Input	The full precision equivalent to expp.
log	log Result, Input	The full precision equivalent to logp.
frc	frc Result, Input	Computes the fractional portion of the x and y components.

Swizzling and Write Masks

As I mentioned earlier, some free operations can be written into vertex shaders. One of the free operations is negation. Inputs to instructions can be negated with the minus sign. The other free operation is swizzling. Swizzling lets you reorder the individual components of the input vectors and duplicate components. For example, constants are stored as a vector of four values. Let's say you are writing a shader that multiplies values by powers of ten (1, 10, 100, and 1,000). You can store all four values in a single constant vector and then use them individually with swizzling. The following shader code assumes that the constant c1 is set to (1, 10, 100, 1000):

```
mul r1, r0, c1.y     ; All components of r0 are multiplied by 10.
mul r1, r0, c1.xxzz  ; The first two components are multiplied by one
                     ; and the last two are multiplied by 100.
mul r1, r0, c1.zzxx  ; The first two components are multiplied by 100
                     ; and the last two are multiplied by one.
mul r1, r0, -c1.w    ; All components are multiplied by -1000.
```

Careful use of swizzling can sometimes save many instructions. Swizzling also lets you use constants more effectively. If you have data that is not vector based, save multiple values in a single vector. This applies equally to constants and vertex data.

For example, you can save several array indices in a single vertex vector and use swizzling to extract each value separately inside of the shader.

The other useful tool is write masking. The format here is similar to swizzling. If you only want the shader to write to specific components, specify those components as follows:

```
mul r1.x, r0, c1.y    ; Only the x component is written to.
mul r1.xw, r0, c1.xxzz ; Only x and w are written to.
```

You are rapidly reaching the point where shader concepts are best explained in context. Next, you'll look at how shaders are actually implemented. You'll continue looking at some of the basics once you begin writing some simple shaders.

Shader Implementation

Before creating the shader, you need to know whether your hardware can handle it. To create a shader, you need a declaration and the code for the shader itself. Like a function declaration, the shader declaration defines the format of the inputs to the shader. Once you have a declaration, you need to compile the shader. Finally, you ask the device to actually create the shader. This produces a shader handle, which can be passed to the SetVertexShader function. Let's walk through each step in detail.

Shaders and the Device

The first thing you should check is what shader version the hardware supports. This book is written with the assumption that your hardware supports at least version 1.1. You can check this with a call to your good friend GetDeviceCaps. Then check the VertexShaderVersion member of the D3DCAPS8 structure:

```
m_pD3D->GetDeviceCaps(D3DADAPTER_DEFAULT,
                      D3DDEVTYPE_HAL, &Caps);
if (Caps.VertexShaderVersion == D3DVS_VERSION(1,1))
```

If you specify a HAL device, it gives you the capabilities of the hardware. If the hardware doesn't support vertex shaders, you can create the device with software vertex processing.

Creating the Declaration

The declaration serves much of the same purpose as the FVF in earlier samples. It lets the shader know what it's dealing with and where it's coming from. Physically, the declaration is an array of DWORDs created with a series of macros. There are nine macros in all, but I am going to concentrate most heavily on three of them.

The first macro defines the stream that will supply the data. In all the previous examples involving the fixed function pipeline, you used stream 0. However, vertex shaders can receive data from multiple streams. This creates opportunities to store different data in different streams and mix and match as the situations change. Setting different stream sources is not as costly as changing the contents of the buffers themselves. This macro takes the following form:

```
D3DVSD_STREAM(StreamNumber)
```

You can find the maximum number of streams in the D3DCAPS8 structure.

The second macro of interest defines the input registers for each element of the vertex. These registers are analogous to the FVF macros defined several chapters ago. This macro takes the following form:

```
D3DVSD_REG(Register, Type)
```

Within the vertex shader code, the registers are defined as v0 through v15. Table 15.4 defines the possible register parameters and their vertex shader reference.

You must give each vertex register a valid type. Table 15.5 shows the valid types.

The final macro defines the end of the declaration. It simply takes the following form:

```
D3DVSD_END()
```

Now that you've defined the macros, let's make more sense of this by looking at a few actual declarations:

```
DWORD Chapter9Declaration[] =
{
        D3DVSD_STREAM(0),
        D3DVSD_REG(D3DVSDE_POSITION, D3DVSDT_FLOAT3),
        D3DVSD_REG(D3DVSDE_DIFFUSE, D3DVSDT_D3DCOLOR),
        D3DVSD_END()
};
```

Table 15.4 Vertex Registers

Parameter	Register Name
D3DVSDE_POSITION	v0
D3DVSDE_BLENDWEIGHT	v1
D3DVSDE_BLENDINDICES	v2
D3DVSDE_NORMAL	v3
D3DVSDE_PSIZE	v4
D3DVSDE_DIFFUSE	v5
D3DVSDE_SPECULAR	v6
D3DVSDE_TEXCOORD0	v7
D3DVSDE_TEXCOORD1	v8
D3DVSDE_TEXCOORD2	v9
D3DVSDE_TEXCOORD3	v10
D3DVSDE_TEXCOORD4	v11
D3DVSDE_TEXCOORD5	v12
D3DVSDE_TEXCOORD6	v13
D3DVSDE_TEXCOORD7	v14

Table 15.5 Register Types

Type	Comments
D3DVSDT_FLOAT4	This is the default format for the vector types.
D3DVSDT_FLOAT3	This is still a 4D vector, but the last component is set to 1.0.
D3DVSDT_FLOAT2	A 4D vector, but the last components are set to 0.0 and 1.0.
D3DVSDT_FLOAT1	Here the vector takes the form of (value, 0.0, 0.0, 1.0).
D3DVSDT_D3DCOLOR	This is the four-byte D3D color format.
D3DVSDT_UBYTE4	This data format is four bytes.

If you had been working with vertex shaders back in Chapter 9, the previous declaration would have been the declaration that matched your simple colored vertices. The following would have been the declaration used in Chapter 12:

```
DWORD Chapter12Declaration[] =
{
      D3DVSD_STREAM(0),
      D3DVSD_REG(D3DVSDE_POSITION, D3DVSDT_FLOAT3),
      D3DVSD_REG(D3DVSDE_TEXCOORD0, D3DVSDT_FLOAT2),
      D3DVSD_END()
};
```

Finally, here is a declaration that uses multiple streams:

```
DWORD MultiStreamDeclaration[] =
{
      D3DVSD_STREAM(0),
      D3DVSD_REG(D3DVSDE_POSITION, D3DVSDT_FLOAT3),
      D3DVSD_REG(D3DVSDE_DIFFUSE, D3DVSDT_D3DCOLOR),
      D3DVSD_STREAM(1),
      D3DVSD_REG(D3DVSDE_TEXCOORD0, D3DVSDT_FLOAT2),
      D3DVSD_END()
};
```

You would use this declaration to draw position and color data from one stream and texture coordinates from the other. Of course, you would need to set both stream sources to valid buffers. Both streams would feed the shader, as shown in Figure15.2.

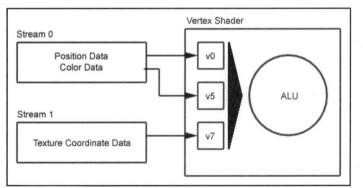

Figure 15.2

Multiple streams into a single shader.

Assembling the Shader

Once the declaration is created, it's time to actually assemble the shader. This is a matter of reading the assembly code from a file or buffer and compiling that into a usable binary form. The easiest way to do this is to use the D3DX library. The two useful functions are D3DXAssembleShader and D3DXAssembleShaderFromFile:

```
HRESULT D3DXAssembleShader(LPCVOID pShaderCode, UINT ShaderCodeLength,
                        DWORD Flags, LPD3DXBUFFER *ppConstants,
                        LPD3DXBUFFER *ppCompiledShader,
                        LPD3DXBUFFER *ppErrors);

HRESULT D3DXAssembleShaderFromFile(LPCSTR pShaderFileName,
                        DWORD Flags,
                        LPD3DXBUFFER *ppConstants,
                        LPD3DXBUFFER *ppCompiledShader,
                        LPD3DXBUFFER *ppErrors);
```

As you can see, the two functions are very similar. The only difference is that one function gets the shader code as input and the other reads the shader code from a file. For the sake of explanation, I describe D3DXAssembleShader. The parameters are listed in Table 15.6.

Table 15.6   D3DXAssembleShader Parameters

Parameter	Comments
pShaderCode	This is a pointer to the source code for the shader. The shader code is a set of the instructions described earlier.
ShaderCodeLength	This is the byte length of the source code buffer.
Flags	This function usually validates the shader code against the capabilities of the device. Flags can disable this validation or include debugging information in the compiled shader, but in most cases, this parameter should be 0.
ppConstants	This is a pointer to a buffer that contains constant data. In most cases, you'll be using a more dynamic way to set constant data, as described later in this chapter. You'll be setting this parameter to NULL.
ppCompiledShader	This is a pointer filled with the compiled shader if this function is successful. This is the pointer that gets passed to the next step in shader creation.
ppErrors	This is a buffer filled with text error messages (if any).

Creating the Shader

If D3DXAssembleShader is successful, the ppCompiledShader parameter contains the compiled shader code. The final step is to pass the compiled shader to the device and create a handle that can be passed to SetVertexShader. You do this with a call to CreateVertexShader:

```
HRESULT IDirect3DDevice8::CreateVertexShader(
                        CONST DWORD *pDeclaration,
                        CONST DWORD *pCompiledShader,
                        DWORD *pShaderHandle, DWORD Usage);
```

This function takes a pointer to the shader declaration and a pointer to the compiled shader data, and creates a shader handle. You can use the Usage parameter to create a shader processed in software.

Using the Shader

Now that you have a shader handle, you can use that handle to set the vertex shader when needed. To do this, call SetVertexShader, but use the shader handle instead of an FVF. Just as the FVF told the hardware how to process vertices in the fixed function pipeline, the shader handle tells the hardware how to process vertices in a shader.

In most cases, you also need to set shader constants. You should set constants before the actual rendering calls they are meant to affect. The values remain in effect until explicitly changed because the shader cannot change them. You set vertex shader constants by calling the appropriately named SetVertexShaderConstant:

```
HRESULT IDirect3DDevice8::SetVertexShaderConstant(DWORD Register,
                                CONST void *pConstantData,
                                DWORD ConstantCount);
```

The Register parameter specifies which constant to set, and the buffer contains the actual data. Remember that constants are each vectors of four FLOAT values. The final ConstantCount parameter specifies the number of vectors. If the constant count is greater than 1, subsequent constants are set to the subsequent vectors. For instance, you could use the following call to set constants c0, c1, c2, and c3:

```
m_pD3DDevice->SetVertexShaderContstant(0, &SomeData, 4);
```

If you're not careful, some calls to SetVertexShaderConstant can overwrite constants set in previous calls. Keep a close eye on when constants are set and whether any calls overlap.

Setting Constants

If you are familiar with vertex shaders already, you may have noticed that I omitted the fact that you can set constants in the vertex shader declaration and in the vertex shader code itself. Personally, I like limiting the mechanisms I use to affect my code unless there is some performance advantage. Placing constant definitions in three different places might be confusing, especially if someone else is trying to follow along. In most cases, some constants need to change fairly frequently, but there is only the slightest overhead associated with setting the more static constants with SetVertexShaderConstant. This book does not use the declarations or code to set constants, but the option is available to you if you choose to do it that way.

After the shader is set and the constants are set, rendering primitives is exactly the same as in previous chapters. Soon, I talk about the basic functionality you need to add to most shaders to make them work, but first let's see how to get rid of a shader when it is no longer useful.

Destroying the Shader

When you are done with a shader (typically at the end of a program), all that you need to do is delete it:

```
HRESULT IDirect3DDevice8::DeleteVertexShader(DWORD ShaderHandle);
```

This call deletes the shader, frees the resources that the shader was using, and allows you to move on with your life.

Using Shaders with Computed Geometry

In some of the samples, you created vertex buffers of computed geometry and filled them with vertices with a set vertex format (FVF). You can use these vertices with a vertex shader if the format described by the FVF matches the format described by the shader declaration. Just set the vertex shader and render the vertex buffer using DrawPrimitive or DrawIndexedPrimitive.

Using Shaders with Meshes

If the mesh is not saved in the format expected by the shader, you might need to change the vertex format before the shader can process the mesh. You do this with `CloneMesh`:

```
HRESULT ID3DXMesh::CloneMesh(DWORD Options, CONST DWORD *pDeclaration,
                    LPDIRECT3DDEVICE8 pD3DDevice,
                    LPD3DXMESH *ppNewMesh);
```

This function creates a new mesh based on the supplied options and declaration. Usually, you call this function, get the resulting mesh, and then release the first mesh. Once the new mesh is created, you should not call `DrawSubset` because that function sets the vertex shader internally. Instead, draw the primitives yourself using the index and vertex buffers owned by the mesh object. You'll see how to do this in Chapter 17.

The Basic Shader

I started out by talking about shaders at the lowest level, describing each individual instruction. Then I talked about shaders at the highest level, talking about how they are created, used, and destroyed. Now I pull it all together and talk about the shader itself. You'll go over some basic operations that nearly every shader does. This will provide the foundation for the more complex shaders you'll see later.

Remember that when you turned your back on the fixed function pipeline, you turned your back on everything it had to offer. Transformations, lighting—everything I have talked about, everything you have worked for—was provided to you. Now you must fend for yourself. You can start with transformations.

Transformations in the Basic Shader

Chapter 9 explained how transformations mapped 3D data onto the 2D screen. The device used the projection, view, and world matrices to convert vertex data to homogeneous screen coordinates. Now you have to do it yourself. The first thing to do is concatenate the matrices:

```
D3DXMATRIX TransformMatrix = WorldMatrix * ViewMatrix *
                    ProjectionMatrix;
```

Although the matrix includes all the transformation data, it is still not ready to use. It is much more useful to take the transpose of the matrix (see Chapter 3). The D3DX library comes in handy once again:

```
D3DXMatrixTranspose(&TransposedMatrix, &TransformMatrix);
```

The transposed matrix is ready to pass into the shader as a set of constants. You will set c0 through c3 with the rows of the matrix:

```
m_pD3DDevice->SetVertexShaderConstant(0, &TransposedMatrix, 4);
```

Once the constants are set, the shader can use them to process the vertices. It now makes sense to look at the code for the vertex shader. You can find each component of the transformed vertex by computing the dot product of the vertex position and each row of the transposed matrix. This was described in Chapter 3. In this case, the four constants are the four rows of the transposed matrix. In Chapter 3, you learned that you could transform a vector by taking the dot product of the vector and the four row vectors. That is exactly what yields the result here. The result is written to the output register oPos. Figure 15.3 reworks the equations from Chapter 3 to show how the constants are set and used.

$$M = \begin{bmatrix} 1 & 0 & 0 & 0 \\ 0 & 1 & 0 & 0 \\ 0 & 0 & 1 & 0 \\ 10 & 20 & 30 & 1 \end{bmatrix} \quad M^T = \begin{bmatrix} 1 & 0 & 0 & 10 \\ 0 & 1 & 0 & 20 \\ 0 & 0 & 1 & 30 \\ 0 & 0 & 0 & 1 \end{bmatrix}$$

Figure 15.3

Transformations based on the transposed transformation matrix.

```
c0 = (1, 0, 0, 10)      oPos.x = v0 • c0
c1 = (0, 1, 0, 20)      oPos.y = v0 • c1
c2 = (0, 0, 1, 30)      oPos.z = v0 • c2
c3 = (0, 0, 0, 1)       oPos.w = v0 • c3
```

The code follows:

```
vs.1.1
dp4 oPos.x, v0, c0
dp4 oPos.y, v0, c1
dp4 oPos.z, v0, c2
dp4 oPos.w, v0, c3
```

There are a bunch of things happening here. The first line identifies the vertex shader version as 1.1. After that, the input vertex is dotted with each of the four rows of the transposed matrix, and the results of each dot product are written to the components of the output register oPos. Most samples set a temporary register and then copy the temporary register to oPos. This isn't particularly useful, and it "costs" an extra instruction count.

Setting Other Vertex Data

In later chapters, you will be processing colors and texture coordinates in interesting ways, for now, you'll just pass the information along. You do this with the mov instruction:

```
mov oD0, v5
```

This line passes the vertex color through the shader unchanged. Even though you don't process the color in any way, you still need to copy the data from the input register to the output register. I revisit the complete shader when I talk about the sample application. First, I discuss performance issues.

Performance Issues

Remember that a vertex shader is run once for every vertex. Therefore, anything that affects many vertices should probably be done once and passed in as a constant. In the basic shader example, you could have concatenated and transposed the matrices inside the shader, but that would have meant repeating the operation many times. Also, remember that you can set constants, render some primitives, set the constants again, and render more primitives. Just remember that there is a cost associated with certain operations. Setting constants isn't that costly, but setting the vertex shader can be. If you are using several vertex shaders, avoid switching between shaders unnecessarily.

In the shader code itself, remember that each instruction takes one cycle of the graphics chip. It's easy to see that the longer the shader, the more time it takes to execute that shader. If you can shave one instruction off a shader, that can actually translate into many saved cycles over the course of the application. Always look for shortcuts within the shader code.

The Code

The code for this chapter is simple and concentrates mostly on setting up a basic vertex shader. You will revisit the application from Chapter 9, only this time the simple transformations will happen in a shader. This should provide the foundation you'll need for the real techniques in the coming chapters. Figure 15.4 shows a screenshot of the application. The application from Chapter 9 showed four different viewports, but this application uses only one of them; from a shader perspective, each one was the same.

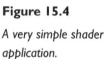

Figure 15.4

A very simple shader application.

As always, you'll start with the header file, BasicShaderApplication.h:

```
class CBasicVertexShaderApplication : public CHostApplication
{
public:
    CBasicVertexShaderApplication();
    virtual ~CBasicVertexShaderApplication();
```

This is the only new function in the application. This function is called every time the device is created or reset. The other functions are duplicates of those from Chapter 9:

```
    HRESULT CreateShader();
    BOOL FillVertexBuffer();
    BOOL CreateVertexBuffer();
    void DestroyVertexBuffer();

    virtual BOOL PostInitialize();
```

```
        virtual BOOL PreTerminate();
        virtual BOOL PreReset();
        virtual BOOL PostReset();
        virtual void Render();


        LPDIRECT3DVERTEXBUFFER8 m_pVertexBuffer;


        D3DXMATRIX m_WorldMatrix;
        D3DXMATRIX m_ViewMatrix;
        D3DXMATRIX m_ProjectionMatrix;
```

The shader handle below identifies the shader when it is created, set, and destroyed.

```
        DWORD m_ShaderHandle;
};
```

Following is the code for the implementation of the new class. This is a revamped version of the code from Chapter 9, so I only discuss the new stuff. If you haven't read the comments from Chapter 9, you might want to do so:

```
#include "BasicVertexShaderApplication.h"
```

You still create an FVF even though it's not being passed to SetVertexShader. The FVF is still used when creating the vertex buffer:

```
#define D3DFVF_SIMPLEVERTEX (D3DFVF_XYZ | D3DFVF_DIFFUSE)


struct SIMPLE_VERTEX
{
        float x, y, z;
        DWORD color;
};
#define NUM_VERTICES 20


CBasicVertexShaderApplication::CBasicVertexShaderApplication()
{
        m_pVertexBuffer = NULL;
}


CBasicVertexShaderApplication::~CBasicVertexShaderApplication()
{
        DestroyVertexBuffer();
```

```
}

BOOL CBasicVertexShaderApplication::PostInitialize()
{
        D3DCAPS8 Caps;
        m_pD3D->GetDeviceCaps(D3DADAPTER_DEFAULT, D3DDEVTYPE_HAL,
         &Caps);
```

The above code decides whether to create the device with hardware vertex shading or software vertex shading. When you call the GetDeviceCaps method of the D3D object and specify the HAL device, the device capabilities returned are the hardware-specific capabilities. If they do not include support for vertex shaders, create the device with software vertex processing. Next, you assume that the hardware and driver at least support vertex shaders in software:

```
        if (Caps.VertexShaderVersion == D3DVS_VERSION(1,1))
        {
                if (FAILED(EasyCreateWindowed(m_hWnd, D3DDEVTYPE_HAL,
                              D3DCREATE_HARDWARE_VERTEXPROCESSING)))
                      return FALSE;
        }
        else
        {
                if (FAILED(EasyCreateWindowed(m_hWnd, D3DDEVTYPE_HAL,
                              D3DCREATE_SOFTWARE_VERTEXPROCESSING)))
                      return FALSE;
        }
        m_pD3DDevice->SetRenderState(D3DRS_LIGHTING, FALSE);

        D3DXMatrixIdentity(&m_ViewMatrix);

        RECT WindowRect;
        GetClientRect(m_hWnd, &WindowRect);
        D3DXMatrixPerspectiveFovLH(&m_ProjectionMatrix,
                        D3DX_PI / 4,
                        (float)(WindowRect.right - WindowRect.left) /
                        (float)(WindowRect.bottom - WindowRect.top),
                        1.0f, 100.0f);
```

Create the shader. If this fails, there's no reason to go on. At this point, the only real reason for failing is that the device has no support for shaders. If so, you might need to create a REF device instead:

```
        if (FAILED(CreateShader()))
                return FALSE;
        return CreateVertexBuffer();
}


BOOL CBasicVertexShaderApplication::PreReset()
{
        DestroyVertexBuffer();
```

In addition to destroying the vertices, you should also delete the vertex shader and free up its resources:

```
        m_pD3DDevice->DeleteVertexShader(m_ShaderHandle);
        return TRUE;
}


BOOL CBasicVertexShaderApplication::PostReset()
{
```

Re-create the shader if the device has been reset:

```
        if (FAILED(CreateShader()))
                return FALSE;
        return CreateVertexBuffer();
}


BOOL CBasicVertexShaderApplication::CreateVertexBuffer()
{
        if (FAILED(m_pD3DDevice->CreateVertexBuffer(NUM_VERTICES *
                                        sizeof(SIMPLE_VERTEX),
                                        D3DUSAGE_WRITEONLY,
                                        D3DFVF_SIMPLEVERTEX,
                                        D3DPOOL_DEFAULT,
                                        &m_pVertexBuffer)))

                return FALSE;

        m_pD3DDevice->SetStreamSource(0, m_pVertexBuffer,
```

```
                                sizeof(SIMPLE_VERTEX));

        FillVertexBuffer();
```

In Chapter 9 you set the vertex shader here because it was the FVF. Now you're using shaders, so you set the vertex shader after the shader is created:

```
        return TRUE;
}


void CBasicVertexShaderApplication::DestroyVertexBuffer()
{
        if (m_pVertexBuffer)
        {
                m_pVertexBuffer->Release();
                m_pVertexBuffer = NULL;
        }
}


void CBasicVertexShaderApplication::Render()
{
        D3DXMATRIX RotationMatrix1;
        D3DXMATRIX RotationMatrix2;
        D3DXMATRIX TranslationMatrix;
        D3DXMATRIX ScalingMatrix;

        D3DXMatrixRotationZ(&RotationMatrix1,
                            (float)GetTickCount() / 1000.0f);
        D3DXMatrixRotationZ(&RotationMatrix2,
                            -(float)GetTickCount() / 1000.0f);
```

In Chapter 9, you used four different viewports to show four different types of transformations. In this chapter, you show only one transformation. Notice that here you set the world matrix, but again, you don't call SetTransform. There's no reason to:

```
        D3DXMatrixTranslation(&TranslationMatrix, 3.0f, 0.0f, 0.0f);
        D3DXMatrixScaling(&ScalingMatrix, 1.0f, 0.5f, 1.0f);

        m_WorldMatrix = ScalingMatrix * RotationMatrix2 *
                        TranslationMatrix * RotationMatrix1;
```

Next, you multiply the three matrices to form the one transform matrix that is sent to the shader. However, the final screen position of the vertex is actually computed using the transpose of the matrix. Because the transpose is the same for all vertices, you do the transpose operation once and pass the result to the shader, setting the first four constant registers to the four rows of the transposed matrix.

```
D3DXMATRIX ShaderMatrix = m_WorldMatrix * m_ViewMatrix *
                          m_ProjectionMatrix;

D3DXMatrixTranspose(&ShaderMatrix, &ShaderMatrix);

m_pD3DDevice->SetVertexShaderConstant(0, &ShaderMatrix, 4);
```

Once the matrix is passed to the shader, you are ready to render:

```
m_pD3DDevice->DrawPrimitive(D3DPT_POINTLIST, 0, NUM_VERTICES);
}


BOOL CBasicVertexShaderApplication::PreTerminate()
{
    DestroyVertexBuffer();

    m_pD3DDevice->DeleteVertexShader(m_ShaderHandle);

    return TRUE;
}


BOOL CBasicVertexShaderApplication::FillVertexBuffer()
{
    if (!m_pVertexBuffer)
        return FALSE;

    SIMPLE_VERTEX *pVertices;

    if (FAILED(m_pVertexBuffer->Lock(0,
                       NUM_VERTICES * sizeof(SIMPLE_VERTEX),
                       (BYTE **)&pVertices,
                       0)))
    {
        DestroyVertexBuffer();
        return FALSE;
```

```
        }

        for (long Index = 0; Index < NUM_VERTICES; Index++)
        {
                float Angle = 2.0f * D3DX_PI *
                                (float)Index / NUM_VERTICES;

                pVertices[Index].x = cos(Angle);
                pVertices[Index].y = sin(Angle);
                pVertices[Index].z = 10.0f;

                pVertices[Index].color = 0xffffffff;
        }

        m_pVertexBuffer->Unlock();

        return TRUE;
}


HRESULT CBasicVertexShaderApplication::CreateShader()
{
```

Because this shader is so simple, it is created in code rather than in a file. The new line characters at the end of each line are for the shader assembler. The shader computes the dot products of the input vector and each row of the transposed matrix and places the results into the components of the output position. It also copies the diffuse color to the output color unchanged. This is the simplest shader that produces transformed colored vertices. Shaders in later chapters are much more involved:

```
        const char BasicShader[] =
        "vs.1.1                 \n"
        "dp4 oPos.x, v0, c0      \n"
        "dp4 oPos.y, v0, c1      \n"
        "dp4 oPos.z, v0, c2      \n"
        "dp4 oPos.w, v0, c3      \n"
        "mov oD0,   v5           \n";
```

This is the shader declaration. It specifies that the vertices used by the shader should have a position vector and a color. Also, these vertices will be taken from stream 0. If there is a mismatch between the shader declaration and the vertex format, the shader will either produce bad data or crash. Neither is a desired result:

```
DWORD Declaration[] =
{
        D3DVSD_STREAM(0),
        D3DVSD_REG(D3DVSDE_POSITION,    D3DVSDT_FLOAT3),
        D3DVSD_REG(D3DVSDE_DIFFUSE,     D3DVSDT_D3DCOLOR),
        D3DVSD_END()
};
ID3DXBuffer* pShaderBuffer;
ID3DXBuffer* pShaderErrors;
```

First, you assemble the shader using the character buffer that contains the shader code. This application has fairly minimal error checking, but in real usage, you might want to check the error buffer if the assembler fails. The result is a compiled shader, which still needs to be instantiated on the device:

```
if (FAILED(D3DXAssembleShader(BasicShader,
                          sizeof(BasicShader) - 1,
                0, NULL, &pShaderBuffer, &pShaderErrors)))
        return E_FAIL;
```

Creating the vertex shader is basically creating an instance of the vertex shader on the device that can be used by the device. You tell the device what inputs the shader expects, and you give it the compiled shader code. The result is a shader handle, which is used as an identifier when you need to set or destroy the shader.

```
if (FAILED(m_pD3DDevice->CreateVertexShader(Declaration,
                (DWORD *)pShaderBuffer->GetBufferPointer(),
                          &m_ShaderHandle, 0)))
        return E_FAIL;
```

The final thing you do is release the buffers that were used during the creation process. After the actual shader is created, there is no more need for these buffers:

```
pShaderBuffer->Release();
```

The last thing you do is set the vertex shader. This application is simple, so you can set the vertex shader here and forget about it. In other applications that use more than one shader, you might need to be more careful about when each shader is active.

```
return m_pD3DDevice->SetVertexShader(m_ShaderHandle);
}
```

In Conclusion...

This chapter really only touches on the basics of shaders. It's important to lay down the basic concepts such as instructions and different register types, but it's difficult to see just how powerful they can be until you look at the techniques in later chapters. If you don't see the power of shaders yet, don't worry: You'll have plenty of time for that. For now, here are the important things to remember:

- Shaders take data from input registers and write to output registers. Along the way, they may use constants and temporary registers to actually do the computations.

- You can use the Address register to index into the constant registers.

- Shaders are limited to 128 instructions.

- The basic shader instructions handle elementary vector manipulation. You can perform higher-order computations with groups of instructions.

- Vertex shader macros provide some shortcuts to commonly used functionality, but be careful not to exceed the instruction count.

- Swizzling, negation, and write masking are "free" operations that can be extremely useful.

- Performance depends on instruction count. Fewer instructions equals better performance.

- It's a good idea to make sure the device supports shaders before creating the device. If the device does not support them with hardware vertex processing, it should support them with software vertex processing.

- The shader declaration specifies the input format of the vertices, much like the FVF. The vertex format must match the declaration or the shader will not work.

- Unlike the fixed function pipeline, vertex shaders can take advantage of data from multiple streams. This can allow you to mix and match different streams containing different vertex elements.

- Shaders must be assembled and then created on the device.

- Rendering primitives with vertex shaders is the same as in previous chapters, assuming the vertex formats match the declaration. Meshes might require changing the vertex format.

- The easiest way for a shader to compute the transformation from object space to camera space is with the transpose of the transformation matrix. The simple shader transformation code shown in this chapter is repeated many times in later chapters.

- Just one more time because it's important: Performance depends on instruction count. Fewer instructions equals better performance.

CHAPTER 16

PIXEL SHADERS

Pixel shaders are analogous to vertex shaders, but they operate on pixels instead of vertices. After vertices are transformed, the triangles are rasterized into pixels that are drawn to the back buffer. Previous chapters discussed how vertex colors and texture operations affect the colors of the final output. In this chapter, I introduce the concepts behind pixel shaders. These ideas are fleshed out more in the actual technique chapters, but this chapter serves as an introduction to the following basic pixel shader concepts:

- Different pixel shader versions.
- Inputs and outputs of a pixel shader.
- Dependent texture reads.
- Pixel shader instructions and instruction pairing.
- Pixel shader modifiers.
- Pixel shader limitations and caveats.
- Determining pixel shader support.
- Assembling and creating pixel shaders.
- A simple pixel shader application.

What Is a Pixel Shader?

In previous chapters, you saw that different color operations influence the way that texture and vertex colors are blended when triangles are rasterized. Texture stage color operations give the programmer a decent amount of control over blending, but they don't provide much in the way of flexibility. Pixel shaders, like vertex shaders, allow a much finer grain of control over how the device deals with data. In the case of pixel shaders, the data in question is a pixel. The shader operates on every pixel that will be rendered to the screen. Note that this is not every pixel of the screen, but rather every pixel of the rendered primitive. Figure 16.1 shows a different view of the later stages of Figure 5.1. As you can see, the shader influences the coloring of a given primitive, but the resulting pixel must still pass the alpha, depth, and stencil tests before it becomes a pixel on the screen.

The point is that the pixel shader operates on every pixel of the rendered primitive, not necessarily every pixel of the output screen or window. This means that the pixel shader influences how a given triangle or object looks. It takes the place of texture blending states and offers a finer level of control over the transparency and

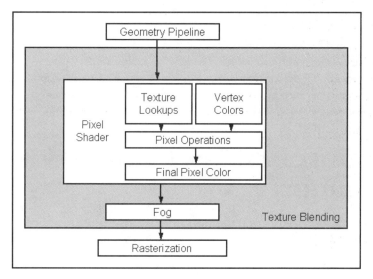

Figure 16.1

A pixel shader's place in the pipeline.

color of whatever object is being drawn. As you'll see in later chapters, this has implications in terms of lighting, shadows, and many other color operations.

Perhaps one of the biggest advantages of pixel shaders is that they simplify the representation of complex texture-blending operations. Texture stage states require you to set texture operations, arguments, blending factors, and several other states. These states remain in effect until they are explicitly changed. The result is that the syntax is sometimes clumsy, and it sometimes is difficult to keep track of all the settings. Pixel shaders replace the calls to SetTextureStageState with a series of relatively straightforward arithmetic instructions with clearly defined arguments. Once you become familiar with pixel shaders, you will find them quite useful.

Pixel Shader Versions

The pixel shader specification is changing more rapidly and significantly than the vertex shader specification. There is a version 1.0, but you should use 1.1 instead. Currently, almost all pixel shader hardware supports version 1.1, but there are hardware implementations for versions 1.2, 1.3, and 1.4. Later versions extend the functionality in many ways, but I chose to limit the techniques in later chapters to version 1.1. In this chapter, I explain the features of all the versions. I note any features that are limited to later versions. Unless I note otherwise, you can assume general comments apply to all versions.

The Inputs, Outputs, and Operation of a Pixel Shader

As with a vertex shader, pixel shader operations depend on a set of inputs, a set of instructions, and registers to hold the final output. Figure 16.2 shows an architectural depiction of a pixel shader.

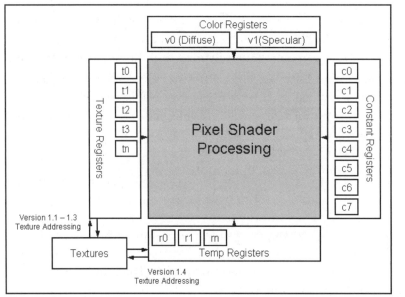

Figure 16.2

Pixel shader architecture.

Following is a breakdown of each component of a pixel shader. I give a brief overview here and then fill in the gaps as the chapter progresses.

Color Registers

The color registers v0 and v1 are the most straightforward inputs. They are four component color values that correspond to the oD0 and oD1 output registers of the vertex shader. These can be useful as colors, texture coordinates, or even vectors that influence the blending or coloring of the final pixel.

Temporary and Output Registers

Similar to the vertex shader registers, the temporary registers hold temporary data between shader instructions. They are four component color values held as floating-point values. Unlike vertex shaders, the r0 value is the final output color value from the shader. You can use the r0 register as a temporary register as well, but whatever r0 is at the end of the shader is what is passed along to the later stages of the pipeline. Also, the values of all the temporary registers are floating-point values within the shader, but r0 is clamped to the range of 0.0 to 1.0 upon leaving the shader.

Constant Registers

Pixel shader constants have exactly the same form and function as vertex shader constants except that the values should be in the range of –1.0 to 1.0. In many cases, you'll see the constants defined in the pixel shader itself. In most pixel shader techniques, the constant value is truly constant, meaning that it never really changes. You can feed changing values to the pixel shader through the vertex shader. If you need to, you can also feed constant values to the pixel shader with API calls.

Texture Registers

The texture registers supply the pixel shader with texture information. Technically, the texture register contains the texture coordinates, but in most cases that information is immediately converted into the color data as sampled from those coordinates. In shader versions 1.1 through 1.3, the texture registers can be read as coordinates and then written with the color data. In version 1.4, they are read only and are used as a parameter to load color data into other registers. The exact function of these registers will become clearer after the discussion on shader instructions. The number of texture registers depends on the number of texture stages.

Dependent Texture Reads

In most cases, you use the texture register to sample data based on the texture coordinates passed from a vertex shader. However, the purpose of some pixel shader instructions is to manipulate texture coordinates in the pixel shader before the actual texture value is read. This is called a dependent texture read because the coordinates used to fetch the texture value depend on some earlier pixel shader operation and not just external factors. Figure 16.3 shows a graphical representation of this.

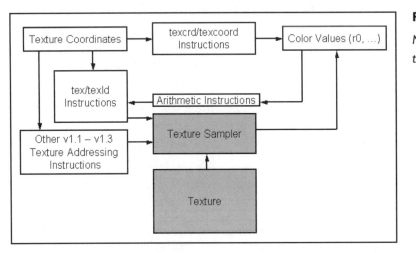

Figure 16.3

Normal and dependent texture reads.

This allows the programmer to build a series of texture stages that provide lookup functionality into each subsequent stage. For instance, there are techniques in which a vertex shader provides texture coordinates into a texture that contains color values used as texture coordinates into another texture. If these are used correctly, they form the basis of mathematical functions that go well beyond the operations made possible by the texture stage states. The next section on instructions covers this in more detail.

Pixel Shader Instructions

Pixel shader instructions operate on input and temporary register values in much the same way as vertex shader instructions. There are a couple of major differences. The first difference is that pixel shaders support a much lower instruction count for each shader. This is a limiting factor, but it makes sense in practical terms because of the frequency of use of a pixel shader. Hardware capabilities aside, you wouldn't want to write a long shader that might have to operate on millions of pixels per frame. The other major factor is support for instruction modifiers. Instruction modifiers can be powerful add-ons to shader instructions. I discuss the modifiers in the next section.

One annoyance is that different pixel shader versions support different instructions to varying degrees. In the following explanations, I list the supporting shader versions for each instruction. If there is no list, you can assume that the instruction is equally supported across all current versions.

There are three general categories of instructions. I'm calling them setup instructions, arithmetic instructions, and texture addressing instructions. The setup instructions category is a bit of a catchall category for the three instructions that don't fit the other categories. Tables 16.1 lists the setup instructions.

Table 16.2 lists the arithmetic instructions. Most of these instructions are at least partially supported in all shader versions. Be careful, because a couple of them are either not supported or they use up more than one instruction count.

Table 16.1   Pixel Shader "Setup" Instructions

Instruction	Comments
ps	The ps instruction tells the shader to compile which version you are using. Currently, the most widely supported version is 1.1, but later versions will soon enjoy wider support.
def	The def instruction defines a constant value as a four-component vector. This is useful for setting values that never change throughout the lifetime of the shader.
phase	This instruction is unique to version 1.4. Version 1.4 lets you split the pixel shader into two different phases of operation, which can effectively double the amount of instructions per pixel shader. Color values set in one phase of the shader carry through to the second phase of the shader, but alpha values are not guaranteed to be intact. If the shader has no phase instruction, the device runs the shader as if it were in the final phase. (1.4 only.)

Table 16.2   Pixel Shader Arithmetic Instructions

Instruction	Format	Comments
mov	mov Result, Input0	Simply move a value from one register to another. This might be useful for moving temporary values to r0 for final output from the shader.
add	add Result, Input0, Input1	Add one register value to another and place the sum in the result register.
sub	sub Result, Input0, Input1	Subtract one value from another and place the result in the result register. Pixel shaders also support register negation, so you can just use the add instruction with a negative input.
mul	mul Result, Input0, Input1	Multiply two values together and place the product in the result register. Like vertex shaders, pixel shaders do not support a division instruction. Any time you need to divide a number, you need to get the reciprocal into the shader.
mad	mad Result, Input0, Input1, Input2	Like the mad vertex shader instruction, this instruction performs a multiply and an add in a single instruction. First, Input0 is multiplied by Input1. Input2 is then added to the product, and the final result is placed in the result register.
dp3	dp3 Result, Input0, Input1	This instruction performs a three-component dot product operation between the values stored in Input0 and Input1. These values are assumed to be vector values, although you might be able to find other uses for it. Chapter 31 makes use of this instruction.
dp4	dp4 Result, Input0, Input1	This is the same as dp3 with four components. This instruction is supported only on versions 1.2 and higher and counts as two instructions in versions 1.2 and 1.3. (1.2, 1.3, 1.4.)

Table 16.2 (continued)

Instruction	Format	Comments
cnd	cnd Result, Input0, Input1, Input2	This conditional instruction sets the values in the result register based on whether the components are greater than 0.5. In version 1.4, this instruction operates on each component separately. If a given component of Input0 is greater than 0.5, that component of the result register is set to the value of that component of Input1; otherwise, the value is retrieved from Input2. Therefore, it is possible for the result vector to be some amalgam of values from Input1 and Input2. In all versions previous to 1.4, the comparison value is limited to one value in r0.a. (1.1, 1.2, 1.3, 1.4 with the aforementioned restrictions.)
cmp	cmp Result, Input0, Input1, Input2	This is similar to cnd, only this time the input components are compared to 0.0. If they are greater than or equal to 0.0, the value from Input1 is chosen; otherwise, the value from Input2 is chosen. This instruction is supported in version 1.2 and above, but it counts as two instructions in versions 1.2 and 1.3. (1.2, 1.3, 1.4 with restrictions.)
lrp	lrp Result, Input0, Input1, Input2	The "lerp" instruction linearly interpolates the values in Input1 and Input2 based on the factors in Input0. For instance, a single component of the result value is computed as Result.r = (Input1.r * Input0.r) + (Input2.r * (1.0 - Input0.r)).
bem	bem Result.rg, Input0, Input1	This instruction is supported by version 1.4 only. It computes a fake environmental bump map value based on the bump matrix texture stage state setting. (1.4 only.)
nop	nop	This instruction literally does nothing.

Instruction Pairing

The pixel shader processes alpha and color data in two different pipelines. It is therefore possible to specify two completely different instructions for the two pipelines that execute simultaneously. For instance, you might want to issue a dp3 instruction for the RGB data but simply move the alpha value from one register to another. You can do this as follows:

```
dp3 r2.rgb, r1, c1
+ mov r0.a, c2
```

There are some limitations as to which instructions you can coissue. A decent rule of thumb is that you can't pair the instructions with the most limitations or caveats. The simple arithmetic instructions should be safe to pair.

Texture Addressing Instructions

The texture addressing instructions can be more powerful than the arithmetic instructions. They can also be more confusing to use. Table 16.3 briefly explains the texture addressing instructions. I explain some of these instructions in more detail in later technique chapters.

With texture addressing instructions, it's frequently difficult to understand when t(n) is used for texture coordinate data and when it contains a color value. To clear that up, here are a few examples of how texture coordinates are related to texture color values and texture output registers.

In the following case, the texture at stage 0 is sampled with the texture coordinates from stage 0. The resulting color value is written to t0. Subsequent instructions that use t0 will be using the sampled color value:

```
tex t0
```

In this example, the t0 register is written with the texture coordinates from stage 0. Subsequent instructions that use t0 will be using the texture coordinate data interpreted as a color value:

```
texcoord t0
```

The next line of code uses the first two texture coordinates from stage 0 as coordinates into the texture at stage 1. The stage 1 texture is sampled, and the resulting color value is written to t1. Subsequent instructions with t1 will be using the color value from the sampled texture of stage 1:

```
texreg2ar t1, t0
```

Table 16.3 Pixel Shader Texture Addressing Instructions

Instruction	Format	Comments
tex	tex t(n)	This instruction loads the value from a given texture stage based on the texture coordinates for that stage. This basically pulls the value in for processing. The tex instruction is not supported in version 1.4. For version 1.4 shaders, use texld. (1.1, 1.2, 1.3.)
texld	texld r(n), t(n)	This instruction loads the color values from a texture into a temporary register. In this case, the texture register t(n) holds the texture coordinates and r(n) holds the actual texture data. Therefore, the line texld r2, t0 takes the texture coordinates from stage 0 and uses them to look up a color value in the texture in stage 2. The color values are written to r2. (1.4 only.)
texcrd	texcrd Result, t(n)	In version 1.4, the texcrd instruction copies the texture coordinate data from t(n) into the result register as color information. In the second phase of the pixel shader, you could use this result register as a source in a call to texld, but only in phase 2. (1.4 only.)
texcoord	texcoord t(n)	This instruction is somewhat of a partner to tex and analogous to texcrd. If the shader calls this instruction rather than tex, the texture coordinate data is loaded instead of the color value. This can be useful for techniques in which the vertex shader passes data into the pixel shader via texture coordinates. (1.1, 1.2, 1.3.)
texreg2ar	texreg2ar t(m), t(n)	This instruction interprets the alpha and red components of the t(n) as u and v texture coordinates. These texture coordinates are used to index into t(m) to retrieve a color value from that texture stage. For example, a vertex shader could set the texture coordinates for stage 0 to (0, 0). The alpha and red components at that point in the texture might both be 0.5. Therefore, you could use the texture coordinates (0.5, 0.5) to find the texel value in the middle of t1. That line in the pixel shader would look like texreg2ar t1, t0. The final texture stage must be greater than the source texture stage. (1.1, 1.2, 1.3.)

Table 16.3 (continued)

Instruction	Format	Comments
texreg2gb	texreg2gb t(m), t(n)	This is the same as texreg2ar, only in this case the green and blue components are used as texture coordinates. (1.1, 1.2, 1.3.)
texreg2rgb	texreg2rgb t(m), t(n)	Again, this is the same as earlier, but it supports three texture coordinates for use in a cube map or 3D texture. (1.2 and 1.3 only.)
texkill	texkill t(n)	This instruction "kills" the current pixel if any of the first three texture coordinates are less than zero. This can be useful for implementing clipping planes in the pixel shader, but it can cause undesired effects if you are using multisampling. In version 1.4 phase 2, the input register can be a temporary register that was set in phase 1.
texm3x2pad	texm3x2pad t(m), t(n)	This instruction does the first half of a 3-by-2 matrix calculation. The values in t(n) (usually a vector) are multiplied by the first three values in the texture coordinates of stage m, which in this case are used as the first row of a 3x2 matrix. You can only use this instruction with either texm3x2tex or texm3x2depth (see later). You can't use it alone. Think of this instruction as the first part of one two-part instruction. (1.1, 1.2, 1.3.)
texm3x2tex	texm3x2tex t(m+1), t(n)	This is the second part of the preceding instruction. The destination register must be from a higher texture stage than the other two stages. This instruction does the second part of the 3x2 matrix multiply. t(n) is multiplied by the second row of the matrix (stored as the texture coordinates for stage m+1). The result is then used as a lookup into the texture at stage m+1. The result of this instruction is that t(m+1) contains the lookup color. This instruction is best explained by example. Chapter 32 concentrates heavily on this and similar instructions. (1.1, 1.2, 1.3.)

Table 16.3   (continued)

Instruction	Format	Comments
texm3x2depth	tex3x2depth t(m+1), t(n)	This is the alternate second half of the tex3x2pad instruction. If you use this instruction, tex3x2pad should have been used to calculate the z value for this particular pixel (based on the first row of the matrix). This instruction computes w using the coordinates from stage m+1 as the second row of the matrix. This instruction then computes z/w and tags that value to be used as an alternate depth value for this pixel. (1.3 only.)
texm3x3pad	tex3x3pad t(m), t(n)	This instruction is exactly the same as tex3x2pad except that it works on a 3x3 matrix. Therefore, you need to make two calls to tex3x3pad before completing the instruction with tex3x3tex, tex3x3spec, or tex3x3vspec. (1.1, 1.2, 1.3.)
texm3x3tex	tex3x3tex t(m+2), t(n)	Like tex3x2tex, this instruction completes a full matrix operation. In this case, it's a full 3x3 matrix multiply. This assumes that it was preceded by two calls to tex3x3pad and that each stage used was higher than the last. The result of the multiplication is used as the texture coordinates to retrieve the texture value from t(m+2). (1.1, 1.2, 1.3.)
texm3x3spec	tex3x3spec t(m+2), t(n), c(n)	This is an alternate to tex3x3tex. The result of the 3x3 matrix multiply is treated as a normal vector for reflection calculations. c(n) stores a constant eye vector, which this instruction reflects about the resulting normal vector. The resulting 3D vector is used as a set of texture coordinates into the texture in stage m+1. You use this instruction for environmental mapping. (1.1, 1.2, 1.3.)
texm3x3vspec	tex3x3vspec t(m+2), t(n)	This is similar to tex3x3spec, but it does not use a constant eye vector. Instead, the eye vector is retrieved from the fourth component of the matrix rows. (1.1, 1,2, 1.3.)

Table 16.3   (continued)

Instruction	Format	Comments
texm3x3	texm3x3 t(m+2), t(n)	This instruction can also complete the three instruction series. This instruction moves the final vector to the output register without doing the texture lookup. (1.2, 1.3.)
texbem	texbem t(m), t(n)	This instruction computes fake environmental bump-mapping information using the bump matrix set by calls to SetTextureStageState. The color values in t(n) are multiplied by the texture matrix, and the result is used to index into the texture at stage m. (1.1, 1.2, 1.3.)
texbem1	texbem1 t(m), t(n)	This is an augmentation of texbem. It performs the same function as texbem but adds a luminance correction from texture stage states.
texdepth	texdepth r(n)	You can only use this instruction in the second phase of a version 1.4 shader. The first phase must fill the r and g components of the register with z and w values. This instruction computes z/w and tags it to be used as the depth value for this pixel. (1.4 phase 2 only.)
texdp3	texdp3 t(m), t(n)	This instruction computes the three component dot product of the data in t(n) and the texture coordinates of t(m). The resulting scalar value is copied to all four components of t(m). (1.2, 1.3.)
texdp3tex	texdp3tex t(m), t(n)	This instruction computes the dot product as the preceding instruction, but the resulting scalar value is used as an 1D texture lookup into the texture at stage m. The resulting color value is written to the t(m) register. (1.2, 1.3.)

In all shader versions prior to 1.4, the t(n) registers can be both read and written. When they are read, the texture coordinate is the data that is read. When they are written to, the written value could contain the sample texture color data or perhaps an interpreted texture coordinate (in the case of texcoord). In version 1.4, the texture registers are only readable. In this case of the texld instruction, the t0 register contains the texture coordinates, and r0 contains the result of using those coordinates to sample into the texture at stage 0:

```
texld r0, t0
```

Later chapters show some of these instructions in action. They should make more sense when you see them used.

The processing functionality is not limited to a set of instructions. Like vertex shaders, pixel shaders provide a host of modifiers that provide many freebies.

Pixel Shader Modifiers

Pixel shaders provide some of the added features of vertex shaders in terms of negation and write masks, but they also provide instruction modifiers for powerful added functionality. Table 16.4 shows the available source register modifiers.

Table 16.4 Pixel Shader Source Register Modifiers

Modifier	Syntax	Comments
Bias	r0_bias	Subtract 0.5 from all four components of the register. You can apply this modifier to any source register.
Invert	1- r0	Subtract the values of the source register from 1.0 before the actual instruction is performed. The contents of the source register are not changed.
Negate	-r0	Negate the components before the instruction. Again, the actual contents of the source register are not changed.
Scale by 2	r0_x2	This modifier multiplies the components by 2.0 before the instruction begins. This modifier is only supported in version 1.4.
Signed scale	r0_bx2	This modifier subtracts 0.5 and multiplies the result by 2. This modifier is most useful when converting values from the color range of 0.0 to 1.0 to the vector range of −1.0 to 1.0.

Pixel shaders also support a less powerful form of swizzling. You can replicate one channel to all color channels before an instruction executes. Like vertex shader swizzling, the underlying register data does not change. Table 16.5 shows the source register selectors.

There is also support for write masks. In all shader versions, you can choose whether to write to all channels, alpha only, or color only. In version 1.4, you can select arbitrary channels to be written to. The syntax is the same as vertex shader write masks, only using the .rgba labeling shown in Table 16.5 rather than .xyzw.

The final modifiers are instruction modifiers. You can think of these modifiers as the final operations that are performed before the result value is set. Table 16.6 describes these modifiers. The examples use the add instruction, but you can use the modifiers with most arithmetic instructions.

Pixel Shader Limitations and Caveats

As with vertex shaders, the primary limitation of pixel shaders is the limit on instruction count. Pixel shaders are significantly more limited than vertex shaders. Versions 1.1, 1.2, and 1.3 have a limit of 4 texture addressing instructions and 8 arithmetic instructions, for a grand total of 12 instructions. Version 1.4 pixel

Table 16.5 Pixel Shader Source Register Selectors

Selector	Syntax	Comments
Replicate Alpha	r0.a	This selector replicates alpha to all components of the input register. This selector is compatible with all shader versions.
Replicate Blue	r0.b	Replicate the blue channel to all of the components. This selector is available on all shader versions 1.1 and higher.
Replicate Green	r0.g	Replicate green to all channels. This is only supported in version 1.4.
Replicate Red	r0.r	Replicate red. This is only available in version 1.4.

Table 16.6 Pixel Shader Instruction Modifiers

Modifier	Syntax	Comments
Multiply by 2	add_x2	This modifier multiplies the result of the instruction by 2.
Multiply by 4	add_x4	This multiplies the result by 4.
Multiply by 8	add_x8	This instruction modifier is only available in version 1.4. It multiplies the result by 8.
Divide by 2	add_d2	This divides the result by 2.
Divide by 4	add_d4	This divides the result by 4 and is only available in version 1.4.
Divide by 8	add_d8	Divide the result by 8. This is also only available in version 1.4.
Saturate	add_sat	Clamp the result to the range of 0.0 to 1.0. The saturate modifier ensures that values stay within the usual color range.

shaders support eight arithmetic instructions and six texture addressing instructions for each of the two phases. This creates a grand total of 28 available instructions. This is more than double the number of instructions available in previous versions but still far below the number of instructions available in a vertex shader.

Although there is a limit on the number of addressing and arithmetic instructions, there is no limit on the number of "setup" instructions. The def, phase, and ps instructions do not use up available instruction count.

Another limitation is the number of available registers. Table 16.7 lists the register limitations for all pixel shader versions.

Table 16.7 Pixel Shader Register Limitations

Register Type	Limit in Versions 1.1-1.3	Limit in Version 1.4
Color register v(n)	2	2 (phase 2)
Texture register t(n)	4	6
Constant register c(n)	8	8
Temporary register r(n)	2	6

Finally, pixel shaders are limited by the hardware they run on. Some pieces of hardware might never support some versions of pixel shaders. Unlike vertex shaders, there is no acceptable software fallback for pixel shader support. If the hardware doesn't support them, the performance is abysmal. You can use the reference device to test shader implementations, but not for production code.

Determining Pixel Shader Support

As with vertex shader support, you can determine pixel shader support with a call to SetDeviceCaps. The Caps structure includes a DWORD member called PixelShaderVersion. The value encodes both the main version number and the subversion number. The best way to resolve the meaning of this value is with the D3DPS_VERSION macro:

```
D3DCAPS8 Caps;
m_pD3D->GetDeviceCaps(D3DADAPTER_DEFAULT, D3DDEVTYPE_HAL,
 &Caps);
if (Caps.PixelShaderVersion == D3DPS_VERSION(1,1))
{
        if (FAILED(EasyCreateWindowed(m_hWnd, D3DDEVTYPE_HAL,
                        D3DCREATE_HARDWARE_VERTEXPROCESSING)))
                return FALSE;
}
```

This is the maximum shader version. Devices that support a given shader version should support earlier versions as well. If the device doesn't support pixel shaders, you might need to implement a fallback technique using texture blending operations, or you might want to disable certain effects altogether. If pixel shaders are supported, you can move forward and actually create the shader.

Assembling, Creating, and Using Pixel Shaders

Assembling a pixel shader is similar to assembling a vertex shader. You should use the same calls to the D3DXAssembleShader functions (see previous chapter). If the syntax is correct, the assembled shader is in the shader buffer. You can use the assembled shader to actually create the shader.

The CreatePixelShader function appears next. It is similar to CreateVertexShader, but it does not require a declaration. Pixel shaders always deal with four-component color values regardless of the texture or buffer format:

```
HRESULT IDirect3DDevice8::CreatePixelShader(CONST
                              DWORD *pAssembledShader,
                              DWORD *pShaderHandle);
```

You can enable the resulting shader handle with calls to SetPixelShader:

```
HRESULT IDirect3DDevice8::SetPixelShader(DWORD ShaderHandle)
```

Calling SetPixelShader is analogous to setting several texture stage states. You can disable the pixel shader by passing NULL to SetPixelShader. You can use texture stage states as usual if there is no current pixel shader. In fact, you might still want to use texture states for very simple operations. For instance, by default the first texture stage modulates the diffuse color. There is no need to implement this operation in a shader; let the default blending operations handle it.

A Very Simple Pixel Shader Application

Unfortunately, I need to explain several vertex shader applications before I can get to really interesting and useful pixel shader applications. Most of the interesting pixel shader applications require a vertex shader to feed the proper data into the pixel shader. In this chapter, I concentrate on a simple application that illustrates some of the basic concepts. After that, Chapter 29 is the first chapter that uses pixel shaders for something useful.

This chapter uses a simple vertex shader to compute per-vertex directional lighting values. These lighting factors are interpolated over the surface of a simple plane. A pixel shader blends a texture with the lighting value, but it also uses a second texture to define an area of the texture that reflects less light. This is an oversimplified version of per-pixel lighting. The vertex shader computes per-vertex lighting, but the pixel shader does one last line of calculations to figure out a lighting value for each pixel. Figure 16.4 shows a screenshot of the application.

To understand what's being fed into the pixel shader, you must first take a look at the vertex shader.

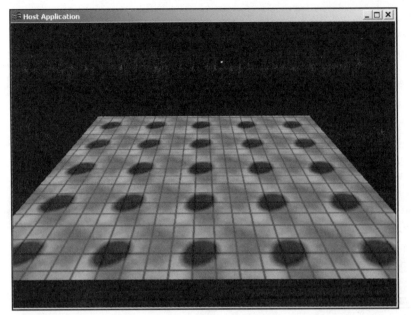

Figure 16.4

Very simple pixel shader application.

Simple Lighting in a Vertex Shader

Chapter 24 goes into detail about how lighting calculations are performed in a vertex shader, so I don't go into all the theory here. This is an extremely simple vertex shader that computes the dot product of a light vector and a vertex normal. I made the vertex shader output slightly convoluted in order to show how to feed values into the pixel shader. Later chapters will show better examples of this. I wanted to show how flexible shader interactions can be. The following shader code comes from PixelSetup.vsh:

```
vs.1.1
```

Output the transformed position. These do not affect the pixel shader in any way:

```
dp4 oPos.x, v0, c0
dp4 oPos.y, v0, c1
dp4 oPos.z, v0, c2
dp4 oPos.w, v0, c3
```

Compute the dot product of the vertex normal and the light vector of a directional light. The value of the dot product is the cosine of the angle between the two vectors. In this context, the dot product is used to determine how much light is reflected off the surface in a simple diffuse lighting model. The light vector is passed to the vertex shader as c4. It's negated to transform it to a "vertex to light" vector. The final output is written to the specular color output oD1. This corresponds to the color input v1 in the pixel shader:

```
dp3 oD1, v3, -c4
```

The c5 constant stores an ambient lighting value. Move this value to oD0 (v0 is the pixel shader). This is where I've made the shader slightly convoluted. Sometimes you could argue that you could add the directional lighting and ambient lighting in the shader. You could argue about what data goes in what register. Remember that the point of this application is to show flexibility instead of proper lighting technique:

```
mov oD0, c5
```

Finally, move the texture coordinates (v7) to the output texture coordinates. This allows the pixel shader to index into the texture properly:

```
mov oT0, v7
```

So the vertex shader sets things up by sending two color values and a set of texture coordinates to the pixel shader. This is shown in Figure 16.5.

The pixel shader does the last line of processing.

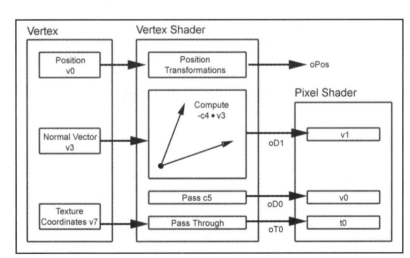

Figure 16.5

Pixel shader setup in a vertex shader.

Simple Blending in a Pixel Shader

Texture stage 0 contains one texture that really serves two purposes. The color channel defines the colors of the object and the alpha channel defines how well each pixel reflects the directional light. Again, keep in mind that this is not the best lighting model in the world. Figure 16.6 shows the color and alpha channels of the texture.

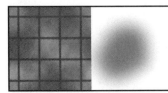

Figure 16.6

*Color and alpha
channels of the texture.*

One of the points here is that the alpha channel is a convenient storage area for values that are not necessarily visible, but necessary for calculations. If you are not explicitly using the alpha channel for transparency data, you can always use it for something else. In this case, I am using it to hold an 8-bit scaling factor for the directional lighting value. The following shader code appears in Simple.psh. The first line tells the shader assembler which shader version this is meant for:

```
ps.1.1
```

This first line loads the texture value into the pixel shader. You can think of this line as using the texture coordinates in t0 as the input and using t0 as an output register for the color values at this particular pixel. After this line, the t0 register contains the sample color values for this pixel based on the texture coordinates that were interpolated from the vertices:

```
tex t0
```

This next line is where all the real work happens. The mad instruction multiplies the interpolated directional lighting value by the scaling factor in the alpha channel of the texture. The ambient lighting value is added to the scaled directional value. This means that the surface is affected by ambient lighting evenly over the surface, but directional lighting is reflected with different intensities for different pixels. It's an odd way to light an object but makes for a simple pixel shader:

```
mad r0, v1, t0.a, v0
```

Once the lighting values are resolved, the final value is modulated by the texture color value. The r0 register is both a temporary register and the output register. In vertex shaders, the output registers are read only. You can't use them as inputs to an instruction. This is not the case in pixel shaders. You can use the r0 register repeatedly, but make sure that the final value is the value you want emitted:

```
mul r0, r0, t0
```

Figure 16.7 shows a close-up of the final output of the application. Notice that the darkened blob matches the shape defined in the alpha channel in Figure 16.6.

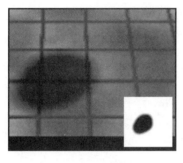

Figure 16.7

Tile with varying directional reflection.

The shaders themselves are pretty simple. The last remaining piece is the application that holds everything together.

Simple Pixel Shader Application

The preceding shaders do most of the interesting work. The main role of the application is to supply the shaders with data and make sure the right shaders are created and active at the right time. In the following code, I show only the new functions. The complete source code appears on the CD (\Code\Chapter16).

First, I extended the PostInitialize function to check for pixel shader support. If the hardware device doesn't support pixel shaders, the application falls back to the reference device. This is good for testing, but in a real application you'd be better off disabling the technique instead of using the reference device:

```
BOOL CTechniqueApplication::PostInitialize()
{
```

Get the caps and check for vertex and pixel shader support with the version macros. All the samples in this book use version 1.1 shaders to maximize the hardware support. If shaders are supported, create a hardware device using the convenience function. Otherwise, create a reference device. Keep in mind that the reference fallback might be extremely slow, especially if you have a slow CPU. If your hardware doesn't support shaders, you might have to wait several seconds before any frames are rendered. Remember to be patient if this is the case:

```
    D3DCAPS8 Caps;
    m_pD3D->GetDeviceCaps(D3DADAPTER_DEFAULT, D3DDEVTYPE_HAL,
```

```
            &Caps);
        if (Caps.VertexShaderVersion == D3DVS_VERSION(1,1) &&
            Caps.VertexShaderVersion == D3DPS_VERSION(1,1))
        {
                if (FAILED(EasyCreateWindowed(m_hWnd, D3DDEVTYPE_HAL,
                            D3DCREATE_HARDWARE_VERTEXPROCESSING)))
                    return FALSE;
        }
        else
        {
                if (FAILED(EasyCreateWindowed(m_hWnd, D3DDEVTYPE_REF,
                            D3DCREATE_SOFTWARE_VERTEXPROCESSING)))
                    return FALSE;
        }
```

SetupDevice and CreatePlaneBuffer do some basic device setup and buffer creation for
a four-point rectangle. They are not shown in this text. There's nothing new going
on there:

```
        SetupDevice();
        if (FAILED(CreatePlaneBuffer()))
                return FALSE;
```

CreateShaders creates both the vertex and the pixel shader. If this function fails, that
probably means that you have a syntax error in your shader. If the shader is correct,
this should never fail because of the fallback to the reference device. If you disable
the reference fallback, this might fail in the case where shaders are not supported:

```
        if (FAILED(CreateShaders()))
                return FALSE;
```

This texture is the one shown in Figure 16.5. Both the color and the reflectance
data are encoded into this single texture:

```
        if (FAILED(D3DXCreateTextureFromFile(m_pD3DDevice,
                                             "Tile.dds",
                                             &m_pTexture)))
                return FALSE;

        return TRUE;
}
```

The CreateShaders function creates the shaders used when the scene is rendered. This code is similar to the code shown in the previous chapter:

```
HRESULT CTechniqueApplication::CreateShaders()
{
    ID3DXBuffer* pShaderBuffer;
    ID3DXBuffer* pShaderErrors;
```

The vertex shader is created and assembled as described in the previous chapter. In a real implementation, you might want to look at the contents of the error buffer if this fails:

```
    if (FAILED(D3DXAssembleShaderFromFile("PixelSetup.vsh",
                                  0, NULL, &pShaderBuffer,
                                  &pShaderErrors)))
        return E_FAIL;

    if (FAILED(m_pD3DDevice->CreateVertexShader(Declaration,
                (DWORD *)pShaderBuffer->GetBufferPointer(),
                &m_SetupShader, 0)))
        return E_FAIL;
```

Release the shader buffer so it can be reused to create the pixel shader. You shouldn't need to release the error buffer because it was not created if you got this far:

```
    pShaderBuffer->Release();
```

The call to create the pixel shader is exactly the same as the call to create the vertex shader. The assembler uses the first version instruction to figure out what type of shader it is and how it should be assembled:

```
    if (FAILED(D3DXAssembleShaderFromFile("Simple.psh",
                                  0, NULL, &pShaderBuffer,
                                  &pShaderErrors)))
        return E_FAIL;
```

The call to CreatePixelShader is similar to the call to CreateVertexShader, but there is no need for a declaration. If everything is successful, you have a valid pixel shader handle to use when rendering:

```
    if (FAILED(m_pD3DDevice->CreatePixelShader(
                (DWORD *)pShaderBuffer->GetBufferPointer(),
```

```
                        &m_SimplePixelShader)))
            return E_FAIL;

    pShaderBuffer->Release();

    return S_OK;
}
```

These lines have taken care of creating the shaders. You should take care to destroy them when the application ends or gets reset. The following code from PreReset shows how to delete the shaders:

```
BOOL CTechniqueApplication::PreReset()
{
```

Make sure the shaders are deleted with calls to DeleteVertexShader and DeletePixelShader. You can create vertex buffers that are automatically re-created when a device is reset, but you must delete and re-create shaders yourself:

```
    m_pD3DDevice->DeleteVertexShader(m_SetupShader);
    m_pD3DDevice->DeletePixelShader(m_SimplePixelShader);

    return TRUE;
}
```

Finally, the render function uses these shaders to do all the interesting work. The following code assumes that all the previous code created the shaders properly:

```
void CTechniqueApplication::Render()
{
```

You must set the vertex shader. In this simple application, you could have set the vertex shader when the shader was created, but I'm putting it here to better illustrate what's going on:

```
    m_pD3DDevice->SetVertexShader(m_SetupShader);
```

The following code animates the light's direction. The math is set up to always point the light down no matter what the animation value is. After the light direction is defined, it is passed to the c4 constant of the shader. In Chapter 24, you'll learn that this is a naïve (and usually incorrect) view of how the light vector relates to the transformations of the object, but it works for this simple application. If you decide to change the world matrix you'll get incorrect results, but that's not terribly important in this context. You'll see what I mean in Chapter 24:

```
float Time = (float)GetTickCount() / 1000.0f;
D3DXVECTOR4 LightDir = D3DXVECTOR4(sin(Time), -fabs(cos(Time)),
                                          0.0f, 0.0f);
m_pD3DDevice->SetVertexShaderConstant(4, &LightDir, 1);
```

Set a small amount of ambient light. The ambient light is passed to the vertex shader and in turn is passed to the pixel shader:

```
D3DXVECTOR4 Ambient     (0.1, 0.1f, 0.1f, 0.0f);
m_pD3DDevice->SetVertexShaderConstant(5, &Ambient, 1);
```

You must always pass the concatenated matrix to the shader. The matrices were set in `SetupDevice`:

```
D3DXMATRIX ShaderMatrix = m_WorldMatrix * m_ViewMatrix *
                m_ProjectionMatrix;
D3DXMatrixTranspose(&ShaderMatrix, &ShaderMatrix);
m_pD3DDevice->SetVertexShaderConstant(0, &ShaderMatrix, 4);
```

Set the texture in stage 0. In this simple case, you could have set the texture when it was loaded, but I am setting it here for clarity:

```
m_pD3DDevice->SetTexture(0, m_pTexture);
```

Set the pixel shader. This shader expects certain input textures and vertex shader values. You could use the pixel shader with a different vertex shader and texture, but the results would be unpredictable and probably wrong:

```
m_pD3DDevice->SetPixelShader(m_SimplePixelShader);
```

Everything is set up, so draw the mesh. In this case, the mesh is a simple textured plane. The mesh contains the texture coordinates that tell the pixel shader how to sample the texture. As with other texturing concepts, bad texture coordinates equal bad output:

```
m_pD3DDevice->SetStreamSource(0, m_pPlaneVertexBuffer,
                                  sizeof(MESH_VERTEX));
m_pD3DDevice->DrawPrimitive(D3DPT_TRIANGLESTRIP, 0, 2);
```

It's usually a good idea to disable the pixel shader when it's not being used. In this case, the pixel shader is always being used, but I added this to demonstrate the importance of disabling the shader. Like texture stage states, the pixel shader affects every pixel until it's explicitly changed. Unlike texture stage states, disabling the shader is much easier than disabling each state separately:

```
m_pD3DDevice->SetPixelShader(0);
}
```

The output of this application has already been shown in Figures 16.4 and 16.6. This sample is a bit contrived and the lighting procedures are not the best in the world, but it does illustrate the basics of how a pixel shader is created, fed by a vertex shader, and used to affect the output of a rendering pass.

In Conclusion...

I'm guessing that many readers are still a bit lost at this point. That's somewhat expected given the novelty of the material. I personally believe that concepts are easier to digest when you see them being used. In this chapter, I wanted to fly through the basic ideas and instruction definitions. Later chapters solidify the ideas with examples.

That said, the next several chapters concentrate heavily on vertex shaders. You'll learn the syntax and many of the concepts behind some interesting and fun techniques. These techniques will get you thinking in terms of shader instructions, limitations, and so on. By the time you get to the first pixel shader in Chapter 29, you should be pretty comfortable thinking about shaders. From there, the transition from vertex shaders to pixel shaders is easier than you may think. So digest what you can here, but remember that the later chapters solidify many of the ideas mentioned here. Before moving on, here's a recap of some of those ideas:

- Pixel shaders replace the more cumbersome texture state methodology with a programmable model similar to vertex shaders.
- It is possible to use pixel shaders and texture-stage blending in the same application. In fact, you should probably use pixel shaders for more complex operations but leave simple operations to the "old way."
- Four pixel shader versions enjoy varying levels of support on different pieces of hardware. Currently, version 1.4 is the most powerful and the least supported. Any hardware that supports pixel shaders at all will support version 1.1.
- Pixel shaders work in much the same way as vertex shaders. Registers are read and written to by shader instructions before they are finally emitted as output.

- Most registers hold color information. The exception is texture registers. Texture registers hold texture coordinate information. Depending on the instruction, you can use it either as a sampled color or as vector data.

- The `ps`, `def`, and `phase` instructions set up the shader and do not count towards the instruction count limit.

- You can use arithmetic instructions to do math operations on color values, and you can usually coissue different instructions for the color and alpha values.

- Texture-addressing instructions are the most powerful instructions. They control how a texture input is interpreted. You can use them to load color values or to do vector and matrix operations based on texture coordinates.

- You can use modifiers to modify instructions, swizzle input registers, and mask output registers. They offer more functionality with less instruction count.

- Pixel shaders are more severely limited by instruction count than are vertex shaders. These limitations are not only on total count but also count on different instruction types and sometimes on specific instructions and modifiers.

- You can determine whether hardware supports pixel shaders by looking at the device caps.

- Pixel shaders are assembled, created, and set much like vertex shaders. There is no need for any sort of declaration when creating a pixel shader.

- For testing, you can always fall back to the reference device, but remember that you'll get miserable performance.

PART FIVE

VERTEX SHADER
TECHNIQUES

In the previous chapters, I created application code that was as optimized as possible while still easy to read. Throughout the rest of the book, I optimize the shaders, but not the application code. I show what goes into the shaders without worrying about the tightness of the application. In most cases, I point out where the code is bad and what you can do to improve it. If you see application code that breaks the optimization rules laid out in previous chapters, assume that the previous chapter was correct.

The samples throughout the rest of the book use an updated application framework to display performance data. The details of that framework are described in Chapters 37 and 38. However, you are shielded from the details so that you can concentrate on the following concepts:

- Chapter 17, "Using Shaders with Meshes," describes how to break meshes out of the fixed-function paradigm and how to deal with the data in a vertex shader. I used this technique as a basis for nearly every subsequent chapter.

- Chapter 18, "Simple and Complex Geometric Manipulation with Vertex Shaders," describes how to perturb vertices with complex functions.

- Chapter 19, "Billboards and Vertex Shaders," explains how to align a surface with a user's viewpoint to create billboard effects.

- Almost everything you see in 3D graphics is in Cartesian coordinates. In Chapter 20, "Working Outside of Cartesian Coordinates," I explain other coordinate systems and how a vertex shader can convert from one system to another.

- Chapter 21, "Bezier Patches," expands on the ideas of geometric manipulation by introducing 3D patches rendered by a vertex shader. And I talk about how to generate dynamic normals for dynamic geometry.

- Matrix palette skinning is a method of animation that can apply multiple transformation matrices to a single object. In Chapter 22, "Character Animation—Matrix Palette Skinning," the palette skinning is done with a vertex shader.

- Chapter 23, "Simple Color Manipulation," teaches you to encode depth values into color values and to adjust transparency for an x-ray effect.

- When you switch to shaders, you lose all the functionality of the fixed-function pipeline, including lighting. In Chapter 24, "Do-It-Yourself Lighting in a Vertex Shader," I explain how to implement all the DirectX lights in a vertex shader.

- Chapter 25, "Cartoon Shading," shows how to implement cartoon shading in a single pass using vector manipulation and two lookup textures.

- Environmental mapping allows objects to reflect the world around them. Chapter 26, "Reflection and Refraction," explains the concepts behind cube maps and using a shader to map them to a surface.

- Shadows are necessary features in today's games. Chapter 27, "Shadows Part 1—Planar Shadows," explains some mathematical concepts behind planes.

- Chapter 28, "Shadows Part 2—Shadow Volumes," introduces a far more powerful shadowing technique.

- Chapter 29, "Shadows Part 3—Shadow Maps," details rendering to a texture and then projecting that texture onto the entire scene. This is the first vertex shader technique that uses a pixel shader.

CHAPTER 17

USING
SHADERS WITH
MESHES

Chapter 15 briefly explained how to prepare mesh objects for use with shaders. This chapter explains more of the details and presents some actual code. This technique really doesn't teach anything new about shaders themselves, but most of the time you'll be using shaders with meshes, so it's important that you take a look at how to reformat meshes so you can apply shaders to them. In this chapter, I will explain the steps needed to reformat and use meshes with shaders. In this chapter, I also discuss the following:

- Learning how meshes store vertex data.
- Mapping materials to vertex colors.
- Using colors to store other vertex data.
- Exploring the performance considerations.
- Implementing code that extracts data from the mesh.

The Basic Idea

There seems to be some misunderstanding about how the D3DX mesh objects work. Some people feel that meshes hide a lot of implementation details or that they make the underlying data harder to access. This really isn't true. For the most part, the D3DX mesh objects can be fairly transparent as long as you know a little bit about how they work. Assuming that you've read the previous chapters, delving into the mesh should be easy.

If you've taken a look at the mesh files on the CD, you may have noticed that all of the .X files are in text format. This makes for a bigger file and longer load times, but it is also easier to see what's in the file. The files contain the position data, the normals, the texture coordinates, and materials. They also contain a section that maps materials to individual faces. When the D3DX library opens a file containing a mesh, it determines the vertex format that matches the data and then loads the data into a vertex buffer. It also creates and populates an index buffer. Finally, it creates an array of the mesh materials and creates an attribute buffer to hold the one-to-one mapping between materials and faces. These arrays are used when the geometry is drawn, as shown in Figure 17.1. Figure 17.2 shows how the individual buffers are related.

After these buffers are loaded, you can use them just as you would any of your own vertex or index buffers.

So far, so good, but there is a wrinkle. If you weren't using shaders, you could just call DrawSubset and the mesh would render correctly in the fixed-function pipeline.

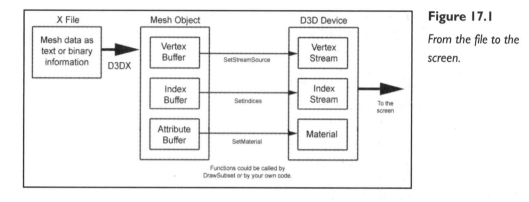

Figure 17.1

From the file to the screen.

Now that you're using shaders, it's very likely that the FVF of the original mesh will not match the format described in the shader declaration. There are a couple ways to address this problem. The first way is to create a shader declaration that you know matches the format of the mesh. This really isn't the best idea because it might force you to create suboptimal shaders. It might also require you to rewrite or at least tweak shaders if the mesh format ever changes.

> **TIP**
>
> Remember, the cloning operation does not create new data. You can clone a mesh format to add vertex normals, but the normals are not generated automatically. Cloning produces more "slots" for data, but it's up to you to fill them.

A better way is to change the mesh format to fit your shader declaration. You do this with the cloning methods described in Chapter 15. These methods create a new mesh that fits a given format, thus making your shader happy, but they are not perfect. If the original mesh object contains more data than the new format needs, the extraneous data is stripped out of the new mesh. However, if the original mesh contains less data, you might need to populate the missing data in code. The sample code for this chapter demonstrates how to do this.

From Materials to Vertex Colors

Most mesh files do not contain vertex colors. Instead, they contain materials that are mapped to faces through the attribute table. If you load a mesh, you can clone it to a format that includes a vertex color, but then you need to fill in the actual color values with more code. To do this, you have to back-track from the attribute buffer. Figure 17.2 shows how the attribute buffer, index buffer, and vertex buffer are interrelated.

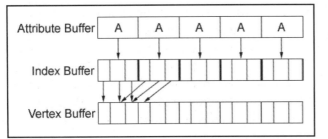

Figure 17.2

The relationships between the buffers.

I haven't talked about any of the mesh optimization methods yet, so you can assume that the attribute buffer and index buffer map to each other linearly. With that assumption, you can walk through the attribute buffer and map a given material to a given face. You'll go through this step-by-step. Let's assume you are only talking about extracting the diffuse color of a material so that you can populate the diffuse color of a vertex. The first code snippet shows how to access the diffuse color of a face from the attribute buffer:

```
DWORD        *pAttribs;
m_pMesh->LockAttributeBuffer(D3DLOCK_READONLY, &pAttribs);
for (long Face = 0; Face < m_pMesh->GetNumFaces(); Face++)
{
        D3DXCOLOR Diffuse =
            (D3DXCOLOR)m_pMeshMaterials[pAttribs[Face]].Diffuse;
}
m_pMesh->UnlockAttributeBuffer();
```

The loop allows you to index into the attribute buffer, which then allows you to index into the material array. Once you retrieve the specific material, you can extract the diffuse color. If you were interested in more of the material properties, you could extract them just as easily. The second code snippet above shows how to actually update the vertex buffer with the color information. The following snippet assumes that the index and vertex buffers have been locked:

```
pMeshVertices[pIndices[Face * 3 + 0]].color = Diffuse;
pMeshVertices[pIndices[Face * 3 + 1]].color = Diffuse;
pMeshVertices[pIndices[Face * 3 + 2]].color = Diffuse;
```

You know each face constitutes a set of three entries in the index buffer. As you loop through each face, the preceding code indexes into the index buffer and uses those values to index into the vertex buffer. You can then set the diffuse color of each vertex to the diffuse color of the material. The source code for this chapter shows the complete procedure.

When you're done, the vertices are individually colored. In fact, you could throw away the attribute table entirely. The code for this chapter reuses the cloned vertex and index buffers contained in the mesh object, but it would be easy to create new vertex and index buffers and copy the mesh data to them. In fact, the D3DX mesh objects are good for loading the data initially, but in some cases they really don't add a lot of value during the actual rendering. In those cases, you could load the mesh, clone it to a new format, copy the buffers, and release the mesh object. This would free up some memory. I'll leave that as an exercise.

From Vertex Colors to Vertex Data

The preceding procedure outlined how to map material values to vertex colors, but if you think out of the box a little bit, you can see some more powerful applications. In many cases, the actual vertex color is not terribly interesting because the real visual impact comes from the texture. Vertices might still be colored by lights and shading, but the actual color stored in the geometry might have limited value in the final output. It might, however, be extremely useful when authoring your geometry in a modeling tool.

In many of the shader chapters, you'll see how data encoded into each vertex helps to determine the effects of animation, warping, and other techniques. Most of that data can be encoded when the model is being crafted. If you're a power user of a tool such as 3DSMAX, you can use scripting or plug-ins to help encode data into a model. For most people, it might be easier to use color. You could decide that different colors correspond to different values or parameters used by the vertex shader. You could easily paint those values on your geometry in your modeling tool and then use them for something else once the model is loaded. For instance, the previous snippets could extract the color from the materials and then use that data to populate the blend weight of vertices. It could then populate the actual color data with white. The idea is that the vertex color can be a valuable visual tool for the artist without affecting what the end user sees. I'm being vague here because there are many possible ways to apply this idea to your own needs.

Performance Considerations

As you will see later, mesh cloning involves a decent amount of code that involves locking and unlocking buffers and moving a lot of data around. It's a fairly expensive operation, but it's difficult to think of any time that you would need to do this while you're actually rendering. You usually do this during initialization.

The one thing to consider here is memory usage. Remember that a cloned mesh is a new mesh. If you clone and then do not release the old mesh, that mesh occupies memory. It could also possibly be in video memory, which is more precious. Also, mesh-specific buffers such as the attribute buffers don't really do anything for you, so you might consider getting rid of the mesh altogether. The one thing to remember is that you are creating new objects. Keep an eye on what is actually being used.

The Implementation

Figure 17.3 shows a screenshot from this chapter's sample application. There's not a whole lot going on, but it does show that the colors were successfully extracted from the materials.

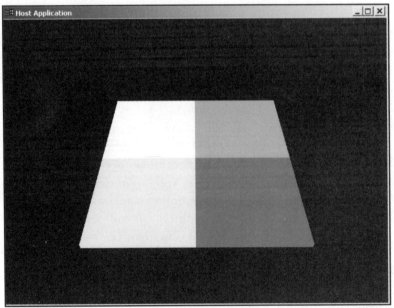

Figure 17.3

The sample application.

There's not much theory behind this technique, so the best way to explain it is to jump right into the code. Many of the pieces borrow heavily from previous chapters, so the explanations concentrate on the new material. Also, the header file for this technique doesn't contain anything conceptually new, so it is omitted here. As usual, the complete code appears on the CD in the \Code\Chapter17 directory. The following code is from \Code\Chapter17\TechniqueApplication.cpp:

```
#include "TechniqueApplication.h"
```

This is the desired vertex format that matches the shader declaration. The .X file contains the position and normal data, but the color data is not part of the vertex format:

```
#define D3DFVF_MESHVERTEX (D3DFVF_XYZ | D3DFVF_NORMAL |
 D3DFVF_DIFFUSE)

struct MESH_VERTEX
{
      float x, y, z;
      float nx, ny, nz;
      DWORD color;
};
CTechniqueApplication::CTechniqueApplication()
{
      m_pMeshVertexBuffer = NULL;
      m_pMeshIndexBuffer  = NULL;
      m_pMesh             = NULL;
      m_pMeshMaterials    = NULL;
      m_NumMaterials      = 0;
      m_ShaderHandle      = 0;
}


CTechniqueApplication::~CTechniqueApplication()
{
}


BOOL CTechniqueApplication::PostInitialize()
{
      D3DCAPS8 Caps;
      m_pD3D->GetDeviceCaps(D3DADAPTER_DEFAULT, D3DDEVTYPE_HAL,
       &Caps);
      if (Caps.VertexShaderVersion == D3DVS_VERSION(1,1))
      {
            if (FAILED(EasyCreateWindowed(m_hWnd, D3DDEVTYPE_HAL,
                 D3DCREATE_HARDWARE_VERTEXPROCESSING)))
                  return FALSE;
      }
      else
      {
```

```
                if (FAILED(EasyCreateWindowed(m_hWnd, D3DDEVTYPE_HAL,
                    D3DCREATE_SOFTWARE_VERTEXPROCESSING)))
                        return FALSE;

        }
```

This will become the usual procedure for device creation in all the shader chapters:

```
        SetupDevice();
        LoadMesh();
        ExtractBuffers();
        CreateShader();

        return TRUE;
}


void CTechniqueApplication::Render()
{
```

This shader setup code is copied from Chapter 15. Again, you are using a very simple shader so that you can focus on meshes:

```
        D3DXMATRIX ShaderMatrix = m_WorldMatrix *
                                    m_ViewMatrix *
                                    m_ProjectionMatrix;

        D3DXMatrixTranspose(&ShaderMatrix, &ShaderMatrix);
        m_pD3DDevice->SetVertexShaderConstant(0, &ShaderMatrix, 4);
```

The stream sources are set when the mesh is loaded, so simply call
DrawIndexedPrimitive after setting the vertex shader. The number of primitives is
derived from the mesh itself. It might be slightly faster to call these methods once
and hold them as variables instead of constantly incurring the overhead of a call to
the mesh object:

```
        m_pD3DDevice->SetVertexShader(m_ShaderHandle);
        m_pD3DDevice->DrawIndexedPrimitive(D3DPT_TRIANGLELIST, 0,
                                    m_pMesh->GetNumVertices(), 0,
                                    m_pMesh->GetNumFaces());

}
HRESULT CTechniqueApplication::LoadMesh()
{
        LPD3DXBUFFER pD3DXMtrlBuffer;
```

```
LPD3DXMESH    pOriginalMesh;

if(FAILED(D3DXLoadMeshFromX("..\\media\\shaders\\Chapter17.x",
                    D3DXMESH_MANAGED,
                    m_pD3DDevice, NULL, &pD3DXMtrlBuffer,
                    &m_NumMaterials, &pOriginalMesh)))
  return FALSE;

D3DXMATERIAL* d3dxMaterials =
     (D3DXMATERIAL*)pD3DXMtrlBuffer->GetBufferPointer();

m_pMeshMaterials = new D3DMATERIAL8[m_NumMaterials];
```

In previous chapters, this code usually included a line that set the ambient color of
the material to match the diffuse color. Because you're not actually using the
materials, you don't need to bother with that anymore. In fact, once you copy the
data into the vertex buffer, the array of materials is just using up memory:

```
for(long MatCount = 0; MatCount < m_NumMaterials; MatCount++)
{
     m_pMeshMaterials[MatCount] =
       d3dxMaterials[MatCount].MatD3D;
}

pD3DXMtrlBuffer->Release();
if (pOriginalMesh->GetFVF() != D3DFVF_MESHVERTEX)
{
```

The mesh included with the sample is not in the same vertex format, so the mesh is
always cloned. The code clones the mesh into another mesh in managed memory
with the new vertex format. It then releases the mesh object that was used to load
the file. The alternative is here just for completeness. If the formats do match, the
mesh is set to the original mesh and you move on:

```
pOriginalMesh->CloneMeshFVF(D3DXMESH_MANAGED,
                     D3DFVF_MESHVERTEX,
                     m_pD3DDevice, &m_pMesh);

pOriginalMesh->Release();
pOriginalMesh = NULL;
}
```

```
        else
                m_pMesh = pOriginalMesh;

        return S_OK;
}
```

Figure 17.4 shows how the newly cloned mesh relates to the old mesh.

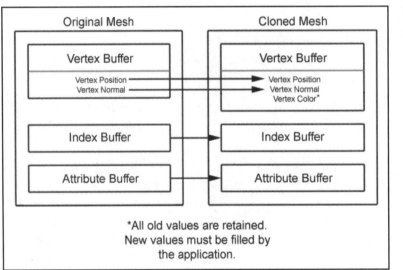

Figure 17.4

Cloning a mesh.

```
BOOL CTechniqueApplication::PreReset()
{
        return TRUE;
}

BOOL CTechniqueApplication::PostReset()
{
        SetupDevice();
        return TRUE;
}



BOOL CTechniqueApplication::PreTerminate()
{
        m_pD3DDevice->DeleteVertexShader(m_ShaderHandle);
```

Remember that the mesh object should still have references to the buffers, so calling Release on them does not necessarily destroy them. They are destroyed when reference counts drop to zero:

```
if (m_pMeshVertexBuffer)
{
        m_pMeshVertexBuffer->Release();
        m_pMeshVertexBuffer = NULL;
}

if (m_pMeshIndexBuffer)
{
        m_pMeshIndexBuffer->Release();
        m_pMeshIndexBuffer  = NULL;
}
if (m_pMesh)
{
        m_pMesh->Release();
        m_pMesh = NULL;
}
```

Theoretically, you could have released the mesh materials earlier in the program. The materials are never actually used in the program (after the vertices are set):

```
if (m_pMeshMaterials)
{
        delete m_pMeshMaterials;
        m_pMeshMaterials = NULL;
}
return TRUE;
}


void CTechniqueApplication::SetupDevice()
{
```

This is the same old thing except for the fact that you don't need to call SetTransform. Calling SetTransform wouldn't really cost you anything, but the point is that it is unnecessary:

```
RECT WindowRect;
GetClientRect(m_hWnd, &WindowRect);
```

```
D3DXMatrixPerspectiveFovLH(&m_ProjectionMatrix,
        D3DX_PI / 4,
        (float)(WindowRect.right - WindowRect.left) /
        (float)(WindowRect.bottom - WindowRect.top),
                1.0f, 1000.0f);


D3DXMatrixLookAtLH(&m_ViewMatrix,
            &D3DXVECTOR3(0.0f, 50.0f, -50.0f),
            &D3DXVECTOR3(0.0f, 0.0f, 0.0f),
            &D3DXVECTOR3(0.0f, 1.0f, 0.0f));


D3DXMatrixIdentity(&m_WorldMatrix);
}
```

This is really the meat of the sample. You start by extracting the vertex and index buffers. This simply gives you a reference. The mesh still has a reference as well, so you can't just destroy them at will. Also, this did not create new buffers; it simply allows access to the existing ones. There are methods for locking the buffers directly, but it is done this way for clarity:

```
HRESULT CTechniqueApplication::ExtractBuffers()
{
    m_pMesh->GetVertexBuffer(&m_pMeshVertexBuffer);
    m_pMesh->GetIndexBuffer(&m_pMeshIndexBuffer);
    MESH_VERTEX *pMeshVertices;
    short       *pIndices;
    DWORD       *pAttribs;
```

The vertex buffer is locked with the default behavior of allowing data to be written. This is because you are going to add a color to each vertex:

```
m_pMeshVertexBuffer->Lock(0,
        m_pMesh->GetNumVertices() * sizeof(MESH_VERTEX),
        (BYTE **)&pMeshVertices, 0);
m_pMeshIndexBuffer->Lock(0, 3 * m_pMesh->GetNumFaces()
                    * sizeof(short),
                (BYTE **)&pIndices, D3DLOCK_READONLY);
```

You're just going to read through the index and attribute buffers, so lock them as read-only. Performance isn't really an issue here, but there's no point to setting them up for writing since you only need to read the data:

```
m_pMesh->LockAttributeBuffer(D3DLOCK_READONLY, &pAttribs);
```

I described this code earlier in the chapter. It's easy to get lost in some of the arrays, but remember that you are looking into the index buffer, which contains the index you then use to access the correct vertex:

```
for (long Face = 0; Face < m_pMesh->GetNumFaces(); Face++)
{
        D3DXCOLOR Diffuse =
        (D3DXCOLOR)m_pMeshMaterials[pAttribs[Face]].Diffuse;

        pMeshVertices[pIndices[Face * 3 + 0]].color = Diffuse;
        pMeshVertices[pIndices[Face * 3 + 1]].color = Diffuse;
        pMeshVertices[pIndices[Face * 3 + 2]].color = Diffuse;
}
```

And of course, you unlock. If you are absolutely, positively sure you weren't going to use them, this is where you can release the array of materials:

```
m_pMeshVertexBuffer->Unlock();
m_pMeshIndexBuffer->Unlock();
m_pMesh->UnlockAttributeBuffer();
m_pD3DDevice->SetStreamSource(0, m_pMeshVertexBuffer,
                             sizeof(MESH_VERTEX));
m_pD3DDevice->SetIndices(m_pMeshIndexBuffer, 0);
return S_OK;
}
```

The process of remapping the vertex data is shown in Figure 17.5.

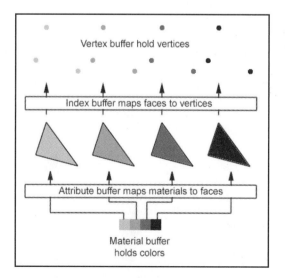

Figure 17.5

Remapping vertex data.

```
HRESULT CTechniqueApplication::CreateShader()
{
      const char BasicShader[] =
      "vs.1.1                \n"
      "dp4 oPos.x, v0, c0     \n"
      "dp4 oPos.y, v0, c1     \n"
      "dp4 oPos.z, v0, c2     \n"
      "dp4 oPos.w, v0, c3     \n"
      "mov oD0,  v5           \n";
```

This declaration does not match the format of the loaded .X file, which is the whole point of this chapter. In this chapter, you supplied the equivalent FVF to the cloning methods, but there are also cloning methods that take declarations as input. This function is just a repeat of what you saw in Chapter 15:

```
      DWORD Declaration[] =
      {
            D3DVSD_STREAM(0),
            D3DVSD_REG(D3DVSDE_POSITION,  D3DVSDT_FLOAT3),
            D3DVSD_REG(D3DVSDE_NORMAL,  D3DVSDT_FLOAT3),
            D3DVSD_REG(D3DVSDE_DIFFUSE,  D3DVSDT_D3DCOLOR),
            D3DVSD_END()
      };
      ID3DXBuffer* pShaderBuffer;
      ID3DXBuffer* pShaderErrors;

      if (FAILED(D3DXAssembleShader(BasicShader,
                  sizeof(BasicShader) - 1,
                  0, NULL, &pShaderBuffer, &pShaderErrors)))
            return E_FAIL;

      if (FAILED(m_pD3DDevice->CreateVertexShader(Declaration,
                  (DWORD *)pShaderBuffer->GetBufferPointer(),
                  &m_ShaderHandle, 0)))
            return E_FAIL;

      pShaderBuffer->Release();

      return m_pD3DDevice->SetVertexShader(m_ShaderHandle);
}
```

In Conclusion...

Okay, so this wasn't really a way-cool special effect, but in many cases it might be an important part of using shaders. Also, I hope it demystifies the mesh objects a little bit by showing how to get at and manipulate the underlying data. This will come in handy in many later chapters. Until then, let's review:

- Shader declarations and vertex formats must match; otherwise, the shader will produce bad results or fail altogether.

- If a mesh is cloned with an expanded FVF, the data might not be filled in even though it may exist somewhere.

- Mesh objects are fairly easy to open up and deconstruct. At the most basic level, they are just the now familiar combination of index and vertex buffers.

- You do not need to use data stored in an .X file in the most obvious ways. Once the file is loaded, feel free to use it however you like. Think out of the box.

- Many of the steps in this procedure produce new data or pointers to old data. If you're not careful, these pointers could cause memory leaks or just waste memory while the program is running.

CHAPTER 18

Simple and Complex Geometric Manipulation with Vertex Shaders

For the first real shader technique, you'll look at how a shader affects the most fundamental aspect of a vertex—its position. It would be socially and ecologically irresponsible to write a book that covered each and every possibility of how you can use a shader to manipulate the vertex position. It would also be difficult to carry that book home from the store. For these reasons, this chapter outlines a couple geometric effects that illustrate the basics of vertex manipulation. The idea is that you can use these ideas to build shaders that specifically fit your needs. You'll look at two shaders, a very simple one and a more complex one.

The first shader scales each vertex along its normal. If this scaling is applied evenly, the effect is akin to inflating a balloon. The second shader is more complex. It ripples the model with a sine wave. This general idea can provide a basis for many effects, such as waves in the ocean, ground tremors, or other warping effects. I also use this chapter to briefly explain how to approximate sine and cosine in a shader. These functions can be useful for a wide variety of applications, and they also demonstrate the kind of higher-order math that is possible with a limited number of instructions. Let's get started.

Expanding Vertices along Their Normals

When a model is scaled with a scaling matrix, the model retains all of its original features, only it gets bigger or smaller. This first technique is more like inflating a balloon. For simple geometry such as a sphere, the effect is the same as a scaling matrix. For other objects, the shader creates a puffy effect. This type of manipulation lends itself well to rendering inflatable objects or trendy winter wear.

It might also be useful when you need to create effects that envelope an object. For instance, many games feature a shield power that creates a shimmering force field around the players and temporarily saves them from the surrounding carnage. One way to implement this effect is to render the player once as usual and then render the player again with this puffed-out effect and the semi-transparent shield texture.

A side effect to this shader could be seen as a good thing or a bad thing, depending on your needs. This side effect appears in Figure 18.1, a screenshot from this chapter's sample application.

When you watch the actual animated application, you see the dumbbell shape expand and contract along its normals. However, the box shape behaves differently. As it

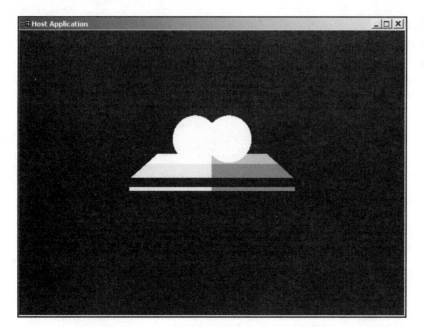

Figure 18.1

Objects scaled along their normals.

expands along its normals, the sides separate. This is because there is a discontinuity between the normals of one side and the normals of another. The top of the box moves up, the bottom moves down, and the sides move to the side. The whole thing breaks apart like a couple in a bad country-western song. This doesn't happen with the dumbbell shape because the vertex normals are interpolated from many faces. It doesn't help that objects loaded with the simple D3DX mesh interfaces use triangle lists that do not share vertices. If this splitting is not the desired behavior, this shader can cause trouble with meshes with sharp corners. However, in some cases, this splitting might be a desired effect. At the end of this chapter, I talk about some ways to augment the sample code to create explosion effects with just a few tweaks of this shader. Before you get into that, look at the shader.

This effect is simple to implement. It has only two new shader instructions in addition to the basic transformation instructions you've seen so far. The first code snippet shows the shader. This shader is written with the assumption that the vertex has a position, a normal vector, and a diffuse color. The shader also assumes that the application set the first four constants to the transformation matrix and a fifth constant to a scaling factor. The scaling factor is used to determine how much scaling is applied:

```
vs.1.1
```

After the obligatory version designation, the vertex normal (which is assumed to be normalized) is multiplied by the scaling factor in c5.

```
mul r0, c5, v3
```

The vector r0 determines how far the vertex is to be moved and in what direction. This vector is then added to the vertex position to create the new vertex position in object space.

```
add r0, r0, v0
```

This new position is transformed to screen coordinates by the matrix, the diffuse color is set, and the shader is complete. Figure 18.2 shows the complete process.

```
dp4 oPos.x, r0, c0
dp4 oPos.y, r0, c1
dp4 oPos.z, r0, c2
dp4 oPos.w, r0, c3
mov oD0,   v5
```

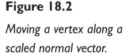

Figure 18.2

Moving a vertex along a scaled normal vector.

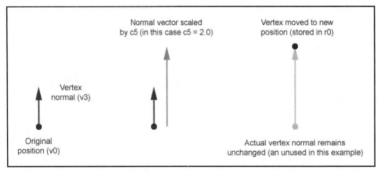

You might contend that the first two instructions of the shader could be collapsed into a single mad instruction that would have eliminated an instruction by combining the multiply and add operations. The reason I did not do this is that there are limitations on how many registers of which type can be accessed by a single instruction. In this case, you cannot reference the v3 and v0 registers with one mad instruction. You could have written those two lines like this:

```
mov r0, v3
mad r0, c5, r0, v0
```

But that wouldn't have saved an instruction count. After you take a look at the more complex technique, I show how the shader is used by the application. You can find this shader in \Media\Shaders\ScaleNormal.vsh on the CD.

Warping Vertices with a Sine Wave

Before you get into the shader, take a look at some of the theory behind this next technique. For those of you who've had higher-level algebra or calculus, this explanation is mostly review. For others, this is a cursory look into the wonderful world of calculus.

This technique warps geometry with a sine wave. It requires you to actually compute the sine of a value within the shader. Calculating the sine of an angle is a nontrivial task, but it can be made easier with a Taylor series approximation. You can write many complex functions as series expansions, where the output of the function is derived from summing the powers of the input variable. A Taylor series is one type of series expansion that has many trigonometric uses, which is exactly what you need for sine. The Taylor series representation of $sin(x)$ follows. (x is in radians.)

$$sin(x) = x - \left(\frac{x^3}{3!} + \frac{x^5}{5!} - \frac{x^7}{7!} \right)$$

Similarly, this is the series representation for cosine:

$$cos(x) = 1 - \left(\frac{x^2}{2!} + \frac{x^4}{4!} - \frac{x^6}{6!} \right)$$

Ideally, these series would be infinitely long to achieve maximum accuracy, but we don't live in an ideal world. Nor do you need maximum accuracy, so you can approximate the value of sine by using a finite number of terms in the series. Figure 18.3 compares the shape of a "real" sine wave against the Taylor series approximations using one to four terms.

The main observation here is that, for decent accuracy, the number of terms you need grows as x gets farther from the origin. In fact, four terms is more than adequate for values near the origin. If the value of x was within the range of –pi to pi, you could have your cake and eat it, too. You could compute a fairly accurate result with a limited number of terms, but to do this, you need to guarantee that x does not fall outside of that range. Luckily, sine is a function that repeats every 2pi radians. Therefore, you can easily map any value of x to its equivalent value near the origin. Once you have x near the origin, you can compute an approximation for $sin(x)$ very easily. The approach is best described by example.

This shader is based on ripple.vsh, a shader included with the DirectX SDK. It has been reworked slightly to eliminate some instructions, but the general idea is the same. This shader has the same inputs as the first shader with three additional

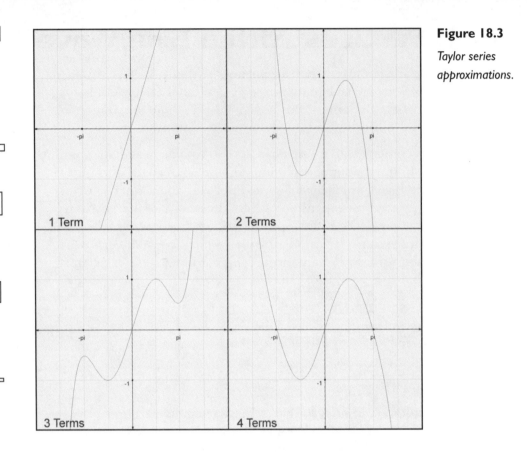

Figure 18.3

Taylor series approximations.

constants. The first new constant, c4, determines the shape of the sine wave. These three values are phase, wavelength, and amplitude, as shown in Figure 18.4.

The phase and wavelength parameters describe how to map a position in model space to a point along the sine wave. (In this case, you are using the x component of the vertex position.) Once that point is determined, the amplitude determines the height of the wave. The final component of c4 is not a wave parameter. It is used to affect the final output color.

The second new constant is c6. It is used in the equation that constrains the input value of $\sin(x)$ to the range of –pi to pi. These values scale and shift the value of x to constrain it to its equivalent value within the limited range.

Finally, c7 contains the first four Taylor coefficients for your sine approximation. These values approximate a sine wave with a limited number of instructions. The following code is the actual shader:

```
vs.1.1
```

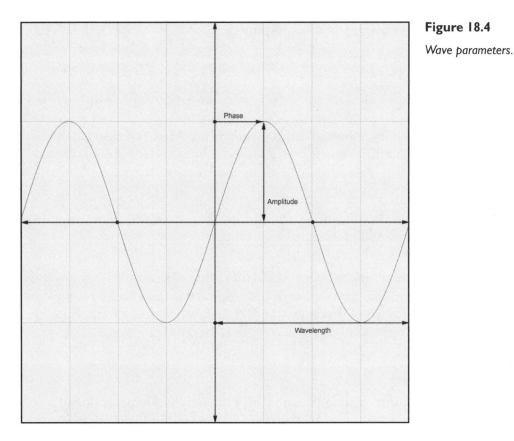

Figure 18.4

Wave parameters.

r0 is used as the final output vector for the vertex, but you are only really changing the y component of this vector. The point of this instruction is to set all the other components:

```
mov r0, v0
```

This instruction applies the wave function shown in Figure 18.3. This enables you to easily reshape the wave or animate it with time by adjusting the phase:

```
mad r1.x, v0.x, c4.y, c4.x
```

This section comes from Ripple.vsh in the SDK. The basic idea is that it shifts the value by pi (c6.x) and divides the result by 2pi (by multiplying by 1/(2pi), the value in c6.y). It then takes the fractional component of that result, multiplies it by 2pi (c6.z) and subtracts pi (c6.x with the negation operator). The result is the equivalent value in the range of –pi to pi.

When the value is constrained, you can compute the Taylor series approximation:

```
add r1.x, r1.x, c6.x
mul r1.x, r1.x, c6.y
frc r1.xy, r1.x
mad r1.x, r1.x, c6.z, -c6.x
```

These first four instructions compute the odd powers of x. The first instruction computes x squared, and that value is then used with the original value to compute the odd powers:

```
mul r2.x, r1.x, r1.x;
mul r1.y, r2.x, r1.x;
mul r1.z, r1.y, r2.x;
mul r1.w, r1.y, r2.x;
```

This second set of instructions computes the actual value of sin(x). First, the two vectors of values are multiplied so that each component of r1 contains a term of the series. Then the dot product of that vector and 1 effectively sums all four components into a single scalar value and outputs it directly into r0:

```
mul r1, r1, c7
dp4 r0.y, r1, c7.x
```

This sets the vertex color by scaling the color with the height. Simply scaling the value normally produces a color in the range of –1.0 to 1.0, but the hardware clamps the value to a range of 0.0 to 1.0. Because the background is black, you want to bias the color a little. You do this by adding the bias factor in c4.w. The downside is that clamping produces oversaturation effects. For example, if a vertex is colored with an RGB value of (1.0, 0.0, 0.0), adding a bias of 0.1 produces a final color of (1.0, 0.1, 0.1). Instead of being full red, the color becomes pink. In this particular sample, you don't really care, but this is something to keep in mind for other effects:

```
mad oD0, v5, r0.y, c4.w
```

This is the last real instruction before the final transformation. This instruction scales the value of sin(x) by the amplitude parameter and adds this value to the original y component of the vertex position:

```
mad r0.y, r0.y, c4.z, v0.y
```

The vertex is finally transformed to screen coordinates. The final output appears in Figure 18.5.

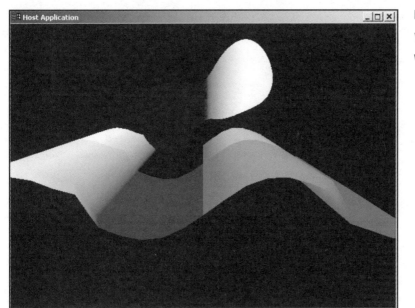

Figure 18.5

Warping with a sine wave.

```
dp4 oPos.x, r0, c0
dp4 oPos.y, r0, c1
dp4 oPos.z, r0, c2
dp4 oPos.w, r0, c3
```

The Implementation

Now that you've seen the shaders, take a look at the actual application code that uses the shaders. Figures 18.1 and 18.5 show the two different modes of this application. You can toggle between the different shaders by pressing the F2 key. In fact, you'll probably notice a slight increase in performance when you switch from the sine shader to the scaling shader. The two modes are identical in terms of vertex count and CPU instructions, but the sine shader has more than twice as many instructions. To reiterate the point, instruction count does matter.

Much of the setup, such as device creation and mesh cloning, is identical to previous chapters, so those functions were omitted here. The complete code is in the \Code\Chapter18 directory on the CD. The next several pages discuss only the newer portions of the code. Following is the listing for TechniqueApplication.cpp:

```
#include "TechniqueApplication.h"
```

This is really the same old vertex format you've been using, but it's important to remember that this is the format actually being sent to your shaders:

```
#define D3DFVF_MESHVERTEX (D3DFVF_XYZ | D3DFVF_NORMAL |
 D3DFVF_DIFFUSE)

struct MESH_VERTEX
{
      float x, y, z;
      float nx, ny, nz;
      DWORD color;
};
```

All the usual suspects are initialized here. In addition to the buffers and mesh objects, you also have two different shader handles for your two shaders, plus a flag that determines which shader should be set for a particular frame:

```
CTechniqueApplication::CTechniqueApplication()
{
      m_pMeshVertexBuffer = NULL;
      m_pMeshIndexBuffer  = NULL;
      m_pMesh             = NULL;
      m_pMeshMaterials    = NULL;
      m_NumMaterials      = 0;
      m_WhichShader       = 0;
      m_SineShaderHandle  = 0;
      m_ScaleShaderHandle = 0;
}
HRESULT CTechniqueApplication::CreateShaders()
{
      DWORD Declaration[] =
      {
            D3DVSD_STREAM(0),
            D3DVSD_REG(D3DVSDE_POSITION, D3DVSDT_FLOAT3),
            D3DVSD_REG(D3DVSDE_NORMAL, D3DVSDT_FLOAT3),
            D3DVSD_REG(D3DVSDE_DIFFUSE, D3DVSDT_D3DCOLOR),
            D3DVSD_END()
      };


      ID3DXBuffer* pShaderBuffer;
      ID3DXBuffer* pShaderErrors;
```

This first block of code creates the sine shader by loading the shader file and using the assembled shader and the declaration to create an instance of the shader on the device:

```
if (FAILED(D3DXAssembleShaderFromFile(
                    "..\\ media\\shaders\\Chapter18_1.vsh",
                    0, NULL, &pShaderBuffer,
                    &pShaderErrors)))
        return E_FAIL;

if (FAILED(m_pD3DDevice->CreateVertexShader(Declaration,
                (DWORD *)pShaderBuffer->GetBufferPointer(),
                &m_SineShaderHandle, 0)))
        return E_FAIL;

pShaderBuffer->Release();
if (FAILED(D3DXAssembleShaderFromFile(
                    "..\\ media\\shaders\\Chapter18_2.vsh",
                    0, NULL, &pShaderBuffer,
                    &pShaderErrors)))
        return E_FAIL;

if (FAILED(m_pD3DDevice->CreateVertexShader(Declaration,
                (DWORD *)pShaderBuffer->GetBufferPointer(),
                &m_ScaleShaderHandle, 0)))
        return E_FAIL;
```

You now have the two different shaders, each with its own shader handle. You can use these handles to switch between shaders as each frame is rendered:

```
pShaderBuffer->Release();
pShaderErrors->Release();
```

This constant contains the first four coefficients in the Taylor series for the sine approximation. If you really want to, you can create several constants containing more of the coefficients, but you really don't need the accuracy. If you're interested, the nVidia developer's site features a document that outlines several ways to calculate sine and cosine. Some of the methods emphasize speed, and others emphasize accuracy. If you have an application that actually uses sine waves or similar functions, it might be a good idea to read that document and others on the developer site:

```
D3DXVECTOR4 Sine(1.0f, -1.0f/6.0f, 1.0f/120.0f, -1.0f/5040.0f);
```

These constants are used by the part of the shader that constrains the value of x to the range of –pi to pi. Again, the nVidia document features an alternative method that takes a slightly different set of constants. It might be worth a look:

```
D3DXVECTOR4 RangeConstants(D3DX_PI, 1.0f/(2.0f*D3DX_PI),
                           2.0f*D3DX_PI, 0.0f);
```

These constants don't change, so you can set them here and forget about them. The only time this might not be true is if several shaders were being used and each shader reused constant registers for its own purposes. In this application, the scaling shader uses c5, and the sine shader uses c4, c6, and c7 and ignores c5, but in other cases, multiple shaders might access the same constants. Setting the constants once and forgetting about them saves a little bit of work in the rendering function, but make sure it doesn't bite you later if your application becomes more complex:

```
m_pD3DDevice->SetVertexShaderConstant(6, &RangeConstants, 1);
m_pD3DDevice->SetVertexShaderConstant(7, &Sine, 1);
return S_OK;
}


void CTechniqueApplication::Render()
{
```

You set up the transformation constants exactly the same way you have in previous chapters. The two shaders both know to use the first four constant registers for the transposed matrix. In this application, you don't change the matrix dynamically, so you can move this code into one of the initialization functions, saving a bit of work here. In this sample, this code was included for clarity:

```
D3DXMATRIX ShaderMatrix = m_WorldMatrix *
                          m_ViewMatrix *
                          m_ProjectionMatrix;

D3DXMatrixTranspose(&ShaderMatrix, &ShaderMatrix);

m_pD3DDevice->SetVertexShaderConstant(0, &ShaderMatrix, 4);
```

This constant contains the parameters of the wave equation and the color bias factor. The phase of the sine wave is set using the tick count, which gives you a simple way to ripple the model over time. Feel free to experiment with different values. Changing the way the phase is computed increases or decreases the rippling effect. Changing the wavelength produces wider rolling waves or tight little waves. Changing the amplitude affects the wave height. One thing that becomes apparent is that there is a relationship between the resolution of the model and the effects of the wave constants. If you decrease the wavelength, the jagged edges of the polygons become more obvious. If you create gentle rolling waves, a lower-resolution mesh might be adequate. Knowing how a shader affects your model can affect how you design the model and how you determine the polygon count of your model:

```
D3DXVECTOR4 Wave((float)GetTickCount() / 100.0f, 0.25f,
  3.0f, 0.1f);
m_pD3DDevice->SetVertexShaderConstant(4, &Wave, 1);
```

Here you set the scale factor used by the scaling shader. The fact that you use the sin() function has nothing to do with the sine shader; it's just an easy way to constrain the scale factor between the values of −3.0 and 3.0. The scale factor is applied to the X,Y,Z components of the position, but the w component is unaffected:

```
float ScaleFactor = 3.0f * sinf((float)GetTickCount() /
  1000.0f);
D3DXVECTOR4 Scale(ScaleFactor, ScaleFactor, ScaleFactor,
  1.0f);
m_pD3DDevice->SetVertexShaderConstant(5, &Scale, 1);
```

The following code sets the shader. To be optimal, this code should probably only set the shader when the user presses the F2 key. Also, you could further optimize by only setting the constants used by that particular shader. Again, the focus here is more on clarity, and these constants do not require a lot of processing anyway:

```
if (!m_WhichShader)
        m_pD3DDevice->SetVertexShader(m_SineShaderHandle);
else
        m_pD3DDevice->SetVertexShader(m_ScaleShaderHandle);
```

The final step is to actually draw the mesh. This code is based on the mesh cloning and rendering technique described in the previous chapter:

```
m_pD3DDevice->SetStreamSource(0, m_pMeshVertexBuffer,
                            sizeof(MESH_VERTEX));
m_pD3DDevice->SetIndices(m_pMeshIndexBuffer, 0);

m_pD3DDevice->DrawIndexedPrimitive(D3DPT_TRIANGLELIST, 0,
                            m_pMesh->GetNumVertices(), 0,
                            m_pMesh->GetNumFaces());
}
```

This is the first chapter that features two shaders in the same sample. Remember to delete both vertex shaders in both this function and PreTerminate:

```
BOOL CTechniqueApplication::PreReset()
{
        m_pD3DDevice->DeleteVertexShader(m_SineShaderHandle);
        m_pD3DDevice->DeleteVertexShader(m_ScaleShaderHandle);

        return TRUE;

}
```

This code toggles between shaders. Another way to do this is to actually set the shader and the related constants in this function instead of once per frame. This sample is set up for clarity, but the alternative is probably better because the shader and constants would only be set when they need to be. I leave it up to you to make the changes.

```
BOOL CTechniqueApplication::HandleMessage(MSG *pMessage)
{
        if (pMessage->message == WM_KEYDOWN &&
         pMessage->wParam == VK_F2)
                m_WhichShader = !m_WhichShader;

        return CHostApplication::HandleMessage(pMessage);

}
```

Ideas for Extensions to the Sample

There are several ways to expand these ideas, depending on what you need to do. Here are a couple ideas to try.

For the scaling shader, clone the mesh to a format that includes a texture coordinate. Then, for each face, encode a random value into the u coordinate. This value is not used for texturing. Instead it is used as another scaling factor in the shader. Now rewrite the shader to include this factor in the scaling calculations. If everything is set up correctly, the mesh "explodes" into its component triangles when it is rescaled. If you want to augment the effect, you can extend the shader to decrease the alpha value of the diffuse color as the scaling factor increases. Also, remember to enable alpha blending. This makes the object explode and gradually fade away.

For the sine wave shader, you can add a factor that decreases the effect of the sine wave as the value of x increases. You can do this either mathematically in the shader or per vertex with a damping factor added to the vertices. This can create the effect of ocean waves rolling to the shore. You can also add a factor that curls the tops of the tall parts of the waves to create a better ocean effect. This effect might require a higher-resolution mesh to really look good. Also, once I describe shader-based lighting techniques, you might want to augment this sample with the correct lighting effects. This involves calculating a new normal for each vertex in the shader. (Hint: It involves computing $\cos(x)$.)

In Conclusion...

As promised, this chapter is not a comprehensive examination of the myriad ways to manipulate a vertex's position, but I hope it gave you some ideas of how to write your own specific shaders. The value of many of these chapters is in exposing you to more shader code to get you comfortable with the structure, the instructions, and the ways to process data with a limited number of instructions. The implementation details of the sine approximation is one of those basic tools that you might not need at the moment but will probably come in handy at one point or another.

If this material is new to you, I highly recommend experimenting with this code before moving on. Experiment with different values for some of the constants. Implement cosine rather than sine. (Remember that it is difficult to distinguish between them unless you use a constant value for the phase.) Also, implement the extension ideas. If you can't quite get them, read on, get more comfortable with shaders, and then come back to this. These examples are not terribly exciting, but I selected them because they serve as good building blocks for cooler effects. If you get comfortable with these shaders, it will become easy to implement your own shaders with more interesting effects. Here are some points to remember:

- Scaling with normals is different from other scaling methods in that it can be used to create an inflation or explosion effect.
- Be careful with objects that have sharp edges. This is a good general rule for life, but in the context of this scaling shader, it could create meshes that break apart when you don't want them to.
- You can exploit the preceding point to create explosion effects if the vertices are set up properly. You can create models of spaceships that explode not with a general explosion graphic, but when the shader tells them to.

- The approximation of sine is just one example of how you can use a series to approximate a complex function. Some functions might require more instructions or more setup than others, but you can apply the approach to a wide range of problems.

- There are limitations to how many times a shader can access some registers with a single instruction. Sometimes this forces you to include more instructions.

- This sample application offers many opportunities for further optimization. The shaders themselves are optimized, but I point out all the places in the code that can be better. Once you understand the sample completely, it is worthwhile to restructure the code. The performance increase will probably not be substantial, but it will get you into the habit of looking for possible optimizations.

CHAPTER 19

BILLBOARDS AND VERTEX SHADERS

If you have played any sort of 3D game at all (and I'm guessing you have…), you have seen billboards. Back in the days of DOOM, most of the objects within a 3D world were actually billboards, sprites that were 2D rectangles aligned with the viewer's line of sight. For objects such as columns or bottles, these sprites would just rotate to face the player. For more complex objects, the actual image changed as the viewer walked around the object, but geometrically it was just a view-aligned rectangle. This works well for objects that are symmetric about at least one axis, such as objects based on cylinders and cones.

Games such as Quake and nearly every first-person game after are full 3D. Monsters and objects consist of real 3D geometry, and the video hardware is more than capable of handling this. However, some objects are still too complex to render in full 3D. That, or they have properties that lend themselves well to the kind of fake 3D you can accomplish with billboards. One such object is an explosion. Creating a real explosion with volumetric fire and smoke can be a costly operation, but you can render an explosion very effectively as a 2D animation that is aligned with the player's view. Another good object to create with a billboard is a tree. Trees are fairly complex objects, and rendering a forest of them can bring video hardware to its proverbial knees. One alternative is to create an image of a tree and render a forest of billboards.

Effects such as the ubiquitous lens-flare effect are rendered with billboards. One tangential note about lens flares is that a lens flare is a byproduct of the camera lens itself. You see lens flares all the time in movies, but you never see a lens flare with the naked eye. In a first-person shooter, a lens flare really doesn't make any sense, but it looks good because we are used to seeing lens flares in movies and TV, and a video game has a very similar form factor. This really has nothing to do with billboards, but given the ubiquity of lens flares, I thought it was an interesting aside. But I digress….

The Basic Idea behind Billboards

Imagine you have an arrow pointing straight out of the top of your head. Now imagine you have another arrow pointing straight out of your right ear. This setup makes it difficult to wear a hat but easy to conceptualize billboards. The arrow pointing up is your up vector; the arrow pointing out of your ear is your right vector. Any surface in the world is considered view aligned if its up and right vectors are parallel to your up and right vectors. This is shown in Figure 19.1.

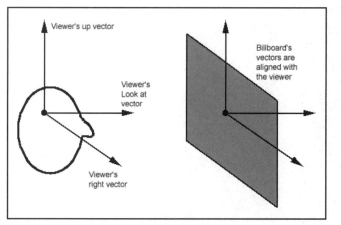

Figure 19.1

A 2D plane aligned with the viewer's direction vectors.

The idea behind billboards is that the surfaces remain view aligned. This means that the surfaces are always manipulated so that they are parallel to your right and up vectors. To put it another way, the surfaces are always perpendicular to your eye vector.

To create a billboard surface, you need to create a 2D rectangle and then align that rectangle with the viewer each time the viewer moves (in most cases, every frame). To do this, you will create a shader that dynamically creates the rectangle based on the right and up view vectors. You don't *need* shaders to implement billboards, but shaders allow you to implement a variety of other features on a per-vertex level without the need to directly manipulate the vertex data on the CPU. Besides, this part is about shaders, so you should be using them.

The Billboard Shader

The sample application for this chapter features a simple street lamp model with a glowing bulb represented with a billboard. The glow is a spherical effect, so it should be easy to create the effect shown in Figure 19.2.

To accomplish this effect, you're going to create a shader that dynamically creates a view-aligned billboard. This is conceptually easy to do on a per-primitive level, but vertex shaders work on individual vertices, so you need a way to encode each vertex with information about the rectangle it is part of. To do this, you will specify a format that includes vertex normals and then use that slot to encode other information. You will use the x component of the vertex normal to encode how far the billboard expands in the direction of the right vector and the y component of the normal to

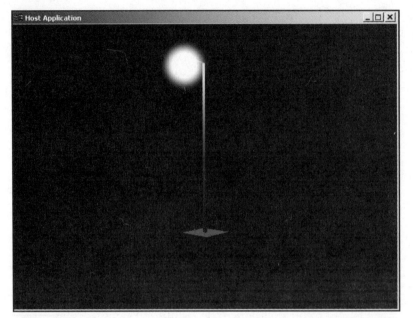

Figure 19.2

Billboard street lamp glow.

control the expansion along the up vector. The position of each vertex is the position of the billboard. All four positions are the same. As the shader processes each vertex, they move to the four corners of the view-aligned rectangle, and the billboard comes alive. That's the role of the vertex information, but you have several constants feeding the shader as well. Each of these pieces is shown in Figure 19.3.

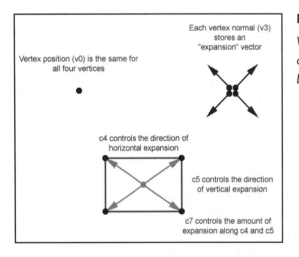

Figure 19.3

Vertex and constant data and the resulting billboard.

The gruesome imagery of arrows poking out of your head should have driven home the point that the billboard technique is based on knowing those two vectors. So before you look at the shader, you have to look at where those vectors come from. This is easy. For most operations, the D3DX library shields you from the intricacies of the transformation matrices, but it turns out that the information you need is stored in the view matrix in a very accessible way. The first three columns of the view matrix are the x-axis, the y-axis, and the z-axis of the viewer. In other words, the right, up, and look at vectors for the viewer are the first, second, and third columns respectively of the view matrix. This is easy to extract. In the shader code later, the shader assumes that the right vector is stored in $c4$ and the up vector is stored in $c5$.

Finally, another wrinkle in this particular example is that the glow of the street lamp originates from the center of a virtual bulb at the end of the lamppost, but the 2D nature of the billboard means that sometimes the end of the post obscures the glow. One way to solve this is to turn off depth testing, but that would mean the glow might obscure the post itself or that you might need to sort the mesh to figure out which objects should obscure others in each frame. This seems like a lot of work, and there is an easier way. To solve this problem, you can also extract the eye vector and store it in $c6$. In addition to aligning the billboard with the right and up vectors, you can also pull the billboard a little closer to the viewer along the eye vector. As long as you don't pull it too far, the glow will always be in front of the end of the post but behind the post itself (when it needs to be). Figure 19.4 shows several frames that demonstrate the point of this.

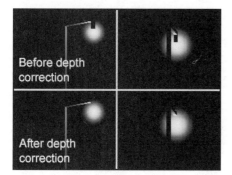

Before depth correction

After depth correction

Figure 19.4

Easy depth correction of the glow.

This is by no means a general point for all billboards, but it does enhance this particular effect. It also shows you how one extra instruction can improve the overall effect without much work. The final extraneous feature of the shader is that it uses a scaling factor in $c7$ to control how the billboard is scaled. This allows the application to dynamically set the size of many billboards by setting one constant. Now that I've defined all the inputs, look at the actual shader (\Media\Shaders\Billboard.vsh):

```
vs.1.1
```

This first instruction multiplies the expansion vector (stored in the vertex normal) by the scaling factor in c7. You use the final result, r2, to dynamically size and align the billboard:

```
mul r2, v3, c7
```

These two lines control the actual alignment and expansion. The first line moves the vertex position along the right vector and places the result in r1. The next line moves r1 along the up vector. The amount of expansion is controlled by the values in r2. The r1 register now contains the aligned and expanded billboard vertex. For a general billboard solution, this is all you need in terms of model space manipulation:

```
mad r1, r2.xxx, c4, v0
mad r1, r2.yyy, c5, r1
```

Figure 19.5 shows these three steps. The figure shows the effect on all three vertices even though the shader works on one vertex at a time.

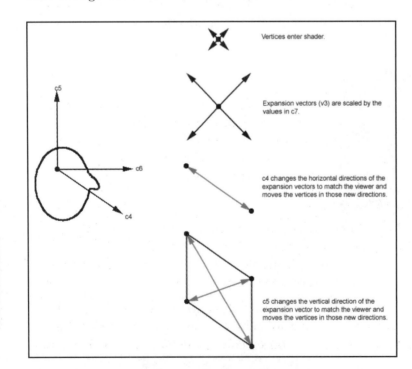

Figure 19.5

Rescaling the billboard with the shader.

Vertices enter shader.

Expansion vectors (v3) are scaled by the values in c7.

c4 changes the horizontal directions of the expansion vectors to match the viewer and moves the vertices in those new directions.

c5 changes the vertical direction of the expansion vector to match the viewer and moves the vertices in those new directions.

This instruction moves the vertex along the eye vector. This part isn't necessary for something like an explosion or a tree, but it is an easy way to control effects such as a glow or a flare:

```
add r1, -c6, r1
```

You may notice that this technique is not exactly correct because the billboard is following the eye vector and not the vector from the billboard to the eye, meaning that it is not exactly moving toward the viewer. However, this is a good approximation for very small offsets and it requires fewer shader instructions.

These final lines transform and emit the final vertex position along with the diffuse color (supplied in v5) and texture coordinates (supplied in v7).

```
dp4 oPos.x, r1, c0
dp4 oPos.y, r1, c1
dp4 oPos.z, r1, c2
dp4 oPos.w, r1, c3
mov oT0, v7
mov oD0, v5
```

This shader might be a little difficult to digest because there are so many interdependencies between the vertex data and the constants. The best way to fill in the missing details is probably to jump right into the application code.

The Implementation

The following is a discussion of the sample code. As is becoming the norm, I do not discuss the header file because there's nothing earth-shattering there. Also, I omitted functions that were discussed heavily in previous chapters. As always, the nitty-gritty details appear in the full source code on the CD. The following is a partial listing from \Code\Chapter19\TechniqueApplication.cpp:

```
#include "TechniqueApplication.h"
```

I have omitted the initialization functions from this listing. The one important point is that you are loading the flare texture from the flare.dds file in the media directory of the CD. This contains a simple gradient circle with an alpha channel. This is a very simple light glow, but it serves the purpose.

The billboard vertex format contains information about the vertex position, the diffuse color, and texture coordinates. It also includes a slot that is nominally for a vertex normal but actually stores information specific to the billboard shader. Also notice that the normal vector has only two elements. This isn't the usual usage, but the shader declaration takes this into account:

```
#define D3DFVF_BBVERTEX (D3DFVF_XYZ | D3DFVF_NORMAL |
                         D3DFVF_DIFFUSE | D3DFVF_TEX1)

struct BB_VERTEX
{
      float x, y, z;
      float RightDir, UpDir;
      DWORD d;
      float u, v;
};
HRESULT CTechniqueApplication::CreateBuffer()
{
```

The following vertex buffer contains the four vertices that make up the single textured quad that will be your billboard lamp glow. You need only four vertices because you have only one quad, but if you had several billboards you could place them all in the same vertex buffer. The way the shader works on a per-vertex level, you could correctly render many different billboards at the same time with the same inputs:

```
    if (FAILED(m_pD3DDevice->CreateVertexBuffer(
                                4 * sizeof(BB_VERTEX),
                                D3DUSAGE_WRITEONLY,
                                D3DFVF_BBVERTEX,
                                D3DPOOL_MANAGED,
                                &m_pVertexBuffer)))
        return E_FAIL;

    BB_VERTEX* pVertices = NULL;
    m_pVertexBuffer->Lock(0, 4 * sizeof(BB_VERTEX),
      (BYTE**)&pVertices, 0);

    memset(pVertices, 0, 4 * sizeof(BB_VERTEX));
```

You set the diffuse color to full white. One easy way to recolor the lamp glow is to change the vertex colors. You can also create fading effects by setting different alpha values for different vertices:

```
    pVertices[0].d = pVertices[1].d =
                    pVertices[2].d = pVertices[3].d = 0xFFFFFFFF;
```

You set each vertex to the same base position. In this case, the position is below the end of the lamp holder. These values are based on the model for the lamppost, which was loaded as a mesh in code not shown here:

```
pVertices[0].x = pVertices[1].x = pVertices[2].x =
pVertices[3].x = 9.0f;
pVertices[0].y = pVertices[1].y =
                   pVertices[2].y = pVertices[3].y = 47.0f;
pVertices[0].z = pVertices[1].z = pVertices[2].z =
pVertices[3].z = 0.0f;
```

This is basic texture mapping. The four corners of the texture are mapped to the four corners of the quad. But the vertex position is the same for all four vertices, so which vertices are in which corner? This question is answered with the data in your vertex normal:

```
pVertices[0].u = pVertices[1].u = 0.0f;
pVertices[2].u = pVertices[3].u = 1.0f;
pVertices[0].v = pVertices[2].v = 1.0f;
pVertices[1].v = pVertices[3].v = 0.0f;
```

Each vertex has the same position, but different factors influence how they move along the up and right view vectors. Once the vertices are moved in the shader, the first vertex is located in the upper left, the second is located in the lower left, and so on. These factors determine how the texture coordinates were set.

You also have opportunities for more effects here. In this example, the billboard expands evenly as a square, but it can expand as a trapezoid or any other four-sided shape. This system allows many possibilities within the same vertex shader:

```
pVertices[0].RightDir = -1.0f; pVertices[0].UpDir =  1.0f;
pVertices[1].RightDir = -1.0f; pVertices[1].UpDir = -1.0f;
pVertices[2].RightDir =  1.0f; pVertices[2].UpDir =  1.0f;
pVertices[3].RightDir =  1.0f; pVertices[3].UpDir = -1.0f;
m_pVertexBuffer->Unlock();

    return S_OK;
}


HRESULT CTechniqueApplication::CreateShader()
{
```

The shader declaration determines the input format of the vertices. One thing to notice here is that the normal vector is declared as a two-component vector. In this specific case, the texture coordinates are closely related to the expansion vectors, so perhaps you could have rewritten the shader to use one input for two purposes? Perhaps, but this way is more flexible and much clearer:

```
DWORD Declaration[] =
{
        D3DVSD_STREAM(0),
        D3DVSD_REG(D3DVSDE_POSITION,  D3DVSDT_FLOAT3),
        D3DVSD_REG(D3DVSDE_NORMAL,    D3DVSDT_FLOAT2),
        D3DVSD_REG(D3DVSDE_DIFFUSE,   D3DVSDT_D3DCOLOR),
        D3DVSD_REG(D3DVSDE_TEXCOORD0, D3DVSDT_FLOAT2),
        D3DVSD_END()
};

ID3DXBuffer* pShaderBuffer;
ID3DXBuffer* pShaderErrors;

if (FAILED(D3DXAssembleShaderFromFile(
                    "..\\media\\Shaders\\Billboard.vsh",
                    0, NULL, &pShaderBuffer, &pShaderErrors)))
        return E_FAIL;

if (FAILED(m_pD3DDevice->CreateVertexShader(Declaration,
                (DWORD *)pShaderBuffer->GetBufferPointer(),
                &m_BillboardShaderHandle, 0)))
        return E_FAIL;

pShaderBuffer->Release();

return S_OK;
}

void CTechniqueApplication::SetupDevice()
{
    RECT WindowRect;
    GetClientRect(m_hWnd, &WindowRect);
    D3DXMatrixPerspectiveFovLH(&m_ProjectionMatrix,
```

```
                    D3DX_PI / 4,
                    (float)(WindowRect.right - WindowRect.left) /
                    (float)(WindowRect.bottom - WindowRect.top),
                            1.0f, 1000.0f);
    m_pD3DDevice->SetTransform(D3DTS_PROJECTION,
     &m_ProjectionMatrix);
```

Many of the shader examples don't call SetTransform because the matrices are passed to the shader via constants. In this example, you rely on the fixed function pipeline to render the lit lamppost:

```
    D3DXMatrixIdentity(&m_WorldMatrix);
    m_pD3DDevice->SetTransform(D3DTS_WORLD, &m_WorldMatrix);
```

The basic device setup is the same, but you have also created a point light that is located at the same position as the lamp glow. This light completes the lamp illusion by correctly lighting the model of the lamppost. Notice that you set this light once and then ignore it. However, the lamp glow in this sample pulses. One exercise to consider is to rework the lighting a little so that the attenuation and range of the point light are synchronized with the pulsing of the lamp glow. This should be an easy thing to change, and I leave it to you to play around with:

> **TIP**
>
> In this particular sample, alpha testing doesn't really have an impact on the overall effect, but if you were creating a forest of trees, you'd want to alpha test so that trees were not obscured by the transparent geometry of closer trees that were rendered first. This is one of the points from Chapter 14, where you saw that alpha testing helps ensure that fully transparent geometry really is transparent.

```
    D3DLIGHT8 PointLight;
    ZeroMemory(&PointLight, sizeof(D3DLIGHT8));
    PointLight.Type          = D3DLIGHT_POINT;
    PointLight.Diffuse.r     = PointLight.Diffuse.g =
                               PointLight.Diffuse.b = 1.0f;
    PointLight.Position      = D3DXVECTOR3(9.0f, 48.0f, 0.0f);
    PointLight.Range         = 50.0f;
    PointLight.Attenuation1  = 0.25f;

    m_pD3DDevice->SetRenderState(D3DRS_LIGHTING, TRUE);
    m_pD3DDevice->SetRenderState(D3DRS_AMBIENT, 0x00222222);
```

```
              m_pD3DDevice->SetLight(0, &PointLight);
              m_pD3DDevice->LightEnable(0, TRUE);
```

To achieve the glow effect, you must enable alpha blending. You also enable alpha testing:

```
              m_pD3DDevice->SetRenderState(D3DRS_CULLMODE, D3DCULL_NONE);
              m_pD3DDevice->SetRenderState(D3DRS_SRCBLEND,
              D3DBLEND_SRCALPHA);
              m_pD3DDevice->SetRenderState(D3DRS_DESTBLEND,
              D3DBLEND_INVSRCALPHA);
              m_pD3DDevice->SetRenderState(D3DRS_ALPHAREF, 0x00000000);
              m_pD3DDevice->SetRenderState(D3DRS_ALPHAFUNC, D3DCMP_GREATER);
}
void CTechniqueApplication::Render()
{
```

This rotates the viewer around the lamppost. Again, you set the transform so that the mesh renders properly. If you'd like to see the billboard from other angles, change this code:

```
              float Time = (float)GetTickCount() / 1000.0f;

              D3DXMatrixLookAtLH(&m_ViewMatrix,
                      &D3DXVECTOR3(-100.0f * sin(Time),
                       20.0f, -100.0f * cos(Time)),
                      &D3DXVECTOR3(0.0f, 20.0f, 0.0f),
                      &D3DXVECTOR3(0.0f, 1.0f, 0.0f));
              m_pD3DDevice->SetTransform(D3DTS_VIEW, &m_ViewMatrix);
```

The lamppost mesh only has one subset and one material. The DrawSubset function also handles setting the vertex shader for the mesh, so you don't need to do this explicitly, but you do need to make sure you set the vertex shader back to the billboard shader when you render the lamp glow:

```
              m_pD3DDevice->SetMaterial(&m_pMeshMaterials[0]);
              m_pMesh->DrawSubset(0);
```

You extract the three view vectors and normalize them. Other billboarding samples retrieve the view matrix by calling GetTransform, but you can directly access your view matrix member variable:

```
              D3DXVECTOR4 Right;
              D3DXVECTOR4 Up;
```

```
D3DXVECTOR4 Eye;
D3DXVec4Normalize(&Right, &D3DXVECTOR4(m_ViewMatrix._11,
                                       m_ViewMatrix._21,
                                       m_ViewMatrix._31,
                                       0.0f));

D3DXVec4Normalize(&Up,    &D3DXVECTOR4(m_ViewMatrix._12,
                                       m_ViewMatrix._22,
                                       m_ViewMatrix._32,
                                       0.0f));

D3DXVec4Normalize(&Eye,   &D3DXVECTOR4(m_ViewMatrix._13,
                                       m_ViewMatrix._23,
                                       m_ViewMatrix._33,
                                       0.0f));
```

Here you set the scale factor that determines the size of the glow. This sample pulses the glow over time to demonstrate the effect, but there can be more uses for this feature. If you want to synchronize the lighting, you change the point light parameters as this value changes:

```
float Pulse = 2.0f * (sin(Time * 2.0f) + 1.0f) + 4.0f;
D3DXVECTOR4 ScaleFactors(Pulse, Pulse, 1.0f, 0.0f);
```

Set the four constants. These change every frame, so they must be reset every frame:

```
m_pD3DDevice->SetVertexShaderConstant(4,  &Right,        1);
m_pD3DDevice->SetVertexShaderConstant(5,  &Up,           1);
m_pD3DDevice->SetVertexShaderConstant(6,  &Eye,          1);
m_pD3DDevice->SetVertexShaderConstant(7,  &ScaleFactors, 1);
D3DXMATRIX ShaderMatrix = m_WorldMatrix *
                          m_ViewMatrix *
                          m_ProjectionMatrix;
```

Set the basic transformation matrix in the usual constants:

```
D3DXMatrixTranspose(&ShaderMatrix, &ShaderMatrix
m_pD3DDevice->SetVertexShaderConstant(0, &ShaderMatrix, 4);
```

You have to make sure to set the shader because it was changed when the mesh was rendered:

```
m_pD3DDevice->SetVertexShader(m_BillboardShaderHandle);
```

Before the billboard is rendered, set the texture and the alpha blending modes. After it is rendered, set the states back to normal so that they don't affect the mesh:

```
m_pD3DDevice->SetTexture(0, m_pLightTexture);
m_pD3DDevice->SetRenderState(D3DRS_ALPHABLENDENABLE, TRUE);
m_pD3DDevice->SetRenderState(D3DRS_ALPHATESTENABLE, TRUE);
m_pD3DDevice->SetStreamSource(0, m_pVertexBuffer,
 sizeof(BB_VERTEX));
m_pD3DDevice->DrawPrimitive(D3DPT_TRIANGLESTRIP, 0, 2);

m_pD3DDevice->SetTexture(0, NULL);
m_pD3DDevice->SetRenderState(D3DRS_ALPHABLENDENABLE, FALSE);
m_pD3DDevice->SetRenderState(D3DRS_ALPHATESTENABLE, FALSE);
}
```

Other Billboard Ideas

Billboards are useful for a wide variety of effects. After you understand the sample, add several more instances of the billboard to the scene. You can even create a row of street lamps with their own glowing lights. Once that is working, switch gears and render a forest with several tree billboards. You'll probably want to turn off the pulsating feature.

Also, experiment with the different parameters that control how the vertices are moved along the view vectors. For instance, instead of a glowing orb, you can set things up so that the street lamp casts a cone of light downward. To do this, you can have the two top vertices stay in the original position and make the other two move downward and sideways to produce the cone. If you try this, remember that this probably looks good from street level, but if you allow the viewer to look at the lamp from above, the effect is ruined pretty quickly.

Another easy effect to try is an explosion. Place several frames of an explosion animation in a single texture. In the shader code, change the texture coordinates based on some constant set by the application. This creates an animated, billboard explosion. If you created the exploding mesh in the previous chapter, mix the two effects. You might have to add something to account for depth testing as you did for the street lamp.

In Conclusion...

Almost all 3D games have some sort of billboard effect. Although billboards don't require shaders, shaders do give you a lot of control over the vertices without requiring any work on the CPU and without the overhead of vertex buffer locking. Implementing this technique in a shader also allows you to experiment with the technique without necessarily affecting the code of the application, which can be helpful if multiple people are working on the project.

Besides illustrating the basics of billboards, this technique is the first technique encoding nonstandard data in a vertex buffer. In the next chapter, you'll look at this idea more closely, but it's worth stressing here. All the vertices had the same position, something you don't normally see. The real position information was stored in the vertex normal slot, which wasn't really used until the shader worked its magic. The point here and in the next chapter is that you can make many effects possible by thinking out of the box. With shaders, you can use any data for anything. I'm getting a little ahead of myself. You'll see more in the next chapter, but I never let you leave a chapter without some review:

- Billboards provide a method for rendering very complex objects with a minimum of geometry.

- Billboards work best on objects that don't change appearance too much as the viewer changes the view angle around a given axis.

- Billboards are aligned with the viewer's up and right vectors. For simple quads, you can build the quad based on those vectors. You do this with a shader and a special vertex format.

- You can extract the individual view vectors from the view matrix. The first three columns of the matrix are the right, up, and eye vectors, respectively.

- The shader provides many opportunities for adding effects, such as dynamically scaling the color or size of the billboard.

- This sample added a depth-correction component to the billboard shader. This is not necessary for all billboards, but it might be a useful technique for any situation where 3D objects overlap with the 2D billboard in a way that ruins the effect.

- If you choose to add more billboards to this application, remember that you can place all of the billboards in the same vertex buffer, although you probably want to render them as one big (indexed) triangle list rather than several triangle strips.

- As usual, take time to experiment with this code before moving on.

CHAPTER 20

WORKING OUTSIDE OF CARTESIAN COORDINATES

I am including this shader technique because it drives home the point that data going into vertex shaders can be loosely typed. This means that vertex shaders let you think "out of the box" and come up with things that might be extremely useful. In this chapter, I demonstrate the following:

- The differences between coordinate systems and what they are good for.
- How to manipulate data in other coordinate systems.
- How to convert from one coordinate system to another in a vertex shader.
- Possible uses for this and similar techniques.

Before you get into any of this, perhaps I should explain the title.

Cartesian and Other Coordinate Systems

In every other chapter in this book, locations within 3D space are defined with the coordinates X, Y, and Z. This system of defining coordinates is called a Cartesian coordinate system, and it is the most common coordinate system in 3D graphics. Defining a point or vector with three coordinates is useful for general 3D tasks, but other coordinate systems are good for more specialized tasks.

One common 2D alternative is the polar coordinate system. As you can see in Figure 20.1, polar coordinates define a point on a 2D plane as an angle and a radius.

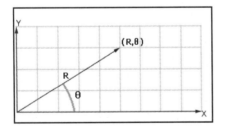

Figure 20.1

Polar coordinates.

Polar coordinates can be useful for defining objects that are circular in nature or for defining the relationship between two objects. For example, if you are flying a jet fighter, it might be more useful to know that the enemy is 45 degrees to your left and one kilometer away than to know his position in Cartesian coordinates.

Mapping between polar coordinates and Cartesian coordinates is easy with some simple trigonometry:

x = r*cos(θ)

y = r*sin(θ)

Why "Cartesian"?

Cartesian coordinates are named after Rene Descartes. Descartes is known for many things, but one of the most famous is his quote, "I think, therefore I am."

Polar coordinates, on the other hand, are not named for anyone in particular, so right now someone out there probably feels very cheated. If I could credit that person with inventing polar coordinates, I would. But, to paraphrase Descartes, it's the thought that counts.

Polar coordinates can be extended to three dimensions in a couple of different ways. You can describe a 3D point in terms of cylindrical or spherical coordinates, as shown in Figure 20.2.

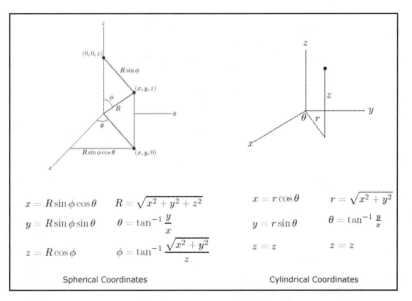

Figure 20.2

Cylindrical and spherical coordinates.

$$x = R\sin\phi\cos\theta \qquad R = \sqrt{x^2 + y^2 + z^2}$$

$$y = R\sin\phi\sin\theta \qquad \theta = \tan^{-1}\frac{y}{x}$$

$$z = R\cos\phi \qquad \phi = \tan^{-1}\frac{\sqrt{x^2 + y^2}}{z}$$

Spherical Coordinates

$$x = r\cos\theta \qquad r = \sqrt{x^2 + y^2}$$

$$y = r\sin\theta \qquad \theta = \tan^{-1}\frac{y}{x}$$

$$z = z \qquad z = z$$

Cylindrical Coordinates

Cylindrical coordinates are more straightforward. They add a height parameter that is exactly the same as the Y value in Cartesian coordinates. Spherical coordinates are a little more involved. Polar coordinates are specified on a plane. The second angular value given in spherical coordinates is the angle from that plane. In the previous example involving a jet fighter, what you really want to know is that the enemy is 45 degrees to your left, 10 degrees above you, and one kilometer away. Oh, and by the way, he just fired a missile. Use the following equations to map between spherical and Cartesian coordinates:

$$x = r*\cos(\theta)$$
$$y = r*\sin(\theta)$$
$$z = r*\cos(\emptyset)$$

There are many other coordinate systems available, but most are not that interesting for graphics applications. Spherical and cylindrical coordinates might not be that interesting either, but they might be useful for some approaches that are more conducive to a representation that includes distance and angles. For example, a model of a helix or spring may be easier to represent as a function of heights and angles rather than X, Y, and Z. Also, the deformation of a sphere might involve computing a new radius as a function of the two angular values. At the end of this chapter, I go into some more scenarios where this might be useful.

Mapping between Coordinate Systems in a Vertex Shader

The shader for this chapter takes a vertex position as input, but that position register does not contain the X,Y,Z coordinates of the point. Instead, it contains cylindrical coordinates in the form of Angle, Radius, and Height. The shader then manipulates these values instead of X,Y,Z values to create a twisting effect. For the purposes of demonstration, I keep the manipulation pretty simple, but the point is that you can easily change the cylindrical coordinates within the shader and then transform them to Cartesian coordinates for final output. Of course, the translation cost is relatively high, but the cost would have been higher if I had transformed from Cartesian to cylindrical, done the manipulation, and then transformed back.

All this is moot if this isn't the type of manipulation you're looking for, but it might be useful for some interesting effects. Most games feature rectangular shapes such as buildings and crates. In the past, rounded organic shapes were just not possible because they required more rendering power, but that rule is changing. I'm imagining possibilities for games that feature more rounded shapes. These shapes and the algorithms that deform them might make more sense in a different coordinate system. Many twisting or squishing effects would be easy to accomplish in cylindrical or spherical coordinates.

The following is the code from NonCartesian.vsh, the shader that handles cylindrical coordinates. The assumed input is the Angle, Radius, and Height data stored in v0 and the diffuse color stored in v5:

```
vs.1.1
```

The first thing the shader does is scale the angle by the value found in c6.x. This changes the angle and produces a twisting effect. A slightly more complex effect could scale the angle as a function of the height or radius. As always, I encourage you to play with these shaders once you understand what they do. You can easily create some interesting effects:

```
mul r1.x, v0.x, c6.x
```

These next four lines compute the first four terms of the sine approximation. If you haven't read the previous chapter, do so now for a full explanation of what's going on here. I don't bother constraining the angle value to the range of –pi to pi. This is because that was handled when the vertex buffer was initially filled with the angle values. You'll see how that was done when you look at the actual application code. In these four lines, the square of the angle value is placed in r2.x, and that value is used as a base to compute the odd powers used in the series:

```
mul r2.x, r1.x, r1.x
mul r1.y, r2.x, r1.x
mul r1.z, r1.y, r2.x
mul r1.w, r1.y, r2.x
```

These next four lines compute the cosine terms. The first term (1.0) is retrieved from c5, and the rest of the terms are even powers of the angle. The value in r2.x comes in handy again:

```
mov r3.x, c5.x
mov r3.y, r2.x
mul r3.z, r2.x, r2.x
mul r3.w, r2.x, r3.z
```

Here I compute the actual value for the sine of the new angle value using the values stored in c4. When this is done, r0.x contains the sine of the angle:

```
mul r1, r1, c4
dp4 r0.x, r1, c5.x
```

Now the cosine is computed and the value is stored in r0.y:

```
mul r3, r3, c5
dp4 r0.y, r3, c5.x
```

Now the radius value is scaled. Again, a more complex scaling function would probably yield more interesting results. In the end, r3.x contains the scaled radius:

```
mul r3.x, v0.y, c6.y
```

Everything is ready to compute the actual Cartesian values. The real X value is the new radius multiplied by the cosine of the new angle. The Y value is the height value multiplied by the height scaler (c6.z). The Z value is the radius multiplied by the sine of the angle. Perhaps a clever way to save an instruction or two would have been to multiply the sine and cosine constants by the radius scaler. That would have saved a couple of instructions here but might not have been a good general solution. In any case, it's something to think about. The final step is to load the w component with the w component stored in the input register:

```
mul r4.x, r3.x, r0.y
mul r4.y, v0.z, c6.z
mul r4.z, r3.x, r0.x
mov r4.w, v0.w
```

Now that the values are in Cartesian coordinates, the shader transforms them for final output to the rest of the pipeline:

```
dp4 oPos.x, r4, c0
dp4 oPos.y, r4, c1
dp4 oPos.z, r4, c2
dp4 oPos.w, r4, c3
```

This shader simply passes the color to the output register. The color could have been a function of the angle, radius, or anything else:

```
mov oD0, v5
```

That's the shader. It's pretty simple. Figure 20.3 shows the procedure graphically. The code is actually quite modular. There is a stage that performs transformations to cylindrical coordinates, one that converts coordinate systems, and one that does any necessary Cartesian processing. You can replace the transformation stages with different code to yield other effects.

I used cylindrical coordinates because they demonstrate the concepts without too much trouble, but you could use spherical coordinates in the same way with the addition of another Taylor series computation.

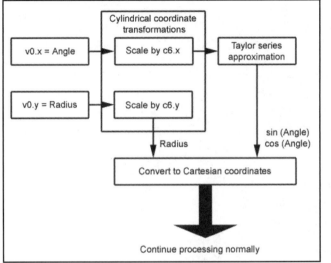

Figure 20.3

The components of the shader.

What about Lighting and Shading?

One notable issue with this shader is the absence of a vertex normal, which is necessary for lighting calculations. The computation of the normals depends on how you manipulate the position. For instance, this shader does not require normals to be recomputed, but a shader that changes radii based on height might need to recompute the vertex normal to produce the correct lighting results. Keep in mind that you could encode a normal in cylindrical coordinates with two values (Angle and Height) because the radius value should always be 1. This can create opportunities for less data transfer and fewer instructions. Once the normals are computed, I'd compute the lighting equations in the more familiar Cartesian space. On the subject of normals, remember that these types of coordinate systems are not limited to position manipulation. Perhaps lighting models or texturing models would benefit from this thinking.

The Application Code

Figure 20.4 shows several frames of the application in action. The model twists and scales over time, creating a different effect that you usually see with other forms of manipulation.

The code for this chapter appears in the \Code\Chapter20 folder. Following the trend from the past couple of chapters, I only highlight code that is new and

Figure 20.4

The application in action.

interesting to the topic at hand. The complete code is on the CD. The header file doesn't specify anything new, so I jump right into Technique.cpp.

This is the vertex format and vertex structure. The format specifies a position, but it doesn't care what kind. The structure names the three members as `Angle`, `Radius`, and `Height`, but these can be in any order as long as you are consistent across the code and the shader. Also, remember that if you try to use this data in the fixed function pipeline, the cylindrical data will be meaningless and produce garbage on the screen:

```
#define D3DFVF_MESHVERTEX (D3DFVF_XYZ | D3DFVF_DIFFUSE)
struct MESH_VERTEX
{
    float Angle, Radius, Height;
    DWORD color;
};
```

The `CreateShaders` function creates the cylindrical shader and sets the constants for the cosine and sine approximations:

```
HRESULT CTechniqueApplication::CreateShaders()
{
```

Notice that the declaration still specifies a position in the usual way. This sets up the shader to expect three floating-point values in v0, but no rule says those values must be X,Y,Z coordinates. That's what I mean when I say that shader values can be loosely typed. The one difference is that you cannot mix and match shaders as easily as you can in some cases. For instance, as long as you are consistent with the declaration and the use of constants, you can sometime trade shaders in and out of applications and get very different (but correct) results just by loading a different shader file. In this case, if you load a shader that expects Cartesian coordinates, you get garbage. If you decide to experiment with vertex normals or texture coordinates, you have to add them to the declaration. Remember that you can probably specify a normal as a two-component vector, thus saving space:

```
DWORD Declaration[] =
{
        D3DVSD_STREAM(0),
        D3DVSD_REG(D3DVSDE_POSITION,D3DVSDT_FLOAT3),
        D3DVSD_REG(D3DVSDE_DIFFUSE, D3DVSDT_D3DCOLOR),
        D3DVSD_END()
};
```

The following lines create the shader in the usual way. Remember that I'm doing less error checking than you probably want to, especially if you are writing applications for a wide variety of users and hardware:

```
ID3DXBuffer* pShaderBuffer;
ID3DXBuffer* pShaderErrors;

if (FAILED(D3DXAssembleShaderFromFile
("..\\media\\shaders\\NonCartesian.vsh",
                                    0, NULL, &pShaderBuffer,
                                    &pShaderErrors)))
        return E_FAIL;

if (FAILED(m_pD3DDevice->CreateVertexShader(Declaration,
                (DWORD *)pShaderBuffer->GetBufferPointer(),
                            &m_CylindricalShader, 0)))
        return E_FAIL;

pShaderBuffer->Release();
```

These lines set the constants used to create the sine and cosine approximations, as described in the previous chapter. You can set these constants once because they are not going to change, but remember not to overwrite them with other constants. Also, remember that one possible optimization of this particular technique might be to scale these constants rather than scale the radius. If you want to save a couple of vertex shader instructions, you may want to try that. If you do, you must recompute and reset these constants every time the radius scaler changes:

```
D3DXVECTOR4 Sine  (1.0f, -1.0f/6.0f, 1.0f/120.0f,
                      -1.0f/5040.0f);
D3DXVECTOR4 Cosine(1.0f, -1.0f/2.0f, 1.0f/24.0f,
                      -1.0f/720.0f);


m_pD3DDevice->SetVertexShaderConstant(4, &Sine,   1);
m_pD3DDevice->SetVertexShaderConstant(5, &Cosine, 1);


return S_OK;
}
```

The ExtractBuffers function extracts the vertex and index buffers from the mesh object and reformats them to cylindrical coordinates. The following code snippet is not the complete listing for this function. Instead, I clipped out the pieces that were discussed in previous chapters so that I can focus on the new parts:

```
HRESULT CTechniqueApplication::ExtractBuffers()
{
```

The following code comes after the vertex buffer is locked and the diffuse color is set based on the material properties of each face. This loop steps through each vertex and converts the coordinates to the cylindrical equivalent. You might want to retain a copy of the model in the usual coordinate system and make a cylindrical version that is only used when the model needs to be warped in a certain way. If that's the case, then I suggest cloning the mesh and keeping two copies. You can also change the declaration to include a three-component set of texture coordinates and store the cylindrical coordinates in those coordinates. The next chapter demonstrates something like that. This method allows you to use a shader that expects Cartesian data in v0 and a shader that expects cylindrical data in v7 (for instance). The advantage to doing it this way is that you can store multiple copies of the data in the same buffer. The disadvantage is that you are carrying more data around in a fairly bloated buffer. The final alternative I mention is that you can specify different data types in different streams. This method can be useful if you have data such as texture coordinates and color data that is consistent despite the coordinate system of the position data. The vertex tweening sample in the DirectX

SDK shows how to feed a vertex shader with multiple streams. Having said all that, this implementation completely replaces the Cartesian data with cylindrical data:

```
for (long Vertex = 0;
     Vertex < m_pMesh->GetNumVertices();
     Vertex++)
{
```

The vertex structure names each member in cylindrical coordinates, but the data is not cylindrical yet. This might be confusing, but the mesh cloning code just places data in a given slot. It has no notion of the meaning of the names of those slots. This code pulls out the data so that it can be reformatted:

```
float TempX = pMeshVertices[Vertex].Angle;
float TempY = pMeshVertices[Vertex].Radius;
float TempZ = pMeshVertices[Vertex].Height;
```

Referring to Figure 20.1, the tangent of an angle is computed as the length of the opposite side of the triangle over the length of the adjacent side of the triangle. Therefore, you can find the angle by taking the arctangent of that ratio. In this case, that means taking the arctangent of Z over X:

```
float Angle = atan(TempZ / TempX);
```

Now that you know the angle, a little bit more trigonometry gives you the radial value. Normally, you find the length of the side of the triangle that is opposite to the angle by multiplying the radius by the sine of the angle. You can move things around to find the radius:

```
float Radius = TempZ / sin(Angle);
```

In the previous chapter, I outlined why you should constrain the value of the angle and how to do it in a shader. For this technique, you don't need to do it in a shader because you can do it here for a one-time cost. The trigonometric functions yield values in the range of 0 to 2pi radians. The following code changes that to the equivalent value in the range of –pi to pi:

```
if (Angle > D3DX_PI)
    Angle -= 2.0f * D3DX_PI;
```

Now that all the values are found, you set the vertex data. The structure names match the data they contain. It's important to remember the order of these values and stay consistent. It might be too easy to forget which value corresponds to v0.x in the shader. Remember that you can play around with the data, but you can also make things confusing for yourself or anyone who reads your code later. If you do use a technique like this, make sure you comment it fairly heavily, or there might be problems down the road:

```
            pMeshVertices[Vertex].Angle  = Angle;
            pMeshVertices[Vertex].Radius = Radius;
            pMeshVertices[Vertex].Height = TempY;
    }
```

The data is now ready to be used. Unlock everything and get ready to render:

```
        m_pMeshVertexBuffer->Unlock();
        m_pMeshIndexBuffer->Unlock();
        m_pMesh->UnlockAttributeBuffer();

        return S_OK;
}
```

The Render function does the actual drawing. It also sets the scaling parameters each frame. In this simple example, it's less than optimal to set the shader and the buffers each time, but I've kept them here to keep things clear. Remember that this application code is not at all optimized:

```
void CTechniqueApplication::Render()
{
```

I'm creating an arbitrary world matrix just to show that the warping is still compatible with the standard transformations. Otherwise, the following lines of code create the world matrix, concatenate the matrices, and feed them to the vertex shader in the normal way. Even though the vertices are not in Cartesian coordinates, the final transformations still are:

```
        D3DXMatrixRotationY(&m_WorldMatrix,
                            (float)GetTickCount() /1000.0f);

        D3DXMATRIX ShaderMatrix = m_WorldMatrix *
                                  m_ViewMatrix *
                                  m_ProjectionMatrix;

        D3DXMatrixTranspose(&ShaderMatrix, &ShaderMatrix);
        m_pD3DDevice->SetVertexShaderConstant(0, &ShaderMatrix, 4);
```

The following values are just simple scaling parameters set to demonstrate how you can use the cylindrical coordinates. As usual, I encourage you to experiment with these values to see how they affect the model. You might also want to implement a more complex manipulator in the shader where the scaling of one attribute is some function of the others. If you do that, you might want to set a shader constant with the constants for that function and implement the function in the shader. This is essentially what the Taylor series part of the shader does. One thing to remember as you experiment with different values is that you should not let the angle fall outside of the range from −pi to pi unless you want to implement the constraints shown in the shader from the last chapter. For example, the angle scaler in the next piece of code does not produce values outside of that range because the sine function is constrained from −1 to 1. However, other scaling functions or functions of other variables could easily produce "bad" angles. This is not a showstopper at all, but it is something to be aware of.

The radius and height scalers have no such problems, although remember that negative angle, radius, or height values could cause the model to collapse and invert on itself. This might be exactly what you are looking for. (Imagine a monster that does this rather than turn around to get you.) In fact, the sample code does this if you watch carefully. If this is not the effect you want, you might need to limit the scaling values to positive values:

```
float AngleScaler  = sin((float)GetTickCount() / 1000.0f);
float RadiusScaler = 2.0f * fabs(sin((float)GetTickCount() /
  1000.0f));
float HeightScaler = 1.0f;
D3DXVECTOR4 Manipulators(AngleScaler, RadiusScaler,
                         HeightScaler, 0.0f);
m_pD3DDevice->SetVertexShaderConstant(6, &Manipulators, 1);
```

Once all of the scaling values are set, the model renders in the usual way. Figure 20.5 shows several frames of where the angle is being scaled. Figure 20.6 shows the radius being scaled. Scaling the radius scales only X and Z because of the nature of cylindrical coordinates. If you are dealing with spherical coordinates, scaling the radius produces results that are very similar to normal Cartesian scaling. If you are comfortable with this code, I suggest implementing a spherical version of this technique:

```
m_pD3DDevice->SetVertexShader(m_CylindricalShader);

m_pD3DDevice->SetStreamSource(0, m_pMeshVertexBuffer,
                              sizeof(MESH_VERTEX));
m_pD3DDevice->SetIndices(m_pMeshIndexBuffer, 0);

m_pD3DDevice->DrawIndexedPrimitive(D3DPT_TRIANGLELIST, 0,
                              m_pMesh->GetNumVertices(), 0,
                              m_pMesh->GetNumFaces());
}
```

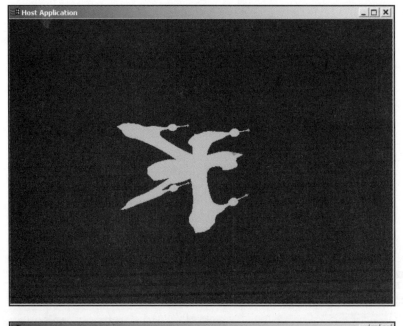

Figure 20.5

Scaling only the angle.

Figure 20.6

Scaling only the radius.

Those are the important parts of the code from this chapter. Remember that there is still code that loads the mesh file, clones it to the new format, and so on. The code snippets make use of variables that were defined or set in code not shown in this text. If you see anything confusing, refer to the complete code listing.

Applications of This Technique

I included this technique as a demonstration of how vertex shaders allow you to completely redefine how you deal with vertex data. My hope is that this will spark ideas that you may not have considered because you weren't thinking out of the box.

Some possible applications for this technique include various kinds of warping. Cylindrical coordinates are good for effects that involve twisting along an axis. One could imagine a cartoon character getting twisted up and then untwisting wildly. I'm also imagining effects such as an energy blot that corkscrews towards the target or a transporter beam that twists and undulates as it beams monsters down to the surface of a planet. Warping in spherical coordinates might be good for effects such as wobbling soap bubbles or other blobby organic effects. As higher polygon counts support shapes that are less rectangular, I can foresee the possible advantage to working in coordinate systems that are less rectangular.

Even if you don't buy that, it's probably a good idea to keep these ideas in the back of your mind. Although there are lots of clones out there, some games really shine when they break the mold. Vertex shaders have led to games that look like cartoons and games with motion and effects that were never really possible before. If you are intent on creating the next Quake clone, this technique will probably not help you, but maybe it will….

In Conclusion...

Almost all of the techniques in this book are techniques that I feel are useful to a wide range of people, either because they demonstrate a commonly desired effect (such as reflection) or because I'm trying to explain a difficult concept (such as Bezier patches). I'm guessing that most people will ignore this chapter because it doesn't answer a specific question or address a specific need, but I still added this chapter because I believe it demonstrates how you can change the way you deal with the hardware. The sample for this chapter was simple so that I could demonstrate the basic idea without getting bogged down in one particular algorithm, but this should still provide a good platform for experimentation. You might also want to compare this technique with some similar techniques found on nVidia's developer site. Sending data to the shader in cylindrical coordinates allows you to create very simple shaders that produce fairly interesting effects.

Here are some points to remember:

- Polar, cylindrical, and spherical coordinate systems all specify positions mainly in terms of angles and radii.

- Deformations in these spaces might be easier to accomplish than the equivalent deformations in Cartesian coordinates.

- Vertex shaders are very loosely typed. They care about the number of registers and the number of values sent to them, but they don't care about how you use them. It's up to you to be consistent.

- You can easily translate from Cartesian to these other coordinate systems and back using the sine and cosine approximations described in the previous chapter.

- If you're careful, you can avoid the vertex shader instructions used to constrain the range of the angle.

- Computing the vertex normals can be either very easy or very difficult depending on how the vertices are manipulated. The next chapter explains how to compute normals as the derivative of your position function.

- Remember that different coordinate systems have a different set of effects that may be good or bad, depending on what you need.

- With this or any other loosely typed technique, remember to comment your code well. Most people have expectations about how things work, and you are breaking those expectations. That's not a bad thing, but make sure you document what's going on.

CHAPTER 21

BEZIER PATCHES

The last couple of chapters have involved shaders that manipulate the position of the vertex according to some function, but each of these shaders has affected the geometry in limited ways. Some situations require a large number of vertices to be set according to some relatively complex function. The temptation is to process the vertices on the CPU where it's easy to implement complex functions. A better way is to use the CPU to define a coarse representation of the basic shape of the geometry and then let the GPU process the larger number of points. You can do this using Bezier patches. This chapter looks at many aspects of Bezier patches, including the following topics:

- The theory behind Bezier curves and patches.
- Computing the normals of a patch (with an extremely brief introduction to calculus).
- Implementing Bezier patches with a shader.
- Setting up patch data to send to a shader.
- Uses for patches in manipulation and level of detail operations.
- Patch representation for complex objects.

Everything in this chapter hinges on you understanding the complex subject of Bezier curves and patches, so bear with me as we delve into some pretty murky depths.

Lines and Curves and Patches, Oh...

Consider Figure 21.1, which is a screenshot from this chapter's sample application.

The original data for this model was a flat 2D plane of many triangles, yet the resulting surface is far more complex than what any of the previous techniques could have produced. The secret behind this technique is that the surface in Figure 21.1 was produced with a Bezier patch. Patches are 3D extensions of Bezier curves, so I start there, but keep the screenshot in mind as you read the following.

> **NOTE**
>
> Some texts use the letters u and or v to represent the range of the curve. I have chosen to use s and t to avoid confusion with the most common texture coordinates u and v. If you see textbooks that use other letters, know that the concepts are exactly the same. They are just using other symbols.

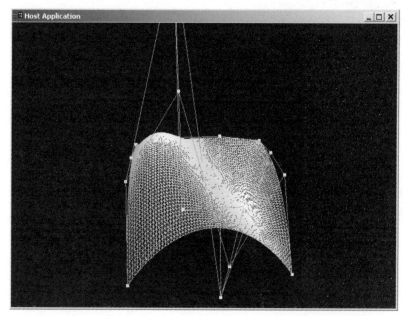

Bezier curves are generally defined as curves that can be described by a set of control points. In most cases, these curves are defined with four control points, as shown in Figure 21.2.

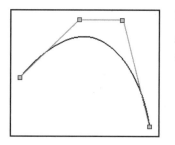

Figure 21.2

A Bezier curve defined with four control points.

These four control points define the curve with P0 and P3 defining the endpoints. If you think of an arbitrary variable s as ranging from 0 to 1 over the length of the curve, you can define the values of the curve as a function of s.

With control points P0-P3 and the range s, the equation for the curve becomes

$$Q(s) = \sum_{i=0}^{3} P_i b_i(s)$$

where $Q(s)$ is the position of a point along the curve and b is a basis function that describes the "weight" of each point in the calculation. For our purposes, the basis functions are the following Bernstein polynomials:

$$b_0 = (1 - s)^3$$
$$b_1 = 3s(1 - s)^2$$
$$b_2 = 3s^2(1 - s)$$
$$b_3 = s^3$$

Putting all this together, the long form of the values along the curve as a function of s is the following dreadful-looking function:

$$Q(s) = p_0(1 - s)^3 + p_1 3s(1 - s)^2 + p_2 3s^2(1 - s) + p_3 s^3$$

In graphical terms, the basis functions are shown in Figure 21.3. As you can see, P0 and P3 are the actual endpoints of the curve, but at every other point, the other control points have some contribution to the value of Q. I marked a couple of points of interest on Figure 21.3.

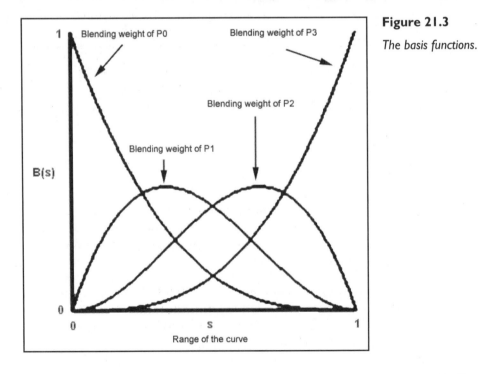

Figure 21.3

The basis functions.

The line at s = a shows where the first two control points have equal influence on the value of Q, and the line at s = b shows where the inner points have equal control and the outer points have equal (but far less) control. At this point, the easiest way to internalize the concepts might be to break out a sheet of paper and a pencil, plot four points, and plot a couple of points along the curve to see for yourself how they work. Take your time; I'll wait.

One of the nice things about these curves is that the math doesn't care how many points you actually plot along the curve. If you plot 10 points, you'll create a rough but accurate curve. If you plot one million points, you will have a very accurate curve, but you will be old and lonely. I revisit this point later when I talk about some level of detail considerations.

La Vie de Msr. Bezier

Bezier developed the idea of Bezier curves while working for Renault. At the time, curves given in engineering drawings were fairly arbitrary and not very consistent. Bezier developed these curves as a way to give a more rigorous definition to the curves in design drawings. This was especially useful when manufacturing CAD/CAM machines emerged. Incidentally, similar ideas were developed by James Ferguson and Paul de Casteljau, but both innovations were kept secret by their employers. Bezier was credited with the curves that now bear his name. Pierre Bezier passed away in 1999.

Extending these ideas to another dimension is a relatively simple matter of extending the four control points to a four-by-four control grid. If we use t to specify the range in the other dimension, the equation for values anywhere in the patch becomes

$$Q(s,t) = \sum_{i=0}^{3} \sum_{j=0}^{3} P_{i,j} b_i(s) b_j(t)$$

In this equation, the basis functions are the same, and all the underlying concepts are the same; I've just extended the ideas into another dimension. Again, if you'd like, plot out a couple points if it helps you internalize the concepts. I refrain from giving the equation in its long form.

You now have an equation that gives you the value of any point in the space of the patch based on the 16 control points within the patch. Soon I show you the shader that makes this possible, but first I have to address the method of deriving the surface normals that is necessary for lighting calculations.

Deriving Surface Normals with "Calculus"

I'm placing calculus in quotes because a full explanation of calculus is well outside the scope of this humble tome. If you already know calculus, you should understand the following ideas, but you'll also see that my explanation is far less than complete. If you have not already studied calculus, please take this quick and dirty explanation with a grain of salt.

There are two branches of calculus, but the one applicable here is differential calculus. If you think of every function as describing some curve on a graph, then you can use differential calculus to find the derivative of that function. The derivative is a new function that describes the slope of the curve at any given point. For the simplest case, consider the function shown in Figure 21.4.

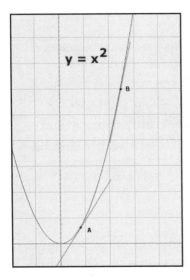

Figure 21.4

Changing slopes on a curve.

As you can see, the slope of the curve at point A is very different from the slope of the curve at point B. To approximate the slope at any given point, you could find the value of the function at point A and the value of the function at a very short distance away. The approximation then takes the form of the following equation:

$$f'(a) = \lim_{h \to 0} \frac{f(a + h) - f(a)}{h}$$

I don't delve into the exact mathematical proof of differential calculus, but the short version of the story is that you find the derivative by shrinking that interval to an infinitesimal value. Figure 21.5 revisits the graph from Figure 21.4. The second graph shows the derivative of the first function. As you can see, as X increases, the slope also increases. You can see this increase on the graph of the derivative.

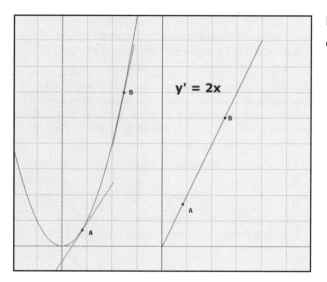

Figure 21.5

Graphing the derivative.

There are many rules for finding different kinds of derivatives, but in this chapter you only need to find the derivatives of the polynomials that define the Bezier patch. Derivatives of simple polynomials take the following form:

if $f(a) = ca^x$,   then

$$\frac{d}{dx} f(a) = f'(a) = xca^{x-1}$$

One thing to remember is that the derivative of a constant is zero. If you plot a constant function, there is no slope. Again, you might want to take a break and sketch out a few of these graphs on graph paper and get a feel for what's going on. Once you try it yourself, it will probably be much clearer. Using these rules, you can compute the following derivatives of the basis functions for a 2D Bezier curve. The derivatives for the other dimension of a 3D patch are analogous:

$$b'_0 = -3(1 - s)^2$$
$$b'_1 = 3 - 12s + 9s^2$$
$$b'_2 = 6s - 9s^2$$
$$b'_3 = 3s^2$$

Derivatives of Other Functions

Please remember that this is only the simplest explanation of how to find the derivative for a simple polynomial and that some functions might not adhere to this simple rule. I don't go into all the rules, but it might be worthwhile to mention the derivatives for sine and cosine. The derivatives for sin(x) and cos(x) are cos(x) and −sin(x), respectively. This becomes pretty apparent if you plot both curves and look at their slopes at various points. If you are interested, you can go back and use this information to compute the proper lighting values for the example from Chapter 18.

You are now very close to being able to compute the normals for a Bezier patch. The derivatives for the basis functions allow you to compute the slopes of the surface in both directions on the patch (s and t in this case). These are the surface tangents, not the normals. That's where the cross product comes in. In Chapter 2, I said that the cross product of two vectors yields the vector that was perpendicular to both. In this case, you want the vector that is perpendicular to the two surface tangents. You can now find the normal vector for any point on the surface of a Bezier patch with the following equation:

$$N(s,t) = \sum_{i=0}^{3}\sum_{j=0}^{3} P_{i,j} b'_i(s) b_j(t) \times \sum_{i=0}^{3}\sum_{j=0}^{3} P_{i,j} b_i(s) b'_j(t)$$

This is relatively difficult to illustrate on a 2D page, but consider the very simple case of a flat control grid producing a flat patch. The surface tangents would then be straight vectors lying on the surface of the plane, and the cross product of those two lines would be a vector pointing straight up from the plane, as shown in Figure 21.6.

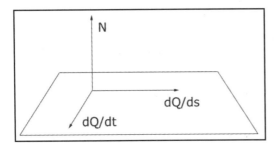

Figure 21.6

A very simple surface normal.

One thing to remember is that order matters when finding the cross product of two vectors. If you compute the cross product in the wrong order, the vector will point the opposite direction. This mistake is fairly easy to identify because your lights show up "backwards."

This all sounds like a lot of work, but it's not really that bad. In the next few pages, I show how you can set up the nasty math once and then control everything else with the control points.

Computing the Patch Values in a Shader

If you compare and contrast my version of this technique with a similar effect found on the nVidia site, you'll see a major difference in the way we handle the basis functions. The nVidia effect encodes the s and t positions in the vertices and then computes the basis functions at the beginning of the shader before applying the control points. My version computes the basis values once when the vertices are loaded and then performs the relatively simple task of multiplying and adding up the influences of all the control points. The tradeoff is that my shader has less computational overhead, but at a higher overall data cost. To be honest, I haven't tested both versions to see which is faster under equal conditions (the effect example handles lighting differently), but a determination of which way is better would have to account for the exact requirements of your project and where bottlenecks are found to occur. In any case, be aware that the tradeoff exists.

The following shader code expects v7 to contain the precomputed basis functions in the s direction and v8 to contain the functions for the t direction. The v9 and v10 input registers also contain the precomputed derivatives used to compute the vertex normal. Also, the positions of the 16 control points are stored in constants c10 through c25. I show you how that data is stored when I get to the application code. The full code appears in Bezier.vsh in the shaders directory:

```
vs.1.1
```

These first lines move the data from the input registers to temporary registers. This makes it easier to use the data because the shader allows better concurrent access to temporary registers than it does to the input registers:

```
mov r7, v7
mov r8, v8

mov r9, v9
mov r10, v10
```

This first chunk of code computes the influence of the S0T0 control point. This is the equivalent to P0 on the Bezier curve, but I name the control points by their s and t values because they are in two dimensions. The block of code multiplies the two precomputed basis functions together and then multiplies that by the position of S0T0 given in the constant c10. It then multiplies each of the precomputed derivatives with the position of the control point. In the case of the tangent vectors, you do not want to multiply the two values together because you must use the final tangent vectors to compute the surface normal. Throughout this shader, r0 is a temporary working variable, r1 contains the vertex position, r2 is the tangent vector in the s direction, and r3 is the tangent vector in the t direction:

> **TIP**
>
> You never want to use more shader instructions than you have to. In some cases, shader limitations will force you to. In this case, the shader cannot access multiple input registers in the same line, so I move the input values into temporary registers. This is one of the few places where you really need to move data without performing some other value added operation.

```
;S0T0 control point
mul r0.x, r7.x, r8.x
mul r1, c10, r0.x

mul r2, c10, r9.x
mul r3, c10, r10.x
```

This next block computes the influence of the S0T1 control point. It multiplies the appropriate basis values and then uses the mad instruction to multiply the control point value and add it to the position stored in r1. The same procedure is repeated for the tangent vectors, but again they are not multiplied together:

```
;S0T1 control point
mul r0.x, r7.x, r8.y
mad r1, c11, r0.x, r1

mad r2, r9.x,  c11, r2
mad r3, r10.y, c11, r3
```

I removed several lines of the shader from this listing because they basically repeat the same operation for each of the control points. You can find the full listing on the CD. At first glance, the lines of code are exactly the same, but remember that each of the four values of r7, r8, r9, and r10 contains separate precomputed basis values. It's extremely important to match the proper control point with the proper basis functions. For instance, S0T0 matched with r7.x and r8.x and now the final point S3T3 matches with r7.w and r8.w:

```
;S3T3 control point
mul r0.x, r7.w, r8.w
mad r1, c25, r0.x, r1

mad r2, r9.w,  c25, r2
mad r3, r10.w, c25, r3
```

The r1 register now contains the interpolated position of this vertex on the Bezier patch. In the application code, I loaded a mesh that was centered on the origin from –0.5 to 0.5, and then I added 0.5 to compute s and t values in the range of 0 to 1. Here, I subtract 0.5 again to undo that correction. This might not be needed for other implementations, but I wanted to add a complication into the mesh-loading process just to show how you might handle something. You could have just as easily derived the s and t values for each vertex in a different way and saved this instruction. I talk more about this when I get into the application code:

```
add r1, r1, c6
```

The following lines compute the cross product in a manner described in some of the nVidia documentation. Shaders provide native support for the dot product, but cross product requires two instructions and some clever swizzling. If you deconstruct these two lines, you can see that it does match the cross product shown in Chapter 2:

```
mul r6, r3.yzxw, r2.zxyw
mad r6, -r2.yzxw, r3.zxyw, r6
```

The r6 register now contains the normal vector. You must normalize it in the usual way before using it in the lighting instructions:

```
dp3 r5.w, r6, r6
rsq r5.w, r5.w
mul r6, r6, r5.w
```

For the sake of simplicity, I am computing only simple diffuse lighting by finding the dot product of the normal and the light vector. There is no reason you couldn't add more, but a full description of lighting in vertex shaders does not appear until Chapter 24:

```
dp3 oD0, r6, -c5
```

The final four lines transform the new vertex position to clip space. You can use the control grid to transform the positions of each point, but the world matrix is still good for positioning, rotating, or scaling the actual mesh:

```
dp4 oPos.x, r1, c0
dp4 oPos.y, r1, c1
dp4 oPos.z, r1, c2
dp4 oPos.w, r1, c3
```

That's the shader (or at least part of it), but the picture isn't really complete until you take a look at the application code. Next, I show you how the application prepares the vertex data, computes the control points, and feeds the shader.

The Bezier Application

This section contains the abridged code for the Bezier application. The application loads the patch vertices from a mesh in a file and creates another set of vertices to use when displaying the control grid. In the render loop, the application sets the 16 control points and feeds them to the shader through a set of 16 constants. It then renders the mesh, and the vertex shader computes the actual vertex positions. See the source code for the complete code listing.

The following structure defines the vertex format for the patch vertices. The shader doesn't actually use the three position values, but I included them here because sometimes you might want to display the original data either to debug or to simply render the existing model. In the following sample, the mesh is a plane of many vertices, but I can also imagine scenarios when you might want to use the control grid to warp a 3D model instead of a simple plane. For instance, you might want to compute the influence of the control points, but instead of setting the position, you could add the interpolated position to the real coordinates. This would allow you to warp a real 3D object using the control grid and the original position, but generating the normals could be a bit tricky. Finally, including the position is convenient when cloning the mesh because the cloning functions have a place to put the position data. For this sample, I could have restructured the vertex format and saved the three unused floats. Also, as I mentioned earlier, I could have encoded the s and t values into the vertex structure and generated the basis values in the shader. In the best case, the vertex structure could have been as small as two floats. This would be nearly one-eighth of amount of data (if the following format were more efficient), but it would require in the neighborhood of 50 percent more shader instructions. Again, there are advantages and disadvantages to either approach. Chances are that the other approach is faster on very fast hardware, but it depends on your exact needs. In any case, be aware that at least two different approaches both use the same underlying concepts:

```
struct BEZIER_VERTEX
{
        float x, y, z;
        float Bs0, Bs1, Bs2, Bs3;
        float Bt0, Bt1, Bt2, Bt3;
        float dBs0, dBs1, dBs2, dBs3;
        float dBt0, dBt1, dBt2, dBt3;
};
```

The following declaration defines the vertex structure for the vertex shader. The unused position information is stored in v0, and the precomputed basis values for both position and tangent vectors are stored as four values in the first four texture coordinate registers. This doesn't mean that you must use these values as texture coordinates; it just defines which registers contain the values:

```
DWORD BezierDeclaration[] =
{
        D3DVSD_STREAM(0),
        D3DVSD_REG(D3DVSDE_POSITION, D3DVSDT_FLOAT3),
        D3DVSD_REG(D3DVSDE_TEXCOORD0,D3DVSDT_FLOAT4),
        D3DVSD_REG(D3DVSDE_TEXCOORD1,D3DVSDT_FLOAT4),
        D3DVSD_REG(D3DVSDE_TEXCOORD2,D3DVSDT_FLOAT4),
        D3DVSD_REG(D3DVSDE_TEXCOORD3,D3DVSDT_FLOAT4),
        D3DVSD_END()
};
```

The following structure renders the control grid. The vertex structure contains the position, and the shader sets the color according to a constant. The extremely simple shader is in the shader directory as BezierControl.vsh:

```
struct CONTROL_VERTEX
{
        float x, y, z;
};
```

This is the FVF and declaration that creates a buffer of the simple control vertices. Rendering the control grid is very simple and could have been done without a shader, but I used a shader to increase your exposure to shader code. Also, you can use the shader to easily set the vertex color with a constant. If I had used the fixed function pipeline, I would have had to add code that sets a material, adjusts lighting, and so on. The shader method is arguably easier:

```
#define D3DFVF_CONTROLVERTEX (D3DFVF_XYZ)

DWORD ControlDeclaration[] =
{
        D3DVSD_STREAM(0),
        D3DVSD_REG(D3DVSDE_POSITION, D3DVSDT_FLOAT3),
        D3DVSD_END()
};
```

The ExtractBuffers function assumes that a mesh has already been loaded and cloned to the Bezier vertex format. In this case, the mesh is a plane of vertices with position values ranging from –0.5 to 0.5 in both the X and the Z directions. If you shift these values by 0.5, it creates a mesh that has a convenient range of 0 to 1, and the shader corrects this shifting by subtracting 0.5 later.

Creating s and t Values

I created a mesh that had convenient values so I could concentrate on more important matters, but using meshes with less convenient values is still easy. For any mesh, you can find the bounding box and use the extents of that box to find s and t values in the range of 0 to 1. For instance, if the mesh has x values that range from 0 to 100, you can create the correct s value by dividing each x value by 100.

I could have just as easily created the vertices in code by creating a vertex buffer and index buffer. It was a little bit less code to create the patch vertices with a mesh, and you will see a how to create the vertex and index buffers in the next function:

```
HRESULT CTechniqueApplication::ExtractBuffers()
{
        m_pMesh->GetVertexBuffer(&m_pMeshVertexBuffer);
        m_pMesh->GetIndexBuffer(&m_pMeshIndexBuffer);

        BEZIER_VERTEX *pMeshVertices;

        m_pMeshVertexBuffer->Lock(0, m_pMesh->GetNumVertices() *
                                sizeof(BEZIER_VERTEX),
                                (BYTE **)&pMeshVertices, 0);

        for (long Vertex = 0;
```

```
        Vertex < m_pMesh->GetNumVertices();
        Vertex++)
{
```

The patch shader works on two dimensions, so I use the x and z coordinates and ignore y. There is nothing about Bezier patches that explicitly forces you to work with a horizontal plane. The vertices and control points could also be vertically oriented. Theoretically, any orientation is fine as long as you are consistent all the way through. Again, the half-unit shift is an idiosyncrasy of the particular mesh I'm using; it is not a general requirement:

```
float S = pMeshVertices[Vertex].x + 0.5;
float T = pMeshVertices[Vertex].z + 0.5;
```

The following four values are the precomputed basis functions for this particular s value. The underlying mesh data does not change, so there is no reason to compute these values each time:

```
pMeshVertices[Vertex].Bs0 = (1.0f - S) * (1.0f - S) *
                            (1.0f - S);
pMeshVertices[Vertex].Bs1 = 3.0f * S * (1.0f - S) *
                            (1.0f - S);
pMeshVertices[Vertex].Bs2 = 3.0f * S * S * (1.0f - S);
pMeshVertices[Vertex].Bs3 = S * S * S;
```

Here the process is repeated for the t value. The basis functions are exactly the same. Only this time, they use the t value instead of the s value:

```
pMeshVertices[Vertex].Bt0 = (1.0f - T) * (1.0f - T) *
                            (1.0f - T);
pMeshVertices[Vertex].Bt1 = 3.0f * T * (1.0f - T) *
                            (1.0f - T);
pMeshVertices[Vertex].Bt2 = 3.0f * T * T * (1.0f - T);
pMeshVertices[Vertex].Bt3 = T * T * T;
```

These next eight lines compute the values of the derivatives of the basis functions. You derive these functions using the rule for simple polynomials. If you expand the basis functions and then take the derivative, you obtain the functions that follow:

```
pMeshVertices[Vertex].dBs0 = (6.0f * S) -
(3.0f * S *S) - 3.0f;
pMeshVertices[Vertex].dBs1 = 3.0f - (12.0f * S) +
                            (9.0f * S * S);
pMeshVertices[Vertex].dBs2 = (6.0f * S) - (9.0f * S * S);
```

```
        pMeshVertices[Vertex].dBs3 = 3.0f * S * S;

        pMeshVertices[Vertex].dBt0 = (6.0f * T) - (3.0f * T *
         T) - 3.0f;
        pMeshVertices[Vertex].dBt1 = 3.0f - (12.0f * T) +
                                     (9.0f * T * T);
        pMeshVertices[Vertex].dBt2 = (6.0f * T) - (9.0f * T * T);
        pMeshVertices[Vertex].dBt3 = 3.0f * T * T;
    }
```

After you have computed the basis values, unlock the buffer. The vertex shader
makes any further changes:

```
        m_pMeshVertexBuffer->Unlock();

        return S_OK;
}
```

CreateGridVisuals creates the simple vertices used to display the control grid. This is
really only a debugging and learning tool, so I don't spend too much time
optimizing their usage:

```
HRESULT CTechniqueApplication::CreateGridVisuals()
{
```

You need 16 vertices to show the 16 control points. You use these vertices to render
both the points and the grid of lines that connect them. They are created in managed
memory so that they do not need to be explicitly recreated if the device is reset:

```
        if (FAILED(m_pD3DDevice->CreateVertexBuffer(16 *
                                        sizeof(CONTROL_VERTEX),
                             0, D3DFVF_CONTROLVERTEX,
                             D3DPOOL_MANAGED,
                             &m_pControlVertexBuffer)))
            return E_FAIL;
```

The index buffer allows you to reuse the 16 vertices to draw the lines that
interconnect the control points. This is not just an optimization; I think it's easier
than creating more points:

```
        if (FAILED(m_pD3DDevice->CreateIndexBuffer(48 * sizeof(short),
                             0, D3DFMT_INDEX16,
                             D3DPOOL_MANAGED,
```

```
                                              &m_pControlIndexBuffer)))
            return E_FAIL;
```

The index buffer contains the data for a line list of interconnections between the control points. You can hardcode these values because they won't ever change. It is also possible to generate these values in a loop, but writing this way is easier to show what is actually going on:

```
        short *pIndex;
        m_pControlIndexBuffer->Lock(0, 48 * sizeof(short),
                              (BYTE**)&pIndex, 0);
        short Indices[] = {0, 1, 1, 2, 2, 3, 4, 5, 5, 6, 6, 7, 8, 9, 9,
              10, 10, 11, 12, 13, 13, 14, 14, 15, 0, 4, 4, 8, 8, 12,
              1, 5, 5, 9, 9, 13, 2, 6, 6, 10, 10, 14, 3, 7, 7,
              11, 11, 15};
        memcpy(pIndex, &Indices, 48 * sizeof(short));
        m_pControlIndexBuffer->Unlock();
}
```

The render function is where the real magic happens. Figures 21.7 and 21.8 show the application in action both in solid and wireframe renderings:

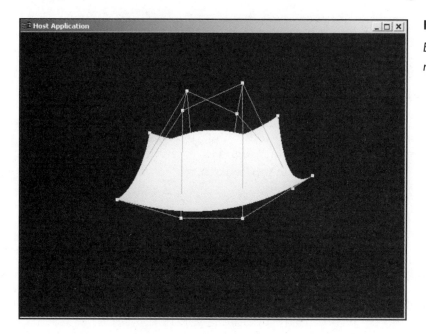

Figure 21.7

Bezier patch solid rendering.

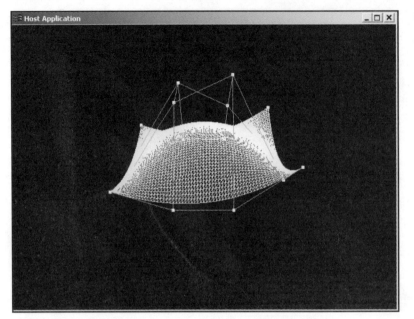
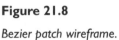

Figure 21.8

Bezier patch wireframe.

```
void CTechniqueApplication::Render()
{
```

The underlying data is based on a very small one-unit array of vertices and corresponding control points. Computing everything with those values is convenient, and the scaling matrix lets you scale the final mesh to any size you need:

```
D3DXMatrixScaling(&m_WorldMatrix, 5.0f, 5.0f, 5.0f);
```

I also added a rotation to the mesh so that you can see the Bezier functionality working with the standard matrix transformations. The rotation matrix is concatenated with the scaling values in the world matrix:

```
D3DXMATRIX Rotation;
D3DXMatrixRotationY(&Rotation, (float)GetTickCount() / 1000.0f);
m_WorldMatrix *= Rotation;
```

Once the new world matrix is computed, you still need to concatenate, transpose, and send the matrix to the vertex shader:

```
D3DXMATRIX ShaderMatrix = m_WorldMatrix *
                          m_ViewMatrix *
```

```
                    m_ProjectionMatrix;

D3DXMatrixTranspose(&ShaderMatrix, &ShaderMatrix);
m_pD3DDevice->SetVertexShaderConstant(0, &ShaderMatrix, 4);
```

The light is shining straight down, and I didn't bother to specify a specific light color or any other attributes. Also, when you get to Chapter 24 you'll see some of the considerations you must take to make sure the lighting is consistent with the matrix transformations. If you want to experiment with this code, you might need to augment it to make the lighting work correctly. See Chapter 24 for more details:

```
D3DXVECTOR4 LightDir(0.0f, -1.0f, 0.0f, 0.0f);
m_pD3DDevice->SetVertexShaderConstant(5, &LightDir, 1);
```

Here I also set the correction values to account for this particular mesh. In other cases, you may be able to save the constant and the instruction count:

```
D3DXVECTOR4 Correction(-0.5f, 0.0f, -0.5f, 0.0f);
m_pD3DDevice->SetVertexShaderConstant(6, &Correction, 1);
```

These warp values are just arbitrary values I picked to animate the control grid. I highly recommend you experiment with these values or any of the control grid parameters. Just remember that if you pull the grid in too many different directions, the patch may be mathematically correct but very ugly. Experiment all you want, but change the code is small increments until you are comfortable with what is going on:

```
float Warp1 = 2.0f * sin((float)GetTickCount() / 1000.0f);
float Warp2 = 2.0f * cos((float)GetTickCount() / 1000.0f);
```

Each of these four blocks of code sets the control-point positions for one row of points. For the sample, I change only the height of the points and keep the other values evenly spaced along the grid:

```
D3DXVECTOR4 ControlS0T0(0.0f, 0.25f * Warp1, 0.0f, 1.0f);
D3DXVECTOR4 ControlS0T1(0.0f, 0.0f, 0.33f, 1.0f);
D3DXVECTOR4 ControlS0T2(0.0f, 0.0f, 0.66f, 1.0f);
D3DXVECTOR4 ControlS0T3(0.0f, 0.25f * Warp1, 1.0f, 1.0f);

D3DXVECTOR4 ControlS1T0(0.33f, 0.0f, 0.0f, 1.0f);
D3DXVECTOR4 ControlS1T1(0.33f, 0.33f * Warp1 + 0.33 * Warp2,
                        0.33f, 1.0f);
```

```
D3DXVECTOR4 ControlS1T2(0.33f, -0.33f * Warp1 + 0.66f * Warp2,
                        0.66f, 1.0f);
D3DXVECTOR4 ControlS1T3(0.33f, 0.0f, 1.0f, 1.0f);


D3DXVECTOR4 ControlS2T0(0.66f, 0.0f, 0.0f, 1.0f);
D3DXVECTOR4 ControlS2T1(0.66f, 0.66f * Warp1 + 0.33 * Warp2,
                        0.33f, 1.0f);
D3DXVECTOR4 ControlS2T2(0.66f, -0.66f * Warp1 + 0.66f * Warp2,
                        0.66f, 1.0f);
D3DXVECTOR4 ControlS2T3(0.66f, 0.0f, 1.0f, 1.0f);


D3DXVECTOR4 ControlS3T0(1.0f, 0.25f * Warp2, 0.0f, 1.0f);
D3DXVECTOR4 ControlS3T1(1.0f, 0.0f, 0.33f, 1.0f);
D3DXVECTOR4 ControlS3T2(1.0f, 0.0f, 0.66f, 1.0f);
D3DXVECTOR4 ControlS3T3(1.0f, 0.25f * Warp2, 1.0f, 1.0f);
```

When the control points are set, each control point is set in the shader. It may have
been more optimal to create an array of 16 vectors and then send the complete
block of vectors in a single call to SetVertexShaderConstant. However, this was a better
way to demonstrate which constant matched with which control point. If you are
interested, you can optimize the way that constants are set:

```
m_pD3DDevice->SetVertexShaderConstant(10, &ControlS0T0, 1);
m_pD3DDevice->SetVertexShaderConstant(11, &ControlS0T1, 1);
m_pD3DDevice->SetVertexShaderConstant(12, &ControlS0T2, 1);
m_pD3DDevice->SetVertexShaderConstant(13, &ControlS0T3, 1);
m_pD3DDevice->SetVertexShaderConstant(14, &ControlS1T0, 1);
m_pD3DDevice->SetVertexShaderConstant(15, &ControlS1T1, 1);
m_pD3DDevice->SetVertexShaderConstant(16, &ControlS1T2, 1);
m_pD3DDevice->SetVertexShaderConstant(17, &ControlS1T3, 1);
m_pD3DDevice->SetVertexShaderConstant(18, &ControlS2T0, 1);
m_pD3DDevice->SetVertexShaderConstant(19, &ControlS2T1, 1);
m_pD3DDevice->SetVertexShaderConstant(20, &ControlS2T2, 1);
m_pD3DDevice->SetVertexShaderConstant(21, &ControlS2T3, 1);
m_pD3DDevice->SetVertexShaderConstant(22, &ControlS3T0, 1);
m_pD3DDevice->SetVertexShaderConstant(23, &ControlS3T1, 1);
m_pD3DDevice->SetVertexShaderConstant(24, &ControlS3T2, 1);
m_pD3DDevice->SetVertexShaderConstant(25, &ControlS3T3, 1);
```

Everything is now ready for some actual rendering. First make sure that the shader is set, and then set the vertex and index buffers:

```
m_pD3DDevice->SetVertexShader(m_BezierShader);

m_pD3DDevice->SetStreamSource(0, m_pMeshVertexBuffer,
                              sizeof(BEZIER_VERTEX));
m_pD3DDevice->SetIndices(m_pMeshIndexBuffer, 0);
```

This line is commented out in the source code, but you can uncomment it if you want to see the mesh rendered in wireframe:

```
//m_pD3DDevice->SetRenderState(D3DRS_FILLMODE,
                               D3DFILL_WIREFRAME);
```

Draw the mesh with the vertex shader. If you enable the preceding line, the output displays the wireframe view of the mesh; otherwise it displays a solid rendering of the mesh:

```
m_pD3DDevice->DrawIndexedPrimitive(D3DPT_TRIANGLELIST, 0,
                                   m_pMesh->GetNumVertices(), 0,
                                   m_pMesh->GetNumFaces());
```

This line ensures that the rendering mode is solid for all subsequent calls. If you want to optimize, you can make sure that this call is enabled only if the wireframe call is enabled:

```
m_pD3DDevice->SetRenderState(D3DRS_FILLMODE, D3DFILL_SOLID);
```

The last thing the render function does is call the function that renders the control grid. You can remove this line if you like:

```
RenderControlGrid();
}
```

The `RenderControlGrid` function is not at all optimized, but it is still useful to see what is going on with the control points:

```
void CTechniqueApplication::RenderControlGrid()
{
```

This code locks the vertex buffer so that it can be filled with control point data. In the next chapter, you'll see a method for accessing specific constants with the address register. I could have done that here and avoided the lock and the need to retrieve the constants, but it seemed overly complicated and there is no real need to optimize this function:

```
CONTROL_VERTEX *pVertices;

m_pControlVertexBuffer->Lock(0, 16 * sizeof(CONTROL_VERTEX),
                             (BYTE **)&pVertices, 0);
```

The loop walks through each vertex and retrieves the value of the constant. This is a bit heavy handed because you just passed the constants into the shader in the previous function. The advantage of this method is that you can be sure the values are consistent. Once the constants are retrieved, they are used to set the vertex position. Note the correction here keeps everything together with the mesh object. I don't go into too much detail, but keep this in mind as you read the next chapter. You could encode each vertex with the address of the constant that it matches to and then rewrite the control grid shader to retrieve the real position from that constant. If you did that, this function would become much simpler:

```
for (long Vertex = 0; Vertex < 16; Vertex++)
{
        D3DXVECTOR4 Temp;
        m_pD3DDevice->GetVertexShaderConstant(10 + Vertex,
                                              &Temp, 1);
        pVertices[Vertex].x = Temp.x - 0.5f;
        pVertices[Vertex].y = Temp.y;
        pVertices[Vertex].z = Temp.z - 0.5f;
}

m_pControlVertexBuffer->Unlock();
```

The control grid shader uses c4 to set the vertex color. The first pass draws all the lines between the control points using a red color.

```
D3DXVECTOR4 LineColor(1.0f, 0.0f, 0.0f, 0.0f);
m_pD3DDevice->SetVertexShaderConstant(4, &LineColor, 1);
```

These next lines set the shader and the proper data sources used for two passes:

```
m_pD3DDevice->SetVertexShader(m_ControlShader);
m_pD3DDevice->SetIndices(m_pControlIndexBuffer, 0);
m_pD3DDevice->SetStreamSource(0, m_pControlVertexBuffer,
                              sizeof(CONTROL_VERTEX));
```

The first rendering call draws the lines:

```
m_pD3DDevice->DrawIndexedPrimitive(D3DPT_LINELIST, 0,
                                   16, 0, 24);
```

These lines now reset the vertex color constant so that the control points can be rendered as yellow points:

```
D3DXVECTOR4 PointColor(1.0f, 1.0f, 0.0f, 0.0f);
m_pD3DDevice->SetVertexShaderConstant(4, &PointColor, 1);
```

Before I render the points, I set the point size. It's possible that some devices might not support this. If that's the case, you may not actually see the points:

```
float PointSize = 5.0f;
m_pD3DDevice->SetRenderState(D3DRS_POINTSIZE,
                             *((DWORD*)&PointSize));
m_pD3DDevice->DrawPrimitive(D3DPT_POINTLIST, 0, 16);
}
```

Uses and Advantages of Bezier Patches

There are many uses for Bezier curves and Bezier patches, but most have to do with the fact that the parametric representation allows you to apply the curve functions to an arbitrary number of vertices. For instance, you could use a lower-resolution mesh in the sample application and get a shape that was correct but much coarser. This lends itself well to the dynamic level of detail meshes.

Imagine a section of terrain defined with a set of Bezier patches that created rolling hills and deep valleys. If you are actually standing in a valley, you might want to render the terrain with a very high number of vertices so that all the edges appear smooth. If you hop into a plane and fly above the valley, you can render the same Bezier patches using fewer vertices. The patch calculations ensure that the general shape of the patches are correct, yet you can save calculations because you don't need as much detail when you are farther away.

This idea is not limited to something like terrain. Most algorithms for higher-order primitives use similar concepts to render 3D objects. For example, you can represent an object as a collection of parametric patches rather than a set of vertices. Using the patches, you can dynamically generate different meshes at any level of detail. This is the basis for hardware implementations as well. Some hardware implementations use lower-resolution meshes to interpolate smoother curved values without the data-transfer overhead of additional vertices. The underlying algorithms might not be exactly the same as the algorithms shown here, but the basic concepts are the same.

Also, as I mentioned earlier, you can use the patches to define how to warp a real 3D object. To do this, use the patch values to increment or scale the vertex positions rather than set them directly. You can use this method to create very organic and smooth warping effects. You can also use it to warp or move materials such as cloth. Imagine a waving flag. You can use the CPU to generate the rough control points of the flag and let the Bezier functionality control the smooth interpolation of the points on the flag. You can also apply this idea to moving capes and so on.

Finally, you can apply the concepts behind this chapter to other areas outside of rendering. For instance, you can describe a path of motion with a Bezier curve and use the basis functions to generate a smooth interpolated position at any time value. This type of approach can be useful for any situation where you might need to derive smooth values from relatively coarse data. Keep in mind that this sample generates a very smooth surface based on only four points.

Connecting Curves and Patches

Many of these ideas involve shapes or paths with more control points. You can specify a Bezier curve with more than 4 control points or a Bezier patch with more than 16, but this often becomes computationally expensive. Instead, you can join curves by having two curves share a common endpoint. This is an acceptable solution, but it can create abrupt transitions if the two curves are very different. You can also join two patches by having them share a common row of four control points, but the same caveat about abrupt transitions also applies.

If you do choose to add more control points, the generalized definition for the set of basis functions is as follows:

$$b_{i,n}(s) = s^i(1 - s)^{(n - i)}n!/i!(n - i)!$$

In Conclusion...

If you have not studied a lot of geometry or calculus, this chapter may have been like drinking from the fire hose. My hope is that I watered down the math enough to make the overall concepts understandable. If you have not studied calculus, you might have to simply trust me about the derivatives, but I do recommend trying a couple simple calculations for yourself. It should be pretty apparent that the methodology works even if you don't understand the underlying mechanics. If you are really interested in learning more, many math resources on the Web attack these subjects from a variety of different angles. Do a couple searches and see which explanations work for you.

In the meantime, I finish this chapter off with a recap of some of the major points:

- Bezier curves and patches let you define curves and surfaces with a very small amount of data.

- The equation for Bezier curves is a function of a set of basis functions and a set of control points.

- You can use the derivatives of the basis functions to find the tangent vectors for a surface. Once those vectors are found, the cross product of two tangent vectors yields the surface normal at a given point.

- Once the control points are found, you can then use a vertex shader to apply the influences of the control points to an arbitrary number of vertices.

- The vertex shader can also compute the surface normal and apply lighting calculations.

- My method involves encoding more data into the vertices and using fewer instructions. A sample effect on the nVidia site does the opposite. There are advantages and disadvantages to each approach.

- Bezier patches are most useful in situations where you want to control a large amount of vertices with a very small amount of changing data.

- Bezier patches are also good when you don't necessarily want the number of vertices to remain constant. This is useful in cases where you want a dynamic level of detail control and you want to render the same general shape with fewer vertices.

- If you want more control over the shape, you can add more control points, but it might be better to connect multiple curves. The result is fewer calculations, but abrupt changes at the interface might be an issue.

CHAPTER 22

Character
Animation—
Matrix
Palette
Skinning

The last several chapters have concentrated on techniques that manipulate vertex positions through a variety of approaches. These techniques are great for many different kinds of special effects, but they are probably not all that useful for modeling how a character walks or how a shark swims. There are many character animation techniques, but I have chosen to concentrate on matrix palette skinning because it illustrates some basic concepts and some interesting shader techniques. I also think that you can extend the idea of palletizing shader constants to many other classes of techniques. This chapter includes discussion on the following:

- Animation techniques and skinning.
- How you use the address register to index into a "palette" of constants.
- The shader implementation of matrix palette skinning.
- The application code that drives the shader.
- Some tips about the "real" implementations of this technique.
- Other uses for palettes.

Character Animation Techniques

There are many techniques for character animation and animation in general. At a high level, the two most common classes of techniques (at least for characters) are key frame animation and skinning. I say "classes of techniques" because there are many different ways to implement each class of technique, either in terms of the mathematical details, the mechanics of the implementation, or both. The SDK and the Web offer many animation samples, so I define some of the different techniques here and point you to the SDK for details.

Key frame animation is perhaps the most straightforward method of animation. Key frames store the position of each vertex in several different poses. Usually these poses are contained in different versions of the mesh. For example, the key frame poses for a running animation might include a mesh with the left leg forward, another with the right leg forward, and so on. Figure 22.1 shows a simple example of this.

You achieve the actual animation by interpolating between key frame poses. The key frames represent poses of the model at certain times. For each interim time, the position of each vertex is interpolated from the two key frames. Figure 22.2 demonstrates this graphically.

This is the technique used in the DolphinVS example in the DirectX SDK. You load three different "poses" of a dolphin mesh, and a vertex shader interpolates between

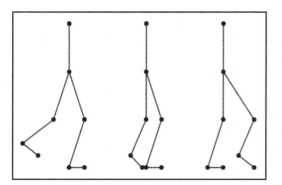

Figure 22.1

Sample poses from a running animation.

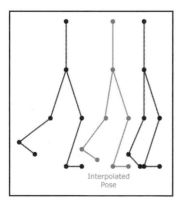

Figure 22.2

Key frame animation.

the different poses. This works well for the simple motions of the dolphin, but not as well for more involved motion such as walking or line dancing. The problem with key frame animation is that complex motion requires many key frames for proper movement. In Figure 22.3, the desired movement is similar to an elbow bending, but the key frame data is too sparse to create the proper movement.

Supplying more key frames could help create the proper effect, but more key frames equals more data. More data means everything from more assets to keep track of to more vertices taking up valuable memory. There are also interpolation approaches that are less linear in nature and that may improve the motion, but they still suffer from needing a fair amount of data to be accurate.

This is where skinning comes in. Skinning treats a mesh as a skin that is attached to a system of bones. The movement of one or more bones influences the movement of each vertex. To illustrate this, flex your arm. Skin on your upper or lower arm moves with your upper or lower arm. Skin on your elbow stretches in relation to both parts of your arm. Okay, you can stop flexing now.

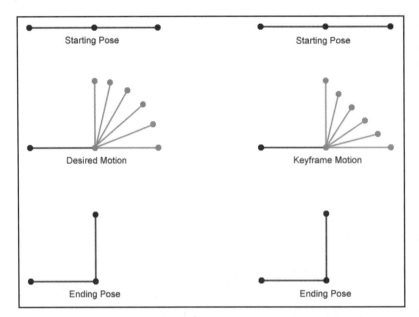

Figure 22.3

Key frame animation with too few key frames.

The skin is usually a mesh of vertices, but the bones are really representations of matrix operations. For instance, each time you flexed your arms, you were really just rotating some points about some axis. This points to a fairly obvious advantage of skinning over key framing. If you revisit the motion from Figure 22.3, you can see that you can represent the elbow motion as one rotation about a given point. Some of the vertices remain stationary while others follow that rotation. The advantage is that you need only one mesh (which saves memory) and some transformation matrices (which are probably faster to process). As time passes, one rotation value is interpolated, and the resulting transformation is applied to the correct vertices. As Figure 22.4 illustrates, the resulting motion is exactly correct with less memory and arguably less processing.

Throughout this chapter and many other samples involving skinning, you might visualize the bones as points and lines, which may lead you to think that the bones are themselves vertices. The bones merely define the motion. They are mathematical constructs. However, it is usually convenient to be able to visualize the bones. To do that, you use vertices, but again, the bones are not necessarily visual entities.

Figure 22.5 shows screenshots from this chapter's sample application. The shot on the left is the skin as it follows the joints. The shot on the right is the same shot showing only the bones. Much like your elbow, the two bones influence the skin at the joints. The rest of the skin follows the closest bone.

Figure 22.4

Skinning animation.

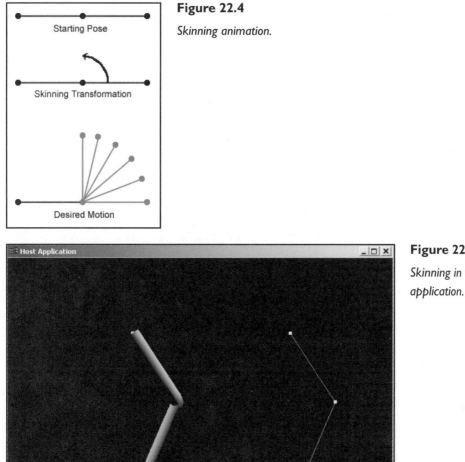

Figure 22.5

Skinning in the sample application.

The screenshots demonstrate that several bones influence the mesh, yet only certain bones affect certain vertices. This is where the idea of matrix palettes comes into play. If you think of a system of bones as a system of matrices, then several matrices affect different parts of the skin mesh. Ignoring efficient implementation details for a moment, you could store all of the matrices and then walk through the vertices deciding which matrices to use to transform a given vertex.

The problem is that efficient implementations work best in large batches. You need a way to send a lot of data through and have the processor decide how to apply the different matrices to the different vertices. The matrix palette method works this way. You store each matrix in a set of constants in the vertex shader. These matrices can be dynamically changed every frame with new constants. The vertices sent to the shader encode additional information that tells the shader which matrices to apply and with how much weight. The shader then indexes to the correct matrix and applies the correct transformations. This is made possible by the address register.

The Address Register

The techniques in the previous chapters used registers to obtain, store, and set values. The address register is peculiar in that its purpose is to provide a way to index into the constant registers. For instance, in previous examples, I showed you shader code where I used a value that was stored in c5. This was explicitly stated as c5 and compiled into the executable shader code as c5. But in some cases you might need the value stored in c6 or c7 and you don't know which beforehand. This is where the address register is useful. In the following code snippet, several values are stored in several constant registers. One of these constants will be added to the vertex normal, but instead of explicitly writing which constant into the shader, you write the index of the constant into v7.x. You set the address register to the value in v7.x and then use it to add the proper constant:

```
mov a0.x, v7.x
add r1, v3, c[a0.x]
```

One thing to remember is that currently, you can set and use only a0.x. The a0 register is the only address register, and you can only use the first component as the index.

The address register is a very important part of the matrix palette skinning shader because it allows the vertex to specify which matrices should be used to transform it. This allows you to encode the matrix addresses into the vertices once and then send the whole vertex buffer to the shader to be rendered. The shader dynamically determines how to apply the transformations on a per-vertex basis. For the rest of the story, take a look at the shader.

Matrix Palette Skinning in a Shader

The following code comes from PaletteSkin.vsh in the shaders directory of the CD. In addition to performing the animation functions, the shader does some very basic lighting calculations with the skinned normal. I comment on that part of the shader here to be complete, but you might need to read Chapter 24 to understand why things are done the way they are.

The shader expects v0 to store the basic vertex position, v3 to store the vertex normal, and v7 to store the matrix information in the format of (First Bone Index, First Bone Weight, Second Bone Index, Second Bone Weight). There's no reason why the vertex couldn't contain more information such as color or texture coordinates, but I omitted those added features here for simplicity. The matrix (bone) information is stored in constant registers. Notice that the shader is completely agnostic about where the bone data is stored. As long as the application is consistent between setting the constants and setting the indices in the vertex, the shader will work, no matter which constants are used:

```
vs.1.1
```

The first line retrieves the index for the first bone from the value stored in v7.x:

```
mov a0.x, v7.x
```

Once the address register is set, you can use it to index into the constant registers. Here you use the address register to designate which three constants are the first three rows of the first transformation matrix. These three lines transform the vertex position by the first bone matrix and store the transformed position in r1:

```
dp4 r1.x, v0, c[a0.x]
dp4 r1.y, v0, c[a0.x + 1]
dp4 r1.z, v0, c[a0.x + 2]
```

Here the same process is repeated for the vertex normal, still using the first bone. The r3 register contains the transformed normal:

```
dp3 r3.x, v3, c[a0.x]
dp3 r3.y, v3, c[a0.x + 1]
dp3 r3.z, v3, c[a0.x + 2]
```

These next several lines repeat the process for the second bone. You set the address register to the value stored in v7.z, which is then used to index to the constants that contain the second bone matrix. The transformed position and normal are stored in r2 and r4:

```
mov a0.x, v7.z
dp4 r2.x, v0, c[a0.x]
dp4 r2.y, v0, c[a0.x + 1]
dp4 r2.z, v0, c[a0.x + 2]
```

```
dp3 r4.x, v3, c[a0.x]
dp3 r4.y, v3, c[a0.x + 1]
dp3 r4.z, v3, c[a0.x + 2]
```

Now, you apply the blending weights to each version of the vertex, and the result is summed to produce the final position. The first line multiplies the first version of the position by the first weight value (v7.y). The next line does the same for the second position and then adds the two results to place the final value in r2. Finally, r2.w is set to 1.0, the value stored in c6.x. Note that vertices only affected by one bone should set the first bone index to that bone and the first weight to 1.0. You can set the second bone to (nearly) any value and the weight to 0.0. This means that single bone vertices waste a lot of shader instructions for the second bone, but this is the best general solution:

```
mul r1.xyz, r1.xyz, v7.y
mad r2.xyz, r2.xyz, v7.w, r1.xyz
mov r2.w, c6.x
```

You repeat the same process to generate the final skinned vertex normal. It is important to skin the normal to get the proper lighting. You don't need to set the w component of the normal because it is never used:

```
mul r3.xyz, r3.xyz, v7.y
mad r4.xyz, r4.xyz, v7.w, r3.xyz
```

You must renormalize the transformed normal by dividing each component by the magnitude of the vector:

```
dp3 r4.w, r4, r4
rsq r4.w, r4.w
mul r4, r4, r4.w
```

You can do the lighting calculations between the object space light direction and the new normal vector. This line computes a basic diffuse lighting value by finding the dot product between the two vectors. This is not a complete lighting solution, but it will suffice for now:

```
dp3 r0.x, r4, -c4
```

Returning back to the position calculations, the final skinned position is transformed into clip space and emitted from the shader. The skinning calculations handle transforming the mesh, but you can still set the world position, rotation, and so on. For instance, you can create a running animation that makes the legs move properly, but you should still translate the model with the world matrix if you want the character to get anywhere:

```
dp4 oPos.x, r2, c0
dp4 oPos.y, r2, c1
dp4 oPos.z, r2, c2
dp4 oPos.w, r2, c3
```

You set the vertex color to the sum of the simple diffuse lighting value and a small amount of ambient light stored in c5:

```
add oD0, r0.x, c5
```

That's the shader. Once you understand the address register, everything else just falls into place. After you take a look at the application code, I describe some other ideas for how you can use palettes.

The Application

The following application is meant to demonstrate the basics of matrix palette skinning without getting into the specifics of how the animation data might be written to a file. The details are different depending on which modeling tool you use, which formats you use, and how you choose to implement your own solution. This application generates a simple model applying simple animations that should be fairly easy to follow. When you are comfortable with the basic concepts, take a look at the skinning code included with the DirectX SDK and with the nVidia Effects Browser. Those samples include descriptions of how to load skinning data from a mesh file.

As usual, the following code is incomplete, but you can find the complete code on the CD:

```
#include "TechniqueApplication.h"
```

This defines the constant that contains the first row of the first matrix. By changing this value, the application should be able to place the matrices in nearly any constant register, and the shader should work as advertised. Of course, you don't want to overwrite other constants or extend past the valid number of constants:

```
#define FIRST_BONE 20.0f
```

This is the structure of the palette skinned vertices. I am storing a position and a vertex normal along with the bone indices and weights:

```
struct PALETTESKIN_VERTEX
{
```

```
        float x, y, z;
        float nx, ny, nz;
        float Bone1, Weight1, Bone2, Weight2;
};
```

The vertex declaration is what tells the shader how the data will be formatted. Here, all the values are stored in stream zero. The position and normal information is stored in the usual registers, and the bone information is stored in the first texture coordinate register. It is very important not to forget to that the texture coordinate is a four-component vector as opposed to the usual two-component u and v coordinate:

```
DWORD PaletteSkinDeclaration[] =
{
        D3DVSD_STREAM(0),
        D3DVSD_REG(D3DVSDE_POSITION, D3DVSDT_FLOAT3),
        D3DVSD_REG(D3DVSDE_NORMAL,   D3DVSDT_FLOAT3),
        D3DVSD_REG(D3DVSDE_TEXCOORD0,D3DVSDT_FLOAT4),
        D3DVSD_END()
};
```

The FVF encodes the same information, and sometimes it's useful to be able to pass the FVF to a function. Notice the texture coordinate size attribute that sets the size of texture coordinate zero to four values:

```
#define D3DFVF_PALETTESKINVERTEX  (D3DFVF_XYZ | D3DFVF_NORMAL | \
                        D3DFVF_TEX0 | D3DFVF_TEXCOORDSIZE4(0))
```

The SetBoneConstants function is called every time the application wants to update the bone matrices. It sets the vertex shader constants that will be used to skin the mesh. If this application used a more complex skinned mesh, a lot of the matrix operations in the function would be performed offline with the modeling tool:

```
void CTechniqueApplication::SetBoneConstants()
{
        D3DXMATRIX Bone1;
        D3DXMATRIX Bone2;
        D3DXMATRIX Bone3;
        D3DXMATRIX Bone4;
```

Once four matrices are created, I use the same old tick-count trick to generate some animation data. Here I generate an angle that will be used to bend the mesh with each bone. Remember that I haven't really optimized any of this application code. Creating new matrix variables every time might not be the best way to go. If you have variables that are reused often, make them class members so they are not re-created all of the time:

```
float Time = (float)GetTickCount() / 2000.0f;
float Angle = (D3DX_PI / 2.0f) * fabs(sin(Time));
```

These values offset the rotation of each bone. Each bone rotates around a different point in the same way that your shoulder is a different rotation point than your elbow. The offset values offset the rotation point before the bone is rotated. Once the bone is rotated, the offset is pulled back so that the vertices are not translated, only rotated:

```
D3DXMATRIX PosOffset;
D3DXMATRIX NegOffset;
D3DXMatrixTranslation(&PosOffset, 0.0f, 0.0f,  12.0f);
D3DXMatrixTranslation(&NegOffset, 0.0f, 0.0f, -12.0f);
```

The rotation matrix is a basis for all of the bone rotations. It is created once and then used to generate each bone's rotation:

```
D3DXMATRIX SimpleRotate;
D3DXMatrixRotationX(&SimpleRotate, Angle);
```

First, you translate the first bone a small amount. This bone is the base for all of the other bones. For instance, if this bone system were an arm, the first bone would be the shoulder or the torso. The movement of each bone in the chain depends upon the movement of the bones further up the chain. In this sample, the chain is pretty simple, but some bone systems can be complex hierarchies where you have a torso that connects to two legs, which each have subparts, and so on. I'm just adding a little motion to the first bone to show how it affects the later bones:

```
D3DXMatrixTranslation(&Bone1, 0.0f, 5.0f * sin(Time), 0.0f);
```

Bone2 builds on the motion of the first bone by rotating by the angle that was set earlier. In this example, the axis of Bone2 is where Bone1 and Bone2 connect, so there is no need to offset the position. Keep in mind that different skeletal systems will have different parameters:

```
Bone2 = SimpleRotate * Bone1;
```

The axis of Bone3 is offset along the "arm." It builds upon Bone2, but only after the axis is offset to the new position. The same procedure is repeated for Bone4. Each bone is constrained to follow its predecessors in the chain. If not, the skeleton would blow up and the character would be very unhappy:

```
Bone3 = SimpleRotate * PosOffset * Bone2;
Bone4 = SimpleRotate * PosOffset * Bone3;
```

Once the bones are rotated, the negative offset is applied to cancel out the translation aspects of the matrix. If you don't do this, the skin will be translated over the offset, which is probably not the desired effect. Note that you can have translation if you want to create a telescoping effect. This is perfect for modeling dishonest wooden boys, but that's not what I'm doing here:

```
Bone3 = NegOffset * Bone3;
Bone4 = NegOffset * NegOffset * Bone4;
```

Each bone matrix now contains the proper transformations. Now that they are built, each matrix is transposed so that the shader can use it:

```
D3DXMatrixTranspose(&Bone1, &Bone1);
D3DXMatrixTranspose(&Bone2, &Bone2);
D3DXMatrixTranspose(&Bone3, &Bone3);
D3DXMatrixTranspose(&Bone4, &Bone4);
```

Each bone is set as a vertex shader constant according to the value that defines the first bone. Each matrix uses four constants. However, calculations really only happen on three of the four rows, so there are opportunities for optimization if you are short on constant space:

```
m_pD3DDevice->SetVertexShaderConstant(FIRST_BONE + 0,
                                      &Bone1, 4);
m_pD3DDevice->SetVertexShaderConstant(FIRST_BONE + 4,
                                      &Bone2, 4);
m_pD3DDevice->SetVertexShaderConstant(FIRST_BONE + 8,
                                      &Bone3, 4);
m_pD3DDevice->SetVertexShaderConstant(FIRST_BONE + 12,
                                      &Bone4, 4);
}
```

You call the ExtractBuffers function after the mesh is loaded. In this application, its main purpose is to set the bones and weights for each vertex:

```
HRESULT CTechniqueApplication::ExtractBuffers()
{
    m_pMesh->GetVertexBuffer(&m_pMeshVertexBuffer);
    m_pMesh->GetIndexBuffer(&m_pMeshIndexBuffer);

    PALETTESKIN_VERTEX *pMeshVertices;
```

This function assumes that the mesh was cloned to the proper vertex format when it was loaded. It locks the buffer in order to analyze the vertices and set the skinning values:

```
m_pMeshVertexBuffer->Lock(0,
                          m_pMesh->GetNumVertices() *
                          sizeof(PALETTESKIN_VERTEX),
                          (BYTE **)&pMeshVertices, 0);
```

Three moving bones are in this system, and each vertex needs to be "attached" to one or more bones. The vertex data is set in two passes just to make the process clearer. In the first pass, the cylinder mesh is divided into three sections of 12 units each, and each section is "attached" to the appropriate bone. Each section is fully attached to one bone, and the second bone weight is set to zero:

```
for (long Vertex = 0;
     Vertex < m_pMesh->GetNumVertices();
     Vertex++)
{
```

You can see that the first bone index is actually the second bone. If there were a body attached to this arm, then I could attach some vertices to the first bone, but as it stands, I'm only really attaching the vertices to the other three bones. Remember, the first bone does influence every other bone in the chain.

The mesh is 36 units long, so the mesh is divided into three sections of 12 units each. No constraint says the bones must be of equal length, so feel free to experiment here if you want. However, you might want to experiment with the bone visualization before changing the mesh because it is easier to see changes or problems with the simpler visualization:

```
if (pMeshVertices[Vertex].z < 12.0f)
{
        pMeshVertices[Vertex].Bone1 = FIRST_BONE + 4.0f;
        pMeshVertices[Vertex].Weight1 = 1.0f;
        pMeshVertices[Vertex].Bone2 = FIRST_BONE + 4.0f;
        pMeshVertices[Vertex].Weight2 = 0.0f;
}
else if (pMeshVertices[Vertex].z < 24.0f)
{
        pMeshVertices[Vertex].Bone1 = FIRST_BONE + 4.0f;
        pMeshVertices[Vertex].Weight1 = 0.0f;
```

```
                    pMeshVertices[Vertex].Bone2 = FIRST_BONE + 8.0f;
                    pMeshVertices[Vertex].Weight2 = 1.0f;
        }
        else
        {
                    pMeshVertices[Vertex].Bone1 = FIRST_BONE + 8.0f;
                    pMeshVertices[Vertex].Weight1 = 0.0f;
                    pMeshVertices[Vertex].Bone2 = FIRST_BONE + 12.0f;
                    pMeshVertices[Vertex].Weight2 = 1.0f;

        }
    }
```

The second pass is concerned with setting the bone influences at the joints. Instead of limiting the effects to one bone, the following code linearly interpolates the influence of the two adjacent bones on vertices near the joint. Figure 22.6 shows this in detail.

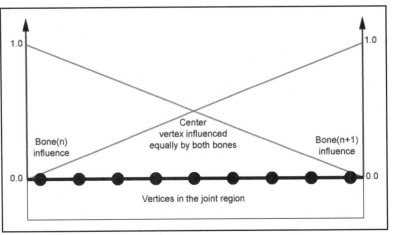

Figure 22.6

Bone influences on joint vertices.

Some schemes may call for something other than linear interpolation, but here it creates the desired effect. Also, you set these weights only for vertices on the outside of the joint. The vertices on the inside are allowed to just fold in on themselves. I did this to demonstrate more fine-grained control. You can set weights wherever and however you deem appropriate:

```
    for (Vertex = 0; Vertex < m_pMesh->GetNumVertices(); Vertex++)
    {
            if (pMeshVertices[Vertex].z > 11.0f &&
                pMeshVertices[Vertex].z < 13.0f &&
```

```
                    pMeshVertices[Vertex].y > 0.0f)
            {
                    float Weight = (pMeshVertices[Vertex].z -
                                    11.0f) / 2.0f;
                    pMeshVertices[Vertex].Bone1 = FIRST_BONE + 4.0f;
                    pMeshVertices[Vertex].Weight1 = 1.0f - Weight;
                    pMeshVertices[Vertex].Bone2 = FIRST_BONE + 8.0f;
                    pMeshVertices[Vertex].Weight2 = Weight;
            }
            if (pMeshVertices[Vertex].z > 23.0f &&
                    pMeshVertices[Vertex].z < 25.0f &&
                    pMeshVertices[Vertex].y > 0.0f)
            {
                    float Weight = (pMeshVertices[Vertex].z -
                                    23.0f) / 2.0f;
                    pMeshVertices[Vertex].Bone1 = FIRST_BONE + 8.0f;
                    pMeshVertices[Vertex].Weight1 = 1.0f - Weight;
                    pMeshVertices[Vertex].Bone2 = FIRST_BONE + 12.0f;
                    pMeshVertices[Vertex].Weight2 = Weight;
            }
    }

    m_pMeshVertexBuffer->Unlock();

    return S_OK;
}
```

The CreateBones function creates the vertices used to render the bone structure. Unlike the Bezier control grid, these vertices are subjected to exactly the same vertex shader as the higher-resolution cylinder mesh. In addition to helping visualize the bones, this also proves a point. The skinning operations work very well across meshes of different levels of detail. Unlike key frame animation, skinning allows you to trade in different meshes if you want, and it does not ruin the animation (assuming the skinning values for all vertices were set properly). Contrast this with the dolphin example in the SDK, which requires that all the vertex streams be consistent with each other. The following code creates and sets four vertices in very much the same way as the first pass for the mesh:

```
HRESULT CTechniqueApplication::CreateBones()
{
```

```
        if (FAILED(m_pD3DDevice->CreateVertexBuffer(
                            4 * sizeof(PALETTESKIN_VERTEX),
                            0, D3DFVF_PALETTESKINVERTEX,
                            D3DPOOL_MANAGED,
                            &m_pBoneVertexBuffer)))
            return E_FAIL;

    PALETTESKIN_VERTEX *pVertices;

    m_pBoneVertexBuffer->Lock(0, 4 * sizeof(PALETTESKIN_VERTEX),
                            (BYTE **)&pVertices, 0);

    pVertices[0].x = 0.0f; pVertices[0].y = 0.0f;
     pVertices[0].z =  0.0f;
    pVertices[1].x = 0.0f; pVertices[1].y = 0.0f;
     pVertices[1].z =  12.0f;
    pVertices[2].x = 0.0f; pVertices[2].y = 0.0f;
     pVertices[2].z =  24.0f;
    pVertices[3].x = 0.0f; pVertices[3].y = 0.0f;
     pVertices[3].z =  36.0f;

    pVertices[0].Bone1 = FIRST_BONE + 0.0f;
     pVertices[0].Weight1 = 1.0f;
    pVertices[0].Bone2 = FIRST_BONE + 0.0f;
     pVertices[0].Weight2 = 0.0f;

    pVertices[1].Bone1 = FIRST_BONE + 4.0f;
     pVertices[1].Weight1 = 1.0f;
    pVertices[1].Bone2 = FIRST_BONE + 4.0f;
     pVertices[1].Weight2 = 0.0f;

    pVertices[2].Bone1 = FIRST_BONE + 8.0f;
     pVertices[2].Weight1 = 1.0f;
    pVertices[2].Bone2 = FIRST_BONE + 8.0f;
     pVertices[2].Weight2 = 0.0f;

    pVertices[3].Bone1 = FIRST_BONE + 12.0f;
     pVertices[3].Weight1 = 1.0f;
    pVertices[3].Bone2 = FIRST_BONE + 12.0f;
```

```
            pVertices[3].Weight2 = 0.0f;

        m_pBoneVertexBuffer->Unlock();

        return S_OK;
}
```

The Render function is fairly simple; it just sets up some vertices and lets the shader do the magic. A call to SetBoneConstants gets everything started:

```
void CTechniqueApplication::Render()
{
        SetBoneConstants();
```

I set the world matrix to a rotation just to prove the point that the skinning operation changes the mesh, but the world matrix can still do the macroscopic transformations such as simple translation and rotation. Once the world matrix is set up, the shader matrix is transposed and sent to the shader:

```
        D3DXMatrixRotationY(&m_WorldMatrix,
                        (float)GetTickCount() /         1000.0f);

        D3DXMATRIX ShaderMatrix = m_WorldMatrix * m_ViewMatrix *
                            m_ProjectionMatrix;

        D3DXMatrixTranspose(&ShaderMatrix, &ShaderMatrix);
        m_pD3DDevice->SetVertexShaderConstant(0, &ShaderMatrix, 4);
```

These constants define the lighting parameters and one convenience constant that holds the values for one and zero:

```
        D3DXVECTOR4 LightDir(0.0f, -1.0f, 0.0f, 0.0f);
        D3DXVECTOR4 Ambient (0.1f,  0.1f, 0.1f, 1.0f);
        D3DXVECTOR4 One     (1.0f,  0.0f, 0.0f, 0.0f);
```

The next block of code will make more sense after you read Chapter 24. You transform the light direction so that it's in the same space as the vertex normal. This is necessary for the shader's dot product calculation:

```
        D3DXMATRIX WorldInverse;
        D3DXMatrixInverse(&WorldInverse, NULL, &m_WorldMatrix);
        D3DXVec4Transform(&LightDir, &LightDir, &WorldInverse);
        D3DXVec4Normalize(&LightDir, &LightDir);
```

Again, these constants don't really change, so you don't need to set them every time. I put them in the render loop so you can easily see where they are coming from:

```
m_pD3DDevice->SetVertexShaderConstant(4, &LightDir, 1);
m_pD3DDevice->SetVertexShaderConstant(5, &Ambient, 1);
m_pD3DDevice->SetVertexShaderConstant(6, &One, 1);
```

Everything is set up for the actual drawing. Again, you could optimize this step if the bones were not in a separate vertex buffer or if the bones were not drawn:

```
m_pD3DDevice->SetVertexShader(m_SkinShader);
m_pD3DDevice->SetStreamSource(0, m_pMeshVertexBuffer,
                              sizeof(PALETTESKIN_VERTEX));
m_pD3DDevice->SetIndices(m_pMeshIndexBuffer, 0);
```

As with the Bezier patches, I included a line of code that you can uncomment to see the wireframe view. By default, I have it commented out. Either way, the mesh is rendered, and the render state is set to ensure that you are not in wireframe mode:

```
//m_pD3DDevice->SetRenderState(D3DRS_FILLMODE,
                              D3DFILL_WIREFRAME);

m_pD3DDevice->DrawIndexedPrimitive(D3DPT_TRIANGLELIST, 0,
                              m_pMesh->GetNumVertices(), 0,
                              m_pMesh->GetNumFaces());

m_pD3DDevice->SetRenderState(D3DRS_FILLMODE, D3DFILL_SOLID);
```

This final line renders the bones. It is more or less a debugging function, and you can comment it out if you want to. Alternately, you could comment out the `DrawIndexedPrimitive` call and render only the bones. This might be advantageous if you start experimenting with other animations:

```
RenderBones();
}
```

The `RenderBones` function renders the bone visualization, which is just a set of vertices sent to the same skinning shader. This function uses the ambient lighting feature of the shader to color the lines and points:

```
void CTechniqueApplication::RenderBones()
{
    D3DXVECTOR4 LineColor (1.0f, 0.0f, 0.0f, 1.0f);
```

```
m_pD3DDevice->SetVertexShaderConstant(5, &LineColor, 1);

m_pD3DDevice->SetStreamSource(0, m_pBoneVertexBuffer,
                                sizeof(PALETTESKIN_VERTEX));

m_pD3DDevice->DrawPrimitive(D3DPT_LINESTRIP, 0, 3);
```

The bones are rendered in two passes. The previous pass rendered red lines, and now the ambient light is reset to render yellow points. Your hardware might not support sized points, but you should still see the lines:

```
D3DXVECTOR4 PointColor (1.0f,  1.0f, 0.0f, 1.0f);
m_pD3DDevice->SetVertexShaderConstant(5, &PointColor, 1);

float PointSize = 5.0f;
m_pD3DDevice->SetRenderState(D3DRS_POINTSIZE,
                                *((DWORD*)&PointSize));
m_pD3DDevice->DrawPrimitive(D3DPT_POINTLIST, 0, 4);
}
```

Run the application and experiment with different parameters. I want to call your attention to one point before I move on. Figure 22.7 shows the wireframe view of the mesh.

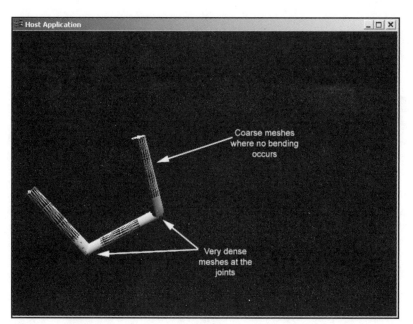

Figure 22.7

Variable resolution in the skin.

As you can see, the mesh becomes much denser at the joints. This is important because you want smooth bends in the joints, but you don't want to make the mesh unnecessarily dense. Most modeling programs let you optimize certain sections of a mesh while keeping other sections dense enough to allow for smooth motion. Keep this in mind as you create your models.

Once you have a grasp on the underlying mechanics of this sample, take some time to look at the samples in the SDK. The SDK samples will provide more information about loading animations stored in files and will give you another viewpoint on the technique.

Other Uses for Palettes

There are many more uses for the address register and for the concept of palettes. Here are just a few ideas.

In discussions about lighting, I mentioned that spot lights are very expensive. You could write a shader that allows a scene to have multiple spot lights but have each mesh specify which spot lights actually cast light onto the mesh. This would allow you to batch multiple lights and multiple meshes but still optimize calculations.

On a similar note, you could also specify which light casts a shadow. In a scene with several lights, you might want to pick the one best light to cast the shadow. That might not be a realistic solution, but it may be good enough and save many expensive calculations.

In the last chapter, I mentioned that you could set up several control points and then use the palette concept to allow different patches to be guided by different control points. This is conceptually similar to index buffers. You are setting up a cluster of data and then indexing higher-level primitives into that cluster. In this case, you are talking about control points and patches rather than vertices and triangles.

There are probably enough examples for me to ramble on for quite some time. The seed I want to plant in your head is that the address register allows you to batch up constants and index into them in interesting ways. If you use this idea correctly, you have a huge amount of control over how the shader influences large batches of data. Keep this in mind as you develop more complex shaders.

In Conclusion...

This chapter is just the tip of the iceberg in terms of all the options available to you when rendering characters. I quickly breezed over the idea of key frame interpolation because I wanted to talk about this technique, but sometimes different techniques are better than others. Become acquainted with the SDK samples from Microsoft, nVidia, and ATI. I want to give you a conceptual base, but they can show you several different ways to build the real implementation.

This is the last shader that focuses on manipulating the vertex position. Before moving on to colors and lighting, check out a quick recap of this chapter:

- There are many different forms of animation, but the two most common are key framing and skinning.
- Key frames usually require several key frames to produce smooth animation during complex motions.
- Skinning usually involves one mesh being attached to a hierarchical set of transformation "bones."
- Skinning can offer a big advantage over key frames because it takes up less storage than multiple copies of a mesh.
- The address register is a unique register that you can use to index into the constant registers.
- Only a0.x is available for use by the shader.
- Matrix palette skinning uses the address register to index into a "palette" of bone matrices. If each vertex knows which bones it's attached to, you can render all the vertices at once, and the shader can resolve skin/bone dependencies.
- The SDK samples include more real-world examples of how you can load an animated character from a file.
- The concept of palettes or the address register in general can be useful for a wide range of applications and effects.

CHAPTER 23

SIMPLE COLOR MANIPULATION

The last five chapters have concentrated on changing the vertex position within a vertex shader. This is extremely useful, but it's only part of the story. Once you figure out where the vertex is, you still need to figure out what it looks like. This chapter demonstrates two techniques that change the vertex color to create some useful effects. It is a warm-up for the next chapter, which concentrates on how to implement lights in a shader. In anticipation of that, this chapter demonstrates the following:

- How to encode depth into the color of the vertex using the data from the clip-space transformation.
- Some potential uses for the depth-encoding technique.
- An easy way to implement an x-ray effect using a shader.
- An introduction to the lit instruction.

Unlike other chapters, this chapter features two different sample programs that highlight different shaders. I fully explain the first depth shader and then follow it with the x-ray shader later in the chapter.

Encoding Depth into the Vertex Color

This first shader is very simple. It uses the z coordinate in clip space to derive a vertex color. This can be useful for a variety of techniques. For example, if you are implementing your own fog effect, you might want to adjust the color of a vertex based on its distance from the viewer. You could also combine the distance calculation with the alpha test to implement some optimizations. For instance, if you figure out that the vertex is far enough away, you might set the alpha component of the vertex color low enough that you know that the object will fail the alpha test.

I revisit this technique in Chapter 29 when I demonstrate shadow mapping. The shadow-mapping technique depends on comparing distances between the vertex and the light from the light's viewpoint and from the viewer's viewpoint. One of the limitations of the depth technique that will become apparent in Chapter 29 is that values stored in the vertex color are ultimately limited by the bit depth of your color format. Within the shader, all values are in the form of floating-point values, but colors are ultimately clamped to the range of 0 to 1 and subject to the limitations of the color format. This means that each component of a 32-bit color can really hold only one of 256 different values between 0 and 1. The resolution of each individual component is only good enough to differentiate between changes greater than 1/256. Therefore, very small differences in the values of a color may actually disappear when the value leaves the shader and becomes an actual color value. Figure 23.1 demonstrates this graphically.

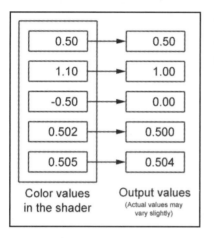

Figure 23.1

Shader color values and real color values.

Color values in the shader		Output values (Actual values may vary slightly)
0.50	→	0.50
1.10	→	1.00
-0.50	→	0.00
0.502	→	0.500
0.505	→	0.504

There are many techniques for circumventing this limitation. Some involve encoding data into more than one of the color channels and then reconstructing the value later. Others involve encoding the depth value into texture coordinates and then using the values from a specially designed texture to actually define the data. Some actually extend that technique to more complex textures such as cube maps. These approaches are effective, but they can be complicated and dependent on the exact needs of a particular application or approach. For that reason, I demonstrate only the simplest approach in hopes that it will lay the groundwork for ideas in using this technique. If you do have uses for this, you might want to investigate approaches that address the issue of bit depth.

Another issue is that future versions of hardware and DirectX are shaping up to include color formats with much higher bit depths. When that happens, many of the complicated techniques become less important. In any case, the following shader encodes distance in the 8 bits of each component of the diffuse color.

The Depth Shader

The depth shader is extremely simple and uses the ubiquitous clip-space transformation to generate the depth value. The computation of the depth value is an almost free side effect of the necessary position transformation. The following code is from EncodeDepth.vsh:

```
vs.1.1
```

The following code is the usual transformation from object space to clip space using the concatenated world, view, and projection matrices. The z component contains the value that would determine the value stored in the depth buffer. This is the value I use for depth. See Chapter 29 for more of a discussion related to depth values. In this shader, I do not output directly to oPos because I need to use the z component and oPos is write-only. I could have written the shader to output the other three components directly to oPos, but that wouldn't have saved any instructions. Besides, the full readable position is now in r1 in case you want to use it for anything else:

```
dp4 r1.x, v0, c0
dp4 r1.y, v0, c1
dp4 r1.z, v0, c2
dp4 r1.w, v0, c3
```

Now emit the transformed position to oPos. This shader doesn't do anything to warp the position:

```
mov oPos, r1
```

As you will see in the application code, c4 contains some depth-encoding parameters that will help you get the most out of the 8 bits available in the current approach. The first component of c4 contains the near plane distance. Anything closer to this is treated as being behind the camera. This is conceptually the same as the near plane of the viewing frustum, although the value can be different from the frustum values in the projection matrix. Setting the near plane distance farther from the camera decreases the range the 8-bit depth value must cover, increasing overall resolution. For instance, if the object is 512 units away and the near plane is at zero, the color can only record new distinct values every two units. If you slide the near plane to be 256 units out, there are distinct color values for every one unit of change. The tradeoff is that a farther near plane might cut off depth values for objects near the camera. I chose the values of these constants for this particular example. You might need different values for different applications. The following line subtracts the near plane distance from the vertex distance:

```
sub r1.z, r1.z, c4.x
```

The last line scales the distance value by the value stored in c4.y. Most of the time, the depth value is greater than 1, which is normally clamped to 1 when it is output from the shader. Scaling the value by some fraction helps to constrain it to the 0 to 1 range and also helps to determine how the bits are used. One aspect that you can implement is the concept of a far plane. This would clamp out values that are farther than your region of interest. The scaling code does that to some extent in that some values still scale to be greater than 1. Again, I chose the values stored in c4 to fit this particular situation:

```
mul oD0, r1.z, c4.y
```

As you can see, this shader is very simple. The depth value is written to all four channels of the color. This is okay if alpha blending is not enabled, but you might need to set the alpha channel separately if blending is enabled. Then again, perhaps your desired effect is that the depth affects the transparency of an object.

One could argue that the shader has ignored the fact that more data can be stored in the other color channels. This is true, but it does depend on the use. For instance, if you are trying to visualize the Z buffer for some reason, you are probably better off with grayscale values because they are generally easier to sort out in your head if you are trying to compare values. If you are feeding the data to some blending operation or pixel shader, you might need to encode things differently to work with the pixel shader. This is why I'm avoiding any particularly clever encoding scheme. The final output of the shader appears in Figure 23.2.

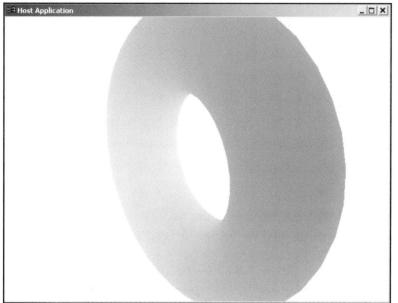

Figure 23.2

The depth encoded model.

The Depth Encoding Application

The depth encoding application is simple. In fact, the render function is really the only function with any new code (besides the shader). The following code snippet is the render function, but the complete application code appears on the CD:

```
void CTechniqueApplication::Render()
{
```

Set the eye position and use that to generate the view matrix. This value and the attributes of the model help determine what the near plane and scaling values should be. The camera is stationary in this sample, but the technique still works if the camera is moving:

```
        D3DXVECTOR4 EyePos(0.0, 10.0f, -30.0f, 0.0f);
        D3DXMatrixLookAtLH(&m_ViewMatrix, &(D3DXVECTOR3)EyePos,
                           &D3DXVECTOR3(0.0f, 0.0f, 0.0f),
                           &D3DXVECTOR3(0.0f, 1.0f, 0.0f));
```

As usual, I rotate the model just to give you something to look at. Once the world matrix is set, the final matrix is built, transposed, and sent off to the shader in the usual way:

```
        D3DXMatrixRotationY(&m_WorldMatrix,
                            (float)GetTickCount() /        1000.0f);

        D3DXMATRIX ShaderMatrix = m_WorldMatrix * m_ViewMatrix *
                                  m_ProjectionMatrix;

        D3DXMatrixTranspose(&ShaderMatrix, &ShaderMatrix);

        m_pD3DDevice->SetVertexShaderConstant(0, &ShaderMatrix, 4);
```

These are the values used to shift and scale the depth values. These could be subject to a lot of tweaking if you want to maximize the utility of the color values. If you are just trying to visualize the Z buffer for your own eyes, the exact values may be less important than if you are trying to use the output in some mathematical operation. The first value stores the near plane distance, and the second value is the scaling value. The other values are convenient constants to have just in case. Remember that you can set different values for different objects, but that might make it difficult to compare the values effectively. This simple example works best if all objects share the same parameters. One potential feature is to encode an object ID into the shaded color. There are definitely more constants available:

```
D3DXVECTOR4 DepthScalers(1.0f, 0.025, 0.0f, 1.0f);

m_pD3DDevice->SetVertexShaderConstant(4, &DepthScalers, 1);
```

Once everything is set up, the model is rendered in the usual fashion. Again, there are optimization opportunities here. There is no reason to reset the shader and the stream in this simple application:

```
m_pD3DDevice->SetVertexShader(m_DepthShader);

m_pD3DDevice->SetStreamSource(0, m_pMeshVertexBuffer,
                              sizeof(MESH_VERTEX));

m_pD3DDevice->SetIndices(m_pMeshIndexBuffer, 0);

m_pD3DDevice->DrawIndexedPrimitive(D3DPT_TRIANGLELIST, 0,
                              m_pMesh->GetNumVertices(), 0,
                              m_pMesh->GetNumFaces());
}
```

Experiment with this shader and change the values of the encoding constants. In Chapter 29, I show you how this effect can be useful, and I discuss some more of the tweaks you could implement.

The X-Ray Shader

The x-ray shader is a fairly simple shader that simulates the effect of x-ray glasses by changing the transparency of vertices directly in front of the eye. Some of the vector manipulation in this shader is similar to the computations you'll see in the next chapter when I demonstrate lighting. This chapter is a stepping stone to some of the more complex calculations you'll see in Chapter 24.

Figure 23.3 shows a screenshot from this application. The area directly in front of the viewer is transparent, but surrounding areas are opaque. As you read through the code, remember that the blending effect is highly dependent on the rendering order. You must render the interior model first for the effect to make sense.

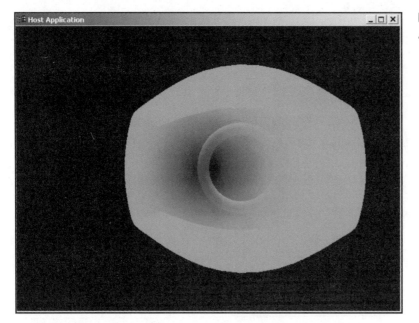

Figure 23.3

"X-ray" glasses.

The following is the shader code from XRayGlasses.vsh. One of the more interesting aspects of the shader is that it uses the `lit` instruction to compute higher powers of the dot product value. In the next chapter, you'll see how `lit` was intended to be used:

```
vs.1.1
```

The shader doesn't affect the position at all, so the shader does the transformation to clip space and emits the position in `oPos`:

```
dp4 oPos.x, v0, c0
dp4 oPos.y, v0, c1
dp4 oPos.z, v0, c2
dp4 oPos.w, v0, c3
```

The constant `c6` contains the eye position in object space. The next chapter goes into more detail about why this is important. In the meantime, the following line of code computes the vector between the eye and the vertex and places the result in `r1`:

```
sub r1, c6, v0
```

The following lines normalize the eye-to-vertex vector:

```
dp3 r1.w, r1, r1
rsq r1.w, r1.w
mul r1, r1, r1.w
```

The following lines compute the dot product of the eye-to-vertex vector and store the result in the first two components of r4. The rest of the shader doesn't use r4.x, but you need to put some value into r4.x for the lit instruction to accept it. Rather than set r4.x somewhere else, you just fill it with the same value as r4.y so that there is some valid value. Once the dot product is computed, r4.w is filled with the exponent value stored in c11.y. The r4 register is then sent to the lit instruction. The main purpose of the lit instruction is to quickly compute powers of the value stored in r4.y and place that value in the z component of the output register. The outcome here is shown in the following equation:

$$r4.z = r4.y^{r4.w}$$

This entire process is shown in Figure 23.4. The dot product defines the difference between the eye-to-vertex vector and the eye direction, which defines the cone of the x-ray effect. Raising the dot product to a higher power helps constrain the effect to a tighter cone. The final value of interest is stored in r4.z:

```
dp3 r4.xy, r1, -c10
mov r4.w, c11.y
lit r4, r4
```

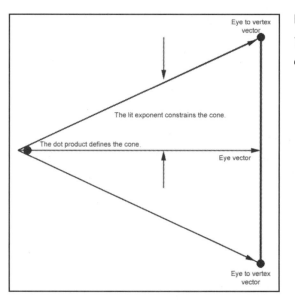

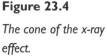

Figure 23.4

The cone of the x-ray effect.

The color values from the vertex color are output in the diffuse color. My original version of this shader included lighting, but I removed it pending the explanation in the next chapter. If you'd like to add more realism with lighting, read the following chapter and add the code to this shader. The process is relatively straightforward because lighting affects the color components, and this shader affects only the alpha component:

```
mov oD0, v5
```

The last line finds the complement of r4.z and uses that to set the alpha component of the output color. Outputting r4.z directly would reverse the effect, making everything outside the code transparent. This might be interesting to incorporate into a spot light effect because you could set things up so that objects outside the spot light are not only unlit, but they fail an alpha test entirely. This would only be really useful in a situation such as a dark cave or somewhere with very little ambient lighting:

```
sub oD0.w, c11.x, r4.z
```

This sample actually uses two shaders, but I discuss the second shader in the next chapter. For now, take a look at the application code.

The X-Ray Application

Like the other sample, the most interesting part of the code for this sample is the Render function. As you look through this function or through the rest of the code on the CD, keep in mind that the full source code loads two objects and creates two shaders. The first shader is the shader described earlier. The second shader implements directional lighting, which is discussed in the next chapter. The following code is the Render function from the x-ray application:

```
void CTechniqueApplication::Render()
{
```

The eye is at a fixed position and it is scanning back and forth, which might produce the mistaken impression that the object is swinging back and forth. The purpose of the scanning is just to give the sample a more dynamic nature. You can move the camera or world any way you want:

```
D3DXVECTOR4 EyePos(0.0, 5.0f, -30.0f, 0.0f);
float EyeScan = 5.0f * sin((float)GetTickCount() / 1000.0f);
D3DXMatrixLookAtLH(&m_ViewMatrix, &(D3DXVECTOR3)EyePos,
                &D3DXVECTOR3(EyeScan, 5.0f, 0.0f),
                &D3DXVECTOR3(0.0f, 1.0f, 0.0f));
```

As usual, set the main transformation matrix:

```
D3DXMATRIX ShaderMatrix = m_WorldMatrix * m_ViewMatrix *
                          m_ProjectionMatrix;
D3DXMatrixTranspose(&ShaderMatrix, &ShaderMatrix);
m_pD3DDevice->SetVertexShaderConstant(0, &ShaderMatrix, 4);
```

Most of the constants are used in the second lighting shader. I explain them in the next chapter. The constant of interest in this chapter is the one that holds the x-ray parameters. The first component stores the value of 1 (c11.x), which is used to compute the complement of the cone value. The second component stores the exponent used by the lit instruction to compute a higher power of the dot product and constrain the cone. The maximum value of this exponent is 127.9961, meaning that this value is right at the edge of the valid range. In a larger scene, you probably do not need this high of a value. If you do, you might need to rework the shader to call the lit instruction twice to compute higher powers:

```
D3DXVECTOR4 LightDir(0.0, -1.0f, 0.0f, 0.0f);
D3DXVECTOR4 LightColor(1.0, 1.0f, 1.0f, 1.0f);
D3DXVECTOR4 Specular(1.0, 1.0f, 1.0f, 100.0f);
D3DXVECTOR4 Ambient(0.1f, 0.1f, 0.1f, 1.0f);
D3DXVECTOR4 XRayParams(1.0f, 127.0f, 1.0, 1.0f);
D3DXMATRIX InverseWorld;
D3DXMATRIX InverseEye;
```

The following lines transform the light direction to object space. This is another explanation saved until the next chapter:

```
D3DXMatrixInverse(&InverseWorld, NULL, &m_WorldMatrix);
D3DXVec4Transform(&LightDir, &LightDir, &InverseWorld);
```

After the D3DX library builds the view matrix, the third column of the matrix contains the direction vector for the eye. The following code extracts that vector from the view matrix and normalizes it:

```
D3DXVECTOR4 EyeDir;
D3DXVec4Normalize(&EyeDir,   &D3DXVECTOR4(m_ViewMatrix._13,
                                          m_ViewMatrix._23,
                                          m_ViewMatrix._33, 0.0f));
```

The eye position and the eye direction are in world space. You need them to be in object space for exactly the same reasons that the light is transformed to object space (as described in the next chapter). As I said, this chapter is supposed to get you really excited about the next chapter. The following code transforms the position and direction of the eye to object space and normalizes the resulting eye direction vector. I don't normalize the position because you don't need to. Some samples do calculations such as this in the vertex shader. Here you can do it once and save the per-vertex calculation:

```
D3DXVec4Transform(&EyePos, &EyePos, &InverseWorld);
D3DXVec4Transform(&EyeDir, &EyeDir, &InverseWorld);
D3DXVec4Normalize(&EyeDir, &EyeDir);
```

Now set the constants so that the shader can use them. Only the lighting shader uses the lighting constants:

```
m_pD3DDevice->SetVertexShaderConstant(5, &LightDir, 1);
m_pD3DDevice->SetVertexShaderConstant(6, &EyePos, 1);
m_pD3DDevice->SetVertexShaderConstant(7, &Specular, 1);
m_pD3DDevice->SetVertexShaderConstant(8, &LightColor, 1);
m_pD3DDevice->SetVertexShaderConstant(9, &Ambient, 1);
m_pD3DDevice->SetVertexShaderConstant(10, &EyeDir, 1);
m_pD3DDevice->SetVertexShaderConstant(11, &XRayParams, 1);
```

The first thing you need to do is draw the interior object. You draw the object using the lighting shader. Once the shader is set, the ring is drawn in the usual way:

```
m_pD3DDevice->SetVertexShader(m_LightingShader);

m_pD3DDevice->SetStreamSource(0, m_pRingVertexBuffer,
                              sizeof(MESH_VERTEX));
m_pD3DDevice->SetIndices(m_pRingIndexBuffer, 0);

m_pD3DDevice->DrawIndexedPrimitive(D3DPT_TRIANGLELIST, 0,
                              m_pRing->GetNumVertices(), 0,
                              m_pRing->GetNumFaces());
```

Finally, you need to draw the outside box. Note that the code to enable alpha blending is not shown here. It is enabled for the entire rendering process, meaning that it might cause inefficiencies when the opaque ring is rendered. Remember that these samples leave a lot of room for optimization. Because the alpha blending has already been set, all you need to do is set the x-ray shader and render the outside object:

```
m_pD3DDevice->SetVertexShader(m_XRayShader);

m_pD3DDevice->SetStreamSource(0, m_pBoxVertexBuffer,
                              sizeof(MESH_VERTEX));
```

```
m_pD3DDevice->SetIndices(m_pBoxIndexBuffer, 0);

m_pD3DDevice->DrawIndexedPrimitive(D3DPT_TRIANGLELIST, 0,
                                   m_pBox->GetNumVertices(), 0,
                                   m_pBox->GetNumFaces());
}
```

One of the details not readily apparent from the code is that this technique works best on models that have a decent amount of vertices to work with. For instance, I call the outer object a box, but it is not a simple cube. I did this to make the scene slightly more interesting, and because the effect, like lighting, is highly dependent on the number of vertices it has to work with. Figure 23.5 shows a screenshot of the outer object rendered in wireframe.

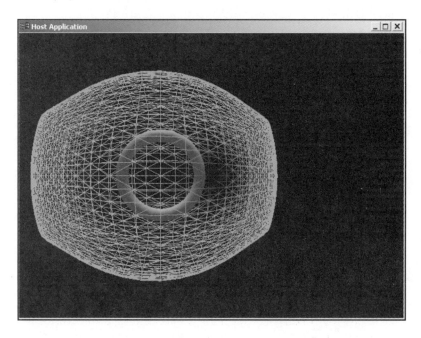

Figure 23.5

A view of the vertices of the outer box.

If the box had been a simple cube, the effect would have been nonexistent because none of the vertices would have fallen within the cone of the x-ray. If one or more had, the effect would have been very coarse and much less interesting. I am trying to set up some of the rationale behind using per-pixel techniques instead of per-vertex techniques. It is several chapters before I talk about pixel shaders, but I want to start planting ideas in your head now.

In Conclusion...

I've probably raised as many questions as answers, especially pertaining to how the vectors are set up for the shader. The next chapter answers those questions and so much more. The purpose of this chapter was to introduce you to some very basic techniques before I delve into the specifics of lighting. I also wanted to show how you could use an instruction such as lit for more than just lighting calculations. Sometimes people get one specific use locked in their heads and have a hard time applying concepts to other techniques. That is the syndrome I'm trying to avoid in this chapter. So before moving on, let me review:

- You can retrieve the depth of a vertex as a byproduct of the standard transformation calculations. There is no need to compute it separately.

- The biggest limitation to encoding depth in color is that the present color formats do not yield accurate results. There are many tricks and hacks to improve this, but the far-term solution involves color formats with higher bit depths.

- Careful choices of shifting and scaling values can lead to better use of the available bits.

- The x-ray shader demonstrates how you can derive color values from vector data. Think of it as a simplified version of some of the lighting techniques.

- The lit instruction has uses beyond lighting. It can be useful in cases where you need to compute powers of other values.

- Many color techniques from lighting to special effects require decent tessellation to get the desired effect. This fact is very apparent in techniques involving lighting and the x-ray effect.

CHAPTER 24

Do-It-Yourself Lighting in a Vertex Shader

I ronically, this chapter features some of the few vertex shaders that actually shade in the usual sense of the word. As you may have noticed in the previous examples, once you enter the wonderful world of shaders, you must do everything yourself. That is the primary reason for implementing lighting in a shader, but there are other reasons as well. For instance, you might want to implement more lights than the standard DirectX lighting model allows. Given the number of constants and instructions available to you, it is quite possible to implement more lights than the DirectX limit allows. You might also want to implement a finer level of control over how the lights work. You might want to implement more complex rules for how things are lit. For example, you may want to light only objects of a given attribute or distance from the viewer. In any case, it is extremely useful and often necessary to implement your own lighting.

This chapter describes the following lighting concepts.

- The difference between object space, world space, and eye space and why it is important.
- Diffuse lighting in a directional lighting model.
- Specular lighting in a directional lighting model.
- Attenuation in a point light model.
- Falloff and other features in a spot light model.
- Opportunities for optimization and features.

The first thing I should do is answer some of the questions raised in the last chapter regarding vector transformation into other spaces.

Converting Light Vectors to Object Space

In the previous chapter, a couple lines of code dealt with inverted matrices and something I kept referring to as object space. I promised I'd explain myself, and I almost always come through on my promises. Sometimes.

Very early in this book, I explained the purpose and computation of a dot product. The dot product and every other vector operation assume that the vectors are given in a consistent coordinate system, but it's not always that easy. Consider the case where an object is sitting in the world, and you have not applied a world matrix transformation. In this case, the world coordinate system and the object coordinate system are effectively the same. An object's normal vectors are almost always given in object coordinates, so in this very specific case, you can correctly compute the dot product of the normal vector and a vector that exists in world space (such as a light vector). This is shown in Figure 24.1.

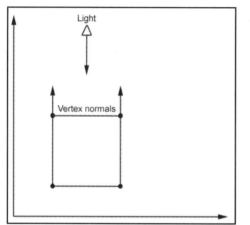
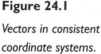

Figure 24.1

Vectors in consistent coordinate systems.

But this is by far the exception that proves the rule. Consider Figure 24.2. Now I have applied some world transformation that has rotated the vertices, but I have not transformed the vertex normals. If you compute the dot product of the light vector and the normal vector, you get an answer, but the effect is incorrect. The top surface of the model is fully lit as if it were directly facing the light, but this is no longer the case.

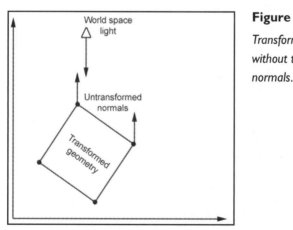

Figure 24.2

Transformed vertices without transformed normals.

There is an easy solution. You can transform the normals as well, which in this case rotates the normal vectors so that you can compute the correct dot product. This is shown in Figure 24.3.

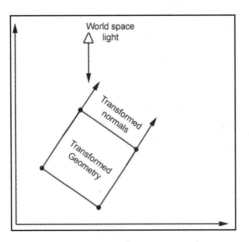

Figure 24.3

Transformed vertices with transformed normals.

Transforming the normals is easy, it's intuitive, and it makes complete sense, but it is not the most optimal solution. Transforming the normal vector costs at least six vertex shader instructions (three to transform and three to normalize). This means that not only are you using up your limited supply of shader instructions, but you are also incurring the overhead of executing those instructions for each and every vertex. There's a better way that has no per-vertex cost at all.

Imagine you are standing on top of the box shown in the previous figures. From your point of view, the two situations can be represented as shown in Figure 24.4. In your frame of reference, it is the light that is moving, not the box.

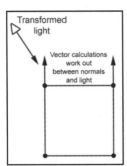

Figure 24.4

World transformations from the object point of view.

In fact, this is exactly the same phenomenon we see here on Earth. From the universal point of view, the Earth is rotating and revolving around the sun. From our point of view, the sun and stars are revolving around us. This is the concept of different reference frames. For our purposes, object space and world space are different reference frames, each with their own interpretations of what is going on.

Reference Frames

The idea of different reference frames is important in physics and other scientific fields. For example, lift is produced as air flows quickly over a wing, yet the same volume of air is nearly motionless with respect to the Earth. The idea that the Earth revolved around the sun instead of the opposite is what got Copernicus and Galileo excommunicated from the church. Long ago, people were locked into the idea of an Earth-centric reference frame and could not see that there might be other reference frames. Today, Galileo and Copernicus are venerated. In their own day, they were excommunicated. I guess it depends on your frame of reference.

You can transform the light into object space rather than transform the vertex normals into world space, and the vector calculations will be correct. As you'll see in the code, one light transformation can affect thousands of vertices. This is much better than transforming thousands of vertices to match one light.

To do this, apply the inverse of the world matrix to the light position and direction. Figure 24.5 shows the process. You use the world matrix to transform the vertex position and orientation, which sets everything up in clip space. You use the inverse of the world matrix to transform the light position, which sets up things for object space lighting calculations. Therefore, you can avoid transforming the normal (unless you have a situation where you need a world space normal, which you'll see in Chapter 26).

If you are not clear on the concept, read on. I explain more as you go through the code.

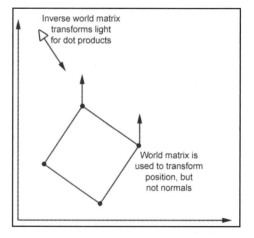

Figure 24.5

The effects of the world and inverse world matrices.

The Directional Light Shader

All three shaders for this chapter are used by one common application, so I explain all three shaders before moving on to the application. The first shader implements one directional light, which is arguably the least complicated light. This code appears in DirLights.vsh:

```
vs.1.1
```

This shader doesn't do anything to warp the vertex position, so you can do the clip space transformation and move on. If you want to add lighting to a shader that does warp the vertex position, you can augment these lines with the warping code and then move on to the lighting. In cases such as Bezier patches, you probably need to properly generate an object space normal before moving on:

```
dp4 oPos.x, v0, c0
dp4 oPos.y, v0, c1
dp4 oPos.z, v0, c2
dp4 oPos.w, v0, c3
```

The constant c5 contains the object space light direction. I chose to specify the light direction as the actual physical direction from the light, but the lighting calculations are based on a vector from the vertex to the light. This is why the values in c5 are negated. Some people choose to define the light differently, eliminating the need for the negation. The final value of the dot product is placed in r0.x. This is all you really need to compute simple diffuse color. Most of the remaining work is for computing specular color:

```
dp3 r0.x, v3, -c5
```

The constant c6 contains the object space eye position. This line computes the vector from the vertex to the eye in object space. Again, computing the vector in object space is cheaper than transforming the normal and calculating in world space:

```
sub r1, c6, v0
```

Now you must normalize the vertex-to-eye vector. When that is complete, the normalized vector is stored in r1:

```
dp3 r1.w, r1, r1
rsq r1.w, r1.w
mul r1, r1, r1.w
```

For specular lighting, you need the half-angle vector between the eye vector and the light direction. Adding the two vectors gives you the right direction, but not the right magnitude. The following lines compute the normalized half-angle vector and place the result in r2:

```
add r2, r1, -c5
dp3 r2.w, r2, r2
rsq r2.w, r2.w
mul r2, r2, r2.w
```

The following line computes the dot product of the object space half-angle vector and the object space vertex normal. The result is placed in the second component of r0:

```
dp3 r0.y, r2, v3
```

The constant c7.w contains the specular power. That value is moved to r0.w:

```
mov r0.w, c7.w
```

The last chapter highlighted the use of the lit instruction for purposes other than lighting. Now I am using it for real lighting calculations. The lit instruction expects "N dot L" to be stored in the x component of the input register, "N dot H" to be stored in the y component, and the specular power to be stored in the w component. If all three are set, the result register stores the "N dot L" value in the y component and "N dot H" to the specular power in the z component of the output register. The preceding code set everything up, so now you can let lit do its job:

```
lit r4, r0
```

The constant c7 stores the specular color for this object. The following line multiplies the specular light contribution by the specular color. Most of the time, the specular color is white, but it doesn't need to be:

```
mul r5, r4.z, c7
```

You multiply the diffuse lighting contribution (r4.y) by the diffuse light color. This yields the diffuse light value for the vertex. You then multiply this value by the diffuse color of the vertex itself and finally add the ambient light color (c9). The register r6 now contains the complete diffuse color of the vertex:

```
mul r6, r4.y, c8
mad r6, r6, v5, c9
```

The last line adds the specular lighting value and outputs the final color. The result is a vertex lit with a simple directional light:

```
add oD0, r5, r6
```

In many cases in this shader, I mentioned that a certain constant held a certain object color or attribute. Remember that you can set these constants before all objects are rendered, some objects are rendered, or even parts of objects are rendered. Those constants define the attributes for whatever vertices are passed into the shader on a given call to DrawPrimitive. If you really want, you can pass the triangles in one at a time and define different lighting constants for each one. This would be extremely bad from an optimization standpoint, but the point is that you have whatever level of control you want or need.

That is the directional light shader. You can activate it in the sample program by pressing the 1 key. Figure 24.6 shows a screenshot.

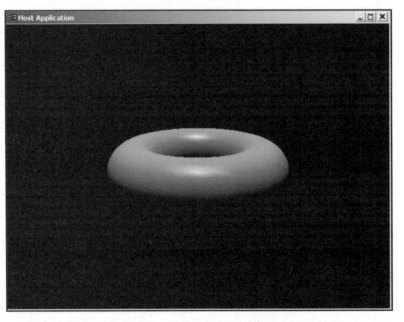

Figure 24.6

Directional lighting.

The Point Light Shader

Following is the shader for a point light. This shader builds from the directional light shader but adds the effects of attenuation and a vertex-to-light direction vector. The shader code is from PointLight.vsh:

```
vs.1.1
```

Output the position:

```
dp4 oPos.x, v0, c0
dp4 oPos.y, v0, c1
```

```
dp4 oPos.z, v0, c2
dp4 oPos.w, v0, c3
```

Compute the vertex-to-light vector and store it in r0. You will use this to get the distance value needed for the attenuation effect. Also, unlike directional lights, point lights require you to find the direction from the vertex to the light. You use this vector for that step as well. Remember that c4 contains the object space position of the light:

```
sub r0, c4, v0
```

The following lines compute the distance squared and the inverse of the distance. These values are used by the dst instruction to generate a distance value:

```
dp3 r1.w, r0, r0
rsq r2.w, r1.w
```

Before moving on to the dst instruction, I use the inverse distance value stored in r2.w to normalize the vertex-to-light vector stored in r0:

```
mul r0, r0, r2.w
```

You use the following lines to compute the attenuation factor. First the dst instruction sets r1 to (1, d, d*d, 1/d). The first three components are exactly what are needed for the attenuation equation (see Chapter 11). You multiply these values by the attenuation factors in c10. Finally, the rcp instruction generates the reciprocal, and you have the attenuation factor stored in r1.w:

```
dst r1, r1.wwww, r2.wwww
dp3 r1.w, r1, c10
rcp r1.w, r1.w
```

Find the dot product of the light vector and the normal vector. This time, the light direction is not based on a constant. Instead, it is based on the direction from the vertex to the point light. This vector is different for different vertices:

```
dp3 r0.x, v3, r0
```

The following four lines find the vertex-to-eye vector and normalize it in the same fashion you saw in the previous shader. The normalized vector is stored in r2:

```
sub r2, c6, v0
dp3 r2.w, r2, r2
rsq r2.w, r2.w
mul r2, r2, r2.w
```

You compute the half-angle vector as you did before. The normalized vector is stored in r3:

```
add r3, r2, r0
dp3 r4.x, r3, r3
rsq r4, r4.x
mul r3, r3, r4
```

Set up and execute the lit instruction as described in the previous shader:

```
dp3 r0.y, r3, v3
mov r0.w, c7.w
lit r4, r0
```

This is where the attenuation comes into play. The following line multiplies all the lighting contributions by the attenuation factor. Unlike the directional light, point lighting is dependent on both the direction and distance of the light to the vertex:

```
mul r4, r4, r1.w
```

The last four lines compute and emit the final vertex color in the same way as the previous shader:

```
mul r5, r4.z, c7
mul r6, r4.y, c8
mad r6, r6, v5, c9
add oD0, r5, r6
```

Figure 24.7 is a screenshot of the point light shader in use. You can activate the point light shader by pressing the 2 key:

The Spot Light Shader

The last shader builds from the previous shader. This time I add the code for the spot light cone. The following shader does not include the ability to use a nonlinear falloff profile for the penumbra because I wanted to keep the shader fairly simple. For complex spot lights, I'd be tempted to recommend a per-pixel approach. You can find the following code in Spotlights.vsh:

```
vs.1.1
```

Output the position:

```
dp4 oPos.x, v0, c0
dp4 oPos.y, v0, c1
```

Figure 24.7

Per-vertex point lighting.

```
dp4 oPos.z, v0, c2
dp4 oPos.w, v0, c3
```

The following block of code is from the previous shader. In the end, r0 contains the normalized vertex-to-light vector, and r1.w contains the attenuation factor:

```
sub r0, c4, v0
dp3 r1.w, r0, r0
rsq r2.w, r1.w
mul r0, r0, r2.w
dst r1, r1.wwww, r2.wwww
dp3 r1.w, r1, c10
rcp r1.w, r1.w
```

Compute the dot product of the vertex-to-light vector with the object space light direction. You use this value to determine where this vertex is in the spot light cone:

```
dp3 r5.x, -r0, c5
```

Once the dot product value is stored in r5.x, subtract it from the spot light umbra value. The x component of c11 contains the cosine of the umbra angle divided by two. Therefore, you can compare the two values as two dot products. If the vertex is outside of the umbra, the value of r5.y is positive; otherwise, it is some negative value:

```
sub r5.y, c11.x, r5.x
```

The following line makes the assumption that the vertex is within the penumbra. The value of r5.y is scaled by 1 / (umbra–penumbra). This produces a linear falloff through the penumbra, but the falloff is in the wrong direction. This line corrects that by negating the value and finding the complement. If you want to control the shape of the falloff, this is where you do it:

```
mad r5.y, -c11.z, r5.y, c11.w
```

If the value was inside the umbra, the result of the previous line is greater than one. The min instruction clamps the value to one for all vertices inside the umbra:

```
min r5.y, r5.y, c11.w
```

The previous lines have derived values for points in the umbra and in the penumbra. This last line computes values for points outside of the spot light cone. Using the original value stored in r5.x, the sge instruction checks whether the vertex is inside the cone. If it is, r6.w is set to one. If not, r6.w is set to zero. The falloff term (r5.y) is then multiplied by r6.w. The falloff term is set to zero for all vertices outside the cone. For all other vertices, the falloff value remains unaffected:

```
sge r6.w, r5.x, c11.y
mul r5.y, r5.y, r6.w
```

The following lines are repeated from the previous shaders. In the end, r4 contains the diffuse and specular lighting contributions:

```
dp3 r0.x, v3, r0
sub r2, c6, v0
dp3 r2.w, r2, r2
rsq r2.w, r2.w
mul r2, r2, r2.w
add r3, r2, r0
dp3 r4.x, r3, r3
rsq r4, r4.x
mul r3, r3, r4
dp3 r0.y, r3, v3
mov r0.w, c7.w
lit r4, r0
```

The first of these two lines attenuates the lighting over distance, as you saw in the previous shader. The second line applies the falloff values that define the spot light cone:

```
mul r4, r4, r1.w
mul r4, r4, r5.y
```

The remaining lines repeat the final color computations from the previous shaders:

```
mul r5, r4.z, c7
mul r6, r4.y, c8
mad r6, r6, v5, c9
add oD0, r5, r6
```

Figure 24.8 shows a screenshot of this shader. You can activate the spot light shader by pressing the 3 key:

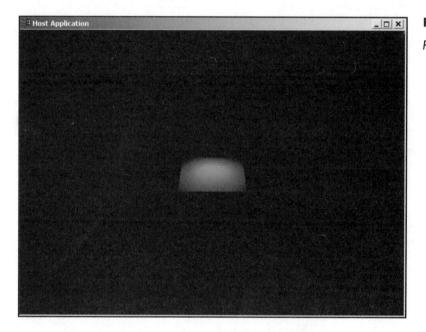

Figure 24.8

Per-vertex spot lighting.

The Application Code

As in the previous chapters, the Render function is by far the most interesting part of the application code. However, there are a couple points to highlight about the rest of the code. The application creates three different vertex shaders and decides which shader to use based on a variable called m_WhichShader. The following function responds to keyboard input and decides which shader is used:

```
BOOL CTechniqueApplication::HandleMessage(MSG *pMessage)
{
        if (pMessage->message == WM_KEYDOWN && pMessage->wParam == '1')
            m_WhichShader = 0;
        if (pMessage->message == WM_KEYDOWN && pMessage->wParam == '2')
```

```
                m_WhichShader = 1;
        if (pMessage->message == WM_KEYDOWN && pMessage->wParam == '3')
                m_WhichShader = 2;


        return CHostApplication::HandleMessage(pMessage);
}
```

One thing to point out here is that I could have just called SetVertexShader with the appropriate shader handle. That would have been slightly more efficient, but I'm trying to make the Render function as clear as possible. Here is the Render function:

```
void CTechniqueApplication::Render()
{
```

The following lines set up the view and world matrices and pass the main transformation matrix to the shader:

```
        D3DXVECTOR4 EyePos(0.0, 10.0f, -50.0f, 0.0f);

        D3DXMatrixLookAtLH(&m_ViewMatrix, &(D3DXVECTOR3)EyePos,
                        &D3DXVECTOR3(0.0f, 0.0f, 0.0f),
                        &D3DXVECTOR3(0.0f, 1.0f, 0.0f));

        D3DXMatrixRotationX(&m_WorldMatrix,
                        (float)GetTickCount() /          1000.0f);

        D3DXMATRIX ShaderMatrix = m_WorldMatrix * m_ViewMatrix *
                                m_ProjectionMatrix;

        D3DXMatrixTranspose(&ShaderMatrix, &ShaderMatrix);

        m_pD3DDevice->SetVertexShaderConstant(0, &ShaderMatrix, 4);
```

These constants set all the properties for the lights. Some of the lighting modes might not use all of the lighting parameters, but they are all set in bulk. As usual, setting these constants to the same values every frame is not very efficient. The constant values are fairly self-explanatory. Some of the more cryptic values are the specular power set in the last component of the specular constant and the attenuation terms that correspond to the values discussed in Chapter 11. Remember that the specular power is subject to the limitations of the lit instruction:

```
        D3DXVECTOR4 LightPos(0.0f, 5.0f, 0.0f, 0.0f);
        D3DXVECTOR4 LightDir(0.0, -1.0f, 0.0f, 0.0f);
```

```
D3DXVECTOR4 LightColor(1.0, 1.0f, 1.0f, 1.0f);
D3DXVECTOR4 Specular(1.0, 1.0f, 1.0f, 100.0f);
D3DXVECTOR4 Ambient(0.01f, 0.01f, 0.01f, 1.0f);
D3DXVECTOR4 Attenuation(1.0f, 0.2f, 0.0f, 0.0f);
```

The falloff constant is cryptic. The first component contains the cosine of the umbra angle divided by two. The second component is a similar value for the penumbra. Note that lower angles have higher cosine values. The third component is the reciprocal of the first component minus the second component. You use this to scale the falloff. Finally, the last component stores the useful value of 1.0:

```
D3DXVECTOR4 Falloff(0.9f, 0.5f, 2.5f, 1.0f);
```

These lines transform the light position and direction to the equivalent object space vectors. First you need to compute the inverse of the world matrix and then use that matrix to transform the vectors. Once everything is transformed, you should still normalize the light direction. Even though these transformations happen on the CPU, it's still more efficient than transforming every vertex normal:

```
D3DXMATRIX InverseWorld;

D3DXMatrixInverse(&InverseWorld, NULL, &m_WorldMatrix);
D3DXVec4Transform(&LightDir, &LightDir, &InverseWorld);
D3DXVec4Transform(&LightPos, &LightPos, &InverseWorld);
D3DXVec4Transform(&EyePos, &EyePos, &InverseWorld);
D3DXVec4Normalize(&LightDir, &LightDir);
```

Feed all the constants to the shader:

```
m_pD3DDevice->SetVertexShaderConstant(4, &LightPos, 1);
m_pD3DDevice->SetVertexShaderConstant(5, &LightDir, 1);
m_pD3DDevice->SetVertexShaderConstant(6, &EyePos, 1);
m_pD3DDevice->SetVertexShaderConstant(7, &Specular, 1);
m_pD3DDevice->SetVertexShaderConstant(8, &LightColor, 1);
m_pD3DDevice->SetVertexShaderConstant(9, &Ambient, 1);
m_pD3DDevice->SetVertexShaderConstant(10, &Attenuation, 1);
m_pD3DDevice->SetVertexShaderConstant(11, &Falloff, 1);
```

Set the shader based on the user input:

```
m_pD3DDevice->SetVertexShader(m_LightShaders[m_WhichShader]);
```

Render the model in the usual fashion:

```
m_pD3DDevice->SetStreamSource(0, m_pMeshVertexBuffer,
                              sizeof(MESH_VERTEX));
m_pD3DDevice->SetIndices(m_pMeshIndexBuffer, 0);

m_pD3DDevice->DrawIndexedPrimitive(D3DPT_TRIANGLELIST, 0,
                                   m_pMesh->GetNumVertices(), 0,
                                   m_pMesh->GetNumFaces());
}
```

That's the application code. As usual, you should experiment with different parameters until you get a good feel for how things work.

Multiple Lights in One Shader

Each of these shaders implements a single light of a single type, but there is nothing to stop you from implementing several lights in the same shader. Your only limitations are the number of constants and instructions.

You might even want to experiment with palettes of lights. You are probably more limited by instruction count than by constant availability. You could conceivably store many lights in the constants and then use a palette scheme to pick the small number of good lights for any given object. I leave that to you to experiment with.

In Conclusion...

Perhaps the most common reason for lighting in a shader is to provide lighting alongside some other shader effect. In fact, if you are just implementing a shader to exactly replicate the DirectX lighting functions, the built-in lights are probably better. In many of the previous chapters, I used very simple lighting so I could concentrate on the other effects. If you'd like, you can go back and add real lighting to the sample programs. Here's the review for this chapter:

- If you are using a shader, you no longer have access to the built-in lighting features of DirectX.
- Vector calculations in object space are much cheaper than converting all normals to other spaces.

- Directional lights are the easiest lights to implement and use the fewest shader instructions.
- You can set lighting constants as often as you need. If you have different lighting properties for different objects, reset the lighting parameters accordingly.
- You can build multiple lights into a single shader. You are only limited by the limits of shaders in general.

CHAPTER 25

CARTOON SHADING

For many years, the holy grail of computer graphics has been the ability to render photorealistic graphics in real time. Ironically, as soon as shaders were available, people began working on interesting rendering effects that were not at all photorealistic. Cartoon or "toon" shading is one of those techniques, and it seems like everyone has an example of this. This chapter discusses the following points:

- Using shaders and textures to support complex rendering algorithms.
- The theory behind toon shading.
- Toon shading in a shader.
- Other uses of the same techniques.

Shaders, Textures, and Complex Functions

The toon shader is one example of a more general class of shaders that implement complex color calculations with the help of a texture lookup. Many techniques use textures that encode the results of complex mathematical functions rather than visual "textures." The shader performs some simple initial calculations and encodes the results into texture coordinates. These texture coordinates serve as lookup values into the results of the complex math. To put it a different way, the vertex shader can compute some values that then serve as parameters to some complex function that would be difficult to implement in a shader.

For instance, imagine you wanted to add the contributions of two lights to light a vertex. You can think of this as the following equation:

$$C = (l_1 \bullet N) + (l_2 \bullet N)$$

The shader would look like the following pseudocode:

```
dp3 r0.x, VERTEX_NORMAL, LIGHT1_DIRECTION
dp3 r0.y, VERTEX_NORMAL, LIGHT2_DIRECTION
add oD0, r0.x, r0.y
```

Now imagine I challenged you to not use the add instruction. You could use the dp3 instruction twice to find the lighting component for each light, but then you'd have no way to add them. This is where the texture comes in.

You know that the dp3 instruction produces some value between zero and one. You also know that you have two lights. Based on this, you can create a two-dimensional texture, as shown in Figure 25.1.

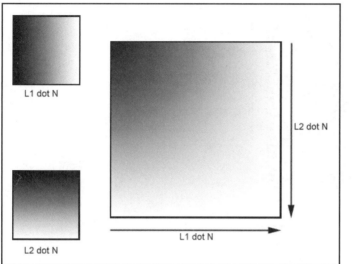

Figure 25.1

Encoding the sum of two values in a texture.

Each texel contains a value for the sum of the two lighting values. The size of the texture affects the accuracy of individual values. A higher-resolution texture encodes more samples of the function. Now, assuming you render your vertices with the proper texture states, you can produce the lighting effect with the following pseudocode:

```
dp3 oT0.x, VERTEX_NORMAL, LIGHT1_DIRECTION
dp3 oT0.y, VERTEX_NORMAL, LIGHT2_DIRECTION
```

This snippet of shader code places the value of the two lighting components into the u and v texture coordinates. These serve as lookup values into the texture, and the final texture value is the sum of the two lighting values. Obviously, this is a contrived example because you never need to do this for such a simple function. You can apply the same concept to more complex functions without any additional cost. For instance, imagine that you need to use the following lighting equation instead of simply summing the two lights:

$$C = \sin(l_1 \cdot N) + \cos(l_2 \cdot N)$$

I discussed the sine and cosine in previous chapters, so you know that you can write shader code for this function, but that requires many instructions in the shader. Instead, you can generate a texture that produces the correct result using exactly the same code snippet shown earlier. Figure 25.2 shows how the results of the preceding equation can be encoded into the color values of a texture. A shader can calculate two dot products and output texture coordinates with fewer instructions than the Taylor series approximation seen in previous chapters.

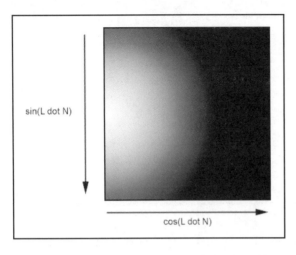

Figure 25.2

Encoding a complex function in a shader.

This type of approach saves shader instructions and is a flexible way to experiment with different approaches. It is also useful when you need to implement functions that are not easy to implement with basic shader instructions. The toon shader is one of these.

Applying the Approach to the Toon Shader (Part 1)

So far, the examples have only been abstract, but the toon shader is a simple example of how these ideas come into play. Figure 25.3 shows an object rendered with directional light in a realistic way and in a cartoon way. Figure 25.3 doesn't "edge" the carton object; I get to that soon.

Figure 25.3

Realistic and toon shading.

If you were to create a spectrum of the values applied to both of these renderings, you would get two very different spectra, as shown in Figure 25.4.

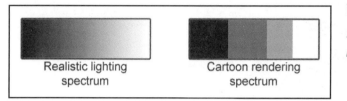

Figure 25.4

Spectra for different renderings.

The realistic rendering uses a smooth range of values to create a smooth-shaded set of surfaces. The cartoon rendering uses a limited set of values with sharp discontinuities between different values.

Technically...

Mathematically speaking, functions with this type of continuity are called step functions. It is possible to implement this function in a shader, but it requires a lot of juggling and jumping through hoops. Any hardware that has good shader support should have very good texture support, so it just makes more sense to use the texture approach. This is especially true with toon shading because a cartoon probably wouldn't use texture states for many other things.

Figure 25.4 has already given away the punch line. If you think of the toon spectrum as a "complex function," then Figure 25.4 shows the lookup texture you need to implement toon shading. In the previous example, I showed you 2D textures as examples. For toon shading, you need values in only one dimension. Figure 25.4 showed the spectra as larger rectangles so that the values would be easy to see, but in reality the texture only needs to be a one-dimensional texture. In practical terms, this means that the texture is one pixel high and a certain number of pixels wide. The width depends on the resolution you need. You can use a four-pixel-wide texture if you have four different values evenly spread over the spectrum. The texture must be wider if you have more values or if the spread is uneven.

I show the exact shader code and discuss the interactions more when I get to the full shader code listing. In the meantime, we still have one more missing piece.

Applying the Approach to the Toon Shader (Part 2)

Figure 25.5 shows a screenshot from this chapter's sample application. It shows the complete toon effect with the proper edging effect. This effect is based on the same lookup concept, but it is not based on lighting.

Figure 25.5

Screenshot with edging.

The edge effect simulates the way a cartoonist would ink the sharp edges and silhouette of the cartoon object. In this case, sharp edges are defined from the perspective of the viewer. To generate the edges, you can compare the vertex normal with the vertex-to-eye vector (in object space). If the two vectors are very similar (the dot product is near 1.0), the vertex is not on an edge. If the two values are not similar (the dot product is near 0.0), the vertex is on an edge. This is shown in Figure 25.6.

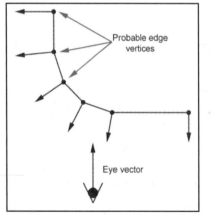

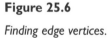

Figure 25.6

Finding edge vertices.

Based on this, you can apply the texture approach and use the dot product of the two vectors as an index into a lookup texture that would modulate the shading texture. The lookup texture could specify a black value for dot products near zero and white for all other values. However, there is a problem with this. If you create a texture that has a small black region, that region has a heavier than needed impact at higher mip map levels. This means that some areas may be darkened more or less than you want them to be. Instead, you can set the mip map levels yourself, weighting the black region differently at each level. This ensures that the edge effect is only applied to the small regions that access the higher mip levels. This excludes large polygons that might have one vertex on the edge and others that are not on the edge, and therefore stretches the edge effect over a wider area. Figure 25.7 shows the different mip levels of the edge texture.

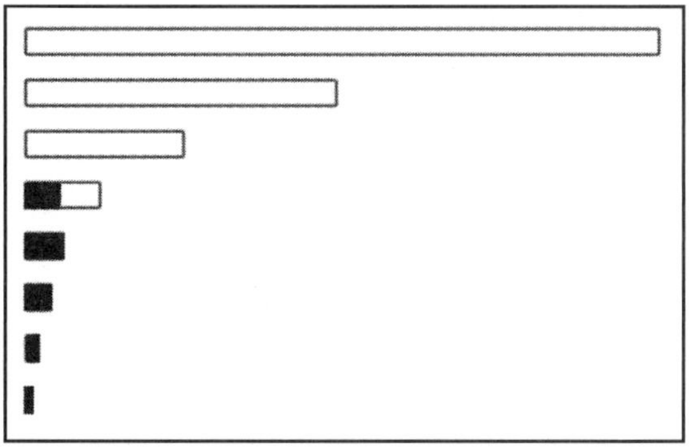

Figure 25.7

Levels of the edge texture.

This texture is similar to the texture used in nVidia's toon effect. You can apply different weights or colors to adjust the edge effect. Greater emphasis on the black regions of lower mip levels results in thicker edges. Slight variations in color or gradation can produce other effects. Feel free to experiment with different texture values, but begin your experiments with small changes. You will find that some small changes have large impacts on the overall effect.

Putting It All Together in a Shader

You now have all the pieces to the puzzle. The following shader code applies both techniques in a single pass using two different textures. This shader is in Toon.vsh. It expects the object space light vector in c5 and the object space eye position in c6:

```
vs.1.1
```

As usual, output the position. You can use the toon shader to supplement any other technique. For example, you can replace these lines with the skinning animation technique to produce a skinned cartoon character—assuming, of course, that the application, mesh, and so on are set up for both techniques:

```
dp4 oPos.x, v0, c0
dp4 oPos.y, v0, c1
dp4 oPos.z, v0, c2
dp4 oPos.w, v0, c3
```

The following line swaps the light direction so that it becomes the vertex-to-light direction and computes the dot product of that and the normal vector. The result is a basic diffuse lighting value, which is stored in the x component of the first texture coordinate. The texture is 1D, so you use only the first component:

```
dp3 oT0.x, v3, -c5
```

These lines compute the normalized vertex-to-eye vector in object space. In the end, r1 contains the normalized vector:

```
sub r1, c6, v0
dp3 r1.w, r1, r1
rsq r1.w, r1.w
mul r1, r1, r1.w
```

The dot product of the normal vector and the eye vector is written to the x component of the second texture coordinate. The device is responsible for setting the proper mip level of the texture. Again, this is a 1D texture. The edge texture is the last texture stage, and it modulates the previous values. Because the texel values are either zero or one, they either set the final color to black or leave it unchanged:

```
dp3 oT1.x, v3, r1
```

Finally, you pass the diffuse color through the shader. The diffuse color defines the overall color of the vertex. The first texture modulates it with a toon shading value. Finally, the edge texture sets it to black if it is on an edge:

```
mov oD0, v5
```

As you can see, it's a pretty simple shader. The application code is fairly simple as well.

The Toon Shading Application

As usual, I include only the code for the Render function here in the text. The only interesting missing piece is that the application loads the two textures during the PostInitialize function. The full source code is available on the CD:

```
void CTechniqueApplication::Render()
{
```

The following lines set up the view and world matrices and transpose them for the shader. You also reuse the eye position later when it is passed to the shader for the edge calculations:

```
D3DXVECTOR4 EyePos(0.0, 10.0f, -20.0f, 0.0f);
D3DXMatrixLookAtLH(&m_ViewMatrix, &(D3DXVECTOR3)EyePos,
                   &D3DXVECTOR3(0.0f, 0.0f, 0.0f),
                   &D3DXVECTOR3(0.0f, 1.0f, 0.0f));

D3DXMatrixRotationY(&m_WorldMatrix,
                    (float)GetTickCount() /          1000.0f);

D3DXMATRIX ShaderMatrix = m_WorldMatrix * m_ViewMatrix *
                          m_ProjectionMatrix;

D3DXMatrixTranspose(&ShaderMatrix, &ShaderMatrix);
m_pD3DDevice->SetVertexShaderConstant(0, &ShaderMatrix, 4);
```

As you have seen in previous chapters, the light direction is given as the true physical light direction, but it is swapped in the shader to give the vertex-to-light direction:

```
D3DXVECTOR4 LightDir(0.0, -1.0f, 0.0f, 0.0f);
```

You transform the light direction and eye position to object space before passing them to the shader. This is necessary for both the shading and edging calculations:

```
D3DXMATRIX InverseWorld;
D3DXMatrixInverse(&InverseWorld, NULL, &m_WorldMatrix);
D3DXVec4Transform(&LightDir, &LightDir, &InverseWorld);
D3DXVec4Transform(&EyePos, &EyePos, &InverseWorld);
```

Pass the constants to the shader. In this case, the light direction never changes, so recomputing and resending the transformed light direction every frame is less than optimal. Feel free to optimize this once you fully understand it:

```
m_pD3DDevice->SetVertexShaderConstant(5, &LightDir, 1);
m_pD3DDevice->SetVertexShaderConstant(6, &EyePos, 1);
```

Set the vertex shader. Again, you can optimize this:

```
m_pD3DDevice->SetVertexShader(m_ToonShader);
```

Setting textures is a mildly expensive operation that you don't need to redo every frame. I do it here for clarity:

```
m_pD3DDevice->SetTexture(0, m_pToonTexture);
m_pD3DDevice->SetTexture(1, m_pEdgeTexture);
```

Setting the texture stage states every frame might be necessary because of the relatively sparse set of states that are recorded and reset by the font class used to render the frame rate. If you try to optimize this by moving these lines, be aware of the interactions between this and the font class.

These lines set the texture to clamp. Any values greater than one or less than zero are treated as one or zero. This makes sense in the context of both shading and edging because you don't want values to wrap to some lower or higher value.

Also, by default, the first texture modulates the diffuse color and other textures are disabled. These lines enable the second texture by setting the color operation to modulate and the mip filter to a linear filter. The linear filter helps to smooth transitions when vertices go from being an edge to not being an edge over the course of an animation:

```
m_pD3DDevice->SetTextureStageState(0, D3DTSS_ADDRESSU,
                                   D3DTADDRESS_CLAMP);
m_pD3DDevice->SetTextureStageState(1, D3DTSS_ADDRESSU,
                                   D3DTADDRESS_CLAMP);
m_pD3DDevice->SetTextureStageState(1, D3DTSS_COLOROP,
                                   D3DTOP_MODULATE);
m_pD3DDevice->SetTextureStageState(1, D3DTSS_MIPFILTER,
                                   D3DTEXF_LINEAR);
```

Now that everything is set up, render the mesh in the usual fashion. In this specific case, setting the stream and index source every frame is redundant:

```
m_pD3DDevice->SetStreamSource(0, m_pMeshVertexBuffer,
                              sizeof(MESH_VERTEX));
```

```
        m_pD3DDevice->SetIndices(m_pMeshIndexBuffer, 0);

        m_pD3DDevice->DrawIndexedPrimitive(D3DPT_TRIANGLELIST, 0,
                                    m_pMesh->GetNumVertices(), 0,
                                    m_pMesh->GetNumFaces());
}
```

One thing that doesn't appear in the code here is the vertex format for the mesh. There are no texture coordinates in the input vertex format even though the shader outputs texture coordinates. Because there are no input values, there is no reason to have them. The types of output information are not dependent on the input formats.

There aren't that many opportunities here for experimentation. Most of the changes would take place in either the shader or the textures.

Ideas for Texture Changes

The sample toon shading texture goes beyond simply changing the intensity of the lit vertex. It also adds a bluish tint. There is no real reason for this beyond proving the point that the texture is capable of changing colors in more interesting ways. You could do a lot by changing the color or alpha values of the texture.

You can also change the number of values in the shading texture. A texture with two values could produce a harsh monochrome effect. A smooth gradient across the texture would produce a normal diffuse lighting effect. Figure 25.8 shows different gradient textures and their effects on the final rendering.

Figure 25.8

Different shading textures.

You could produce interesting effects by transitioning between these different textures. One way to do this is to create a 2D texture with different 1D textures in each row. Then, the shader could change the v coordinate for the texture based on some constant. This could create an effect such as a character going from normal shading to cartoon shading as you run through the different texture rows.

Ideas for Shader Changes

Many other shaders use the basic ideas behind the toon shader. If you look at the nVidia Effects Browser, you will see many shaders based upon this idea of using a texture to encode more complex functions. For instance, the Membrane effect is based on the idea that some materials are more transparent when they are viewed directly than when they are viewed at an angle. The dot product of the eye vector and the normal vector is used as an index value into different textures that simulate different materials. Other effects simulate more complex vector interactions.

In many ways, the next chapter is based on the same underlying idea, only it uses a cube map texture rather than a standard texture. You'll see many of the same concepts feeding into the reflection shader.

In Conclusion...

Even if you never write a game or application that uses a cartoon style, there are many ideas to take away from this chapter. Many functions or techniques that could be implemented using shader instructions just make more sense encoded into a texture. Sometimes, a texture-based solution is also a more flexible solution. I have not included other chapters of this type because I believe they are all fundamentally the same. Once you understand these basic ideas, it's just a matter of applying different math functions in the same basic shader and application code.

These ideas also feed well into pixel shaders. Many pixel shader techniques are based on using textures as lookup tables. In some cases, texel values from one texture serve as lookup values into another texture. I get into this more with some of the pixel shader techniques.

Finally, many advanced features on the horizon might make these things even more interesting. For instance, it is probable that you'll see displacement maps in the future. These textures displace vertex positions based on texel values. It's possible that this can create opportunities for interesting shaders such as a texture-based

Bezier patch modeler. Other advances such as higher-precision textures might make these approaches much better. But these things are not quite a reality yet. While we're all waiting, I review:

- Textures can texture an object, but they can also store the values for complex functions. They can be powerful tools when used with the proper shader and texture stage states.

- 2D textures can encode functions with two variables. 1D functions can encode functions with one variable. The next chapter shows how you use a 3D texture coordinate.

- Toon shading is based on the idea that shading in a cartoon is not smooth. You can use a texture to encode discontinuities in the shading. The texture coordinate is based on the same dot product you saw for simple diffuse lighting.

- The edges of a toon are rendered with a texture that encodes black values for texture coordinates near zero. This is used as a lookup table for the dot product of the eye vector and the normal vector.

- The edge texture encodes the edge lookup differently in different mip levels. This ensures that the edge effect is only seen on vertices that are on the edge and that access higher mip levels.

- Different textures have different effects on the final outcome of this technique. You should experiment with different textures.

- This technique is conceptually the same as many other techniques that use textures as lookup tables. Spend some time looking at other techniques to get more ideas about how they are implemented and to see how powerful the basic technique is.

CHAPTER 26

REFLECTION AND REFRACTION

Y ou've seen that much of the realistic effect of 3D graphics comes from using enough vertices to make a smooth model, using the proper lighting models, or using a high-resolution texture. One thing that's been missing is the idea of reflection. If you look around the real world, you see that many objects are more reflective than you might think. Adding reflections to some objects adds an extra dimension to the object and minimizes that fake lifeless look that some renderings have. This chapter focuses on reflection and refraction with the following points:

- Environmental mapping and cube maps.
- Dynamic cube maps.
- The reflection/refraction vertex shader.
- How to use cube maps to texture the environment.
- Other uses of environmental mapping and cube maps.

Environmental Mapping and Cube Maps

Environmental mapping is a type of texture mapping with the primary purpose of adding environmental effects to objects. In most cases, the environmental effect is reflection, but at the end of the chapter I talk about a few more effects. There are several types of environmental maps, but the most common and easiest to use is a cube map.

If you want to talk about mapping the environment onto an object, you have to figure out a way to represent the environment. Conceptually, cube maps represent the environment as six sides of a cube that surrounds one or more of the objects in your scene. In practice, a cube map is a specialized DirectX texture object that represents each of the six cube sides in a separate texture surface, as shown in Figure 26.1.

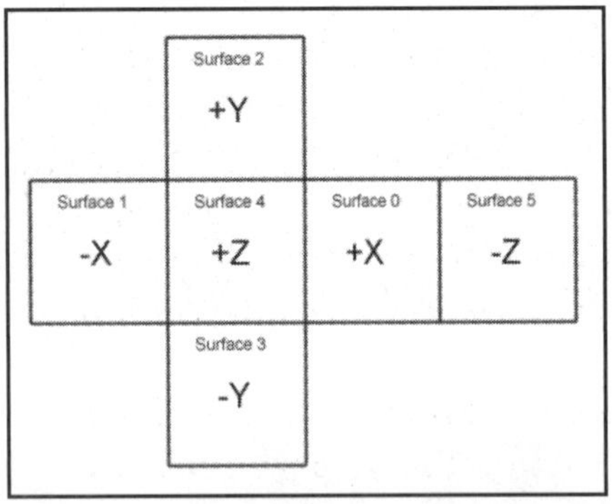

Figure 26.1

A cube map texture.

Think of the texture coordinates used to access this texture as 3D vectors. If you think of the texture coordinate as a 3D vector pointing from the center of the cube out toward the sides, the point where the vector intersects a cube wall is the matching texel for that texture coordinate. I explain this more when you get to the actual vector math of reflection.

The cube map texture is represented by the IDirect3DCubeTexture8 interface. As you will see, the D3DX functions make loading a cube map just as easy as loading a normal texture. The best way to create a cube map is with the DirectX texture tool. The texture tool lets you load each side of the cube map from a separate image and save the complete cube map as one .dds file. If you need only static cube maps and you use the D3DX libraries to load them, you never need to deal with the specifics of a cube map. The only time you do is with dynamic cube maps.

Changing Cube Maps Dynamically

Imagine you have a racing game and the cars are racing through a tunnel. If the tunnel never changes, you could have a cube map of the tunnel that you load once and use throughout the game. This would create a decent effect of the tunnel walls reflected on the car as it drives along, but what happens when another car passes? This is where dynamic cube maps come in.

To keep the example easy, imagine the tunnel runs straight along the positive Z axis. If the car is driving alone, you can use the loaded cube map. If a second car begins closing in from behind (the negative Z direction), you can update the cube map by changing the view matrix so that the camera is looking back towards the second car and render the scene into the –Z face of the cube map. Then, you can render the scene as usual, using the updated cube map to generate the correct reflection of the second car closing in on the back bumper. As the second car passes on the left (+X direction), you can change the

> **NOTE**
>
> I'm not going to go into detail about rendering to a texture because that is covered in Chapter 36. Chapter 36 also includes the code snippets to access the faces of a cube map. For now, keep in mind that a cube map can be dynamic, but a fully dynamic cube map requires six passes to update the cube map, plus whatever passes you need to actually render the scene. This can get expensive, so it's advantageous to update only the faces that need updating.

camera to look in the +X direction and render the scene into the +X face of the cube map. Then again, render the real scene normally. In this scenario, each car might have its own cube map textures that represent the proper reflections from their points of view.

One thing to keep in mind when updating a cube map is that the cube map faces do not need to be in the same resolution as the actual scene. For instance, if your game is running at 1024×768, you can probably still get by with a cube map with sides that are 256×256 or smaller. You'll see in the sample application that reflections are distorted enough that higher-resolution cube maps are usually a waste of memory.

Computing Reflection Vectors

So far I've been talking about reflections, but I haven't really explained what reflections are and how you should use cube maps to show them. Now it's time to delve back into a little vector math.

You've actually been using reflection since the earliest chapter on lighting. Diffuse lighting is based on the fact that light reflects imperfectly off of uneven surfaces. In the diffuse lighting model, light that strikes a surface scatters in all directions. Perfect reflection is different. In the ideal case, the angle of reflectance equals the angle of incidence. To put it a different way, a ray bounces off of a surface in an equal but opposite direction, as shown in Figure 26.2.

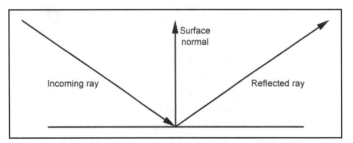

Figure 26.2

Perfect reflection of incoming light.

I touched on this with specular lighting, but the half-vector approximation provided an easy way to avoid a true reflectance calculation. Now I need to talk about the real equation for reflection.

Upon Reflection...

A recent study found that a significant number of college students thought that people see by shooting some sort of ray out of their eyes. The following algorithms would seem to support that notion, but it is very much untrue. We see reflections because images and light strike a surface and reflect back to our eyes. The following algorithms work because we are essentially working backwards and finding the vector that would have lined up with our eyes in the real world.

Ultimately, you need a vector that will serve as the texture coordinate vector into the cube map. For reflection, this vector will be the reflection of the eye vector about the vertex normal, as shown in Figure 26.3.

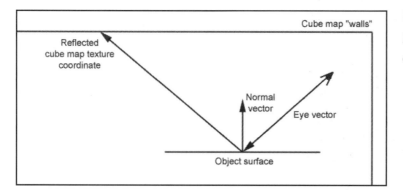

Figure 26.3

Reflection into a cube map.

For a given world space eye vector and world space normal vector, the reflected vector serves as the correct texture coordinate into the cube map. You need an equation that gives the equal and opposite reflection vector based on a vertex normal and an eye vector. Ideally, that equation should be based on shader-friendly operations such as the dot product. The following equation satisfies those requirements and yields the correct reflected vector:

$$R = E - 2N(E \cdot N)$$

WARNING

In nearly every other chapter, the eye vector has usually meant the vertex-to-eye vector. That orientation made sense in the context of comparing the vector to the normal. In this case, the eye vector is the eye-to-vertex vector, which makes more sense when generating the cube map texture coordinate.

Many texts and Web sites include a rigorous mathematical proof of the preceding formula. I think it might be easier to provide a kind of "proof by inspection." If you are mathematically inclined, many sources provide a trigonometric breakdown. Note that the vectors must be normalized for this to work. You'll see why when I talk about refraction.

Based on what you know about dot products and vectors, you can see from Figure 26.3 that the dot product of the normal vector and the eye vector is negative for any vertex facing the eye. The subtraction in the equation swaps the vector back in the same direction as the normal. Figure 26.4 shows part of the equation broken down into steps.

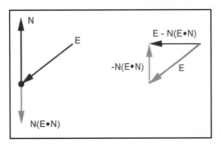

Figure 26.4

Reflection equation

in steps.

As Figure 26.4 shows, if you multiply the normal vector by the dot product of the eye vector and the normal vector and subtract that vector from the eye vector, you get a vector that is halfway between the eye vector and the proper reflection vector. So you can get the reflection vector by doubling the vector that is subtracted from the eye vector. This is shown in Figure 26.5.

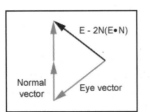

Figure 26.5

The final reflection

equation.

Figure 26.5 shows the final reflection vector. This vector is the correct texture coordinate into the cube map, provided the input vectors are in world space and they are both normalized. I talk about more of the details in the actual shader code.

Computing Approximate Refraction Vectors

The following is based on an approximation found in one of the nVidia effects. In the real world, light rays that pass through one medium into another are bent at the interface between the two mediums. This is called refraction. The most common example of this is when you stand at the edge of the water and look at a fish below the surface, as shown in Figure 26.6.

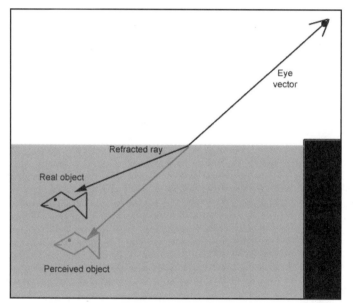

Figure 26.6

Refraction between water and air.

You see the fish as if it were straight in front of you, but it is actually in a slightly different position. This is because light reflected off of the fish bends as it leaves the water. The water also causes the light to bend differently as the shape of the surface of the water changes. This is why it is difficult to see into rippling water.

Normally, refraction vectors are calculated as a function of the properties of the surface and the indices of refraction of the two materials. If you want to model proper refraction, you still need to do that, but most of the time you just need an approximate refraction effect more than a physically accurate one. You can create an approximate refraction effect using the reflection equation and a scaled (but not renormalized) normal vector.

Snell's Law

The actual law governing refraction is called Snell's Law. Snell's Law states that the ratio of the sines of the incoming and outgoing angles (relative to the surface normal) is equal to the ratio of the indices of refraction of the two materials. A rigorous implementation of refraction would take all these factors into account. The problem with such an approach is that you don't have any sense of the volume of the object. This means that you can't follow the complete path of the light as it passes through the object. Therefore, any solution will be an approximation unless you get into ray tracing. That's a whole other ball of wax.

Incidentally, Snell discovered the phenomenon, but the most common form of Snell's Law was actually published first by Descartes.

Shortening the normal has the effect of not reversing the reflection vector. Figure 26.7 is the same as Figure 26.5, only this time the normal has been rescaled. As you can see, the refraction vector continues in roughly the same direction as the eye vector, only it is bent slightly.

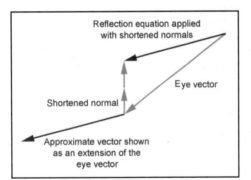

Figure 26.7

Refraction approximation.

Mathematically, it's easy to see that if the normal were shortened to a zero length, the refraction vector would be the same as the eye vector. When you get to the actual sample code, experiment with different values of the refraction constant. You will find that higher values of the constant (near 1.0) result in something that looks very much like reflection, whereas lower values (near zero) are closer to the eye vector and may cause a zooming effect. As always, experiment.

The Reflection/Refraction Vertex Shader

The following shader code implements both the reflection and the refraction effects in a single pass using two sets of texture coordinates. This shader expects the vertices to contain normal and position information. The texture coordinates are set in the shader and do not need to be part of the input vertex format. Also, this shader is the first shader that transforms the normals to world space. The transposed world matrix must be in constants c4 through c7. The shader is in ReflectRefract.vsh:

```
vs.1.1
```

Set the position. You could append this code to one of the warping effects from previous chapters. The reflection and refraction effects work with any other effect that generates proper vertex positions and normals:

```
dp4 oPos.x, v0, c0
dp4 oPos.y, v0, c1
dp4 oPos.z, v0, c2
dp4 oPos.w, v0, c3
```

The following six lines transform both the vertex position and vertex normal to world space so you can use them in the world space reflection equation. I considered the approach of finding a final object space reflection vector and then transforming that to world space. If the shader only did reflection, that approach would save an instruction or two. This approach is slightly better when you are computing both reflection and refraction vectors because you can transform the normal once versus transforming two result vectors:

```
dp4 r0.x, v0, c4
dp4 r0.y, v0, c5
dp4 r0.z, v0, c6

dp3 r1.x, v3, c4
dp3 r1.y, v3, c5
dp3 r1.z, v3, c6
```

You must normalize the normal vector before any of the next steps will work. The refraction approximation shows that you can have unpredictable effects if the normal is not re-normalized:

```
dp3 r1.w, r1, r1
rsq r1.w, r1.w
mul r1, r1, r1.w
```

This code computes the world space eye-to-vertex vector and normalizes it. Remember that this is the opposite of the vertex-to-eye vectors of previous chapters. Once you have the normalized eye vector, you have all the inputs for the reflection equation:

```
sub r2, r0.xyz, c8.xyz
dp3 r2.w, r2, r2
rsq r2.w, r2.w
mul r2, r2, r2.w
```

First, find the dot product of the normal and eye vectors and double it. This is the first part of the shader implementation of the reflection equation:

```
dp3 r3, r2, r1
add r3, r3, r3
```

You use the `mad` instruction to multiply the normal vector by the negated value of `r3`, and you add that value to the eye vector stored in `r2`. The result is written to the first three components of the first texture coordinate. This concludes the reflection portion of the program:

```
mad oT0.xyz, r1, -r3, r2
```

The refraction calculations start by scaling the world space normal by the scaling value in `c10.x`. Different values produce very different effects:

```
mul r1, r1, c10.xxxx
```

The refraction calculation is repeated, only this time it uses the shortened vertex normal. The final value is written into the second set of texture coordinates. The texture stage states control how the two effects are blended together:

```
dp3 r3, r2, r1
add r3, r3, r3
mad oT1.xyz, r1, -r3, r2
```

The application also uses another shader to draw the environment box. This shader is in EnvironmentBox.vsh. It just does the basic position transformation and passes the untransformed position vector to the output texture coordinate vector, as shown next. This works because the same direction vectors that define the eight corners of the cube model also define the eight corners of the cube map. This means that you can texture the sides of a cube without using separate textures or texture coordinates. This saves texture memory and vertex memory:

```
vs.1.1
dp4 oPos.x, v0, c0
dp4 oPos.y, v0, c1
dp4 oPos.z, v0, c2
dp4 oPos.w, v0, c3
mov oT0.xyz, v0.xyz
```

Figure 26.8 shows the final output of the shader using a test cube map. When you are debugging, you might want to create a texture that makes it easy to see what is going on. This might be especially useful when trying new refraction values. The test cube map is in the media directory as TestCube.dds.

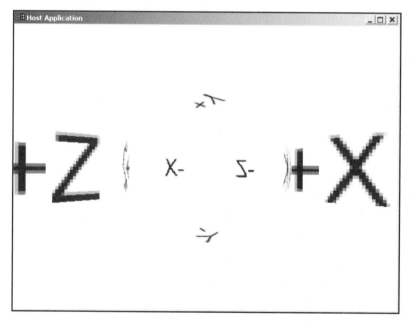

Figure 26.8

Sample application with test cube map.

The Application Code

This application has a couple of interesting points beyond the Render function. Unlike some of the sample applications, this code reuses the cube map to texture the environment as well as the reflection and refraction effects. You'll see how in the following code. This text presents bits and pieces of the code, but the full code is available on the CD.

The following snippets are the vertex formats and the associated declarations. You use the mesh vertex for the reflecting object (in this case a sphere) and the box vertex to render the environment box. These are the minimal formats, but you could add more attributes such as texture coordinates for simple textures or vertex colors. The mesh vertex format does not include a texture coordinate because the 3D texture coordinates are derived in the shader. The box vertex format also foregoes the 3D texture coordinates because the box shader uses the position vector as a texture coordinate:

```
struct MESH_VERTEX
{
        float x, y, z;
        float nx, ny, nz;
};

struct BOX_VERTEX
{
        float x, y, z;
};

DWORD Declaration[] =
{
        D3DVSD_STREAM(0),
        D3DVSD_REG(D3DVSDE_POSITION,D3DVSDT_FLOAT3),
        D3DVSD_REG(D3DVSDE_NORMAL,  D3DVSDT_FLOAT3),
        D3DVSD_END()
};

DWORD BoxDeclaration[] =
{
        D3DVSD_STREAM(0),
        D3DVSD_REG(D3DVSDE_POSITION,    D3DVSDT_FLOAT3),
        D3DVSD_END()
};
```

This is the very small portion of the PostInitialize function that loads the cube map texture. As you can see, loading a cube map is just as easy as loading a normal texture. In fact, all the basic texture code is the same:

```
BOOL CTechniqueApplication::PostInitialize()
{
        if (FAILED(D3DXCreateCubeTextureFromFile(m_pD3DDevice,
                                              "cubemap.dds",
                                              &m_pCubeTexture)))
                return FALSE;

        return TRUE;
}
```

The following code is the initialization function for the environment box. SetupEnvironment creates a vertex buffer and a cube that will be used to draw the environment. You should take some care to match the environment cube size with the object size. For instance, if the environmental cube was significantly larger than the refractive object, the refractive effect might not work in the way you want it to. This isn't too much of an issue with reflection, but it is something to keep in mind:

```
HRESULT CTechniqueApplication::SetupEnvironment()
{
```

Create the buffer in managed memory to make it easier to reset the device. There are eight vertices, one for each corner of the cube:

```
        if (FAILED(m_pD3DDevice->CreateVertexBuffer(8 *
                                              sizeof(BOX_VERTEX),
                                        0, D3DFVF_BOXVERTEX,
                                        D3DPOOL_MANAGED,
                                        &m_pBoxVertexBuffer)))
                return E_FAIL;
```

Lock the vertex buffer just this once so that you can write the position and texture coordinate values:

```
        BOX_VERTEX *pVertices;
        m_pBoxVertexBuffer->Lock(0, 8 * sizeof(BOX_VERTEX),
                            (BYTE **)&pVertices, 0);
```

These lines create each of the eight corners. I chose the size of the cube to match up nicely with the sphere mesh. In reality, you'd probably never draw this except for debugging. These values also serve as the texture coordinates into the cube map texture. Other samples load six additional textures and then use the standard 2D texture coordinates to texture map the environment cube. This sample reuses the cube map texture (saving texture memory) and reuses the position vector (saving vertex buffer memory). This approach might not work in all cases, but it's something to think about as you look at other samples:

```
pVertices[0].x = -2.0f; pVertices[0].y = -2.0f;
 pVertices[0].z =  2.0f;
pVertices[1].x = -2.0f; pVertices[1].y =  2.0f;
 pVertices[1].z =  2.0f;
pVertices[2].x =  2.0f; pVertices[2].y = -2.0f;
 pVertices[2].z =  2.0f;
pVertices[3].x =  2.0f; pVertices[3].y =  2.0f;
 pVertices[3].z =  2.0f;
pVertices[4].x =  2.0f; pVertices[4].y = -2.0f;
 pVertices[4].z = -2.0f;
pVertices[5].x =  2.0f; pVertices[5].y =  2.0f;
 pVertices[5].z = -2.0f;
pVertices[6].x = -2.0f; pVertices[6].y = -2.0f;
 pVertices[6].z = -2.0f;
pVertices[7].x = -2.0f; pVertices[7].y =  2.0f;
 pVertices[7].z = -2.0f;
m_pBoxVertexBuffer->Unlock();
```

The index buffer contains 18 entries. Ten of the entries define the four sides of the cube in the form of a triangle strip. The eight remaining vertices store the top and bottom of the cube in the form of two small triangle strips. This is more efficient than a 36 entry index buffer for a triangle list:

```
if (FAILED(m_pD3DDevice->CreateIndexBuffer(18 * sizeof(short),
                                  0, D3DFMT_INDEX16,
                                  D3DPOOL_MANAGED,
                                  &m_pBoxIndexBuffer)))
        return E_FAIL;
```

Lock the buffer and set the 18 entries by hand. These values will probably never change, so hardcoding them is not a bad idea:

```
short *pIndex;
m_pBoxIndexBuffer->Lock(0, 18 * sizeof(short),
  (BYTE**)&pIndex, 0);
```

```
short Indices[] = {0, 1, 2, 3, 4, 5, 6, 7, 0, 1, 1,
                   7, 3, 5, 0, 2, 6, 4};
memcpy(pIndex, &Indices, 18 * sizeof(short));
m_pBoxIndexBuffer->Unlock();

return S_OK;
}
```

The following code is for the Render function. Keep in mind that you could optimize many aspects of this function in a real application:

```
void CTechniqueApplication::Render()
{
```

Set both of the textures to the same cube map texture. Even though there are two different effects, both effects use the same texture:

```
m_pD3DDevice->SetTexture(0, m_pCubeTexture);
m_pD3DDevice->SetTexture(1, m_pCubeTexture);
```

These texture stage states tell the first texture stage to use the first texture as is, ignoring any other influences such as diffuse color (which is not used in this application anyway). The second texture is blended based on the value of the alpha channel of the texture factor. This allows you to decide how transparent the object is. Currently, the texture factor is set up to create the illusion that the object is slightly more transparent than opaque and reflective. Figure 26.9 shows the effect of different texture factor values:

```
m_pD3DDevice->SetTextureStageState(0, D3DTSS_COLOROP,
                                   D3DTOP_SELECTARG1);
m_pD3DDevice->SetTextureStageState(1, D3DTSS_COLOROP,
                                   D3DTOP_BLENDFACTORALPHA);
m_pD3DDevice->SetRenderState(D3DRS_TEXTUREFACTOR, 0x88ffffff);
```

Figure 26.9

The effects of different blending factors.

These lines enable mip mapping in the cube map:

```
m_pD3DDevice->SetTextureStageState(0, D3DTSS_MIPFILTER,
                                    D3DTEXF_LINEAR);
m_pD3DDevice->SetTextureStageState(1, D3DTSS_MIPFILTER,
                                    D3DTEXF_LINEAR);
```

The following lines set up the view matrix so that the eye is orbiting around the object looking in toward the center. The eye position is also set to a constant to be used in the reflection calculations:

```
float Time = (float)GetTickCount() / 5000.0f;
D3DXVECTOR4 EyePos(2.0f * sin(Time), 0.0f, 2.0f * cos(Time), 0.0f);
D3DXMatrixLookAtLH(&m_ViewMatrix, &(D3DXVECTOR3)EyePos,
                    &D3DXVECTOR3(0.0f, 0.0f, 0.0f),
                    &D3DXVECTOR3(0.0f, 1.0f, 0.0f));
```

In the following code, the world matrix is set to spin the object. This line makes sure that the room isn't spinning. Once the matrices are set up, they are passed to the shader:

```
D3DXMatrixIdentity(&m_WorldMatrix);


D3DXMATRIX ShaderMatrix = m_WorldMatrix * m_ViewMatrix *
                            m_ProjectionMatrix;
D3DXMatrixTranspose(&ShaderMatrix, &ShaderMatrix);
m_pD3DDevice->SetVertexShaderConstant(0, &ShaderMatrix, 4);
```

First, render the environment box. This code sets the streams and then renders the box as three different triangle strips. In the SetupEnvironment code, I mentioned that this is the most efficient representation, but it is possible that it would be better to set up the index buffer as a triangle list and call DrawIndexedPrimitive only once. I'm just pointing out the possibility that one type of efficiency can lead to worse inefficiencies down the line. In this simple example, it doesn't really matter, but you might want to experiment with the different approaches:

```
m_pD3DDevice->SetVertexShader(m_EnvironmentShader);
m_pD3DDevice->SetStreamSource(0, m_pBoxVertexBuffer,
                                sizeof(BOX_VERTEX));
m_pD3DDevice->SetIndices(m_pBoxIndexBuffer, 0);
m_pD3DDevice->DrawIndexedPrimitive(D3DPT_TRIANGLESTRIP, 0, 8, 0, 8);
m_pD3DDevice->DrawIndexedPrimitive(D3DPT_TRIANGLESTRIP, 0, 8, 10, 2);
m_pD3DDevice->DrawIndexedPrimitive(D3DPT_TRIANGLESTRIP, 0, 8, 14, 2);
```

After the environment is rendered, it's time to render the actual object. The first thing I do is spin the object just to show that the vector math works out. For a sphere, it's difficult to tell that anything is rotating, but you can experiment with different models if you like. Once the matrix is set up, the shader matrix is updated and sent to the shader:

```
D3DXMatrixRotationY(&m_WorldMatrix, (float)GetTickCount() /
  1000.0f);

ShaderMatrix = m_WorldMatrix * m_ViewMatrix *
               m_ProjectionMatrix;
D3DXMatrixTranspose(&ShaderMatrix, &ShaderMatrix);
m_pD3DDevice->SetVertexShaderConstant(0, &ShaderMatrix, 4);
```

The world matrix is transposed and sent to the shader. The shader uses the world matrix to transform the vertex normal to world space. This is something I tried to avoid in the lighting chapters, but it makes sense here:

```
D3DXMATRIX TransposedWorld;
D3DXMatrixTranspose(&TransposedWorld, &m_WorldMatrix);
m_pD3DDevice->SetVertexShaderConstant(4, &TransposedWorld, 4);
```

The final constant is the refraction value used to scale the normal in the refraction calculation. This is the value that you should experiment with:

```
D3DXVECTOR4 Refraction(0.4f, 0.0f, 0.0f, 0.0f);
```

Once all the constants are defined, send them all to the shader and render the object in the usual way. The textures were set at the beginning of the function:

```
m_pD3DDevice->SetVertexShaderConstant(8, &EyePos, 1);
m_pD3DDevice->SetVertexShaderConstant(9, &One, 1);
m_pD3DDevice->SetVertexShaderConstant(10, &Refraction, 1);

m_pD3DDevice->SetVertexShader(m_ReflectRefractShader);

m_pD3DDevice->SetStreamSource(0, m_pMeshVertexBuffer,
                              sizeof(MESH_VERTEX));
m_pD3DDevice->SetIndices(m_pMeshIndexBuffer, 0);

m_pD3DDevice->DrawIndexedPrimitive(D3DPT_TRIANGLELIST, 0,
                              m_pMesh->GetNumVertices(), 0,
                              m_pMesh->GetNumFaces());
```

These lines are a byproduct of the fact that the font-rendering functions save a limited number of states. I created the limitations for the state blocks partly on purpose. I wanted to show that different parts of code affect each other in unpredictable ways. In this instance, the second texture stage affects the color of the rendered text if it is not set to NULL:

```
m_pD3DDevice->SetTextureStageState(0, D3DTSS_MIPFILTER,
                                   D3DTEXF_NONE);
m_pD3DDevice->SetTextureStageState(1, D3DTSS_MIPFILTER,
                                   D3DTEXF_NONE);
m_pD3DDevice->SetTexture(1, NULL);
}
```

That's it for the application code. Figure 26.10 shows the application in action.

Figure 26.10

The reflection/refraction application.

Other Uses for Cube Maps

Many uses for cube maps fall outside of the bounds of reflection and refraction. In the previous chapter, I talked about using textures as a lookup table for complex functions of one or two variables. Cube maps add the possibility of a third variable, and some techniques use a cube map as a lookup table.

There are also techniques for encoding better depth values into a cube map to help get around the problem of low bit depths, as described in Chapter 23. These techniques are fairly complex and intensive. In Chapter 29, I show you a way to render shadows using a depth approach. If you are casting shadows from a point light, you need to use a cube map to figure out how the omnidirectional light intersects different objects.

On the subject of lighting, an effect called hemispherical lighting uses a cube map to derive environmental lighting values. The idea is that surfaces facing upward are receiving more light than surfaces facing downward. In a sense, this is the same as reflection, but the focus is more on the intensity of light than on reflected images.

This is just a taste of what some people are doing with cube maps. One of the points with many of these chapters is to show how you can use a technique in new ways if you're willing to think out of the box. Sometimes, this can lead to a technique that is just showing off some quirk of the hardware, but other times it can lead to something very effective.

In Conclusion...

In this chapter, I've introduced many new concepts very quickly. I didn't give a comprehensive overview of the cube map interface because it is largely the same as the other textures I've described at length. The one subject I revisit is the idea of a dynamic texture. I discuss that more when I talk about rendering to a texture.

The other new introduction is the math behind reflection and refraction calculations. I've provided as many visual explanations as I could, but some of the math might still be confusing. If you need to, I recommend sitting down with a sheet of paper and drawing out the vectors. Once you try it yourself, it should be much easier. Now I review some of the more interesting points:

- Cube maps represent the environment that surrounds an object. You can think of the object as being inside of a box, reflecting the insides of the four walls.
- You can update a cube map by rendering to one or more of the six individual sides.
- The texture coordinates for a cube map are actually 3D vectors that point from the center out of the box and onto one of the sides.
- A reflected vector leaves the surface at exactly the opposite angle it came in.
- Contrary to popular belief, human beings do not shoot rays from their eyes, but it would be really cool if they did!

- Refraction is the phenomenon that occurs when light passes from one medium to another. The light is bent a certain amount depending on the difference between the two mediums.

- You can approximate the effect of refraction by using the reflection equation with a shortened normal vector.

- There are many uses for cube maps beyond environmental mapping.

CHAPTER 27

Shadows Part 1— Planar Shadows

The last chapter covered the subtle but important effect of reflection. This chapter is the first of three chapters that add shadows using techniques that advance in difficulty. The following is not really a shader technique, but the other two are so it makes sense to put them together in a group. It's also possible that you will need to add shadows to other techniques that do include shaders. This chapter discusses the following:

- Defining planar shadows.
- Defining a plane with the plane equation.
- Setting up matrices for planar shadows.
- Applying the stencil buffer.
- The limitations of the effect.

Of the three techniques, this is the easiest to implement and the least flexible. It involves casting shadows onto a flat plane.

Casting Shadows on a Plane

Figure 27.1 shows some simple representations of shadows cast when a single object comes between a single light source and a flat plane.

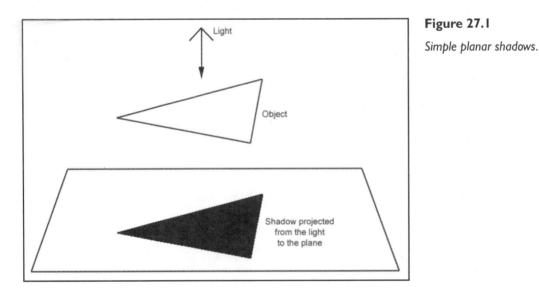

Figure 27.1

Simple planar shadows.

A shadow is cast when the object blocks some of the rays of light but not others. In real terms, the shadow is the area where no light is projected onto the plane, but you can also think of a shadow as a projection of the object from the light onto the flat plane. Once you consider that, a few pieces begin to fall into place.

Everything you have seen so far ends with a finished scene being projected from a 3D space onto the final 2D output plane of your monitor, so you know that a 3D model can be projected onto a 2D plane. You also know that transformations are not a one-shot deal. You can project a model onto a 2D plane, but there is nothing to stop you from projecting that image back onto the proper area of the screen so that it can be seen.

This is the heart of planar shadows. In this chapter, I show you how geometry can be projected from a light to a plane such that it can be used to create shadows on that plane. To do this, I have to introduce several new concepts, beginning with the mathematical definition of a plane.

The Plane Equation

Before you can do anything with a plane, you must have a way to represent it mathematically. You can define any plane in space with the following equation:

$$Ax + By + Cz = D$$

The values of A, B, and C are the three components of the normal vector of the surface. This defines how the plane is oriented in space. The final D variable defines where in space the plane is. You can think of D as the position of the plane along the normal. Increasing or decreasing D "slides" the plane up or down along the vector defined by A, B, and C. This is shown in Figure 27.2.

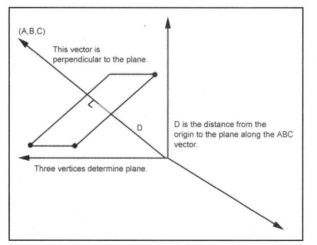

(A,B,C)

This vector is
perpendicular to the plane.

D

D is the distance from the
origin to the plane along the ABC
vector.

Three vertices determine plane.

Figure 27.2

The coefficients of the plane equation.

So the first step in deriving the equation for a given plane is to find the vector that is normal to the plane. You've already seen some of the pieces of this in earlier chapters. You need three points to represent a plane, which is why the basic primitive for surfaces is the triangle. The three points of the triangle define three vectors between each set of points, as shown in Figure 27.3.

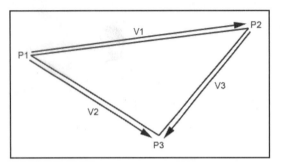

Figure 27.3

Three points on a plane.

You can find the normal vector of this plane if you take the cross product of any two of the three vectors. In Figure 27.3, the cross product of V1 and V2 would yield the normal. Remember that the order of the cross product matters. The cross product of V2 and V1 would yield a vector pointing in the equal but opposite direction. When you take the cross product, order the operands so that the angle between the first vector and the second vector is the least of the two choices.

The components of the normal vector define the A, B, and C variables. You find the D variable by plugging the values of any of the three points into the equation. This will yield the value of D, and the plane equation will be complete. This entire process is shown with the following equations:

$$Ax + By + Cz = D$$
$$N = (P2 - P1) \times (P3 - P1)$$
$$A = N.x$$
$$B = N.y$$
$$C = N.z$$
$$D = A(P1.x) + B(P1.y) + C(P1.z)$$

The plane equation serves as the basis for many important mathematical operations. For example, you can use the equation to find out whether a given point is on the plane. If you plug the point into the equation and the result is zero, then the point is on the plane. If not, the result is the perpendicular distance between the plane and the point. More useful algorithms compute the intersection of a line and a point and others. These are all built around the plane equation. For this chapter, the focus is on projecting geometry onto the plane. For that, you need a matrix based on the plane equation.

The Shadow Matrix

Every transformation and projection involves matrices. This is no exception. You need a matrix that will project the shadow onto the plane based on the light position. The D3DX library provides a handy function to generate the matrix, D3DXMatrixShadow:

```
D3DXMATRIX* D3DXMatrixShadow(D3DXMATRIX* pShadowMatrix,
                    CONST D3DXVECTOR4* pLightPosition,
                    CONST D3DXPLANE* pTargetPlane);
```

This function takes the light position and plane equation as input and creates a matrix that will flatten the geometry onto the plane as if it were being projected from the light. Once the matrix is created, it can be inserted into the string of concatenated matrices, as shown in the following code snippet:

```
D3DXMatrixShadow(&ShadowMatrix, &LightPosition, &ShadowPlane);
ShaderMatrix = m_WorldMatrix * ShadowMatrix *
            m_ViewMatrix * ProjectionMatrix;
```

This flattens the vertices on the plane before the world matrix applies any final world transformations. You can think of the shadow matrix as a component of the world matrix. The "flattening" effect is just another combination of the translations, rotations, and scaling built into every other matrix.

Figure 27.4 shows the final outcome. This is a screenshot of the application, but the full shadow effect is disabled to show the flattening effect.

The flattened geometry serves as a template for the shadow. The matrix can set things up to draw the flattened geometry, but you really need the stencil buffer to make everything work.

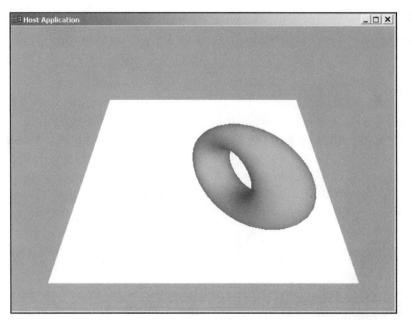

Figure 27.4

Flattened geometry.

The Stencil Buffer and Shadows

I cover the stencil buffer more thoroughly in Chapter 40. You might want to skip ahead to that chapter if you have never worked with the stencil buffer before. Assuming you have some sort of familiarity with stencil buffers, the rest of the technique continues as follows.

The shadow matrix takes care of flattening the geometry, but flattened geometry does not a shadow make. You could render the geometry in black, creating a completely black shadow, but this isn't realistic because it would completely obscure any textures or detail on the ground plane. You could render the geometry as a semitransparent black color, but overlapping triangles might over-darken some areas and not others. What you really need is a way to render a semitransparent darkness in the shape of the shadow. This is where the stencil buffer comes in.

As you'll see soon, the application begins by rendering a ground plane. This draws the plane and also increments the stencil values of the new pixels. This ensures that the shadow is not cast outside of the plane. If the plane modeled the edge of a cliff, you wouldn't want shadows hanging off of the cliff.

Next, the application renders the flattened geometry, but only the pixels where the stencil buffer was incremented. Any new pixels increment the stencil buffer again.

Before doing this, you set the device to make sure that the color values are unaffected. The flattened geometry is drawn, but only to the stencil buffer. It is not drawn in the visible sense of being drawn to the color buffer.

Finally, you draw a semitransparent black plane, but only in the areas where the stencil buffer was incremented by both of the previous steps. Some implementations cover the entire screen with a transparent black quad. This application simply redraws the ground plane. This works out well for a sample with one plane, but the other approach might be better in more involved cases. The next chapter uses the full-screen quad approach for more complex shadows. Figure 27.5 shows the steps of the algorithm and Figure 27.6 shows the final rendering.

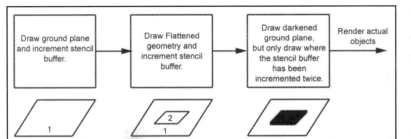

Figure 27.5

Planar shadow rendering steps.

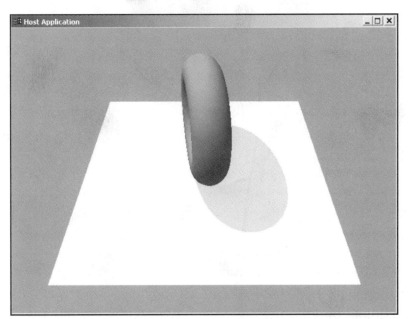

Figure 27.6

Planar shadows.

Figure 27.6 reveals several limitations of this technique, but I discuss that after I walk you through the application code. This application uses a simple shader, but the shader only computes simple diffuse lighting as you've seen many times. Instead of looking at the shader, I jump right into the code.

The Planar Shadow Application

This application introduces several new features, so the amount of source code I've included here is greater than in previous chapters. As I've mentioned before, if you are not familiar with stencil buffers, you might want to read through Chapter 40 before moving on. You don't need to be an expert; you just need to understand what a stencil buffer is designed to do.

Speaking of stencil buffers, I should revisit a small part of the initialization functions created back in Chapter 7. This is the first time an application has needed it, but the samples have been creating stencil buffers all along. The following line is taken from the application-creation functions in the CHostApplication base class. It creates a depth/stencil buffer with 24 bits of depth and 8 bits reserved for the stencil buffer. Eight bits are more than enough for this technique, but more advanced techniques might need more bits of stencil:

```
m_PresentParameters.AutoDepthStencilFormat =
  D3DFMT_D24S8;
```

So the stencil buffer is available in all the sample applications if you want to add shadows to any of the other samples. If you do, one of the things you should remember is that you must clear the stencil buffer just as you do the depth and color buffers. This application has a tweaked PreRender function that handles clearing the stencil buffer:

```
void CTechniqueApplication::PreRender()
{
```

This clears the color and depth buffers and also clears the stencil buffer to a value of zero. You can clear the stencil buffer to a different default value by changing the last parameter of the Clear function. This application also clears the color buffer to a different color than black, so it is easy to see where the shadow is and isn't being drawn:

```
m_pD3DDevice->Clear(0, NULL,
               D3DCLEAR_TARGET | D3DCLEAR_ZBUFFER |
               D3DCLEAR_STENCIL, D3DCOLOR_XRGB(100, 100, 200),
               1.0f, 0);
```

Any application that implements a new version of PreRender must include a call to
BeginScene in the PreRender function. If not, the rest of the framework fails to
render properly:

```
m_pD3DDevice->BeginScene();


return;
}
```

The next step is to create a simple mesh for the plane. You can load this plane from
a mesh file, but this technique only works if the final geometry of the shadowed
surface is a flat plane. For instance, you cannot load a plane from a mesh file and
warp it with the Bezier shader and expect shadows to work properly. If you need to
cast shadows on complex surfaces, you have to use one of the two shadow
techniques in the next chapters. I am including the plane-creation function because
there are a few minor tricks in the code. As usual, a few tweaks could probably make
the code more optimal:

```
HRESULT CTechniqueApplication::CreatePlaneBuffer()
{
```

The vertex buffer holds four vertices. You need only three points to define a plane
mathematically, but a plane still looks better with four points. It's important that all
four points are actually coplanar. If not, the shadow is still drawn, but it might cut
through the mesh or hang off of it. This is the primary limitation of planar shadows:

```
    if (FAILED(m_pD3DDevice->CreateVertexBuffer(4 *
                                        sizeof(MESH_VERTEX),
                            0, D3DFVF_MESHVERTEX,
                            D3DPOOL_MANAGED,
                            &m_pPlaneVertexBuffer)))
        return E_FAIL;

    MESH_VERTEX *pVertices;

    m_pPlaneVertexBuffer->Lock(0, 4 * sizeof(MESH_VERTEX),
                        (BYTE **)&pVertices, 0);
```

Once the vertex buffer is locked, set all the values equal to zero. If you don't see a
value set in the following code, you can assume that the value has been set to zero:

```
    memset(pVertices, 0x00, 4 * sizeof(MESH_VERTEX));
```

This creates a mesh that is 60 units square. Notice that I am setting the X and Z values of the position and the Y value of the normal. I can do this because all other values are zero. Some could argue that this is an example of code that is confusing to read. There are some examples like this on the Web and in various pieces of source code. Be careful when reading over someone else's code. This was easy for me to write but could be confusing to read:

```
pVertices[0].x = -30.0f; pVertices[0].ny = 1.0f;
 pVertices[0].z = -30.0f;
pVertices[1].x = -30.0f; pVertices[1].ny = 1.0f;
 pVertices[1].z =  30.0f;
pVertices[2].x =  30.0f; pVertices[2].ny = 1.0f;
 pVertices[2].z = -30.0f;
pVertices[3].x =  30.0f; pVertices[3].ny = 1.0f;
 pVertices[3].z =  30.0f;
```

Here I set the vertex color to white, but I set the alpha channel to zero. Normally, this means that the plane is fully transparent and that it does not show up when alpha blending is enabled. This is true, but it also allows me to play a few tricks with the shader. I return to this point in the shadow rendering code:

```
pVertices[0].color = pVertices[1].color =
                     pVertices[2].color =
                     pVertices[3].color = 0x00ffffff;

m_pPlaneVertexBuffer->Unlock();

return S_OK;
}
```

More code loads the mesh, extracts the buffers, creates the simple shader, and so on, but none of that is new at this point. The real new material is in the function called RenderPlaneAndShadow. This function takes care of rendering everything but the final visible mesh of the shadow-casting object. As usual, there might be plenty of room for optimization in this function:

```
void CTechniqueApplication::RenderPlaneAndShadow()
{
```

This first block of code sets up the stencil buffer for the first time the plane is drawn. The stencil buffer is enabled and the compare function is set up to always update any drawn pixels. If a pixel is drawn, the stencil buffer value at that pixel is incremented. This is the first stencil operation that occurs after the stencil buffer is cleared, so the stencil values are set to one for all pixels that make up the plane. The stencil buffer remains enabled for most of this function:

```
m_pD3DDevice->SetRenderState(D3DRS_STENCILENABLE,    TRUE);
m_pD3DDevice->SetRenderState(D3DRS_STENCILFUNC,
                             D3DCMP_ALWAYS);
m_pD3DDevice->SetRenderState(D3DRS_STENCILPASS,
                             D3DSTENCILOP_INCR);
```

The Render function (described later) sets the world matrix, but the application only uses that matrix to affect the position and orientation of the mesh, not the plane. Therefore, you set the shader matrix for the plane using only the view and projection matrices. This is equivalent to using an identity world matrix:

```
D3DXMATRIX ShaderMatrix = m_ViewMatrix * m_ProjectionMatrix;
D3DXMatrixTranspose(&ShaderMatrix, &ShaderMatrix);
m_pD3DDevice->SetVertexShaderConstant(0, &ShaderMatrix, 4);
```

The light moves back and forth in a line above the mesh, as shown in Figure 27.7. This is to show the effect that the light position has on the shadow. Once the light is moved across the sky, the direction is set to point it toward the origin. This light vector is fed to the shader to provide simple shading support for the plane:

```
float Time = (float)GetTickCount() / 1000.0f;
D3DXVECTOR4 LightPosition(150.0f * sin(Time), 70.0f,
                          0.0f, 1.0f);
D3DXVECTOR4 LightDir = D3DXVECTOR4(0.0f, 0.0f, 0.0f, 0.0f) -
                       LightPosition;
D3DXVec4Normalize(&LightDir, &LightDir);
m_pD3DDevice->SetVertexShaderConstant(4, &LightDir, 1);
```

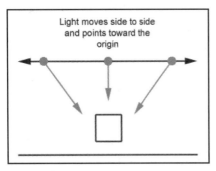

Figure 27.7

The light's path in the "sky."

Render the plane as a triangle strip. This sets the stencil buffer to one everywhere the plane is drawn:

```
m_pD3DDevice->SetStreamSource(0, m_pPlaneVertexBuffer,
                              sizeof(MESH_VERTEX));
m_pD3DDevice->DrawPrimitive(D3DPT_TRIANGLESTRIP, 0, 2);
```

Now it's time to create the shadow matrix. The shadow plane is set to match the plane defined in the vertex buffer. It is a simple plane that faces straight up and is sitting on the origin. I recommend experimenting with other planes and applying what you know about the plane equation. Remember that the plane used in the equation should match the plane in the vertex buffer. You feed the light position and the shadow plane to the D3DXMatrixShadow function. D3DX sets the matrix so that the light is pointing toward the mesh and that the shadow is projected onto the plane. This makes the most sense in the context of a point light source:

```
D3DXMATRIX  ShadowMatrix;
D3DXPLANE   ShadowPlane(0.0f, 1.0f, 0.0f, 0.0);
D3DXMatrixShadow(&ShadowMatrix, &LightPosition, &ShadowPlane);
```

Once the shadow matrix is computed, it is used to set the concatenated shader matrix. The shadow matrix creates the projected effect, and the world matrix applies world transformations in the usual way. You then send the concatenated matrix to the shader. The shader has no knowledge of the shadow effect; that is part of the transformation matrix. This makes it easy to use planar shadows with shaders that warp the geometry of a mesh:

```
ShaderMatrix = m_WorldMatrix * ShadowMatrix *
               m_ViewMatrix * m_ProjectionMatrix;
D3DXMatrixTranspose(&ShaderMatrix, &ShaderMatrix);
m_pD3DDevice->SetVertexShaderConstant(0, &ShaderMatrix, 4);
```

Once the constants are set up, the mesh is set up to be rendered in the usual way. This raises one optimization point. This effect requires the mesh to be rendered twice. If you have detailed geometry, this can be a heavy operation. You might want to consider using a second low-resolution version of the mesh to cast shadows. In many cases, you can get away with this because you cannot see much of the detail in the shadow. Chances are pretty good that a low-resolution mesh would speed things up without making a noticeable visual difference. In any case, when you are rendering the shadow pass, remember to disable textures, pixel shaders, lighting, and any other effects that might impact performance for no visual benefit:

```
m_pD3DDevice->SetStreamSource(0, m_pMeshVertexBuffer,
                                sizeof(MESH_VERTEX));
m_pD3DDevice->SetIndices(m_pMeshIndexBuffer, 0);
```

Before rendering the shadow pass, disable the depth test and set the stencil test so that new pixels are only drawn if the reference value (zero) is less than that pixel's stencil value. If the new pixel is drawn, increment the stencil value. Disabling the depth test eliminates any visual artifacts that might otherwise occur if the planar shadow is too close to the plane. You can also eliminate this problem by setting the Z bias or by tweaking the D variable in the plane equation. In this simple example, it's easier to disable the depth test. That could also lead to modest performance gains:

```
m_pD3DDevice->SetRenderState(D3DRS_ZENABLE,    FALSE);
m_pD3DDevice->SetRenderState(D3DRS_STENCILPASS,
                                D3DSTENCILOP_INCR);
m_pD3DDevice->SetRenderState(D3DRS_STENCILFUNC,  D3DCMP_LESS);
m_pD3DDevice->SetRenderState(D3DRS_STENCILREF,   0);
```

You can disable changes to the color buffer by enabling alpha blending and setting the blend operations so that color values are always blended completely transparently. New hardware supports a render state that explicitly disables color buffer writing, but this feature is not yet universally available. Until it is, this is a good method:

```
m_pD3DDevice->SetRenderState(D3DRS_ALPHABLENDENABLE,   TRUE);
m_pD3DDevice->SetRenderState(D3DRS_SRCBLEND,  D3DBLEND_ZERO);
m_pD3DDevice->SetRenderState(D3DRS_DESTBLEND, D3DBLEND_ONE);
```

With the previous settings, the rendered mesh does not update the color buffer or the depth buffer, and it only updates the stencil buffer in the areas where the plane was drawn. In the places the mesh is drawn, the stencil buffer is incremented to a value of two:

```
m_pD3DDevice->DrawIndexedPrimitive(D3DPT_TRIANGLELIST, 0,
                                  m_pMesh->GetNumVertices(), 0,
                                  m_pMesh->GetNumFaces());
```

The following is a hack, but it's a good way to reuse buffers without making changes. The basic shader does some simple diffuse lighting calculations with ambient lighting. The light direction is set here so that the light is facing directly away from the plane. This means that the plane is rendered as black. The ambient light is set to black, but the alpha value is set to some small value. The reasoning is this: The plane vertices were set with a fully transparent alpha value. The first pass of the plane was rendered with alpha blending disabled so the transparency didn't matter. Now the plane is rendered again, and the diffuse light value is black. The ambient value is added in, but it is also black. Because the original alpha value of the vertices was zero, it is set to the alpha value of the ambient light. All of this allows you to reuse the plane vertices to render both a white, lit plane and a black semitransparent plane without locking and setting the vertex values. In this case, the ambient alpha value is essentially the complement of the ambient light intensity. If you set the alpha component to 1.0, you are making it full black as if there were no ambient light. If the alpha value is 0.0, this means that the ambient light is at full brightness and there is no shadow:

```
D3DXVECTOR4 HackLightDir(0.0, 1.0f, 0.0f, 0.0f);
D3DXVECTOR4 Ambient (0.0,  0.0f, 0.0f, 0.25f);
m_pD3DDevice->SetVertexShaderConstant(4, &HackLightDir, 1);
m_pD3DDevice->SetVertexShaderConstant(5, &Ambient, 1);
```

The stencil test is set up so that the plane is only drawn where the reference value (one) is less than the current stencil value. The stencil value was incremented twice in any area where the shadow appears, so the plane is drawn only in those areas. Remember that the depth test is still disabled, so the two passes of the plane should not interfere with each other:

```
m_pD3DDevice->SetRenderState(D3DRS_STENCILFUNC,  D3DCMP_LESS);
m_pD3DDevice->SetRenderState(D3DRS_STENCILREF,   1);
```

These are the "normal" alpha blending modes. You use them to blend the shadow plane with the first plane:

```
m_pD3DDevice->SetRenderState(D3DRS_SRCBLEND,
                            D3DBLEND_SRCALPHA);
```

```
m_pD3DDevice->SetRenderState(D3DRS_DESTBLEND,
                               D3DBLEND_INVSRCALPHA);
```

All the modes are set. Reset the matrices and redraw the plane:

```
ShaderMatrix = m_ViewMatrix * m_ProjectionMatrix;
D3DXMatrixTranspose(&ShaderMatrix, &ShaderMatrix);
m_pD3DDevice->SetVertexShaderConstant(0, &ShaderMatrix, 4);
m_pD3DDevice->SetStreamSource(0, m_pPlaneVertexBuffer,
                               sizeof(MESH_VERTEX));
m_pD3DDevice->DrawPrimitive(D3DPT_TRIANGLESTRIP, 0, 2);
```

Reset all the tests to their normal settings so that the real mesh can be rendered:

```
m_pD3DDevice->SetRenderState(D3DRS_ZENABLE,          TRUE);
m_pD3DDevice->SetRenderState(D3DRS_STENCILENABLE,    FALSE);
m_pD3DDevice->SetRenderState(D3DRS_ALPHABLENDENABLE, FALSE);
```

Pass the light direction into the shader so that it will correctly render the real mesh:

```
D3DXMATRIX InverseWorld;
D3DXMatrixInverse(&InverseWorld, NULL, &m_WorldMatrix);
D3DXVec4Transform(&LightDir, &LightDir, &InverseWorld);
D3DXVec4Normalize(&LightDir, &LightDir);
m_pD3DDevice->SetVertexShaderConstant(4, &LightDir, 1);
}
```

Remember that this function has not yet rendered the mesh, only the plane and the shadow. Figure 27.8 shows the output of this function.

The RenderPlaneAndShadow function is called by the Render function before the mesh is visibly rendered. This is the Render function:

```
void CTechniqueApplication::Render()
{
```

The Render function takes care of setting the view and world matrices along with the shader, but it doesn't set the shader constants until after RenderPlaneAndShadow does what it needs to do:

```
D3DXVECTOR4 EyePos(0.0, 60.0f, -60.0f, 0.0f);
D3DXMatrixLookAtLH(&m_ViewMatrix, &(D3DXVECTOR3)EyePos,
                    &D3DXVECTOR3(0.0f, 0.0f, 0.0f),
```

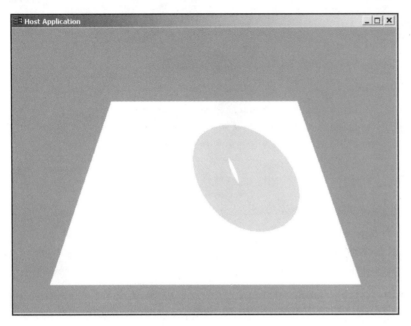

Figure 27.8

The shadow and the plane.

```
                                  &D3DXVECTOR3(0.0f, 1.0f, 0.0f));


        m_pD3DDevice->SetVertexShader(m_BasicShader);

        D3DXMATRIX Rotation;
        D3DXMATRIX Translation;

        D3DXMatrixRotationY(&Rotation,
                            (float)GetTickCount() /1000.0f);
        D3DXMatrixTranslation(&Translation, 0.0f, 10.0f, 0.0f);
        m_WorldMatrix = Rotation * Translation;
```

Once everything is set up, the Render function relies on RenderPlaneAndShadow to do the dirty work. By the time control is returned to the Render function, the light direction constant has been set and it is time to render the mesh:

```
        RenderPlaneAndShadow();
```

Set a small amount of ambient light. The rest of the lighting was set in the other function. The one problem here is that it's possible to decouple the lighting applied to the plane from the lighting applied to the mesh. You might want to consolidate all the lighting functions in one place or leave them separate so that you can tweak them if need be:

```
D3DXVECTOR4 Ambient    (0.1,  0.1f, 0.1f, 0.0f);
m_pD3DDevice->SetVertexShaderConstant(5, &Ambient, 1);
```

Once everything is set up, the last pass of the mesh is rendered to create the visible model. Figure 27.7 in the next section shows the final output of the application, and I use it to discuss some of the limitations of the technique:

```
D3DXMATRIX ShaderMatrix = m_WorldMatrix * m_ViewMatrix *
                          m_ProjectionMatrix;
D3DXMatrixTranspose(&ShaderMatrix, &ShaderMatrix);
m_pD3DDevice->SetVertexShaderConstant(0, &ShaderMatrix, 4);

m_pD3DDevice->SetStreamSource(0, m_pMeshVertexBuffer,
                              sizeof(MESH_VERTEX));
m_pD3DDevice->SetIndices(m_pMeshIndexBuffer, 0);
m_pD3DDevice->DrawIndexedPrimitive(D3DPT_TRIANGLELIST, 0,
                                   m_pMesh->GetNumVertices(), 0,
                                   m_pMesh->GetNumFaces());
}
```

Limitations and Areas for Improvement

Figure 27.9 shows the final output of the application. This screenshot is a little different from Figure 27.6 in that it shows how the shadow is confined to the plane. This is good, but there are plenty of things wrong with this picture.

One of the first things you might notice is that the area of the shadow is still influenced by the diffuse lighting calculations. As the light moves across the sky, it lights the plane, including the area that is in shadow. This is incorrect. If the area is in shadow, it should not be influenced by the light's direction. Instead, the area should be completely dark except for whatever ambient lighting is present. The incorrect lighting comes from the fact that the plane is lit with diffuse lighting and then artificially darkened with shadow technique. This is the downside of many shadow methods. One possible solution is to draw the second plane/shadow pass with a shader that accounts for the light direction and darkens the shadow to counter the effects of the first lighting pass. For instance, the shader could tell that

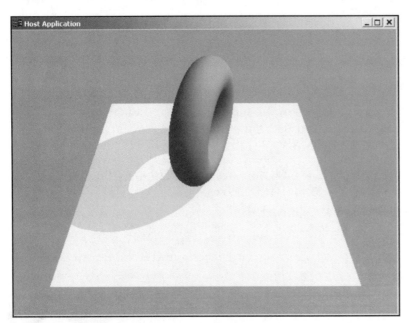

Figure 27.9

The application in action.

the light direction brightened the plane and could darken the shadow pass accordingly. As the light moved back and forth, the shader could make sure that the shadow brightness remained constant. I didn't include this in the example because I wanted to keep things simple and highlight the limitations of the basic technique.

The biggest limitation of this technique is that it only works with shadows projected on a flat plane. This means that the technique is not adequate for shadowing objects on rugged terrain or other complex geometry. If the triangles that make up the terrain are big enough, you might be able to cast shadows on specific planes, but this could get tricky. The plane's limitation also means that objects do not cast shadows on each other. You can render a scene with multiple objects casting shadows on the same ground plane, but the objects do not cast shadows on other objects. If the objects are separated enough, this might be okay, but your eye is very good at telling you when something isn't right.

In addition to objects not shadowing each other, the objects do not shadow themselves. If you have fairly simple convex objects this might not be a problem, but you can see from Figure 27.9 that the upper parts of the object should be casting shadows on the lower portions of the object. Sometimes this isn't a problem, but it can be a little disconcerting.

You could add more to this technique in terms of shadowing multiple planes. For instance, if you had an object in a square room, you could do a separate pass for each wall and treat each wall as a separate plane. This simply involves repeating the technique for each wall of the room. If you choose to do this, it might actually make more sense to draw into the stencil buffer for all the walls and then render one full-screen black quad instead of separate planar quads. The only problem with rendering one full-screen quad is that you won't be able to implement the shadow brightness correction shader I talked about earlier.

The final limitation is true for any multipass technique. The geometry is rendered at least twice, so if you have complex geometry, you might notice a performance penalty. You can improve performance by using a less detailed model for the shadow pass. In most cases, the shadow does not reveal the lack of detail as long as you don't take too much detail out of the mesh.

In many cases, these limitations are not showstoppers. Especially in action games, the player is less concerned with scrutinizing the shadows and is more concerned with finding their buddies and introducing them to Mr. Rocket Launcher. Simple planar shadows, despite all their limitations, are a relatively simple way to provide a visual cue that tells the viewer how far the object is from the ground.

In Conclusion...

This is the first of three shadow techniques, and it is the most simple. You don't need a shader, but a shader could definitely help with controlling the shadow color. Once you understand the basic technique, change the shadow pass in the way I described. In the next chapter, I describe a much better technique that actually uses a shader to greatly simplify an old technique. Before moving on, here's a review of the important points:

- The plane equation is based on the plane's normal vector and its position along that vector.
- You can derive the plane equation from three points.
- The shadow matrix transforms the vertices so that the vertices appear to be flattened and projected onto a plane.
- The D3DX library provides a handy function for building the shadow matrix.
- The flattened geometry isn't actually drawn to the screen in a visible way. It is written to the stencil buffer to create a stencil for the darkened plane.
- The first step draws the visible plane and preloads the stencil buffer with a value of one.

- The second step renders the flattened geometry. The flattened geometry writes only to the stencil buffer, and it writes only in the areas where the plane was written. You can disable the depth test to prevent interference between the plane and the shadow model.

- The third step renders a semitransparent black plane, but the new plane is only rendered in the areas where the flattened geometry was written.

- Finally, the actual object is rendered using whatever visible effects you need.

- This technique darkens the plane in a way that is completely disconnected from the lighting pass. The effect is that the plane is lit and then darkened, which is not correct. You could improve this technique by using a shader on the third pass that takes the planar lighting into account and adjusts the shadow brightness accordingly.

- The technique only allows for shadows cast onto a plane. Rendering shadows of multiple objects is legal, but the objects do not cast shadows on each other. Sometimes this (incorrect) effect is not really noticeable. It depends on the exact situation.

- This technique does not allow objects to self-shadow. Again, this might not even be noticeable with certain objects.

- You can extend and repeat the technique for multiple planes. This could be helpful when casting shadows on multiple walls in a room. It might even help with casting shadows on a handful of planes on terrain.

- Remember that the mesh used to create the shadow need not be the mesh used when drawing the visible object. The different passes change the vertex streams anyway, so there's no penalty for substituting different-resolution meshes.

CHAPTER 28

SHADOWS PART 2—SHADOW VOLUMES

Planar shadows are more or less a mathematical trick that exploits the fact you can use matrix operations to project geometry onto a plane other than the screen. The technique is not based on any of the physical realities of shadows, which is why the shadows only work on the plane. Shadow volumes are different in that they account for the fact that light (and therefore shadow) occupies a volume of space, and it affects any objects in that volume. This chapter explains this technique with the following points:

- The shadow volume approach.
- The vertex shader for this technique.
- The application code that works with the shader.
- The advantages over planar shadows.
- The limitations of the technique.

In terms of functionality and flexibility, shadow volumes are a dramatic leap over planar shadows, but the approach is also more complex.

Shadow Volumes Explained

Shadow volumes take into account the fact that lights occupy a given volume of space. On a misty day, you can sometimes see clearly defined cones of light coming from the headlights of a car. Shadows are the same way. They are essentially voids within that volume of light, so they occupy a volume themselves. Anything within the volume of light is lit. Anything within the volume of the shadow is not lit. Figure 28.1 shows a conceptual drawing of this.

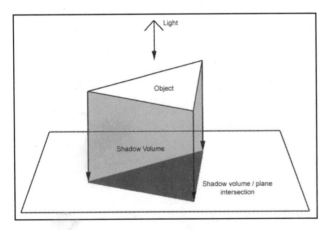

Figure 28.1

Shadow volume of a plane on a plane.

By now you have seen that a directional light lights everything in a scene, regardless of where it is or what's around it. Point lights and spot lights also light everything in the scene within the bounds of their attenuation and falloff parameters. There is no built-in notion of how objects interrelate to block light from each other. That's something you have to build in yourself. It turns out that shaders make this relatively easy.

The traditional way of computing a shadow volume was this. First, given a light position and direction and a mesh, you had to compute the silhouette edges of the mesh from the perspective of the light. In some ways, this was conceptually similar to planar shadows in that you had to figure out what that object looked like from the perspective of the light. Unlike the planar technique, it wasn't enough to flatten the geometry. You actually had to analyze the mesh on the CPU and figure out which vertices constituted edges and which did not. There were algorithms to make this faster, but it was still a fairly heavy operation.

Once the silhouette was computed, you could extrude that shape away from the light, thereby defining the volume of the shadow where the mesh was blocking the light. This was the heart of the shadow volume technique. Before moving on in the explanation, let me switch gears and explain how this first part has been improved with vertex shaders. Then I explain the rest of the technique.

Vertex shaders have greatly simplified the silhouette and extrusion step. Instead of calculating the silhouette and extruding, the shader can do both in one step. The shader figures out which vertices are facing away from the light, and it pushes those vertices away from the light along the light vector. All other vertices remain unchanged. If the mesh is tessellated enough, the result is the extruded shadow volume. If the mesh is not very tessellated, there might be visual artifacts. I explain this more at the end of the chapter. Figure 28.2 shows a shadow volume extruded from an object.

In Figure 28.2, the light is coming from the upper right and casting a shadow down and to the left. The volume in this shot is only partially extruded so that you can see the effect. Figure 28.3 shows a simplified diagram. Vertices that face away from the light are pushed along the light direction. Other vertices are unaffected.

Normally, you want to extrude the volume enough so that it intersects all the objects in the scene. The exact amount of extrusion depends on the size of your scene and how far you need the shadow volume to extend. The shadow volume is really a scene space operation, so there is no real cost associated with shadowing very distant objects other than the fact that you might not want the shadow to affect something that is very far away. One thing to notice in Figure 28.2 is that one of the meshes is extruding a volume and the other is not. You can apply the technique to

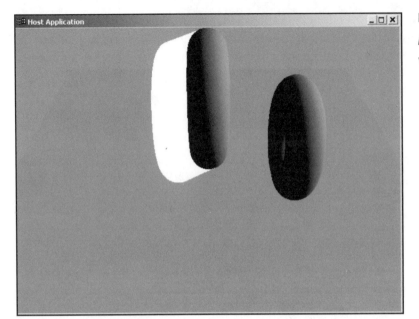

Figure 28.2

Partially extruded volume.

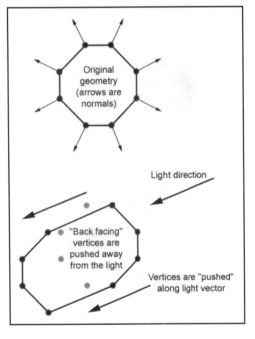

Figure 28.3

Extruded vertices.

every object in the scene, but I chose to apply the shadow technique to only one object in order to simplify the code and to show the difference. When you get to the code, I point out how to enable shadows for the other object.

Once the shadow is extruded, the technique becomes another stencil buffer effect, but it requires more rendering passes of the model. Normally, the rendering passes do not write to the color buffer until the actual shadow pass. I took the following screenshots with the color buffer enabled to show you how the effect works.

With planar shadows, the actual visible model was drawn after all the shadow passes were done. This technique does the opposite. As Figure 28.4 shows, the visible objects are drawn first. This pass writes to the color buffer and the depth buffer, just like any normal rendering pass.

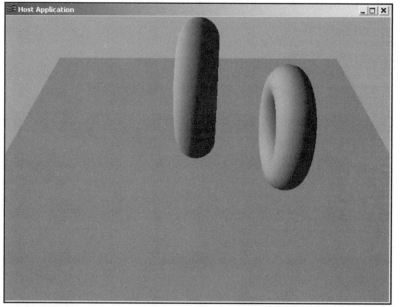

Figure 28.4

The first "normal" pass.

The second pass uses the extrusion shader, but it draws only the front-facing triangles of the object casting the shadow. It doesn't write to the color buffer or the depth buffer, but it does increment the stencil buffer. Figure 28.5 shows the front faces extruded away from the object. Notice that the volume is now fully extruded.

The third pass renders the extruded volume again, but this time it renders only the back-facing triangles of the mesh. Again, the color and depth values remain unchanged, but the stencil buffer values are decremented. Figure 28.6 shows the back-facing triangles. (The front-facing pass was disabled for this figure.)

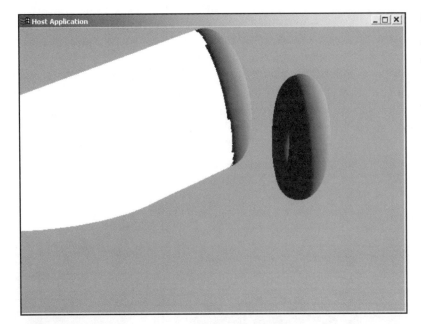

Figure 28.5

Drawing the front faces of the shadow volume.

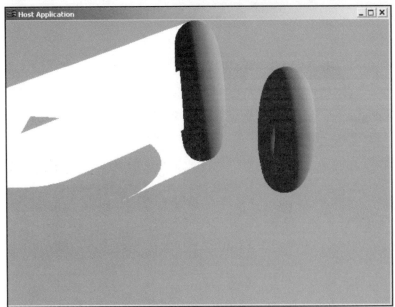

Figure 28.6

Drawing the back faces of the shadow volume.

If you compare Figures 28.5 and 28.6, you can see that the objects in the scene intersect the front- and back-facing triangles differently. Think of the front- and back-facing triangles as the near and far walls of the shadow volume. If you can look through the volume and see both the near and the far walls, that means there is nothing inside the volume at that particular point, so there is nothing to receive the shadow. If you look through the volume and you cannot see the back wall, you know that there is something inside the volume and it should receive a shadow. Figure 28.7 demonstrates this.

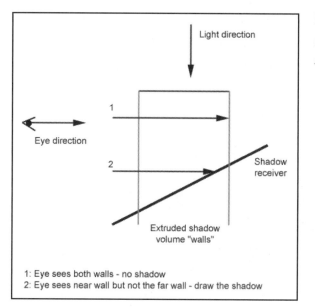

Figure 28.7

Looking through the shadow volume.

This is the reason for rendering the front and back faces in multiple passes. The first pass increments the stencil buffer for the entire volume. The back face pass decrements the stencil value for every pixel that is not blocked by some object in the stencil volume. Assuming the stencil values started at zero, any pixel with a stencil value of one is a pixel where you can see into but not out of the shadow volume. This pixel is therefore in shadow.

The only step remaining is to draw the shadow itself. In the last chapter, you could draw the plane because the shadow was cast only on the plane. Now, you should draw a large back quad over the entire screen, using the stencil buffer to define the shadowed pixels. This works out well for complex shadows, but there is no way to correct for the lighting effects as I mentioned in the last chapter. Figure 28.8 shows each step. The final output appears in Figure 28.9.

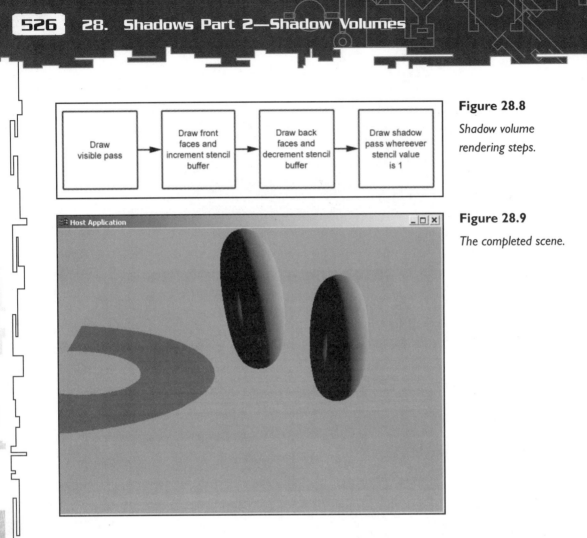

Figure 28.8

Shadow volume rendering steps.

Figure 28.9

The completed scene.

Figure 28.10 shows the exact same procedure, only now the light has been moved to the opposite side so that the shadow is cast on the other object. As you can see, the shadow falls correctly on the other object and is not limited to the ground plane. In fact, the ground plane could be a fairly complex object such as terrain or a Bezier patch.

That's the basics for the technique. Each of the actual shadow passes is based on one shader that handles the extrusion.

The Shadow Volume Shader

The shader is pretty straightforward, especially when you compare it to other shadow volume generation techniques. All it needs is the object space light position

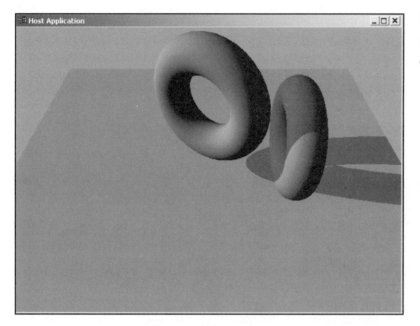

Figure 28.10

Shadows on other objects.

and direction, and from that it can correctly extrude the shadow volume. This shader appears in ShadowVolume.vsh:

```
vs.1.1
```

First, find the dot product of the vertex normal and the light direction and store the value in r0.x. You use this to figure out whether the vertex is facing away from the light:

```
dp3 r0.x, v3, -c4
```

Also, find the vector from the light to the vertex. If the vertex is facing away from the light, the vertex is pushed along this vector. In this example, I don't bother to normalize the direction vector because it is only used to push the vertex. It's not used in dot product calculations with other instructions that might work better with a normalized vector. The only consequence of not normalizing the vector is that the vertex might get pushed farther than expected. In this case, it doesn't matter because the vertex is being pushed way out of the scene anyway. It might matter if you want a finer grain of control over the push distance. If that's the case, you should probably add code to normalize the vector:

```
sub r1, v0, c7
```

The slt instruction checks whether the dot product of the vertex normal and the light direction is negative by comparing it to the value of zero in c8.y. If it is negative, r2.x is set to one. If it's not, r2.x is set to zero. That value is then multiplied by the push distance stored in c8.x, and the new value is stored in r2.x. Finally, the push distance is multiplied by the vector from the light to the vertex, and the whole thing is added to the original vertex position. This means that if the vertex is facing toward the light, r2.x is set to zero and the mad instruction has no effect on the position. If r2.x is negative, the position is offset along the light-to-vertex vector. The actual distance is not necessarily known because the light-to-vertex vector was not normalized. In the end, the back-facing vertices are pushed some distance away from the light. In this sample, the distance is more than adequate to cover all objects in the scene:

```
slt r2.x, r0.x, c8.y
mul r2.x, r2.x, c8.x
mad r3, r2.x, r1, v0
```

These lines have either pushed the vertex from the light or just passed the original position through. In either case, the final transformation is applied, and the vertex is output in clip space. There are no color calculations because these passes only update the stencil buffer:

```
dp4 oPos.x, r3, c0
dp4 oPos.y, r3, c1
dp4 oPos.z, r3, c2
dp4 oPos.w, r3, c3
```

For a relatively complex technique, the shader is actually fairly straightforward. Like the last technique, most of the actual complexity appears in the application.

The Shadow Volume Application

Like the last technique, this technique uses multiple passes that write to the stencil buffer. If you haven't read the previous chapter, I strongly recommend you do that now. This is only a small portion of the code, but it does cover all the new concepts. The complete code is on the CD.

The first order of business is defining the vertex formats. Nothing really new here except the "mask" vertices are in the transformed format. This allows you to set up the full screen shadow mask using the screen coordinates. There's no point in doing anything fancier:

```
#define D3DFVF_MESHVERTEX (D3DFVF_XYZ | D3DFVF_NORMAL |
                           D3DFVF_DIFFUSE)
```

```
#define D3DFVF_MASKVERTEX (D3DFVF_XYZRHW | D3DFVF_DIFFUSE)

struct MESH_VERTEX
{
        float x, y, z;
        float nx, ny, nz;
        DWORD color;
};

struct MASK_VERTEX
{
        float x, y, z, rhw;
        DWORD color;
};
```

Once the vertex format is set up, you need to create a simple vertex buffer with the full-screen mask vertices. You do this in `CreatePlaneBuffers`. Only part of the function appears here. The full source code includes the code to create the ground plane, which is the same code from the previous chapter:

```
HRESULT CTechniqueApplication::CreatePlaneBuffers()
{
        if (FAILED(m_pD3DDevice->CreateVertexBuffer(4 *
                                                sizeof(MASK_VERTEX),
                                     0, D3DFVF_MASKVERTEX,
                                     D3DPOOL_MANAGED,
                                     &m_pMaskVertexBuffer)))
                return E_FAIL;

        MASK_VERTEX *pMaskVertices;

        m_pMaskVertexBuffer->Lock(0, 4 * sizeof(MASK_VERTEX),
                                (BYTE **)&pMaskVertices, 0);
```

`memset` sets all the values in the vertex buffer to zero. If any values are not set, they can be assumed to be zero:

```
        memset(pMaskVertices, 0x00, 4 * sizeof(MASK_VERTEX));
```

Set the vertices to match the screen extents. This probably isn't the best general code. The vertex buffer is created as a managed buffer so that it does not need re-creating if the device is reset. This could be a problem if you build this into an application that allows the user to choose a new device at a new resolution. As it is right now, this rectangle would be too small if the device were reset at a higher resolution. That's something to check when using transformed vertices. As it stands, this creates a full-screen rectangle:

```
pMaskVertices[0].x = 0.0f; pMaskVertices[0].y = 0.0f;
pMaskVertices[1].x = (float)m_WindowWidth;
pMaskVertices[1].y = 0.0f;
pMaskVertices[2].x = 0.0f;
pMaskVertices[2].y = (float)m_WindowHeight;
pMaskVertices[3].x = (float)m_WindowWidth;
pMaskVertices[3].y = (float)m_WindowHeight;
```

This sets the color to black and half transparent. This alpha value should be related to the ambient light intensity. The brighter the ambient light, the more transparent the shadow should be. If the ambient light intensity is dynamic, you might want to make this value more dynamic. You could do this with some of the state settings described in earlier chapters. In the meantime, a simple transparency setting is probably good enough for most applications:

```
pMaskVertices[0].color = pMaskVertices[1].color =
                        pMaskVertices[2].color =
                        pMaskVertices[3].color = 0x80000000;

m_pMaskVertexBuffer->Unlock();

return S_OK;
}
```

As usual, the bulk of the actual work happens in the Render function. I wrote this application with only one shadow casting object to keep the code to a minimum. As I walk through the code, I talk about how to make all the objects cast shadows:

```
void CTechniqueApplication::Render()
{
        D3DXVECTOR4 EyePos(0.0, 60.0f, -60.0f, 0.0f);
        D3DXMatrixLookAtLH(&m_ViewMatrix, &(D3DXVECTOR3)EyePos,
                        &D3DXVECTOR3(0.0f, 0.0f, 0.0f),
                        &D3DXVECTOR3(0.0f, 1.0f, 0.0f));
```

The light follows the same path as the light in the previous chapter. It moves side to side above the scene and always aims toward the origin of the scene:

```
float Time = (float)GetTickCount() / 2000.0f;
D3DXVECTOR4 LightPos(150.0f * sin(Time), 90.0f, 0.0f, 1.0f);

D3DXVECTOR4 LightDir = D3DXVECTOR4(0.0f, 0.0f, 0.0f, 0.0f) -
                       LightPos;
D3DXVec4Normalize(&LightDir, &LightDir);
```

By default I have no ambient lighting, but the basic shader does add it if you need ambient lighting. Like the last sample, this sample uses a basic diffuse lighting calculation to do the visible pass of the objects:

```
D3DXVECTOR4 Ambient    (0.0f, 0.0f, 0.0f, 0.0f);
m_pD3DDevice->SetVertexShaderConstant(5, &Ambient, 1);
```

This next constant defines the distance that the vertices are pushed. This value depends heavily on the units in your scene and the distance you want the shadow volume to travel. For instance, if you have a space battle with giant battle cruisers projecting shadows on far-off planets, you probably want to increase this value. Remember that the current shader does not normalize the light-to-vertex vector, so the actual distance that the vertex is pushed is almost certainly not going to be equal to this value, but the value does provide a rough idea of the range. If you need a specific value, normalize the vector in the shader. In the battle cruiser example, it might not make sense to cast a shadow on a planet that is very far in the distance. In that case, you may want to more carefully control the depth of the shadow volume:

```
D3DXVECTOR4 PushDistance(100.0f, 0.0f, 0.0f, 0.0f);
m_pD3DDevice->SetVertexShaderConstant(8, &PushDistance, 1);
```

The first pass renders the objects in the usual, visible way. The shader does simple diffuse lighting calculations based on the preceding light constants:

```
m_pD3DDevice->SetVertexShader(m_BasicShader);
```

This sample uses a depth bias value to make sure that the shadow passes behave well with the visible pass. When you render multiple passes of the same geometry, rounding errors and other quirks of the depth buffer can cause stippling effects where some pixels pass the depth test and others don't. Setting the Z bias ensures that one pass always "wins" even though they both have extremely similar depth values. In this case, the visible model is set to always be on top of the shadow passes.

This does two things. First, it prevents the shadow passes from always overlaying the object, which creates a shadow "film" over the entire object. Figure 28.11 shows the application with this Z bias turned off. Notice that the shadow is still correct, but the entire shadow caster is also in shadow. You want self-shadowing, but that's too much.

Figure 28.11

Shadows without Z biasing.

It also minimizes the amount of popping and other visual artifacts that can occur when there is "Z fighting" between the passes:

```
m_pD3DDevice->SetRenderState(D3DRS_ZBIAS, 1);
```

First, render the plane. Unlike the last chapter, there is nothing special about the plane. This time it's just another mesh in the scene:

```
RenderPlane();
```

This scene draws two instances of the same object. There's no reason they need to be the same other than the fact that I'm trying to keep the code as simple as possible. This first object is just there to show shadows on a second object. The object is moved over, and all the constants are set for the usual rendering. You must reset constants any time the world matrix changes because the shader expects object space vectors. If you choose to add more objects, make sure that the constants are set correctly:

```
D3DXMATRIX Rotation;
D3DXMATRIX Translation;

D3DXMatrixTranslation(&m_WorldMatrix, 20.0f, 10.0f, 0.0f);
D3DXMATRIX ShaderMatrix = m_WorldMatrix * m_ViewMatrix *
                          m_ProjectionMatrix;
D3DXMatrixTranspose(&ShaderMatrix, &ShaderMatrix);
m_pD3DDevice->SetVertexShaderConstant(0, &ShaderMatrix, 4);

D3DXMATRIX InverseWorld;
D3DXMatrixInverse(&InverseWorld, NULL, &m_WorldMatrix);
D3DXVec4Transform(&LightDir, &LightDir, &InverseWorld);
D3DXVec4Normalize(&LightDir, &LightDir);
m_pD3DDevice->SetVertexShaderConstant(4, &LightDir, 1);

D3DXVec4Transform(&LightPos, &LightPos, &InverseWorld);
m_pD3DDevice->SetVertexShaderConstant(7, &LightPos, 1);

m_pD3DDevice->SetStreamSource(0, m_pMeshVertexBuffer,
                              sizeof(MESH_VERTEX));
m_pD3DDevice->SetIndices(m_pMeshIndexBuffer, 0);
m_pD3DDevice->DrawIndexedPrimitive(D3DPT_TRIANGLELIST, 0,
                              m_pMesh->GetNumVertices(), 0,
                              m_pMesh->GetNumFaces());
```

This second call to DrawIndexedPrimitive is actually the first pass of the shadow casting object. I rotated it and raised it above the first object so that you can see the shadow projected down on the first object. When the world matrix is changed, you should recompute and reset all object space vectors:

```
D3DXMatrixRotationY(&Rotation, (float)GetTickCount() / 1000.0f);
D3DXMatrixTranslation(&Translation, 0.0f, 20.0f, 0.0f);
m_WorldMatrix = Rotation * Translation;

ShaderMatrix = m_WorldMatrix * m_ViewMatrix *
               m_ProjectionMatrix;
D3DXMatrixTranspose(&ShaderMatrix, &ShaderMatrix);
```

```
m_pD3DDevice->SetVertexShaderConstant(0, &ShaderMatrix, 4);
D3DXMatrixInverse(&InverseWorld, NULL, &m_WorldMatrix);
D3DXVec4Transform(&LightDir, &LightDir, &InverseWorld);
D3DXVec4Normalize(&LightDir, &LightDir);
m_pD3DDevice->SetVertexShaderConstant(4, &LightDir, 1);
D3DXVec4Transform(&LightPos, &LightPos, &InverseWorld);
m_pD3DDevice->SetVertexShaderConstant(7, &LightPos, 1);

m_pD3DDevice->SetStreamSource(0, m_pMeshVertexBuffer,
                                   sizeof(MESH_VERTEX));
m_pD3DDevice->SetIndices(m_pMeshIndexBuffer, 0);
m_pD3DDevice->DrawIndexedPrimitive(D3DPT_TRIANGLELIST, 0,
                                m_pMesh->GetNumVertices(), 0,
                                m_pMesh->GetNumFaces());
```

Now the actual shadow passes begin. First, clear the stencil buffer. You could have cleared the stencil buffer when the color buffer was cleared. You also need to enable the stencil test. The stencil test always passes in this first pass. Any new pixels are incremented in the stencil buffer:

```
m_pD3DDevice->Clear(0, NULL, D3DCLEAR_STENCIL, 0, 1.0f, 0);
m_pD3DDevice->SetRenderState(D3DRS_STENCILENABLE, TRUE);
m_pD3DDevice->SetRenderState(D3DRS_STENCILFUNC,
                             D3DCMP_ALWAYS);
m_pD3DDevice->SetRenderState(D3DRS_STENCILPASS,
                             D3DSTENCILOP_INCR);
```

Disable writing to the depth buffer. This keeps multiple passes from interfering with each other. It also alleviates the need for the hardware to do the stencil test, which means that it gives a slight performance boost:

```
m_pD3DDevice->SetRenderState(D3DRS_ZWRITEENABLE, FALSE);
```

These lines disable writing to the color buffer as discussed in the previous chapter. There is a render state that specifically does this, but this method works on all hardware:

```
m_pD3DDevice->SetRenderState(D3DRS_ALPHABLENDENABLE, TRUE);
m_pD3DDevice->SetRenderState(D3DRS_SRCBLEND,  D3DBLEND_ZERO);
m_pD3DDevice->SetRenderState(D3DRS_DESTBLEND, D3DBLEND_ONE);
```

The two shadow passes use the shadow volume extrusion shader defined earlier in this chapter:

```
m_pD3DDevice->SetVertexShader(m_VolumeShader);
```

The visible pass had a Z bias of one. Setting the Z bias to zero ensures that the shadow pass does not interfere with the actual object where the two overlap exactly. The shadow pass still overlaps in places where the depth values are not very close. This does not interfere with self shadowing; it just makes things cleaner:

```
m_pD3DDevice->SetRenderState(D3DRS_ZBIAS, 0);
```

This first shadow pass draws only the front-facing polygons of the model. Stencil values are incremented wherever the front faces are drawn. If you want to cast shadows from multiple objects, this is where you do it. You must reset the world matrices, reset the shader constants, and call DrawIndexedPrimitive for each of the shadow casters. If shadows overlap, each volume increments the stencil value. This is the desired effect, but you need to make sure that you draw both the front and back faces for each object:

```
m_pD3DDevice->SetRenderState(D3DRS_CULLMODE, D3DCULL_CCW);
m_pD3DDevice->DrawIndexedPrimitive(D3DPT_TRIANGLELIST, 0,
                              m_pMesh->GetNumVertices(), 0,
                              m_pMesh->GetNumFaces());
```

The second shadow pass draws the back-facing triangles and decrements the values wherever they are drawn. If multiple objects are casting shadows, they either match each increment with a decrement (if the area is not in any shadow), or they have more increments than decrements (if the area is in shadow from one or more objects):

```
m_pD3DDevice->SetRenderState(D3DRS_CULLMODE,      D3DCULL_CW);
m_pD3DDevice->SetRenderState(D3DRS_STENCILPASS,
                              D3DSTENCILOP_DECR);
m_pD3DDevice->DrawIndexedPrimitive(D3DPT_TRIANGLELIST, 0,
                              m_pMesh->GetNumVertices(), 0,
                              m_pMesh->GetNumFaces());
```

The two shadow passes have set up the stencil buffer; it's now time to draw the full-screen black quad. First you set the stencil test to pass if the current stencil value is greater than or equal to one. If an area is in several shadows, the stencil value is greater than one. This operation doesn't overwrite the stencil value:

```
m_pD3DDevice->SetRenderState(D3DRS_STENCILFUNC,
                              D3DCMP_LESSEQUAL);
m_pD3DDevice->SetRenderState(D3DRS_STENCILPASS,
                              D3DSTENCILOP_KEEP);
m_pD3DDevice->SetRenderState(D3DRS_STENCILREF,    1);
```

Turn off the depth test, and set the blending modes to allow for alpha blending. If you want to be able to set the alpha value of the rectangle, this is where you do it:

```
m_pD3DDevice->SetRenderState(D3DRS_ZENABLE, FALSE);
m_pD3DDevice->SetRenderState(D3DRS_CULLMODE, D3DCULL_NONE);
m_pD3DDevice->SetRenderState(D3DRS_SRCBLEND, D3DBLEND_SRCALPHA);
m_pD3DDevice->SetRenderState(D3DRS_DESTBLEND,
                             D3DBLEND_INVSRCALPHA);
```

Draw the big black rectangle. All objects in the scene get the same amount of darkening. This is not really accurate, but the effect is usually good enough for gaming. This operation doesn't use a shader; the rectangle is drawn to the screen using the preset values:

```
m_pD3DDevice->SetVertexShader(D3DFVF_MASKVERTEX);
m_pD3DDevice->SetStreamSource(0, m_pMaskVertexBuffer,
                              sizeof(MASK_VERTEX));
m_pD3DDevice->DrawPrimitive(D3DPT_TRIANGLESTRIP, 0, 2);
```

The scene is now complete, and the shadows have been rendered. Before moving on, make sure that all the tests are set back to their default values:

```
m_pD3DDevice->SetRenderState(D3DRS_ZENABLE, TRUE);
m_pD3DDevice->SetRenderState(D3DRS_STENCILENABLE, FALSE);
m_pD3DDevice->SetRenderState(D3DRS_ZWRITEENABLE, TRUE);
m_pD3DDevice->SetRenderState(D3DRS_ALPHABLENDENABLE, FALSE);
}
```

That's the application. As I mentioned, you can easily cast shadows from both objects in the scene. I omitted that to make the code more compact because there would be a lot of repetition. I also didn't add code for multiple lights. You can add shadows for multiple lights. The only problem is that multiple lights mean multiple passes. You might have to decide which light should cast the shadow based on proximity, brightness, and so on.

Advantages and Disadvantages of Shadow Volumes

Shadow volumes require an extra pass versus planar shadows, but the advantages of this technique are well worth it. This is a more flexible and widely applicable shadowing technique. That extra pass buys you self-shadowing, interobject shadowing, and independence from simple planes.

If your geometry is detailed, that extra pass could be costly. You still have the possibility of creating a less dense mesh, but you should be more careful. This technique requires a decently tessellated mesh. If your mesh is too simple, you might get a lot of visual artifacts. However, if your mesh is extremely dense, you might be able to strike a happy medium with an optimized shadow caster. The problem with coarse meshes is that you might not have enough vertices to push over the light vector and still maintain the correct shape of the silhouette. Figure 28.12 shows this effect with a low-resolution mesh.

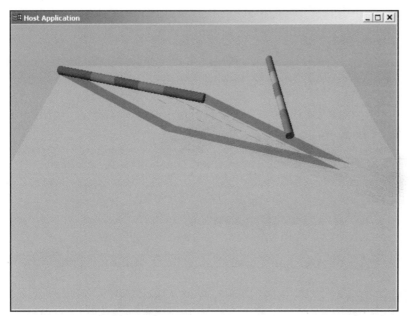

Figure 28.12

Incorrect volume for low tessellation mesh.

If the mesh is something like a cube and it doesn't need more triangles, you can solve this problem by adding degenerate triangles. The degenerate triangles allow the shader to push vertices around without distorting the rest of the mesh. You can see this solution in nVidia's shadow volume effect.

For all its advantages over planar shadows, this effect is still far from perfect. One notable problem is that the shadows all have hard, sometimes blocky edges. This isn't realistic, but it can't be helped too easily. The shadow edges are defined where the shadow volume triangles intersect the other triangles in the scene. These intersection lines are hard edges. In the next chapter, you'll see another technique that creates opportunities for soft edges.

Another problem is that this technique is still based on darkening geometry that has already been lit by the same light being blocked out. This isn't correct. In the previous chapter, I talked about a way to correct for this by playing with the alpha value of the darkening plane. In this case, there is no good way to do that because the darkening plane covers the entire screen.

One possible solution, albeit a heavy one, is to render the entire scene with only ambient light and again with other lights enabled. Then, render all the passes you need to build the correct stencil buffer and use the stencil buffer to blend the ambient rendering with the lit rendering. That solution is essentially the same as this technique, but the "mask" would contain the ambient rendering instead of a simple black quad. There would also be opportunities to soften the shadows. Such a technique would be very nice but very expensive on current hardware. When I talk about full-screen motion blur, you will see some of the pieces of such a technique in action.

In Conclusion...

As with any technique, you should consider the trade-offs when using shadow volumes. The effect isn't perfect, but it is nicer than planar shadows and better for real-world applications. Also, the shader is simple enough that the technique is not too expensive on current hardware. Shadow volumes do have the limitation of hard-edged shadows, but that's usually a problem most people can live with.

In the next chapter, you'll see the third and final shadowing technique. That technique is very different and provides its own advantages and trade-offs. Before moving on, let me quickly review the shadow volume technique:

- Shadow volumes are based on the fact that shadows occupy a given volume of space. Any objects that intersect that volume are in shadow.
- The shadow volume shader finds faces that are facing away from the light and pushes them away in the direction of the light-to-vertex vector. This requires that the model be fairly well tessellated.
- The shadow volume is drawn in two passes. If any pixels of the far faces are blocked out, that means there is an object within the volume and those pixels should be in shadow.
- The Z bias factor in the application code ensures the shadow passes don't overwrite the faces that are not pushed away by the shader.

- This technique suffers from the same "light and then darken" problem I showed you in the last chapter. This effect is incorrect, but in most cases the viewer can't point it out.
- The edges of shadow volume shadows are almost by definition hard and angular. The next chapter shows one technique that can produce soft edges.

CHAPTER 29

Shadows
Part 3—
Shadow Maps

Planar shadows exploited a mathematical reality of matrix transformation. Shadow volumes acknowledged the fact that shadows occupy a given volume of space. This third technique actually casts shadows from the light. Well, sort of.... This is the last of the three shadow techniques. It is also the first chapter that includes the use of pixel shaders. If you don't have hardware that supports pixel shaders, you might not be able to run the application, but you can still read up on the following concepts:

- The basics of shadow mapping.
- Rendering distance to a render target.
- Setting up a texture matrix for projected textures.
- Implementing a depth-comparing shader.
- Implementing the pixel shader.
- Setting the passes in the application.
- Limitations and areas for improvement.

Even if your current hardware doesn't support pixel shaders, read through the following section to see how shadow maps work and how they differ from the other techniques.

The Shadow Map Concept

Like many of the other techniques, the basic idea behind shadow mapping is fairly simple once you take a good look at it. Shadow maps are based on the fact that the distance from the light to the shadow caster is shorter than the distance between the light and the shadow receiver (along a single vector). Figure 29.1 illustrates this concept.

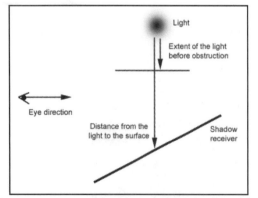

Figure 29.1

Distances from a light.

For any given point in space, you can compute the vector between that point and the light and the length of that vector. The length of that vector is the ideal unobstructed distance between the light and the point. Now, imagine standing on the light and following the same vector toward the point. If the distance between you and the point is the same as the first distance, you know you are getting an unobstructed view, and likewise the light is also unobstructed. This means that the point is not in shadow (at least with respect to that light source). If an object is between the light and the point, the distance between the light and the object is shorter than the distance from the light to the original point of interest. If there is an object closer to the light along the same vector, that object must be blocking the light. This means that the point is in a shadow. So you need a way to figure out the unobstructed distance and the real distance between the point and the light.

> **NOTE**
>
> Any nVidia-based hardware that supports pixel shaders also supports shadow maps in hardware. The nVidia hardware renders shadow maps using the depth buffer natively instead of requiring a depth-encoding shader. If you have hardware that supports hardware shadow mapping, that probably is the better way to go. This chapter does not assume hardware shadow mapping for a couple of reasons. The first is that this technique is more general to a wider range of hardware. I want to be able to show the basic technique without relying on a given feature of a given card. Also, a basic technique leads to other derivations for other effects. Finally, if you understand the basic concept, it is easy to retrofit this code to use the nVidia features. You do not need hardware shadow maps, but this technique really only makes sense on pixel shader hardware.

This is where the depth shader from Chapter 23 comes in. In Chapter 23, you saw that you could create a shader that would render the distance as a color. This capability is perfect for the shadow mapping technique.

This technique requires two passes of the entire scene. The first pass renders the scene from the light's point of view. The scene is not rendered to the normal back buffer. Instead, it is rendered to a texture that is used in the second pass. The second pass renders the scene to the back buffer and uses the camera's point of view. The shader computes the distance from each vertex to the camera and encodes that in one of the color channels using the depth shader technique. It also textures the entire scene with the texture that was generated in the first pass, as shown in Figure 29.2.

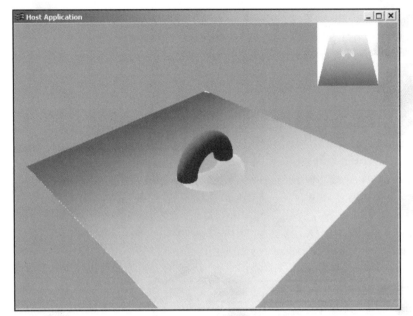

Figure 29.2

The light texture applied to the scene.

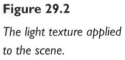

You can then use a pixel shader to compare the unobstructed distance (stored in the color value) with the light-based distance (stored in the texture). This happens on a per-pixel basis. If the color value is greater than the texture value, the pixel shader knows that the pixel is in shadow, and it can set the color accordingly. If the two values are equal or within a small threshold, the pixel shader knows that the pixel is not shadowed. This entire procedure is still at the mercy of all the bit depth issues discussed in Chapter 23, but careful selections of the encoding parameters can usually help.

The fact that this technique requires two passes shows one of the possible advantages of this technique. Shadow volumes require three passes to get the final output. This technique saves a pass but requires more texture and pixel processing. If your application is geometry limited, this might be the better technique. If your application does many stages of multitexturing or if it is otherwise limited by pixel operations, then this might not be a better bet. This technique is also limited by its dependence on pixel shaders and hardware shadow buffers.

Conceptually, that's the technique in a nutshell. You saw how to compute depth values in Chapter 23. This technique uses a couple new tools to compare those values and color a pixel accordingly. The next several pages talk about some of the new concepts you need to understand to make this work.

Rendering the Light Viewpoint to a Texture

Chapter 33 covers the mechanics of rendering to a texture, so I do not go into many of those details here, but I want to discuss some of the limitations and potential problems with respect to this technique. If you are unfamiliar with render targets, now might be a good time to skip ahead to Chapter 33 to see the specifics of rendering to a texture.

This technique uses a render-to-texture pass to create a texture that will eventually be mapped over the entire scene. This means that the texture must be fairly high resolution because it might cover a large area. The texture used to produce Figure 29.2 was a fairly high resolution of 1,024x1,024. Figure 29.3 is the same screen shot, only this time the texture is a very low resolution of 32x32.

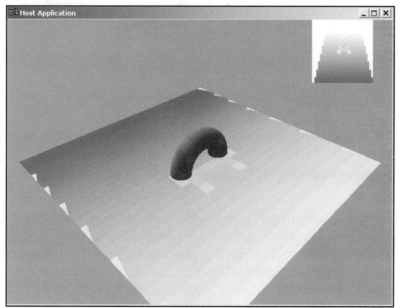

Figure 29.3

Low-resolution light texture.

In both screen shots, the pixel shader has not been used to create the actual shadow effect; you are only seeing the texture mapped onto the scene. The impact of the lower resolution is clear. When the pixel shader does compare the distances, the lower-resolution texture creates a blocky and jagged shadow. This is usually not the desired effect, although you might be constrained to something like this if you are short on texture memory or horsepower. In reality, the 32x32 texture is a worst case. Figure 29.4 shows the screen shot again, this time with a 256x256 texture.

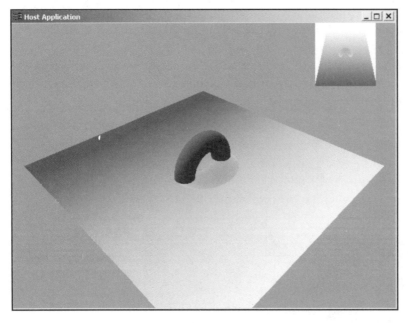

Figure 29.4

Medium-resolution light texture.

As you can see, the resulting image is nearly as good as the one shown in Figure 29.2, and the texture is 1/16 the size of the original texture. The bottom line is that this is yet another instance where you might need to experiment to find the best trade-off between quality and performance.

The real hardware shadow maps available on the geForce3 are subject to the same limitations and trade-offs. Hardware shadow buffers use the depth buffer directly, but you still need to specify the size of the depth buffer used in the render-to-texture pass. In any case, be aware that you need a decently sized texture, although in some cases the necessary resolution might be lower than you think. Once you have the texture, you still need to map it onto the geometry.

Texture Mapping the World

Chapter 23 told you how to render a scene with encoded depth information. Chapter 33 walks through the steps of rendering to a texture. The previous page talked about choosing the correct texture size. Now you have all the pieces: You just need to map them onto the world correctly.

Stepping back for a second, remember that the final renderings of any of the previous applications are based on transformations that map some vertex to somewhere in the view space of the camera. When you look at any given pixel, you are seeing data that the transformation operations mapped to that pixel. There is a mathematical relationship between a position on a screen and a vector through space. The same is true for a texture that has been used as a render target. Each texel on that texture is based in part on a set of transformations.

To understand what I'm getting at, consider the scene in Figure 29.5. This figure shows a simple scene and the light's view of that scene.

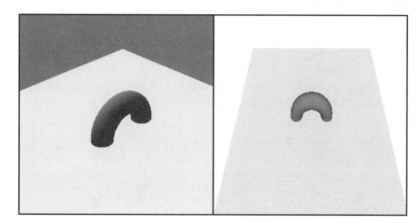

Figure 29.5

Camera view and light view of a simple scene.

The camera's view of the scene is based on a set of matrices that correspond to the position and orientation of the camera. The same is true for the light's point of view. In the case of the light, the transformations have placed the square in the upper left of the texture and the square in the lower right. Now, imagine that you want to render the plane again, only this time you want to project the texture onto the plane. You have most of the pieces that make this a piece of cake.

When you render the scene again, the vertex positions are transformed to the clip space positions using the camera transformations. The only new part is the texture mapping operation, but there's actually nothing new about that. The texture coordinates are based on the vertex position and the light's transformations. You apply the exact same transformations as you did for the light's point of view that created the texture in the first place. When the texture was rendered, the far-right vertex was mapped to the upper left of the texture. Now, the texture coordinate of the far-right vertex is mapped to the upper left of the texture as shown in Figure 29.6.

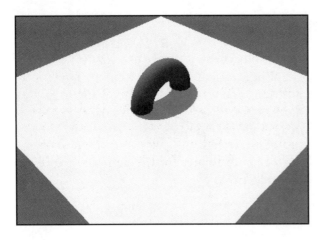

Figure 29.6

Light view mapped to camera view.

Everything is as it should be. Well, almost. The one missing piece is that texture coordinates are based on a range of zero to one, and this is not the range of the clip space transformations. You need to tweak the transformation matrix to account for this. The matrix must provide a final operation that offsets and scales the other transformations to the equivalent texture coordinates. The following code snippet shows how to build such a matrix:

```
D3DXMATRIX TextureMatrix;
float Offset = 0.5f + (0.5f / (float)TEX_DIMENSION);
ZeroMemory(&TextureMatrix, sizeof(D3DXMATRIX));
TextureMatrix._11 =  0.5f;
TextureMatrix._22 = -0.5f;
TextureMatrix._33 =  1.0f;
TextureMatrix._41 =  Offset;
TextureMatrix._42 =  Offset;
TextureMatrix._44 =  1.0f;
```

After the texture matrix is created, it can augment the standard concatenated shader matrix:

```
D3DXMATRIX TextureShaderMatrix = m_WorldMatrix *
                                 LightViewMatrix *
                       m_ProjectionMatrix * TextureMatrix;
```

Now the shader can compute texture matrices that correctly index into the texture matrix for any point in the world. Obviously, this only makes sense if the texture itself has been rendered with the same light view transformations. Assuming that's true, the following shader should create the values needed for comparison in the pixel shader.

The Depth Comparison Vertex Shader

The first pass in this technique renders to the target texture with the depth-encoding shader from Chapter 23. That shader is not covered here. The following shader is used in the second pass. It encodes the vertex-to-light distance into the specular color output register and a simple diffuse lighting color into the diffuse output register. It also sets the proper texture coordinates for the light texture. This shader is in the media directory as CompareDepth.vsh:

```
vs.1.1

dp4 oPos.x, v0, c0
dp4 oPos.y, v0, c1
dp4 oPos.z, v0, c2
dp4 oPos.w, v0, c3
```

This code is copied from the EncodeDepth shader. It computes the ideal distance between the light and the vertex. It then subtracts the new plane distance and multiplies by the scaling factor. The near plane and scaling factors must be the same for both the light pass and this pass. If the two values are different, there can be no basis for comparison. The final depth value is written to r1.z:

```
dp4 r1.z, v0, c12
sub r1.z, r1.z, c4.x
mul r1.z, r1.z, c4.y
```

Output the distance to the specular output register. The pixel shader will use this when it compares against the distance value in the texture:

```
mov oD1, r1.zzzz
```

Again, the lighting in this example is very simple. This is just a diffuse lighting factor plus an ambient lighting component:

```
dp3 r0, -c5, v3
mad oD0, v5, r0, c6
```

These lines compute the texture coordinates as described earlier in this chapter. Earlier in the shader, the vertex position was computed using the camera transformations in constants c0 through c3. The texture coordinates are based on the light transformations found in constants c20 through c23. These constants contain the matrix concatenated from the light matrices and the texture correction matrix. This shader computes the proper light view texture coordinates for any object in the scene as long as the proper constants remain consistent across both passes:

```
dp4 oT0.x, v0, c20
dp4 oT0.y, v0, c21
dp4 oT0.z, v0, c22
dp4 oT0.w, v0, c23
```

That's the extent of the comparison shader. The primary purpose of this shader is to properly set up the values that feed into the pixel shader. The pixel shader is where most of the actual effect takes place.

The Shadow Mapping Pixel Shader

This is the first pixel shader of the book. The preceding vertex shader has set up all the inputs to the shader. The only thing the pixel shader needs to do is decide whether a given pixel is in shadow. This pixel shader uses one texture and the diffuse and specular colors, but it still leaves some texture stages free for real textures, colors, and light maps. This shader is in the media directory as ShadowMap.psh:

```
ps.1.1
```

The first thing you need to do is define a set of constants. The first constant provides a bias value. The cnd instruction compares values against 0.5, so you need to bias comparison values by that value. The second two constants either turn on or turn off the lighting value for any given pixel. This shader is set up to fully darken any geometry that is in shadow, but you could include another constant to simulate ambient lighting:

```
def c0, 0.5, 0.5, 0.5, 0.5
def c1, 1.0, 1.0, 1.0, 1.0
def c2, 0.0, 0.0, 0.0, 0.0
```

The one and only texture is the texture that contains the light distance values:

```
tex t0
```

Start the comparison by subtracting the light distance from the ideal distance. The result is either zero or some positive value:

```
sub r1, v1, t0
```

Continue the comparison by adding 0.5 and writing the result to r0.a. Version 1.1 pixel shaders can only use r0.a in the cnd instruction, so you need to write to that component. Writing to r0.a requires the blue read modifier. All of the components are the same, so this is not a problem. Depth values that use more components might need to do more processing:

```
add r0.a, r1.b, c0.b
```

Compare `r0.a` with 0.5. If `r0.a` is greater than 0.5, the final output value is set to zero and the pixel is in shadow. If the value of `r0.a` is 0.5, the final output is set to 1.0 and the pixel receives the full lighting value:

```
cnd r0, r0.a, c2, c1
```

Finally, the value of `r0` is multiplied by the lighting value. This turns the lighting either on or off for each pixel:

```
mul r0, r0, v0
```

The pixel shader operates on every pixel, so it's important to keep the shader short and sweet. The only thing left to do now is write the application.

The Shadow Map Application

The two shaders do most of the interesting work, but the application has a few interesting bits. I haven't been including explanations of the header files, but this technique does define some interesting new members in terms of the render target texture. The following is an excerpt from this application's header file. The full source code appears on the CD:

```
class CTechniqueApplication : public CHostApplication
{
public:
```

The render target textures are created in the `SetupDevice` function and destroyed in `CleanUpTarget`. The `CreateShaders` function is mostly the same as in the previous techniques, only this time the `CreateShaders` function also creates the pixel shader. This function fails if pixel shaders are not supported:

```
    HRESULT SetupDevice();
    void CleanUpTarget();
    HRESULT CreateShaders();
```

This vertex buffer renders the small rectangle that is used to verify the texture:

```
    LPDIRECT3DVERTEXBUFFER8 m_pTestVertexBuffer;
```

These next five member variables are all used in the render-to-texture operation. The first variable is the only actual texture object. The first surface is the actual surface data for the texture. This is the object that's actually used as the target, but the parent texture is used when it comes time to texture the objects in the scene. The m_pShadowZSurface is the surface that provides a Z buffer when rendering to the texture. In this sample, the Z surface isn't actually used, but it could be used in place of the color buffer on hardware that supports hardware shadow mapping. Finally, the last two surfaces are the actual back and depth buffers created by the device. Once the device is active, the application obtains a copy of these so that it knows what to switch back to after the render-to-texture pass is complete. The application doesn't create new versions of these; it just keeps track of pointers so that it can switch back and forth:

```
LPDIRECT3DTEXTURE8 m_pShadowTexture;
LPDIRECT3DSURFACE8 m_pShadowTextureSurface;
LPDIRECT3DSURFACE8 m_pShadowZSurface;
LPDIRECT3DSURFACE8 m_pBackBuffer;
LPDIRECT3DSURFACE8 m_pZBuffer;
```

This application uses three shaders. The comparison shader was discussed earlier in this chapter, and the distance shader was discussed in Chapter 23. The pixel shader was also discussed earlier in this chapter:

```
DWORD m_CompareShader;
DWORD m_DistanceShader;
DWORD m_PixelShader;
};
```

Those are the newly defined members of this application. Now take a look at some of the functions in the application code itself. The following is an excerpt from the CreateShaders function. After creating the two vertex shaders, the function loads and creates the pixel shader:

```
HRESULT CTechniqueApplication::CreateShaders()
{
    ID3DXBuffer* pShaderBuffer;
    ID3DXBuffer* pShaderErrors;
```

The pixel shader is assembled in exactly the same way you've created all the vertex shaders. The first line in the shader defines what kind of shader it is, and the assembler works from there:

```
if (FAILED(D3DXAssembleShaderFromFile(
                            "..\\media\\shaders\\ShadowMap.psh",
                            0, NULL, &pShaderBuffer,
```

```
                                        &pShaderErrors)))
            return E_FAIL;
```

Pixel shader creation is a little bit easier than vertex shader creation. There is no
vertex format declaration, so the only thing you need to do is supply the assembled
code. This function returns a handle that you can use to set the pixel shader when
it's needed:

```
    if (FAILED(m_pD3DDevice->CreatePixelShader(
                (DWORD *)pShaderBuffer->GetBufferPointer(),
                &m_PixelShader)))
    {
```

If the pixel shader cannot be created, it is probably because your hardware can't
support it. If that's the case, this sample will run very slowly. You could try changing
the code to use the reference device, but be warned that the experience can be
painful:

```
            return E_FAIL;
    }
    pShaderBuffer->Release();

    return S_OK;
}
```

In addition to setting up the shaders, the application also needs to create the
render target objects. This happens in SetupDevice because it would need to be
redone if the device was restored. I removed some of the basic setup from the
following code:

```
HRESULT CTechniqueApplication::SetupDevice()
{
```

First, create a texture to be the render target. The best dimensions for this texture
are probably 256x256 or higher. Only one mip level is specified because only one
would ever be used. The render target flag tells the device to set up this texture as a
valid render target. Without this flag, rendering to the texture would fail. If your
hardware supports vertex and pixel shaders, it should have no problem with render
targets. Also, the format is given as a color-only format:

```
    if (FAILED(D3DXCreateTexture(m_pD3DDevice, TEX_DIMENSION,
                    TEX_DIMENSION,
                1, D3DUSAGE_RENDERTARGET, D3DFMT_X8R8G8B8,
```

```
                            D3DPOOL_DEFAULT, &m_pShadowTexture)))
            return E_FAIL;
```

You also need to create a surface that will serve as the depth buffer when rendering to the texture. This application doesn't use the contents of this buffer, but some applications or techniques might. The depth buffer is given the same dimensions as the render target texture:

```
    if (FAILED(m_pD3DDevice->CreateDepthStencilSurface(TEX_DIMENSION,
                                        TEX_DIMENSION,
                                        D3DFMT_D24S8,
                                        D3DMULTISAMPLE_NONE,
                                        &m_pShadowZSurface)))
            return E_FAIL;
```

The target texture was created, but the render target functions require a surface, not a texture. Here I extract the surface from the texture. The render operation renders to a surface, but that surface is still the underlying data structure for the texture. You still need to use the texture interface when using the data as a texture:

```
    if (FAILED(m_pShadowTexture->GetSurfaceLevel(0,
                                    &m_pShadowTextureSurface)))
            return E_FAIL;
```

Finally, the application asks the device for pointers to its default back buffer and depth buffer. These pointers are used only to swap back to the default buffers after the render-to-texture pass. If the device is reset, these pointers will be invalid:

```
    if (FAILED(m_pD3DDevice->GetRenderTarget(&m_pBackBuffer)))
            return E_FAIL;
    if (FAILED(m_pD3DDevice->GetDepthStencilSurface(&m_pZBuffer)))
            return E_FAIL;

    return S_OK;
}
```

Before moving on to the Render function, I mention a couple of items that are fairly important but that don't really need source code to explain. It's important to remember that you must clean up these new objects as you do any of the other objects. The code provides clean-up using the typical sequence you've seen of releasing them if they are valid pointers. For the pixel shader, the shader handle is passed to DeletePixelShader.

This code also creates a vertex buffer to hold the small debug window for the texture. This is a rectangle created with transformed coordinates. The code is exactly like the full-screen quad from the previous chapter, only this time the quad is smaller. The only purpose of the quad is to show the texture without the influence of texture matrices and strange texture states. This can be useful for debugging.

As usual, Render does most of the real work. This code comes with my usual caveat about possible optimizations. Once you understand the code, you can probably restructure it to make it cleaner and possibly slightly faster:

```
void CTechniqueApplication::Render()
{
```

The following code builds the texture matrix as described earlier in this chapter. I added this code to the Render function to make it more visible, but there is no point in creating this matrix every time. It is slightly better to create it at the start of the application and whenever the texture dimensions are set:

```
D3DXMATRIX TextureMatrix;
float Offset = 0.5f + (0.5f / (float)TEX_DIMENSION);
ZeroMemory(&TextureMatrix, sizeof(D3DXMATRIX));
TextureMatrix._11 =  0.5f;
TextureMatrix._22 = -0.5f;
TextureMatrix._33 =  1.0f;
TextureMatrix._41 =  Offset;
TextureMatrix._42 =  Offset;
TextureMatrix._44 =  1.0f;
```

This code sets up the lighting parameters. The time is used to provide some simple animation. In this case, the light moves slowly toward and away from the center of the world. The light position is used to build a view matrix. Usually, you only need the light's position and direction because you are doing vector operations. In this case, you need to be able to render a scene from the light's viewpoint. That requires a full-fledged view matrix:

```
D3DXMATRIX LightViewMatrix;
float Time = (float)GetTickCount() / 2000.0f;
D3DXVECTOR4 LightPos(-25.0f * sin(Time) - 50.0f, 90.0f,
                     0.0f, 1.0f);

D3DXMatrixLookAtLH(&LightViewMatrix, &(D3DXVECTOR3)LightPos,
                   &D3DXVECTOR3(0.0f, 0.0f, 0.0f),
                   &D3DXVECTOR3(0.0f, 1.0f, 0.0f));
```

In addition to the light's view matrix, you still need the light direction for simple lighting calculations. You set the light direction to point at the origin and normalize the vector before sending it off to the shader. At the same time, the application sets a small ambient value:

```
D3DXVECTOR4 LightDir = D3DXVECTOR4(0.0f, 0.0f, 0.0f, 0.0f) -
                       LightPos;
D3DXVec4Normalize(&LightDir, &LightDir);
m_pD3DDevice->SetVertexShaderConstant(5, &LightDir, 1);
D3DXVECTOR4 Ambient    (0.1f,  0.1f, 0.1f, 0.0f);
m_pD3DDevice->SetVertexShaderConstant(6, &Ambient, 1);
```

You use the eye position to create a view matrix for the final rendering. You could have created the matrix once when the application started if you didn't include animation:

```
D3DXVECTOR4 EyePos(75.0, 75.0f, -75.0f, 0.0f);
D3DXMatrixLookAtLH(&m_ViewMatrix, &(D3DXVECTOR3)EyePos,
                   &D3DXVECTOR3(0.0f, 0.0f, 0.0f),
                   &D3DXVECTOR3(0.0f, 1.0f, 0.0f));
```

The light shader matrix is the matrix used to render the scene from the light's point of view. The eye shader matrix is the usual camera transformation matrix. The texture shader matrix is the same as the light shader matrix except that it does the texture coordinate correction transformation. This matrix is used in the comparison shader:

```
D3DXMATRIX LightShaderMatrix = m_WorldMatrix * LightViewMatrix *
                               m_ProjectionMatrix;

D3DXMATRIX EyeShaderMatrix =   m_WorldMatrix * m_ViewMatrix *
                               m_ProjectionMatrix;

D3DXMATRIX TextureShaderMatrix = m_WorldMatrix *
                                 LightViewMatrix *
                          m_ProjectionMatrix * TextureMatrix;

D3DXMatrixTranspose(&LightShaderMatrix,   &LightShaderMatrix);
D3DXMatrixTranspose(&EyeShaderMatrix,     &EyeShaderMatrix);
D3DXMatrixTranspose(&TextureShaderMatrix, &TextureShaderMatrix);
```

The distance scaling values help to get the most out of the 8 bits that are available using this simple distance encoding technique. Chapter 23 talks at length about the importance of choosing the right values. These values are going to be heavily dependent on the size of the objects in your scene, the distance from the objects to the camera, and other factors:

```
D3DXVECTOR4 DistanceScalers(75.0f, 0.025f, 0.0f, 1.0f);
m_pD3DDevice->SetVertexShaderConstant(4, &DistanceScalers, 1);
```

The texture is disabled for the first pass. In any case, you would not want to texture any objects during the first pass because textures would corrupt the depth data being written to the color buffer of the render target:

```
m_pD3DDevice->SetTexture(0, NULL);
```

For the first pass, use the simple distance shader discussed in Chapter 23:

```
m_pD3DDevice->SetVertexShader(m_DistanceShader);
```

The first pass is rendered to a texture, and that texture probably has very different dimensions from the normal output window of the application. The following code saves a copy of the current viewport and creates a new one based on the texture dimensions. Again, you can probably put this code elsewhere once you understand the flow of the technique. If you move the viewport creation code, remember to not move the last line that actually sets the new viewport. Once the new viewport is set, the rendering matches the dimensions of the texture:

```
D3DVIEWPORT8 NormalViewport;
m_pD3DDevice->GetViewport(&NormalViewport);

D3DVIEWPORT8 ShadowViewport;
ShadowViewport.X = 0;
ShadowViewport.Y = 0;
ShadowViewport.Width  = TEX_DIMENSION;
ShadowViewport.Height = TEX_DIMENSION;
ShadowViewport.MinZ = 0.0f;
ShadowViewport.MaxZ = 1.0f;
m_pD3DDevice->SetViewport(&ShadowViewport);
```

This is a very important stage. You must set the render target to the target texture. Once the target is set, you need to clear the buffers. This application still calls clear before every frame, but that call clears the default back buffer, not this render target. The target is cleared to white, which is the farthest distance for the distance shader:

```
m_pD3DDevice->SetRenderTarget(m_pShadowTextureSurface,
                             m_pShadowZSurface);
m_pD3DDevice->Clear(0, NULL, D3DCLEAR_TARGET |
```

```
                       D3DCLEAR_ZBUFFER,
                       D3DCOLOR_XRGB(255, 255, 255), 1.0f, 0);
```

Once everything is set up, set the main transformation matrix to the light's view and prepare to render the scene:

```
    m_pD3DDevice->SetVertexShaderConstant(0, &LightShaderMatrix, 4);
```

RenderPlane is a function that renders the simple ground plane for the scene. I put it into another function now that many samples have illustrated this:

```
    RenderPlane();
```

You also want to render every object in the scene. This example has only one object, but if there are more, you should render them all. If not, the shadows will probably not be correct because you have no way of accurately knowing whether some objects were obstructed:

```
    m_pD3DDevice->SetStreamSource(0, m_pMeshVertexBuffer,
                                  sizeof(MESH_VERTEX));
    m_pD3DDevice->SetIndices(m_pMeshIndexBuffer, 0);
    m_pD3DDevice->DrawIndexedPrimitive(D3DPT_TRIANGLELIST, 0,
                                  m_pMesh->GetNumVertices(), 0,
                                  m_pMesh->GetNumFaces());
```

The render target texture now contains the depth-encoded scene from the viewpoint of the light. Now it's time to use that texture to shadow the real scene. The first thing you should do is restore the default render targets and the default viewport. Once you do that, the device is back to the usual state and you can render normally:

```
    m_pD3DDevice->SetRenderTarget(m_pBackBuffer, m_pZBuffer);
    m_pD3DDevice->SetViewport(&NormalViewport);
```

This pass requires a new vertex shader and a new pixel shader. This pixel shader is applied to the entire scene. If you have objects with different texturing or lighting requirements, you probably need to augment the pixel or vertex shader to accommodate that:

```
    m_pD3DDevice->SetVertexShader(m_CompareShader);
    m_pD3DDevice->SetPixelShader(m_PixelShader);
```

The texture stage states set the texture to clamp on anything outside the zero-to-one range. Wrapping of any sort really doesn't make sense in this context:

```
    m_pD3DDevice->SetTextureStageState(0, D3DTSS_ADDRESSU,
                                  D3DTADDRESS_CLAMP);
```

```
m_pD3DDevice->SetTextureStageState(0, D3DTSS_ADDRESSV,
                                   D3DTADDRESS_CLAMP);
```

After all the work that went into creating the light depth texture, don't forget to set it. If you use other textures in the scene, you might want to use a different texture stage for the light depth texture. If you do move the texture to a different stage, remember to set the stage states and pixel shader to match:

```
m_pD3DDevice->SetTexture(0, m_pShadowTexture);
```

All of the shaders from this book have reserved c0 through c3 for the main transformation matrix. In this pass, set that matrix to the eye's point of view. Place the texture-corrected light view matrix in c20 through c23. The light parameters were set earlier in the function, so you are now ready to render:

```
m_pD3DDevice->SetVertexShaderConstant(0, &EyeShaderMatrix, 4);
m_pD3DDevice->SetVertexShaderConstant(20,
  &TextureShaderMatrix, 4);
```

Render all the objects again in the usual fashion. In this case, all objects must use the same vertex shader. However, the vertex shader just sets up the data that is eventually used by the pixel shader. You could build similar functionality into several vertex shaders. For instance, if you had a skinned character running across Bezier terrain, you could build the proper instructions into both of those shaders and still get the proper results:

```
RenderPlane();

m_pD3DDevice->SetStreamSource(0, m_pMeshVertexBuffer,
                             sizeof(MESH_VERTEX));
m_pD3DDevice->SetIndices(m_pMeshIndexBuffer, 0);
m_pD3DDevice->DrawIndexedPrimitive(D3DPT_TRIANGLELIST, 0,
                                   m_pMesh->GetNumVertices(), 0,
                                   m_pMesh->GetNumFaces());
```

The scene is not complete. Disable the pixel shader so it does not have an effect on either the debug window or the frame rate display:

```
m_pD3DDevice->SetPixelShader(NULL);
```

The following code draws the small debug panel in the corner of the application. The depth test is disabled so that it renders over everything on the screen. After the panel is drawn, the render states are set back to normal:

```
m_pD3DDevice->SetRenderState(D3DRS_CULLMODE, D3DCULL_NONE);
m_pD3DDevice->SetRenderState(D3DRS_ZENABLE, FALSE);
```

```
        m_pD3DDevice->SetVertexShader(D3DFVF_TESTVERTEX);
        m_pD3DDevice->SetStreamSource(0, m_pTestVertexBuffer,
                                      sizeof(TEST_VERTEX));
        m_pD3DDevice->DrawPrimitive(D3DPT_TRIANGLESTRIP, 0, 2);

        m_pD3DDevice->SetRenderState(D3DRS_CULLMODE, D3DCULL_CCW);
        m_pD3DDevice->SetRenderState(D3DRS_ZENABLE, TRUE);
}
```

That's the bulk of the shadow mapping application. The final output appears in Figure 29.7.

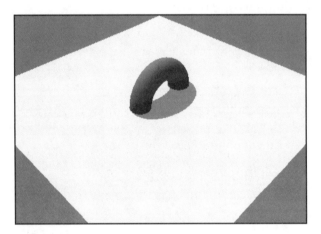

Figure 29.7

The final output with mapped shadows.

Limitations and Improvements

The most obvious limitation of this technique is its dependence on pixel shader support. Eventually such hardware will reach the masses, but in the meantime, shadow volumes are still the better choice. Another limitation is the complication associated with trying to encode better distance data into the texture. This is made easier with features such as hardware shadow buffers or higher precision formats, but these are also not ubiquitous.

Despite its limitations, this technique does offer advantages over the others. Shadowing between objects and themselves is built into this technique. Also, the per-pixel nature of the shadows opens up opportunities for softer shadows. Chapter 36 shows you how to use a jittered texture in multiple stages to blur the final output. You can use the same blurring effect to create softer shadows.

Also, the fact that this technique requires fewer passes might lead to some improvements for some situations. The overall advantage depends on how much geometry you have in your scene and how much pixel processing power you can use to compensate for that.

In Conclusion...

You now have three different shadowing techniques in your toolbox. All have their advantages and disadvantages. This technique is perhaps the most cutting edge in terms of implementation, but it's a double-edged sword. It will probably be a while before high-performance support for this technique is universal.

This chapter showed the first pixel shader technique and the last vertex shader technique. There are many more pixel shader techniques coming up next, so if you have any questions about how the pixel shader works, read on. However, before you jump ahead, let me review:

- Shadow mapping exploits the fact that objects obstruct the light as it travels through space.
- You can check for obstructions by comparing the ideal distance from a point to the light with the distance measured from the light's perspective.
- You can obtain the light values by rendering the light's view to a texture using the depth-encoding shader.
- The overall effect of shadow mapping is very dependent on the resolution of the texture render target.
- You can use the texture matrix to transform texture coordinates. In this case, it maps screen output coordinates to their equivalent texture coordinate values.
- You use a vertex shader to set up data that is sent to the pixel shader, but the pixel shader is where the effect actually happens.
- The most limiting factor with this technique is the current lack of widespread hardware support.

Part Six

Pixel Shader
Techniques

The previous section introduced several techniques based on per-vertex operations. This next section covers per-pixel techniques. In some cases, the end result is roughly the same, but pixel shaders offer more flexibility.

The same caveat from the last section holds true here as well. Much of the actual application code is not optimized, but I point out the flaws wherever possible. Also, some of these techniques use shader versions that might not be supported on your hardware. In that case, they should run with the reference device, albeit very slowly.

It may seem that this list doesn't include many pixel shader effects. There are two reasons for this. The first is that these chapters each include more than one effect. The other reason is that pixel shaders are used more in the next section, but the focus is less on pixel shaders and more on higher-level concepts:

- The problem with implementing spot lights and point lights in a vertex shader is that the vertices need to be fairly dense to get good results. Chapter 30, "Per-Pixel Lighting," introduces per-pixel methods that give good results for any geometric density.

- Bump mapping allows you to create correctly lit physical details without added geometry. Chapter 31, "Per-Pixel Lighting—Bump Mapping," explains the concepts behind setting up and rendering bump-mapped geometry.

- Chapter 32, "Per-Vertex Techniques Done per Pixel," revisits reflection and cartoon rendering from a per-pixel point of view. The samples demonstrate how to integrate the older techniques with per-pixel lighting to create better effects.

CHAPTER 30

PER-PIXEL LIGHTING

his is the last of the chapters that discuss lighting. So far, I have talked about lighting theory, DirectX lights, lighting in vertex shaders, and a little about lightmapping. In this chapter, I talk more about lightmapping, but the real focus is on dynamic per-pixel lighting. This requires revisiting some old topics and introducing some new ones, including the following:

- Simple light maps.
- The theory behind dynamic per-pixel lighting.
- Implementation of a per-pixel spot light.
- Implementation of a per-pixel point light.
- Limitations of the techniques.

The bulk of this chapter is based on pixel shader techniques, but a form of per-pixel lighting that predates pixel shaders is very useful today. I start with light maps.

Simple Light Maps

Light maps were used as a texturing technique long before the advent of vertex or pixel shaders. The idea behind a light map was simple. Each object would be textured with at least two different textures. One texture was a texture in the normal sense. It defined the appearance of the object. The other texture was a light map. This texture defined the intensity of the light at each texel. The light map values modulated the texture map values, meaning that they were multiplied together. Therefore, dark areas of the light map darkened the base texture, and light areas lightened the base texture. The result was usually much better than simple vertex lighting.

You can construct light maps in a variety of ways. For "first-person shooter" games, some techniques involve using a tool at design time to compute the light maps using radiosity calculations that would be far too slow to compute in real time. These tools compute the lighting values and store them in light maps that are applied to walls of the level. In a sense, this lets you have your cake and eat it too because you get the smoothness of high-fidelity lighting without the runtime computation cost.

Another simpler technique works well for defining the shape of lights along a wall or other areas. Figure 30.1 shows a wall texture and the light map for the shape of the light from a wall lamp. You can apply the two textures with very basic texture coordinates.

Figure 30.1

Lightmapping a wall.

This technique doesn't have all the subtleties of a true radiosity light map, but it is fairly easy to animate. For instance, if the player shoots at the wall lamp (not shown in the figure), you can make the light map swing back and forth with a texture transformation. If the player keeps shooting, you can turn the light off by setting the texture coordinates such that a black region of the light map was stretched over the entire section of wall.

In any case, light maps required at least two textures. If a system did not support multitexturing, the scene had to be rendered in two passes. One pass would render the scene with the base textures; the other pass would render the light-mapped scene and modulate the two results. The effect was the same, but the frame rate was effectively halved. Multitexturing hardware greatly improved the situation by allowing the system to render with both textures at the same time and setting the color operation to modulate the two textures. Most DX7-class hardware was very capable of supporting multiple textures, making light maps accessible to most people.

DirectX 8.0 introduced the idea of pixel shaders, which represents the next step for lighting and manipulation on a pixel level. This opens things up to more complex and dynamic methods of per-pixel lighting.

Per-Pixel Lighting with Pixel Shaders

As earlier examples showed, the advantage of vertex lighting is that it is fairly easy to dynamically compute lighting values on a per-vertex basis using low-cost vector operations. The disadvantage of vertex lighting is that smooth lighting effects such as point lights or spot lights require many vertices to give the proper effect. For lightmapping, the tradeoff works in the opposite way. The lighting effects are very smooth, even with few vertices. The downside is that the light map doesn't really define the light itself, so it is very difficult to get dynamic shape and attenuation effects. For instance, Figure 30.1 shows the cone of a spot light cast onto the wall, but you could not use that same light map to define the way the spot light affects other objects from other angles.

This is where pixel shaders come in handy. With the right combination of vertex shaders, pixel shaders, and textures, you can create very smooth lighting effects on any sort of geometry in real time. The advantage of pixel shaders over DX7 texture operations is that pixel shaders allow much more control over the pixel operations and the way that texture values are manipulated within the shader. For example, texture stage states allow you to set the color operations, but those operations affect each color component equally. Pixel shaders allow you to use different components in different ways. This creates more options for the way you can encode and derive lighting values.

Per Pixel?

The "per-pixel" label can be a bit of a misnomer. One reading implies that every pixel in a scene can have its own unique lighting value. This could be the case, but as Chapter 29 showed, it depends on the resolution of the textures involved. Pixel shaders work on a per-pixel level, but ultimately it is a texture that defines the lighting values. Very low textures produce low-resolution results. For instance, if you use a 2x2 texture and light a quad with these techniques, you get a result that is analogous to per-vertex lighting. Obviously, this is a worst-case scenario, but it does show how the texture can limit "per-pixel" effects.

Very high-resolution textures might not be helpful either (at least at current bit depths). If the pixel values are only 8-bit and you are encoding intensity values, only 256 unique values are possible. Any texture larger than 256x256 is a waste of memory unless you are encoding values in some more clever way.

Lighting in a scene is based on the distance of the light from any particular object and the orientation of that light with respect to that object. In a per-vertex lighting scheme, the "object" in question is a vertex. Lighting values are computed on a per-vertex basis and interpolated across the mesh.

In a per-pixel scheme, you'd like the "object" to be each individual pixel on the mesh rather than each vertex. But your mesh is still defined by vertices, so the challenge becomes how to map vertex data to pixel data. The answer is fairly simple. Instead of interpolating a lighting color value between the vertices, interpolate one or more of the lighting parameters. A pixel shader can then use this parameter to compute lighting values on a per-pixel basis. In the case of the point light, the parameter in question is the distance between the pixel and the light because point lighting is most concerned with attenuation over distance. For the spot light technique, both distance and angle are encoded, although the angle encoding is a side effect of projective texturing.

What about Directional Lights?

You might notice that there is no per-pixel example for directional lights. This is because there is no difference between per-vertex and per-pixel lighting for simple lighting cases. When I get to bump mapping, things change because angles change on a per-pixel basis. I discuss directional lights in the bump mapping chapters (Chapter 31).

Per-Pixel Spot Lights

Per-vertex spot lights are computationally expensive because of the shape of the umbra and penumbra. Per-vertex spot lighting requires a decent number of vertices to even see the effect of the different regions of the light. The example from Chapter 11 showed that the overall spot light effect was heavily dependent on the density of the mesh being lit. As graphics cards get better, geometry is becoming denser, but in some cases the geometry will always be sparse. For instance, a flat wall of a maze will always be a low-resolution mesh, but you might want to allow for cool flashlight effects on the wall. This is the type of situation where per-pixel spot lights come in handy.

The per-pixel spot light technique is similar to the shadow mapping technique from the previous chapter in that it involves projecting a texture from the light source onto the scene. In this case, the texture is not some rendered distance image; it is an image of the spot light itself.

The heart of a per-pixel spot light scheme is a texture that defines the shape of light cast from the spot light. A per-vertex scheme requires computations to determine whether a vertex is within the umbra or penumbra. If it is within the penumbra, you must determine a falloff value. In some ways, the per-pixel method is much less complex because all of those computations are explicitly built into the spot light texture. Figure 30.2 shows one example of a spot light texture.

Figure 30.2

A spot light cross section.

In Chapter 24, the falloff function within the penumbra was linear in order to simplify the calculations. In this case, the falloff function could be whatever shape you need it to be. You could even add effects such as ripples within the penumbra or anything else you want. In fact, the spot light doesn't even need to be round. You could create effects such as stage lights by using different shapes and falloff functions.

In any case, most spot light cross section images should be centered in the texture and fill the bounds of the texture. However, the edge texels should all be black. As you'll see in the code, the texture stage states are set to clamp the texture. The edge texels are stretched over all areas not within the spot light cone. If any of these texels are not black, you will probably get strange banding effects when those texels are stretched.

The texture defines the cross section of the spot light, but the light is actually cast in a cone. The next task is to define the cone of the spot light. The projective texturing matrices handle this. In the previous chapter, I showed you how to set up and render an image from the light's point of view. In that case, the light was acting as a camera. The projection matrix determined the field of view of the light/camera. In this case, the projection matrix defines the cone of the light.

Recall that the projection matrix defines the viewing frustum, which is a pyramidal shape defined by the clipping planes and the field of view. When the projection matrix is used as part of a projective texturing matrix, the frustum defines the shape of the projection. With a circular spot light, the circular cross section defines the conical region of the projection frustum, as shown in Figure 30.3.

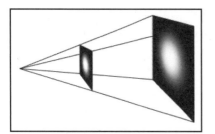

Figure 30.3

Projective spot light cone.

This is why the spot light image should fill the bounds of the texture. If it fills the texture, the field of view of the projection matrix defines the angle of the penumbra and the umbra. If you increase the FOV, the spot light angles increase accordingly. This is what I meant before when I said that the angle values were a side effect of projective texturing. All you need to do is project the spot light texture onto the geometry. If a given pixel is within the umbra, it is textured by the umbra. If it is outside the cone, it is textured with the clamped edge value. The angular computations are side effects of the texture and the projection matrix. They do not need to be explicitly computed.

So at this point, I have defined a spot light cross section and the methodology behind producing the spot light cone. I explain the projective texturing details while walking through the code. This nearly completes the spot light effect, and at this point you don't really need a pixel shader. Figure 30.4 shows the spot light hitting the floor at a slight angle. Notice how the spot light has the correct umbra and penumbra and how both are slightly distorted due to the fact that it is hitting the floor at an angle.

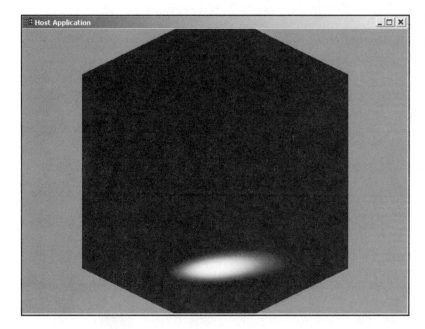

Figure 30.4

Spot light in action.

There is one feature missing. The current setup does not allow for attenuation over distance. This would be okay if the distances in the screenshot were significantly small relative to the range of the light, but it's not too difficult to do it right.

You can add attenuation to the technique by encoding the distance into vertices and letting those values interpolate over the pixels. To do this, compute the distance from each vertex to the light in the vertex shader. Then, normalize that distance by dividing it by the light's range. If the attenuation function was linear, you could easily encode this into the diffuse color and use it to modulate the texture values. You could also encode the attenuation function into a 1D texture, as shown in Figure 30.5. Pixels near the light are modulated by 1.0; pixels outside of the range receive the clamped attenuation value of 0.0.

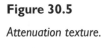

Figure 30.5

Attenuation texture.

The advantage of the texture method is that it is very easy to encode a nonlinear attenuation function. Instead of a smooth linear gradient, use some other gradient. The disadvantage of using another texture is that it costs more texture memory. Using the diffuse color output denies the use of a diffuse color.

Instead of using a second texture, encode the attenuation factor into the alpha channel of the 2D spot light texture. Simply stretch the 1D texture to fill the 2D texture. The alpha channel was already present, so the additional data doesn't "cost" any more. You can use the same texture for multiple stages without actually loading multiple textures. This texture is used as a lookup table for the pixel shader. Shown next are the vertex and pixel shaders for the per-pixel spot light technique.

Per-Pixel Spot Light Vertex Shader

The pixel shader does per-pixel calculations, but most of the setup happens in the vertex shader. Ultimately, the shader computes values based on textures and colors, and the vertex shader is needed to compute the proper texture coordinates and colors that will feed the pixel shader. The following spot light shader appears in PerPixelSpotlight.vsh:

```
vs.1.1
```

Begin by outputting the transformed position values. This technique is compatible with any of the geometry warping shaders. Just remember, the projective texturing portion of this shader is based on assumption that the geometry is not being warped. If you change the geometry, be sure to account for that in the projective texturing phase:

```
dp4 oPos.x, v0, c0
dp4 oPos.y, v0, c1
dp4 oPos.z, v0, c2
dp4 oPos.w, v0, c3
```

This next block of code transforms the input vertex position by the projective texturing matrices and sets the values of the first texture coordinate. This operation is similar to the clip space transformation earlier, only in this case the transformations map the vertex to texture space. I explain the actual texture matrix in the application code. You need all four coordinates to properly project the matrix:

```
dp4 oT0.x, v0, c4
dp4 oT0.y, v0, c5
dp4 oT0.z, v0, c6
dp4 oT0.w, v0, c7
```

The following lines compute the distance from the object space light (c8) to the vertex. Once the vector is found, the dot product instruction is used to square it. The shader then gets the reciprocal square root and gets the reciprocal of that to end up with a distance value:

```
sub r0, v0, c8
dp3 r0.w, r0, r0
rsq r1.w, r0.w
rcp r1.w, r1.w
```

The x component of c9 contains the inverse of the range of the light. This is multiplied by the distance value to obtain the attenuation lookup value. The final value is written to the first component of the second texture coordinate. All other components are set to zero:

```
mul oT1, r1.wwww, c9.xyyy
```

Finally, output the diffuse color as usual. If the attenuation function was linear, you could easily use this value to modulate the spot light value without a pixel shader. In fact, that is shown next:

```
mov oD0, v5
```

The following line is an alternative to the last few lines of the preceding shader. It encodes the attenuation factor into the diffuse color, which frees up a texture stage. This works best with linear attenuation. The distance value is scaled by the range, and this value is subtracted from 1.0 (c9.w). The diffuse color now stores the attenuation factor:

```
mad oD0, r1.w, -c9.x, c9.w
```

Figure 30.6 shows the application with the diffuse attenuation method.

The sample application is very simple, but you could enable more texture stages for more effects. The following pixel shader is used for the two-texture method.

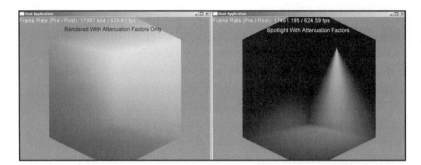

Figure 30.6

Attenuated light.

Per-Pixel Spot Light Pixel Shader

As Figure 30.6 showed, you can build a per-pixel spot light effect without a pixel shader, but a pixel shader is necessary for more complex attenuation functions. You might also need to get into pixel shaders if you want to combine the spot light effect with other effects such as bump mapping. For now, the spot light pixel shader is very simple. The following shader is from Spotlight.psh:

```
ps.1.1
```

The actual texture used by both texture stages is the same, but you still need to specify both. The tex instruction loads the texel values into the shader:

```
tex t0
tex t1
```

The shader really consists of only two lines. The first line multiplies the spot light value by the attenuation factor in the alpha channel of the second texture stage. These are two different stages with different texture coordinates. The second line multiplies the result by the diffuse color. This shader only works correctly if you have not enabled the alternate diffuse color technique in the vertex shader:

```
mul r0, t0, t1.a
mul r0, r0, v0
```

Figure 30.7 shows the spot light with a texture-based attenuation function. This function creates a light that retains its full brightness throughout the first half of its range and then falls off linearly over the second half. The attenuation function doesn't really make any sense because no real light would do this, but it does show off the versatility of the texture-based attenuation.

Of course, these shaders require constants and matrices that are set up by the application.

Figure 30.7

Texture attenuated light.

Per-Pixel Spot Light Application

As usual, I'm showing only the Render function here in the text, but some other aspects of the code are worth mentioning. The first is that both the vertex and pixel shaders are created. If your hardware does not support pixel shaders, you need to change to a reference device. It also creates a very simple cube that is four units on a side. This cube provides the walls for the spot light to shine on, but the technique would work for any collection of objects.

The usual caveat applies here. I wrote the following code more for completeness than for efficiency:

```
void CTechniqueApplication::Render()
{
```

Set the spot light texture to both stages. The second texture stage is only used in the pixel shader technique. Both texture stages are set to clamp values outside of the 0.0 to 1.0 range. Anything outside of the cone of the spot light is set to the edge values of the texture. This is why it is important to set the edge texels to black:

```
        m_pD3DDevice->SetTexture(0, m_pSpotLightTexture);
        m_pD3DDevice->SetTextureStageState(0, D3DTSS_ADDRESSU,
                                           D3DTADDRESS_CLAMP);
        m_pD3DDevice->SetTextureStageState(0, D3DTSS_ADDRESSV,
                                           D3DTADDRESS_CLAMP);

        m_pD3DDevice->SetTexture(1, m_pSpotLightTexture);
        m_pD3DDevice->SetTextureStageState(1, D3DTSS_ADDRESSU,
                                           D3DTADDRESS_CLAMP);
        m_pD3DDevice->SetTextureStageState(1, D3DTSS_ADDRESSV,
                                           D3DTADDRESS_CLAMP);
```

If you don't want to use the pixel shader, comment out this line. Otherwise, this line enables the pixel shader:

```
        m_pD3DDevice->SetPixelShader(m_AttenuationShader);
```

The time variable is just a convenience variable for animation. If you'd like, you can move the light, rotate it, and so on. This is the best way to see different attenuation and projection effects:

```
float Time = (float)GetTickCount() / 1000.0f;
```

Set up the shader matrices. The current code doesn't set any world transformations, but you could if you wanted. If you choose to move the eye position, the device takes care of culling the walls that face away from the viewer. If you don't see any lighting, it's probable that you have the light shining on one of the culled walls. If you don't see any effects, try moving or rotating the light:

```
D3DXVECTOR3 EyePos(5.0f, 0.0f, 5.0f);
D3DXMatrixLookAtLH(&m_ViewMatrix, &EyePos,
                   &D3DXVECTOR3(0.0f, 0.0f, 0.0f),
                   &D3DXVECTOR3(0.0f, 1.0f, 0.0f));
D3DXMATRIX ShaderMatrix = m_WorldMatrix * m_ViewMatrix *
                          m_ProjectionMatrix;
D3DXMatrixTranspose(&ShaderMatrix, &ShaderMatrix);
m_pD3DDevice->SetVertexShaderConstant(0, &ShaderMatrix, 4);
```

The second set of matrices is used for the texture projection. When you are rendering to the screen, the view and projection matrices define the position of the vertex on the screen. When you are projecting a texture, the matrices define the position of the vertex in the texture. This is effectively the texture coordinate, so the result is that the vertex is properly textured with the projected texture.

In this case, the FOV of the projection matrix defines the angle of the spot light cone. Everything outside of this cone is mapped to some point outside of the normal texture coordinates. Clamping ensures that those points remain unlit:

```
D3DXMATRIX LightProjection;
D3DXMatrixPerspectiveFovLH(&LightProjection, D3DX_PI / 2.0f,
                           1.0f, 1.0f, 1000.0f);
```

The LightView matrix defines the position and direction of the spot light. In this case, the light swings to and from the wall of the cube. Notice that the up vector is not set to the standard positive Y direction. If the light is facing straight down, it doesn't make sense that the up vector would be straight up:

```
D3DXMATRIX LightView;
D3DXVECTOR4 LightPos(-2.0f, 2.0f, 0.0f, 0.0f);
D3DXMatrixLookAtLH(&LightView, &(D3DXVECTOR3)LightPos,
```

```
                    &D3DXVECTOR3(sin(Time), -1.0f, 0.0f),
                    &D3DXVECTOR3(1.0f, 0.0f, 0.0f));
```

I described the function of the texture matrix in the previous chapter. The function of this matrix is to correct for the fact that textures are not centered about the origin. This matrix offsets values to account for the 0.0 to 1.0 range of the texture. The value of 128.0 is based on the assumption that the texture is 128x128. You might need to set this to a different value for different textures. You could also query the actual texture to find the correct dimensions:

```
D3DXMATRIX TextureMatrix;
float Offset = 0.5f + (0.5f / 128.0f);

ZeroMemory(&TextureMatrix, sizeof(D3DXMATRIX));
TextureMatrix._11 =  0.5f;
TextureMatrix._22 = -0.5f;
TextureMatrix._33 =  1.0f;
TextureMatrix._41 =  Offset;
TextureMatrix._42 =  Offset;
TextureMatrix._44 =  1.0f;
```

Concatenate the matrices and send the complete matrix to the shader. Note the concatenation order:

```
D3DXMATRIX LightMatrix = m_WorldMatrix * LightView *
                          LightProjection * TextureMatrix;
D3DXMatrixTranspose(&LightMatrix, &LightMatrix);
m_pD3DDevice->SetVertexShaderConstant(4, &LightMatrix, 4);
```

Transform the light to object space. The current application code doesn't feature a world transformation, so this is a bit of a waste, but it is needed if you add a transformation:

```
D3DXMATRIX InversesWorld;
D3DXMatrixInverse(&InversesWorld, NULL, &m_WorldMatrix);
D3DXVec3Transform(&LightPos, &(D3DXVECTOR3)LightPos,
                  &InversesWorld);
m_pD3DDevice->SetVertexShaderConstant(8, &LightPos, 1);
```

The range constant contains the inverse of the range value because there is no divide instruction in the shader. Remember that the current cube is only four units on a side. Take this into account when setting the range of the light:

```
D3DXVECTOR4 Range(1.0f / 5.5f, 0.0f, 0.0f, 1.0f);
m_pD3DDevice->SetVertexShaderConstant(9, &Range, 1);
```

Draw the cube with the spot light vertex shader. The cube is rendered as a set of triangle strips, but it could have been rendered from a mesh object:

```
m_pD3DDevice->SetVertexShader(m_ProjectionShader);
m_pD3DDevice->SetStreamSource(0, m_pBoxVertexBuffer,
 sizeof(BOX_VERTEX));
m_pD3DDevice->SetIndices(m_pBoxIndexBuffer, 0);
m_pD3DDevice->DrawIndexedPrimitive(D3DPT_TRIANGLESTRIP,
                                 0, 8, 0, 8);
m_pD3DDevice->DrawIndexedPrimitive(D3DPT_TRIANGLESTRIP,
                                 0, 8, 10, 2);
m_pD3DDevice->DrawIndexedPrimitive(D3DPT_TRIANGLESTRIP,
                                 0, 8, 14, 2);
```

If you use the pixel shader, you must disable it before moving on. If not, the font drawing code uses the spot light shader:

```
m_pD3DDevice->SetPixelShader(NULL);
}
```

These three components work together to create the effect. The application feeds the vertex shader, which in turn feeds the pixel shader. The pixel shader does the final per-pixel calculations. You can set up the same system for point lights.

Per-Pixel Point Lights

The technique for point lights is conceptually the same, but the actual implementation is different. Point lights are omnidirectional, so the only real effect is attenuation over distance. A handful of different techniques model the attenuation of a point light, but I chose to concentrate on one that uses the following intensity function:

$$L = 1 - \frac{D^2}{R} = 1 - \left[\frac{x^2}{R} + \frac{y^2}{R} + \frac{z^2}{R} \right]$$

The attenuation texture for the spot light was a linear gradient in one direction because attenuation changes over the vector of the spot light. Point lights are different in that there is no single vector for the light. For this reason, the attenuation gradient should be bidirectional, as illustrated in Figure 30.8.

Figure 30.8

Attenuation gradients.

The equation shows three different factors in the attenuation function. Therefore, you must map this gradient to three different dimensions. You could create a three-dimensional texture, but they are very heavy and not widely supported. Instead, you could map two of the three factors to a 2D texture and map the last factor to the alpha channel of the same texture. The final texture is shown in Figure 30.9.

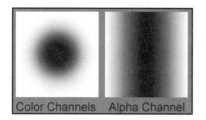

Figure 30.9

Attenuation texture.

As with spot lights, the point light texture is the heart of the technique, but it still requires a set of shaders to make it happen.

Per-Pixel Point-Light Vertex Shader

The point light pixel shader is somewhat similar to the spot light shader, but it doesn't use projective texturing. Instead, it sets up the texture coordinates into the attenuation texture. The following shader is in PerPixelPointLight.vsh:

```
vs.1.1
```

Output the position. Again, you could supplement this with warping code:

```
dp4 oPos.x, v0, c0
dp4 oPos.y, v0, c1
dp4 oPos.z, v0, c2
dp4 oPos.w, v0, c3
```

Get the vector between the vertex and the object space light position. If the vertex position is changed, you must take that into account:

```
sub r0, v0, c8
```

Each component of the vector is divided by the range value. This is different from the spot light shader in that you use the components of the vector instead of the distance:

```
mul r0, r0, c9.x
```

The result of the previous operation is a vector of values in the range of –1.0 to 1.0. This value must be mapped to the 0.0 to 1.0 range of texture coordinates. You do this range correction by dividing each component by 2 and adding 0.5:

```
mad r0, r0, c9.yyyy, c9.yyyy
```

Map the first two components to the texture coordinates of the first texture. This accounts for the first two attenuation factors:

```
mov oT0.xy, r0.xy
```

Map the third component to the first texture coordinate of the second texture. This represents the last of the three attenuation factors:

```
mov oT1.x, r0.z
```

Finally, move the diffuse color out of the shader:

```
mov oD0, v5
```

This shader feeds the pixel shader with the correct texture coordinates. You could do this technique without a pixel shader, but I like to concentrate on shaders. If you wanted to implement a version that did not use shaders, you could use a third texture or color channel for the value of 1.0 and use the subtraction color operation to compute the attenuation values with the texture stage states. The following is the pixel shader implementation.

Per-Pixel Point-Light Pixel Shader

The use of constants by this shader eliminates the need to use up other texture or color channels for the point-light function. The pixel shader performs the subtraction shown in the attenuation equation:

```
ps.1.1
```

The constant c0 provides the value of 1.0 for the attenuation equation. The two tex instructions load the proper texture values from the attenuation texture. The same texture object feeds both texture stages:

```
def c0, 1.0, 1.0, 1.0, 1.0
tex t0
tex t1
```

The following lines subtract the first two attenuation factors from 1.0 based on the RGB values of t0. Then the third factor is taken from t1.a and subtracted from the previous result. Finally, the result is used to modulate the diffuse color, and the value is output from the shader. If you use other texture stages, they too could be modulated:

```
sub r0, c0, t0
sub r0, r0, t1.a
mul r0, r0, v0
```

Per-Pixel Point-Light Application

Without the need for projective texturing, the Render function is very simple. The following code comes from the point-lighting application, but most of the basic setup features are the same as those for the spot light application:

```
void CTechniqueApplication::Render()
{
```

The point-light attenuation texture represents the range of the point light, so anything outside of the range should be clamped to the edge values. Unlike the spot light texture, Figure 30.9 shows that the edge values are set to 1.0. In this case, that makes sense because the attenuation equation is based on subtraction from 1.0. Therefore, anything outside the range results in a value of 1.0.

```
        m_pD3DDevice->SetTexture(0, m_pPointLightTexture);
        m_pD3DDevice->SetTextureStageState(0, D3DTSS_ADDRESSU,
                                    D3DTADDRESS_CLAMP);
        m_pD3DDevice->SetTextureStageState(0, D3DTSS_ADDRESSV,
                                    D3DTADDRESS_CLAMP);

        m_pD3DDevice->SetTexture(1, m_pPointLightTexture);
        m_pD3DDevice->SetTextureStageState(1, D3DTSS_ADDRESSU,
                                    D3DTADDRESS_CLAMP);
        m_pD3DDevice->SetTextureStageState(1, D3DTSS_ADDRESSV,
                                    D3DTADDRESS_CLAMP);
```

Set the pixel shader:

```
        m_pD3DDevice->SetPixelShader(m_AttenuationShader);
```

Set the shader matrices:

```
        D3DXVECTOR3 EyePos(10.0f, 0.0f, 10.0f);
        D3DXMatrixLookAtLH(&m_ViewMatrix, &EyePos,
```

```
                             &D3DXVECTOR3(0.0f, 0.0f, 0.0f),
                             &D3DXVECTOR3(0.0f, 1.0f, 0.0f));
        D3DXMATRIX ShaderMatrix = m_WorldMatrix * m_ViewMatrix *
                             m_ProjectionMatrix;
        D3DXMatrixTranspose(&ShaderMatrix, &ShaderMatrix);
        m_pD3DDevice->SetVertexShaderConstant(0, &ShaderMatrix, 4);
```

Animate the light and convert the light to object space:

```
        float Time = (float)GetTickCount() / 5000.0f;
        D3DXVECTOR4 LightPos(sin(Time), 0.0f, 0.0f, 0.0f);
        D3DXMATRIX InversesWorld;
        D3DXMatrixInverse(&InversesWorld, NULL, &m_WorldMatrix);
        D3DXVec3Transform(&LightPos, &(D3DXVECTOR3)LightPos,
                          &InversesWorld);
        m_pD3DDevice->SetVertexShaderConstant(8, &LightPos, 1);
```

Set the range parameter. Remember that the cube is only four units to a side:

```
        D3DXVECTOR4 Range(1.0f / 4.0f, 0.5f, 0.0f, 0.0f);
        m_pD3DDevice->SetVertexShaderConstant(9, &Range, 1);
```

Once everything is set up, render the cube:

```
        m_pD3DDevice->SetVertexShader(m_PointLightShader);
        m_pD3DDevice->SetStreamSource(0, m_pBoxVertexBuffer,
                                   sizeof(BOX_VERTEX));
        m_pD3DDevice->SetIndices(m_pBoxIndexBuffer, 0);
        m_pD3DDevice->DrawIndexedPrimitive(D3DPT_TRIANGLESTRIP,
                                   0, 8, 0, 8);
        m_pD3DDevice->DrawIndexedPrimitive(D3DPT_TRIANGLESTRIP,
                                   0, 8, 10, 2);
        m_pD3DDevice->DrawIndexedPrimitive(D3DPT_TRIANGLESTRIP,
                                   0, 8, 14, 2);
```

Finally, disable the pixel shader:

```
        m_pD3DDevice->SetPixelShader(NULL);
}
```

Figure 30.10 shows the point-light application in action.

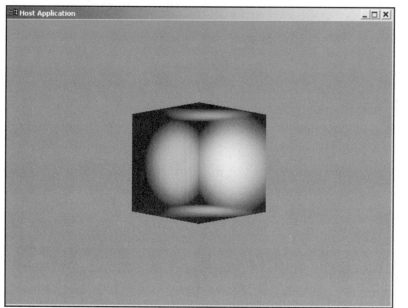

Figure 30.10

Point lighting.

Limitations

One of the major limitations of these techniques is the dependence on pixel shaders and the fact that they use up many texture stages. You can solve the first problem with alternate techniques that are less dependent on shaders, but the stage usage is difficult to overcome. On current hardware, it is very difficult to render a scene with bump mapping, environment mapping, a base texture, and more than one per-pixel light. In fact, you might have difficulty implementing those features at all (at least in one pass).

Another limitation that's peculiar to spot lights is the fact that the texture is projected in two directions, as shown in Figure 30.11. This is a difficult-to-avoid mathematical reality of projective textures.

This can be a problem in some situations, but many times you can work around it. For instance, if you use a spot light as a flashlight for the viewer, the texture is projected behind the viewer. In other cases, the back-projected texture can go off into space and be attenuated down to nothing before it strikes anything that might give it away.

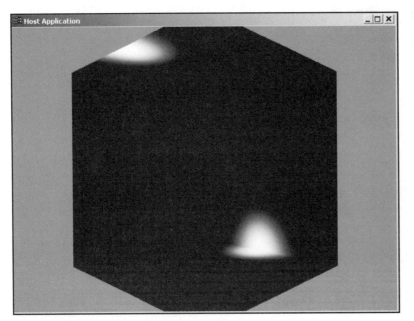

Figure 30.11

Projective texture issues.

In Conclusion...

Per-pixel lighting eliminates many of the constraints and limitations of per-vertex lighting. It also gives you more flexibility in terms of the exact shapes and attenuation functions for the lights. You can implement fairly complex effects with almost no additional computational cost.

This does come at a price. With per-vertex lighting, you can have many more lights in a single scene because the limitation is on vertex shader instructions. With per-pixel lighting, the limitation is on texture stages, of which there are far fewer. It is very difficult to implement many texture-based effects in the same scene in the same pass. Even if the number of texture stages doesn't limit you, you might still be limited by the fact that pixel shader hardware is not yet ubiquitous.

Having said all that, per-pixel lighting techniques are still valuable to study and understand. At the very least, they are another example of the types of things you can do in a pixel shader. They are also worth learning because all indications point to future hardware having more texture stages and much more pixel shader support. The pixel shader support includes features such as added instruction count and higher-level instructions. It may be awhile before this type of lighting replaces per-vertex lighting, but it is always a possibility. In the meantime, here's a breakdown of the major points of this chapter:

- Lightmapping involves multitexturing an object with one or more textures that modulate the color values of the object with precomputed lighting values. I didn't include an actual sample application because it is simply a straightforward matter of applying two textures to an object.

- Per-pixel lighting is different from the other lighting techniques in this book in that it not as constrained by the number of available vertices. Instead of interpolating final light values across a surface, a vertex shader can be set up to interpolate lighting parameters across a surface. You can use those parameters to look up an intensity value within a texture. In many cases, this lookup functionality is made possible with pixel shaders.

- "Per pixel" refers to the fact that pixel shaders operate on every pixel, but the actual lighting values are highly dependent on the resolution of the textures being used.

- The heart of the per-pixel spot light technique is the spot light texture that defines the umbra and penumbra as well as the attenuation function. This texture is projected onto the scene in a sense that very much mimics the way it is projected in physical reality.

- The projection matrix defines the cone of the spot light just as it defines the pyramidal viewing frustum. The FOV of the projection matrix defines the penumbra angle of the light if the texture is created properly. The angle of the umbra is dependent on its relative size in the texture.

- The spot light vertex shader performs the projective texturing calculations and encodes the distance into a texture coordinate that indexes into the attenuation texture.

- The spot light also projects backwards. If you choose to use this technique, you must somehow take that into account.

- The point-light technique is also based on a texture, but the point-light texture encodes the intensity values for the attenuation function. Each of these values is subtracted from 1.0 to yield an attenuation value.

- The point-light vertex shader encodes both the length and the direction of the distance vector into the texture coordinates. These texture coordinates index to the three factors of the attenuation equation.

- You can do both of these techniques without pixel shaders, but shaders do provide a cleaner and more flexible solution.

CHAPTER 31

PER-PIXEL LIGHTING— LIGHTING— BUMP MAPPING

In the previous chapter, you saw a per-pixel technique that computed lighting values for each pixel, but these lighting values were still dependent on the overall geometry of the vertices. In this chapter, I describe bump mapping, which is a method for describing geometrical features in a texture. I cover the following points:

- The concepts behind bump mapping.
- Creating and using normal maps.
- Creating texture space vectors for texturing.
- Bump mapping with texture stage states.
- Bump mapping with a pixel shader.
- Limitations and areas for improvement.

Bump Mapping Concepts

The idea behind bump mapping is not complex at all. It's basically an extension of the per-vertex lighting concepts. Consider Figure 31.1. By now, you understand how lighting calculations work with vertex normals. For directional lights, the light vector is compared to the normal vector, which yields a per-vertex intensity value. Each intensity value is interpolated across the triangle. Any lighting features are dependent on the resolution of the mesh.

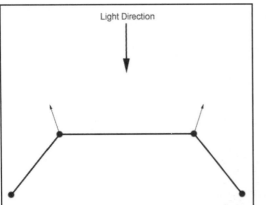

Figure 31.1

Lighting with vertex normals.

Things change in Figure 31.2. As you've seen in previous chapters, textures aren't just for pretty pictures anymore. In this case, a texture is mapped onto the surface. The texture contains normal data for pixels on that surface.

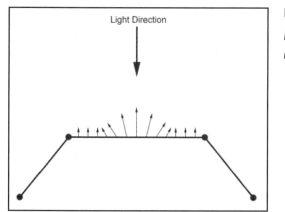

Figure 31.2

Lighting with pixel normals.

Figure 31.2 shows the normals for a bump on the surface. The normals point one way as if the bump were sloping up, they point straight up at the top of the bump, and they point the other way as the bump slopes down. Notice that I did not draw an actual bump on the surface. That's because it's not really there. Bump mapping is a lighting trick. The lighting intensity value is derived as if there were a bump there, but there's no actual change in elevation. Figure 31.3 shows a close-up from one of this chapter's applications. As you can see, the solid rendered view shows a nicely shaded bump. The wireframe view reveals that there is no bump at all.

Figure 31.3

Bump solid and wireframe views.

In a sense, you already know how to do bump mapping. You know that directional lighting involves getting the dot product of the light vector and the normal vector. Bump mapping works exactly the same way. There are, however, many implementation details I must describe to fill in the gaps, but it's important to keep in mind that this is just directional lighting with different normals. These normals are taken from a normal map.

Creating and Using Normal Maps

Normal maps are not special textures in the sense that cube maps are specialized textures, but they do hold specialized data. The RGB channels of each texel hold the normalized X,Y,Z normal vector for that particular point. These normals are usually derived from another texture, the height map.

A height map is usually a grayscale texture that encodes height information as intensity. Height maps are often used in terrain rendering, where they provide a compact way to represent the heights of points on a mesh. In most cases, an intensity of 0.0 (black) relates to a height of 0.0 above the ground plane, and an intensity of 1.0 (white) relates to the full height. (The value is scaled by an actual height range.) Figure 31.4 shows a height map and the equivalent mesh.

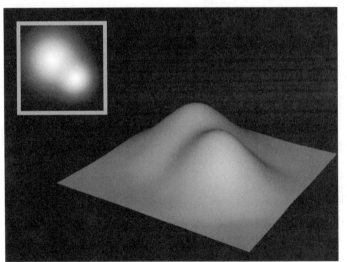

Figure 31.4

Height map applied to a mesh.

The normals in the normal map are based on changes in the height information. In Chapter 21, I talked a little about how to compute the slope of a line and I had to fall back to calculus to compute the slope at any given point, but in this case it's just a matter of arithmetic. Figure 31.5 shows a simple 1D representation of one row of a height map. You can derive the slopes of the values from one texel to another by simply subtracting one texel value from the next. Each texel is actually connected to two slopes, the slope to the left and the slope to the right (in this simple 1D case). You can average the slope at each texel from the two slopes. This is conceptually the same as averaging vertex normals in a mesh. In the simple 1D case, the normal vector is at a right angle to the slope vector.

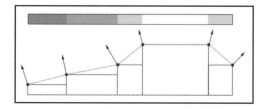

Figure 31.5

1D normals from a 1D height map.

In the 2D case, things get a little more complicated. You can find the slopes along the two axes, but then you need to compute the cross product of those two vectors to get the normal vector. Once you find the normal vector, normalize it. This vector contains values in the range of −1 to 1. You need to save these values to color channels that have a range of 0 to 1, so you must multiply the values by 0.5 and add 0.5. The values are then in the proper range, and you can save the X,Y,Z components to the RGB components of the normal map.

This can seem like a daunting task, but tools generate the normal maps for you. In fact, these tools often average the texel normal across many of the surrounding texels to create a smooth normal. Unless you need dynamic normal maps, I recommend using one of these tools.

TIP

If you're a Photoshop user, you can use the nVidia normal map plug-in to generate normal maps from height maps. This can be downloaded from nVidia's site.

Figure 31.6 shows a height map and the resulting normal map. This is a grayscale image of a normal map, so it is probably not very illustrative, but the normal map contains the vector information resulting from the height map.

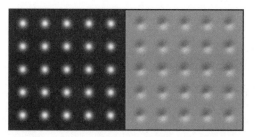

Figure 31.6

Height map and normal map.

In the end, the normal map contains the normal vectors you can use in the dot product calculations, but the two vectors must be in the same space. As you saw in earlier chapters, vectors must be in the same space if you want the dot product result to be meaningful. In most of the earlier examples, I transformed light vectors to object space. That way, I could use the vertex normals without additional transformations. In this case, the normals are in the texture, not the object. If object-based normals worked best with object space calculations, it makes sense to work with texture-based normals in texture space.

Creating Texture Space Basis Vectors

You already know how to convert light vectors to object space. You still need one additional transformation to transform those vectors into tangent space. The key is the fact that the vertices contain both object space positions and texture space texture coordinates. Using this information, you can derive a set of three per-vertex basis vectors for the object space to texture space transformation. These basis vectors serve as the columns for a transformation matrix that transforms object space vectors to texture space vectors. This is not as bad as it sounds.

The basis vectors are two vectors that describe principle axes and a normal vector that is the cross product of those two vectors. The principle axes describe how the texture coordinates change with respect to the object space position. For that, you need values that describe the change in u with respect to X,Y,Z and the change in v with respect to X,Y,Z (the texture gradients). This is illustrated in Figure 31.7.

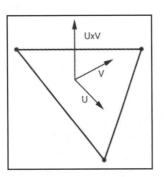

Figure 31.7

Per-triangle basis vectors.

The math you need for finding these vectors is similar to the vector operations used to solve the plane equations in Chapter 27, but with a twist. You can start with the following plane equations:

$$A1x + B1u + C1v + D1 = 0$$
$$A2y + B2u + C2v + D2 = 0$$
$$A3z + B3u + C3v + D3 = 0$$

In Chapter 27, the plane equations were based on the X,Y,Z values of the three vertices on a given triangle. These plane equations are computed in exactly the same way, although you use the u and v values in place of some of the X,Y,Z values. Once you solve for the plane equations, you can solve for the individual gradient components:

$$U = \left[\frac{du}{dx}, \frac{du}{dy}, \frac{du}{dz}\right] = \left[\frac{-A1}{B1}, \frac{-A2}{B2}, \frac{-A3}{B3}\right]$$

$$V = \left[\frac{dv}{dx}, \frac{dv}{dy}, \frac{dv}{dz}\right] = \left[\frac{-A1}{C1}, \frac{-A2}{C2}, \frac{-A3}{C3}\right]$$

Read the du/dx notation as "the change in u with respect to changes in x." These are the six components you need for the two vectors that describe how the texture coordinates are related to object space positions. These two vectors are denoted here as U and V. The third basis vector is the cross product:

$$U \times X = \left[\frac{du}{dx}, \frac{du}{dy}, \frac{du}{dz}\right] \times \left[\frac{dv}{dx}, \frac{dv}{dy}, \frac{dv}{dz}\right]$$

These basis vectors are the columns of a matrix used to transform vectors to tangent space. The matrix is next:

$$\begin{bmatrix} U.x & V.x & U \times V.x \\ U.y & V.y & U \times V.y \\ U.z & V.z & U \times V.z \end{bmatrix}$$

At this point, your head might be swimming a little. If you don't quite understand the mathematics yet, the source code will probably clear things up a lot. At this point, just understand that the U and V vectors describe the relationship between texture coordinates and object space position coordinates for a given triangle. This relationship can be expressed as a transformation matrix that is used to transform object space vectors to texture space vectors based on that relationship.

Per-Vertex Basis Vectors

So far, I have only described basis vectors on a per-triangle basis. Computing basis vectors per vertex would create much smoother basis vectors (analogous to smoother per-vertex normal vectors), but I chose to only illustrate the per-triangle technique both here and in the code. Extending this to a per-vertex technique is simple and is just a matter of averaging triangle vectors. For each vertex, find all the triangles that include that vertex. Then average the basis vectors of those triangles. Mathematically, this is more or less a matter of arithmetic, so I chose not to obscure the more complex calculations. As you will see, this method yields an acceptable result, but you still may want to average the vectors in your own code.

At this point, you have a normal map that describes the normals for the lighting calculations and a transformation matrix that maps object space light vectors into that normal map. Now, you just need code to bring it all together.

Bump Mapping Vertex Shader

Like the previous technique, the bump mapping technique relies on a vertex shader to do the first set of vector calculations. This chapter presents two final applications. The first application does not use a pixel shader; the second one does. Both applications use the same vertex shader. This shader is on the CD as BumpMap.vsh:

```
vs.1.1
```

As usual, emit the transformed position. This shader is based on the assumption that the object is a rigid body. If it is not and you are warping the object in some way, you might need to recompute the basis vectors in the shader. Once you understand the basic concepts from this code, take a look at the skinning examples in the SDK. Some examples compute basis vectors on the fly, but that greatly increases instruction count. If you can, precompute them:

```
dp4 oPos.x, v0, c0
dp4 oPos.y, v0, c1
dp4 oPos.z, v0, c2
dp4 oPos.w, v0, c3
```

The v8, v9, and v10 input registers contain the three rows of the texture space transformation matrix. Transform the object space light vector to texture space using this matrix. As usual, I negate the light vector to create a vertex-to-light direction instead of light-to-vertex:

```
dp3 r0.x, v8.xyz,  -c4
dp3 r0.y, v9.xyz,  -c4
dp3 r0.z, v10.xyz, -c4
```

Once the vector is transformed, normalize it. If you do not, the vector will not match up to the normal map properly and things will not work:

```
dp3 r0.w, r0, r0
rsq r0.w, r0.w
mul r0, r0, r0.w
```

The normalized vector includes values in the range of –1 to 1. You use the mad instruction to multiply the result by 0.5 (c6.x) and add 0.5, placing the values in the range of 0 to 1. This matches the values in the normal map, which are also in the range of 0 to 1. The final value is emitted in the diffuse color channel as the transformed per-pixel light vector. The alpha channel is not explicitly set. It is not used in the lighting calculation:

```
mad oD0, r0, c6.x, c6.x
```

This final line emits the texture coordinates for the normal map. As usual, I omitted eye candy to reduce the code to the barest minimum needed to demonstrate the technique. In real practice, you'd probably want to add more textures for actual visible properties. There is nothing about bump mapping that would prohibit more textures. It is also possible that you might want to add more features that allow for other types of lighting or a little bit of ambient lighting. You can do this, but remember that, in some cases, other forms of lighting can interfere with the bump mapping effect:

```
mov oT0, v7
```

This vertex shader sets up the color values for texture operations or a pixel shader. First, I talk about the application that uses color operations. After that, I talk about the pixel shader version. Both versions use the same code to find the basis vectors, so read the following section even if you're going to use pixel shaders:

Bump Mapping without a Pixel Shader

This first application uses the vertex shader to set up the texture and diffuse color, but it does the dot product operation with texture stage state settings. This happens in the Render function, but before I get to that, I show the code that's needed to generate per-triangle basis vectors. The basis vectors are stored in the following vertex format:

```
DWORD Declaration[] =
{
        D3DVSD_STREAM(0),
        D3DVSD_REG(D3DVSDE_POSITION,   D3DVSDT_FLOAT3),
        D3DVSD_REG(D3DVSDE_NORMAL,     D3DVSDT_FLOAT3),
        D3DVSD_REG(D3DVSDE_TEXCOORD0, D3DVSDT_FLOAT2),
        D3DVSD_REG(D3DVSDE_TEXCOORD1, D3DVSDT_FLOAT3),
        D3DVSD_REG(D3DVSDE_TEXCOORD2, D3DVSDT_FLOAT3),
        D3DVSD_REG(D3DVSDE_TEXCOORD3, D3DVSDT_FLOAT3),
        D3DVSD_END()
};
```

The three basis vectors are stored in unused texture coordinate registers. If you choose to use more textures, you might need to shuffle these registers around to accommodate both the basis vectors and real texture coordinates. The vectors don't need to be stored in any specific register. As long as you're consistent, you can store them in any unused register:

```
struct MESH_VERTEX
{
        float x, y, z;
        float nx, ny, nz;
        float u, v;
        float Ux, Uy, Uz;
        float Vx, Vy, Vz;
        float UVx, UVy, UVz;
};
```

The uppercase U and V vectors are the texture gradient vectors on the surface of the triangle. The UV vector is actually "U cross V," which is perpendicular to the two surface vectors.

Keep in mind that the following code only computes basis vectors per triangle and then assigns those vectors to each of the three vertices of the triangle. If a vertex is used by multiple triangles (which is true in most cases), the vectors are overwritten by each subsequent triangle. The results are acceptable, but you will probably want to average them instead of overwriting them:

```
HRESULT CTechniqueApplication::ExtractBuffers()
{
        m_pMesh->GetVertexBuffer(&m_pMeshVertexBuffer);
        m_pMesh->GetIndexBuffer(&m_pMeshIndexBuffer);

        MESH_VERTEX *pMeshVertices;
        short       *pIndices;
```

Lock the vertex buffer and the index buffer. You need to be able to write the new basis vectors to the vertex buffer, but you only need to read from the index buffer. This doesn't need to be optimized too much because you should only be doing this at the start of the application:

```
        m_pMeshVertexBuffer->Lock(0,
                            m_pMesh->GetNumVertices() *
                            sizeof(MESH_VERTEX),
                            (BYTE **)&pMeshVertices, 0);

        m_pMeshIndexBuffer->Lock(0, 3 * m_pMesh->GetNumFaces() *
                            sizeof(short),
                            (BYTE **)&pIndices, D3DLOCK_READONLY);
```

Each set of basis vectors is found on a per-triangle basis, so you need to walk through the mesh one face at a time. The index buffer holds sets of three vertices for each face, so this walks through the index buffer accordingly. The index value indexes into the index buffer, and that value is used to retrieve the three actual vertices:

```
        for (long i = 0; i < m_pMesh->GetNumFaces() * 3; i += 3)
        {
                MESH_VERTEX *pVertex1 = &pMeshVertices[pIndices[i]];
                MESH_VERTEX *pVertex2 = &pMeshVertices[pIndices[i + 1]];
                MESH_VERTEX *pVertex3 = &pMeshVertices[pIndices[i + 2]];
```

For the plane equation, you need to compute two sides of the triangle. These vectors are crossed to get the plane equation values. In this case, you need to compute three different plane equations in terms of X, Y, and Z. This first block of code computes the plane equation in terms of X. Pay careful attention to the components that are used in the side vectors:

```
D3DXVECTOR3 Side1 = D3DXVECTOR3(
                        pVertex2->x - pVertex1->x,
                        pVertex2->u - pVertex1->u,
                        pVertex2->v - pVertex1->v);

D3DXVECTOR3 Side2 = D3DXVECTOR3(
                                pVertex3->x - pVertex1->x,
                        pVertex3->u - pVertex1->u,
                        pVertex3->v - pVertex1->v);
```

The cross product yields the normal to the two side vectors. The normal provides the actual values in the plane equation:

```
D3DXVECTOR3 CrossProduct;
D3DXVec3Cross(&CrossProduct, &Side1, &Side2);
```

The U and V vectors are the texture gradients across this face. They are eventually written to the vertices, but only after they are fully derived:

```
D3DXVECTOR3 U;
D3DXVECTOR3 V;
```

The cross product is a D3DXVECTOR3 with named X,Y,Z components, but in this case, the vector is actually X,U,V. Find the x component of each texture gradient by dividing the appropriate component by the x component:

```
U.x = -CrossProduct.y / CrossProduct.x;
V.x = -CrossProduct.z / CrossProduct.x;
```

Repeat the same sequence of operations for the y component of the U and V vectors:

```
Side1 = D3DXVECTOR3(pVertex2->y - pVertex1->y,
                        pVertex2->u - pVertex1->u,
                        pVertex2->v - pVertex1->v);

Side2 = D3DXVECTOR3(pVertex3->y - pVertex1->y,
                        pVertex3->u - pVertex1->u,
                        pVertex3->v - pVertex1->v);

D3DXVec3Cross(&CrossProduct, &Side1, &Side2);
```

In this case, the X,Y,Z of the cross product is really Y,U,V because of the way the side vectors were set up. Don't be confused by the changing meaning of the components of the cross product:

```
U.y = -CrossProduct.y / CrossProduct.x;
V.y = -CrossProduct.z / CrossProduct.x;
```

Repeat the sequence one last time for the z component of the two basis vectors:

```
Side1 = D3DXVECTOR3(pVertex2->z - pVertex1->z,
                    pVertex2->u - pVertex1->u,
                    pVertex2->v - pVertex1->v);

Side2 = D3DXVECTOR3(pVertex3->z - pVertex1->z,
                    pVertex3->u - pVertex1->u,
                    pVertex3->v - pVertex1->v);

D3DXVec3Cross(&CrossProduct, &Side1, &Side2);
```

Again, the cross product X,Y,Z is really Z,U,V. Once this last component is set, the U and V vectors are complete:

```
U.z = -CrossProduct.y / CrossProduct.x;
V.z = -CrossProduct.z / CrossProduct.x;
```

Normalize the two vectors:

```
D3DXVec3Normalize(&U, &U);
D3DXVec3Normalize(&V, &V);
```

Get the cross product. This is the normal vector to the two gradients:

```
D3DXVECTOR3 UxV;
D3DXVec3Cross(&UxV, &U, &V);
```

The basis vector normal should be pointing in roughly the same direction as the vertex normal. If the basis normal is facing in the opposite direction, you should probably flip the direction by negating the vector:

```
if (D3DXVec3Dot(&UxV, &D3DXVECTOR3(pVertex1->nx,
                pVertex1->ny, pVertex1->nz)) < 0.0f)
    UxV = -UxV;
```

Now that you have all three components, write the vectors to the three vertices. In many cases, these vertices are overwritten several times as different triangles write new information:

```
pVertex1->Ux  = pVertex2->Ux  = pVertex3->Ux  = U.x;
pVertex1->Uy  = pVertex2->Uy  = pVertex3->Uy  = U.y;
pVertex1->Uz  = pVertex2->Uz  = pVertex3->Uz  = U.z;
pVertex1->Vx  = pVertex2->Vx  = pVertex3->Vx  = V.x;
pVertex1->Vy  = pVertex2->Vy  = pVertex3->Vy  = V.y;
pVertex1->Vz  = pVertex2->Vz  = pVertex3->Vz  = V.z;
pVertex1->UVx = pVertex2->UVx = pVertex3->UVx = UxV.x;
pVertex1->UVy = pVertex2->UVy = pVertex3->UVy = UxV.y;
pVertex1->UVz = pVertex2->UVz = pVertex3->UVz = UxV.z;
}
```

Unlock the buffers. You're ready to go:

```
m_pMeshVertexBuffer->Unlock();
m_pMeshIndexBuffer->Unlock();

return S_OK;
}
```

Your Good Friend D3DX

I wanted to include the code for generating the basis functions because I personally understand things much better if I can see what's going on. In the next chapter, I show you how to use D3DX to generate the gradients.

The ExtractBuffers function sets up the vertices. The application also loads the bump map texture and creates the vertex shader. The rest is done by the Render function:

```
void CTechniqueApplication::Render()
{
    D3DXVECTOR4 EyePos(-60.0, 30.0f, 0.0f, 0.0f);
    D3DXMatrixLookAtLH(&m_ViewMatrix, &(D3DXVECTOR3)EyePos,
                       &D3DXVECTOR3(0.0f, 0.0f, 0.0f),
                       &D3DXVECTOR3(0.0f, 1.0f, 0.0f));
```

Set the vertex shader that was described earlier in this chapter:

```
    m_pD3DDevice->SetVertexShader(m_BumpShader);
```

Sweep the light back and forth over the object. I included a few mathematical hoops so that the light is always shining down. Once you have the light position, transform it by the inverse of the world matrix to place the light vector in object space. The vertex shader will do all of its operations in object space, and the pixel operations take place in texture space:

```
float Time = (float)GetTickCount() / 1000.0f;
D3DXVECTOR4 LightDir = D3DXVECTOR4(sin(Time),
                                   -fabs(cos(Time)),
                                   0.0f, 0.0f);
D3DXMATRIX InverseWorld;
D3DXMatrixInverse(&InverseWorld, NULL, &m_WorldMatrix);
D3DXVec3Transform(&LightDir, &(D3DXVECTOR3)LightDir,
                  &InverseWorld);
m_pD3DDevice->SetVertexShaderConstant(4, &LightDir, 1);
```

Send the usual shader matrix to the shader. This matrix is used for position transformations, but all other transformations are done with the basis vectors included with the vertices:

```
D3DXMATRIX ShaderMatrix = m_WorldMatrix * m_ViewMatrix *
                                   m_ProjectionMatrix;
D3DXMatrixTranspose(&ShaderMatrix, &ShaderMatrix);
m_pD3DDevice->SetVertexShaderConstant(0, &ShaderMatrix, 4);
```

The value of 0.5 is used to scale and bias the texture coordinates as described in the vertex shader explanation:

```
D3DXVECTOR4 Helpers (0.5f, 0.0, 0.0f, 0.0f);
m_pD3DDevice->SetVertexShaderConstant(6, &Helpers, 1);
```

Set the texture to the normal map. If you need to use more textures, you can enable them here in different texture stages. Once the texture is set, set the texture stage states. In this case, the texture pipeline treats the diffuse and texture color values as vectors and computes the dot product between them. The final value is output to the pixel. If you use more textures, you might want the output of this operation to modulate some other visible texture:

```
m_pD3DDevice->SetTexture(0, m_pNormalMap);

m_pD3DDevice->SetTextureStageState(0, D3DTSS_COLORARG1,
                                   D3DTA_TEXTURE);
m_pD3DDevice->SetTextureStageState(0, D3DTSS_COLORARG2,
```

```
                                        D3DTA_DIFFUSE);
    m_pD3DDevice->SetTextureStageState(0, D3DTSS_COLOROP,
                                        D3DTOP_DOTPRODUCT3);
```

Render the mesh in the usual way:

```
    m_pD3DDevice->SetStreamSource(0, m_pMeshVertexBuffer,
                                  sizeof(MESH_VERTEX));
    m_pD3DDevice->SetIndices(m_pMeshIndexBuffer, 0);

    m_pD3DDevice->DrawIndexedPrimitive(D3DPT_TRIANGLELIST, 0,
                                  m_pMesh->GetNumVertices(), 0,
                                  m_pMesh->GetNumFaces());
```

Reset the color operation to modulate. This ensures that the texture state does not adversely affect other rendering operations:

```
    m_pD3DDevice->SetTextureStageState(0, D3DTSS_COLOROP,
                                        D3DTOP_MODULATE);
}
```

The final output is shown in Figure 31.8. The lighting on the bumps is very realistic, but there is no actual change in geometry.

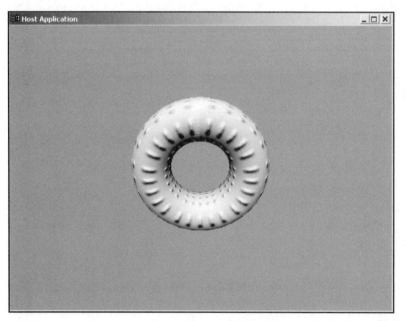

Figure 31.8

Bump mapped torus.

As an alternative, you can bypass the texture stage states and do the bump mapping pixel operations in a pixel shader.

Bump Mapping Pixel Shader

The dot product texture operation is usually adequate for bump mapping, but a bump mapping pixel shader is still interesting because it is a more flexible mechanism. The following shader does essentially the same operation with a few minor tweaks. The shader is in BumpMapping.psh:

```
ps.1.1
```

The first line defines a constant value for a small amount of ambient light. This is useful because you can add more data through constants without using up more texture stages or color channels. If a lighting factor is constant, add it as a constant instead of an input:

```
def c0, 0.01, 0.01, 0.01, 0.0
```

I also added a constant that can be tweaked to change the intensity and color of the light:

```
def c1, 0.5, 0.5, 0.5, 0.0
```

Load the value from the normal map:

```
tex t0
```

Compute the dot product of the vector from the diffuse color channel and the vector stored in the normal map. The _bx2 modifier changes color values from the range of 0 to 1 to the range of –1 to 1. This is the exact opposite of what you need to do in the vertex shader. The vertex shader changes the range of the vector components to accommodate the color register, and the pixel shader changes it back before doing the actual dot product calculation. Remember that you are not necessarily limited by the limitations of a particular register. There are probably ways of working around limitations. The _sat modifier clamps the result to a range between 0 and 1. The result of this operation is the intensity of the transformed directional light for this pixel:

```
dp3_sat r0, t0_bx2, v0_bx2
```

The mad instruction multiplies the light intensity by the light color defined by c1. It adds the ambient light defined by c0. The _sat modifier clamps the result. The final output is then emitted from the shader:

```
mad_sat r0, r0, c1, c0
```

Figure 31.9 shows the result of this pixel shader approach. In this scene, the ambient light causes the image to appear a little washed out, but more textures greatly improve the appearance.

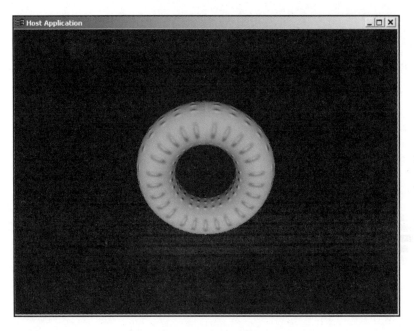

Figure 31.9

Bump mapped torus with a pixel shader.

The code for the pixel shader application is similar to the code from the previous application. Following is the code from the Render function:

```
void CTechniqueApplication::Render()
{
    // Matrix setup is the same as in the last application

    m_pD3DDevice->SetTexture(0, m_pNormalMap);
```

Set the pixel shader. This application created the pixel shader in CreateShaders. Setting the pixel shader replaces all the SetTextureStageState calls, and the operations of the shader are only active while the shader is active. This means that there is no risk of states "hanging around" as long as you know which shader (if any) is currently set:

```
    m_pD3DDevice->SetPixelShader(m_BumpPixelShader);

    m_pD3DDevice->SetStreamSource(0, m_pMeshVertexBuffer,
                                  sizeof(MESH_VERTEX));
```

```
m_pD3DDevice->SetIndices(m_pMeshIndexBuffer, 0);

m_pD3DDevice->DrawIndexedPrimitive(D3DPT_TRIANGLELIST, 0,
                               m_pMesh->GetNumVertices(), 0,
                               m_pMesh->GetNumFaces());
```

Make sure to disable the pixel shader so that it doesn't interfere with other processes. In this case, the pixel shader could affect the text rendering:

```
m_pD3DDevice->SetPixelShader(0);
}
```

Limitations and Areas for Improvement

You can improve a couple of areas in the preceding technique. First of all, I encourage you to experiment with per-vertex basis vectors. Averaging the basis vectors should be relatively easy now that you have the per-triangle vectors.

Another limitation related to the basis vectors is that they're static. If the geometry of the object changes, the basis vectors should change as well. If you are implementing skinning shaders with bump maps, you need to take this into account. In most cases, you can transform the basis vectors with the same transformation matrices used to transform the vertex position.

The number of textures and texture operations needed for a single light precludes the inclusion of several lights in a scene. You can work around this. You can provide several per-vertex lights in a scene and select the most appropriate one to provide the bump effect. You can also create a vector that averages all the lighting directions in the scene and use that average vector to do the bump calculations.

One area of improvement relates to dynamic bump mapping. One easy way to make the textures more dynamic might be to move the textures across the surface with texture transformations. You might want to be careful with scaling operations because they may affect the texture gradients. Another way to create dynamic bumps is to change the actual bump map texture. This could create very nice water or environmental effects. This requires locking and manipulating the texture on the fly, which is a fairly expensive operation but possible with current hardware. You can also experiment with loading several different normal map textures as frames of an animation.

In Conclusion...

My intention with this chapter was to provide the basics of bump mapping, but there are several holes that you might need to fill for specific applications. Any further manipulations of the basis vectors are based on the same underlying technique. You have all the pieces in this chapter, but you might just need to put them together in different ways.

Bump mapping is useful for creating added visual detail without getting into a lot of geometry. Even if hardware could handle more geometry, this technique might still be valuable because you can get the same effect with fewer assets and less data overhead. I'm only scratching the surface of the functionality.

This chapter provided the basics, but several other chapters provide useful augmentations. For instance, the next chapter extends this technique to include reflection. The same transformations applied to the vertex positions in Chapters 21 and 22 could be applied to the basis vectors to account for object animation. As you read other chapters, keep an eye out for how you can make the different techniques interact with bump mapping. In the meantime, here's a bit of nostalgia:

- Bump mapping is only a per-pixel illusion. Vector operations affect the light calculations, but the actual geometry of an object does not change.

- Normal maps are derived from height maps. You can find the differences between each pixel and the surrounding pixels and use this information to derive per-pixel normals.

- An easier way to build a normal map is to let tools do it for you. A Photoshop plug-in from nVidia will build a normal map from a height map.

- You must perform lighting calculations with vectors that are all in the same space. For bump mapping, the logical space is "texture space."

- The texture space basis vectors provide the mapping between object space positions and texture space positions. These vectors make up the rows of the matrix that transforms object space light vectors into object space light vectors.

- The current application computes per-triangle basis vectors and places these in each vertex. True per-vertex vectors may produce smoother results.

- The bump mapping vertex shader transforms the light to texture space for each vertex. This vector is then encoded into the diffuse color output of the shader for use by either texture blending operations or a pixel shader.

- The default texture blending operations can compute the bump mapping result with the DOT3 color operation. This operation computes the three-component dot product of the vector stored in the normal map and the vector stored in the diffuse color.

- The pixel shader method provides more flexibility. You could add ambient color, more textures or texture operations, and conceivably more lights.

- There are many possible enhancements to this technique, depending on your needs. Dynamic normal maps could provide rippling water effects or maybe even bullet holes in a wall. This technique could interface well with many other techniques in this book.

CHAPTER 32

Per-Vertex Techniques Done per Pixel

I n this chapter, I'd like to revisit a couple of the techniques from previous chapters and show how you can do them per pixel. The purpose is twofold. The per-pixel techniques could be useful as actual techniques, but they also provide a convenient context in which to describe some new pixel shader concepts and better explain some old ones. Some of those concepts include the following:

- Using D3DX to compute texture space basis vectors.
- Performing per-pixel reflection with bump mapping.
- Describing how the texm3x3 pixel shader instructions operate.
- Adding lighting to per-pixel reflection.
- Performing per-pixel toon shading with bump mapping.
- Introducing several version 1.4 shader instructions and techniques.

This chapter has two sample applications. The first sample shows how to do per-pixel reflection. The second sample shows how to do per-pixel toon shading. The second sample is one of the few places I use a version 1.4 pixel shader. The first technique uses version 1.1.

Per-Pixel Reflection

Chapter 26 explained how you can use a vertex shader to compute reflection and refraction texture coordinates that index into a cube map texture. You can use the per-vertex technique to create very convincing reflection effects on simple geometry, but it quickly falls apart if the object is bump mapped in any way. Reflection is similar to lighting in that the results are based on vector operations. Therefore, the same vectors you use to generate bump map lighting should be used to generate bump map reflection. If they aren't, the reflection effect does not account for the surface bumps. Figure 32.1 shows a screenshot of per-pixel reflection. As you can see, the reflections are properly bent around the bumps on the surface of the object. Remember, the geometry is still not directly affected. The effect is strictly the result of pixel operations.

The heart of the per-pixel reflection technique is a series of pixel shader instructions that do matrix operations on the normal vector and the eye vector. I described these instructions in Chapter 16, but I couldn't get into many of the details because I hadn't yet described vertex shaders and many of the vector operations you need to do before getting to the pixel shader. Now you've seen many vertex shaders, so it's time to talk about some of the more interesting shader instructions.

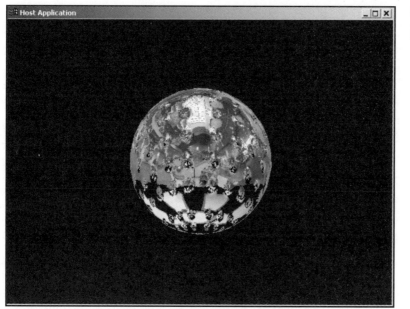

Figure 32.1

Per-pixel reflection.

Using texm3x3pad

One of the more mysterious of the pixel shader instructions described in Chapter 16 was the texm3x3pad instruction and the accompanying finishing instructions. These instructions have no direct counterpart in the vertex shader instruction set, and they can often be somewhat confusing. I shed some light on it here. No pun intended!

The purpose of these pixel shader instructions is to perform a 3×3 matrix multiply of a 3-component vector and a 3×3 matrix. The vector is stored in a color value, and the three rows of the matrix are contained in three sets of texture coordinates. The typical usage of the instructions looks something like this:

```
texm3x3pad    t1,   t0
texm3x3pad    t2,   t0
texm3x3tex    t3,   t0
```

The closest equivalent in the vertex shader world is the following set of instructions that you should now be fairly familiar with:

```
dp4 oPos.x, v0, c0
dp4 oPos.y, v0, c1
dp4 oPos.z, v0, c2
```

In the next vertex shader snippet, the vector v0 is multiplied by the 3x3 matrix stored in c0 through c2. The result of the operation is stored in oPos. Now, I don't mean that this vertex shader snippet is exactly equivalent to the pixel shader snippet. I just wanted to show you that functionally the two snippets are similar. Syntactically they are different, but you can use what you know about vertex shaders to decode the pixel shader snippet.

The key to pulling everything together is to realize that there is more happening than you can see in the shader code. If you write vertex shaders without macros, you can see exactly everything that's happening with every instruction. Some pixel shader instructions are more like vertex shader macros. There is more going on than meets the eye. In this case, the pad instructions perform the first two steps of the multiplication. The last instruction (in this case, texm3x3tex) performs the final step of the matrix multiplication plus some additional operations. In the case of texm3x3tex, the final transformed vector is used as a texture coordinate to index into the texture at stage 3. The resulting color value is written to the t3 register. You could translate the preceding pixel shader snippet to the following pseudocode:

```
dp3 TEMP.x, color of t0 (rgb = xyz), texture coordinate from
                                    stage 1 (uvw = xyz)
dp3 TEMP.y, color of t0 (rgb = xyz), texture coordinate from
                                    stage 2 (uvw = xyz)
dp3 TEMP.z, color of t0 (rgb = xyz), texture coordinate from
                                    stage 3 (uvw = xyz)
COLOR = sample from texture at stage 3 using TEMP as texture coordinate
mov t3, COLOR
```

This is why you cannot use the pad instruction separately. It doesn't actually output anything. The output is dependent upon the finishing instruction.

There are finishing instructions other than texm3x3tex. The texm3x3spec and texm3x3vspec instructions both perform the additional operation of reflecting an eye vector about the resulting normal vector. You can obtain the eye vector from either a constant (texm3x3spec) or the fourth component of the input texture coordinates (texm3x3vspec). The following pseudocode shows this. In this case, EYE is either a constant or the last row, depending on the instruction:

```
dp3 TEMP.x, color of t0 (rgb = xyz), texture coordinate from
                                    stage 1 (uvw = xyz)
dp3 TEMP.y, color of t0 (rgb = xyz), texture coordinate from
                                    stage 2 (uvw = xyz)
dp3 TEMP.Z, color of t0 (rgb = xyz), texture coordinate from
```

```
                          stage 3 (uvw = xyz)
normalize TEMP
TEMP = Reflect EYE about TEMP
COLOR = sample from texture at stage 3 using TEMP as texture coordinate
mov t3, COLOR
```

As you can see, these instructions do a fair amount of work in a limited number of instructions. Pixel shader instructions are far more instruction-limited than vertex shaders, but they have a couple of instructions that really do a lot.

Having said all that, version 1.4 shaders do away with the pad instructions. Version 1.4 shaders have much better swizzling and write masking support, making it possible to use a syntax that is much like the series of dp3 instructions in vertex shaders. The finishing instructions are also replaced by a better mechanism for dependent reads. You can compute several lookup vectors in the first phase of a shader and then do dependent reads in the second phase based on those vectors. I'm not going to spend much time with version 1.4, but if you understand vertex shaders, you are far along in understanding the 1.4 methodology.

These instructions are highly dependent on correct input from a vertex shader. I explain the full reflective pixel shader, but first you need to understand what is sent to the pixel shader.

The Reflective Bump Mapping Vertex Shader

The following vertex shader includes elements from the reflection vertex shader in Chapter 26 and the bump map shader from Chapter 31. In Chapter 31, the vector operations happened in object space. With the reflection shader, the reflection calculations happen in world space to account for the environmental mapping. The lighting calculations still take space in object space. It's okay to do different operations in different spaces as long as any single operation does not use vectors from different spaces. The following shader code is from ReflectiveBumpMap.vsh:

```
vs.1.1

dp4 oPos.x, v0, c0
dp4 oPos.y, v0, c1
dp4 oPos.z, v0, c2
dp4 oPos.w, v0, c3
```

The following nine lines transform the basis vectors from object space vectors to world space vectors so that they can properly interact with the environmental cube map. It is possible to save these instructions by transforming the texture coordinates to object space, but that requires more instructions in the pixel shader. In most cases, including a few more instructions in the vertex shader is probably better than including a few more instructions in the pixel shader. This is also true in the sense that a few more instructions in the application are usually better than a few more instructions in the vertex shader. Always keep in mind which operation executes more often.

The resulting vectors are written to the first three components of oT1 through oT3. These three texture coordinates are used as the matrix in the 3×3 matrix multiplication step of the pixel shader. The transformation converts texture space normals to world space normals so that the world space eye vector can be reflected properly:

```
dp3 oT1.x, v8,  c10
dp3 oT1.y, v9,  c10
dp3 oT1.z, v10, c10

dp3 oT2.x, v8,  c11
dp3 oT2.y, v9,  c11
dp3 oT2.z, v10, c11

dp3 oT3.x, v8,  c12
dp3 oT3.y, v9,  c12
dp3 oT3.z, v10, c12
```

Lighting calculations still performed in object space. Here the light vector is transformed from object space to texture space. The r0 register contains the texture space light vector:

```
dp3 r0.x, v8.xyz,  -c4
dp3 r0.y, v9.xyz,  -c4
dp3 r0.z, v10.xyz, -c4
```

Normalize the texture space light vector:

```
dp3 r0.w, r0, r0
rsq r0.w, r0.w
mul r0, r0, r0.w
```

Place the vector in the color compatible 0.0 to 1.0 range. The pixel shader _bx2 modifier puts it back into the −1.0 to 1.0 range before it is actually used. The value is then written to the diffuse color channel. Make sure you do this before moving on because the next section of code reuses r0. You don't have to reuse r0. The point is that you can:

```
mad oD0, r0, c6.x, c6.x
```

Transform the position to world space in preparation for world space eye vector calculations:

```
dp3 r0.x, v0, c10
dp3 r0.y, v0, c11
dp3 r0.z, v0, c12
```

Subtract the world space position from the world space eye position to get the eye vector:

```
sub r1.xyz, c5.xyz, r0.xyz
```

Normalize the eye vector:

```
dp3 r1.w, r1.xyz, r1.xyz
rsq r1.w, r1.w
mul r1.xyz, r1, r1.w
```

Write the three components of the normalized eye vector into the last component of each of the three texture coordinates. The texm3x3vspec instruction obtains the 3×3 matrix from the first three components and the eye vector from the fourth components. Therefore, oT1, oT2, and oT3 now contain all the vector and matrix data needed to perform the reflection operation:

```
mov oT1.w, r1.x
mov oT2.w, r1.y
mov oT3.w, r1.z
```

The last step is to pass the standard texture coordinates through to oT0. This is for the normal map. This is the only set of texture coordinates that is actually used as texture coordinates. The rest of the stages use texture coordinates as a means to pass data to the pixel shader:

```
mov oT0.xy, v7.xy
```

So in terms of pixel shader input, oT0 contains the texture coordinates needed to properly position the normal map on the object, and the other three texture stages hold the transformation data needed for the per-pixel reflection lookup. All of this feeds the shader.

The Reflective Bump Mapping Pixel Shader

This pixel shader includes the lighting calculation shown in the last chapter and the new reflection mapping courtesy of the texm3x3 functions. This shader is on the CD as ReflectiveBumpMapping.psh:

```
ps.1.1
```

Define a small amount of ambient light in a constant. If the object is reflective enough to reflect a lit scene, it would probably never be too dark:

```
def c0, 0.1, 0.1, 0.1, 1.0
```

Load the color data from the normal map. Again, you can interpret this instruction as "use the t0 texture coordinate to sample color data into t0":

```
tex t0
```

This operation works as described earlier in the chapter. The _bx2 modifier places the normal components in the range of −1 to 1. The matrix components are already in that range. The code converts the pixel normal to a world space normal and reflects the world space eye vector about the new normal. This value is then used to look up a value from the texture in stage 3 (the cube map), and the resulting color value is written to the t3 register. This completes the actual reflection. The rest of the shader is used for lighting:

```
texm3x3pad    t1,   t0_bx2
texm3x3pad    t2,   t0_bx2
texm3x3vspec t3,   t0_bx2
```

Get the dot product of the texture space light vector and the value from the normal map. The value is written to r0. At this point, the diffuse lighting is done:

```
dp3_sat r0, t0_bx2, v0_bx2
```

Add a bit of ambient light so that the object never goes completely dark:

```
add_sat r0, r0, c0
```

Finally, modulate the reflected value by the lighting value and output from the shader:

```
mul r0, r0, t3
```

Figure 32.2 shows the output of per-pixel reflection and lighting.

All the interesting bits are done. The only thing left is the application.

Figure 32.2

Per-pixel reflection with lighting.

Reflective Bump Mapping Application

The application is very similar to the application from the previous chapter. The one major change that's worth mentioning is that I replaced the handmade basis vector computation with a call to the D3DX library. D3DX includes a function for computing per-vertex basis vectors.

Remember that the previous chapter only computed per-triangle basis vectors. I wanted to describe the operation

> **NOTE**
>
> **All of the techniques so far should work equally well with DirectX 8.0 or 8.1. In this case I am using a D3DX function from DirectX 8.1. If you haven't upgraded, you may have problems with this particular application. I'd recommend upgrading.**

without relying on a "black box," but now that you've seen how it's done, you can offload most of the work onto D3DXComputeTangent:

```
HRESULT D3DXComputeTangent(LPD3DXMESH OriginalMesh,
                    DWORD GradientTextureStage,
            LPD3DXMESH OutputMesh, DWORD UvectorTextureStage,
```

```
        DWORD VvectorTextureStage, DWORD WrapCoordinates,
        DWORD *pAdjacency);
```

This function takes an input and an output mesh (they can be the same) and generates the texture gradients based on the texture coordinates. You need to specify which set of texture coordinates contains the actual coordinate data and which set of texture coordinates should be filled with the U and V texture gradients. You also need to specify whether or not D3DX should wrap texture coordinates. This is a DWORD parameter, but it's really only true or false, depending on what you need. Finally, the function can return adjacency information. In most cases, this parameter can be NULL.

This function computes the U and V gradients, but not the UxV vector. You still need to do a little work, as shown in the code from ExtractBuffers:

```
HRESULT CTechniqueApplication::ExtractBuffers()
{
```

Let D3DX do most of the dirty work. In this case, I pass in the same mesh for both input and output. Texture stage 0 contains the actual texture coordinates, and I want the D3DX function to right the resulting per-vertex vectors into stages 1 and 2. I'm also telling it to wrap the coordinates and that I don't care about adjacency:

```
        D3DXComputeTangent(m_pMesh, 0, m_pMesh, 1, 2, TRUE, NULL);
```

Now I get the vertex and index buffers. You still need to manipulate the vertices, but the index buffer is only for rendering later:

```
        m_pMesh->GetVertexBuffer(&m_pMeshVertexBuffer);
        m_pMesh->GetIndexBuffer(&m_pMeshIndexBuffer);

        MESH_VERTEX *pMeshVertices;

        m_pMeshVertexBuffer->Lock(0,
                m_pMesh->GetNumVertices() * sizeof(MESH_VERTEX),
                (BYTE **)&pMeshVertices, 0);
```

In the previous code, I walked through the indices to compute per-triangle vectors. In this case, all the data is per vertex, so there is no need to deal with the index buffer at all. You only need to get the cross product of the texture gradients:

```
        for (long i = 0; i < m_pMesh->GetNumVertices(); i++)
        {
                MESH_VERTEX *pVertex = &pMeshVertices[i];
```

The D3DX function has already placed the gradients in stages 1 and 2. The vertex format names these U and V. I'm creating new vectors here just to clarify things:

```
D3DXVECTOR3 U(pVertex->Ux, pVertex->Uy, pVertex->Uz);
D3DXVECTOR3 V(pVertex->Vx, pVertex->Vy, pVertex->Vz);
```

Compute the cross product of the two vectors:

```
D3DXVECTOR3 UxV;
D3DXVec3Cross(&UxV, &U, &V);
```

It's probably still a good idea to make sure the vectors are pointing in the right direction. If not, swap the cross product around:

```
if (D3DXVec3Dot(&UxV, &D3DXVECTOR3(pVertex->nx,
                    pVertex->ny, pVertex->nz)) < 0.0f)
    UxV = -UxV;
```

Everything is complete; set the cross product and move on to the next vertex:

```
        pVertex->UVx = UxV.x;
        pVertex->UVy = UxV.y;
        pVertex->UVz = UxV.z;
    }
```

Remember to unlock your vertex buffer before completing the function:

```
    m_pMeshVertexBuffer->Unlock();

    return S_OK;
}
```

As you can see, using D3DX makes computation much easier. This is why I was reluctant to go into all the details of how to average the per-triangle vectors. It's important that you know how the gradients are computed, but once you understand it, you should let D3DX do the work.

Debugging Fun for the Whole Family

If you are so inclined, you might want to add the D3DX function to the code from Chapter 31 and compare vector values in the debugger. Many of the values will be close, but some might be quite different because of the difference between averaged and per-triangle calculations. It may also be interesting to visually compare the difference between the two techniques. You might see some difference with the lighting samples, but the reflection samples will probably obscure most of the differences.

The application also creates the two shaders shown earlier and loads the cube map texture. Once everything is loaded, Render does all the work:

```
void CTechniqueApplication::Render()
{
```

Set the eye position and use it to build the view matrix. You also need to pass it along to the shader. The eye position is in world coordinates:

```
D3DXVECTOR4 EyePos(-60.0, 30.0f, 0.0f, 0.0f);

D3DXMatrixLookAtLH(&m_ViewMatrix, &(D3DXVECTOR3)EyePos,
                   &D3DXVECTOR3(0.0f, 0.0f, 0.0f),
                   &D3DXVECTOR3(0.0f, 1.0f, 0.0f));

m_pD3DDevice->SetVertexShaderConstant(5, &EyePos, 1);
```

Set the vertex shader to the bump mapping shader shown earlier. Create the concatenated and transposed shader matrix and pass it through to the shader:

```
m_pD3DDevice->SetVertexShader(m_BumpShader);
D3DXMATRIX ShaderMatrix = m_WorldMatrix * m_ViewMatrix *
                          m_ProjectionMatrix;
D3DXMatrixTranspose(&ShaderMatrix, &ShaderMatrix);
m_pD3DDevice->SetVertexShaderConstant(0, &ShaderMatrix, 4);
```

I'm animating the light slightly just to demonstrate the changes in lighting. The light always faces down and sweeps back and forth over the object:

```
float Time = (float)GetTickCount() / 1000.0f;
D3DXVECTOR4 LightDir = D3DXVECTOR4(sin(Time),
                                   -fabs(cos(Time)), 0.0f, 0.0f);
```

Find the inverse of the world matrix and use it to convert the light to object space coordinates. The vertex shader then converts the light to texture space and encodes that vector into the diffuse color of each vertex:

```
D3DXMATRIX InverseWorld;
D3DXMatrixInverse(&InverseWorld, NULL, &m_WorldMatrix);
D3DXVec3Transform(&LightDir, &(D3DXVECTOR3)LightDir,
                  &InverseWorld);
m_pD3DDevice->SetVertexShaderConstant(4, &LightDir, 1);
```

The world space eye calculations require the vertex to be transformed to world space coordinates. Therefore, you need to pass the world matrix into the shader separately from the concatenated matrix. The transposed world matrix is held in constant c10:

```
D3DXMatrixTranspose(&m_WorldMatrix, &m_WorldMatrix);
m_pD3DDevice->SetVertexShaderConstant(10, &m_WorldMatrix, 4);
```

The c6 register contains the 0.5 value needed to transform vector values to the range of 0.0 to 1.0. Only one of the components is used. You could use the others for other purposes if you needed them:

```
D3DXVECTOR4 Helpers (0.5f, 0.0f, 0.0f, 0.0f);
m_pD3DDevice->SetVertexShaderConstant(6, &Helpers, 1);
```

This is where things get a little more interesting. One requirement of the texm3x3 instructions is that the stages used in matrix operations and the final lookup are in ascending order. To satisfy this, the normal map is placed in stage 0 and the cube map is in stage 3. Stages 1 and 2 should not contain textures (at least for this example). Instead, their primary purpose is to hold matrix rows as texture coordinates:

```
m_pD3DDevice->SetTexture(0, m_pNormalMap);
m_pD3DDevice->SetTexture(1, NULL);
m_pD3DDevice->SetTexture(2, NULL);
m_pD3DDevice->SetTexture(3, m_pCubeTexture);
```

Enable the bump mapping pixel shader. The pixel shader defines how the texture stages interact:

```
m_pD3DDevice->SetPixelShader(m_BumpPixelShader);
```

Everything is now in place. Render the object as usual:

```
m_pD3DDevice->SetStreamSource(0, m_pMeshVertexBuffer,
                              sizeof(MESH_VERTEX));
m_pD3DDevice->SetIndices(m_pMeshIndexBuffer, 0);
m_pD3DDevice->DrawIndexedPrimitive(D3DPT_TRIANGLELIST, 0,
                        m_pMesh->GetNumVertices(), 0,
                        m_pMesh->GetNumFaces());
```

Always make sure to clean up after yourself. Remember that disabling a pixel shader basically enables any texture stage states. You might want to keep track of what is currently enabled:

```
m_pD3DDevice->SetPixelShader(0);
}
```

The output of this application was shown in Figure 32.2. In earlier chapters, the application was responsible for nearly everything. Now, everything happens in the shaders and the application is mostly responsible for setup.

Upon Reflection on Refraction

I originally intended to add a refraction component to this example. If you move to version 1.4, there are enough instruction slots to handle it. I chose not to add this because the bump mapping really shows the limitations of the refraction technique. Real refraction is dependent on how light passes through the complete object. Adding bumps to the surface changes the refraction but doesn't account for the fact that bumps on the opposite side of the solid have an effect as well. In the end, I chose to scrap the refraction section and concentrate on a version 1.1 shader.

One of the primary purposes of this sample was to demonstrate some of the pixel shader instructions beyond simple arithmetic. Now I'm going to change gears and demonstrate some of the features of version 1.4.

Per-Pixel Toon Shading

In Chapter 25, I introduced the technique of toon shading. The technique was based on a moderately easy vertex shader and some texturing tricks. In this section, I want to revisit toon shading, but I want to do it in a pixel shader. In most cases, the pixel shader technique is far more complex than you need, but it's necessary if you want bumps in your toon. It also provides a good context for talking about version 1.4 shaders. It might be possible to do this in 1.1, but it's nice to have the added instruction count. The following sample also uses some swizzling features that are not available in earlier versions.

I should revisit some of the basic toon shading concepts. In Chapter 25, I did toon shading in one pass, but with two distinct modes of shading. The first mode used a texture to quantize illumination values down to a very limited number of shades. The illumination was used as a per-vertex lookup into a 1D texture. The second mode used the dot product of the eye vector and the normal vector to define the edges of the object. The eye-normal dot product indexed into a separate 1D texture and relied on mip levels to get around some of the limitations of per-vertex processing.

A pixel-based toon shading technique doesn't need any texture workarounds because the vector calculations happen on a pixel level. In fact, this particular technique doesn't use any textures at all (except for the normal map). I could probably simplify the technique if it did use textures, but I wanted to show off some features of version 1.4 shaders.

Before jumping into the pixel shader, you should take a look at the vertex shader.

Per-Pixel Toon Vertex Shader

The following shader incorporates elements from Chapters 25 and 31 and this chapter. It transforms both eye and light vectors from object space to texture space and passes them on to the pixel shader for processing. The shader is on the CD as PerPixelToon.vsh:

```
vs.1.1

dp4 oPos.x, v0, c0
dp4 oPos.y, v0, c1
dp4 oPos.z, v0, c2
dp4 oPos.w, v0, c3
```

Transform the object space light vector to a texture space vector with the basis vectors. This is the same vertex shader lighting calculation shown in earlier examples. The real change comes in the pixel shader:

```
dp3 r0.x, v8.xyz,  -c4
dp3 r0.y, v9.xyz,  -c4
dp3 r0.z, v10.xyz, -c4
```

As usual, make sure the transformed vector is normalized:

```
dp3 r0.w, r0, r0
rsq r0.w, r0.w
mul r0, r0, r0.w
```

Convert the vector value to the 0 to 1 range, and store the final value in the diffuse color register. This is v0 in the pixel shader:

```
mad oD0, r0, c6.x, c6.x
```

Get the vector from the vertex to the eye in object space. The c5 register contains the object space eye position:

```
sub r1, c5, v0
```

Transform the eye vector from object space to texture space with the basis vectors:

```
dp3 r0.x, v8.xyz,  r1
dp3 r0.y, v9.xyz,  r1
dp3 r0.z, v10.xyz, r1
```

Normalize the resulting transformed vector:

```
dp3 r0.w, r0, r0
rsq r0.w, r0.w
mul r0, r0, r0.w
```

Convert the range of the vector and store it in the specular color output. This becomes the v1 input to the pixel shader:

```
mad oD1, r0, c6.x, c6.x
```

Output the texture coordinates for the normal map:

```
mov oT0.xy, v7.xy
```

As you can see, there are no visible textures in use here. The pixel shader uses the normal map and two texture space vectors stored in the color registers.

Per-Pixel Toon Pixel Shader

As I mentioned earlier, this might not be the best demonstration of the easiest or even the best way to do this, but it does allow me to demonstrate a couple of new features within the context of a well-understood technique. If you're interested, you might want to experiment with this shader to see whether you can optimize it more with textures. As it stands, I think it's pretty well optimized for textureless operation. The shader is on the CD as PerPixelToon.psh. If your hardware doesn't support version 1.4, the application runs with the reference device:

```
ps.1.4
```

I wanted to do the technique without any textures other than the normal map. To do this, it's necessary to define the toon gradient in constants rather than a texture. I chose to implement a three-level gradient as defined by c0. The red component defines the lower bound of the top value of the gradient. Any lighting value that is greater than c0.r gets set to the highest color value in the gradient. The green or blue components define the upper bound of the lowest value of the gradient. Anything below this level gets set to the lowest color value. All other values are set to the middle color value of the gradient. The shader is currently set up to use the blue component, but you could switch or you could change these values to get different effects. The application could also set pixel shader constants to dynamically define toon shading values:

```
def c0, 0.8, 0.5, 0.3, 1.0
```

Constants c1, c2, and c3 are the actual color values of the three levels of the toon gradient. The way they are currently set up, they match the values of c0 with a bias toward red. You can change these values to whatever you want:

```
def c1, 0.8, 0.5, 0.5, 1.0
def c2, 0.5, 0.2, 0.2, 1.0
def c3, 0.3, 0.1, 0.1, 1.0
```

The c4 constant defines the value that is used to determine whether a given pixel is an edge pixel. This technique is a per-pixel technique, so you can test for edges on a per-pixel basis. In some ways, this is more straightforward than the mip mapping technique from Chapter 25. Lowering these values creates thinner edges:

```
def c4, 0.3, 0.3, 0.3, 1.0
```

These values define the two options for edge values. If the value is on an edge, it is modulated by c5; otherwise it is modulated by c6. You can change the color of an edge by changing c5:

```
def c5, 0.0, 0.0, 0.0, 1.0
def c6, 1.0, 1.0, 1.0, 1.0
```

The constants define many of the colors. The rest of the data comes from the normal map and the input colors. The texld instruction loads the normal map value into r0:

```
texld  r0, t0
```

The technique begins with the usual dot product of the texture space light vector and the normal vector. The same scalar result is written to each component of r3:

```
dp3_sat r3, r0_bx2, v0_bx2
```

These lines handle the actual toon shading. Each component of r3 is the same and subtraction is a per-component operation. After the subtraction operation, the red channel of the r4 register contains the difference between the dot product and the upper gradient value. The blue component of r4 contains the difference between the dot product and the lower gradient value:

```
sub r4, r3, c0
```

The first compare instruction coupled with the subtraction compares the lighting value with the upper bound of the toon gradient. If the lighting intensity is greater than $c0.r$, the value of $r4.r$ is greater than 0.0, and r5 is set to c1. If the lighting intensity is less than $c0.r$, $r4.r$ is less than 0.0, and r5 is set to c2. The source register selection capabilities of 1.4 make this operation much easier than it would have been in a 1.1 shader:

```
cmp r5, r4.r, c1, c2
```

The second compare instruction only resets the toon value for the lower part of the gradient. If the lighting intensity was greater than $c0.b$, the value of $r4.b$ is positive, and r4 retains the value set to r5 by the last instruction. If the lighting intensity was less than $c0.b$, the value is set to c3:

```
cmp r4, r4.b, r5, c3
```

These lines complete the first step of the toon shading process. Figure 32.3 shows the result of this first part of the shader.

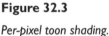

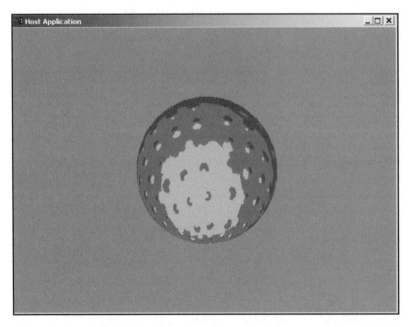

Figure 32.3

Per-pixel toon shading.

The remaining lines handle the edging of the object. This first line computes the dot product of the texture space eye vector and the pixel normal:

```
dp3_sat r1, r0_bx2, v1_bx2
```

This next step is similar to the preceding steps. If the dot product value is less than the threshold set by c6, the shader determines that this pixel is part of the edge, and r1 is set to the edge color (black, in this case). If not, r1 is set to white, meaning that it does not affect the color when the edge factor is modulated with the previous result:

```
sub r1, r1, c4
cmp r1.rgb, r1, c6, c5
```

Output the final value from the shader. In this case, the pixel value is modulated by the edge value before the shader ends:

```
mul r0, r4, r1
```

Figure 32.4 shows the output of the full shader. The edges are fairly thick because the threshold value was set fairly high.

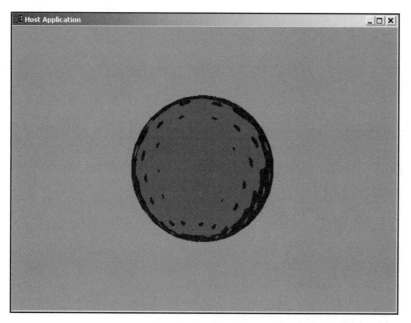

Figure 32.4

Per-pixel toon shading with edging.

This shader offers more dynamic flexibility than the texture-based toon shader. The fact that the gradient values are defined by constants allows the application to change them on the fly.

Per-Pixel Toon Application

The application for this sample is similar to the applications of the previous samples, so I only show the Render code. The most interesting aspect is the ability to change toon values on the fly:

```
void CTechniqueApplication::Render()
{
        D3DXVECTOR4 EyePos(-60.0, 30.0f, 0.0f, 0.0f);

        D3DXMatrixLookAtLH(&m_ViewMatrix, &(D3DXVECTOR3)EyePos,
                        &D3DXVECTOR3(0.0f, 0.0f, 0.0f),
                        &D3DXVECTOR3(0.0f, 1.0f, 0.0f));

        m_pD3DDevice->SetVertexShader(m_ToonShader);

        D3DXMATRIX ShaderMatrix = m_WorldMatrix * m_ViewMatrix *
                                m_ProjectionMatrix;
        D3DXMatrixTranspose(&ShaderMatrix, &ShaderMatrix);
        m_pD3DDevice->SetVertexShaderConstant(0, &ShaderMatrix, 4);
```

Set the light direction and transform it to object space before passing it to the vertex shader:

```
        float Time = (float)GetTickCount() / 1000.0f;
        D3DXVECTOR4 LightDir = D3DXVECTOR4(sin(Time),
                                        -fabs(cos(Time)), 0.0f, 0.0f);
        D3DXMATRIX InverseWorld;
        D3DXMatrixInverse(&InverseWorld, NULL, &m_WorldMatrix);
        D3DXVec3Transform(&LightDir, &(D3DXVECTOR3)LightDir,
                        &InverseWorld);
        m_pD3DDevice->SetVertexShaderConstant(4, &LightDir, 1);
```

Transform the eye position to object space and pass it to the vertex shader:

```
        D3DXVec3Transform(&EyePos, &(D3DXVECTOR3)EyePos, &InverseWorld);
        m_pD3DDevice->SetVertexShaderConstant(5, &EyePos, 1);

        D3DXVECTOR4 Helpers (0.5f, 0.0f, 0.0f, 0.0f);
```

```
m_pD3DDevice->SetVertexShaderConstant(6, &Helpers, 1);

m_pD3DDevice->SetTexture(0, m_pNormalMap);
m_pD3DDevice->SetPixelShader(m_ToonPixelShader);
```

Here I call `SetPixelShaderConstant` and set a new value for the upper value of the toon gradient. The value here sets the color to black. This isn't great for a toon effect, but it makes the point. Disable this line to see the basic effect. The application can change all of the parameters of the toon shader on the fly. It can change the edge thickness, edge color, and all the colors and parameters of the lighting gradient. The vertex shader toon technique is much simpler than this sample, but this technique is more flexible. A simple operation such as changing edge thickness would have been difficult in the texture-based method because of the mip map considerations. When pixel shader support becomes more widespread, this might be a better alternative for toon shading:

```
D3DXVECTOR4 Color (0.0f, 0.0f, 0.0f, 0.0f);
m_pD3DDevice->SetPixelShaderConstant(1, &Color, 1);
```

The rest of the application is the same as the last several samples:

```
m_pD3DDevice->SetStreamSource(0, m_pMeshVertexBuffer,
                              sizeof(MESH_VERTEX));
m_pD3DDevice->SetIndices(m_pMeshIndexBuffer, 0);
m_pD3DDevice->DrawIndexedPrimitive(D3DPT_TRIANGLELIST, 0,
                              m_pMesh->GetNumVertices(), 0,
                              m_pMesh->GetNumFaces());

m_pD3DDevice->SetPixelShader(0);
}
```

Figure 32.5 shows the effect of changing the color gradient in the application. I chose the black color to better demonstrate the change in a grayscale figure. For a better effect, you'd probably want to experiment with different colors.

In Conclusion...

This chapter presented two very different techniques, but the underlying purpose was to demonstrate other pixel shader features. In that respect, the two techniques were related. As usual, I hope that these techniques provide a basis for experimentation. Although I didn't stress it too much, you might want to pay

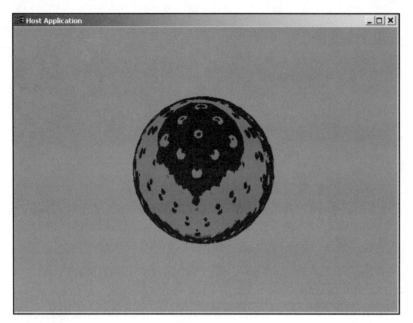

Figure 32.5

Changing the toon colors.

careful attention to some of the differences in the way version 1.4 handles texture input or the added functionality of source selectors. You might also want to experiment with implementing per-pixel reflection with version 1.4 instructions. Here's a breakdown of some of the more interesting bits from this chapter:

- The version 1.1 matrix instructions require that you use several instructions together. Unlike vertex shader instructions, some pixel shader instructions hide some of the calculation and data flow.

- The matrix operations are based on both color data and texture coordinate data, and the texture stages should be in ascending order.

- The texm3x3vspec instruction expects an eye vector in the last column of the transformation matrix. This is reflected about the pixel normal.

- The D3DX library provides a very easy way to calculate per-vertex basis vectors.

- You can do toon shading in a pixel shader, and this technique supports toon-shaded bumps.

- Edges are computed on a per-pixel basis, so there is no need for a mip mapped edge texture.

- A toon pixel shader that doesn't use textures is more flexible than the texture-based approach, but not widely supported. You can use calls to SetPixelShaderConstant to dynamically reconfigure nearly all aspects of the shader.

Part Seven

Other Useful Techniques

The two previous parts focused heavily on specific shader techniques. This last section focuses on higher-level techniques that may or may not use shaders. Some of these chapters provide further explanation of concepts introduced earlier. Others are advanced topics. All are interesting and useful in their own way:

- Chapter 33, "Rendering to a Texture—Full-Screen Motion Blur," explains how to render to a texture render target, which is the basis for other techniques in this book. The example demonstrates how to use render targets and transparency for a full-screen motion blur effect.

- People frequently ask how to do 2D rendering now that DirectDraw is no longer an official version of the API. In Chapter 34, "2D Rendering—Just Drop a 'D'," I explain how to do 2D rendering, as well as some of the performance implications. I also dispel some of the myths about 2D in 3D.

- Chapter 35, "DirectShow: Using Video as a Texture," explains how to use DirectShow to incorporate video and other forms of streaming into your scenes. I also talk about some situations where video as a texture might be useful.

- Chapter 36, "Image Processing with Pixel Shaders," introduces many image-processing effects implemented as pixel shaders. You can use these effects to change the mood or the general look and feel of a scene.

- There are many bad ways to draw text in Direct3D. In Chapter 37, "A Much Better Way to Draw Text," I introduce a general framework for drawing text. This framework is used in all the examples to display the frame rate.

- There are a couple of different ways to implement timing in your applications. In Chapter 38, "Perfect Timing," I introduce two different methods of timing. All the samples use these methods.

- I introduced stencil buffers in Chapter 27, but with very little explanation. Chapter 39, "The Stencil Buffer," explains how you use stencil buffers.

- Chapter 40, "Picking: A Plethora of Practical Picking Procedures," looks at several techniques for picking objects in a scene. The focus is on a pixel-picking technique that works well with vertex shaders.

CHAPTER 33

Rendering to a Texture— Full-Screen Motion Blur

The ability to render to a texture is a powerful thing. You saw a technique in Chapter 29 that required a render-to-texture operation to do shadowing, but I held off on a full description so that I could concentrate on the actual shadowing concepts. In this chapter, I discuss the intricacies of rendering to a texture. The sample application presents an approach to motion blurring, but I cover other concepts as well. Specifically, this chapter covers the following:

- Creating a texture as a render target.
- Creating a texture as a depth stencil target.
- Obtaining surfaces from texture render targets.
- Rendering to a simple 2D texture.
- Rendering to a dynamic cube map.
- The theory and concepts behind motion blur.
- Implementing full-screen motion blur as a post-processing technique.
- Performance implications.
- Other uses for dynamic textures.

Rendering to a texture is relatively easy, but first you need to create a texture that is a valid render target.

Creating a Texture as a Render Target

Chapter 12 talked at length about how textures are created and how they are structured, so you already know how to create textures. Chapter 29 created a render target texture with little regard for whether the device supported render targets. The assumption was that any hardware that could support pixel shaders and other features of shadow mapping should be able to support render target textures.

In reality, you should probably verify support before you actually use such a feature. You can check for support of render targets with a call to `CheckDeviceFormat`:

```
HRESULT IDirect3D8::CheckDeviceFormat(UINT Adapter,
                        D3DDEVTYPE DeviceType,
                    D3DFORMAT AdapterFormat,
                        DWORD Usage,
                    D3DRESOURCETYPE ResourceType,
                    D3DFORMAT CheckFormat);
```

A call to CheckDeviceFormat tells you whether a given device supports a given usage for a given format. The first three parameters should match the parameters used to create your device. You should set the usage parameter in this case to D3DUSAGE_RENDERTARGET because you are interested in finding out whether this device supports a render target texture. Likewise, set the resource type to D3DRTYPE_TEXTURE if you are interested in creating a simple 2D texture. Finally, set the format to whichever format you want the texture to be. In this book, I have stuck to 32-bit formats.

If the format is not supported, the call returns a failure code, and the specific device does not support the given combination of usage and format. If the format is supported, the call returns D3D_OK, and you are good to go.

Once you check the support, you can create a texture using either the methods of the D3D device or the D3DX texture-creation functions. Either way, the major difference between this and any other texture creation call is the inclusion of the render target usage flag. Following is a code snippet from the sample application:

```
if (FAILED(D3DXCreateTexture(m_pD3DDevice, TEX_DIMENSION,
    TEX_DIMENSION, 1, D3DUSAGE_RENDERTARGET, D3DFMT_X8R8G8B8,
    D3DPOOL_DEFAULT, &m_pDisplayTexture)))
        return E_FAIL;
```

This code is asking for a new texture to be used as a render target. It specifies the dimensions and the fact that it needs only one mip level. It also specifies a 32-bit format. Finally, the texture should be created in the default memory pool. This means the texture cannot be locked, but you very rarely need to do that anyway. If everything is successful, D3DXCreateTexture returns a valid texture object. You can use this texture as a target for color information, but you might also want a texture that can receive depth information.

Currently, support for depth stencil textures is not widely available, so verify the support with a call to CheckDeviceFormat. If depth stencil textures are available, the call to create one is similar to the preceding code:

```
if (FAILED(D3DXCreateTexture(m_pD3DDevice, TEX_DIMENSION,
    TEX_DIMENSION, 1, D3DUSAGE_DEPTHSTENCIL, D3DFMT_D24S8,
    D3DPOOL_DEFAULT, &m_pZTexture)))
        return E_FAIL;
```

This creates a texture that can receive depth stencil information. Notice that the format must match a valid depth stencil format. The bit depth of the format should also be the same as the bit depth of the color render target. For instance, the first code snippet asked for a 32-bit texture, so the depth stencil buffer should be a total of 32 bits. If one of the two were 16 bits, the other should match.

You can use both of these calls to create textures to be used as render targets. However, the device doesn't render to textures; it renders to surfaces.

Obtaining Surfaces from Texture Render Targets

As described in Chapter 12, a texture object is a wrapper that extends the basic functionality of a surface (or a set of surfaces, in the case of a cube map). So you can obtain a render target surface from a texture by asking for one of its surface levels. You do this with GetSurfaceLevel. The following code retrieves the surface from the texture that was created in the preceding code:

```
if (FAILED(m_pDisplayTexture->GetSurfaceLevel(0,
        &m_pDisplayTextureSurface)))
    return E_FAIL;
```

The code requests the first mip level. The creation code requested only one mip level, so there is only one surface. You can use this surface as a render target for rendering operations. If you create a texture and don't specify the render target usage, you can still retrieve the surface, but you cannot successfully pass the surface to the device as a render target. This code snippet works equally well for both color and depth stencil surfaces.

If you do not create a depth stencil texture, you still want to create a target depth surface to use when rendering to your target texture. In fact, the only time you need to worry about a depth stencil texture is when you actually want to use it to texture other objects in other rendering passes. If not, you can just create a depth surface:

```
if (FAILED(m_pD3DDevice->CreateDepthStencilSurface(
                                            TEX_DIMENSION,
                    TEX_DIMENSION,
                    D3DFMT_D24S8,
                    D3DMULTISAMPLE_NONE,
                    &m_pDisplayZSurface)))
    return E_FAIL;
```

You can use this surface to provide depth buffer support when rendering to your render target texture. This surface should be the same dimensions and format as your render target.

While I'm on the subject of obtaining surfaces, it's probably a good idea to talk about retrieving the current targets of the device. This is important because you want to restore the actual device render target when you are done rendering to your texture. To do this, you need a pointer to the original color buffer and depth buffer:

```
if (FAILED(m_pD3DDevice->GetRenderTarget(&m_pBackBuffer)))
        return E_FAIL;


if (FAILED(m_pD3DDevice->GetDepthStencilSurface(&m_pZBuffer)))
        return E_FAIL;
```

You can retrieve these pointers once at the beginning of the application and hold them until the end of the application or until the device is reset. Retrieving them once at the beginning saves a little bit of processing during the render loop. But remember, these pointers will probably become invalid if the device is reset.

You now have all the pieces you need to begin rendering to a texture. You have the texture itself, the texture surface, and a depth surface that is either a simple surface or a part of a depth texture. You are ready to render.

Rendering to a Texture Render Target

Rendering to a new render target is relatively straightforward once you have all the pieces. The one potential stumbling point concerns viewports. When you switch to a new render target, the viewport is automatically set to match the dimensions of the new target. Sometimes that's the desired effect; other times it's not. If the target texture is larger than the actual back buffer, you might want to set the viewport to match the real screen size (as shown next). If it's smaller than the real back buffer, you might want to scale the viewport accordingly. Frequently, a viewport size is set to match the size of the screen, as shown in Figure 33.1, meaning that the render target is only partially filled with the rendered image.

In many cases that's exactly what you want, but you see the resulting blank spaces if the texture is wrapped. In any case, be aware that the size and shape of the viewport has an effect on how the image is rendered and how the texture looks when it is mapped onto an object.

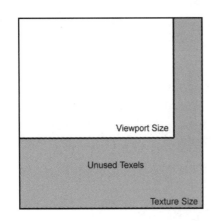

Figure 33.1

Setting the viewport to match the screen size.

The following code shows how to render to the surface obtained earlier:

```
m_pD3DDevice->SetRenderTarget(m_pDisplayTextureSurface,
                              m_pDisplayZSurface);

m_pD3DDevice->Clear(0, NULL, D3DCLEAR_TARGET | D3DCLEAR_ZBUFFER,
                    D3DCOLOR_XRGB(100, 100, 200), 1.0f, 0);

// Render something

m_pD3DDevice->SetRenderTarget(m_pBackBuffer, m_pZBuffer);
```

The real application code later in this chapter discusses this step in more depth, including the details of setting the viewport. Remember that the new target may contain old data. Clearing the real render target does not clear the texture target. You can use the target texture to texture objects once the target is set back to the real back buffer.

Rendering to a Dynamic Cube Map

Chapters 26 and 32 used cube maps to reflect the environment around a shiny object. In those examples, the cube map was a static texture, but often you want to properly reflect a dynamic scene. To do this, you need to render the scene to the faces of the cube map. The underlying idea is exactly the same as rendering to the single surface of a 2D texture. The only difference is that a cube map has six different faces.

As with a normal 2D texture, you can create a cube map render target with the render target usage flag. This creates six different surfaces for the cube map, and all

of them are valid render targets. You can retrieve a single surface with a call to
`GetCubeMapSurface`:

```
HRESULT IDirect3DCubeTexture8::GetCubeMapSurface(
                        D3DCUBEMAP_FACES FaceType,
            UINT Level, IDirect3DSurface8** ppCubeMapSurface);
```

This function is basically the same as `GetSurfaceLevel`, but it takes the additional
parameter of the face type. The `D3DCUBEMAP_FACES` type is an enumerated type that
contains members for each of the six faces. Next is a sample call to `GetCubeMapSurface`
to retrieve the positive X surface:

```
m_pCubeMap->GetCubeMapSurface(D3DCUBEMAP_FACE_POSITIVE_X, 0,
                        &pCubeFace);
```

Once you have the face, you can render to it as you do any other surface, but you
probably want to render to all six surfaces to get a fully updated cube map. For each
face, retrieve the surface and set it to your render target. Then, use the view matrix
to position the camera in the same position as the reflective object. Change the
orientation of the camera to point in the direction that matches the current face.
For instance, if you are rendering to the positive X face, the camera should be
pointed in the positive X direction. Also, set your projection matrix to a 90 degree
field of view and a one-to-one aspect ratio. Finally, do not change the viewport. In
this case, you want to render to the entire face. Once everything is set up, render
the scene but do not render the reflective object. Repeat this sequence for all six
faces of the cube map, as shown in Figure 33.2.

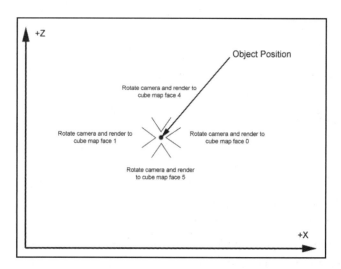

Figure 33.2

Rendering to a cube map.

After all six faces are rendered, set the render target back to the back buffer, set the projection matrix back to normal, and render the scene from the user's point of view using the cube map to texture the reflective object.

This can be a costly operation. As described, you would have to render the scene at least seven different times to complete the final rendering. In many cases, this is prohibitively expensive. One way around this is to update the cube faces less frequently. This would save horsepower, but it might not give the effect you need because reflected objects may appear to stutter across the object.

Another solution is to update only the textures that contain dynamic data. For instance, if there is activity only on the +X side of the object, only update the +X face. If you want to be really clever, only update the faces that the viewer can actually see. Depending on the shape of the reflective object, this might be difficult because it is hard to determine what the viewer can and cannot see.

One final suggestion might be to render the scene using much lower-resolution meshes and textures. In many cases, the curves of the reflective object make it difficult to see many details anyway. The downside is that such a solution might require more assets to track and maintain.

These are just a handful of suggestions. Chances are that a real solution contains elements of all three. The correct solution depends on your requirements. I am not including a sample application for dynamic cube maps. The SDK contains a cube map sample with a biplane flying around a teapot. That application contains a straightforward example of how to render to the faces of the cube.

Motion Blur

For this chapter's sample application, I chose to implement a motion-blur technique that uses texture render targets to create a full-screen motion-blur effect. It is implemented a little differently than other motion-blur effects, but I think it creates an interesting effect and leaves a lot of room for extended special effects. Before I talk about the actual application, I should talk a little about motion blur as a concept.

Early in the days of film, experiments showed that people saw smooth motion if the frame rate of the film was at least 16 frames per second. Later, this frame rate was increased to 24 frames per second, but this had more to do with the requirements for sound than jerkiness in the image. Current movie frame rates are 24 frames per second, and televisions run at 30 frames per second (25 for PAL systems). Why is it that Quake looks terrible at 24 frames per second?

The answer lies in the difference between virtual images and real images exposed on film. Cameras work by opening a shutter for a finite amount of time and exposing a single frame of film. The shutter closes, the film advances one frame, and the process is repeated. The process is not instantaneous. If an object is moving while the shutter is open, that object appears blurred in the frame because it was in several different positions during the exposure. Figure 33.3 shows one such blurred image.

Figure 33.3

Motion blur of a moving circle.

The amount of blurring depends on the speed of the object and the length of the exposure. When you take a photograph, your body is moving slightly, but the effect on the final photograph is not apparent because the shutter speed is very fast. If you take the same picture at night with a very slow shutter speed, those movements almost certainly blur the image.

The problem with virtual images is that they are too good. A 3D rendering is instantaneous. World transformations place an object in a very specific location for every given frame. You can animate an object over a series of frames, but there is no apparent motion on any single frame. Figure 33.4 shows two screenshots. In one of the shots, the object is spinning rapidly around the Y axis. In the other, the object is completely motionless. I let you decide which is which.

Figure 33.4

Virtual images in motion.

This is why Quake looks silky smooth only at very high frame rates. The higher the frame rate, the more the illusion is filled in by our brains or by latencies in the computer screen itself. The purpose of motion blur is to reproduce the blurring effect to give the illusion of smoother motion. You can use this technique for other effects as well.

Motion Blur as a Post-Processing Technique

If you are familiar with OpenGL, you are probably familiar with the accumulation buffer. The accumulation buffer is a specialized back buffer that allows images to be accumulated together with multiple rendering passes. For motion blur, you use the accumulation buffer to render the scene multiple times per frame so that moving objects blur. The final motion-blurred image is then copied to the front buffer for final output. This technique produces great results, but accelerated support for the accumulation buffer is not widespread, so the technique is not widely used.

DirectX has no accumulation buffer, but you can accumulate scenes to the back buffer using alpha effects. One solution is to render the scene with multiple passes and adjust the transparency of each object on each pass. After several passes, you use a call to Present() to display the resulting image. This technique still requires the additional processing overhead from rendering geometry multiple times, and it also could interfere with any transparency effects that are part of the normal scene.

Instead, I'm proposing that motion blur be an entirely "post-processing" technique, meaning that the image is rendered once per frame and then you perform some operations to produce the blurring effect. The implementation is fairly easy.

In all the examples so far, the back buffer is cleared before the next frame is rendered so that you don't see any of the previous contents. In this case, I do not clear the back buffer. You can use the previous frame to simulate the motion blur. You can render the next frame with a small amount of transparency and blend the old frame with the new frame, giving the appearance of motion blur to any moving object. The problem is that you can't just adjust transparency and render a new frame on top of the old frame because any changes in transparency affect the look of the scene. For instance, a semitransparent object creates a nice blurring effect with the previously rendered frame, but it also shows up as a semitransparent object.

This is where the render target is important. With every frame, the scene is rendered to a render target texture. That rendering pass renders all the objects in the normal way without any manipulation of transparency. Once the scene is rendered to a texture, the texture is used to texture a full-screen quad. You can adjust the transparency of the full-screen rectangle so that it blends with the previous image (which was never cleared). This produces a very fast accumulation effect and does not require multiple geometry passes. You could argue that the results are not quite as good as rendering multiple passes per frame, but this technique wins on performance. Figure 33.5 shows the same scene as Figure 33.4, only this time the motion-blur effect has been added to improve the illusion of motion.

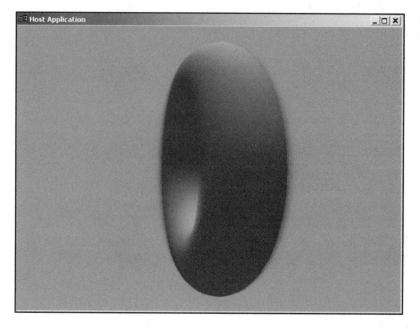

Figure 33.5

Virtual object in motion.

This technique doesn't use any interesting shaders, so the implementation details begin with the application code. Chapter 36 talks about how you can use pixel shaders with this technique, but for now the interesting effect is a product of render targets, transparency, and the old contents of the back buffer.

The Motion-Blur Application

This application renders the scene as does any other application. The difference is that it renders the scene to a target texture. The texture is applied to a quad, and that is the object actually drawn to the screen. The blur effect works if you don't clear the back buffer each frame. This blends the current scene with the previous scene, blurring any motion.

In this chapter, you can't use the `EasyCreateWindowed` convenience function because that function creates a device that discards the back buffer every time the screen is drawn. In this case you need the back buffer, so you have to create a device that holds onto the contents. Following is a partial listing for `PostInitialize`. The only difference between this code and the other creation functions is that this creates a device that copies the back buffer instead of discarding it:

```
BOOL CTechniqueApplication::PostInitialize()
{
    D3DDISPLAYMODE CurrentMode;
    if (SUCCEEDED(m_pD3D->GetAdapterDisplayMode(D3DADAPTER_DEFAULT,
                                        &CurrentMode)))
    {
        ZeroMemory(&m_PresentParameters,
                    sizeof(D3DPRESENT_PARAMETERS));
        m_PresentParameters.Windowed = TRUE;
```

This is the important bit. Make sure the contents remain intact between frames:

```
        m_PresentParameters.SwapEffect = D3DSWAPEFFECT_COPY;
        m_PresentParameters.BackBufferFormat = CurrentMode.Format;
        m_PresentParameters.EnableAutoDepthStencil = TRUE;
        m_PresentParameters.AutoDepthStencilFormat = D3DFMT_D24S8;
        m_CreationParameters.AdapterOrdinal = D3DADAPTER_DEFAULT;
        m_CreationParameters.DeviceType    = D3DDEVTYPE_HAL;
        m_CreationParameters.hFocusWindow  = m_hWnd;
```

I moved the shader verification down and used it to set the behavior. In other cases, you might want to also verify whether you should be using the HAL device or REF:

```
        D3DCAPS8 Caps;
        m_pD3D->GetDeviceCaps(D3DADAPTER_DEFAULT,
         D3DDEVTYPE_HAL, &Caps);
        if (Caps.VertexShaderVersion == D3DVS_VERSION(1,1))
            m_CreationParameters.BehaviorFlags =
                    D3DCREATE_HARDWARE_VERTEXPROCESSING;
        else
            m_CreationParameters.BehaviorFlags =
                    D3DCREATE_SOFTWARE_VERTEXPROCESSING;

        if (FAILED(CreateDevice(&m_CreationParameters,
                            &m_PresentParameters)))
```

```
                return FALSE;
    }
```

The next step is to create render target textures. The textures are created in SetupDevice because they must be re-created every time the device is created or reset:

```
HRESULT CTechniqueApplication::SetupDevice()
{
```

Set up the projection matrix based on the properties on the display window. In this sample, I defined the texture dimensions with a constant width and height, but you could use the window rectangle to define a texture size based on the window dimensions. For instance, if the window is 640x480, you can specify a 1,024x512 texture:

```
    RECT WindowRect;
    GetClientRect(m_hWnd, &WindowRect);
    D3DXMatrixPerspectiveFovLH(&m_ProjectionMatrix, D3DX_PI / 4,
                   (float)(WindowRect.right - WindowRect.left) /
                   (float)(WindowRect.bottom - WindowRect.top),
                   1.0f, 1000.0f);


    D3DXMatrixIdentity(&m_WorldMatrix);
```

Create a texture using the function call described earlier in this chapter. You might want to be smarter about how you pick the texture dimensions. In this sample, the dimensions are set to 1,024x1,024, but larger application resolutions might demand larger textures. Because the sample application is 640x480, you would still be safe with a 1,024x512 texture. Furthermore, some cards support textures with dimensions that are not powers of two. In that case, you could create a texture that is exactly the same size as the output window:

```
    if (FAILED(D3DXCreateTexture(m_pD3DDevice, TEX_DIMENSION,
        TEX_DIMENSION, 1, D3DUSAGE_RENDERTARGET, D3DFMT_X8R8G8B8,
        D3DPOOL_DEFAULT, &m_pDisplayTexture)))
            return E_FAIL;
```

Retrieve the surface from the texture. This surface serves as the actual render target. You only use the texture interface to apply the contents of the surface on a textured object:

```
    if (FAILED(m_pDisplayTexture->GetSurfaceLevel(0,
                &m_pDisplayTextureSurface)))
            return E_FAIL;
```

Create a depth stencil surface that is exactly the same size as the render target texture. You don't need to use the depth information as a texture, so there is no need to create this as a texture. In fact, you never need to use the contents of the buffer yourself. Simply create a surface to serve as a depth buffer for the render target:

```
if (FAILED(m_pD3DDevice->CreateDepthStencilSurface(
                                                    TEX_DIMENSION,
                            TEX_DIMENSION,
                            D3DFMT_D24S8,
                            D3DMULTISAMPLE_NONE,
                            &m_pDisplayZSurface)))
        return E_FAIL;
```

Retrieve pointers to the current back buffers of the device. These pointers are valid over the lifetime of the device. As you will see later, you do want to release these objects before ending the application:

```
if (FAILED(m_pD3DDevice->GetRenderTarget(&m_pBackBuffer)))
        return E_FAIL;

if (FAILED(m_pD3DDevice->GetDepthStencilSurface(&m_pZBuffer)))
        return E_FAIL;

    return S_OK;
}
```

The next step is to create the vertex buffer for the textured quad that will be visible on the screen. This isn't very different from some of the 2D quads you've seen in Chapter 29 and elsewhere. The important point is that this function uses the properties of the viewport to set the positions and texture coordinates:

```
HRESULT CTechniqueApplication::CreateDisplayBuffer()
{
```

You create the quad with a vertex buffer of four transformed vertices. Give the positions as screen coordinates:

```
if (FAILED(m_pD3DDevice->CreateVertexBuffer(4 *
                                            sizeof(DISPLAY_VERTEX),
                        0, D3DFVF_DISPLAYVERTEX,
                        D3DPOOL_MANAGED,
                        &m_pDisplayVertexBuffer)))
```

```
        return E_FAIL;

DISPLAY_VERTEX *pDisplayVertices;

m_pDisplayVertexBuffer->Lock(0, 4 * sizeof(DISPLAY_VERTEX),
                            (BYTE **)&pDisplayVertices, 0);
```

You use the viewport parameters to size the quad and set the texture coordinates. If you change the viewport for some reason, you need to change the vertices accordingly. For instance, you might need to change this code if you are rendering to several different viewports, as shown in some of the very early chapters:

```
D3DVIEWPORT8 Viewport;
m_pD3DDevice->GetViewport(&Viewport);
DWORD X1 = Viewport.X;
DWORD Y1 = Viewport.Y;
DWORD X2 = Viewport.X + Viewport.Width;
DWORD Y2 = Viewport.Y + Viewport.Height;
```

The maximum texture coordinates are expressed as the ratios of the viewport dimensions and the texture dimensions. As you will see, the Render function renders to a section of the texture equal to the viewport dimensions. Here, you set the texture coordinates to ensure that the textured quad shows only that section of the texture:

```
float UMax = (float)Viewport.Width  / (float)TEX_DIMENSION;
float VMax = (float)Viewport.Height / (float)TEX_DIMENSION;
```

Set the four vertices based on the data derived here. This quad is drawn as a two-element triangle strip. The z and rhw values of all the vertices are set to 1.0:

```
pDisplayVertices[0].x = X1;       pDisplayVertices[0].y = Y1;
pDisplayVertices[0].z = 1.0f;     pDisplayVertices[0].rhw = 1.0f;
pDisplayVertices[0].u = 0.0f;     pDisplayVertices[0].v = 0.0f;

pDisplayVertices[1].x = X1;       pDisplayVertices[1].y = Y2;
pDisplayVertices[1].u = 0.0f;     pDisplayVertices[1].v = VMax;
pDisplayVertices[1].z = 1.0f;     pDisplayVertices[1].rhw = 1.0f;

pDisplayVertices[2].x = X2;       pDisplayVertices[2].y = Y1;
pDisplayVertices[2].u = UMax;     pDisplayVertices[2].v = 0.0f;
```

```
        pDisplayVertices[2].z = 1.0f;   pDisplayVertices[2].rhw = 1.0f;

        pDisplayVertices[3].x = X2;     pDisplayVertices[3].y = Y2;
        pDisplayVertices[3].u = UMax;   pDisplayVertices[3].v = VMax;
        pDisplayVertices[3].z = 1.0f;   pDisplayVertices[3].rhw = 1.0f;

        m_pDisplayVertexBuffer->Unlock();

        return S_OK;
}
```

Before getting into the actual rendering code, I want to show how you clean up the
targets. The application still handles the release of the vertex buffers, textures, and
other objects, but I placed the clean-up of the new render target objects in a
separate function:

```
void CTechniqueApplication::CleanUpTarget()
{
```

First, release the surface of the render target texture. This decreases the reference
count so that it gets destroyed when the texture is destroyed:

```
        if (m_pDisplayTextureSurface)
        {
                m_pDisplayTextureSurface->Release();
                m_pDisplayTextureSurface = NULL;
        }
```

Releasing the texture should destroy the texture object. This also destroys all the
related objects. The texture object is now unusable:

```
        if (m_pDisplayTexture)
        {
                m_pDisplayTexture->Release();
                m_pDisplayTexture = NULL;
        }
```

Release the depth surface. Again, this destroys the surface and frees up all of its
resources:

```
        if (m_pDisplayZSurface)
        {
                m_pDisplayZSurface->Release();
```

```
            m_pDisplayZSurface = NULL;
    }
```

Finally, release the pointers to the back buffers that were created by the device. This probably does not destroy these objects because the device itself still holds references to these objects. However, releasing your reference allows the device to destroy these objects properly when the device is destroyed:

```
    if (m_pBackBuffer)
    {
            m_pBackBuffer->Release();
            m_pBackBuffer = NULL;
    }

    if (m_pZBuffer)
    {
            m_pZBuffer->Release();
            m_pZBuffer = NULL;
    }
}
```

Everything is set up to begin rendering. I have overridden the PreRender function to remove the call to Clear. The old frame remains in the back buffer and the new frame is blended on top of it:

```
void CTechniqueApplication::PreRender()
{
    // Don't Clear...

    m_pD3DDevice->BeginScene();

    return;
}
```

As usual, Render does most of the real work. The scene is rendered to the render target texture, and the texture is applied to a full-screen quad for final output to the screen. Render does use a vertex shader, but it is the basic directional lighting shader found in Basic.vsh and used in many previous chapters:

```
void CTechniqueApplication::Render()
{
```

The scene, animation, lighting, and vertex shader parameters are all initialized and passed to the shader in the normal way. This is an important point. This technique doesn't affect anything about the way the scene is rendered. Therefore, you can implement the motion-blur effect completely separately from all of the other effects in the scene. In contrast, a true multipass technique might require every vertex and pixel shader to have some notion of the transparency needed to blend multiple passes. It could be difficult to add this effect without an overhaul of many of the other features of the scene. This technique allows you to enable or disable motion blur very easily without changing the way the objects in the scene are rendered. In fact, you could add features into the framework that completely hide the details of motion blur. You would just fill in the Render function as you've seen in all the other samples, and the framework could take care of the render target switching and the final quad rendering:

```
D3DXMatrixLookAtLH(&m_ViewMatrix,
                   &D3DXVECTOR3(0.0, 0.0f, -40.0f),
                   &D3DXVECTOR3(0.0f, 0.0f, 0.0f),
                   &D3DXVECTOR3(0.0f, 1.0f, 0.0f));


D3DXMATRIX Rotation;
D3DXMATRIX Translation;

D3DXMatrixRotationY(&Rotation, (float)GetTickCount() / 1000.0f);
D3DXMatrixTranslation(&Translation, 0.0f, 0.0f, 0.0f);
m_WorldMatrix = Rotation * Translation;

D3DXVECTOR4 Ambient    (0.1,  0.1f, 0.1f, 0.0f);
m_pD3DDevice->SetVertexShaderConstant(5, &Ambient, 1);


D3DXVECTOR4 LightDir = D3DXVECTOR4(0.0f, -1.0f, 0.0f, 0.0f);
D3DXMATRIX InverseWorld;
D3DXMatrixInverse(&InverseWorld, NULL, &m_WorldMatrix);
D3DXVec4Transform(&LightDir, &LightDir, &InverseWorld);
D3DXVec4Normalize(&LightDir, &LightDir);
m_pD3DDevice->SetVertexShaderConstant(4, &LightDir, 1);


D3DXMATRIX ShaderMatrix = m_WorldMatrix * m_ViewMatrix *
                          m_ProjectionMatrix;
D3DXMatrixTranspose(&ShaderMatrix, &ShaderMatrix);
m_pD3DDevice->SetVertexShaderConstant(0, &ShaderMatrix, 4);
```

The initial setup is done, and it's time to render the scene. First, get the current viewport. This viewport sets the viewport of the render target:

```
D3DVIEWPORT8 NormalViewport;
m_pD3DDevice->GetViewport(&NormalViewport);
```

Set the render target to the new surfaces that were created in SetupDevice:

```
m_pD3DDevice->SetRenderTarget(m_pDisplayTextureSurface,
                              m_pDisplayZSurface);
```

Clear the buffers of the new render target. The back buffer of the device is never cleared, but the texture render target is. The render target always contains the newest frame, but the last step of the technique blends that new data with the old data:

```
m_pD3DDevice->Clear(0, NULL, D3DCLEAR_TARGET | D3DCLEAR_ZBUFFER,
                    D3DCOLOR_XRGB(100, 100, 200), 1.0f, 0);
```

Set the viewport to match the real viewport. This code assumes that the texture is at least as big as the actual viewport. If you make the window bigger or the texture smaller, this function might fail or at least fail to do what you want it to. Keep this in mind if you change the window or texture size. The texture must be at least as big as this viewport:

```
m_pD3DDevice->SetViewport(&NormalViewport);
```

Render the scene as usual:

```
m_pD3DDevice->SetVertexShader(m_BasicShader);
m_pD3DDevice->SetStreamSource(0, m_pMeshVertexBuffer,
                              sizeof(MESH_VERTEX));
m_pD3DDevice->SetIndices(m_pMeshIndexBuffer, 0);
m_pD3DDevice->DrawIndexedPrimitive(D3DPT_TRIANGLELIST, 0,
                                   m_pMesh->GetNumVertices(), 0,
                                   m_pMesh->GetNumFaces());
```

The scene is now complete, and the texture holds the current frame. Change the render target back to the real back buffer before completing the final pass:

```
m_pD3DDevice->SetRenderTarget(m_pBackBuffer, m_pZBuffer);
```

Set the current texture to the render target texture. Also, set the level of transparency based on the texture factor. This allows you to modify the amount of blending dynamically. Changing the texture factor changes the amount of blur in the scene:

```
m_pD3DDevice->SetTexture(0, m_pDisplayTexture);
m_pD3DDevice->SetTextureStageState(0, D3DTSS_ALPHAARG1,
```

```
                                    D3DTA_TFACTOR);
        m_pD3DDevice->SetRenderState(D3DRS_TEXTUREFACTOR, 0xaaffffff);
```

Enable alpha blending:

```
        m_pD3DDevice->SetRenderState(D3DRS_ALPHABLENDENABLE,  TRUE);
        m_pD3DDevice->SetRenderState(D3DRS_SRCBLEND,  D3DBLEND_SRCALPHA);
        m_pD3DDevice->SetRenderState(D3DRS_DESTBLEND,
         D3DBLEND_INVSRCALPHA);
```

With 2D quads, I always turn off culling and depth testing to make sure that everything is drawn:

```
        m_pD3DDevice->SetRenderState(D3DRS_CULLMODE, D3DCULL_NONE);
        m_pD3DDevice->SetRenderState(D3DRS_ZENABLE, FALSE);
```

Draw the 2D quad to the entire screen:

```
        m_pD3DDevice->SetVertexShader(D3DFVF_DISPLAYVERTEX);
        m_pD3DDevice->SetStreamSource(0, m_pDisplayVertexBuffer,
                                sizeof(DISPLAY_VERTEX));
        m_pD3DDevice->DrawPrimitive(D3DPT_TRIANGLESTRIP, 0, 2);
```

The following lines are clean-up code. They reset many of the states back to their default mode and finish the technique. The screen is updated with the blended frames:

```
        m_pD3DDevice->SetRenderState(D3DRS_CULLMODE, D3DCULL_CCW);
        m_pD3DDevice->SetRenderState(D3DRS_ZENABLE, TRUE);
        m_pD3DDevice->SetRenderState(D3DRS_ALPHABLENDENABLE,  FALSE);
        m_pD3DDevice->SetTexture(0, NULL);
        m_pD3DDevice->SetTextureStageState(0, D3DTSS_ALPHAARG1,
                                    D3DTA_TEXTURE);
}
```

This technique works by blending data across multiple frames instead of making multiple passes in the same frame. The level of transparency of the final quad controls the blurring effect. A less transparent quad overwrites the old data more quickly, causing less blur. A more transparent quad overwrites the data very slowly, and the blurring effect is more pronounced. Figure 33.6 shows a screenshot with only a little bit of blurring. Figure 33.7 shows a more extreme blurring effect.

The scene in Figure 33.6 is probably close to the type of effect you would want to simulate normal motion blur. The scene in Figure 33.7 is probably not a great

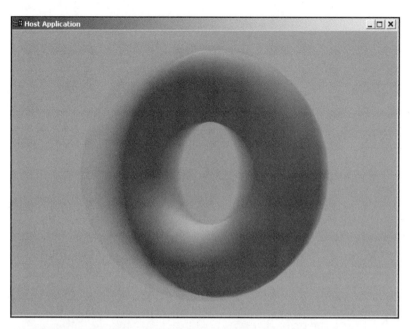

Figure 33.6

Moderate motion-blur effect.

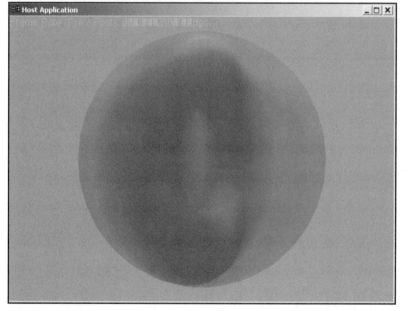

Figure 33.7

Extreme blurring effect.

motion-blur effect, but it might be a useful special effect. For instance, it might be the kind of effect that's good for accelerating into hyperspace. It could also be useful if your character is hit by a blow dart with a poisonous neurological chemical. It is also a great basis for a mesmerizing screensaver.

Performance Implications

You get performance hits in a couple of different places. First, there is a cost associated with changing the render target. The other cost is in rendering the final quad. The actual cost of this depends heavily on the hardware you are using and the complexity of the scene. For instance, I used this technique on a geForce2MX machine with a simple scene (this example), and I got a nearly 50 percent performance hit. The same technique was applied to a very complex scene on a geForce3 with less than a 5 percent performance hit. One point here is that the cost is relative. If your application is fairly complex and runs at a lower frame rate, you see less of an absolute change in the number of frames per second. If you have a very simple scene, the absolute change in frame rate is much more noticeable.

So is the performance hit bad? I don't think so. Compare it to other multipass techniques. If you render the complete scene three times, you get approximately one-third the number of frames. You also introduce complexities into the rendering process. Any additional performance-heavy features have triple the impact. This technique incurs a potentially heavy one-time performance hit, but the cost of switching render targets is the same whether your scene is simple or complex. The 50 percent hit was a worst-case scenario. Very simple scenes are sensitive to any changes. Complex scenes wash out the performance hit.

The construction of this technique makes it very modular. You can easily trade it in and out depending on the performance hit. In fact, it's possible that you will want to disable it and enable it as the scene changes in complexity. The rationale might be that faster frame rates need motion blur less. Slower frame rates might need it more, and the effect might be worthwhile even if it slows the frame rate even more.

In Conclusion...

The purpose of this chapter was really threefold. I wanted to explain the method for creating and using texture render targets. I also wanted to put them to good use with a full-screen motion-blur technique that is modular and extendable. Finally, I wanted to show that this technique can be useful for post-processing effects beyond motion blur. Figure 33.7 showed that simple changes to the technique produce very different results. Chapter 36 talks about other post-processing techniques that might be useful for adding new effects and moods to your application. I highly recommend experimenting with this technique to understand both the performance implications and the potential applications of this technique. To get you started, here are a few of the key points:

- Render target textures are not supported in all formats on all hardware. Use `CheckDeviceFormat` to check for support.

- Render target textures are created just as any other texture, but you need to specify the render target usage flag.

- The device renders to surfaces, not textures. Get the surface from the texture after it is created.

- Pay careful attention to your viewport when changing render targets.

- You can change the contents of a cube map if it was created as a render target. Get each surface, set it as a render target, and render the scene in that direction from the position of the reflective object. Make sure that your camera is set to a 90 degree field of view and that the aspect ratio is 1. Repeat for every surface that must be updated.

- Motion blur helps to give the impression that objects are actually moving.

- Many motion-blur techniques are multipass techniques. This technique renders the scene in a single pass but blends multiple frames to achieve the effect.

- The performance penalties associated with this technique are probably lighter than other techniques. Don't let the performance hit in simple scenes scare you away. The proportional hit change decreases as scene complexity increases.

- This technique has several uses beyond motion blur. The render-to-texture aspect proves very useful when implementing some of the techniques of Chapter 36.

CHAPTER 34

2D Rendering— Just Drop a "D"

As of DirectX 8.0, the 2D API known as DirectDraw is no longer part of the current DirectX API set. The graphics APIs were merged into a single API known as DirectX Graphics. This book mentions the Direct3D moniker many times, but DirectX Graphics is really the official name, and it is not at all limited to 3D. This chapter describes how to construct a simple wrapper class for 2D functionality. I cover the following concepts:

- The rationale behind the consolidation and loss of DirectDraw.
- Setting up a 2D drawing environment with a 3D API.
- Constructing a sprite class for 2D sprites.
- Using the sprite class in a sample application.
- Performance implications and advantages.
- Possible extensions.

Alas, Poor DirectDraw. I Knew It...

This is where I step onto my soapbox. Here is the rationale for the loss of DirectDraw as I understand it. When DirectDraw was created, the hardware of the time was primarily rated on its ability to "blit" pixels very quickly. This means that the metric for what made a card good was its ability to move large blocks of pixels from one area of memory to another. This boils down to the ability to paint bitmap rectangles on a 2D surface as quickly as possible.

Then along came 3D games. Suddenly, gaming cards were judged more on their ability to rasterize 3D triangles and texture them on the fly. The interesting specifications changed from blitting speed to number of triangles per second or number of texels per second. This was gradually expanded to hardware T&L and eventually to shaders. The whole idea of putting time, energy, and silicon into faster 2D operations became a losing proposition. As time passed, the hardware that inspired the design of DirectDraw became obsolete (in terms of technology and increasingly in terms of install base).

Many people find fault in Microsoft for dropping DirectDraw, but it actually makes a lot of sense in the context of the hardware. When versions of DirectX are released, they are aimed at current and future pieces of hardware. When DirectX 8.0 was released, most if not all major hardware manufacturers were concentrating heavily on 3D functionality and not the blitting paradigm. There was no indication that the direction of graphics technology would reverse. So the API was consolidated into one API that concentrated on a 3D paradigm.

This is not to say that the API cannot or should not be used for 2D applications. The fact that an API is focused on vectors, matrices, and textures does not preclude its usage for 2D. This is also true with OpenGL. OpenGL includes a subset of functions that operate very much like DirectDraw blitting functions, but they are rarely hardware accelerated. Therefore, the only way to get good 2D performance with OpenGL is to use the 3D aspects of the API. The same is now true with DirectX. One unfortunate difference is that few OpenGL functions actually include "3D" in the names. In DirectX, "3D" is part of the name of nearly every interface, and I think this scares away a lot of 2D programmers.

I am confused and surprised by the backlash against the consolidation of the two APIs. Many people feel that 2D games necessitate the use of the older API. Those people will swear up and down that DirectDraw is better for 2D and then spend months trying to optimize alpha blending. Most 2D operations are just as fast using Direct3D as they were with DirectDraw, and most extended features such as alpha blending are extremely fast compared to the DirectDraw equivalent. Frankly, I see little point to learning DirectDraw unless you need to support legacy code or you are aiming for very old hardware.

On the Other Hand...

I understand some people have older pieces of hardware that might not be capable of fast 3D operations. Those people may be very tempted to learn DirectDraw. At the time of this writing, many Internet stores sell hardware T&L cards for less than the price of this book. The adage about time equaling money is true. You can spend months learning an old API. That would be far more expensive than one of these cheaper cards.

So in the end you have a consolidated API that is set up for 3D, but you want to use it for 2D. For the remainder of this chapter, I step off my soapbox and show you how.

Step 1: Lose a "D"

When it comes down to it, the difference between 2D and 3D is an extra D. If you can just lose one of those Ds, things get back to 2D and you can begin drawing. In fact, losing that extra D is pretty easy.

In the context of 3D rendering, your drawing area is some three-dimensional space. That 3D space is mapped to your 2D screen with your three matrices. The world and view matrix take care of positioning an object in relation to the viewer, but it is really the projection matrix that determines how the objects are mapped from 3D to 2D space. Therefore, the projection matrix holds the key to losing a D.

In standard 3D drawing, the projection matrix is defined so that it determines the amount of perspective in the scene. Perspective is the phenomenon that determines the 2D position of an object on the screen as a function of distance. Figure 34.1 shows the perspective phenomenon of lines converging into the distance.

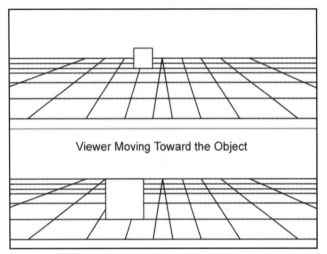

Figure 34.1

Perspective and its effect on rendered objects.

In the two scenes, the object is at the same position in space, but the viewer is nearer in the second frame. Perspective has a definite effect on the size and position of the object when it is drawn on the screen. To put it differently, the 2D position of the object on the screen is dependent on the object's position along the third dimension pointing into the screen. That's the dimension you have to lose.

The secret is a special projection matrix called an orthogonal matrix. A scene rendered with an orthogonal projection matrix is not affected by perspective. Figure 34.2 shows the same scene as Figure 34.1 but with an orthogonal projection matrix. The lines do not converge to a vanishing point and the size of the object doesn't change with distance.

So what's the difference between Figure 34.1 and Figure 34.2? There is one less D in Figure 34.2. For all practical purposes, Figure 34.2 is a 2D drawing.

In terms of implementation, you can set up an orthogonal matrix with one of several D3DX functions. The most straightforward is the D3DXMatrixOrthoLH function:

```
D3DXMATRIX* D3DXMatrixOrthoLH(D3DXMATRIX* pOut, FLOAT Width,
          FLOAT Height, FLOAT NearDistance, FLOAT FarDistance);
```

This function creates an orthogonal projection matrix for a 2D space of a given width and height, as shown in Figure 34.3. The 2D space is centered on (0, 0) and

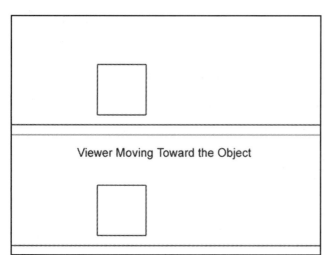

Figure 34.2

Scene with an orthogonal projection matrix.

Viewer Moving Toward the Object

the extents are +/- half of the width and height. The distance parameters define the bounds of the space, but the distance does not affect the size of position of the rendered object.

Figure 34.3

Default 2D layout.

+Height/2

-Width/2

0

+Width/2

-Height/2

If for some reason you don't want the (0, 0) point in the middle of the screen, you can use D3DXMatrixOrthoOffCenterLH to construct the matrix:

```
D3DXMATRIX* D3DXMatrixOrthoOffCenterLH(D3DXMATRIX* pOut, FLOAT Left,
                    FLOAT Right, FLOAT Bottom, FLOAT Top,
                    FLOAT NearDistance, FLOAT FarDistance);
```

This function allows you to set up a matrix with an arbitrary origin. This can be extremely useful if you want to replicate the usual 2D graphics where the origin is in the upper left of the screen. Figure 34.4 shows the 2D space constructed with the following call:

```
D3DXMatrixOrthoOffCenterLH(&Out, 0.0f, 640.0f, 480.0f, 0.0f,
                           0.0f, 1.0f);
```

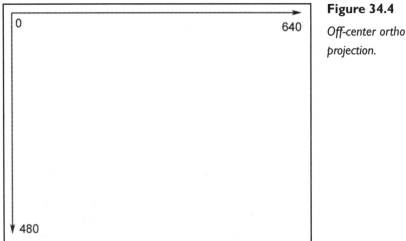

Figure 34.4

Off-center ortho projection.

This raises a potentially interesting question. What should the width and height be? In Figure 34.4, I used a width and height that matched the pixel width and height of a 640x480 screen. You could do something like this and then draw all of your objects with dimensions given in terms of pixels. Another alternative is to use 1.0 for your width and height. This creates a space in which things can be sized proportionately to any screen size. Remember, the projection matrix doesn't set the actual size of the window. It controls the way in which positions are mapped to pixel values on the screen. Therefore, different values have different effects on the way things are drawn.

If you create a projection matrix based on pixel values, you should give all of your object positions and sizes as pixel values. If you want an object to be half as wide as a 640x480 screen, its width should be 320. The problem arises if you change the screen resolution from 640x480 to 1,024x768. Now, the 320 wide object is far less than one-half of the width of the screen. In cases like this, it might be better to use 1.0 as the width and height when you create your projection matrix. Then, specify 0.5 for the object's width. This way, the object is always half of the screen width no matter what the resolution is. I'm getting a little ahead of myself. This will all be a little clearer after I talk about the actual sprite objects.

Sprites—Image Is Everything

Now that you have a 2D drawing environment, you need something to draw. In this chapter, the point is to draw a 2D sprite instead of a 3D mesh object. At this point you could ask why I'm not using the `ID3DXSprite` interface.

There are several reasons I am not using `ID3DXSprite`. The first reason is that I want to show how things are done, much as Chapter 31 showed how to compute texture space vectors before offloading it to D3DX in Chapter 32. Another reason is that a home-brewed solution is ultimately more flexible than the ready-made solution. It's usually not a good idea to reinvent the wheel, but in this case the wheel is easy to reinvent. It is much easier to add other effects later if you understand the underlying theory. For example, you might possibly want to add vertex shader, pixel shader, or other texturing effects to your 2D sprites. Building your own class makes it easier to implement and control these extended features.

For the Object Inclined

The following explanation and sample application does not wrap the sprite functionality into a separate class because I didn't want to confuse the concepts of sprite rendering with the concepts of good object-oriented design. If you are an object-oriented type of person, I highly suggest you wrap much of this functionality into a new class.

The purpose of a sprite is to display a texture on the screen, so the first step in building your own sprite object is to load a texture. You load the texture as you would any other texture using the D3DX functions. The one suggestion is that you might want to get the width and height of the texture. This may be useful for setting the position of the vertices later. Once the texture is loaded, you can retrieve the dimensions of the texture with a call to `GetLevelDesc`:

```
HRESULT IDirect3DTexture8::GetLevelDesc(UINT Level,
                                        D3DSURFACE_DESC* pDesc);
```

The surface description parameter contains the width and height of the texture. You'll see later how this can be useful.

You will probably want to create the textures with dimensions that are powers-of-two. If you don't, the D3DX functions create a power-of-two texture anyway and stretch the image to fill the texture. If this is the case, you might want to load the image with `D3DXCreateTextureFromFileEx` and check the `D3DXIMAGE_INFO` structure to find the real image dimensions. These dimensions could prove very useful when sizing the sprite.

If your sprite has any transparent regions, you probably want to create those in your image editor. The `D3DXCreateTextureFromFileEx` function does allow you to specify a color key parameter, but color key is a binary operation. Creating the transparency in an editor allows you to create much smoother edges and ultimately a much better sprite. Once the texture is loaded, you need something to texture.

Using Vertices in 2D

Some programmers feel that 2D programming should not include vertices. However, there's little difference between setting four corners of a rectangle for a blitting function and setting four vertices for a textured quad. I create 2D sprites as textured quads with the following vertex format:

```
#define D3DFVF_SPRITEVERTEX (D3DFVF_XYZ | D3DFVF_TEX1)

struct SPRITE_VERTEX
{
        float x, y, z;
        float u, v;
};
```

You've seen many bits and pieces of this in earlier chapters. This is the smallest vertex format that will position a 2D texture on the screen. You can definitely add more data if you want to use diffuse colors or more textures, but this is a good starting point.

Once you define your vertex format, you can create a vertex buffer and create four points for the sprite. For my applications, I tend to create one vertex buffer that will be used for all sprites. Therefore, I create one "unit square" with sides that are equal to one unit. This allows me to dynamically resize the sprite to any new size with a scaling matrix. The following code is from the sample application, and it is used to create that reusable unit square:

```
HRESULT CTechniqueApplication::CreateSpriteBuffer()
{
```

Create a vertex buffer that holds four vertices. Currently, the sprite is created in managed memory to ease some of the maintenance. You might want to try other memory pools and see how it affects performance:

```
        if (FAILED(m_pD3DDevice->CreateVertexBuffer(4 *
                                                sizeof(SPRITE_VERTEX),
```

```
                          0, D3DFVF_SPRITEVERTEX,
                          D3DPOOL_MANAGED,
                          &m_pSpriteVertexBuffer)))
            return E_FAIL;

    SPRITE_VERTEX *pSpriteVertices;
```

Lock the vertex buffer and create the four vertices. The way things are currently set up, the vertex buffer contains the points of a square that is one unit long on both sides and centered around the origin. This means that any translation matrices applied to this sprite will translate the center of the sprite. If you want the base point of the sprite to be in another location on the sprite, you can rework the vertex positions accordingly. The fact that this is a "unit square" allows the user to easily change the size with a scaling matrix. The values in the scaling matrix are basically the new width and height of the sprite. This works equally well whether you are dealing with a pixel-based projection matrix or a proportional scaling matrix. Also, the z value of each vertex is set to the farthest distance from the camera. If you want to, you can enable depth buffering and change this value with the scaling matrices. This will allow depth effects with the 2D sprites.

The texture coordinates are also set to use the whole texture. The sample does not show this, but you could use texture matrices to dynamically reset the texture coordinates. The point is that you don't need to lock the buffer every frame. You can change the data with the transformation matrices:

```
    m_pSpriteVertexBuffer->Lock(0, 4 * sizeof(SPRITE_VERTEX),
                          (BYTE **)&pSpriteVertices, 0);

    pSpriteVertices[0].x = -0.5f;    pSpriteVertices[0].y =  -0.5f;
    pSpriteVertices[0].z =  1.0f;
    pSpriteVertices[0].u =  0.0f;    pSpriteVertices[0].v =   0.0f;

    pSpriteVertices[1].x = -0.5f;    pSpriteVertices[1].y =   0.5f;
    pSpriteVertices[1].z =  1.0f;
    pSpriteVertices[1].u =  0.0f;    pSpriteVertices[1].v =   1.0f;

    pSpriteVertices[2].x =  0.5f;    pSpriteVertices[2].y =  -0.5f;
    pSpriteVertices[2].z =  1.0f;
    pSpriteVertices[2].u =  1.0f;    pSpriteVertices[2].v =   0.0f;

    pSpriteVertices[3].x =  0.5f;    pSpriteVertices[3].y =   0.5f;
```

```
            pSpriteVertices[3].z =  1.0f;
            pSpriteVertices[3].u =  1.0f;    pSpriteVertices[3].v =   1.0f;

        m_pSpriteVertexBuffer->Unlock();
```

If you are only using 2D vertices, you can set the vertex shader once and use it throughout the application. You can also set the stream source once because every sprite is based on the same vertex buffer:

```
        m_pD3DDevice->SetVertexShader(D3DFVF_SPRITEVERTEX);
        m_pD3DDevice->SetStreamSource(0, m_pSpriteVertexBuffer,
                                     sizeof(SPRITE_VERTEX));

        return S_OK;
}
```

Once you've created the texture and the vertex buffer, the only step left is to create the application that actually renders the sprites.

A Very Simple 2D Application

You've already seen the key aspects of the 2D technique. The application just pulls everything together. Remember, if you are an object-oriented person, much of this functionality can be wrapped into a sprite class.

The SetupDevice function handles all the initial setup. Most of the matrices are set to identity matrices. Two projection matrices are created. One matrix is created for pixel-based rendering, and the other is set up for proportional rendering:

```
HRESULT CTechniqueApplication::SetupDevice()
{
```

The pixel-based projection matrix is based on the dimensions of the output window. You should use pixel-based dimensions when this matrix is active:

```
        RECT WindowRect;
        GetClientRect(m_hWnd, &WindowRect);
        D3DXMatrixOrthoLH(&m_PixelProjection, (float)WindowRect.right,
                        (float)WindowRect.bottom, 0.0f, 100.0f);
```

The proportional matrix lets you size sprites according to how much of the screen they should occupy. This works out well for full-screen backgrounds or GUI elements that occupy set portions of the screen:

```
D3DXMatrixOrthoLH(&m_ProportionalProjection, float)1.0f,
                  (float)1.0f, 0.0f, 100.0f);
```

The view matrix is set straight ahead looking down the positive Z axis. In most cases, you don't want to change the view matrix at all. It might make sense to manipulate the view matrix for certain scrolling operations, but I prefer to do all the processing on the sprites and leave the view matrix as it is:

```
D3DXMatrixIdentity(&m_ViewMatrix);
m_pD3DDevice->SetTransform(D3DTS_VIEW,  &m_ViewMatrix);
```

This sample application also uses three matrices that define the transformations on the sprite. These are the sorts of variables that it makes sense to wrap into the sprite class:

```
D3DXMatrixIdentity(&m_SpriteTranslation);
D3DXMatrixIdentity(&m_SpriteRotation);
D3DXMatrixIdentity(&m_SpriteScaling);
```

Turn off lighting and culling. They are not needed here:

```
m_pD3DDevice->SetRenderState(D3DRS_LIGHTING, FALSE);
m_pD3DDevice->SetRenderState(D3DRS_CULLMODE, D3DCULL_NONE);
return S_OK;
}
```

TranslateSprite is the first of three functions that make sense as member functions of a sprite class. TranslateSprite sets the position of the origin of the sprite, which is currently set to the middle of the sprite. If you want to translate the upper left of the sprite, either you can change the way the sprite vertices are set or you can change the translate function to include more translations, as shown in Figure 34.5:

```
void CTechniqueApplication::TranslateSprite(float X, float Y, float Z)
{
    D3DXMatrixTranslation(&m_SpriteTranslation, X, Y, Z);
}
```

The RotateSprite function rotates the sprite around the center of the sprite. This function rotates the sprite around the Z axis. If you rotate the sprite around the

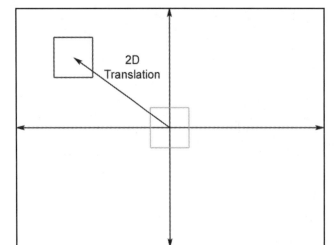

Figure 34.5

Changing the sprite origin.

other axes, the effect is similar to shrinking and expanding the sprite perpendicular to that axis:

```
void CTechniqueApplication::RotateSprite(float Angle)
{
        D3DXMatrixRotationZ(&m_SpriteRotation, Angle);
}
```

The ScaleSprite function scales the width and height of the sprite. As long as the sprite is a unit square, this function sizes the sprite. If the current projection matrix is pixel based, the values passed to this function should be in pixels; otherwise, they should be fractional values:

```
void CTechniqueApplication::ScaleSprite(float X, float Y)
{
        D3DXMatrixScaling(&m_SpriteScaling, X, Y, 1.0f);
}
```

The DrawSprite function concatenates the three matrices and draws the sprite as two textured triangles. This is the simplest case. You can add more transformation matrices if you want more complex transformations, such as orbiting:

```
void CTechniqueApplication::DrawSprite()
{
        m_pD3DDevice->SetTransform(D3DTS_WORLD,
                                &(m_SpriteScaling * m_SpriteRotation *
```

```
                                   m_SpriteTranslation));

        m_pD3DDevice->DrawPrimitive(D3DPT_TRIANGLESTRIP, 0, 2);
}
```

This application is set up to draw sprites in one of two ways. You could call all of the matrix functions followed by a call to DrawSprite, or you could pass all the settings to DrawSpriteEx and do everything in one shot. It might be slightly better to only change the matrices you need to change, but in the end it really doesn't matter. This function is the easier one to use:

```
void CTechniqueApplication::DrawSpriteEx(float X, float Y, float Z,
                                         float Angle, float XScale,
                                         float YScale)
{
        TranslateSprite(X, Y, Z);
        RotateSprite(Angle);
        ScaleSprite(XScale, YScale);

        DrawSprite();
}
```

The Render function renders a couple of sprites to show off the technique:

```
void CTechniqueApplication::Render()
{
```

The first step draws a full-screen background. This is the kind of thing that works very well with a proportional matrix because the background fills the window no matter what the resolution is:

```
        m_pD3DDevice->SetTransform(D3DTS_PROJECTION,
                                   &m_ProportionalProjection);
```

Set the texture to the background texture (loaded in code not shown here in the text). Also, turn off alpha blending. I talk more about performance implications later, but in general you don't want to enable any pixel-based tests that you don't actually need. Alpha blending is not needed for the background because it needs to fill the whole screen. Also, the background image probably has the highest number of pixels, meaning that unneeded tests and blending would be that much more expensive:

```
        m_pD3DDevice->SetTexture(0, m_pBackTexture);
        m_pD3DDevice->SetRenderState(D3DRS_ALPHABLENDENABLE,   FALSE);
```

Draw the background as a full-screen sprite. The projection matrix is set up so that a scale of (1.0, 1.0) fills the window no matter what the resolution is. There is no need to move or rotate the background:

```
DrawSpriteEx(0.0f, 0.0f, 0.0f, 0.0f, 1.0f, 1.0f);
```

The second part of the function draws a couple of sprites over the background. These sprites are sized with pixel dimensions, so set the projection matrix accordingly. This is where the call to `GetLevelDesc` or the dimensions of the `D3DXIMAGE_INFO` structure might be valuable because you'll know the proper pixel size of the texture:

```
m_pD3DDevice->SetTransform(D3DTS_PROJECTION,
 &m_PixelProjection);
```

Set the texture to the sprite texture that was loaded in code not included in this text. The full source code is included on the CD:

```
m_pD3DDevice->SetTexture(0, m_pSpriteTexture);
```

Enable alpha blending so that transparent regions of the sprite appear transparent. This is only one of the many places where Direct3D shines when compared to DirectDraw. Fast alpha blending is difficult in DirectDraw. In Direct3D, transparency is achieved with three lines of code—fewer if the blending modes have already been set! This is one of the reasons I am so opinionated about the differences between Direct3D and DirectDraw. DirectDraw might have an easier learning curve for simple 2D operations, but Direct3D quickly catches up and surpasses DirectDraw when it comes to more advanced functionality. The irony of that statement is that transparency is not even an advanced function in the context of Direct3D:

```
m_pD3DDevice->SetRenderState(D3DRS_ALPHABLENDENABLE, TRUE);
m_pD3DDevice->SetRenderState(D3DRS_SRCBLEND, D3DBLEND_SRCALPHA);
m_pD3DDevice->SetRenderState(D3DRS_DESTBLEND,
                             D3DBLEND_INVSRCALPHA);
```

This next sprite is drawn using the more drawn-out approach. I wanted to show this just for completeness, but you'll probably find `DrawSpriteEx` more useful. This sprite is moved horizontally and rotated:

```
TranslateSprite(200.0f, 0.0f, 0.0f);
RotateSprite((float)GetTickCount() / 1000.0f);
ScaleSprite(100.0f, 200.0f);
DrawSprite();
```

Finally, draw one more sprite using the complete function. Keep in mind that all three sprites used the same vertex buffer:

```
DrawSpriteEx(-320.0f, 0.0f, 0.0f, 0.0f, 100.0f, 50.0f);
}
```

Figure 34.6 shows a screenshot of the application. Notice the frame rate. The application draws a full-screen texture and a couple of transparent sprites at more than 100 frames per second. Notice the pre-present frame rate. This application doesn't tax the graphics card at all.

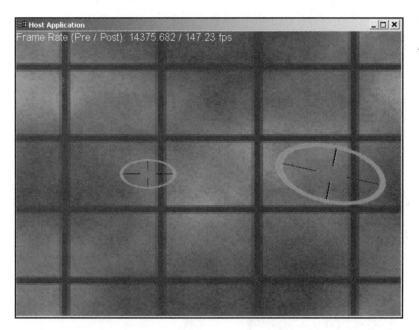

Figure 34.6

Application in action.

Performance Implications

You may have noticed that I have not talked about locking and copying texture buffers at all. Some people who are experienced with DirectDraw approach Direct3D and want to start locking and copying rectangles from texture buffers to the back buffer. This is one of the slowest approaches. In a very few instances, you might need to change the contents of a texture with a function such as CopyRects. The next chapter outlines one such situation, but these are few and far between. You almost never want to update the back buffer with a direct copy. The current graphics hardware is not really optimized for direct buffer copies because this is rarely applicable in the context of 3D. Therefore, cards are set up to quickly manipulate vertices and apply textures to the resulting surfaces. It's possible that if all the brainpower that went into 3D acceleration went into 2D acceleration, the resulting card would be better for straight 2D, but that hasn't happened. Remember the things that the graphics card is good at. It's very good at drawing textured quads, so do things that way and reap all the benefits of the API.

You may have also noticed that I use matrices to transform the positions of the sprites instead of using transformed vertices. Some people believe there is a performance hit there because the card is forced to do the transformations. Also, I am sending the triangles to the card in very small batches of two at a time. This is a very inefficient way to render triangles. Instead, it's better to batch up all your triangles at once and send them to the card in much larger sets. In some ways, the technique I've just outlined breaks many of the optimization rules of earlier chapters, but I do this for a couple of reasons.

One reason is that I find people lock the vertex buffers more often than they really should. Newer people often start with 2D drawing, and as a teacher, I want to introduce them to matrices as soon as possible. Transformed vertices require the application to lock the vertex buffer every time the sprites are moved. That might make sense for simple 2D sprites, but it doesn't translate well to larger 3D meshes.

Another reason is that locking the vertex buffer incurs a performance cost. The vertex buffers are small in most 2D applications, but it turns out that you break about even. For my applications, I've found that the two techniques are roughly equivalent in terms of speed. You can either lock the vertex buffer and incur a cost there, or you can do things my way and incur costs in terms of processing and inefficiency. Figure 34.7 shows one interesting point for consideration. The frame rate numbers in Figure 34.7 are different from what you see in Figure 34.6. The only real difference between the two is that Figure 34.7 was generated by locking the vertex buffer.

As you can see, the final frame rates are pretty much the same, but the pre-present rate is much slower with transformed vertices than with the method described here. Locking the vertex buffer has taken a large toll on the time it actually takes to prepare the frame. If I change the code so that it doesn't lock the buffer, the numbers more closely match the numbers on the left. The cost of Lock has little adverse effect here, but it could be worse in other applications.

Also, I'm just partial to transforming vertices with matrices and hardware rather than doing things on the CPU. I'm willing to live with small potential performance hits to get the benefit of the easy matrix operations. Also, this simple example is not the best for performance testing because the CPU isn't really doing anything at all.

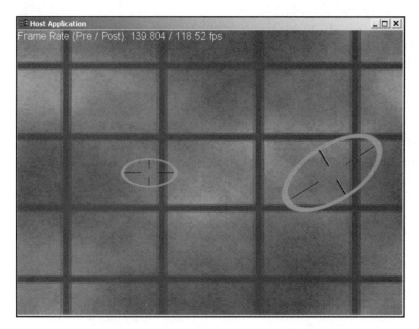

Figure 34.7

Performance differences.

You might find that you don't have spare CPU horsepower once you implement AI, pathfinding, and so on.

One final positive aspect of my method is that it is very easy to add and remove sprites because everything reuses a single vertex buffer. If you place all the sprites in a larger vertex buffer, you might need to resize the buffer or keep more careful track of which vertices to actually render. For instance, if there are three sprites in a buffer and the middle one is no longer needed, you might be forced to work around the defunct vertices. Both of these incur some performance cost. One approach is to meld the two methods. Create a vertex buffer large enough to hold many sprites and then fill these vertices on an as-needed basis based on data held in another array. This way, you can avoid resizing the buffer, and you never need to work around defunct sprite vertices.

So what's the "right" answer? It really depends on what you're doing. I've found that the matrix transformation is much better in some of my programs and transformed vertices are a little bit better in others. For instance, on a geForce2 laptop, using transformed vertices adds 1 to 2 fps in this sample application over the matrix method described here. Given the fact that the results could swing in favor of either method, I chose to stick to what I thought was the easiest method to use. It makes for a good general solution. Other applications might find much more pronounced differences between the two approaches, and differences in hardware will probably add another factor to the equation. If you really want to squeeze every last frame out of your application, I strongly recommend experimenting with both methods and finding the method that gives you the best results. It's also fairly easy to write an abstraction layer that lets you switch back and forth easily.

I have not included the code for transformed vertices to this application. Many applications in previous chapters use transformed vertices. Most recently, Chapter 29 used them to draw the preview rectangle for the shadow map texture. In Chapter 37, I explain how to use them to draw text. It's very easy to change the vertex format and add a few more lines to the `CreateSpriteBuffer` function. Just remember that you cannot use the projection matrix tricks once you work with transformed matrices. You should give all vertex coordinates in pixel-based screen coordinates. Change the "unit square" quad to something much larger.

Also, remember that most 2D applications should never tax the card in terms of geometric processing. They will almost be limited by pixel constraints such as fill rate and alpha blending. If you are blending large full-screen textures, you are processing millions of pixels and tens of vertices. Leaving alpha blending enabled more often than you need to is usually costlier than the small amount of geometric processing. Even extraneous calls to `SetTexture` can greatly affect performance. In that sense, you should worry more about the efficiency of pixel operations and worry less about the vertices.

Large textures equal large amounts of pixels to be manipulated, filtered, and blended. If you load a 2,048x2,048 texture and try to use it as a sprite, the performance will be very slow. This is not a limitation of the API; it is the reality of bus speeds and memory bandwidth. Keep careful track of the size of the sprites you are using because it affects performance. Also, remember that the amount of memory used by the texture has nothing to do with the file size. A 10KB JPEG might take up a lot of texture memory when it's loaded as a 32-bit uncompressed texture. The larger the texture, the more memory is filled. In addition to filling the memory, a large texture incurs performance costs because it means that more bytes are moving through the bus and through the pipeline.

Experiment with the vertex format, but don't forget about the pixel load. Make sure you watch where you are alpha blending and use alpha testing if it makes sense. Also, disable added tests such as the depth test or the stencil test if you know you're not going to need them.

Possible Extensions

Now that you are using a 3D API, you are free to use all the features the 3D API gives you. As you've seen, alpha blending is a lot easier in Direct3D, but you can also do other things.

One point to remember is that you are no longer limited to moving simple rectangles. Alpha channels help you make arbitrary shapes in a texture, but you can also make arbitrary shapes with vertices. In some of the earlier chapters, I showed you how to create circles and other shapes with collections of triangles. You can still do this in a 2D world. In fact, you might find that you can implement very simple sprites as shapes with no texture at all.

You might also find that a rectangle made with more than two triangles might yield better effects. For instance, you could have a spaceship sprite textured onto a rectangle made with a triangle list. If the spaceship is shot, you could have all of the triangles fly off in different directions and fade away. You can create explosion effects without actually making an explosion texture. Throw in some point lists for particles, and you can create explosion geometry that works well for any spaceship sprite texture.

Using pixel shaders, you have some real possibilities for cool lighting effects. One of the trends I've seen lately is the move from 2D sprites to real 3D models in RTS games. The 3D models are great for lighting effects, but they never look as good as a nice 2D sprite. I would really like to see a game mix 2D sprites with normal maps and pixel shaders. This would allow designers to create nice artwork and get the benefits of lighting effects on a per-pixel basis. They could create the sprite texture and a matching normal map. As a light moves past the sprite, a pixel shader could compute per-pixel lighting.

There are many possibilities available within the context of Direct3D. I'm just scratching the surface here, but the point is that you could apply many of the 3D effects discussed in earlier chapters to 2D games. You might have to think carefully about the exact implementation details, but the potential is huge.

In Conclusion...

In this chapter, I tried desperately to make the point that DirectDraw users should move to Direct3D. In a very few cases DirectDraw still makes sense for legacy support, but those cases are disappearing every day. Nowhere is it written in stone that 2D equals "rectangular blit." With current hardware, 2D really means "2D textured quad." This chapter outlined one approach for 2D rendering using 3D concepts such as matrices and presented some possible alternatives that may or may not increase performance.

Many of my numbers and opinions are based on the performance of my particular applications and my hardware. It is possible you may find that my way works poorly on older hardware or that your application fares better with a different approach. A 2D vertex shader approach would preclude the use of transformed vertices. A static 2D GUI would not benefit at all from the matrix approach. Alter the method to fit your specific needs. Here are some things to review:

- Don't let the "3D" in Direct3D scare you. The change to DirectX Graphics was a move towards a consolidated API. The new API doesn't include a Blit function, but this does not preclude its use for 2D.

- Direct3D incorporates features such as alpha blending that should make it extremely attractive to 2D programmers.

- Good Direct3D hardware is becoming inexpensive. If at all possible, don't let the limitations of an old card stop you from learning new skills.

- 2D is just a subset of 3D. Use an orthogonal projection matrix to eliminate the extra D. You do not need it with transformed vertices because their positions should be in pixel coordinates.

- You can create different projection matrices for different drawing modes. You can set the origin in the middle of the screen or any arbitrary point. You can also set up the matrix to express vertex positions in either pixel coordinates or fractions of the screen size.

- Sprites are 2D quads with textures. Textures for 2D sprites are exactly the same as other textures. However, you want to pay careful attention to the size of the texture if you want the sprite to match the texture size. You can get the size of the texture by calling GetLevelDesc, and you can get the size of the original image if you load the texture with D3DXCreateTextureFromFileEx and check the D3DXIMAGE_INFO structure.

- I create the sprite quad as a single reusable triangle strip of two triangles. I create my quad as a square with one-unit length sides so I can use a scaling matrix to size the sprite dynamically. I then reuse this vertex buffer for all sprites. If you choose to use transformed vertices, you might want to place the vertices for all the sprites in the same vertex buffer. This will allow you to draw several sprites in one call to DrawPrimitive.

- There are many potential areas for performance optimization. If you'd like, see how the numbers work out for both transformed vertices and my method. Apply what you've learned to your own application, and see what works best.

- Remember that performance depend heavily on the textures you use. Pay careful attention to the sizes of the textures.

- Disable any pixel-based tests that are not being used. The performance impact of blending is not too high, but it does make a difference.

- Look for ways to use the previous 3D techniques to augment 2D games. In many instances, pixel shader and even vertex shader techniques could create interesting effects.

CHAPTER 35

DirectShow:
Using Video
as a Texture

The ability to use a video as a texture is very useful in some instances. You might want to build a cut-scene player into your 3D engine and keep it consistent with the 3D paradigm. You might also want to place video onto 3D objects in a scene. Your character can walk past a security monitor and view videos to find clues about a killer. Or you may just want to use video files as a way to store animated textures that are used to texture a scene. A video file provides a convenient and compact way to store many frames of an animation for anything from a simple video to an animated normal map.

It's up to you to decide how to best apply this fairly powerful medium. In many of these later chapters, the point is less to illustrate a specific effect and more to provide a platform for several effects. That "platform" is based on the following concepts:

- DirectShow and how it works.
- Implementing a texture video filter.
- Applying video textures to 3D objects.
- More potential applications of the technique.

There are a couple of different ways to read an AVI file and extract video information. However, DirectX provides an API that handles AVI files and other forms of streaming media. This technique uses DirectShow to read and manipulate information from AVI files.

DirectShow in a Nutshell

A complete explanation of DirectShow would require a whole other book. The following explanation provides enough details to explain how you can use video files as textures in a 3D or 2D application. I only cover AVI files, but the same concepts apply to data coming from MPEG files, and even DVDs and video capture devices.

The purpose of the DirectShow API is to provide a means for high-quality playback and manipulation of streaming media. Streaming media takes many forms. It can be a streaming audio file, a streaming video feed, data streaming from a video capture device, or data coming from a whole host of different sources. Regardless of the media type, most instances of streaming media must be manipulated before they are finally output to the user. Applications must be able to extract data from several different file formats, decompress the data, reformat the data, and sometimes even decrypt the data. The architecture of DirectShow provides the means to incorporate all of these manipulations as *filters* in a *filter graph*. Filters are individual software components that handle one or more of the manipulations mentioned here. Filter graphs are collections of filters that are interconnected to provide a path from the media source format to the final output. Figure 35.1 shows a sample filter graph that was built to read and output the contents of an AVI file. This filter graph was automatically constructed by Microsoft's GraphEdit tool, which can be found in the SDK.

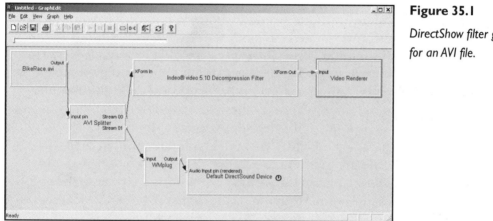

Figure 35.1

DirectShow filter graph for an AVI file.

In the figure, the source filter on the far left is used to open the file and read data. The file is sent to an AVI splitter filter, which separates the video stream from the audio stream. At this point, the video stream is compressed with the Indeo compressor, so the stream is sent to an Indeo decompression filter for decompression. The decompressor decompresses the file, and the final image is converted to a 24-bit RGB bitmap. That bitmap is sent to a video output filter for display. On the audio side, the audio stream is sent to an audio filter and sent to the DirectSound device for final output. Data is passed through input and output *pins*. The pins are connection points that either accept data in a given format or output data in a given format. Pins can only be connected if their formats match.

All about AVI

The AVI file format was Microsoft's first major video storage format. AVI stands for Audio Video Interleaved. AVI files store both audio and video data in an interleaved format, which helps with synchronization. One little-known (and even less frequently used) fact is that AVI files can store all sorts of interleaved data. It is possible to write extra audio streams, text data, or even raw binary data to an AVI file. The reason this feature is not used is that no AVI players support reading that data, but you could write your own player to read and interpret those other data streams.

This is the basic setup for a typical AVI filter graph, but you can do much more. Sometimes, the output player needs a different format for display. This requires another filter in the graph to handle format conversion. You can also incorporate filters that do image processing or other special effects operations on the source data. In this chapter, I explain how to write an output filter that creates a texture with the video data. That texture can then be applied however you want.

Building filter graphs might appear to be a difficult task. It looks like you need to know what sorts of transforms you need to apply to the data. This is much easier than it appears thanks to another DirectShow interface called a *graph builder*. The graph builder interface can create filter graphs automatically for a given media file. It does this by looking at the output format of the source filter and the input requirements of the output filter. Whenever these formats don't match up, the graph builder tries to incorporate filters that provide the correct data transformations. For example, in Figure 35.1, the graph builder used the Indeo decompressor to reconcile the differences between the Indeo-compressed input stream and the 24-bit RGB requirements of the output device. However, the graph builder is currently incapable of performing magic. If you request a format that is not supported by any installed DirectShow filters, the graph builder will be incapable of building the filter graph. You might need to build additional data transforms into your filter or provide additional data transform filters. For example, the decompressor supplies 24-bit RGB images, but you really want 32-bit textures. Instead of asking for 32-bit images, the texture filter does a very small amount of data conversion.

So the filters are components that aid in the transformation from bits in a source stream to some final output format. A filter graph is an arrangement of filters that serves as a pipeline for that transformation, and a graph builder is an interface that aids in the construction of filter graphs. This is by no means a complete explanation of DirectShow, but it provides enough of a foundation to go further.

I Want My MP3

I would like to concentrate on the video aspects of DirectShow, but it is probably worthwhile to talk a little bit about the audio aspects of DirectShow as well. Notice that most of the preceding discussion talked about "streaming media" as opposed to "streaming video." This is because nearly all the DirectShow concepts in this chapter apply equally well to audio. I'm not going to spend any real time talking about audio but you should keep audio in mind as I walk through the source code. You can use the graph builder interface to "render" audio files as well as video files. Figure 35.2 shows a screenshot of the filter graph needed to render an MP3 file. Notice the similarities between this filter graph and the audio portion of the AVI filter graph.

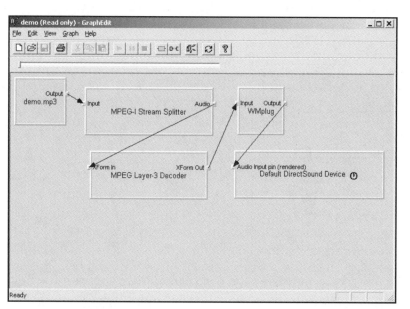

Figure 35.2

Filter graph for an MP3 file.

As I walk through the video code, I point out the concepts and features that are applicable to audio rendering.

The Operation of the Video-to-Texture Filter

The source code for this chapter is based heavily on the Texture 3D sample in the SDK. I changed some things around to clarify, enhance performance, and protect the innocent.

The purpose of this technique is to provide a means to turn video data from an AVI file into a texture that you can use in 3D scenes. To do this, you need to create an output filter for the video data. An output filter isn't really any different from any other filter except that it has no output pin. The graph ends and the graph builder assumes the data will be used somehow. The GraphEdit tool uses a video window as the default output, but it could just as easily write the data to another file, to a network device, or in this case, to the surface of a texture.

The easiest way to deal with AVI data is to let some upstream filter handle all of the decompression and other data transformations. The final output of most of these filters is a 24-bit RGB bitmap, so you need to build a filter that accepts that format as input. This allows the graph builder to connect the texture filter to the upstream filters. Figure 35.3 shows a conceptual diagram of the texture filter.

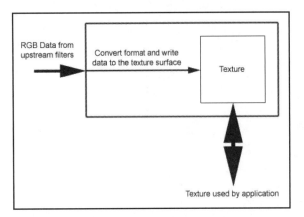

Figure 35.3

The texture filter.

Once that is taken care of, you can construct the complete filter graph with the help of the graph builder. The graph builder includes a mechanism with which the application can supply two pins and the graph builder finds the right sequence of intermediate filters. In the case of an AVI file, the resulting filter graph will probably look something like Figure 35.4.

This looks a lot like the filter shown in Figure 35.1, only this time the final filter is the texture filter. Also, I added the audio path in this sample so that you can see the complete AVI solution. If you are using an AVI file for video only, the audio path is not necessary.

Once the graph builder builds the complete graph, the application can tell the filter graph to begin reading data from the source file and pumping it through the filter graph pipeline. When the filter graph is given the go ahead, it begins pumping data from the source file through the filters to the texture filter. The filter graph handles all the timing and synchronization, pumping the data through at a pace that matches the specified frame rate of the video file.

After the video file travels through the intermediate filters, the filter passes the RGB data to the texture filter. The texture filter locks the surface of the texture and writes the video frame to that surface. The texture now contains the video frame.

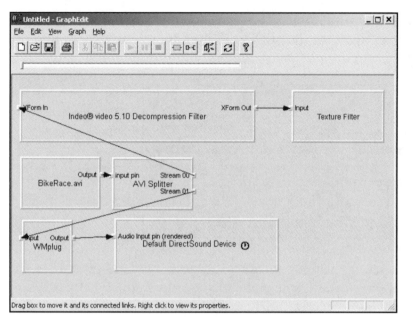

Figure 35.4

The AVI-file-to-texture filter graph.

You can apply the texture to geometry just as you do any other texture. The texture holds the video data until the filter graph passes a new frame to the texture filter. When that happens, the process is repeated and the texture is updated.

This implementation adds one more feature. After each frame is sent to the texture, the texture filter checks to see whether the video has ended. If so, the texture filter seeks back to the beginning of the file and loops the video.

Preparing to Build the Texture Class

The DirectShow SDK includes the source code for several DirectShow base classes. The source code for these base classes has not been compiled and can be found in the [SDK_PATH]\samples\Multimedia\DirectShow\BaseClasses directory. These base classes are useful for developing DirectShow filters, but you must compile the source code before you can use the classes.

To compile the classes using Microsoft Visual C++, load the workspace for the base classes and press F7 to compile the code. The code should compile without any problems, and the base classes should be ready to use by your own project. You do not need to explicitly deal with these files yourself. Instead, the video texture will be based on a class found in the base class directory. The compiler will find the correct files, provided you tell it where to look.

Before you can compile your own project, you must add the base class directory to your library and include directories. Figure 35.5 shows screenshots of my path options dialog.

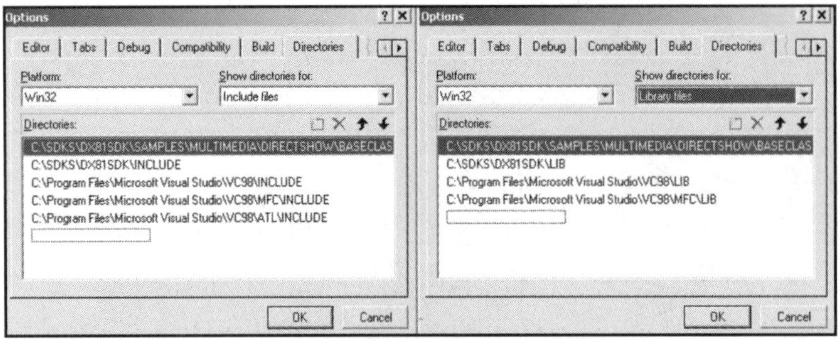

Figure 35.5

Setting the paths for the DirectShow base classes.

Place these directories before the other include paths. It is very important that they are first in the order of directories. Some of the include files in the other paths interfere with the DirectShow include files. Placing the base classes directory first forces the compiler to use the base class files instead of the other files. The order is necessary for code that uses these base classes, but it does not interfere with other code. After these paths are set, you're ready to build the texture filter class.

The Texture Filter Class

I now outline the implementation of the texture filter class. I kept object-oriented design to a minimum, but this is a situation where it makes a lot of sense to place the filter in its own class. A self-contained texture class allows you to wrap all the DirectShow functionality into one class and compartmentalize the implementation details.

First, take a look at the header file for the class. It appears on the CD as DirectXVideoTexture.h. This header file defines the interface and member variables of the texture filter.

The first lines include the standard DirectX 8.0 include files. These are needed for the definition of the texture interface, the device interface, and a couple of D3D structures:

```
#include <d3d8.h>
#include <d3dx8.h>
```

Include two more header files. The first one is for general COM support. The other defines some of the streaming media interfaces:

```
#include <atlbase.h>
#include <streams.h>
```

DirectShow filters all have a unique ID that distinguishes them from other filters. You can generate a unique ID with ID-generating tools included with Developer's Studio:

```
struct __declspec(uuid("{71771540-2017-11cf-ae26-0020afd79769}"))
                                        CLSID_VideoTexture;
```

The CDirectXVideoTexture is based on CBaseVideoRenderer, which is one of the base classes compiled in the previous section. CBaseVideoRenderer handles all the basic functions of a video output renderer. The texture filter class inherits this functionality but writes the video to a texture rather than output the data in other ways:

```
class CDirectXVideoTexture : public CBaseVideoRenderer
{
public:
        CDirectXVideoTexture();
        virtual ~CDirectXVideoTexture();
```

Applications using this class can create a video texture with a call to CreateFromAVIFile. The inputs of this function are a pointer to the device and a file name. This function loads the specified file and begins updating the texture. This class needs access to the device to create a texture object:

```
        HRESULT CreateFromAVIFile(LPDIRECT3DDEVICE8 pDevice,
                                TCHAR *pFileName);
```

The application can call the CheckForLoop function to check whether the filter graph has reached the end of the video file. If so, the application may choose to play the file again:

```
        void CheckForLoop();
```

These functions are called by the filter graph when the graph is being created or when the frames are ready to render. I fully explain them later:

```
        HRESULT CheckMediaType(const CMediaType *pmt);
        HRESULT SetMediaType(const CMediaType *pmt);
        HRESULT DoRenderSample(IMediaSample *pMediaSample);
```

These member variables keep track of the properties of the texture and the video. These properties are used when the video is copied to the texture. The application can also use these properties to set the proper texture coordinates for the vertices. If the texture is larger than the video, you might want to make sure that the texture coordinates are set accordingly. Many times you might not want to wrap the texture because that will reveal blank spaces:

```
long      m_VideoWidth;
long      m_VideoHeight;
long      m_TextureWidth;
long      m_TextureHeight;
long      m_VideoPitch;
D3DFORMAT m_VideoFormat;
```

You use these interfaces to build and control the DirectShow filter graph. These interfaces are explained fully in the implementation file:

```
CComPtr<IGraphBuilder>      m_pGraphBuilder;
CComPtr<IMediaControl>      m_pMediaControl;
CComPtr<IMediaEvent>        m_pMediaEvent;
CComPtr<IMediaPosition>     m_pMediaPosition;
```

The texture variable holds the actual texture that is updated with the video. The device object creates the texture and may be useful for other operations:

```
LPDIRECT3DTEXTURE8 m_pTexture;
LPDIRECT3DDEVICE8  m_pDevice;
};
```

The following comes from DirectXTexture.cpp. The first function is the constructor. It sets all of the interface pointers to NULL. More interestingly, the constructor calls the constructor for the base class and passes the unique ID and a name for the filter. This handles the actual creation of the filter, but the texture is not created until the application calls CreateFromAVIFile:

```
CDirectXVideoTexture::CDirectXVideoTexture() :
                CBaseVideoRenderer(__uuidof(CLSID_VideoTexture),
            NAME("Video Texture"), NULL, NULL)
{
    m_pMediaControl  = NULL;
    m_pMediaPosition = NULL;
    m_pMediaEvent    = NULL;
```

```
            m_pGraphBuilder  = NULL;
            m_pTexture       = NULL;
}
```

This function creates the texture and the filter graph. It also starts the filter graph and begins reading from the video file:

```
HRESULT CDirectXVideoTexture::CreateFromAVIFile(
                    LPDIRECT3DDEVICE8 pDevice, TCHAR *pFileName)
{
```

Keep track of the device. It might come in handy later. This could lead to some problems if the device is somehow destroyed and re-created. Keep this in mind if you need to re-create the device:

```
        m_pDevice = pDevice;
```

The DirectShow interfaces require double-byte strings. Convert the file name to a wide character so you can pass it to the source filter:

```
        WCHAR wFileName[MAX_PATH];
        MultiByteToWideChar(CP_ACP, 0, pFileName, -1,
         wFileName, MAX_PATH);
```

These three objects connect the filters. They are explained in the setup sequence later:

```
        CComPtr<IPin>          pPinIn;
        CComPtr<IBaseFilter>   pSourceFilter;
        CComPtr<IPin>          pPinOut;
```

Add a reference to this object. You need this because the filter graph releases this object when the graph is destroyed. If you don't add an extra reference count, this object is destroyed in the middle of its own destructor. That's bad:

```
        AddRef();
```

CoInitialize initializes the COM subsystem and allows the use of COM interfaces. You need this before building the filter graph:

```
        CoInitialize(NULL) ;
```

The first step is to create the graph builder object. The graph builder does most of the hard work to build the filter graph. In this case, the graph builder and the filter graph are essentially the same object. The rest of the steps are implemented as a cascading series of nested `if` statements. I took out most of the indentations here in the text, but the source code on the CD has an easier-to-follow layout:

```
if (SUCCEEDED(CoCreateInstance(CLSID_FilterGraph, NULL,
                    CLSCTX_INPROC_SERVER, IID_IFilterGraph,
                    (void **)&m_pGraphBuilder)))
{
```

Add this filter to the filter graph. This adds the filter to the collection of available filters so that it can be connected to the rest of the filter graph:

```
if (SUCCEEDED(m_pGraphBuilder->AddFilter(this,
                                L"TEXTURERENDERER")))
{
```

Add a source filter for the AVI file. The graph builder finds the correct source filter for the AVI file, and this source filter feeds the rest of the filter graph:

```
if (SUCCEEDED(m_pGraphBuilder->AddSourceFilter (
              wFileName, L"SOURCE", &pSourceFilter)))
{
```

Find the input pin of this filter. In this case, the `FindPin` function is part of this filter and is implemented by the base class. So this call to `FindPin` is calling the `FindPin` function of this object:

```
if (SUCCEEDED(FindPin(L"In", &pPinIn)))
{
```

Use `FindPin` to find the output pin of the source filter:

```
if (SUCCEEDED(pSourceFilter->FindPin(L"Output", &pPinOut)))
{
```

The input pin of this class is very likely not of the same format as the output pin of the source filter. This is where the graph builder proves valuable. Pass other pins to the graph builder's `Connect` function, and the graph builder finds the set of filters that translates from one format to the other. It also connects those filters in a contiguous series of filters that, in this case, end with the texture filter. Assuming this function is successful, the filter graph is now ready to render video:

```
if (SUCCEEDED(m_pGraphBuilder->Connect(pPinOut, pPinIn)))
{
```

Once the filter graph is created, you can retrieve a set of interfaces that is used to control the filter graph. The media control interface controls the filter graph. You can use it to start the filter graph, stop the graph, and set the playback speed. The media event interface checks whether the video has ended. If it has, the media position interface backtracks to the beginning of the file:

```
m_pGraphBuilder.QueryInterface(&m_pMediaControl);
m_pGraphBuilder.QueryInterface(&m_pMediaEvent);
m_pGraphBuilder.QueryInterface(&m_pMediaPosition);
```

The filter graph is now ready to supply video data. If you need only video, you can ignore the following code. The next several lines set up the audio portion of the filter graph and give some clues into audio filter graphs.

If there is an audio stream, the graph builder adds an AVI splitter to the filter graph, but the audio path is not created when the filters are connected. If you want to enable audio, you must complete the audio portion of the filter graph:

```
CComPtr<IBaseFilter>    pSplitterFilter;
CComPtr<IPin>           pAudioPin;
```

Ask the filter graph for a pointer to the splitter filter if one exists. If there is no audio stream, the following lines of code fail and the filter graph processes the video stream only:

```
if (SUCCEEDED(m_pGraphBuilder->FindFilterByName(
            L"AVI Splitter", &pSplitterFilter)))
{
```

If there is a splitter filter, get the first audio pin. There are functions for finding pins of a given format and media type, but I hardcoded the name of the filter based on the results of GraphEdit as shown in Figure 35.1. Different file types may require different parameters:

```
if (SUCCEEDED(pSplitterFilter->FindPin(L"Stream 01",
                                        &pAudioPin)))
```

If the pin is retrieved, use the Render method of the graph builder to build a path to a default output filter. The graph builder provides an easy way to build a default path with minimal hassle. This is useful for other DirectShow media types. For instance, you can load an MP3 file by creating a source file as shown earlier. Then, retrieve the output pin and let the graph builder build the filter graph to a sound output filter:

```
m_pGraphBuilder->Render(pAudioPin);
}
```

Use the media control interface to begin reading the video file. This is called regardless of whether the audio pathway was successfully built. At this point, the filter graph is ready to begin supplying data:

```
                if (SUCCEEDED(m_pMediaControl->Run()))
                        return S_OK;
        }
        }
        }
        }
        }
        }

        return E_FAIL;
}
```

It looks like the process is simple, but there is a little more going on behind the scenes. When the graph builder attempts to build the filter graph, it must verify the data formats of the pins. It does this with calls to CheckMediaType. The filter must decide whether it can accept a given format:

```
HRESULT CDirectXVideoTexture::CheckMediaType(const CMediaType
                                                    *pMediaType)

{
```

If the data format isn't video, this filter isn't interested:

```
        if(*pMediaType->FormatType() != FORMAT_VideoInfo)
                return E_INVALIDARG;
```

This filter only accepts video data in 24-bit RGB format. If the graph builder queries this format, the function returns a success code. All other formats result in failure and the graph builder must try a different format. For instance, if the video is compressed, the graph builder asks this filter whether it can handle the compressed data. This filter returns a failure code, and the graph builder adds a decompressor and tries again with the uncompressed format:

```
        if(IsEqualGUID(*pMediaType->Type(),    MEDIATYPE_Video)  &&
           IsEqualGUID(*pMediaType->Subtype(), MEDIASUBTYPE_RGB24))
                return S_OK;

    return E_FAIL;
}
```

SetMediaType is called when the graph builder has built the complete graph. It tells the filter that the graph is done and informs the graph of the final data format. In this case, only 24-bit formats are used, so I don't even bother checking the format. If for some reason you chose to support additional formats (such as 16-bit), you might need to check the media type to see what the graph builder chose:

```
HRESULT CDirectXVideoTexture::SetMediaType(const CMediaType
                                              *pMediaType)
{
```

Extract the properties of the video from the properties of the media type. Depending on the compression, the height could be a negative number. Get the absolute value:

```
    VIDEOINFO *pVideoFormat = (VIDEOINFO *)pMediaType->Format();
    m_VideoWidth  = pVideoFormat->bmiHeader.biWidth;
    m_VideoHeight = abs(pVideoFormat->bmiHeader.biHeight);
```

The following equation sets the pitch of the video frame based on the width and the fact that the format is 24-bit RGB data:

```
    m_VideoPitch = (m_VideoWidth * 3 + 3) & ~(3);
```

Use the properties of the video to create a texture with one mip map level:

```
    if(FAILED(D3DXCreateTexture(m_pDevice, m_VideoWidth,
                m_VideoHeight, 1, 0, D3DFMT_A8R8G8B8, D3DPOOL_MANAGED,
                &m_pTexture)))
        return E_FAIL;
```

D3DXCreateTexture can actually change many of the properties of the texture. Use GetLevelDesc to find the actual properties of the texture. If the D3DX changes the format, return a failure because the update code will not process the data correctly:

```
    D3DSURFACE_DESC SurfaceDescription;
    m_pTexture->GetLevelDesc(0, &SurfaceDescription);
    if (SurfaceDescription.Format != D3DFMT_A8R8G8B8)
        return VFW_E_TYPE_NOT_ACCEPTED;

    m_TextureWidth  = SurfaceDescription.Width;
    m_TextureHeight = SurfaceDescription.Height;

    return S_OK;
}
```

SetMediaType and CheckMediaType are called during the course of the CreateFromAVIFile function. All of these functions are used in the setup of the filter graph. Once the filter graph is built, the CreateFromAVIFile function starts reading the file. When a frame of video is extracted from the file, it is sent through the filter graph until it finally ends up in the filter. The filter graph passes the data to this filter with a call to DoRenderSample. It is then used to update the texture:

```
HRESULT CDirectXVideoTexture::DoRenderSample(IMediaSample * pSample)
{
        BYTE  *pVideoBuffer;
        BYTE  *pTextureBuffer;
        long  TexturePitch;
```

Get a pointer to the video data. The format of this data is the same as the format passed to SetMediaType:

```
        pSample->GetPointer(&pVideoBuffer);
```

Lock the complete texture so that it can be updated:

```
        D3DLOCKED_RECT LockedRect;
        if (FAILED(m_pTexture->LockRect(0, &LockedRect, 0, 0)))
                return E_FAIL;
```

Retrieve the texture buffer from the D3DLOCKED_RECT structure. Also, retrieve the pitch of the texture. This is used to correctly walk through the texture buffer:

```
        pTextureBuffer = static_cast<byte *>(LockedRect.pBits);
        TexturePitch = LockedRect.Pitch;
```

This loop walks through both the texture buffer and the video buffer and copies pixel values from one to the other. This isn't as efficient as a bulk copy, but the conversion from 24- to 32-bit forces you to do this pixel by pixel:

```
        for(long y = 0; y < m_VideoHeight; y++)
        {
                BYTE *pVideoRowStart = pVideoBuffer;
                BYTE *pTextureRowStart = pTextureBuffer;
```

Walk through the buffers row by row. This is a good way to walk through the buffers because it allows you to account for pitch:

```
                for (int x = 0; x < m_VideoWidth; x++)
                {
```

Copy the RGB values and set the alpha value to full opacity. If you wanted, you could manipulate color values here:

```
pTextureBuffer[0] = pVideoBuffer[0];
pTextureBuffer[1] = pVideoBuffer[1];
pTextureBuffer[2] = pVideoBuffer[2];
pTextureBuffer[3] = 0xff;
```

The texture uses four bytes for every pixel. The video frame uses three. Walk through the buffers accordingly:

```
pTextureBuffer += 4;
pVideoBuffer   += 3;
      }
```

At the end of each row, account for the pitch of both the texture and the video before moving to the next row:

```
pVideoBuffer   = pVideoRowStart   + m_VideoPitch;
pTextureBuffer = pTextureRowStart + TexturePitch;
   }
```

At the end of the loop, the texture has been fully updated. Unlock the texture and exit. You can now use the texture to texture objects in the scene:

```
if (FAILED(m_pTexture->UnlockRect(0)))
        return E_FAIL;

    return S_OK;
}
```

The application can call CheckForLoop to see whether the video is complete. In the current implementation, the function automatically sets the position back to the beginning if the video has reached the end:

```
void CDirectXVideoTexture::CheckForLoop()
{
      long lEventCode;
      long lParam1;
      long lParam2;
```

Use the media event interface to check for a completion event. If there has been a completion event, use the media position interface to "rewind" the file:

```
m_pMediaEvent->GetEvent(&lEventCode, &lParam1, &lParam2, 0);
if (EC_COMPLETE == lEventCode)
```

```
        m_pMediaPosition->put_CurrentPosition(0);
}
```

Currently, the filter graph runs until this object is destroyed. You might want to expand this class to include more control options:

```
CDirectXVideoTexture::~CDirectXVideoTexture()
{
```

Use the media control interface to stop the filter graph:

```
    if (m_pMediaControl)
            m_pMediaControl->Stop();
```

Release the graph builder. The graph builder releases all of the filters that are currently in the filter graph. This is why I added the call to `AddRef` earlier. If you don't, this object is destroyed in the middle of this function call. Destroying an object in the middle of its own function is a very bad idea:

```
    if (m_pGraphBuilder)
            m_pGraphBuilder.Release();
```

Destroy the actual texture object:

```
    if (m_pTexture)
    {
            m_pTexture->Release();
            m_pTexture = NULL;
    }
}
```

This video texture class wraps all the DirectShow functionality into a single object and shields the implementation details from the application. This greatly simplifies the application.

The Video Texture Application

The application for this chapter extends the sprite application from the previous chapter. The only thing that changes is the texture that is applied to the sprites. In this case, the video texture is used. The application code is very simple because most of the work was done in the video texture class, so all we have to do here is put it together.

The `PostInitialize` function creates a video texture instead of the standard texture:

```
BOOL CTechniqueApplication::PostInitialize()
{
        if (FAILED(EasyCreateWindowed(m_hWnd, D3DDEVTYPE_HAL,
                          D3DCREATE_HARDWARE_VERTEXPROCESSING)))
                return FALSE;

        SetupDevice();
```

Call `CreateFromAVIFile` to create the texture. The rest of the initialize code is the same as that in the last chapter:

```
        if (FAILED(m_VideoTexture.CreateFromAVIFile(m_pD3DDevice,
                                                "test.avi")))
                return FALSE;

        if (FAILED(CreateSpriteBuffer()))
                return FALSE;

        return TRUE;
}
```

The `Render` function uses the texture to paint a sprite. Other than that, this is just a pared-down version of the `Render` function from the previous chapter:

```
void CTechniqueApplication::Render()
{
        m_pD3DDevice->SetTransform(D3DTS_PROJECTION,
         &m_PercentProjection);
```

The actual texture variable is a public member of the video texture class. You can directly access it to set the current texture. A C++ guru might want to augment the video texture class so that you can transparently use it as a texture:

```
        m_pD3DDevice->SetTexture(0, m_VideoTexture.m_pTexture);
```

Check to see whether the video has reached the end. If it has, the `CheckForLoop` function restarts it:

```
        m_VideoTexture.CheckForLoop();

        DrawSpriteEx(0.0f, 0.0f, 0.0f, 0.0f, 1.0f, 1.0f);
}
```

Figure 35.6 shows the application in action. A still picture doesn't really show anything, but the frame rate might be interesting.

Frame Rate (Pre / Post): 15563.239 / 134.64 fps

Figure 35.6

The video application.

The frame rate shows that this scene is rendering much faster than the frame rate of the video. This reveals the fact there is plenty of leftover horsepower for image manipulation. The next chapter shows how you can use pixel shaders to process pixel data in videos or 3D scenes.

In Conclusion...

I think video files may be an overlooked media type for 3D engines. 3D graphics are becoming extremely lifelike, but there are still times you might want to show video in a 3D scene. For some people, 3D can be a tool for manipulating video as a goal unto itself. You can imagine the advantage of using blending techniques and mesh warping techniques to create a hardware-accelerated morphing effect. Morphing seems to be no longer en vogue, but it might be interesting.

My purpose here is to explain the basics of how to get video into the 3D paradigm. What you do now is up to you. Everything you've learned in this book could be applied to video, or you could use video to feed the technique. In any case, I just open doors. It's up to you to walk through them. Before you walk away, remember these main points:

- DirectShow is a streaming media API. Many of the steps used to set up the video technique are also used to read other types of media.
- DirectShow handles streaming media manipulation with filters and filter graphs. The filters handle data transformation services, and filter graphs are constructed to bind these services together.
- The graph builder interface provides many services for building filter graphs.
- The filter graph passes transformed data to the final output filter. In this case, the texture filter is the final filter.
- The texture filter can lock a texture and copy the image data to the texture.
- Once the video data is copied, you use the texture just as you do any other texture.

CHAPTER 36

Image Processing with Pixel Shaders

C hapter 33 introduced motion blur as a "post-processing" technique. In this chapter, I describe several image-processing techniques that you can also do as a final rendering step. Image processing encompasses many techniques, but I concentrate on the following:

- The motivation for image processing as a post-processing technique.
- The implementation for a series of simple color manipulations with pixel shaders.
- Applying color curve textures as color manipulators.
- The theory behind convolution filters.
- The implementation of an edge-finding filter using multiple texture stages.
- Performance considerations.

It doesn't make sense to get too far into implementation details without first explaining why you would want to do this.

The Advantage of Post Processing

There are a couple of different reasons to take a look at image processing. The first reason is that games and other forms of interactive media are becoming more cinematographic. The mood and tone of a scene is becoming just as important as the number of polygons rendered. It's beginning to make sense to implement filtering and processing techniques for the same reasons that a video-editing application supplies video filters. Adjusting the brightness and contrast of a scene can create a dark and foreboding atmosphere. Grayscaling or sepia-toning a scene can give an antiqued feel.

Arguably, you can implement many of these effects when the scene is rendered. A film noir game can use all black-and-white textures. You can make changes to brightness with changes to lighting. The advantage of a post-processing technique is that you can render your scene normally and make changes only in the final pass. Imagine a game with a time-traveling hero. When the hero is in the present, you render the scene as normal. When the hero goes back in time, you render the scene in black and white to serve as a visual cue to the player. Rather than use two sets of textures (color and black-and-white), render the scene normally in both cases, but use a black-and-white post-processing filter when rendering the past. Some people may find these techniques extremely useful. Others may find them completely useless. As hardware capabilities and player expectations increase, I'm betting these techniques will become more interesting and necessary.

Another reason for exploring these techniques is the usefulness of image processing itself. Normally, image-processing algorithms are implemented either on the CPU or on specialized processing hardware. The capabilities of today's consumer-grade graphics hardware open up many possibilities. For some, it's interesting to figure out just how to use these new capabilities.

Full-Screen Color Manipulations with Pixel Shaders

For the next several pages, I describe a series of pixel shaders that you can use to manipulate the colors of a scene to alter the tone or the look and feel. These shaders are some of the easier image-processing techniques in that they work on each pixel individually. Near the end of this chapter, I describe image-processing techniques that process blocks of pixels for more advanced effects.

Throughout this chapter, I used the video application (Chapter 35) as a starting point because video allows me to show complex scenes without drawing and transforming models in an actual 3D scene. Remember that you can easily apply the same techniques to 3D scenes using the methodology introduced in Chapter 33. Once the scene is rendered to a texture, you can apply that texture to a full-screen quad and render it out to the screen. These pixel shaders would be applied during that final pass. Therefore, you could remove the transparency manipulations from Chapter 33, introduce these pixel shaders, and use these techniques as post-processing filters on your 3D scene.

The following is a series of descriptions of techniques followed by the pixel shader and a few screenshots. In most cases, I do not show the actual application code because it is essentially the same as the code from either Chapter 33 or Chapter 35 with the addition of the pixel shader.

A Black-and-White Filter

The ability to change an entire scene to black and white can be useful for establishing that a game or a single scene is happening in the past. If you are telling a story with cut scenes, a black-and-white scene can establish the difference between flashback scenes and events in the present. It can also establish a particular genre for the game. In a detective game, the switch to black and white can be the difference between a modern mystery and the film noir style of the 40s and 50s.

The pixel shader for converting to black and white is simple. All colors in the scene are averaged together to form a single intensity value that is then written equally to all three color channels to produce a final grayscale color. The simplest approach (in terms of a pixel shader) is to average all three color channels equally. However, a better approach it to weight the color channels based on inherent differences in the intensities of the three different colors. The unevenly weighted formula looks like this:

$$I = 0.3R + 0.59G + 0.11B$$

You can do this calculation in one line of a pixel shader using the dot product operation. The pixel shader is therefore very simple:

```
ps.1.1
```

I defined c1 as the weighting vector for the intensity calculation. If you would like to change the weights, change them here, but remember that the sum of the three color weights should equal 1.0. The alpha channel isn't used:

```
def c1, 0.30, 0.59, 0.11, 1.0
```

Load the texture and compute the dot product of the color and the weighting vector. The dot product operation multiplies each channel by the appropriate weight and sums the results. The resulting value is then written to all of the channels of the output color. This produces a final grayscale color on the screen:

```
tex t0
dp3 r0, t0, c1
```

I wasn't going to show a screenshot of this technique because all the figures in this book are grayscale! However, the next several techniques manipulate the colors in more interesting ways, so I wanted to show a screenshot to establish what the scene normally looks like. Refer to Figure 36.1 as the baseline image for the following techniques.

Adjusting Brightness

This section presents a generally handy technique that you can use to adjust the brightness of the entire scene, independent of lighting settings. This can be useful for fading a scene to either black or white. It may also be useful for altering the

Figure 36.1

A scene in black and white.

player's perception of a world if he has been hit on the head or exposed to a bright flash. In any case, the shader is extremely simple:

```
ps.1.1
```

This shader assumes that the application has set adjustment values in c0. These values are added to the texture color. Positive values of c0 raise the brightness, and negative values lower the brightness. These values should be within the range of –1.0 to 1.0. If you set all the adjustment values evenly, this shader affects the overall brightness of the scene. If you want, you can provide different adjustment values for each of the color channels. You could use this to adjust the color balance of the scene rather than simply fade the colors evenly:

```
tex t0
add r0, t0, c0
```

Figure 36.2 shows a scene that has been brightened considerably. Notice that bright areas of the scene begin to wash out as the brightness is raised. If the brightness is increased, this eventually produces a fade-to-white effect as all the colors saturate and become white.

Figure 36.3 shows a different use for the same pixel shader. In this shot, I decreased the intensity of the red and green channels and left the blue channel unaffected.

Figure 36.2

Brightening a scene.

Figure 36.3

Looking at a single color channel.

The resulting picture is on the blue component of the scene. This effect obviously doesn't show up well in a grayscale figure, but you should be able to see the sparseness in the non-blue areas.

Inverting the Scene

An inverted picture is also known as the negative of the picture. I think this can be useful in cases where you want to create the impression of a bright flash of light. If you flash or strobe this effect, it could provide an interesting feel.

Inverting an image is easy. Color values are inverted about the center value, meaning that a value that is X amount higher than 0.5 becomes X amount lower than 0.5, and vice versa. You can do this in a single line with the invert source modifier:

```
ps.1.1
```

Load the color value from the texture and copy it to r0 using the invert source modifier. This flips the values and produces a negative image:

```
tex t0
mov r0, 1-t0
```

Figure 36.4 shows the negative image of the scene.

Figure 36.4

Inverted image.

Solarizing an Image

Solarization is an effect that mimics the effects of exposing a photo to bright light during the development process. It is similar to inversion, but only values greater than 0.5 are inverted. This produces an interesting look because all the bright areas become very dark and other areas remain unchanged.

This is also the first of the image-processing shaders written with version 1.4. This is because 1.4 has better support for the cnd instruction. It allows me to operate on all channels individually in one instruction:

```
ps.1.4
```

In version 1.4, tex is replaced with texld. The texture value is written to r0:

```
texld r0, t0
```

The cnd instruction compares values to 0.5. If an individual color value is greater than 0.5, this shader replaces that color value with an inverted value. If not, the value remains the same. Prior versions test only r0.a, which means that it would be impossible to do a per-channel solarization effect in a single instruction. I tried to limit myself to earlier versions whenever possible, but version 1.4 makes a lot more sense in this case:

```
cnd r0, r0, 1-r0, r0
```

Figure 36.5 shows the solarized image. Notice that much of the image remains unchanged, but brighter values are inverted.

Figure 36.5

Solarized image.

Adjusting Contrast

The adjust contrast effect should really be a partner to the adjust brightness effect because many times the two work hand in hand. However, the adjust contrast effect is more complex than adjusting brightness. Conceptually, it's not difficult to understand, but it necessitates a complex shader.

Conceptually, raising the contrast is just a matter of making bright areas brighter and dark areas darker. This means that values greater than 0.5 should be increased and values less than 0.5 should be decreased. Lowering the contrast is a little different. In this case, color values are moving closer to 0.5. Values less than 0.5 should be increased, but only up to 0.5. Values greater than 0.5 should be decreased, but only down to 0.5. Both cases are shown in Figure 36.6.

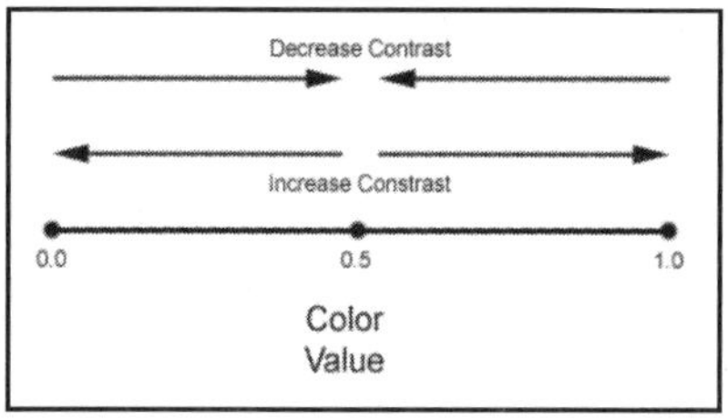

Figure 36.6

Adjusting contrast of a color value.

This creates a challenge when creating a pixel shader. It's easy to raise contrast. Values can be increased or decreased, and the shader automatically clamps the values to the correct range. Lowering contrast is more difficult because there is no easy way to limit the values to 0.5. The following shader gets most of its complexity from the fact that you can raise or lower contrast in the same shader. It might actually make more sense to chop this into two shaders (one for increasing contrast and one for decreasing). This may lower the overall complexity, and it will definitely decrease the instruction count. Right now, the shader runs through all of the instructions regardless of whether it is increasing or decreasing the contrast. The added complexity and instruction count requires a version 1.4 shader:

```
ps.1.4
```

The application supplies an adjustment vector in c0 with values ranging from –1.0 to 1.0. Negative values decrease contrast. Positive values increase contrast. The c1 constant is used later to reverse the effects of a biasing operation:

```
def c1, 0.5, 0.5, 0.5, 1.0
```

Load the texture value into r0:

```
texld r0, t0
```

This first phase handles the case of decreasing contrast. In this case, the values in c0 are assumed to be negative. This line handles the case of r0 values greater than 0.5. It scales and biases the values in r0 to put them in the range of –1.0 to 1.0. It then adds the (negative) c0 values and clamps the result to a range of 0.0 to 1.0. The result is written to r1. If c0 is negative and if r0 is greater than 0.5, this value eventually becomes the reduced contrast value in the range of 0.5 to 1.0 after rescaling and biasing:

```
add_sat r1,  r0_bx2, c0
```

This line handles the case of r0 values less than 0.5. It scales and biases r0 and negates the result. This makes negative values positive, which is needed in the final clamp step. The (negative) value of c0 is added to this, bringing the value closer to 0.0. The _sat modifier ensures that it doesn't travel past 0.0. This value is placed in r2. If c0 is negative and if r0 is less then 0.5, this value eventually becomes the reduced contrast value in the range of 0.0 to 0.5 after rescaling and biasing:

```
add_sat r2, -r0_bx2, c0
```

This line determines which of the two results to use based on the values in r0. If r0 is greater than 0.5, r1 is chosen; otherwise choose the negated values in r2. Negating r2 swaps the values back to negative values. The result is written to r3, but not before it is divided by 2.0. This is the first step toward reversing the effects of the _bx2 modifier:

```
cnd_d2 r3, r0, r1, -r2
```

The last line in this phase completes the reversal of _bx2 by adding 0.5 to all the components. The final values in r3 have been decreased in contrast and are back in the range of 0.0 to 1.0. If the values in c0 are less then zero, the values of r3 are the final output value. If the values of c0 are all positive, this shader just wasted a lot of processing:

```
add     r3, r3, c1
```

Switching phases gives you more available instruction count. The next phase handles the case of increasing contrast:

```
phase
```

Increasing contrast is far easier and doesn't require as many modifiers. First, add the values of c0 to r0 and place the result in r1. This value is used if r0 is greater than 0.5:

```
add r1.rgb, r0, c0
```

Subtract the values of `c0` from `r0` and place the result in `r2`. If the values in `r0` are less than 0.5, this is used as the increased contrast color:

```
sub r2.rgb, r0, c0
```

Choose one of the two cases based on whether `r0` is greater than 0.5. If the values in `c0` are greater than 0.0, the values of `r1` are used in the final output color:

```
cnd r1.rgb, r0, r1, r2
```

The `r1` constant now holds values that assume increasing contrast. The `r3` register holds values that assume decreasing contrast. Now, check the value of `c0` to determine which result to use. In this case, the alpha value of `r3` was lost in the phase change, so you need to coissue two instructions. The RGB values are set to the results in either `r1` or `r3`, and the transparency is taken from `c0`:

```
cmp r0.rgb, c0, r1, r3
+mov r0.a, c0.a
```

This shader handles both cases of increasing and decreasing contrast, but at a considerable performance hit. If you break the shader into two different shaders, you might get a performance boost, but you need to manage two different shaders.

Figure 36.7 shows the scene with heavily increased contrast. Figure 36.8 shown heavily decreased contrast.

Figure 36.7

Increasing the contrast of a scene.

Figure 36.8

Decreasing the contrast of a scene.

Sepia-Toning an Image

The last of the simple color manipulators is a shader that can convert images to sepia-toned images similar to old photographs. There are a couple of different ways to do this. I chose to implement this as a straight arithmetic operation, although better results might be achievable with a color lookup. This shader converts all colors to grayscale and then multiplies the resulting color by a sepia color. This shader can be written with version 1.1 instructions::

```
ps.1.1
```

The first constant is used by the shader to convert the color image to grayscale. The second constant is the sepia tone used to recolor the image:

```
def c1, 0.3, 0.6, 0.1, 1.0
def c2, 0.9, 0.7, 0.3, 1.0
```

```
tex t0
```

Once the texture value is loaded, convert the color value to grayscale:

```
dp3 r0, t0, c1
```

Multiply the resulting value by the sepia color to get the final value:

```
mul r0, r0, c2
```

In print, the resulting screenshot looks nearly the same as black and white, so I am not including a screenshot for this technique. Also, as you read the next section, keep sepia-toning in mind. You could implement sepia tones using color curves.

Using Color Curves to Manipulate Color

All of the preceding techniques manipulate colors with arithmetic functions. For simple manipulation, that's the best way to go, but more complex manipulation requires a more flexible mechanism. One such mechanism is a color curve. A color curve is the graphical representation of a function that maps some value to some new value. The idea is that the curve represents the new color (y axis) for every old color (x axis). Figure 36.9 shows two such curves. The top curve is a basic equality function. The new color equals the old color. The bottom curve is the curve for the invert technique. Low color values are changed to high color values and vice versa.

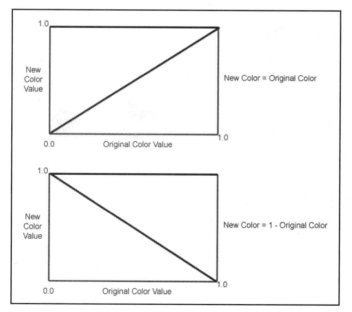

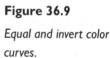

Figure 36.9

Equal and invert color curves.

Figure 36.10 demonstrates some of the curves of the previous techniques. The brightness curve shifts the whole line upward and clamps any values that would exceed 1.0. The solarize curve inverts values greater than 0.5.

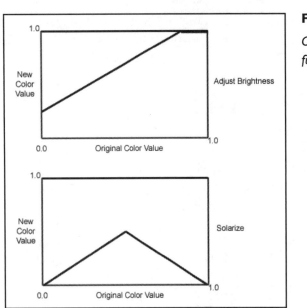

Figure 36.10

Color curves for simple functions.

These techniques were all implemented easily with the arithmetic pixel shader instructions. There was no need to talk about color curves, but consider Figure 36.11.

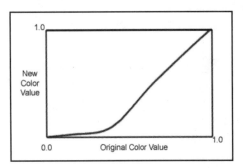

Figure 36.11

Darkening lower range values.

The curve in Figure 36.11 darkens lower color values in a nonlinear curve. This curve would be extremely difficult to implement with a limited number of pixel shader instructions. If you want this level of control over the color values, you need a way to use these color curves. You can do this with dependent texture reads. You can represent any curve as a grayscale gradient texture. If you treat the original color as a texture coordinate into the gradient, a dependent texture read will output a new value based on the gradient. Figure 36.12 shows a graphical representation of this.

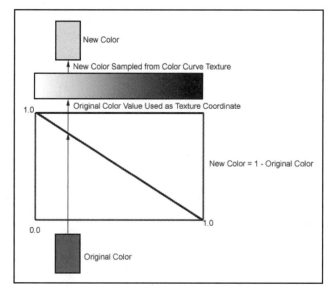

Figure 36.12

Dependent reads from a color curve texture.

The following shader implements the procedure shown in Figure 36.12 using dependent texture reads in a version 1.4 shader. This shader allows different curves for the different RGB channels, but in most cases, you'd use the same curve for all three channels. I'm ignoring alpha, but you could use a fourth curve to manipulate alpha values if you wanted to do that:

```
ps.1.4
```

The following constants are used as write masks for texture coordinates. The shader uses the original color as texture coordinates, but the color curve is a 1D texture. Therefore, you need to map the green and blue values to the first component before they are used as texture coordinates. These masks help to do that:

```
def c1, 1.0, 0.0, 0.0, 0.0
def c2, 0.0, 1.0, 0.0, 0.0
def c3, 0.0, 0.0, 1.0, 0.0
```

Load the original color value into r0:

```
texld r0, t0
```

These lines use the write masks to write the component values into all the channels of r1 through r3. The first channel is the only one of interest when reading the 1D textures, but the important part is that r1 contains the original red value, r2 contains the original green value, and r3 contains the original blue value in all four channels. Incidentally, this shader is one of the few shaders that I know could be optimized, but that I left as is. For instance, there is no real need to do the first dp3 operation. The red value is already in the first channel. Also, this code assumes three distinct textures for the three color curves. You could place the red and green curves into a single 2D texture. This would save at least three lines. I am keeping the shader as is for clarity:

```
dp3   r1, r0, c1
dp3   r2, r0, c2
dp3   r3, r0, c3
```

The r1 through r3 registers now contain the three 1D texture coordinates that can be used as lookup values into the color curve textures. In the next phase, these registers are used as texture coordinates for dependent texture reads:

```
phase
```

Load the new values from the three color curve textures based on the coordinates in r1 through r3. After these three lines, the coordinate data in these textures is replaced with the new color values:

```
texld r1, r1
texld r2, r2
texld r3, r3
```

Assemble the resulting channels into a complete output color. I copied the blue information to the alpha channel simply because the shader requires some alpha value and I don't care which one it is. In the end, r0 contains the final remapped color:

```
mov r0.r,   r0.r, r1.r
mov r0.g,   r0.g, r2.g
mov r0.ba,  r0.b, r3.b
```

This shader derives new color values from a color curve texture. In most cases, the color curve texture should be 256x1 to provide a one-to-one mapping between old 8-bit values and new 8-bit values. However, you might want to use lower-resolution curves if you want to quantize the image down to a fewer number of colors. Also, the texture should be a grayscale gradient. For per-channel lookups, the resulting value is the intensity of each individual channel, so grayscale values make sense.

You could also simplify the shader to work only with grayscale input values as shown next. The combination of this shader with a low-resolution color curve could produce an effect very similar to the cartoon-rendering effect:

```
ps.1.4
```

You use the c1 constant to get the grayscale values using the simple average of all the color values. I included this other formula just for the sake of showing the difference:

```
def c1, 0.33, 0.33, 0.33, 0.0
```

Load the texture value and compute the average value. All the same gray values are written to all the channels of r1:

```
texld r0, t0
dp3   r1, r0, c1
```

Change the phase so that you can do dependent texture reads with a temporary register:

```
Phase
```

All of the channels are the same, so there is no need to do a per-channel curve lookup. When the new value is retrieved, copy it to r0 for output:

```
texld r1, r1
mov r0, r1
```

Also, doing lookups on one grayscale value makes it easy to implement techniques such as sepia-toning. Use the shader to convert the pixel to black and white, and use that single value to index into a gradient that is not black and white. In the case of sepia-toning, the gradient could be a dark- to light-brown gradient. The advantage of doing it this way is that the gradient need not be linear.

There is one final wrinkle to all this. For the pixel shader to do anything meaningful, it needs color curve textures to work with. With the current shader, you should set these curves to stages 1 through 3. Also, you should set the stage states to clamp the texture coordinates. This prevents misreads at the extremes that could be caused by rounding errors or arithmetic operations. The following snippet of code sets the color curve textures for this shader:

```
m_pD3DDevice->SetTexture(1, m_pColorCurve);
m_pD3DDevice->SetTexture(2, m_pColorCurve);
m_pD3DDevice->SetTexture(3, m_pColorCurve);
m_pD3DDevice->SetTextureStageState(1, D3DTSS_ADDRESSU,
                                   D3DTADDRESS_CLAMP);
m_pD3DDevice->SetTextureStageState(1, D3DTSS_ADDRESSV,
                                   D3DTADDRESS_CLAMP);
m_pD3DDevice->SetTextureStageState(2, D3DTSS_ADDRESSU,
                                   D3DTADDRESS_CLAMP);
m_pD3DDevice->SetTextureStageState(2, D3DTSS_ADDRESSV,
```

```
                                       D3DTADDRESS_CLAMP);
        m_pD3DDevice->SetTextureStageState(3, D3DTSS_ADDRESSU,
                                       D3DTADDRESS_CLAMP);
        m_pD3DDevice->SetTextureStageState(3, D3DTSS_ADDRESSV,
                                       D3DTADDRESS_CLAMP);
```

Figures 36.13, 36.14, and 36.15 show color curves with their matching gradients and output results.

Figure 36.13

Accentuating values in a given range.

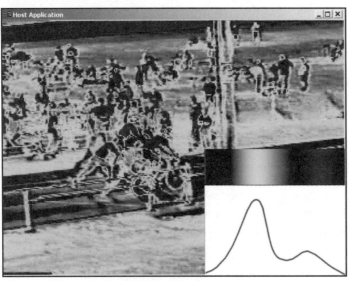

Figure 36.14

Playing with color values.

Figure 36.15

Removing a range of colors.

Image Processing with Convolution Kernels

This section presents the last type of image-processing technique I discuss here. Unlike the other techniques, this section deals with operations on blocks of pixels. This is useful for blurring, finding edges, embossing, sharpening, and many operations that require an analysis of the relationship between neighboring color values.

The following discussion is very light on the actual theory behind why these things work the way they do. A full explanation would require a digression into theory and mathematics that becomes ugly fairly quickly. Instead, I explain things in practical terms.

For many image-processing techniques, you might see the term "convolution kernel" or something similar. This refers to a way of representing how adjacent pixels are processed to obtain a final pixel value. Usually, kernels are 3x3 or larger squares that define the factors in an equation that determines the value of the center pixel. For instance, Figure 36.16 shows kernels for a blur filter.

These filters blur an image by averaging the values in a block of pixels and writing the resulting average to the center pixel. This essentially lessens the differences between adjacent pixels, which causes a blurring effect.

Conversely, Figure 36.17 shows a kernel for a edge-finding filter.

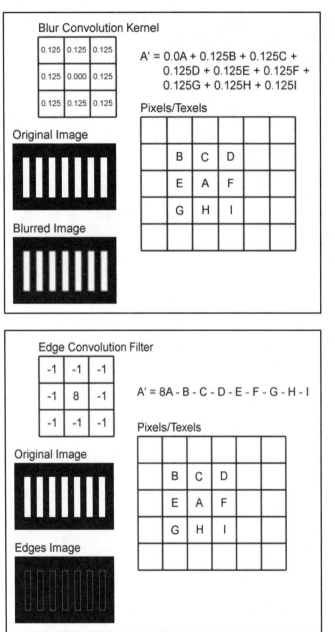

Figure 36.16

Convolution kernels for a blur filter.

Figure 36.17

Edge-finding kernel.

In this case, the values of the surrounding pixels are subtracted from the center pixel. If the adjacent pixels are the same color, the result is a black image. If adjacent pixels are different, the result is some nonzero value, which shows up as an edge. You can build similar kernels for sharpening and other operations.

So what does this have to do with shaders? Typically, image-processing operations are done on the CPU. You load a bitmap into memory and then walk through each pixel. For each pixel, you compute a new value based on the coefficients in the kernel and the values of the neighboring pixels. This can be very fast but doesn't lend itself very well to real-time 3D rendering.

Newer graphics hardware has many texture pipelines that you can manipulate and blend with pixel shaders. This creates the opportunity to do these operations on the hardware with the minimum of transfer over the bus. You can also use the built-in features of the card to maximize performance. Unfortunately, the hardware cannot handle the nine texture stages needed to implement a full 3x3 convolution kernel, but you can cheat a little bit. Figure 36.18 shows a simplified edge-finding kernel using only three texture stages. This finds only vertical edges, but that's good enough to demonstrate the technique.

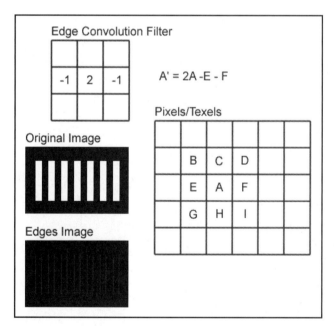

Figure 36.18

Simplified edge-finding kernel.

Now, you need a way to do per-pixel calculations across multiple texels. The trick is to load the same image into multiple texture stages and use slight changes to texture coordinates so that neighboring texels line up with each other. To do this, simply shift the texture coordinates by one texel width. The following code comes from the sample application. The 2D textured quad is set up with three sets of texture coordinates. The latter two sets are ignored by the other techniques, but they are necessary for convolutions. This snippet sets the three sets of texture coordinates for one of the four vertices. The first set of coordinates is the default set and defines the center of the kernel:

```
pSpriteVertices[0].u1 =  0.0f;   pSpriteVertices[0].v1 =  0.0f;
```

The second set of coordinates shifts the texture one texel to the left. This has the effect of overlapping the center pixel with the pixel to its right. The texture is 1,024 texels wide. Other widths would require other shifting values. I explicitly put the value here for clarity. The texture is not shifted vertically at all:

```
pSpriteVertices[0].u2 = pSpriteVertices[0].u1 - 1.0f / 1024.0f;
pSpriteVertices[0].v2 = pSpriteVertices[0].v1;
```

The third set of texture coordinates shifts the texture one texel to the right. This overlaps the center pixel with the pixel to its left. Again, the vertical texture coordinate is unchanged:

```
pSpriteVertices[0].u3 = pSpriteVertices[0].u1 + 1.0f / 1024.0f;
pSpriteVertices[0].v3 = pSpriteVertices[0].v1;
```

The texture coordinates are now set up so that three texture stages can feed the pixel shader with the three values required by the kernel. The last step is to set the texture in the texture stages. The following snippet comes from the Render function:

```
m_pD3DDevice->SetTexture(0, m_VideoTexture.m_pTexture);
m_pD3DDevice->SetTexture(1, m_VideoTexture.m_pTexture);
m_pD3DDevice->SetTexture(2, m_VideoTexture.m_pTexture);
```

So for any given pixel processed by the pixel shader, you have access to the center pixel value and the values of the pixels to its right and left. You can now implement the kernel from Figure 36.18. The following pixel shader code does just that. I supplied both a 1.1 shader and a 1.4 shader:

```
ps.1.4
```

Load the three texel values:

```
texld r0, t0
texld r1, t1
texld r2, t2
```

The version 1.4 shader saves one instruction by using the _x2 source modifier. The first line subtracts the value of one of the side texels from the doubled value of the center pixel. The result is written to r3. The second line subtracts the second side texel from that value and outputs the result in r0:

```
sub r3, r0_x2, r1
sub r0, r3, r2
```

The version 1.1 shader is basically the same, except that you can't use the _x2 source modifier:

```
ps.1.1
```

Load the three values with the tex instruction instead of the texld instruction:

```
tex t0
tex t1
tex t2
```

Double the value in t0 using the mov instruction and the _x2 instruction modifier. Actually, you could save an instruction by using a constant and the mad instruction. The constant would hold 2.0 and the mad instruction to multiply the t0 value before adding a negated t1. I decided to leave the shader like this to show the compatibility differences between the _x2 source modifier and the _x2 instruction modifier. This shader does the same dual-subtraction operation before the final value is output in r0:

```
mov_x2 r0, t0
sub r0, r0, t1
sub r0, r0, t2
```

If you'd like, you could add more instructions to brighten the result or highlight the edges. This could be augmented with either the contrast shader or the color curve technique to help accentuate the edges. Figure 36.19 shows the results of the current implementation.

For further explanations, see the FilterBlit example included with the nVidia EffectsBrowser. Also, ATI's Web site features some documentation on implementing other filters with more texture stages.

Figure 36.19

Results of the edge kernel.

Performance Considerations

If you apply these techniques to a 3D scene, the performance hit should be roughly equivalent to the performance hit of Chapter 33. The pixel shaders might be more complicated here, but these techniques usually do not need to enable alpha blending (unless you are also implementing motion blur as in Chapter 33). I admit that there still might not be enough spare horsepower to justify these techniques, but they might be worth it in some cases. They might also allow you to optimize other areas such as lighting if you know that the post-processing technique will obscure some effects.

Of course, the performance hit will be very high if you try to run a version 1.4 shader on hardware that does not support it. At the moment, many of these techniques do not enjoy ubiquitous support, but they will in the future.

One final performance point to remember: This technique is independent of scene complexity. The technique "costs" the same regardless of how many polygons you have.

In Conclusion...

Some of these techniques might be a bit premature in terms of their actual usefulness. However, I envision a time in the very near future when these techniques might become very important. 3D graphics seem to be following a trend that looks more like movie production. At first, people just wanted to get graphics on the screen. Then they started to worry about lighting and shadow. From there, they started to worry about higher-level lighting concepts such as atmosphere and ambience. At some point, these post-production features will be useful and usable to help produce more tone and depth in the scene. While we all wait for that to happen, I rattle off some points to remember:

- The techniques herein all depend on dealing with data that is in a texture. If you are applying these techniques to video, use the basic framework from Chapter 35. If you are applying these techniques to 3D scenes, use the render target framework described in Chapter 33.

- You can do many simple color manipulations with the arithmetic pixel shader instructions. The limitation of these instructions is the same as any pixel shader. You are limited by instruction count and to operations that are mostly linear in nature.

- Using color curves as a lookup technique frees you from the linearity limitation. You can encode all sorts of functions into color curve textures. You can implement most of the simple manipulations as color curves, although changing a shader parameter is easier than updating a texture for the parameterized techniques (brightness and contrast).

- Convolution kernels provide a way of representing operations done on multiple adjacent pixels. Many interesting techniques are possible, but the principle limitation is the number of available texture stages.

- The performance cost of these techniques remains constant despite changes in scene complexity.

CHAPTER 37

A Much Better Way to Draw Text

I see many questions from people asking how to draw text in a DirectX application. Usually, developers draw text to display the status of the application and statistics such as frame rate. Most of the time, their approach involves retrieving a surface, getting the device context of that surface, and then drawing the text with GDI calls. GDI is short for graphics device interface, the graphics library used for "normal" Windows drawing (windows, toolbars, and so on).

Using GDI calls is perhaps the worst way to draw text in terms of performance. When you create a Direct3D device, the device sets itself up to be good at rendering and not much else. When you use GDI calls, the device must drop everything, do the GDI stuff, and then regroup to continue the normal rendering. This process takes more time than you really want to spend. The ironic side is that many people use GDI calls to display the frame rate, but those calls have quite a negative impact on performance. There's got to be a better way.

As you know by now, the device is very good at rendering geometry and textures. If you can render text using Direct3D geometry and texturing concepts, it should be easy and fast to display anything you want. In this chapter, I go over a text drawing technique that uses GDI once to draw text into a texture and then uses textured triangles to actually display the text on the screen. This technique borrows heavily from the `CD3DFont` class included with the SDK. There aren't too many different ways to skin this cat, but I've restructured the class to make some things clearer and added some features that make it easier to see what's going on. Once you understand the basic idea, you might want to look at `CD3DFont` because it includes more functionality. This chapter contains these basic text functions.

- Drawing text to a texture with GDI calls.
- Rendering text as textured faces.
- Managing state changes.
- Potential effects and performance tips.

The Basic Idea

People use GDI calls to render text because that's really the only easy way to do it in the Windows environment. There are ways to draw text without GDI calls, but they are much harder to implement. The trick here is that you are going to use the GDI to create the actual characters of a font, but that happens only once. After the characters are drawn, you are going to copy them to a texture and render triangles using that texture.

I start by giving an extremely brief explanation of how the GDI works. In the wonderful world of GDI, the equivalent to a Direct3D device is the device context (DC). A DC is similar to a device in that it manages everything that is drawn in a given window or desktop. Also, several steps set up the DC for drawing, much like `SetStreamSource` identifies the vertex buffer used for rendering. The DC must also have a bitmap that represents the target surface for the drawing. If you get a DC of a window, Windows has created a bitmap for the window. If you create a DC yourself, you need to create a bitmap and tell the DC about it. Once everything is set up, you can use GDI calls to draw the font into the bitmap. After that, you can copy the bitmap to a texture, destroy all the GDI objects, and use that texture for rendering.

If you want to be able to render any arbitrary text string, you need to render every printable character to the texture. For English applications, this usually includes ANSI characters 32 through 127. Other character sets might require a different range of characters. Figure 37.1 shows an example of a texture filled with all the printable characters in 16-point Arial.

Figure 37.1

Printable characters in a texture.

To use this texture effectively, you need to know the texture coordinates of the bounding box of each character. When I discuss the actual code, I show you how to do this. Once you know all the coordinates of each character, you have everything you need to draw the characters whenever and wherever you want.

The location of the characters is the final piece of the puzzle. This technique uses transformed vertices because I'm making the assumption that this font will be used for onscreen messages. You can use untransformed vertices and then transform them with transformation matrices, but I omitted that step here for simplicity. I use triangle lists to create two triangles per character. The location of the vertices depends on the starting point of the text and the width of each character. So the texture coordinates serve a dual purpose. You use them to index into the texture, but you can also use them to find the width in pixels of each character. You draw the text by looping through each individual character and building the correct vertex buffer. The CD3DFont class does this dynamically each time the text is drawn. This technique includes an option for creating a vertex buffer for static text that can be created once but rendered many times.

The end result is a flexible and fast technique for rendering text. Of course, there's still a cost associated with rendering textured vertices (as with anything), but it is far better than using GDI calls every frame.

The Implementation

This is the implementation for CDirectXFont. The sample code for this chapter includes a simple application that demonstrates how to use the font class, but the base class for each technique chapter includes the font class so that it can display frame rate. If you want to add more text to the technique chapters, either you can use the existing font to render more text, or you can create another font object. Each instance of CDirectXFont encapsulates one font of a given typeface and size. If you want to use multiple typefaces or sizes, you need to use more than one instance of CDirectXFont.

I begin by describing DirectXFont.h. The header defines the methods that can be called by the application to render both static and dynamic text.

The font class uses transformed vertices. As I mentioned earlier, you can just as easily use untransformed vertices if you want to apply transformation matrices. If you do, you can easily incorporate effects such as scrolling and scaling. For the sake of simplicity, I stick to transformed vertices.

The vertices also include a color. It is used to set the color of the text dynamically. The color does not depend on the texture. Instead, you can set any color and use stage states to blend properly. Finally, there are coordinates for texture mapping:

```
struct FONTVERTEX
{
     float x, y, z, rhw;
     DWORD color;
     float u, v;
};

#define D3DFVF_FONTVERTEX (D3DFVF_XYZRHW | D3DFVF_DIFFUSE |
```

```
                              D3DFVF_TEX1)
class CDirectXFont
{
public:
```

The constructor and destructor don't really do anything. All initialization and destruction should be handled by other methods. That way, the font can be reinitialized if the device is lost:

```
        CDirectXFont();
        virtual ~CDirectXFont();
```

You use the CreateFont method to create a font of a given typeface and size. This size represents the "native" size drawn into the texture, but you can scale the final size by changing the height of the rendered triangles:

```
        HRESULT CreateFont(LPDIRECT3DDEVICE8 pDevice, TCHAR *pFontName,
                           long FontSize);
```

You use the DrawText method to render text dynamically. This is necessary for text that changes every frame, such as frame rate data:

```
        void DrawText(float XPosition, float YPosition, TCHAR *pText,
                 DWORD Color);
```

You use the following three methods for text that doesn't change very often, such as menus or labels. CreateStaticText creates a vertex buffer that you can reuse as often as needed without locking and recreating it. DrawStaticText draws that static vertex buffer. It can render any subset of that buffer, creating the opportunity for some effects. Finally, DestroyStaticText simply destroys that buffer. The application can destroy that buffer itself, but this way is a bit cleaner:

```
        LPDIRECT3DVERTEXBUFFER8 CreateStaticText(float XPosition,
                                                 float YPosition,
                                                 TCHAR *pText, DWORD Color);
        void DrawStaticText(LPDIRECT3DVERTEXBUFFER8 pStaticText,
          long StartChar,
                          long NumChars);
        void DestroyStaticText(LPDIRECT3DVERTEXBUFFER8 pBuffer);
```

DestroyFont cleans up objects related to the font. The main object is the texture that holds the characters:

```
        void DestroyFont();
```

`DrawDebug` is a simple method that draws the entire font texture on a large square. This can be useful for debugging purposes if the text doesn't look right:

```
void DrawDebug(float XPosition, float YPosition);
```

These protected methods shouldn't be called by the application. They are internal helper functions and variables. The two protected methods are helper functions for the more repetitive steps in creating the text vertex buffers:

```
protected:
        void FillCharacter(TCHAR Character, FONTVERTEX **ppVertices,
                        float XStartPosition, float *pXPosition,
                        float *pYPosition, DWORD Color);
        void FillVertex(FONTVERTEX *pVertex, float x, float y, float u,
                        float v, DWORD color);
```

The array of texture coordinates records the four texture coordinates of each character. You use the texture size variable to do conversion from texture coordinates to pixel sizes or vice versa. For instance, texture coordinates are stored as fractional values that allow you to index into the texture. Multiplying those values by the texture size gives you the width of a character in pixels:

```
long m_TextureSize;
float               m_TexCoords[96][4];
```

These are your Direct3D-specific objects. There is one texture object to hold the character set (from Figure 37.1), a reusable vertex buffer for dynamic text strings, and a pointer to the application's current Direct3D device:

```
LPDIRECT3DTEXTURE8      m_pTexture;
LPDIRECT3DVERTEXBUFFER8 m_pVertexBuffer;
LPDIRECT3DDEVICE8       m_pDevice;
```

The final member variables are handles to saved state blocks. You use these state blocks to set the correct render states for text rendering and then restore the device to its previous state:

```
DWORD m_TextStates;
DWORD m_SavedStates;
};
```

The following is the code from `DirectXFont.cpp`. It is very similar to the code from the SDK, but I have made some changes and stripped out everything but the basic functionality. Once you are comfortable with this code, take a look at the code for `CD3DFont` in the SDK. The implementation is slightly different, and there are a few more features:

```
#include "DirectXFont.h"
```

Define the maximum number of characters to render in a single vertex buffer. If you know that the strings you will render are going to be consistently longer, you might want to increase these numbers, but in most cases, you won't have very long dynamic text. You should probably use static text for longer strings that don't often change:

```
#define MAX_TEXT_LENGTH 100
#define MAX_TEXT_VERTICES MAX_TEXT_LENGTH * 6


CDirectXFont::CDirectXFont()
{
        m_TextureSize   = 0;
        m_pTexture      = NULL;
        m_pVertexBuffer = NULL;
}


CDirectXFont::~CDirectXFont()
{
        DestroyFont();
}
```

The `CreateFont` method is really the heart of this technique. It uses GDI commands, but if the class is used properly, the font is created only once when the application initializes. It uses GDI to render the characters to a texture. That texture is used for all subsequent rendering:

```
HRESULT CDirectXFont::CreateFont(LPDIRECT3DDEVICE8 pDevice,
                                 TCHAR *pFontName, long FontSize)

{
```

Keep a pointer to the device that is used in more rendering calls. If the device is reset, the application must call `CreateFont` again or this device pointer may be invalid:

```
        m_pDevice = pDevice;
```

The first step is to create a device context. The following code creates a DC that is compatible with the desktop, so it uses all the system defaults. The DC is then given the attributes for white characters on a black background, aligned to the tops of the characters:

```
HDC hDC = CreateCompatibleDC(NULL);
SetTextColor(hDC, RGB(255,255,255));
SetBkColor(hDC, 0x00000000);
SetTextAlign(hDC, TA_TOP);
SetMapMode(hDC, MM_TEXT);
```

The screen resolution is 72 dots per inch. The next line uses the properties of the device context to convert the font size in points to the font size in pixels. Points are a convenient unit for printing, but pixels make more sense for on-screen text:

```
INT FontHeight = MulDiv(FontSize,
                        (INT)GetDeviceCaps(hDC,
                        LOGPIXELSY), 72);
```

The CreateFont Win32 API call creates the font object that the GDI uses to draw text. Many of these parameters are default settings. The ANTIALIASED_QUALITY flag will try to create smooth, antialiased text, but there is no guarantee that it will be able to:

```
HFONT hFont = ::CreateFont(FontHeight, 0, 0, 0, 0, 0, FALSE,
                   FALSE, DEFAULT_CHARSET, OUT_DEFAULT_PRECIS,
                   CLIP_DEFAULT_PRECIS, ANTIALIASED_QUALITY,
                   VARIABLE_PITCH, pFontName);
if(NULL == hFont)
        return E_FAIL;
```

Before you can use the font, it must be selected into the device context as the current font. It's a good idea to keep track of the old font so that the DC can be restored to its original state before it is destroyed:

```
HFONT hOldFont = (HFONT)SelectObject(hDC, hFont);
```

The following code selects a texture size based on the font size. If the texture is too big, you'll waste memory. If it's too small, the text won't fit in the texture. These values work pretty well, but extreme cases might require more tweaking:

```
if (FontSize > 40)
        m_TextureSize = 1024;
else if (FontSize > 20)
        m_TextureSize = 512;
else
        m_TextureSize = 256;
```

The following code creates the bitmap that will serve as the actual rendering surface for the GDI text. Once the text is created, it is copied from this bitmap to an actual texture. One parameter to note is the negative bitmap height. This value is negative because bitmaps are normally mapped bottom-to-top. The negative value forces the bitmap to map top-to-bottom, which is usually more familiar to people. This has no impact on performance. Also, this bitmap is set as a full 32-bit bitmap, although the GDI text functions do not write an alpha channel. Once the bitmap is created, it is selected into the DC:

```
DWORD      *pBitmapBits;
BITMAPINFO BitmapInfo;
ZeroMemory(&BitmapInfo.bmiHeader,     sizeof(BITMAPINFOHEADER));
BitmapInfo.bmiHeader.biSize         = sizeof(BITMAPINFOHEADER);
BitmapInfo.bmiHeader.biWidth        =  (int)m_TextureSize;
BitmapInfo.bmiHeader.biHeight       = -(int)m_TextureSize;
BitmapInfo.bmiHeader.biPlanes       = 1;
BitmapInfo.bmiHeader.biCompression  = BI_RGB;
BitmapInfo.bmiHeader.biBitCount     = 32;

HBITMAP hBitmap = CreateDIBSection(hDC, &BitmapInfo,
                                   DIB_RGB_COLORS,
                                   (VOID**)&pBitmapBits,
                                   NULL, 0);

HBITMAP hOldBitmap = (HBITMAP)SelectObject(hDC, hBitmap);

long XPos = 0;
long YPos = 0;
SIZE CharExtent;
long CharIndex;
```

The following code generates the texture coordinates for each character before the texture is even created. It loops through each printable character and finds its dimensions in pixels. It uses this information to write the character in the DC and updates the array of coordinates. One small point to notice is that this code creates a space of 10 pixels between each character while the CD3DFont class has only one pixel of spacing. The added spacing minimizes the possibility of individual characters interfering with each other:

```
for(char CurrentChar = 32; CurrentChar < 127; CurrentChar++)
{
```

```
GetTextExtentPoint32(hDC, (LPCTSTR)&CurrentChar, 1,
                          &CharExtent);

if(XPos + CharExtent.cx + 1 > m_TextureSize)
{
      XPos  = 0;
      YPos += FontHeight + 1;
}

ExtTextOut(hDC, XPos, YPos, ETO_OPAQUE, NULL,
                  (LPCTSTR)&CurrentChar, 1, NULL);

CharIndex = CurrentChar - 32;

m_TexCoords[CharIndex][0] = (float)XPos /
 (float)m_TextureSize;
m_TexCoords[CharIndex][1] = (float)YPos /
 (float)m_TextureSize;
m_TexCoords[CharIndex][2] = (float)(XPos +
              CharExtent.cx) / (float)m_TextureSize;
m_TexCoords[CharIndex][3] = (float)(YPos +
              CharExtent.cy) / (float)m_TextureSize;

XPos += CharExtent.cx + 10;
}
```

The following code creates the actual texture. The `CD3DFont` class uses a 16-bit texture, which uses less memory. I chose to use a 32-bit texture here to simplify the code that copies the contents of the bitmap to the texture. You might want to use a 16-bit texture once you understand the code:

```
if (FAILED(pDevice->CreateTexture(m_TextureSize,
                       m_TextureSize, 1,
                       0, D3DFMT_A8R8G8B8, D3DPOOL_MANAGED,
                       &m_pTexture)))
      return E_FAIL;

D3DLOCKED_RECT LockedRect;
m_pTexture->LockRect(0, &LockedRect, 0, 0);
```

Now the texture is locked and the contents are copied into the texture. The bitmap is grayscale, so the code walks through each 32-bit pixel and writes the same value to all four channels of the texture:

```
for (long Index = 0; Index < m_TextureSize * m_TextureSize * 4;
    Index += 4)
{
        BYTE Value = (BYTE)*((BYTE *)pBitmapBits + Index);
        *((BYTE *)LockedRect.pBits + Index + 0) = Value;
        *((BYTE *)LockedRect.pBits + Index + 1) = Value;
        *((BYTE *)LockedRect.pBits + Index + 2) = Value;
        *((BYTE *)LockedRect.pBits + Index + 3) = Value;
}

m_pTexture->UnlockRect(0);
```

The following code restores the device context to its original state and then destroys it. This marks the last of the GDI calls. From here, all the rendering takes place in DirectX:

```
SelectObject(hDC, hOldBitmap);
DeleteObject(hBitmap);
SelectObject(hDC, hOldFont);
DeleteObject(hFont);
DeleteDC(hDC);
```

Create the vertex buffer that will hold the dynamic text. No actual values are set here. They'll be set when the text is actually created and rendered:

```
if(FAILED(pDevice->CreateVertexBuffer(
                    MAX_TEXT_VERTICES * sizeof(FONTVERTEX),
                    D3DUSAGE_WRITEONLY | D3DUSAGE_DYNAMIC,
                    D3DFVF_FONTVERTEX, D3DPOOL_DEFAULT,
                    &m_pVertexBuffer)))
        return E_FAIL;
```

This code sets up a state block used when the text is rendered. The code creates one block for text rendering and another to save the existing states. A state block records only the states that are listed when the block is created. Even though the values of the saved state block change when the states are recorded, this code creates the slots that are filled. I created a simplified state block to minimize the number of state changes, but you might want to look at CD3DFont for a comprehensive list of states:

```
for(long Block = 0; Block < 2; Block++)
{
```

```
            m_pDevice->BeginStateBlock();
            m_pDevice->SetTexture(0, m_pTexture);
            m_pDevice->SetRenderState(D3DRS_ALPHABLENDENABLE, TRUE);
            m_pDevice->SetRenderState(D3DRS_SRCBLEND,
                                      D3DBLEND_SRCALPHA);
            m_pDevice->SetRenderState(D3DRS_DESTBLEND,
                                      D3DBLEND_INVSRCALPHA);
            m_pDevice->SetRenderState(D3DRS_ALPHATESTENABLE,  TRUE);
            m_pDevice->SetRenderState(D3DRS_ALPHAREF,         0x10);
            m_pDevice->SetRenderState(D3DRS_ALPHAFUNC,
                                      D3DCMP_GREATEREQUAL);
            m_pDevice->SetRenderState(D3DRS_ZENABLE,          FALSE);
            m_pDevice->SetVertexShader(D3DFVF_FONTVERTEX);
            m_pDevice->SetStreamSource(0, m_pVertexBuffer,
                                       sizeof(FONTVERTEX));


            if(Block == 0)
                    m_pDevice->EndStateBlock(&m_TextStates);
            else
                    m_pDevice->EndStateBlock(&m_SavedStates);

    }


    return S_OK;
}
```

DrawDebug creates a simple textured quad that displays the entire texture. This can be useful for verifying that the texture was created correctly. The quad is set up to be an arbitrary size of 300 pixels, so the texture is scaled. Scaling artifacts might not give an accurate representation of quality. If you want to see the real quality, change the quad size to the texture size, but remember that larger textures might not fit in a smaller window:

```
void CDirectXFont::DrawDebug(float XPosition, float YPosition)
{
    if(m_pTexture == NULL)
            return;

    m_pDevice->SetRenderState(D3DRS_CULLMODE, D3DCULL_NONE);
    m_pDevice->SetTexture(0, m_pTexture);
```

```
m_pDevice->SetVertexShader(D3DFVF_FONTVERTEX);
m_pDevice->SetStreamSource(0, m_pVertexBuffer,
                           sizeof(FONTVERTEX));


FONTVERTEX* pVertices = NULL;
m_pVertexBuffer->Lock(0, 0, (BYTE**)&pVertices,
                      D3DLOCK_DISCARD);


pVertices[0].x = XPosition;
pVertices[0].y = YPosition;
pVertices[0].z = 1.0f;
pVertices[0].u = 0.0f;
pVertices[0].v = 0.0f;


pVertices[1].x = XPosition;
pVertices[1].y = YPosition + 300.0f;
pVertices[1].z = 1.0f;
pVertices[1].u = 0.0f;
pVertices[1].v = 1.0f;


pVertices[2].x = XPosition + 300.0f;
pVertices[2].y = YPosition;
pVertices[2].z = 1.0f;
pVertices[2].u = 1.0f;
pVertices[2].v = 0.0f;


pVertices[3].x = XPosition + 300.0f;
pVertices[3].y = YPosition + 300.0f;
pVertices[3].z = 1.0f;
pVertices[3].u = 1.0f;
pVertices[3].v = 1.0f;


pVertices[0].rhw = pVertices[1].rhw =
pVertices[2].rhw =
pVertices[3].rhw = 1.0f;


pVertices[0].color = pVertices[1].color =
pVertices[2].color =
```

```
            pVertices[3].color = 0xffffffff;

            m_pVertexBuffer->Unlock();

            m_pDevice->DrawPrimitive(D3DPT_TRIANGLESTRIP, 0, 2);
}
```

The following code renders dynamic text to a position on the screen:

```
void CDirectXFont::DrawText(float XPosition, float YPosition,
                            TCHAR *pText, DWORD Color)
{
        if(m_pTexture == NULL)
                return;
```

Before rendering anything, record the current device states and apply the states needed for texture rendering:

```
        m_pDevice->CaptureStateBlock(m_SavedStates);
        m_pDevice->ApplyStateBlock(m_TextStates);

        float XStartPosition = XPosition;

        FONTVERTEX* pVertices = NULL;
        DWORD       NumTriangles = 0;
        m_pVertexBuffer->Lock(0, 0, (BYTE**)&pVertices,
                            D3DLOCK_DISCARD);
```

Walk through each character and add it to the vertex buffer. In most of the samples, I avoided locking vertex buffers, but in this case, it really can't be avoided. Sometimes locking makes the most sense:

```
        while(*pText)
        {
```

This function adds six vertices to the vertex buffer based on the screen position and texture coordinates of each character. See the FillCharacter function later in this chapter for a full explanation:

```
                FillCharacter(*pText++, &pVertices, XStartPosition,
                            &XPosition, &YPosition, Color);
```

Each character consists of two characters. If the number of characters begins to exceed the size of the vertex buffer, unlock the vertex buffer and render what you have so far. Once it's rendered, you can lock and refill the buffer with the remaining characters:

```
NumTriangles += 2;

if(NumTriangles * 3 > (MAX_TEXT_VERTICES - 6))
{
        m_pVertexBuffer->Unlock();
        m_pDevice->DrawPrimitive(D3DPT_TRIANGLELIST, 0,
                                NumTriangles);
        pVertices = NULL;
        m_pVertexBuffer->Lock(0, 0, (BYTE**)&pVertices,
                                D3DLOCK_DISCARD);
        NumTriangles = 0;
    }
}


m_pVertexBuffer->Unlock();
```

If there are characters to render, render them now. The technique uses triangle lists rather than strips because strips share vertices between primitives and this would create issues with the texture coordinates. Once the characters are rendered, restore the device states and return to the application:

```
if(NumTriangles > 0)
        m_pDevice->DrawPrimitive(D3DPT_TRIANGLELIST, 0,
                                NumTriangles);

m_pDevice->ApplyStateBlock(m_SavedStates);
}
```

CreateStaticText creates a reusable vertex buffer for text that doesn't change very often. It follows the exact same steps as DrawText, only this time the vertex buffer is created dynamically. The length of the vertex buffer depends on the length of the text:

```
LPDIRECT3DVERTEXBUFFER8 CDirectXFont::CreateStaticText(

                                        float XPosition,
                                float YPosition,
                                TCHAR *pText,
                                DWORD Color)

{
```

```
        long NumChars = strlen(pText);


        LPDIRECT3DVERTEXBUFFER8 pStaticBuffer;

        if(FAILED(m_pDevice->CreateVertexBuffer(
                            NumChars * 6 * sizeof(FONTVERTEX),
                            D3DUSAGE_WRITEONLY | D3DUSAGE_DYNAMIC,
                            D3DFVF_FONTVERTEX, D3DPOOL_DEFAULT,
                            &pStaticBuffer)))
                return NULL;


        float XStartPosition = XPosition;

        FONTVERTEX* pVertices = NULL;
        pStaticBuffer->Lock(0, 0, (BYTE**)&pVertices, D3DLOCK_DISCARD);

        while(*pText)
        {
                FillCharacter(*pText++, &pVertices, XStartPosition,
                            &XPosition, &YPosition, Color);
        }

        pStaticBuffer->Unlock();

        return pStaticBuffer;
}
```

DrawStaticText repeats the drawing steps outlined in DrawText, but it can draw any
vertex buffer containing static text. The application can make several different
static text buffers and render each one with this call. Also, you can render
substrings but change the other parameters:

```
void CDirectXFont::DrawStaticText(LPDIRECT3DVERTEXBUFFER8
                    pStaticText, long StartChar, long NumChars)
{
        if(m_pTexture == NULL && pStaticText == NULL)
            return;

        m_pDevice->CaptureStateBlock(m_SavedStates);
        m_pDevice->ApplyStateBlock(m_TextStates);
```

The default state block sets the vertex buffer in addition to all the device states. The following line corrects for this by setting the stream source to the static text buffer:

```
m_pDevice->SetStreamSource(0, pStaticText, sizeof(FONTVERTEX));
m_pDevice->DrawPrimitive(D3DPT_TRIANGLELIST, 6 * StartChar,
                         NumChars * 2);

m_pDevice->ApplyStateBlock(m_SavedStates);
}
```

DestroyStaticText simply releases the vertex buffer. The application can just as easily do this step, but this way lets you compartmentalize. If the implementation changes, you can change the destroy function without changing the application:

```
void CDirectXFont::DestroyStaticText(LPDIRECT3DVERTEXBUFFER8 pBuffer)
{
        if (pBuffer)
        {
                pBuffer->Release();
                pBuffer = NULL;
        }
}
```

DestroyFont destroys the internal vertex buffer and character texture. The application should call this method before the device is reset or destroyed:

```
void CDirectXFont::DestroyFont()
{
        if (m_pVertexBuffer)
        {
                m_pVertexBuffer->Release();
                m_pVertexBuffer = NULL;
        }

        if (m_pTexture)
        {
                m_pTexture->Release();
                m_pTexture = NULL;
        }
}
```

FillCharacter is a helper function that fills the vertices for each individual character. If the character is a new line, the function moves the drawing position down and to the beginning of the new line. If the character is outside the range of printable characters, the function skips it.

You need to offset the character index to account for the fact that printable characters start at character 32, but the array of texture coordinates starts at 0. Once the array index is found, you can get all four corners from the array. You use the coordinates for texturing and determining the pixel width of each character. This is nice for non-fixed width fonts. Once all the data is determined, the function creates the six vertices that make up the two triangles that make up the one quad that lives in the house that I built. After all is said and done, the current horizontal position is incremented by this character's width:

```
void CDirectXFont::FillCharacter(TCHAR Character,
                                 FONTVERTEX **ppVertices,
                       float XStartPosition, float *pXPosition,
                       float *pYPosition, DWORD Color)
{
    if(Character == ('\n'))
    {
        *pXPosition = XStartPosition;
        *pYPosition += (long)((m_TexCoords[0][3] -
                m_TexCoords[0][1]) * (float)m_TextureSize);
    }

    if(Character < (' '))
        return;

    long CharIndex = Character - 32;

    FLOAT UMin = m_TexCoords[CharIndex][0];
    FLOAT VMin = m_TexCoords[CharIndex][1];
    FLOAT UMax = m_TexCoords[CharIndex][2];
    FLOAT VMax = m_TexCoords[CharIndex][3];

    float Width  = (UMax - UMin) * (float)m_TextureSize;
    float Height = (VMax - VMin) * (float)m_TextureSize;

    FillVertex((*ppVertices)++, *pXPosition, *pYPosition + Height,
                    UMin, VMax, Color);
    FillVertex((*ppVertices)++, *pXPosition, *pYPosition,
```

```
                              UMin, VMin, Color);
        FillVertex((*ppVertices)++, *pXPosition + Width, *pYPosition,
                              UMax, VMin, Color);

        FillVertex((*ppVertices)++, *pXPosition + Width, *pYPosition,
                              UMax, VMin, Color);
        FillVertex((*ppVertices)++, *pXPosition + Width, *pYPosition +
                              Height, UMax, VMax, Color);
        FillVertex((*ppVertices)++, *pXPosition , *pYPosition + Height,
                              UMin, VMax, Color);

        *pXPosition += Width;
}
```

FillVertex does just that. In CD3DFont, this method is a macro. I thought it was slightly more clear to make it a method:

```
void CDirectXFont::FillVertex(FONTVERTEX *pVertex, float x, float y,
                              float u, float v, DWORD Color)
{
        pVertex->x     = x;
        pVertex->y     = y;
        pVertex->z     = 1.0f;
        pVertex->rhw   = 1.0f;
        pVertex->color = Color;
        pVertex->u     = u;
        pVertex->v     = v;
}
```

The final tidbit of source code is from the sample application itself. By now, you should be familiar with the basic structure of the sample applications, so I included only the parts of the code that deal with the new font class. Of course, the full listing is available on the CD.

In the sample, I create a simple static text string. In real life, this is probably read from a file or generated, or whatever. It's also a good idea to keep track of the string length:

```
#define STATIC_TEXT    "Static Buffer"
#define STATIC_LENGTH strlen(STATIC_TEXT)
```

The application calls this method when the device is created or reset. The method creates a 20-point Arial font and a text buffer for the static text. If you want several fonts, you need to create several instances of CDirectXFont objects. Also, the color of a static text string is set when it is created. If you want to change colors frequently, use the dynamic text:

```
void CBasicTextApplication::CreateTextObjects()
{
        m_Font.CreateFont(m_pD3DDevice, "Arial", 20);

        m_pStaticTextBuffer = m_Font.CreateStaticText(0.0f, 0.0f,
                                        STATIC_TEXT, 0xff00ff00);
}
```

This is just a simple example of how to render text. The text being rendered dynamically isn't really dynamic at all, but this is just an example. Every technique application includes the code that displays the frame rate. Look at the code in the application base class to see text that is actually generated on the fly.

The nasty looking code after DrawText is basically using the current time to select a character from the static text buffer. The multiplication, division, and sine operations ensure that the character is within the valid range determined by the text length. You use this value to draw one character from the static text buffer. This creates a scanning effect across the string. It's just a simple example of how you can use a static buffer in a dynamic way:

```
void CBasicTextApplication::Render()
{
        m_Font.DrawText(0.0f, 50.0f, "12345\nThis is a test.",
                        0xffffaaaa);

        long Character = (long)((sin((float)GetTickCount() / 200.0f)
                        + 1.0) / 2.0f * (float)STATIC_LENGTH);
        m_Font.DrawStaticText(m_pStaticTextBuffer, Character, 1);

        m_Font.DrawDebug(0, 100);
}
```

This last method is called when the device is reset or terminated. It destroys all font-related objects:

```
void CBasicTextApplication::DestroyTextObjects()
{
        m_Font.DestroyStaticText(m_pStaticTextBuffer);
        m_Font.DestroyFont();
}
```

In Conclusion...

If you are reading through these chapters sequentially, you probably already noticed that this font class is used in every technique chapter. This is the best general method to render text. Tweaks and improvements could probably enhance very specific applications, but I leave that for you to decide. In any case, the important point to remember here is that using GDI every frame is bad. Here are some other quick points to remember:

- GDI calls are the best and easiest way to generate characters, but limit GDI calls to time-insensitive areas such as initialization.

- Once the text is drawn to the texture, the characters themselves are static. Resizing or stretching them might cause visual artifacts.

- The texture size depends on the font size. If you don't need a large font, don't use one because it eats texture memory. Also, it is not implemented here, but you can create smaller fonts and then scale them by stretching them with larger quads. This yields better efficiency at the cost of quality.

- Use the static text method for text that doesn't change often. This gives you slightly better performance.

- If you want to apply transformations, don't use transformed vertices. The difference in performance is probably not worth worrying about, and you'll still be able to use all the translation, rotation, and scaling functionality.

- You can use state blocks to record and restore device states. In this example, the application can be totally unaware of the states needed to render text.

- Once you are comfortable with this code, take a look at `CD3DFont`. It includes more functionality. Also, this code was simplified for clarity in some areas (such as the number of states in the state blocks). The differences between this implementation and `CD3DFont` might be important for your application.

CHAPTER 38

PERFECT TIMING

Another question I see a lot has to do with timing. Most timing issues fall into one of two categories, timing for animations or timing for statistics, such as frame rate. There are actually many different ways to get timing information, but this chapter outlines how to use the two I find most useful.

I go over low-resolution timing and high-resolution timing. Each one has pros and cons. After that, I briefly discuss how you can use timing to drive animation that is time-based rather than frame-based. Finally, I go over a sample application that uses the different methods. The techniques outlined in this chapter are used in every technique chapter to display the frame rate, so if you're reading sequentially, you may have already seen the code in action. First, I discuss these general concepts.

- Low-resolution timing.
- High-resolution timing.
- Basic animation.

Low-Resolution Timing

The phrase "low resolution" might be a bit of a misnomer. By low resolution, I mean a timer with a resolution of one millisecond. This is our old friend `GetTickCount`. Each call to `GetTickCount` retrieves the number of milliseconds that have elapsed since the system was started. In general, the actual value returned by `GetTickCount` isn't particularly useful, but you can compare two values to figure out how many milliseconds have passed. I show you more about this when I get to the actual sample code.

This resolution is usually more than adequate for animation. If your game is running at 100 frames per second, each frame takes 10 milliseconds of time. This is more than enough to generate accurate timing for animation. In fact, this resolution is probably acceptable for any frame rate up to 500fps. Given that your monitor refresh rate won't hit 500Hz any time soon, you are probably in safe territory.

However, this resolution is not really adequate for measuring very fast operations. For example, a single frame may render in 10ms, but each individual call to `DrawPrimitive` probably executes in far less time than that. Also, your frame rate might be constrained by the refresh rate of your monitor, but if you want to measure the actual rendering time, you might need a higher-resolution timer.

High-Resolution Timing

I hope your performance is good enough that you'll need to measure it with a higher-resolution timer. You can get higher resolution using the system's high-resolution performance counter. As with `GetTickCount`, you can use the performance counter to retrieve a number of ticks that have elapsed. Unlike `GetTickCount`, performance-counter ticks are not guaranteed to equal a given length of time. Instead, the performance counter runs on a frequency that varies across systems. The following code shows how to retrieve the performance frequency:

```
__int64 m_HighResFrequency;
QueryPerformanceFrequency((LARGE_INTEGER *)&m_HighResFrequency);
```

The frequency is returned as a 64-bit integer. You can use this frequency to convert counter ticks to seconds. The following code computes how many microseconds are represented by the current value of the performance counter:

```
__int64 m_HighResTime;
QueryPerformanceCounter((LARGE_INTEGER *)&m_HighResTime);
long NumMicroseconds = m_HighResTime /
                       m_HighResFrequency * 1000000;
```

The resolution of the performance counter probably isn't one microsecond, but it is usually much better than one millisecond. This is overkill for animation, but it is very good for looking at the performance of a set of operations. I like to use the higher-resolution timer to measure frame rate because you are more likely to actually see small variations in frame rates as you change parameters in the application. Higher resolution means that you also see every little hiccup in the system, but in general you can pick out trends through the noise.

The one caveat about using the performance counter versus using `GetTickCount` is that it takes much longer to query the high precision value. I don't mean that it really impacts application performance, but it does impact how you should use the performance counter.

To illustrate this, assume that a single call to `QueryPerformanceCounter` takes longer than a single call to `GetTickCount`. If you want to time a call to `GetTickCount`, you can wrap it with calls to `QueryPerformanceCounter`, but this does not give you a good result because the result is influenced heavily by the time it takes to call `QueryPerformanceCounter`. Instead, it is much better to time 100 calls to `GetTickCount` and divide the result by 100 to get the average execution time. That way, the impact of `QueryPerformanceCounter` gets washed out.

The point is that the performance counter can give you a very high-resolution result, but this doesn't necessarily mean that you can use it to effectively measure very small increments. It's usually more useful when measuring small incremental changes to larger values. I use the word "large" here in a relative sense. Large values could mean a couple of milliseconds.

Throughout the application chapters, I use the performance counter to measure frame rate. The higher resolution makes it easy to see very small differences. For instance, add a line or two to any vertex shader and you should see a very small difference in the frame rate. It might be hard to see in the lower decimal places, but you can usually see the trend if you look hard enough.

Some General Words about Animation

I'm talking about animation in the context of the timing chapter because I feel that the two ideas are inextricably related. Many times I see questions about locking the frame rate so that a game doesn't run too fast on a faster system. In general, I think this is a horrible idea. If a future system can run at a silky smooth 1,000fps, why would you artificially limit it to 60fps?

I'll step off my soapbox long enough to say that I have limited frame rate myself on occasion. Sometimes I've needed to control the frame rate in order to direct computing resources to another task. I was synchronizing 3D content to video running at 30fps. If I let the 3D rendering run as fast as possible, it slowed down the video codec. I controlled the frame rate so that the video could run more smoothly. Besides, there was no point to rendering faster than the video could play, especially if it was detrimental to the video.

The point is that in some specific cases locking the frame rate is desirable, but I'd say they were by far the exception rather than the rule. I think most of these animation problems happen when people base their animation on frames. They might tell objects to move a given distance per frame. As the frame rate increases, the object speeds up and people begin looking for ways to lock the frame rate. Instead, base your animations on time.

For instance, I can set up a 3D world where the basic unit of distance is measured in pixels, meters, miles, or leagues. Miles might make the most sense for a racing game, and leagues might make more sense if you are under the sea. In any case, you can now tell your objects to move a given distance in a given length of time. In physics terms, this is the object's speed, or if you define a direction it's the object's velocity. Now, for any arbitrary span of time, you can find the distance the object should travel.

For the sake of simplicity, imagine you are writing a side-scrolling game and you want an object to move 100 pixels per second. If you are running a slower machine, you might get 10fps, meaning that the object moves 10 pixels per frame. Let's assume you find that unacceptable, so you upgrade your video card and you now get 100fps. The object moves at the same speed, but it moves only one pixel per frame. The motion is much smoother, but it isn't faster. Your friend might have a system that runs at 1000fps, and the object still moves one pixel per frame (because that's the best you can do).

This brings me to another point. I have seen some people jump through a lot of hoops to keep track of fractional values because mathematically the object was supposed to move one and a half pixels, but it can move only one—so they keep track of the half pixel so they can correct for it in the next frame. In most cases, this should not be an issue. In fact, in a 3D game, it is very difficult to determine how a 3D movement mapped or didn't map to a given pixel movement because rounding errors, filtering, and antialiasing have some effects. However, if it is an issue, I recommend timing everything relative to some starting point, such as the time the game started or when the object was created. That way, the values at each frame are not dependent on anything that happened in the last frames. Any rounding errors get washed out in the end.

This leads into one final point. So far, I have talked about animation in terms of absolute speed and velocity. Another method of controlling animation is called key framing. Key framing involves moving an object from point A to point B in a given amount of time. At each increment, the movement is interpolated based on the elapsed time, the two points, and the total time. This is represented by the following equation:

$$C = \frac{B - A}{T} t$$

Again, this movement should be based on time, not frames. Also, the motion should be based on some consistent starting time (usually the time of the first key frame). That way, rounding errors are washed out across frames rather than accumulating over time.

This was just a cursory discussion of animation. Many resources discuss animation in more detail, but I wanted to cover a few points that come up repeatedly in questions. The point to remember here is that any animation technique you choose to implement should be based on time rather than frames. And really, this chapter is all about time.

The Implementation

The following is a look at a sample application that illustrates how to use the timing functions. I have also built these ideas into the revised base class at the heart of all the techniques, but I have chosen to illustrate them in a separate application for simplicity. Almost all of the discussion here pertains to how these functions are used in the base class. The only real difference is that the timing calls in this application are in the Render method, whereas the base class wraps these calls around the Render method.

In addition to illustrating the basic ideas behind timing, this application illustrates the effects of animating with a variable frame rate. The easiest way to get something on the screen is to call DrawDebug with the font. Once that is rendered, the application sleeps for a short random length of time before rendering the next frame. The textured quad moves across the screen at a set rate even though the frame rate is constantly in flux.

First, let me explain BasicTimingApplication.h. As usual, I stripped out most of the material that isn't new, but the complete code is on the CD:

```
class CBasicTimingApplication : public CHostApplication
{
public:
```

These first four member variables keep track of the low-resolution timing statistics. If you use any of the code in the technique chapters for your own purposes, you can use these variables to help drive your animations. I do not use them in the samples because I want to make sure you can see where the values are coming from. The start time records the time that the application started, and the current time records the start time of each frame. The last frame time is an elapsed time rather than an absolute time. It records how many milliseconds elapsed while the last frame was being rendered. You use this value to compute the low-resolution frame rate. This is an instantaneous value that could change every frame:

```
long      m_LowResStartTime;
long      m_LowResCurrentTime;
float     m_LowResLastFrameTime;
float     m_LowResFPS;
```

The next set of variables are the high-resolution equivalents to the preceding variables. The only differences are the high-resolution frequency used to compute the times and a temporary variable. You need the temporary variable because the high-performance counter functions require an input variable, so something must be passed in and returned before you can compute values:

```
__int64 m_HighResFrequency;
__int64 m_HighResTemp;

__int64 m_HighResStartTime;
__int64 m_HighResCurrentTime;
double m_HighResLastFrameTime;
double m_HighResFPS;
```

This is the font used to render the statistics to the screen and a text buffer for output:

```
CDirectXFont m_Font;
char m_Output[256];
};
```

The following code is from BasicTimingApplication.cpp. This is a partial listing. The full listing includes the functions that destroy and create the font if the device is reset.

This application includes the standard I/O header, which is needed for the functions that help create the output text string:

```
#include "stdio.h"

BOOL CBasicTimingApplication::PostInitialize()
{
    if (FAILED(EasyCreateWindowed(m_hWnd, D3DDEVTYPE_HAL,
                        D3DCREATE_HARDWARE_VERTEXPROCESSING)))
        return FALSE;

    m_Font.CreateFont(m_pD3DDevice, "Arial", 20);
```

The following code gets the start time of the application. It also sets the current time so that the first frame can compute a reasonable (but fairly meaningless) last frame time:

```
    m_LowResStartTime = GetTickCount();
    m_LowResCurrentTime = m_LowResStartTime;

    QueryPerformanceFrequency(
```

```
                              (LARGE_INTEGER*)&m_HighResFrequency);
        QueryPerformanceCounter((LARGE_INTEGER *)&m_HighResStartTime);
        m_HighResCurrentTime = m_HighResStartTime;

        return TRUE;
}


void CBasicTimingApplication::Render()
{
```

The following code gets the elapsed time of the last frame and uses this value to compute the low-resolution frame rate. This frame rate includes the time it takes to actually present the back buffer. In most cases, this time is much greater than the time it takes to make the rendering calls. After everything is computed, it renders the results to the screen. The low-resolution statistics are measured in milliseconds:

```
        m_LowResLastFrameTime = (float)(GetTickCount() -
                            m_LowResCurrentTime) / 1000.0f;
        m_LowResCurrentTime = GetTickCount();

        m_LowResFPS = 1.0f / (float)m_LowResLastFrameTime;

        sprintf(m_Output, "Low Res Frame Rate (everything):
                %3.2f fps", m_LowResFPS);
        m_Font.DrawText(0.0f, 0.0f, m_Output, 0xffffffff);
```

Now the same steps are repeated for the high-resolution statistics. These values are measured in microseconds:

```
        QueryPerformanceCounter((LARGE_INTEGER *)&m_HighResTemp);
        m_HighResLastFrameTime = (double)(m_HighResTemp -
                        m_HighResCurrentTime) /
                        (double)m_HighResFrequency * 1000000.0;
        QueryPerformanceCounter((LARGE_INTEGER
         *)&m_HighResCurrentTime);

        m_HighResFPS = 1000000.0 / m_HighResLastFrameTime;

        sprintf(m_Output, "High Res Frame Rate (everything):
                %3.3lf fps", m_HighResFPS);
        m_Font.DrawText(0.0f, 60.0f, m_Output, 0xffffffff);
```

You use the timing statistics to animate the textured quad. The frame rate isn't really constant because of the properties of a sine wave, but the point is that the frame rate is constrained by time:

```
float XPosition = 320.0f + 320.0f *
        (float)sin(m_LowResCurrentTime / 1000.0f);
m_Font.DrawDebug(XPosition, 150.0f);
```

Once the quad is rendered, the application pauses for up to 50 milliseconds:

```
long Slowdown = (long)((float)rand() /
 (float)RAND_MAX * 50.0f);
Sleep(Slowdown);
```

The following lines compute the time elapsed since the beginning of this frame. This effectively times the rendering calls. The low-resolution statistics will probably not be adequate, but I include them here for completeness:

```
m_LowResLastFrameTime = (float)(GetTickCount() -
                m_LowResCurrentTime) / 1000.0f;

m_LowResFPS = 1.0f / (float)m_LowResLastFrameTime;

sprintf(m_Output, "Low Res Frame Rate (single frame):
        %3.2f fps", m_LowResFPS);
m_Font.DrawText(0.0f, 30.0f, m_Output, 0xffffffff);

QueryPerformanceCounter((LARGE_INTEGER *)&m_HighResTemp);
m_HighResLastFrameTime = (double)(m_HighResTemp -
        m_HighResCurrentTime) / (double)m_HighResFrequency * 1000000.0;

m_HighResFPS = 1000000.0 / m_HighResLastFrameTime;

sprintf(m_Output, "High Res Frame Rate (single frame):
        %3.3lf fps", m_HighResFPS);
m_Font.DrawText(0.0f, 90.0f, m_Output, 0xffffffff);
}
```

In Conclusion...

There are several different ways to measure time. The main point of this chapter is that sometimes different tasks require different timers. You can use the high-performance counter to control animations, but it's probably overkill. You can use the low-resolution timer to get statistics, but it would be difficult to see small changes. Here are a few points to remember:

- The low-resolution timer is more than adequate for animation.
- The high-resolution timer is better for statistics such as frame rate.
- You can't really use the high-resolution timer to measure very short time spans. However, you can use it to see small changes in longer time spans.
- Animations should be based on time, not on frame rate. In most cases, there is no reason to limit frame rate.
- You can avoid rounding errors between frames by computing the elapsed time relative to the starting time, not the previous frame.
- This code is included with every technique sample. Take a look at those samples for a better idea of how a base class can hide the intricacies of timing.

CHAPTER 39

THE STENCIL BUFFER

In Chapter 27, I introduced stencil testing, but I wanted to focus more on the shadow techniques without getting into the specifics of the stencil buffer. In this chapter, I explain the stencil buffer more fully, without the confusion of other techniques. This chapter discusses the following topics:

- The point and purpose of the stencil buffer and stencil testing.
- Stencil buffer render states.
- Stencil buffer comparison functions.
- Stencil buffer operations.
- Using the stencil buffer to create a zoom effect.

The Purpose of the Stencil Buffer and Stencil Test

I would guess that you have used stencils in real life at one time or another. Usually, you encounter stencils in the context of painting. You can buy stencils of letters, shapes, or symbols. If you want to paint a perfect circle, you can buy or make a sheet of paper that has a circular hole in the middle of it. Place the sheet against the surface you want to paint, paint in the hole, and you miraculously have a perfect painted circle. The stencil blocks any paint that slops over the side. In this case, the stencil defines the areas where paint is and is not allowed to affect the surface.

This is the function of the stencil buffer and the stencil test. Stencil testing determines where a rendering operation can and cannot paint new pixels. At the most basic level, the stencil test is similar to the depth test. Both operations compare incoming pixels to values in a buffer. If the new value passes the comparison test, the operation may write a new value to all or some of the buffers. If it fails the comparison test, the pixel value is discarded, and (in most, but not all cases) the buffers remain unchanged.

Updating Multiple Buffers

Remember, you can write to some buffers and not others. In most cases, you wouldn't need to write to the depth buffer and not the color buffer, but this is frequently the case with stencil buffers. Now that you have three buffers to worry about (color, depth, and stencil), remember that you can update them independently.

The major difference between the stencil test and the depth test is that the stencil test does not rely on depth values when testing the pixels. Instead, stencil testing relies on user-defined reference values and stencil operations to update the values in the buffer. This makes stencil testing more flexible than depth testing. When used properly, the stencil test can be a powerful tool.

Consider Figure 39.1. The figure represents the contents of the stencil buffer. Two triangles have been rendered. In both cases, the color buffer was not updated, but the stencil buffer value was incremented every time a new pixel was drawn.

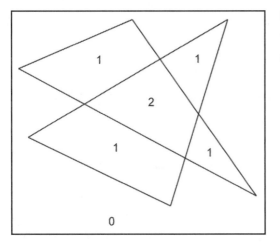

Figure 39.1

Two triangles updating a stencil buffer.

This becomes the basis of a kind of "paint-by-numbers" operation. Once you set values in a stencil buffer, you can enable color buffer updates and set the stencil test to allow drawing only in certain areas. Figure 39.2 shows the effects of different stencil test settings.

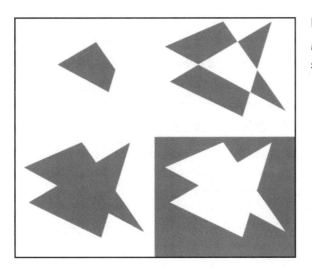

Figure 39.2

Drawing with different stencil tests.

The tests described in Figure 39.2 are actually set with different render states. The rest of this chapter walks through and describes each of those states.

Stencil Buffer Render States

I created all of the samples so far with depth buffer formats that reserve 8 bits for the stencil buffer. You can't enable stencil testing unless you have successfully created a depth buffer with a format that includes bits for the stencil buffer. It's been many chapters since I talked about creating a device with the correct formats. The following code snippet is from EasyCreateWindowed. You use these settings to create a windowed device that supports stencil testing:

```
ZeroMemory(&m_PresentParameters, sizeof(D3DPRESENT_PARAMETERS));
m_PresentParameters.Windowed = TRUE;
m_PresentParameters.SwapEffect = D3DSWAPEFFECT_DISCARD;
m_PresentParameters.BackBufferFormat = CurrentMode.Format;
m_PresentParameters.EnableAutoDepthStencil = TRUE;
m_PresentParameters.AutoDepthStencilFormat = D3DFMT_D24S8;
```

Once the device is created, you control all stencil testing modes, functions, and variables with calls to SetRenderState on that device.

Enabling the Stencil Buffer

The first state you need to worry about is the state that enables stencil testing. The stencil test is disabled by default, even if the stencil buffer exists. The code to enable the stencil test is similar to the code that enables all of the other tests:

```
m_pD3DDevice->SetRenderState(D3DRS_STENCILENABLE,   TRUE);
```

As usual, you should disable tests that you don't need active. When you are not using stencil testing, set this state to FALSE.

Setting a Test Reference Value

Once the test is enabled, it functions much as the other pixel tests do. Incoming data is compared with the data that already exists in the buffer. With depth testing, the incoming data is the distance from the pixel to the view. With alpha testing, the incoming data comes from the alpha value of the incoming pixel. Stencil testing is a little bit different in that the incoming stencil values are set directly by the application, as opposed to indirectly by depth or alpha calculations. This value is the stencil reference value, and you set it with the D3DRS_STENCILREF render state:

```
m_pD3DDevice->SetRenderState(D3DRS_STENCILREF,    1);
```

The default value of this state is 0, but you can set it to any range supported by the number of bits in the stencil buffer. The applications in this book use an 8-bit stencil buffer, so the reference value can be any value from 0 to 255.

Setting the Comparison Function

Once you set the reference value, you still need to define the comparison function that will compare this value to the value already in the stencil buffer. These comparison functions are the same set of functions described in Chapter 14. Table 39.1 reiterates them.

You set the comparison function with the following call to SetRenderState. The default function is D3DCMP_ALWAYS:

```
m_pD3DDevice->SetRenderState(D3DRS_STENCILFUNC,   D3DCMP_LESS);
```

Table 39.1   D3DCMPFUNC Values

Value	Comments
D3DCMP_NEVER	The stencil test never passes.
D3DCMP_LESS	The test passes if the reference value is less than the value in the buffer.
D3DCMP_EQUAL	The test passes if the reference value is equal to the value in the buffer.
D3DCMP_LESSEQUAL	The test passes if the reference value is less than or equal to the value in the buffer.
D3DCMP_GREATER	The test passes if the reference value is greater than the value in the buffer.
D3DCMP_NOTEQUAL	The test passes if the reference value is not equal to the value in the buffer.
D3DCMP_GREATEREQUAL	The test passes if the reference value is greater than or equal to the value in the buffer.
D3DCMP_ALWAYS	The test always passes.

Setting the Update Operations

Once the test is set, it has only two possible outcomes. The comparison test can either pass or fail. The consequences of either outcome are determined by two more render states. The D3DRS_STENCILFAIL and D3DRS_STENCILPASS settings specify how the stencil buffer is affected by the test results. Table 39.2 shows the possible settings of both of these render states.

Refer back to Figure 39.1. You could achieve those results with the following snippet of code:

```
m_pD3DDevice->SetRenderState(D3DRS_STENCILENABLE,    TRUE);
m_pD3DDevice->SetRenderState(D3DRS_STENCILFUNC,
                             D3DCMP_ALWAYS);
m_pD3DDevice->SetRenderState(D3DRS_STENCILPASS,
                             D3DSTENCILOP_INCR);
```

The snippet enables the stencil test and sets the comparison function so that the test always passes. When it does pass, the stencil buffer values are incremented. As Figure 39.1 shows, each triangle increments the stencil buffer values. Where they intersect, the value is incremented twice to equal 2.

Table 39.2   D3DSTENCILOP Values

Value	Comments
D3DSTENCILOP_KEEP	The old stencil buffer value is kept.
D3DSTENCILOP_ZERO	The stencil buffer value is set to zero.
D3DSTENCILOP_REPLACE	The stencil buffer value is replaced with the reference value.
D3DSTENCILOP_INCR	The stencil buffer value is incremented. If the new value exceeds the maximum value, the value wraps down to zero.
D3DSTENCILOP_INCRSAT	The stencil buffer value is incremented. Unlike the previous setting, values that exceed the maximum are clamped to the maximum.
D3DSTENCILOP_DECR	The stencil buffer value is decremented. If the new value is less than zero, it is wrapped to the maximum value.
D3DSTENCILOP_DECRSAT	The stencil buffer value is decremented. Unlike the previous setting, values that are less than zero are clamped to zero.
D3DSTENCILOP_INVERT	The value of the stencil buffer is inverted.

There is one more operation you can set. You can also define what the device should do if the stencil test passes, but the depth test fails. This might be necessary because you may not want to update the stencil buffer if a pixel is behind something else. Sometimes, this doesn't matter. In fact, if you were rendering the scenes in Figures 39.1 and 39.2, you might not want to enable the depth test at all. However, if you do need to account for the depth test, you can do so with the D3DRS_STENCILZFAIL render state. The following line keeps the old stencil value if the incoming pixel fails the depth test:

```
m_pD3DDevice->SetRenderState(D3DRS_STENCILZFAIL,
    D3DSTENCILOP_KEEP);
```

The tests and operations control how and when values are compared and changed. If needed, you can also control the data with masks.

Stencil Masks

The stencil tests support two types of masks. You can use D3DRS_STENCILMASK to mask the reference value and current buffer value. You use D3DRS_STENCILWRITEMASK to mask the values to be written to the stencil buffer. These masks are useful if you want to control the significant bits of the values. In most techniques, the default values of 0xFFFFFFFF are adequate, and you can deal with the values themselves.

These are all the render states you need to use the stencil buffer. In most cases, techniques involve a two-stage process. One set of stencil states is defined, and data is written to the stencil buffer. Frequently, the color buffer is not updated. The first pass only defines the contents of the stencil buffer. Then, a second set of stencil states is defined, and some visible geometry is rendered. This was the case in the shadow chapters. The application for this chapter demonstrates stenciling techniques without the added complexity of shadowing operations.

Stenciled Sniper Scope

Figure 39.3 shows a screenshot from this chapter's sample application. It shows a simple scene with a zoomed sniper-scope effect in the lower-right corner. The objects themselves are not rendered in any special way, but constraining the zoomed view to a circular window takes a little bit of work. It's easy with the stencil test.

Much of the code for this chapter should now be familiar to you, so I show you only the portions that deal with the stencil buffer. The application is created as usual.

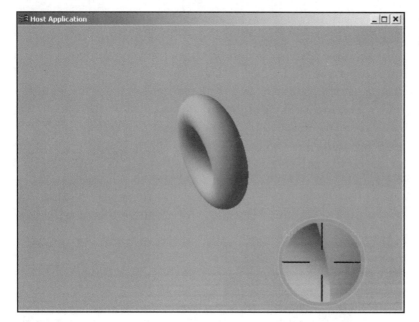

Figure 39.3

A stenciled sniper scope.

The mesh and crosshair textures are loaded. The application also creates a second vertex buffer that will be used to render a circle as a triangle fan. The application uses this fan to create the circle that will serve as a stencil when the zoomed view is drawn. Once everything is set up, it's time to render.

The first new piece of code is in PreRender. There isn't much going on here, but it is important to remember to also clear the stencil buffer, unless you need the old values. In this case, the stencil buffer values are cleared to zero:

```
void CTechniqueApplication::PreRender()
{
    m_pD3DDevice->Clear(0, NULL,
                    D3DCLEAR_TARGET | D3DCLEAR_ZBUFFER |
                    D3DCLEAR_STENCIL,
                    D3DCOLOR_XRGB(100, 100, 200), 1.0f, 0);

    m_pD3DDevice->BeginScene();
    return;
}
```

The real work happens in Render. The Render function renders the scene in two passes. The first pass renders the model in the normal viewport with the normal view settings. The second pass changes the viewport, adjusts the zoom, and renders the scene again. I omitted the code for the first pass because there is absolutely nothing new to see there:

```
void CTechniqueApplication::Render()
{
```

I omitted at least half the code from this function because it doesn't demonstrate anything new. However, remember that the first half of the code does set data that is used here. Features such as the world matrix, the light position, and other factors are set in the omitted code. See the code on the CD for the complete listing.

The first thing I do is clear the depth buffer. This second pass is really a completely separate drawing. Make sure that the old depth values don't interfere:

```
m_pD3DDevice->Clear(0, NULL, D3DCLEAR_ZBUFFER,
                    D3DCOLOR_XRGB(0, 0, 0), 1.0f, 0);
```

Once you clear the buffer, prepare to resize the viewport by saving a copy of the old one. Changing the viewport allows you to resize and reposition the rendered scene without changing the camera position. As you'll soon see, changing the viewport allows you to keep almost everything else the same:

```
D3DVIEWPORT8 NormalViewport;
m_pD3DDevice->GetViewport(&NormalViewport);
```

I just picked an arbitrary size for the new viewport. It really could be anything. However, if you do choose to change it, you might need to update the positions of the vertices that draw the stenciled circle:

```
D3DVIEWPORT8 ZoomViewport;
ZoomViewport.X = 400;
ZoomViewport.Y = 300;
ZoomViewport.Width  = 200;
ZoomViewport.Height = 150;
ZoomViewport.MinZ = 0.0f;
ZoomViewport.MaxZ = 1.0f;
m_pD3DDevice->SetViewport(&ZoomViewport);
```

The new viewport allows you to draw the same scene from the same position with everything the same except for the final screen position. That's almost what you want. You achieve the zoom effect by changing the field of view of the projection matrix. Again, this value is arbitrary. Feel free to experiment:

```
D3DXMATRIX ZoomProjection;
D3DXMatrixPerspectiveFovLH(&ZoomProjection,
                          D3DX_PI / 32, 1.5f, 1.0f, 1000.0f);
```

A change in the projection matrix necessitates an update to the shader matrix. Otherwise, everything is the same as in the first pass:

```
ShaderMatrix = m_WorldMatrix * m_ViewMatrix * ZoomProjection;
D3DXMatrixTranspose(&ShaderMatrix, &ShaderMatrix);
m_pD3DDevice->SetVertexShaderConstant(0, &ShaderMatrix, 4);
```

This is where I begin to draw the circle shape to the stencil buffer. I turn off culling and depth testing and turn on the stencil test. The stencil test is set up to always pass and to increment the stencil values. When the circle is drawn, all stencil values in that area are incremented to one:

```
m_pD3DDevice->SetRenderState(D3DRS_CULLMODE, D3DCULL_NONE);
m_pD3DDevice->SetRenderState(D3DRS_ZENABLE, FALSE);
m_pD3DDevice->SetRenderState(D3DRS_STENCILENABLE,   TRUE);
m_pD3DDevice->SetRenderState(D3DRS_STENCILFUNC,
  D3DCMP_ALWAYS);
m_pD3DDevice->SetRenderState(D3DRS_STENCILPASS,
                            D3DSTENCILOP_INCR);
```

I also disable writes to the color buffer. Newer hardware supports an easier way to do this:

```
m_pD3DDevice->SetRenderState(D3DRS_ALPHABLENDENABLE,   TRUE);
m_pD3DDevice->SetRenderState(D3DRS_SRCBLEND,  D3DBLEND_ZERO);
m_pD3DDevice->SetRenderState(D3DRS_DESTBLEND, D3DBLEND_ONE);
```

Now the circle is drawn. The color buffer is unaffected, and the stencil buffer is incremented everywhere the circle is drawn:

```
m_pD3DDevice->SetVertexShader(D3DFVF_STENCILVERTEX);
m_pD3DDevice->SetStreamSource(0, m_pStencilVertexBuffer,
                             sizeof(STENCIL_VERTEX));
m_pD3DDevice->DrawPrimitive(D3DPT_TRIANGLEFAN, 0,
  CIRCLE_RES - 2);
```

Figure 39.4 is a screenshot of the current state of the application *with color writing enabled.* This is essentially a glimpse of the stencil buffer. The same circular pattern exists in the stencil buffer.

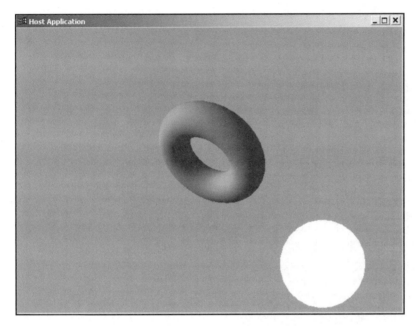

Figure 39.4

Drawing the stencil shape.

Now the render states are reset to the usual settings. You enable color writes as well as depth testing:

```
m_pD3DDevice->SetRenderState(D3DRS_ALPHABLENDENABLE,   FALSE);
m_pD3DDevice->SetRenderState(D3DRS_SRCBLEND,   D3DBLEND_SRCALPHA);
m_pD3DDevice->SetRenderState(D3DRS_DESTBLEND,
                              D3DBLEND_INVSRCALPHA);
m_pD3DDevice->SetRenderState(D3DRS_CULLMODE, D3DCULL_CCW);
m_pD3DDevice->SetRenderState(D3DRS_ZENABLE, TRUE);
```

Reset the stencil tests for the second stage. Now the stencil buffer only passes if the new pixels have a lower value than the current values. In this case, the reference value for the incoming pixels is set to zero, so the stencil test only passes where the circle has set the stencil values to one:

```
m_pD3DDevice->SetRenderState(D3DRS_STENCILFUNC,   D3DCMP_LESS);
m_pD3DDevice->SetRenderState(D3DRS_STENCILREF,   0);
```

Render the scene in the usual way:

```
m_pD3DDevice->SetVertexShader(m_BasicShader);
m_pD3DDevice->SetStreamSource(0, m_pMeshVertexBuffer,
                              sizeof(MESH_VERTEX));
m_pD3DDevice->SetIndices(m_pMeshIndexBuffer, 0);
m_pD3DDevice->DrawIndexedPrimitive(D3DPT_TRIANGLELIST, 0,
                              m_pMesh->GetNumVertices(), 0,
                              m_pMesh->GetNumFaces());
```

I included Figure 39.5 to show you a close-up of this pass before the crosshair texture is applied. As you can see, the quality of the circle is limited by the quality of the mesh. In this close-up, you can see the shape of the geometry used to define the stencil.

Figure 39.5

Zoomed pass with stencil.

This last pass redraws the stencil circle, only this time it is textured with a crosshair image. The edges of the crosshair are opaque, but most of it is transparent and shows the zoomed pass. The texture completes the effect, instead of having a second viewport floating in space:

```
m_pD3DDevice->SetRenderState(D3DRS_STENCILENABLE,   FALSE);

m_pD3DDevice->SetTexture(0, m_pCrossHairTexture);
m_pD3DDevice->SetRenderState(D3DRS_ALPHABLENDENABLE,   TRUE);
m_pD3DDevice->SetRenderState(D3DRS_CULLMODE, D3DCULL_NONE);
m_pD3DDevice->SetRenderState(D3DRS_ZENABLE, FALSE);
```

```
m_pD3DDevice->SetVertexShader(D3DFVF_STENCILVERTEX);
m_pD3DDevice->SetStreamSource(0, m_pStencilVertexBuffer,
                            sizeof(STENCIL_VERTEX));
m_pD3DDevice->DrawPrimitive(D3DPT_TRIANGLESTRIP, CIRCLE_RES, 2);
```

In the end, restore all the settings. It's very important to restore the viewport. If you don't, other passes are affected by the change:

```
m_pD3DDevice->SetTexture(0, NULL);
m_pD3DDevice->SetRenderState(D3DRS_CULLMODE, D3DCULL_CCW);
m_pD3DDevice->SetRenderState(D3DRS_ZENABLE, TRUE);
m_pD3DDevice->SetRenderState(D3DRS_ALPHABLENDENABLE,  FALSE);
m_pD3DDevice->SetViewport(&NormalViewport);
}
```

This technique allows you to draw a zoomed scope in the same window as the normal scene with minimal fuss. You might want to experiment with more shapes and operations. For example, you could render two intersecting circles for a binocular effect. You could use more complex stencil operations and more geometry to define more complex shapes.

In Conclusion...

The stencil test can be a powerful tool. You have seen how you can use it to create great-looking shadows in Chapters 27 and 28. In this chapter, I have shown how you can use it to render more complex shapes. I have seen many requests from people for efficient ways to render the intersections or unions of complex shapes. Sometimes, you need to know what the actual shape is, and that necessitates a geometric approach. Other times, you just need to get something on the screen. In this case, the stencil test comes in very handy.

As you think of nifty stencil techniques, keep the following in mind:

- The stencil tests can define what gets drawn and what doesn't with the help of shapes that are rendered into the stencil buffer. This is useful when rendering complex shapes or rendering to a nonrectangular viewport.
- The stencil test is much like the depth test. Incoming values are compared against current values to decide whether or not a new pixel is drawn.
- Applications must create a stencil-enabled depth buffer before they can use it.

- All stencil settings and operations are set as render states.
- The reference value for stencil tests are not computed; they are application-supplied with the D3DRS_STENCILREF render state.
- When stencil testing, clear the stencil buffer when you clear the other buffers.

CHAPTER 40

Picking!
A Plethora
of Practical
Picking
Procedures

E very application so far has focused on output to the user. In this final chapter, I switch things around and talk about methods of obtaining input from the user. Input can mean a couple of different things. Many books talk about DirectInput as a low-level way to get data from input devices such as mice, keyboards, and joysticks. DirectInput is great, but I want to spend some time talking about how to figure out what the user is trying to point at with that device. This is usually called picking, and there are several ways to handle it. In this chapter, I talk about the following:

- Very simple 2D picking.
- Ray picking.
- Ray picking applied to terrain following.
- Per-pixel picking.
- Other uses for the techniques.
- Performance considerations.

I start with a method that works pretty well for 2D interface elements such as buttons, list boxes, and more.

Very Simple 2D Picking

This technique is very simple, but very important. A 3D game still has interface elements that are 2D. They might be buttons on a pre-game GUI interface or in-game elements such as maps and menus. In either case, you can respond to input easily if you know where the interface elements are on the screen. This is presumably easy to determine because you were the one who put them there.

I start with the assumption that the elements are rectangular, but I expand that a little later. Figure 40.1 shows a screenshot of a GUI for a game. Each GUI element is rectangular or at least close to rectangular.

Because the elements are rectangular, it's easy to figure out how to match the position of a cursor with a particular element. Any time you need to know which element the cursor is touching (such as when the user clicks a mouse button), check to see which rectangle the cursor is inside. Loop through all the rectangles, checking whether the cursor is within the bounds of each. If the cursor is within the bounds of a given rectangle (meaning it is within the bounds of a GUI object), trigger the appropriate response. Figure 40.2 shows this.

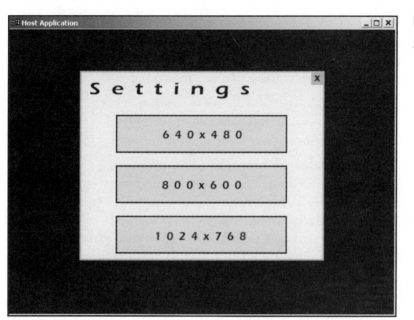

Figure 40.1

Simple sample GUI.

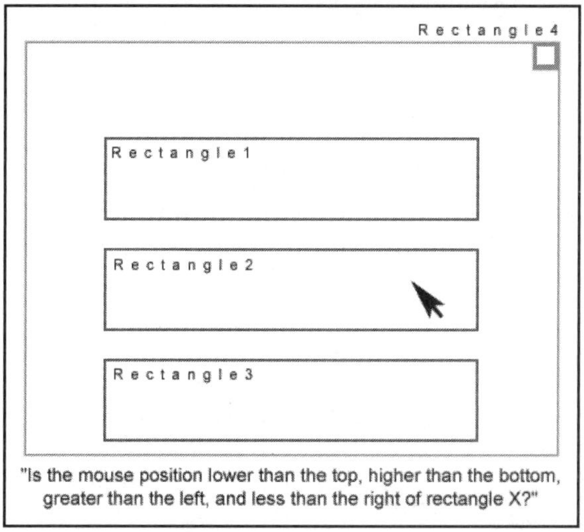

Figure 40.2

Rectangle test.

All of this is contingent upon having a set of rectangles that match the dimensions of the GUI elements and that you can easily compare to the cursor position. You could compare the mouse position with the actual vertex positions in the vertex buffer, but I don't really recommend this. Instead, you can avoid any vertex buffer overhead by storing the rectangles in a separate array that only contains rectangle position data and that is not managed by Direct3D. Also, depending on your matrix setup, your actual vertex positions might not be in screen or window coordinates. The information in the array should probably be in screen coordinates. Once the array is set up, it should be easy to loop through, find a matching rectangle (if any), and respond.

With much of this, I'm assuming that the GUI elements are not actively moving around the screen. If they move, you have to update the rectangles accordingly. In most cases, moving buttons and list boxes are more annoying than useful.

In many cases, button, knobs, and dials are circular. There are two ways to handle them. You can use the rectangular technique and use bounding squares to test whether the cursor is in the circle. This is an inexact technique. The corners of the square are not really parts of the circle. Therefore, you could get bad results. Another option is to compare the radius of the circle to the distance from the click point to the center of the circle. If the distance is smaller than the radius, the point is within the circle, as shown in Figure 40.3.

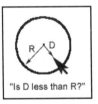

Figure 40.3

Circle test.

These techniques work well for simple stationary GUI elements. If you are using interface elements that are either not stationary or not simple, you might want to use one of the more advanced techniques.

Ray Picking

The SDK contains a sample called Pick that does a good job of demonstrating ray picking. Instead of duplicating the example, I briefly explain what the sample is doing and then show another use for ray picking. My sample demonstrates terrain following, not user input, but many of the implementation details are the same.

Vectors represent a direction in space without a definite beginning or end. You can think of a ray as a vector that has a distinct starting point. In the 3D case, you can think of any pick point on the screen as the beginning of a ray that shoots into the scene. The starting position and direction of that ray depend on the view and projection matrices used when the scene was drawn. Figure 40.4 shows this.

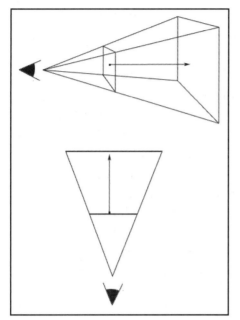

Figure 40.4

Projecting a ray into a scene.

For example, many of the examples in this book use the D3DX "look-at" functions to build the view matrix. In many cases, the camera is looking at the origin. In these instances, the pixel in the center of the viewport represents the start of a ray extending from the near plane of the camera, through the origin, and beyond.

That's the simplest case. You know that the center point aligns with the look-at point because that's what the camera is pointed toward. You also know that the center point of the screen matches the center of the camera and that it is not affected by perspective. In some cases, you might be able to use this information directly without any additional matrix manipulation. For example, consider a first-person shooter game. The crosshair of the gun is in the middle of the screen. Therefore, any shots fired from the gun follow the eye-direction vector (ignoring wind, physics, and so on). You've seen how to extract the eye direction from the view matrix (in Chapter 25 and elsewhere). In this special case, the only missing piece to a ray-picking technique is the method of finding which objects the ray intersects.

For any other point on the screen, you need to account for perspective and the mapping between window coordinates and a screen-space vector. You can find the screen-space vector with the following equations:

$$X_{screen} = \frac{\dfrac{2*X_{window}}{Width_{window}} - 1}{Projection.11}$$

$$Y_{screen} = \frac{\dfrac{2*Y_{window}}{Height_{window}} - 1}{Projection.22}$$

$$Z_{screen} = 1.0$$

This gives you a vector that accounts for the field of view and aspect ratio properties of the projection matrix. In short, the direction of this vector is affected by the amount of perspective in the scene. This vector still needs to be mapped into 3D space so that you can test it against objects in that space. This is where the view matrix comes in. The view matrix contains the camera position, which serves as the origin of the ray. The view matrix also contains the direction of the camera. You can use the inverse of the view matrix to map the screen space ray vector into 3D space using the following equation:

$$Ray_{world} = (WorldMatrix*ViewMatrix)^{-1}*(X,Y,Z)_{screen}$$

The Pick example in the SDK demonstrates this very well and continues the example to show how you can use that ray to find intersections with objects. Once you have a ray, you can see whether it intersects with an object by testing whether the ray intersects with any of the individual triangles of the object. Rather than develop your own ray-triangle intersection routines, you can use D3DX to once again do the heavy lifting. D3DX includes three functions that are useful for finding intersections. Table 40.1 describes them.

Table 40.1   Intersection Functions

Function	Purpose
D3DXIntersectTri	Determine if and where a ray intersects with a given triangle.
D3DXIntersectSubset	Determine if and where a ray intersects a given subset of a mesh object.
D3DXIntersectMesh	Determine if and where a ray intersects a whole mesh object.

All three functions return a Boolean value that indicates whether the ray intersects the object. In some cases, this might be enough. You might just want to know which object the ray hit. In other cases, you might want to know where the ray hit. One reason for this might be to compute damage based on where an object was hit by a projectile. The first sample application for this chapter shows another use for the actual position.

Terrain Following with Ray Picking

The Pick example does a good job of demonstrating how you can use ray picking as a user-interface technique. Rather than duplicate the Pick example, I wanted to show how ray picking is useful for other methods. This is a departure from the input aspects of this chapter, but it still demonstrates several points about ray picking without rehashing the SDK example.

In this example, I want to move a box along an extremely simple piece of terrain. The terrain model is overly simple for the subject of terrain rendering, but it is useful enough for the subject of terrain following. The problem, as shown in Figure 40.5, is that the terrain is very uneven. I want the box to travel along the terrain and align properly with whichever face it is traveling over.

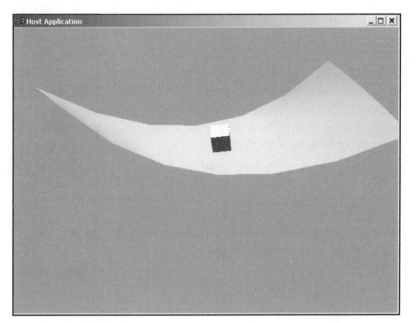

Figure 40.5

Box traveling over terrain.

First, consider the motion of the box. You can try to model the motion of the box as some function of the slopes and continuity of the terrain mesh, but this is a lot of work. Instead, model the motion of the box in a 2D plane above the terrain. As the box moves, find the height of the mesh at that new point. You now have a third dimension, and you can properly position the box in 3D space. This is the equivalent to lifting the box up, moving it in 2D, dropping it onto the terrain, and repeating. I show this process graphically in Figure 40.6.

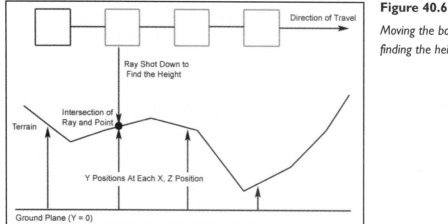

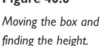

Figure 40.6

Moving the box and finding the height.

This is where the ray-picking technique comes in handy, because the first step is to determine which triangle the box is sitting on. Figure 40.6 shows several positions for the box and the accompanying vectors down to the surface of the terrain. These two pieces of data make up a ray. The position of the box far above the terrain is the starting point of the ray. The direction is straight down. Each time the object moves, you can use this ray to figure out where to place the box along the terrain. The following code snippet shows how to do this. The function takes the 2D position of the box as input and returns the height along the terrain:

```
float CTechniqueApplication::GetHeightAt(float X, float Z)
{
        BOOL Intersection;
```

The start of the ray is positioned high above the maximum height of the terrain, and the direction of the ray is pointing straight down:

```
        D3DXVECTOR3 RayStart(X, 10000.0f, Z);
        D3DXVECTOR3 RayDir(0.0f, -1.0f, 0.0f);

        DWORD FaceIndex;
        float U, V, Distance;
```

```
ID3DXBuffer*      pHitList;
DWORD             HitCount;
```

The `D3DXIntersect` function finds all the intersection points of the ray with the mesh. If the terrain is a simple surface, there should only be one intersection point. If the terrain has caves or other overlapping surfaces, you might need to figure out which layer the box should be on. The function returns the index to the face nearest to the origin. The U and V values are barycentric hit coordinates, not texture coordinates. You use them to figure out the exact location of the intersection:

```
D3DXIntersect(m_pTerrainMesh, &RayStart, &RayDir, &Intersection,
        &FaceIndex, &U, &V, &Distance, &pHitList, &HitCount);
```

With terrain, there should always be at least one intersection. If not, the object has fallen off the ends of the earth, disproving Columbus, and generally making everyone a little uneasy:

```
if (Intersection)
{
    MESH_VERTEX *pMeshVertices;
    short       *pIndices;
```

Lock the vertex and index buffer. You use these buffers to map the face index and barycentric coordinates to real 3D coordinates. Incidentally, you could maintain a separate array of data that matches the data stored in these buffers but that is not managed by the device. That would allow you to do these calculations without locking the real vertex and index buffers, but you would have to deal with duplicate data:

```
m_pTerrainVertexBuffer->Lock(0,
m_pTerrainMesh->GetNumVertices() * sizeof(MESH_VERTEX),
(BYTE **)&pMeshVertices, D3DLOCK_READONLY);

m_pTerrainIndexBuffer->Lock(0,
    3 * m_pTerrainMesh->GetNumFaces() * sizeof(short),
    (BYTE **)&pIndices, D3DLOCK_READONLY);
```

Use the vertex and index buffers to map the face index to a set of three vertices:

```
MESH_VERTEX Vertex0 = pMeshVertices[pIndices[FaceIndex
                                        * 3 + 0]];
MESH_VERTEX Vertex1 = pMeshVertices[pIndices[FaceIndex
                                        * 3 + 1]];
MESH_VERTEX Vertex2 = pMeshVertices[pIndices[FaceIndex
                                        * 3 + 2]];
```

There is no need to hold onto the buffers any longer:

```
m_pTerrainVertexBuffer->Unlock();
m_pTerrainIndexBuffer->Unlock();
```

I map the data back to D3DX vectors. This is not really necessary, and there are ways to avoid it, but the focus here is on clarity rather than performance:

```
D3DXVECTOR3 V0(Vertex0.x, Vertex0.y, Vertex0.z);
D3DXVECTOR3 V1(Vertex1.x, Vertex1.y, Vertex1.z);
D3DXVECTOR3 V2(Vertex2.x, Vertex2.y, Vertex2.z);
```

Use the vertices and the barycentric coordinates to derive the real 3D intersection point. This point should have the same X and Z positions as the input to this function. The height is determined from the position and slope of the intersecting triangle. This function returns that height value:

```
D3DXVECTOR3 IntersectionPoint = V0 + U * (V1 - V0) +
                                    V * (V2 - V0);

        return IntersectionPoint.y;
    }
```

This should never happen, but if it does, return zero:

```
    else
        return 0.0f;
}
```

At this point, the box moves along the terrain, matching the height, as shown in Figure 40.7.

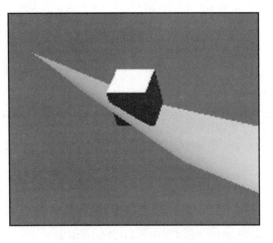

Figure 40.7

Box with correct height values.

As you can see, the box matches the height, but it is not aligned with the ground. To do that, you must rotate the box to match the angle of the triangle. This is fairly easy to do with some of the vector operations from the early chapters. You can think of the box as having a normal vector that points straight in the air. The current triangle also has a normal vector that points up from the plane of the triangle. Both of these vectors are at some orientation in 3D space. The trick is to rotate the box so that the box normal matches the triangle's normal vector. To do this, you need to use the cross product, dot product, and quaternions (at least conceptually). The following code snippet is an addition to the previous snippet. The CD includes the properly assembled code. This snippet begins at the point where the intersection point was calculated:

```
D3DXVECTOR3 IntersectionPoint = V0 + U * (V1 - V0) +
                                V * (V2 - V0);
```

Use the three vertices of the triangle to derive the plane equation. The first three parameters of the plane equation are the three components of the normal vector of the surface:

```
D3DXPLANE Plane;
D3DXPlaneFromPoints(&Plane, &V0, &V1, &V2);
D3DXVECTOR3 PlaneNormal(Plane.a, Plane.b, Plane.c);
```

Also, define the normal vector of the box:

```
D3DXVECTOR3 CubeNormal(0.0f, 1.0f, 0.0f);
```

Use the cross product to get the vector that is perpendicular to both normal vectors. This third vector serves as an axis of rotation. You can think of the axis vector as defining a plane on which both normal vectors lie. Rotating around some angle on that plane transforms one vector into the other:

```
D3DXVECTOR3 Axis;
D3DXVec3Cross(&Axis, &CubeNormal, &PlaneNormal);
```

Use the dot product to determine the angle between the two vectors. As you may recall from Chapter 2, you can use a quaternion to represent transformations in terms of an axis and an angle about that axis. You now have the two pieces needed to build a quaternion:

```
float Angle = acos(D3DXVec3Dot(&CubeNormal,
                               &PlaneNormal));
```

Did I say quaternion? I lied. Conceptually, I am using quaternions in that I am creating a matrix based on an axis and an angle instead of three angles, but the results are computed directly into matrix form to fit nicely with the other matrix-concatenation code. I could have built a quaternion and converted it to a matrix, but in this simple case, that would have been wasteful. No actual quaternions were harmed during the making of this code. However, the CD does include an extended sample that does use quaternions because rotations are being interpolated:

```
D3DXMatrixRotationAxis(pRotation, &Axis, Angle);
```

This code augments the previous snippet by providing a rotation matrix that can be used to align the box to the terrain. Figure 40.8 shows this.

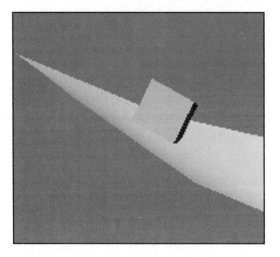

Figure 40.8

Box with correct alignment.

In terms of terrain and terrain following, these are oversimplified examples, but I wanted to show picking in another context. For a better example of following, see the extended sample on the CD. It still leaves a lot to be covered, but it should get you started in the right direction.

This technique and the Pick example in the SDK provide a decent method for picking objects based on their geometric data, but there are limitations. Many of the vertex shader examples manipulate geometry on the card. You can't easily get a hold of that data without jeopardizing performance. You may also have situations where transparency affects what the user is seeing. Geometric methods based on vertex data begin falling apart in these situations. For this, you might need to look at what the user is seeing.

A Picture Perfect Per-Pixel Picking Procedure

As useful as the ray-picking method is, it still has some decent limitations. Most notably, it is difficult to do intersection tests on data that's changed in the hardware. Usually, you can get around this by manipulating very low-density bounding boxes on the CPU and using these for intersection tests, but that can lead to annoying results because it's an approximate technique. Instead, I like the idea of letting the hardware do most of the work for you. Using a per-pixel approach, you can see exactly what the user sees and use that for picking. This involves another rendering pass.

Conceptually, the technique is much easier to grasp than the ray approach. Usually, the user is picking something based on what he sees. He may be picking a button, choosing a unit, or aiming at an enemy. It's up to you to figure out what is being clicked. You need to figure out what is being shown at that particular pixel. As it turns out, you have a lot of hardware that is dedicated to putting certain things on certain pixels. You need a way to ask the hardware what was drawn at a particular pixel.

The way to do this is to draw another pass of the scene that is used exclusively for picking. This pass should disable textures, lights, pixel shaders, and, in some cases, alpha blending. (I get to this in a bit.) You should enable any geometric manipulation but disable any color manipulation. Instead, each object should be colored with an identifying value and the scene should be rendered to an off-screen surface. Once the scene is rendered, you can lock the surface and read a selected pixel or group of pixels. The color of the pixel reveals the ID of the object. This yields perfect results because it "sees" exactly the same objects the user sees. This is made possible by a vertex shader that colors objects according to some ID. The only wrinkle might be transparency. The user might click on a window, but in the user's mind, she might think she's clicking on the object behind the window. In some cases, you might want to use the transparency values but turn alpha blending off and alpha testing on. This step lets transparent objects be transparent to this technique. If the window is clear enough, it fails the alpha test, and the only color retrieved is the ID for the object behind the window.

The Per-Pixel Pick Vertex Shader

The following vertex shader appears in PerPixelPick.vsh. This is an extremely simple shader that colors a set of vertices according to some ID:

```
vs.1.1
```

This simple shader just does the matrix transformations. In a more involved example, you would replace these lines with whatever processing you need. For example, you might want to create a picking version of a skinning shader that does all the skinning transformations but remove all the lighting, texturing, and other operations:

```
dp4 oPos.x, v0, c0
dp4 oPos.y, v0, c1
dp4 oPos.z, v0, c2
dp4 oPos.w, v0, c3
```

The only thing that should affect color is the constant that holds the object ID. This is the color that is read back, so you don't want it influenced by textures, lighting, or other color-related operations. If you want to maintain alpha values, you might want to take the color data from the ID constant and the alpha channel from whatever alpha data or operations affect transparency. For example, you could set up the X-ray glasses shader from Chapter 23 to allow the user to click on the inside object wherever the outer object was transparent enough:

```
mov oD0, c4
```

As you can see, the shader is pretty simple. In this technique, most of the real work is handled by the application itself.

Per-Pixel Pick Application

This entire technique is based on being able to read back what has been written to the render target, so the first thing you must do is create a target for the ID render pass:

```
HRESULT CTechniqueApplication::SetupDevice()
{
    RECT WindowRect;
    GetClientRect(m_hWnd, &WindowRect);
    D3DXMatrixPerspectiveFovLH(&m_ProjectionMatrix, D3DX_PI / 4,
                    (float)(WindowRect.right - WindowRect.left) /
                    (float)(WindowRect.bottom - WindowRect.top),
                    1.0f, 1000.0f);

    D3DXMatrixIdentity(&m_WorldMatrix);
```

In Chapter 33, you saw how to create a render target texture. You needed a texture because the technique used the rendered scene as a texture on the second pass. In this chapter, you do not use the render target to texture polygons. The application only needs to read pixel values. In this case, you only need to create a render target surface. The same caveats for rendering to a texture apply here. In most cases, you want the target to be at least big enough to hold the entire scene. You could create a smaller target and render a smaller scene, but you would lose the true pixel accuracy. Also, you want to make sure that multisampling is not enabled because that affects the color values at the edges of objects:

```
if (FAILED(m_pD3DDevice->CreateRenderTarget(TARGET_DIMENSION,
                                            TARGET_DIMENSION,
                                            D3DFMT_X8R8G8B8,
                                            D3DMULTISAMPLE_NONE,
                                            TRUE, &m_pPickSurface)))
        return E_FAIL;
```

Create a depth surface with the same size. This is the same code in Chapter 33 and elsewhere:

```
if (FAILED(m_pD3DDevice->CreateDepthStencilSurface(TARGET_DIMENSION,
                                            TARGET_DIMENSION,
                                            D3DFMT_D24S8,
                                            D3DMULTISAMPLE_NONE,
                                            &m_pPickZSurface)))
        return E_FAIL;
```

Finally, keep track of the true back buffers for easy switching between rendering passes:

```
if (FAILED(m_pD3DDevice->GetRenderTarget(&m_pBackBuffer)))
        return E_FAIL;

if (FAILED(m_pD3DDevice->GetDepthStencilSurface(&m_pZBuffer)))
        return E_FAIL;

    return S_OK;
}
```

You now have a valid render target, but you only use that when the user actually picks something. In the meantime, you can render the scene as you normally do. This is the only technique that doesn't include the full Render function because this technique doesn't directly affect the rendered scene the user sees.

So you can render in a loop as normal, but you need a way to respond to user input. This is where you could use the DirectInput API to get data from all sorts of input devices. For this sample, I'm responding to simple windows messages. I have overridden the `HandleMessage` function to respond to left mouse clicks:

```
BOOL CTechniqueApplication::HandleMessage(MSG *pMessage)
{
        if (pMessage->message == WM_LBUTTONDOWN)
        {
```

If the message is a left-click message, the `lParam` parameter of the message structure contains the X and Y window coordinates for the mouse pointer. These coordinates are stored as two words in a double-word parameter. The `LOWORD` and `HIWORD` macros extract the two coordinates, which are then passed to the `GetPickObject` function:

```
        m_CurrentObject = GetPickObject(LOWORD(pMessage->lParam),
                                        HIWORD(pMessage->lParam));
        }
```

If this is not a left-click message, pass the message to the base class for further processing:

```
        return CHostApplication::HandleMessage(pMessage);
}
```

The `GetPickObject` function returns the ID of the picked object based on the X and Y mouse coordinates. It does this using the per-pixel technique described earlier:

```
long CTechniqueApplication::GetPickObject(long X, long Y)
{
```

Get the size of the current viewport so that the target viewport can be set to match. With a texture, this wasn't as important because sometimes you want to fill the entire texture. In this case, you are comparing coordinates in both viewports, so you should really be consistent. You could deal with differently sized viewports and scale accordingly, but that over-complicates this example:

```
        D3DVIEWPORT8 NormalViewport;
        m_pD3DDevice->GetViewport(&NormalViewport);
```

This rendering pass is only used in response to a pick event. When this pass is used, the data is only rendered to the render target. Only the real `Render` function renders to the screen:

```
        m_pD3DDevice->SetRenderTarget(m_pPickSurface, m_pPickZSurface);
```

Clear the render target and set the clear color to black. In this example, I begin object IDs with 1, so black represents the absence of a picked object:

```
m_pD3DDevice->Clear(0, NULL, D3DCLEAR_TARGET | D3DCLEAR_ZBUFFER,
                    D3DCOLOR_XRGB(0, 0, 0), 1.0f, 0);
```

Set the viewport to match the real viewport:

```
m_pD3DDevice->SetViewport(&NormalViewport);
```

The following code should match the real rendering pass in the sense that objects should be positioned and manipulated based on the same parameters as in the Render function. If not, the picked object will not match what the user sees. I do not include the complete Render function here in the text, but it is similar to what you see here with a few important exceptions. Although I do not do it explicitly here, remember that you should disable all textures and pixel shaders in this pass:

```
D3DXMatrixLookAtLH(&m_ViewMatrix,
                   &D3DXVECTOR3(0.0, 0.0f, -100.0f),
                   &D3DXVECTOR3(0.0f, 0.0f, 0.0f),
                   &D3DXVECTOR3(0.0f, 1.0f, 0.0f));
```

Use the simple pick shader described earlier:

```
m_pD3DDevice->SetVertexShader(m_PickShader);

D3DXMATRIX Rotation;
D3DXMATRIX Translation;
D3DXMatrixRotationY(&Rotation, (float)GetTickCount() / 1000.0f);
```

Normally, the PreRender function in the simple framework takes care of calling BeginScene. In this case, the rendering takes place outside of the normal framework, so you need to make sure you call BeginScene.

```
m_pD3DDevice->BeginScene();
```

This is the same code as the Render function. I am rendering three interlocking rings that each rotate through each other. This demonstrates that this pick method works on objects that have complicated intersections:

```
for (long i = 0; i < 3; i++)
{
```

I position the rings in a row. The rotation was computed earlier:

```
D3DXMatrixTranslation(&Translation, (float)i * 10.0f -
                      10.0f, 0.0f, 0.0f);
m_WorldMatrix = Rotation * Translation;
```

The object ID is held in the red component of the object color. Object IDs start at 1, with ID 0 as the background. As this is currently set up, you could have up to 256 objects. However, you could use multiple color channels for many more objects. You could also encode more data into the other color channels. For instance, the red channel could hold the object ID, the green channel could hold a sub-object ID (such as an arm or a leg), and the blue channel could hold something else. If you wanted, you could augment the vertex shader so that the shader had more control over color values. The shader could encode distance into the blue channel. If this color was read back, the application could quickly determine that you clicked on "Object 12, on the arm, from 100 units away."

Having said all that, this simple example places the object ID in the red channel:

```
D3DXVECTOR4 PickConstants(((float)i + 1.0f) / 255.0f,
                          0.0f, 0.0f, 0.0f);
m_pD3DDevice->SetVertexShaderConstant(4,
                                      &PickConstants, 1);
```

The rest of this loop renders the object as usual. This loop is repeated three times to draw three objects:

```
D3DXMATRIX ShaderMatrix = m_WorldMatrix * m_ViewMatrix *
                          m_ProjectionMatrix;
D3DXMatrixTranspose(&ShaderMatrix, &ShaderMatrix);
m_pD3DDevice->SetVertexShaderConstant(0,
 &ShaderMatrix, 4);

HRESULT hr = m_pD3DDevice->SetStreamSource(0,
 m_pMeshVertexBuffer,
                                 sizeof(MESH_VERTEX));
hr = m_pD3DDevice->SetIndices(m_pMeshIndexBuffer, 0);
hr = m_pD3DDevice->DrawIndexedPrimitive(D3DPT_TRIANGLELIST,
        0, m_pMesh->GetNumVertices(),
        0,
        m_pMesh->GetNumFaces());
}
```

Make sure you call EndScene once the scene is done:

```
m_pD3DDevice->EndScene();
```

Figure 40.9 shows a screenshot of what the render target contains at this point. I greatly increased the contrast of this screenshot to show what would otherwise be very small changes in color. Notice there are no lighting effects or any other visual effects present in this pass.

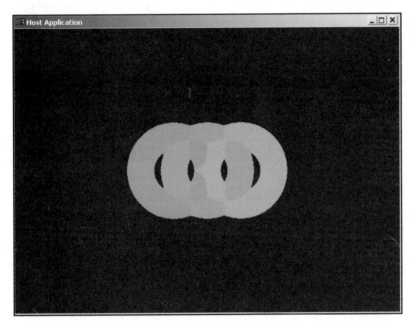

Figure 40.9

Contents of the render target.

Set the render target back to the normal back buffer:

```
m_pD3DDevice->SetRenderTarget(m_pBackBuffer, m_pZBuffer);
```

You need to lock the render target before you can read the values. I set things up here to only read the one pixel of interest. On my particular hardware, I've noticed that locking one pixel has the same impact on performance as locking the whole surface. I'm not sure whether this is true for all hardware. I have noticed that my OpenGL version benefits greatly from a smaller rectangle, so my advice is to lock only the pixels you need:

```
RECT MouseRect;
MouseRect.left = X; MouseRect.right  = X + 1;
MouseRect.top = Y;  MouseRect.bottom = Y + 1;
```

If something goes wrong with the lock operation, I return zero. This is equivalent to clicking on nothing. If you were really concerned with error checking, you might want to return a value in the negative range if an actual error occurs:

```
D3DLOCKED_RECT LockedRect;
if (FAILED(m_pPickSurface->LockRect(&LockedRect, &MouseRect,
                                    D3DLOCK_READONLY)))
        return 0;
```

Retrieve the object ID from the locked rectangle by looking at the color values of the pixel:

```
BYTE  *pPickValue;
pPickValue = static_cast<byte *>(LockedRect.pBits);
long ObjectID = *(pPickValue + 2);
```

Unlock the rectangle and give up control of the surface:

```
if (FAILED(m_pPickSurface->UnlockRect()))
        return 0;
```

Return the ID of the selected object or zero if there was no object selected. If you choose to encode more data, make sure you return it or deal with it properly:

```
return ObjectID;
}
```

If an object is selected, the ID of the object is stored in a member variable called m_CurrentObject. The next code is a small snippet from Render. I wanted to give you visual feedback, so I increased the ambient lighting that affects the selected object. In other cases, you might want to process the pick in some other way.

By default, set a small ambient value that will affect all objects:

```
float AmbientValue = 0.1f;
```

This code is part of a loop that is similar to the loop that draws the three objects as shown in the GetPickObject function. Therefore, if the current object is this object, set the ambient lighting value higher. This affects only the one picked object. See the complete code listing on the CD for more context:

```
if (m_CurrentObject == i + 1)
        AmbientValue = 0.5;
```

Set the ambient value and render as usual:

```
D3DXVECTOR4 Ambient(AmbientValue,  AmbientValue,
                    AmbientValue, 0.0f);
m_pD3DDevice->SetVertexShaderConstant(5, &Ambient, 1);
```

Figure 40.10 shows the scene with all the normal rendering effects. The middle ring was selected with this picking technique. You might want to experiment with this and watch how you can get extremely accurate picks, even when selecting areas where objects intersect.

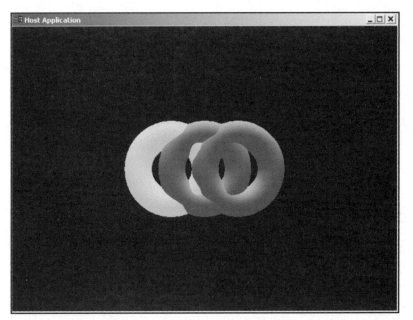

Figure 40.10

Shot with selected object.

Other Uses for Per-Pixel Picking

The ray-picking technique I described works very well for picking waypoints on terrain. If you combine the ray from the SDK pick sample with my code for finding heights on a terrain, you can easily set 3D waypoints for objects moving along a 3D terrain. The ray-based approach is useful for many applications, whether the rays are based on some viewport click point or any other ray traveling through space.

I alluded to this before, but you could encode more data into the picking color for the per-pixel picking technique. If you combine an object ID with a distance value, you might be able to take advantage of the accuracy of the per-pixel technique with the geometric features of a ray-picking technique.

There are many advantages to the per-pixel approach, mostly because of the accuracy and the ability to account for geometry changes on the graphics hardware. This could come in extremely useful when used with N patches because geometry is actually being generated on the card.

There are other uses as well. One technique I particularly like is one outlined by Jeff Lander in the September 2000 issue of *Game Developer*, in which he describes a 3D painting program. He applies a texture to a 3D object, and the texture coordinates are used as the diffuse color for the vertices during the pick operation. The device takes care of interpolating the colors across the polygons, which means that each pixel of the model is correctly encoded with an interpolated texture coordinate. When the user wants to paint on the surface of the model, he clicks on the area he wants to paint. The pick operation reads the color of the picked pixel and converts that to a set of texture coordinates. These coordinates are used to index into the texture, and the texture is updated with whatever painting operation is currently in effect, which in turn is visible on the model. (This technique originally appeared in a 1990 SIGGRAPH paper by Pat Hanrahan and Paul Haeberli.)

Performance Issues

I like the per-pixel technique, but it does have a downside in terms of performance. Reading a render target is still a fairly expensive operation, but the effect isn't too bad if you're only responding to the occasional click. At the moment, reading the render target is one performance-sensitive operation that can't really be avoided. The good news is that this cost is constant no matter how complex the scene is.

The other potential performance hit comes from the fact that you need to render the scene in an extra pass, but this might not be as costly as you think. First of all, the picking pass should disable textures, lighting, pixel shaders, and all other forms of color processing. This should account for a lot of savings in terms of time spent rendering the pick pass. You can also avoid rendering any object that cannot be picked. For instance, if the user can only pick other players, you might be able to get by rendering only the player models. However, if the players can be behind walls, you must render those walls as well to get the proper occlusion of players. You can definitely avoid rendering lens flares, sky boxes, and so on.

So, two distinct factors affect performance. In this simple example, the picking operation cuts the frame rate approximately in half, but the majority of the cost comes from the fact that you are rendering two nearly identical passes. In more realistic, complex scenes, the pick pass might be much less complex than the visible pass, meaning that the proportional performance hit is not as large. This technique bears experimentation, but the point is that you should not be discouraged by the performance specs from this simple application. A 50 percent hit in this example does not necessarily mean that you will get a 50 percent hit in real applications. As always, you should experiment.

In Conclusion...

I presented three picking techniques here, but my focus was on the per-pixel technique. The 2D pick is just a matter of testing to see whether the 2D pick point is in a 2D rectangle. With the ray-picking technique, I feel that the SDK code does a good job of demonstrating the basics, so I chose to digress to a terrain-following example using ray picking. Again, I strongly suggest you look at the SDK sample.

Finally, I wanted to demonstrate the per-pixel picking technique. I like this technique because of its accuracy, but you don't always need that much accuracy. I also like it for the flexibility. Vertex shaders create testing scenarios that would be difficult with ray picking. They become easy with per-pixel picking. However, you might need to experiment to see whether you can accept the performance issues.

Here are some things to consider:

- Simple 2D picking is just a matter of checking whether your pick point is within the rectangle or circle of an interface element.
- Ray picking involves shooting a ray through space and finding intersection points between that ray and the triangles in your scene.
- Refer to the Pick sample in the SDK for the code that determines the ray shooting into the scene from the viewport.
- The D3DX library supplies three functions that you can use to test for intersections.
- The per-pixel technique involves rendering a pick pass that encodes object IDs as colors. The application can then read a specific pixel to determine which object was really visible at the pick point.

- The advantage of the per-pixel technique is that it is highly accurate, even with warping techniques that happen in vertex shaders.

- Reading a render target is expensive, but the performance cost is constant for any scene complexity.

- When rendering the picking pass, you can get by with rendering only objects that can be picked and any objects that potentially block them. You do not need to render the entire scene.

IN CONCLUSION...

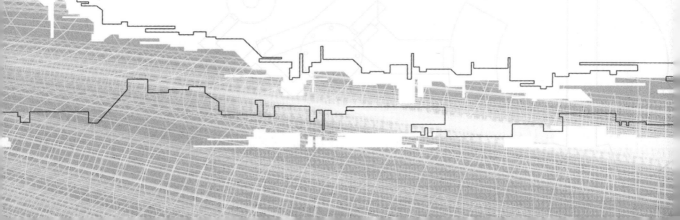

In this book, you have seen many techniques that range from basic vertex buffer creation to using vertex and pixel shaders. Each chapter illustrates a specific point, and I tried to demonstrate those points in the sample code and applications. I hope that you will work with the code and adapt it to your own needs.

Today's hardware is capable of some incredible things. This book focused heavily on shaders to demonstrate how much the hardware can do for you. I don't expect every technique to be useful to everyone. However, every technique was chosen to demonstrate the flexibility and capabilities of the hardware. Every technique includes pieces that can be mixed and matched to solve your own unique puzzle. You just need to remember a couple of points.

Remember that vertex shaders give you a huge amount of control over all the properties of the vertices that are moving through the pipeline. This creates the ability to manipulate geometry, color, and textures completely in hardware. Don't take my techniques at face value. Look at them as starting points. Use the groundwork I've laid out here to develop your own cool techniques and effects.

Pixel shaders also provide an amazing amount of control over what you can put on the screen. Many of the techniques I demonstrated here may not run very quickly on your current hardware, but the graphics industry changes rapidly. Effects that you see in movies today will be run in real time tomorrow. I encourage you to begin learning about pixel shaders even if your hardware doesn't support them. Someday, your hardware will support them and you want to be ready.

Finally, remember that the later chapters of the book were more concerned with illustrating a given point than achieving the best performance. Many shortcuts will depend on your own needs and constraints. Never abandon a specific effect if you don't get good performance the first time out. The most interesting effects are often the hardest to implement correctly. Almost nothing about this field is easy, but the hard work is very rewarding when you see the image on the screen.

Many books concentrate on cool effects that you can copy and paste into your own code with a limited understanding of how they work. My primary goal was to provide you with the basic concepts that you could use to build your own techniques. I can't stress enough how important it is that you experiment with the code. Modify it, take it apart, see how it works, and change it to fit your needs. I provided the basics, but I defer to your creativity to produce the stunning effects. Once you start, you will notice a snowball effect. You will find that you can put more and more pieces together in more interesting ways. The fun is in creating something that you have built based on your skills, experience, and available tools. Enjoy!

Index

Symbols

1D texture coordinates, 196

2D

animation, 3D comparison, 354

picking, 774-776

rendering

applications, 667-671

blitting pixels, 658-659

DirectDraw, 658

OpenGL, 659

orthogonal matrices, 660-662

overview, 659-662

performance, 671-674

sprites, 663-664

T&L cards, 659

vertices, 664-666

3D

animation, 2D comparison, 354-355

history

consoles, 5-6

DirectX, 6-7

movies, 6

PCs, 4-5

objects, warping, 396

vectors, 15-16

4D vectors, 16-17

16-bit color, 32-33

32-bit color, 32-33

A

accumulation buffer (OpenGL), 642

adapters, querying, 72

adding

matrices, 23

vectors, 12

address registers

matrix palette skinning, 416-419

vertex shaders, 263

addressing

instructions (pixel shaders), 298-303

modes

stage states, 233

textures, 220-221

algorithms

Painters Algorithm, 239

rendering, 466-468

alpha blending

code, 245-255

enabling, 243-244

performance, 245

alpha channels, 33. *See also* transparency

blending, 241-244

color keys, 242

pixel shaders, 304

rendering transparency, 241-244

stage states, 216-218

texture tool, 242

alpha tests

blending colors, 244

code, 245-255

pipeline, 50

polygons (depth buffers), 244

ALU (Arithmetic Logic Unit), 262

Ambient function, 515

ambient lighting, 34-35

diffuse, 151

realism, 167

angles

FOV, 120-122

ratio to indices, 486

animation. *See also* images; objects; primitives

key frame, 412-413

mipmaps, 200

rotation (quaternions), 16-17

skinning, 413-416

address registers, 416-419

applications, 419-430

code, 419-430

vertex shaders, 416-419

timing

frame rates, 752-753

high-resolution, 751-752

low-resolution, 750

performance counters, 751-752

anisotropic filters, 223-224

application.cpp file, 63-65

application.h header, 60-61, 79-81

applications. *See also* CHostApplication class

Bezier patches, 396-407

building, 59

application.cpp, 63-65

application.h, 60-61, 79-81

constructors, 60

creating, 63-65

defining classes, 60-61, 80-81

defining windows, 59-60

destructors, 60

executable.cpp, 61-62

executable.h, 59-60

instantiating, 61-62

message handling, 60-62

overview, 67

windows, 63-65

bump mapping

pixel shaders, 603-605

applications (continued)
  reflection, 617-622
  vertex shaders, 596-603
 compiling, 65-67
 DirectShow
  textures, 696-698
  video, 696-698
 implementing application.cpp,
   82-90
 lighting
  fixed function lighting, 168-184
  point lighting (per-pixel
   lighting), 581-583
  spot lighting (per-pixel
   lighting), 575-578
  streetlamps, 359-366
 matrix palettes (skinning), 419-430
 meshes
  behavior, 176
  vertex shaders, 326-334
 motion blur, 643-654
 per-pixel picking, 786-793
 planes (shadows), 506-515
 rendering (2D), 667-671
 running, 65-67
 shaders
  depth shader, 438-439
  lighting, 459-462
  per-pixel toon shaders, 628-629
  pixel shaders, 311-316
  shadow volume shader, 528-536
  toon shaders, 473-475
  vertex shaders, sine waves,
   345-350
  x-ray shader, 442-445
 shadow mapping, 551-560
 stage states, 225-234
 testing, 245-255
 textures, 199-211
 timing, frame rates, 754-757
 transformations, building, 125-130
ApplyStateBlock functions, 740
architecture, pixel shaders, 292
arguments, stage states, 217

Arithmetic Logic Unit (ALU), 262
arithmetic vectors, 11-12
artifacts, troubleshooting, 194
assembling
 pixel shaders, 306-307
 vertex shaders, 271-272
attenuation, 38-39
 directional lighting, 163, 178
 point lighting, 164
attribute buffers, 324
audio. *See* streaming media
**AVI (Audio Video Interleaved)
 files,** 680-682
axes
 rotation (quaternions), 16-17
 rotation matrix, 25-26
 twisting, 383

B

back buffer (pipeline), 50
backward lighting, troubleshooting,
 392
basis functions (Bezier curves), 388
basis vectors
 bump mapping, 605
 texture space, 592-594
batching performance, 105-106, 143
BeginScene function, 77, 85, 507
behavior, meshes, 176
Bezier curves, 386-389
 basis functions, 388
 Bezier patches, 408
 control points, 387
Bezier patches
 advantages, 407-408
 Bezier curves, 408
 flags, 408
 terrain, 407
 uses, 407-408
 vertex shaders
  applications, 396-407
  code, 396-407
  computing, 393-396
Bezier, Pierre, 389

bias
 pixel shaders, 303
 textures, 224
billboards
 explosions, 366
 lighting (streetlamps), 355-359
 vectors, 357
 vertices, 354-355
 vertex shaders
  code, 359-366
  creating, 355-359
binary files, 56
black-and-white filter, 703-704
blackness
 textures (toon shaders), 471
 troubleshooting, 127
blending
 alpha blending
  code, 245-255
  enabling, 243-244
  performance, 245
 alpha channels, 241-244
 colors, alpha tests, 244
 pixel shaders, 309-311
 SDK, 225
 stage states, 215-216
  color arguments, 217
  color operations, 216-217
  triadic operations, 218
blitting pixels (2D rendering),
 658-659
bones. *See* skinning
borders, 220-221
bounding boxes, meshes, 398
brightness (pixel shaders), 704-706
bubbles, wobbling, 383
buffers
 accumulation (OpenGL), 642
 back buffer (pipeline), 50
 depth
  clearing, 241
  overview, 239-240
  polygons (alpha tests), 244
  render states, 239-240

W buffering, 240
Z bias, 241
devices, 74-75
frame (pipeline), 50
index
  buffer relationships, 324
  offsets, 152
  releasing, 151
  rendering primitives, 139-141
locking, performance, 671-674
relationships, 324
static, vertices, 100
stencil
  comparison function, 763
  overview, 760-762
  planes (shadows), 504-506
  reference value, 762-763
  render states, 762-765
  stencil masks, 765
  stencil testing, 762
  update operations, 764-765
  zooming, 765-771
vertex
  buffer relationships, 324
  building, 106-112
  circles, 172
  curves, 172
  destroying, 101, 106-107
  filling, 106-107
  flags, 100, 102
  lighting, 170-171
  locking, 101-102, 111
  MemoryPool parameter, 100-101
  optimizing, 109
  overview, 112-113
  performance, 98, 105
  setting, 101-102
  static, 100
building
applications, 59
  application.cpp, 63-65
  application.h, 60-61, 79-81
  constructors, 60
  creating, 63-65

defining classes, 60-61, 80-81
defining windows, 59-60
destructors, 60
executable.cpp, 61-62
executable.h, 59-60
instantiating, 61-62
message handling, 60-62
overview, 67
transformations, 125-130
windows, 63-65
CBasicTimingApplication class, 754-757
CBasicVertexShaderApplication class, 277-285
CDirectXFont class, 730-746
CDirectXVideoTexture class, 685-696
CGeometryApplication class, 144-159
CHostApplication class, 60-65
CLightingApplication class, 170-184
CTechniqueApplication class, 326-334
CTestingApplication class, 245-255
CTextureApplication class, 199-211
CTextureStateApplication class, 225-234
CTransformApplication class, 125-130
CVertexApplication class, 106-112
IDirect3DDevice8
  creating device, 73-75
  creating object, 71
  destroying device, 77
  querying hardware, 72-73
  resetting device, 76-77
vertex buffers, 106-112
view transformations, 118-120
world transformations, 118-120
bump mapping
basis vectors
  texture space, 592-594
  troubleshooting, 605
lighting, 588-590

meshes, 590-592
pixel shaders
  applications, 603-605
  reflection, 616
  reflection application, 617-622
  stage states, 218
  textures, 590-592
  vertex shaders, 594-595
  applications, 596-603
  reflection, 613-615
bytes, surfaces, 189

C

C++ matrices, 27
calculations, lighting output, 33
calculus
differential, 390-393
Taylor series
  cosines, 341
  sine waves, 341-345
  spherical coordinates, 374
cameras. *See also* transformations
view transformations, 173
virtual, view frustums, 120-122
CaptureStateBlock function, 740
Carmack, John, 6
Cartesian coordinate system
defined, 10
overview, 370-372
cartoons. *See* toon shaders
Casteljau, Paul de, 389
CBaseVideoRenderer function, 688
CBasicTimingApplication class, 754-757
CBasicVertexShaderApplication class, 277-285
CDirectXFont class, 730-746
CDirectXVideoTexture class, 685-696
CGeometryApplication class, 144-159
channels, 33
CheckMediaType function, 687, 692
CHostApplication class, 60-65. *See also* applications

CHostApplication function, 60, 62

circles (vertex buffer), 172

clamping textures, 220-221

classes

  CBasicTimingApplication, 754-757

  CBasicVertexShaderApplication, 277-285

  CDirectXFont, 730-746

  CDirectXVideoTexture, 685-696

  CGeometryApplication, 144-159

  CHostApplication, 60-65. *See also* applications

  CLightingApplication, 170-184

  CTechniqueApplication, 326-334

  CTestingApplication, 245-255

  CTextureApplication, 199-211

  CTextureStateApplication, 225-234

  CTransformApplication, 125-130

  CVertexApplication

    building, 106-112

    constructor, 107

    defining, 107

    destructor, 107

    initializing, 107

    locking buffers, 111

    optimizing, 109

  defining, 60-61, 80-81

  instantiating, 61-62

Clear function, 78-79

clearing

  depth buffers, 241

  IDirect3DDevice8, 78-79

  matrices, 24

CLightingApplication class, 170-184

clipper (pipeline), 48

CloneMesh function, 275

CloneMeshFVF function, 329-331

cloning

  meshes, 329-331

  vertex shaders, 322-323

CMYK (cyan, magenta, yellow, black), 32

CoCreateInstance function, 690

code

  alpha blending, 245-255

alpha testing, 245-255

applications, textures, 199-211

Bezier patches, 396-407

coordinate systems, 375-383

cube maps, reflection/refraction, 490-496

depth testing, 245-255

fixed function lighting applications, 170-184

functions, writing, 17

matrix palettes (skinning), 419-430

meshes, rendering, 144-159

pixel shaders, 311-316

planes (shadows), 506-515

primitives, rendering, 144-159

shaders, lighting, 459-462

shadow mapping, 551-560

stage states, 225-234

toon shaders, 473-475

vertex shaders, 277-285

  billboards, 359-366

vertices (sine waves), 345-350

color, 162

  16-bit, 32-33

  32-bit, 32-33

  alpha channels, 33

    blending, 241-244

    color keys, 242

    pixel shaders, 304

    rendering transparency, 241-244

    stage states, 216-218

    texture tool, 242

  ambient (diffuse), 151

  blending (alpha tests), 244

  channels, 33

  CMYK, 32

  floating-point values, 33

  HSB, 32

  intensity, 38-39, 162

  lighting, 33, 162

  meshes (vertex shaders), 323-325

  normalized, 33

  overview, 41-42

  palettes, 33

  pixel shaders, 304, 703

black-and-white filter, 703-704

brightness, 704-706

color curves, 713-719

color registers, 292

contrast, 709-712

convolution kernels, 719-724

inverting, 707

performance, 724

sepia-tone, 712-713

solarizing, 707-708

  quantizing, 33

  RGB, 32

  RGBA, 33

  stage states, 215-216

    color arguments, 217

    color operations, 216-217

    triadic operations, 218

  textures

    borders, 221

    modulation, 198-199

  vertices, 323-325

    depth shader, 434-439

    white, 179

color curves (pixel shaders), 713-719

color keys (alpha channels), 242

color registers (pixel shaders), 292

Common files, 57

comparison function (stencil buffer), 763

compiling applications, 65-67

computing Bezier patches, 393-396

concatenating matrices, 26-27

cones (spot lights), 165-166

console history, 5-6

constants

  registers

    pixel shaders, 293

    vertex shaders, 263

  setting, 274

constructors

  CVertexApplication class, 107

  defining, 60

contrast (pixel shaders), 709-712

control points (Bezier curves), 387

convolution kernels, 719-724

coordinates. *See also* vectors
  Cartesian system
    defined, 10
    overview, 370-372
  cylindrical, 371
  homogenous, 23
  polar, 370
  spherical, 371, 374
  textures, 194-199
    1D, 196
    stage states, 219-221
  variables, troubleshooting, 386
  vectors, 10-11
  vertex shaders
    code, 375-383
    lighting, 375
    mapping, 372-375
    shading, 375
  vertices
    scaling, 208
    setting, 206-207
Copernicus, Nicolaus, 451
corners (normals), smoothing, 138
cos function, 403
cosines (Tayor series), 341
CreateBones function, 425
CreateCustomTexture function, 201, 203
CreateDepthStencilSurface function, 554, 636
CreateDevice function, 73-75, 80, 86-87
CreateFont function, 731
CreateFromAVIFile function, 687, 689
CreateGeometry function, 145, 201
CreateGridVisuals function, 400
CreateIndexBuffer function, 140, 150
CreatePixelShader function, 307, 313, 553
CreatePlaneBuffer function, 507
CreateShader function, 278, 281, 312-313, 552
CreateSpriteBuffer function, 664, 673

CreateStaticText function, 731
CreateTextObjects function, 746
CreateTexture function, 192
CreateVertexBuffer function, 98, 100, 107, 109, 149, 278
CreateVertexShader function, 273-274
CreateWindow function, 64, 83
creating
  pixel shaders, 306-307
  textures, 191-194
  vertex shaders, 273-274
    billboards, 355-359
cross products, 15-16
CTechniqueApplication class, 326-334
CTestingApplication class, 245-255
CTextureApplication class, 199-211
CTextureApplication function, 201
CTextureStateApplication class, 225-234
CTransformApplication class, 125-130
cube maps
  depth testing, troubleshooting, 240
  dynamic, 481-482
    rendering textures, 638-640
  environmental mapping, 480-481
  hemispherical lighting, 497
  vectors
    eye, 483
    reflection, 482-484
    refraction, 485-486
  vertex shaders
    code, 490-496
    reflection, 487-489
    refraction, 487-489
CubeNormal function, 783
cubic filters, 223
culling (triangle strips), 148
cursors, 2D picking, 774-776
curves
  Bezier, 386-389
    basis functions, 388
    control points, 387

rendering, 172
slopes (derivatives), 390-393
CVertexApplication class
  building, 106-112
  constructor, 107
  defining, 107
  destructor, 107
  initializing, 107
  locking buffers, 111
  optimizing, 109
CVertexApplication function, 107
cyan, magenta, yellow, black (CMYK), 32
cylindrical coordinates, 371

D

D3DCOLORVALUE data type, 38, 40
D3DLIGHT8 structure, 162-163, 168-169
D3DLIGHTTYPE data type, 38, 40
D3DMATRIX data type, 27
D3DMatrixIdentity function, 28, 148, 173
D3DMatrixMultiply function, 28
D3DMatrixPerspectiveFovLH function, 148
D3DMatrixRotationX function, 28
D3DMatrixRotationY function, 28
D3DMatrixRotationZ function, 28, 129
D3DMatrixScaling function, 28
D3DMatrixTranslation function, 28
D3DRM, D3DX comparison, 7
D3DSHADEMODE data type, 41
D3DVECTOR data type, 40
D3DVIEWPORT8 structure, 125
D3DX
  D3DRM comparison, 7
  data types, 17, 19
    matrices, 27-28
    vectors, 17-19
  functions, 17, 19
    matrices, 27-28
    vectors, 17-19

D3DXAssembleShader function, 272, 285, 306

D3DXAssembleShaderFromFile function, 272, 313

D3DXComputeTangent function, 617

D3DXCreateCubeTextureFromFile function, 491

D3DXCreateTextureFromFile function, 193-194, 242

D3DXCreateTextureFromFileEx function, 193-194

D3DXIntersect function, 781

D3DXLoadMeshFrom function, 150

D3DXLoadMeshFromX function, 141

D3DXMATRIX data type, 27

D3DXMatrixLookAtLH function, 173

D3DXMatrixOrthoLH function, 121-122, 660

D3DXMatrixOrthoOffCenterLH function, 122, 661-662

D3DXMatrixPerspectiveFovLH function, 121-122, 174

D3DXMatrixPerspectiveLH function, 122

D3DXMatrixPerspectiveOffCenterLH function, 122

D3DXMatrixRotationYawPitchRoll function, 152

D3DXMatrixScaling function, 129, 182, 208

D3DXMatrixShadow function, 503

D3DXMatrixTranslation function, 129, 181

D3DXMatrixTranspose function, 276, 283

D3DXPlaneFromPoints function, 783

D3DXQUATERNION data type, 18

D3DXQuaternionRotateAxis function, 18

D3DXToRadian function, 178

D3DXToRadian macro, 178

D3DXVec3Add function, 18

D3DXVec3Cross function, 18, 598

D3DXVec3Dot function, 18

D3DXVec3Length function, 18

D3DXVec3Normalize function, 18

D3DXVec3Subtract function, 18

D3DXVecNormalize function, 365

D3DXVECTOR2 data type, 18

D3DXVECTOR3 data type, 18

D3DXVECTOR3 function, 598

D3DXVECTOR4 data type, 18

darkness (mipmaps), weighting, 471

data

    meshes, vertex shaders, 325

    pixels, mapping, 124-125

    vertices, remapping, 333

data structures, instances, 97-98

data types

    D3DCOLORVALUE, 40

    D3DLIGHTTYPE, 38, 40

    D3DMATRIX, 27

    D3DSHADEMODE, 41

    D3DVECTOR, 40

    D3DX, 17, 19

        matrices, 27-28

        vectors, 17-19

    D3DXMATRIX, 27

    D3DXQUATERNION, 18

    D3DXVECTOR2, 18

    D3DXVECTOR3, 18

    D3DXVECTOR4, 18

    FLOAT, 40

    lighting, 39-40

declaring vertex shaders, 269-271

defining

    classes, 60-61, 80-81

    constructors, 60

    CVertexApplication class, 107

    destructors, 60

    message handling, 60-62

    windows, 59-60

DefWindowProc function, 65, 86

degenerate triangles, 138

delete function, 62

DeletePixelShader function, 314

DeleteVertexShader function, 274, 283, 314

dependency, texture reads, 293-294

depth buffers

    clearing, 241

    overview, 239-240

    polygons (alpha tests), 244

    render states, 239-240

    W buffering, 240

    Z bias, 241

depth comparison vertex shaders, 549

depth shaders

    shadow maps, 543

    vertex color, 434-439

depth testing

    code, 245-255

    cube mapping, 240

    overview, 239-240

    performance, 245

    pipeline, 50

    vertex shaders, 357

derivatives (curve slopes), 390-393

deriving surface normals, 390-393

Descartes, Rene, 371, 486

DestroyDevice function, 80, 85, 87

DestroyFont function, 731

DestroyGeometry function, 145, 147, 201

destroying

    devices, 77

    textures, 205

    vertex buffers, 101, 106-107

    vertex shaders, 274

DestroyLightVisuals function, 170, 174

DestroyStaticText function, 731

DestroyTextObjects function, 746

DestroyVertexBuffer function, 107-109, 278

DestroyWindow function, 64

destructors

    CVertexApplication class, 107

    defining, 60

devices

    buffering, 74-75

    building

        creating device, 73-75

creating object, 71

destroying device, 77

querying hardware, 72-73

resetting device, 76-77

clearing, 78-79

floating-point numbers, 74

lighting

querying, 167

setting up, 167-168

multiple threads, 74

overview, 91

performance, 74

rendering, 77-78

states

lighting, 167

resetting, 148

textures, 196-197

types, 70-71

vertex shaders, 268

vertices, processing, 74

windows, 75

differential calculus, 390-393

diffuse lighting, 35-36

ambient, 151

dimensions, textures, 190-192

Direct3D files, 57

Direct3DCreate8 function, 71, 86

DirectDraw, 7

2D rendering, 658

directional light shader, 452-454

directional lighting, 38-39

attenuation, 163, 178

per-pixel lighting, 569

point lighting comparison, 164

setting up, 163

sunlight, 163

directories, setting up, 58

DirectShow

CDirectXVideoTexture class, 685-696

filters, 680-682

streaming media, 680-682

graph builder, 682

GraphEdit tool, 681

interleaving, 681

texture filter, 683-685

textures, 696-698

video, 696-698

DirectX

history, 6-7

OpenGL comparison, 7

DirectX8 files, 56

DirectXEULAs files, 57

DispatchMessage function, 64, 85

distance, lighting, 38-39

DistanceScalers function, 557

Doc files, 56

documentation, DX8SDK, 56

DoRenderSample function, 687, 694

dot products, vectors, 13-14

double precision (floating-point numbers), 74

DrawDebug function, 732

DrawIndexedPrimitive function, 140

drawing

performance, 105

text, 728-746

DrawPrimitive function, 103-104, 129-130, 152-158

DrawSprite function, 668

DrawSpriteEx function, 669

DrawStaticText function, 731

DrawSubset function, 143, 153

DrawText function, 731

DX8SDK

documentation, 56

files, 56-57

installing, 56

DXUtils files, 56

dynamic cube maps, 481-482

rendering textures, 638-640

E

EasyCreateFullScreen function, 80, 89

EasyCreateWindowed function, 80, 84, 89

edges, vertices (toon shaders), 470-471

effects

Membrane, 476

ocean, 351

emissive lighting, 34-35

enabling alpha blending, 243-244

end user license agreements, 57

EndScene function, 77, 86

EntryMessageHandler function, 62

EnumAdapterModes function, 72, 88

EnumerateModes function, 80, 87

environmental mapping (cube maps), 480-481

equations, matrices, 22-23

EULAs (end user license agreements), 57

executable.cpp file, 61-62

executable.h header, 59-60

explosions

billboards, 366

meshes, 350

performance, 354

ExtractBuffers function, 398

extrusion, 521-523

eye vectors (cube maps), 483

F

falloff (spot lights), 165-166

fans, triangle

index buffers, 139-141

rendering, 137, 155

Ferguson, James, 389

field-of-view (FOV), 120-122

angles, 120-122

zooming, 131

files

application.cpp, 63-65

implementing, 82-90

bin, 56

Common, 57

Direct3D, 57

directories, 58

DirectX8, 56

DirectXEULAs, 57

Doc, 56

DX8SDK, 56-57

files (continued)
DXUtils, 56
executable.cpp, 61-62
header
application.h, 60-61, 79-81
executable.h, 59-60
Include files, 57
VertexApplication.h, 107
Include, 57
Lib, 57
Multimedia, 57
Samples, 57
utilities, 56
.X, 56
rendering, 141-143
utilities, 141
FillCharacter function, 732
filling vertex buffers, 106-107
FillVertex function, 745
FillVertexBuffer function, 107, 110,
145, 154, 278
filters
black-and-white, 703-704
DirectShow, 680-682
texture filter, 683-685
stage states, 222-225
anisotropic filters, 223-224
bias, 224
flat cubic filters, 223
Glaussian cubic filters, 223
levels, 224
linear filters, 223
magnifying, 222
minifying, 224
modes, 229
point filters, 223
FindFilterByName function, 691
FindPin function, 690
fixed function lighting, 162-163
applications, 168-169
code, 170-184
overview, 184-185
flags
Bezier patches, 408

FVFs, precedence, 97, 99
vertex buffers, 100-102
flares (point lighting), 164
flashlight lighting, 38-39
flat cubic filters (textures), 223
flat shading, 41
Flexible Vertex Formats (FVFs)
flags precedence, 97, 99
performance, 105
FLOAT data type, 40
floating-point values
color, 33
devices, 74
memset, 508
fog (pipeline), 49
fonts, creating, 728-746
force fields, 338
formats
FVF flags precedence, 97, 99
performance, 105
textures, 192
FOV (field-of-view), 120-122
angles, 120-122
zooming, 131
frame buffer (pipeline), 50
frames
frame rates
applications, 754-757
timing, 752-753
key frame animation, 412-413
reference, lighting, 450
**frustums, projection
transformations,** 120-122
functions
Ambient, 515
ApplyStateBlock, 740
basis (Bezier curves), 388
BeginScene, 77, 85, 507
CaptureStateBlock, 740
CBaseVideoRenderer, 688
CheckMediaType, 687, 692
CHostApplication, 60, 62
Clear, 78-79
CloneMesh, 275

CloneMeshFVF, 329-331
CoCreateInstance, 690
comparison (stencil buffer), 763
cos, 403
CreateBones, 425
CreateCustomTexture, 201, 203
CreateDepthStencilSurface,
554, 636
CreateDevice, 73-75, 80, 86-87
CreateFont, 731
CreateFromAVIFile, 687, 689
CreateGeometry, 145, 201
CreateGridVisuals, 400
CreateIndexBuffer, 140, 150
CreatePixelShader, 307, 313, 553
CreatePlaneBuffer, 507
CreateShader, 278, 281,
312-313, 552
CreateSpriteBuffer, 664, 673
CreateStaticText, 731
CreateTextObjects, 746
CreateTexture, 192
CreateVertexBuffer, 98, 100, 107,
109, 149, 278
CreateVertexShader, 273-274
CreateWindow, 64, 83
CTextureApplication, 201
CubeNormal, 783
CVertexApplication, 107
D3DMatrixIdentity, 28, 148, 173
D3DMatrixMultiply, 28
D3DMatrixPerspectiveFovLH, 148
D3DMatrixRotationX, 28
D3DMatrixRotationY, 28
D3DMatrixRotationZ, 28, 129
D3DMatrixScaling, 28
D3DMatrixTranslation, 28
D3DX, 17, 19
matrices, 27-28
vectors, 17-19
D3DXAssembleShader, 272,
285, 306
D3DXAssembleShaderFromFile,
272, 313
D3DXComputeTangent, 617

D3DXCreateCubeTextureFromFile, 491

D3DXCreateTextureFromFile, 193-194, 242

D3DXCreateTextureFromFileEx, 193-194

D3DXIntersect, 781

D3DXLoadMeshFrom, 150

D3DXLoadMeshFromX, 141

D3DXMatrixLookAtLH, 173

D3DXMatrixOrthoLH, 121-122, 660

D3DXMatrixOrthoOffCenterLH, 122, 661-662

D3DXMatrixPerspectiveFovLH, 121-122, 174

D3DXMatrixPerspectiveLH, 122

D3DXMatrixPerspectiveOffCenterLH, 122

D3DXMatrixRotationYawPitchRoll, 152

D3DXMatrixScaling, 129, 182, 208

D3DXMatrixShadow, 503

D3DXMatrixTranslation, 129, 181

D3DXMatrixTranspose, 276, 283

D3DXPlaneFromPoints, 783

D3DXQuaternionRotateAxis, 18

D3DXToRadian, 178

D3DXVec3Add, 18

D3DXVec3Cross, 18, 598

D3DXVec3Dot, 18

D3DXVec3Length, 18

D3DXVec3Normalize, 18

D3DXVec3Subtract, 18

D3DXVec4Normalize, 365

D3DXVECTOR3, 598

DefWindowProc, 65, 86

delete, 62

DeletePixelShader, 314

DeleteVertexShader, 274, 283, 314

DestroyDevice, 80, 85, 87

DestroyFont, 731

DestroyGeometry, 145, 147, 201

DestroyLightVisuals, 170, 174

DestroyStaticText, 731

DestroyTextObjects, 746

DestroyVertexBuffer, 107-109, 278

DestroyWindow, 64

Direct3DCreate8, 71, 86

DispatchMessage, 64, 85

DistanceScalers, 557

DoRenderSample, 687, 694

DrawDebug, 732

DrawIndexedPrimitive, 140

DrawPrimitive, 103-104, 129-130, 152-158

DrawSprite, 668

DrawSpriteEx, 669

DrawStaticText, 731

DrawSubset, 143, 153

DrawText, 731

EasyCreateFullScreen, 80, 89

EasyCreateWindowed, 80, 84, 89

EndScene, 77, 86

EntryMessageHandler, 62

EnumAdapterModes, 72, 88

EnumerateModes, 80, 87

ExtractBuffers, 398

FillCharacter, 732

FillVertex, 745

FillVertexBuffer, 107, 110, 145, 154, 278

FindFilterByName, 691

FindPin, 690

GetAdapterDisplayMode, 89

GetAdapterModeCount, 72, 87

GetClientRect, 128, 148

GetCubeMapSurface, 639

GetDepthStencilSurface, 637

GetDesktopWindow, 83

GetDeviceCaps, 72, 167

GetHeightAt, 780

GetLevelCount, 192

GetLevelDesc, 192

GetModuleHandle, 83

GetNumFaces, 333

GetPickObject, 788

GetPointer, 694

GetRenderTarget, 554, 637

GetStencilDepthSurface, 554

GetSurfaceLevel, 193, 209

GetTickCount, 129, 750

GetViewpoint, 557

GetViewport, 125, 127, 129

Go, 61-62, 83

HackLight, 512

HandleMessage, 81, 90, 170-171

InitializeD3D, 79, 83, 86

InitializeFan, 146, 154-155

InitializeIndexed, 146, 154, 158

InitializeLights, 146, 148, 158-159, 170, 174

InitializeLightVisuals, 170

InitializeList, 146, 154, 157-158

InitializeStrip, 146, 154, 156-157

InitializeViewports, 126-127

LightDir, 403

LightEnable, 159, 167, 174

LoadMesh, 145, 148, 150, 176

Lock, 101-102, 111

LockAttributeBuffer, 324

LockRect, 193, 210

MessageHandler, 60-62, 86

MulDiv, 734

PeekMessage, 64, 84-85

PickConstants, 790

PlaneNormal, 783

Pop, 123

PostInitialize, 81, 84, 90

PostQuitMessage, 65, 86

PostRender, 80, 84-85, 90

PostReset, 81, 90

PostTerminate, 81, 85, 90

PreInitialize, 81, 83, 90

PreRender, 80-81, 84-85, 90

PreReset, 81, 84, 90

Present, 77, 86, 642

PreTerminate, 81, 85, 90

Push, 123

PushDistance, 531

QueryPerformanceCounter, 751

QueryPerformanceFrequency, 751

RangeConstants, 348

functions (continued)

Release, 77, 86-87, 101

Render, 81, 84, 90

RenderBones, 428

RenderControlGrid, 405

RenderLightVisuals, 170

RenderMesh, 145, 153

RenderPlane, 532

RenderPlaneAndShadow, 509, 513-514

Reset, 76-77, 88

RestoreDevice, 80, 84, 88

RotateSprite, 668

Scale, 349

ScaleSprite, 668

SetBkColor, 734

SetBufferPointer, 150

SetIndices, 140, 152

SetLight, 159, 167

message handling, 177

SetMapMode, 734

SetMaterial, 152-153

SetMediaType, 687, 693

SetPixelShader, 307, 315

SetRenderState, 148, 159, 167

SetRenderTarget, 557

SetStreamSource, 103-104, 109, 152

SetTextAlign, 734

SetTextColor, 734

SetTextExtentPoint32, 736

SetTexture, 197-198

SetTextureStageState, 204, 214-215, 224, 229

SetTransform, 122-123, 128-130, 148

SetupDevice, 145, 148-149, 170, 201

SetupEnvironment, 491

SetVertexShader, 103-104, 109, 152, 273-274, 285

SetVertexShaderConstant, 273-274, 283, 348, 404

SetViewport, 125, 129-130

ShadowPlane, 510

ShowWindow, 64, 83

sin, 349, 403

sinf, 349

switch, 65, 86

TestCooperativeLevel, 76-77, 88

TranslateMessage, 64, 85

TranslateSprite, 667

Unlock, 102

UnlockRect, 193

VerifyModes, 226, 228

Wave, 349

WinMain, 59-60, 62

writing, 17

XRayParams, 443

ZeroMemory, 89, 159, 163

FVFs (Flexible Vertex Formats)

flags precedence, 97, 99

performance, 105

G

Galilei, Galileo, 451

Game Developer magazine, 794

Gauss, Carl Friedrich, 222

Gaussian cubic filters, 223

GDI, rendering text, 728-746

geForce, 4-5

GetAdapterDisplayMode function, 89

GetAdapterModeCount function, 72, 87

GetClientRect function, 128, 148

GetCubeMapSurface function, 639

GetDepthStencilSurface function, 637

GetDesktopWindow function, 83

GetDeviceCaps function, 72, 167

GetHeightAt function, 780

GetLevelCount function, 192

GetLevelDesc function, 192

GetModuleHandle function, 83

GetNumFaces function, 333

GetPickObject function, 788

GetPointer function, 694

GetRenderTarget function, 554, 637

GetStencilDepthSurface function, 554

GetSurfaceLevel function, 193, 209

GetTickCount function, 129, 750

GetViewpoint function, 557

GetViewport function, 125, 127, 129

Go function, 61-62, 83

Gouraud shading, 41

GPU (graphics processing unit), 4-5

graph builder (DirectShow), 682

GraphEdit tool, 681

graphics cards, 190

H

H (halfway vector), 36-37

HackLight function, 512

Haeberli, Paul, 794

HAL (hardware abstraction layer), 70

halfway vector (H), 36-37

HandleMessage function, 81, 90, 170-171

handles (windows), 64

Hanrahan, Pat, 794

hardware, querying, 72-73

hardware abstraction layer (HAL), 70

header files

application.h, 60-61, 79-81

executable.h, 59-60

Include files, 57

VertexApplication.h, 107

height (textures), 192

hemispherical lighting (cube maps), 497

higher-order surfaces, 46

high-resolution timing, 751-752

history

consoles, 5-6

DirectX, 6-7

movies, 6

PCs, 4-5

homogenous coordinates, 23

HSB (hue, saturation, brightness), 32

I

ID3DMatrixStack interface, 123

ID3DXSprite interface, 663

identity matrix, 24

IDEs, setting up directories, 58

IDirect3DBaseTexture8 interface, 191

IDirect3DCubeTexture8 interface, 481

IDirect3DDevice8

buffering, 74-75

building

creating device, 73-75

creating object, 71

destroying device, 77

querying hardware, 72-73

resetting device, 76-77

clearing, 78-79

floating-point numbers, 74

multiple threads, 74

overview, 91

performance, 74

rendering, 77-78

types, 70-71

vertices, processing, 74

windows, 75

IDirect3DTexture8 interface, 191

images. *See also* animation; objects; primitives

motion blur

applications, 643-654

rendering, 640-642

post processing, 702-703

rotation (quaternions), 16-17

sprites, 2D rendering, 663-664

implementing

applications, 82-90

vertex shaders, 268

Include Files, 57

incrementing

lights, 175

meshes, 175

index buffers

buffer relationships, 324

offsets, 152

releasing, 151

rendering primitives, 139-141

indices, ratio to angles, 486

inflating objects, 338

inheritance (textures), 191

InitializeD3D function, 79, 83, 86

InitializeFan function, 146, 154-155

InitializeIndexed function, 146, 154, 158

InitializeLights function, 146, 148, 158-159, 170, 174

InitializeLightVisuals function, 170

InitializeList function, 146, 154, 157-158

InitializeStrip function, 146, 154, 156-157

InitializeViewports function, 126-127

initializing

CVertexApplication class, 107

light, 158-159, 170

meshes, 152

input

keyboards, lighting, 170-171

picking

2D, 774-776

ray, 776-779

pixel shaders, 292

installing DX8SDK, 56

instances, data structures, 97-98

instantiating classes, 61-62

instructions

pixel shaders, 294-297, 305

addressing, 298-303

pairing, 298

slt, 527

texm3x3pad, 611-613

vertex shaders, 264-267

intensity (lighting), 38-39, 162

interfaces

ID3DMatrixStack, 123

ID3DXSprite, 663

IDirect3DBaseTexture8, 191

IDirect3DCubeTexture8, 481

IDirect3DTexture8, 191

interleaving (synchronization), 681

inverse world matrices, 451

inverting pixel shaders, 303, 707

invisibility. *See* transparency

J-K

kernels, convolution, 719-724

key frame animation, 412-413

keyboard input, lighting, 170-171

L

Lander, Jeff, 794

leaks, memory, 205

length (vectors), 11

levels, textures, 224

getting, 193

mipmaps, 190-191, 208-209

number, 192

Lib files, 57

libraries, 57

license agreements, end user, 57

light maps, 566-567

LightDir function, 403

LightEnable function, 159, 167, 174

lighting. *See also* textures

ambient, 34-35

diffuse, 151

realism, 167

attenuated, 38-39

backward, troubleshooting, 392

blackness, troubleshooting, 127

bump mapping overview, 588-590

calculations, output, 33

changing structure, 167

color, 33, 162

coordinate systems (vertex shaders), 375

cube maps

eye vectors, 483

hemispherical, 497

reflection vectors, 482-484

refraction vectors, 485-486

D3DLIGHT8 structure, 162-163

data types, 39-40

devices

querying, 167

setting up, 167-168

state, 167

diffuse, 35-36

lighting (continued)

directional, 38-39

attenuation, 163, 178

setting up, 163

sunlight, 163

directional light shader, 452-454

distance, 38-39

emissive, 34-35

fixed function, 162-163

applications, 168-169

code, 170-184

overview, 184-185

flashlights, 38-39

incrementing, 175

initializing, 158-159, 170

intensity, 38-39, 162

message handling (keyboard input), 170-171

optimizing, 177

overview, 41-42

penumbra, 38-39

performance, 143-144

per-pixel. *See* per-pixel lighting

pipeline, 46

pixel shaders, 308-309

point, 38-39

attenuation, 164

directional comparison, 164

flares, 164

moving, 177

setting up, 163-165

torches, 164

point light shader, 454-456

reference frames, 450

reflection, per-pixel, 610

rendering

number of vertices, 172

spectra, 468

toon shaders, 468-471

shaders

applications, 459-462

code, 459-462

palettes, 462

shading, 39, 41

flat, 41

Gouraud, 41

shadows. *See* shadows

sophisticated, 39

specular, 36-38

halfway vector (H), 36-37

power (P), 36

reflected light (R), 36-37

viewer (V), 36

spot lights, 38-39

cones, 165-166

falloff, 165-166

moving, 181

penumbra, 165-166

performance, 430

Phi, 165-166

scaling, 179-183

setting up, 165-166

Theta, 165-166

umbra, 165-166

spot light shader, 456-459

streetlamps

applications, 359-366

billboards, 355-359

surfaces, direction, 13

T&L (transformation and lighting), 46

cards (2D rendering), 659

pipeline, 46

texture space (basis vectors), 592-294

torches, 38-39

umbra, 38-39

vectors. *See* vectors

vertex buffers, 170-171

vertex shaders, 308-309

vertices, 135

object space, 448-451

viewpoints, rendering, 545-546

water, 485

world matrices, 451

linear filters, 223

lists, triangle

index buffers, 139-141

rendering, 136-137, 157-158

triangle strips comparison, 158

loading

meshes, 141-143, 150

textures, 193-194

LoadMesh function, 145, 148, 150, 176

Lock function, 101-102, 111

LockAttributeBuffer function, 324

locking buffers, 101-102, 111

flags, 102

performance, 671-674

LockRect function, 193, 210

loops (message pumps), 64

low-resolution timing, 750

M

macros

D3DXToRadian, 178

random numbers, 108

vertex shaders, 264-267, 269-271

magazine, *Game Developer,* 794

magnifying textures, 222

magnitude (vectors), 11

mapping

bump. *See* bump mapping

coordinate systems (vertex shaders), 372-375

cube maps. *See* cube maps

data (pixels), 124-125

shadow maps. *See* shadow maps

masks

stencil, 765

write

pixel shaders, 304

vertex shaders, 267-268

materials. *See* meshes

matrices. *See also* transformations

adding, 23

C++, 27

clearing, 24

concatenating, 26-27

D3DX data types, 27-28

D3DX functions, 27-28

defined, 22

equations, 22-23

homogenous coordinates, 23
identity, 24
matrix palettes, 415-416
   address registers, 416-419
   applications, 419-430
   code, 419-430
   vertex shaders, 416-419
multiplying, 22-23
OpenGL, 23
orthogonal (2D rendering),
   660-662
overview, 28-29
rotation, 25-26
scaling, 25
translation, 24
matrix palettes, 415-416
   address registers, 416-419
   applications, 419-430
   code, 419-430
   vertex shaders, 416-419
Membrane effect, 476
memory
   surfaces, 189
   textures, 189
      performance, 194, 198
   troubleshooting leaks, 205
**MemoryPool parameter (vertex
   buffers),** 100-101
memset (floating-point values), 508
meshes
   application behavior, 176
   bounding box values, 398
   bump mapping, 590-592
   cloning, 329-331
   exploding, 350
   incrementing, 175
   loading, 141-143, 150
   performance, 143
   rendering, 141-143
      code, 144-159
      initializing, 152
      sophisticated, 144-159
   skinning, 413-416
      address registers, 416-419
      applications, 419-430

code, 419-430
   vertex shaders, 416-419
transformations
   rotating, 151
   spinning, 151
TRUFORM (pipeline), 46
vertex shaders, 275
   application, 326-334
   cloning, 322-323
   color, 323-325
   data, 325
   performance, 325-326
message handling
   defining, 60-62
   keyboard input, 170-171
   message pumps, 64
   SetLight function, 177
message pumps, 64
MessageHandler function, 60-62, 86
minifying textures, 224
mipmaps
   animated, 200
   darkness, weighting, 471
   defined, 190
   filters, 222-225
      anisotropic, 223-224
      bias, 224
      flat cubic filters, 223
      Gaussian cubic filters, 223
      levels, 224
      linear filters, 223
      magnifying, 222
      minifying, 224
      point filters, 223
   levels, 208-209
   textures, 190-191
mirroring textures, 220-221
modes
   addressing
      stage states, 233
      textures, 220-221
   filters, 229
modifiers, pixel shaders, 303-305
modulation, textures, 198-199

motion blur
   applications, 643-654
   images, rendering, 640-642
   performance, 654
   render targets, 640-642
      post-processing, 642-643
mouse cursor, 2D picking, 774-776
movies, history, 6
moving
   objects (translation matrix), 24
   point lighting, 177
   spot lighting, 181
MulDiv function, 734
multim im parvo, 190
Multimedia files, 57
multiple threads, 74
multiplying
   matrices, 22-23
   vectors, 12
multitexturing
   pipeline, 48-49
   stage states, 215-216
   textures, 199

N

N patches (pipeline), 46
negating
   pixel shaders, 303
   vertex shaders, 267-268
normal vectors. *See* surfaces
normalized color, 33
normalizing vectors, 11
normals
   corners, smoothing, 138
   surface, deriving, 390-393
   vectors, transforming, 450
   vertices
      scaling, 338-340
      surfaces, 135
numbers
   floating-point
      color, 33
      devices, 74
      memset, 508

numbers (continued)
  random macro, 108
  textures
    devices, 196
    levels, 192
  vertices, lighting, 172
nVidia
  Effects Browser Membrane effect, 476
  shadow maps, 543

O

object space, lighting vertices, 448-451
objects. *See also* animation; images; primitives
  3D, warping, 396
  color, 33
  corners, smoothing normals, 138
  IDirect3DDevice8, 71
  inflating, 338
  lighting. *See* lighting
  moving (translation matrix), 24
  rotating (rotation matrix), 25-26
  rotation
    precedence, 119
    quaternions, 16-17
  scaling
    precedence, 120
    scaling matrix, 25
  translation, precedence, 119
ocean effects, 351
offsets (index buffers), 152
OpenGL
  2D rendering, 659
  accumulation buffer, 642
  DirectX comparison, 7
  matrices, 23
operations
  pixel shaders, 292
  transformations
    precedence, 118-120
    sophisticated, 125-130

stage states
  color, 216-217
  triadic, 218
  update (stencil buffer), 764-765
optimizing
  CVertexApplication class, 109
  lighting, 177
  performance. *See* performance
  vertex buffers, 109
orientation. *See* transformations
orthogonal matrices (2D rendering), 660-662
output
  lighting calculations, 33
  pixel shaders, 292-293
  vertex shaders, 263

P

P (power), 36
Painters Algorithm, 239
painting, 66-67
pairing instructions (pixel shaders), 298
palettes
  color, 33
  matrix palettes (skinning), 415-416
    address registers, 416-419
    applications, 419-430
    code, 419-430
    vertex shaders, 416-419
  shaders, lighting, 462
parameters
  D3DX functions, 17-19
    matrices, 27-28
    vectors, 17-19
  MemoryPool (vertex buffers), 100-101
patches (Bezier)
  advantages, 407-408
  Beziercurves, 408
  flags, 408
  terrain, 407
  uses, 407-408

vertex shaders
  applications, 396-407
  code, 396-407
  computing, 393-396
paths, setting up, 58
PCs, history, 4-5
PeekMessage function, 64, 84-85
penumbra
  lighting, 38-39
  spot lights, 165-166
performance (optimizing). *See also* troubleshooting
  3D geometry, 2D animation comparison, 354
  alpha blending, 245
  batching, 105-106, 143
  buffers, locking, 671-674
  counters
    applications, 754-757
    frame rates, 752-753
    high-resolution timing, 751-752
  depth testing, 245
  devices, 74
  drawing, 105
  explosions, 354
  formats, 105
  FVFs, 105
  higher-order surfaces, 46
  lighting, 143-144
    shadows, 430
    spot lights, 430
  memory, textures, 194
  meshes, 143, 325-326
  motion blur, 654
  picking, 794-795
  pipeline, 50-51
  pixel shaders, 724
  querying hardware, 72
  rendering, 105
    2D, 671-674
    primitives, 143
    vertices, 143
  stream sources, 105
  textures, 198

transformations, 132
vertex buffers, 98, 105
vertex shaders, 105, 277
vertices, 98
performance counters
applications, 754-757
frame rates, 752-753
high-resolution timing, 751-752
per-pixel lighting
directional lighting, 569
pixel shaders, 567-569
point lighting, 578-579
applications, 581-583
pixel shaders, 580-581
vertex shaders, 579-580
spot lighting, 569-572
applications, 575-578
pixel shaders, 574-575
vertex shaders, 572-574
troubleshooting, 583
per-pixel picking, 785
applications, 786-793
vertex shaders, 785-786
per-pixel reflection, 610
per-pixel toon pixel shaders, 624-629
per-pixel toon shading, 622-623
per-pixel toon vertex shaders, 623-624
Phi (spot lights), 165-166
PickConstants function, 790
picking
2D, 774-776
performance, 794-795
per-pixel, 785
applications, 786-793
vertex shaders, 785-786
ray, 776-784
pipeline
alpha tests, 50
clipper, 48
depth tests, 50
fog, 49
frame buffer, 50
higher-order surfaces, 46

lighting, 46
multitexturing, 48-49
overview, 51-52
performance, 50-51
pixel shaders, 49, 291
stencil tests, 50
steps, 44-45
T&L, 46
transformations, 46
vertex shaders, 47-48
vertices, 45-46
pitch, 189
pixel shaders
alpha channels, 304
applications, 311-316
architecture, 292
assembling, 306-307
bias, 303
blending, 309-311
bump mapping
applications, 603-605
reflection, 616
code, 311-316
color, 304, 703
black-and-white filter, 703-704
brightness, 704-706
color curves, 713-719
contrast, 709-712
convolution kernels, 719-724
inverting, 707
performance, 724
sepia-tone, 712-713
solarizing, 707-708
creating, 306-307
defined, 290-291
input, 292
instructions, 294-297, 305
addressing, 298-303
pairing, 298
inverting, 303
lighting, 308-309
limitations, 305-306
modifiers, 303-305
negating, 303

operation, 292
output, 292-293
overview, 316-317
per-pixel lighting, 567-569
pipeline, 49, 291
point lighting
applications, 581-583
per-pixel lighting, 580-581
registers, 292-293, 303-305
scaling, 303
selectors, 304
shadow mapping, 550-551
spot light
applications, 575-578
per-pixel lighting, 574-575
stage states, 225
support, 306, 311
swizzling, 304
texm3x3pad instruction, 611-613
texture reads, dependency, 293-294
toon
applications, 628-629
per-pixel, 624-627
using, 306-307
versions, 291
vertex shaders relationship, 307-309
write masks, 304
pixels
blitting (2D rendering), 658-659
data mapping, 124-125
pixel shaders. *See* pixel shaders
PlaneNormal function, 783
planes
shadows, 500-501
applications, 506-515
code, 506-515
stencil buffers, 504-506
stencil test, 512
transformations, 503
troubleshooting, 515-517
vectors, 501-503
view frustums, 120-122
point filters, 223

point light shader, 454-456

point lighting, 38-39

  attenuation, 164

  directional lighting comparison, 164

  flares, 164

  moving, 177

  per-pixel lighting, 578-579

    applications, 581-583

    pixel shaders, 580-581

    vertex shaders, 579-580

  setting up, 163-165

  torches, 164

points (Bezier curves), 387

polar coordinates, 370

polygons (depth buffers), 244

Pop function, 123

positions. *See* transformations

PostInitialize function, 81, 84, 90

post-processing

  images, 702-703

  textures (motion blur), 642-643

PostQuitMessage function, 65, 86

PostRender function, 80, 84-85, 90

PostReset function, 81, 90

PostTerminate function, 81, 85, 90

power (P), 36

precedence

  flags (FVFs), 97, 99

  scaling, 120

  transformations

    examples, 125-130

    operations, 118-120

PreInitialize function, 81, 83, 90

PreRender function, 80-81, 84-85, 90

PreReset function, 81, 84, 90

Present function, 77, 86, 642

PreTerminate function, 81, 85, 90

primitives. *See also* animation; images; objects

  corners, smoothing normals, 138

  culling, 148

  rendering

    code, 144-159

    comparison, 158

index buffers, 139-141

  performance, 143

  sophisticated, 144-159

  triangle fans, 137

  triangle lists, 136-137

  triangle strips, 137-139

  vertices, 103-104

processes (devices), 74

products. *See* cross products; dot products

projection transformation

  right-handed, 121

  view frustums, 120-122

pumps (message pumps), 64

Push function, 123

PushDistance function, 531

Pythagorean theorem, 11

Q

quantizing color, 33

quaternions (vectors), 16-17

querying

  adapters, 72

  devices, 167

  hardware (IDirect3DDevice8), 72-73

  video cards, 72

QueryPerformanceCounter function, 751

QueryPerformanceFrequency function, 751

R

R (reflected light), 36-37

random number macro, 108

RangeConstants function, 348

ratio, sine angles to indices, 486

ray picking, 776-784

reads, texture, 293-294

realism, ambient lighting, 167

red, green, blue (RGB), 32

REF, 70

reference frames (lighting), 450

reference value (stencil buffer), 762-763

reflected light (R), 36-37

reflection

  bump mapping

    application, 617-622

    pixel shaders, 616

    vertex shaders, 613-615

  per-pixel, 610

  vectors (cube maps), 482-484

  vertex shaders

    code, 490-496

    cube maps, 487-489

refraction

  vectors (cube maps), 485-486

  vertex shaders

    code, 490-496

    cube maps, 487-489

registers

  address (matrix palette skinning), 416-419

  pixel shaders, 292-293, 303-305

  vertex shaders, 262-263, 269-271

relationships (buffers), 324

Release function, 77, 86-87, 101

releasing index buffers, 151

remapping vertices, 333

Render function, 81, 84, 90

render states

  depth buffers, 239-240

  stencil buffer, 762-765

render targets

  motion blur, 640-642

    performance, 654

    post-processing, 642-643

  textures, 634-636

    rendering, 637-638

    surfaces, 636-637

RenderBones function, 428

RenderControlGrid function, 405

rendering

  2D

    applications, 667-671

    blitting pixels, 658-659

    DirectDraw, 658

    OpenGL, 659

    orthogonal matrices, 660-662

overview, 659-662

performance, 671-674

sprites, 663-664

T&L cards, 659

vertices, 664-666

algorithms, shaders, 466-468

alpha channels (transparency), 241-244

circles, 172

curves, 172

IDirect3DDevice8, 77-78

lighting

number of vertices, 172

spectra, 468

toon shaders, 468-471

meshes, 141-143

code, 144-159

initializing, 152

sophisticated, 144-159

motion blur

applications, 643-654

images, 640-642

performance, 105

primitives

comparison, 158

index buffers, 139-141

performance, 143

sophisticated, 144-159

render targets, 637-638

surfaces, 135-136

text, 728-746

textures

dynamic cube maps, 638-640

lighting viewpoints, 545-546

triangle fans, 137, 155

triangle lists, 136-137, 157-158

triangle strips, 137-139, 156-157

vertices

performance, 143

primitives, 103-104

stream sources, 103-104

vertex shaders, 103-104

.X files, 141-143

RenderLightVisuals function, 170

RenderMesh function, 145, 153

RenderPlane function, 532

RenderPlaneAndShadow function, 509, 513-514

Reset function, 76-77, 88

resetting

device states, 148

devices, 76-77

RestoreDevice function, 80, 84, 88

RGB (red, green, blue), 32

RGBA color, 33

right-handed projection transformations, 121

RotateSprite function, 668

rotation

axes (quaternions), 16-17

meshes (transformations), 151

objects (rotation matrix), 25-26

translation precedence, 119

rotation matrix, 25-26

running applications, 65-67

S

Samples files, 57

scalars, vector comparison, 10

Scale function, 349

ScaleSprite function, 668

scaling

pixel shaders, 303

precedence, 120

spot lighting, 179-183

textures, 190-191

vertices

coordinates, 208

normals, 338-340

scaling matrix, 25

screens, color, 703

black-and-white filter, 703-704

brightness, 704-706

color curves, 713-719

contrast, 709-712

convolution kernels, 719-724

inverting, 707

performance, 724

sepia-tone, 712-713

solarizing, 707-708

SDK (DX8SDK)

blending, 225

documentation, 56

files, 56-57

GraphEdit tool, 681

installing, 56

texture tool, 242

.X files utility, 141

selectors (pixel shaders), 304

sepia-tone (pixel shaders), 712-713

SetBkColor function, 734

SetBufferPointer function, 150

SetIndices function, 140, 152

SetLight function, 159, 167

message handling, 177

SetMapMode function, 734

SetMaterial function, 152-153

SetMediaType function, 687, 693

SetPixelShader function, 307, 315

SetRenderState function, 148, 159, 167

SetRenderTarget function, 557

SetStreamSource function, 103-104, 109, 152

SetTextAlign function, 734

SetTextColor function, 734

SetTextExtentPoint32 function, 736

SetTexture function, 197-198

SetTextureStageState function, 204, 214-215, 224, 229

setting

constants (vertex shaders), 274

device states, 148

stage states, 214-215

transformations, 122-123

vertex buffers, 101-102

vertices, coordinates, 206-207

white, 179

setting up

devices, lighting, 167-168

directional lighting, 163

file directories, 58

point lighting, 163-165

spot lights, 165-166

SetTransform function, 122-123, 128-130, 148

SetupDevice function, 145, 148-149, 170, 201

SetupEnvironment function, 491

SetVertexShader function, 103-104, 109, 152, 273-274, 285

SetVertexShaderConstant function, 273-274, 283, 348, 404

SetViewport function, 125, 129-130

shaders
  depth comparison vertex shaders, 549
  depth shaders
    shadow maps, 543
    vertex color, 434-439
  directional light shader, 452-454
  lighting
    applications, 459-462
    code, 459-462
    palettes, 462
  pixel. *See* pixel shaders
  point light shader, 454-456
  shadow volume, 526-528
    application, 528-536
    troubleshooting, 536-538
  spot light shader, 456-459
  textures
    rendering algorithms, 466-468
  toon. *See* toon shaders
  vertex. *See* vertex shaders
  x-ray
    application, 442-445
    vertex transparency, 439-442

shading
  coordinate systems, 375
  flat, 41
  Gouraud, 41
  surfaces, 39, 41

shadow maps
  applications, 551-560
  code, 551-560
  depth shaders, 543
  nVidia, 543
  overview, 542-544

pixel shaders, 550-551
  textures
    lighting viewpoints, 545-546
    mapping, 546-548
  troubleshooting, 560
  vertex shaders, depth comparison, 549

shadow volume shader, 526-528
  application, 528-536
  troubleshooting, 536-538

shadow volumes, 520-526

ShadowPlane function, 510

shadows
  performance, 430
  planes, 500-501
    applications, 506-515
    code, 506-515
    stencil buffers, 504-506
    stencil test, 512
    transformations, 503
    troubleshooting, 515-517
    vectors, 501-503
  shadow volume shader, 526-528
    application, 528-536
    troubleshooting, 536-538
  volumes, 520-526

shields (force fields), 338

ShowWindow function, 64, 83

sin function, 349, 403

sine waves
  angles to indices ratio, 486
  Taylor series, 341-345
  vertices
    code, 345-350
    warping, 341-345

sinf function, 349

sizing. *See* scaling

skinning, 413-416
  address registers, 416-419
  applications, 419-430
  code, 419-430
  vertex shaders, 416-419

slopes (curves), derivatives, 390-393

slt instruction, 527

Snell's Law, 486

sniper scopes, 765-771

software, SW devices, 70

solarizing (pixel shaders), 707-708

Sony PS2 history, 5-6

sources (streams)
  performance, 105
  rendering vertices, 103-104

space, object, 448-451

spectra (toon shaders), 468

specular lighting, 36-38
  halfway vector (H), 36-37
  power (P), 36
  reflected light (R), 36-37
  viewer (V), 36

spheres
  coordinates, 371, 374
  hemispherical lighting, 497

spinning meshes, 151

spot light shader, 456-459

spot lights
  cones, 165-166
  falloff, 165-166
  lighting, 38-39
  moving, 181
  penumbra, 165-166
  performance, 430
  per-pixel lighting, 569-572
    applications, 575-578
    pixel shaders, 574-575
    vertex shaders, 572-574
  Phi, 165-166
  scaling, 179-183
  setting up, 165-166
  Theta, 165-166
  umbra, 165-166

sprites, rendering, 663-664

stacks (transformations), 123-124

stage states
  addressing modes, 233
  blending, 215-216
    color arguments, 217
    color operations, 216-217
    triadic operations, 218

border color, 221
bump mapping, 218
code, 225-234
color, 215-216
filter modes, 229
filters, 222-225
    anisotropic, 223-224
    bias, 224
    flat cubic filters, 223
    Gaussian cubic filters, 223
    levels, 224
    linear filters, 223
    magnifying, 222
    minifying, 224
    point filters, 223
multitexturing, 215-216
pixel shaders, 225
setting, 214-215
support, 214
texture coordinates, 219-221
vertex shaders, 225
stages, textures, 197
states
devices
    lighting, 167
    resetting, 148
render
    depth buffers, 239-240
    stencil buffer, 762-765
stage
    addressing modes, 233
    blending, 215-218
    border color, 221
    bump mapping, 218
    code, 225-234
    color, 215-216
    filter modes, 229
    filters, 222-225
    multitexturing, 215-216
    pixel shaders, 225
    setting, 214-215
    support, 214
    texture coordinates, 219-221
    vertex shaders, 225

static vertex buffers, 100
stencil buffers
    comparison function, 763
    overview, 760-762
    planes (shadows), 504-506
    reference value, 762-763
    render states, 762-765
    stencil masks, 765
    stencil testing, 762
    update operations, 764-765
    zooming, 765-771
stencil masks, 765
stencil tests
    overview, 760-762
    pipeline, 50
    planes (shadows), 512
    stencil buffer, 762
steps (pipeline), 44-45
stream sources
    performance, 105
    rendering vertices, 103-104
streaming media
    AVI files, 680-682
    graph builder, 682
    GraphEdit tool, 681
    interleaving, 681
streetlamps
    applications, 359-366
    billboards, 355-359
strips, triangle
    culling, 148
    index buffers, 139-141
    rendering, 137-139, 156-157
    triangle lists comparison, 158
structure, lighting, 167
structures
    D3DLIGHT8, 162-163, 168-169
    D3DVIEWPORT8, 125
sunlight (directional lighting), 163
support
    pixel shaders, 306, 311
    stage states, 214
surfaces. *See also* textures
    dimensions, 190

higher-order
    N patches, 46
    performance, 46
    pipeline, 46
    TRUFORM meshes, 46
lighting. *See* lighting
memory, 189
normals, deriving, 390-393
pitch, 189
render targets, 636-637
rendering, 135-136
shading, 39, 41
textures, 189
vertices, 134-135
SW, defined, 70
switch function, 65, 86
swizzling
    pixel shaders, 304
    vertex shaders, 267-268
synchronization, interleaving, 681

T

T&L (transformation and lighting), 46
    cards (2D rendering), 659
    pipeline, 46
targets, render
    motion blur, 640-642
        performance, 654
        post-processing, 642-643
    textures, 634-636
        rendering, 637-638
        surfaces, 636-637
Taylor series
    cosines, 341
    sine waves, 341-345
    spherical coordinates, 374
temporary registers
    pixel shaders, 293
    vertex shaders, 263
terrain
    Bezier patches, 407
    ray picking, 779-784

TestCooperativeLevel function, 76-77, 88

testing

alpha tests

blending colors, 244

code, 245-255

pipeline, 50

polygons (depth buffers), 244

applications, 245-255

depth testing

code, 245-255

cube mapping, 240

overview, 239-240

performance, 245

pipeline, 50

vertex shaders, 357

stencil tests

overview, 760-762

pipeline, 50

planes (shadows), 512

stencil buffer, 762

texels (texture elements), 189

texm3x3pad instruction, 611-613

text, rendering, 728-746

texture filter (DirectShow), 683-685

texture reads (pixel shaders), 293-294

texture registers

pixel shaders, 293

texture space

basis vectors, 592-294

texture tool

alpha channels, 242

textures. *See also* lighting; surfaces

addressing

modes, 220-221

pixel shaders, 298-303

applications

code, 199-211

DirectShow, 696-698

motion blur, 643-654

acts, 194

mapping, 590-592

VideoTexture class,

clamping, 220-221

color

blackness (toon shaders), 471

borders, 220-221

modulation, 198-199

coordinates, 194-199

1D, 196

stage states, 219-221

creating, 191-194

destroying, 205

devices, 196-197

dimensions, 190, 192

filters, 222-225

anisotropic, 223-224

bias, 224

flat cubic filters, 223

Gaussian cubic filters, 223

levels, 224

linear filters, 223

magnifying, 222

minifying, 224

point filters, 223

formats, 192

inheritance, 191

levels

getting, 193

mipmaps, 190-191

number, 192

light maps, 566-567

loading, 193-194

mapping, shadow maps, 546-548

memory, 189

performance, 194, 198

mipmaps

animated, 200

defined, 190

levels, 208-209

mirroring, 220-221

multitexturing, 199

pipeline, 48-49

overview, 211-212

render targets, 634-636

rendering, 637-638

surfaces, 636-637

rendering

algorithms, 466-468

dynamic cube maps, 638-640

lighting viewpoints, 545-546

motion blur, 640-642

text, 728-746

scaling, 190-191

stage states

addressing modes, 233

blending, 215-218

border color, 221

bump mapping, 218

code, 225-234

color, 215-216

filter modes, 229

filters, 222-225

multitexturing, 215-216

pixel shaders, 225

setting, 214-215

support, 214

texture coordinates, 219-221

vertex shaders, 225

stages, 197

surfaces, 189

testing, 245-255

texels, 189

texture reads, 293-294

tiling, 200-221

toon shaders, 475-476

usage, 192

wrapping, 220-221

theorem, Pythagorean, 11

Theta (spot lights), 165-166

threads, multiple, 74

tiling textures, 200-221

timing

applications, 754-757

frame rates, 752-753

high-resolution, 751-752

low-resolution, 750

tool, GraphEdit, 681

toon shaders

applications, 473-475

code, 473-475

lighting
  rendering, 468-471
  spectra, 468
overview, 471-472
shading per-pixel, 622-623
textures, 475-476
  blackness, 471
toon pixel shaders
  applications, 628-629
  per-pixel, 624-627
toon vertex shaders, 623-624
vertices, edges, 470-471
torches
lighting, 38-39
point lighting, 164
transformation and lighting (T&L), 46
cards (2D rendering), 659
pipeline, 46
transformations. *See also* matrices
applications, 125-130
meshes, rotating, 151
operations
  precedence, 118-120
  sophisticated, 125-130
overview, 116-117, 132
performance, 132
pipeline, 46
planes (shadows), 503
precedence, 125-130
projection
  right-handed, 121
  view frustums, 120-122
setting, 122-123
stacks, 123-124
vertex shaders, 275-277
view, 117
  building, 118-120
  cameras, 173
viewports, 124-125
world, 117-120
zooming, 131
transforming lighting, 450
transforms. *See* transformations

TranslateMessage function, 64, 85
TranslateSprite function, 667
translation, rotation precedence, 119
translation matrix, 24
transparency. *See also* alpha
      channels
  x-ray shader, 439-442
  x-ray shader application, 442-445
triangle fans
  index buffers, 139-141
  rendering, 137, 155
triangle lists
  index buffers, 139-141
  rendering, 136-137, 157-158
  triangle strips comparison, 158
triangle strips
  culling, 148
  index buffers, 139-141
  rendering, 137-139, 156-157
  triangle lists comparison, 158
triangles, degenerate, 138
troubleshooting. *See also*
      performance
  bump mapping, basis vectors, 605
  coordinates, variables, 386
  depth testing
    cube mapping, 240
    vertex shaders, 357
  lighting
    backward, 392
    blackness, 127
  matrices, concatenating, 26
  memory leaks, 205
  per-pixel lighting
    applications, 583
  planes (shadows), 515-517
  shadow mapping, 560
  shadow volume shader, 536-538
  textures
    artifacts, 194
    blackness, 471
    destroying, 205
  triangle strips, 138
TRUFORM meshes (pipeline), 46

twisting axes, 383
types, devices, 70-71

U

umbra
  lighting, 38-39
  spot lights, 165-166
unit vectors, normalized, 11
Unlock function, 102
UnlockRect function, 193
update operations (stencil buffer),
      764-765
user license agreements, 57
using
  Bezier patches, 407-408
  pixel shaders, 306-307
  textures, 192
utilities
  files, 56
  .X files, 141

V

V (viewer), 36
values
  floating-point
    color, 33
    devices, 74
    memset, 508
  meshes, bounding boxes, 398
  reference (stencil buffer), 762-763
vector shaders, 623-624
vectors. *See also* coordinates
  3D, 15-16
  4D, 16-17
  adding, 12
  arithmetic, 11-12
  billboards, 357
  coordinates, 10-11
  cross products, 15-16
  D3DX data types, 17-19
  D3DX functions, 17-19
  defined, 10-11
  direction, 11
  dot products, 13-14

vectors (continued)

cube maps

eye vectors, 483

reflection, 482-484

refraction, 485-486

halfway (H), 36-37

lighting. *See* lighting

magnitude, 11

multiplying, 12

normals. *See also* surfaces

lighting, 33

transforming, 450

normalized unit vectors, 11

overview, 19

planes (shadows), 501-503

quaternions, 16-17

scalars comparison, 10

VerifyModes function, 226-228

versions (pixel shaders), 291

vertex buffers. *See also* buffers

buffer relationships, 324

building, 106-112

circles, 172

curves, 172

destroying, 101, 106-107

filling, 106-107

flags, 100, 102

lighting, 170-171

locking, 101-102, 111

MemoryPool parameter, 100-101

optimizing, 109

overview, 112-113

performance, 98, 105

setting, 101-102

static, 100

vertex shaders

ALU, 262

assembling, 271-272

Bezier patches

applications, 396-407

code, 396-407

computing, 393-396

billboards

code, 359-366

creating, 355-359

bump mapping, 594-595

applications, 596-603

reflection, 613-615

code, 277-285

constants, setting, 274

coordinate systems

code, 375-383

lighting, 375

mapping, 372-375

shading, 375

creating, 273-274

declaring, 269-271

defined, 260-261

depth comparison, shadow maps, 549

depth testing, 357

destroying, 274

device, 268

extrusion, 521-523

implementing, 268

instructions, 264-267

lighting, 308-309

macros, 264-267, 269-271

matrix palettes (skinning), 416-419

meshes, 275

application, 326-334

cloning, 322-323

color, 323-325

data, 325

performance, 325-326

negation, 267-268

normals, scaling, 338-340

overview, 286-287

performance, 105, 277

per-pixel picking, 785-786

pipeline, 47-48

pixel shaders relationship, 307-309

point lighting (per-pixel), 579-580

reflection

code, 490-496

cube maps, 487-489

refraction

code, 490-496

cube maps, 487-489

registers, 262-263, 269-271

rendering vertices, 103-104

shadow volume, 526-528

application, 528-536

troubleshooting, 536-538

sine waves, 345-350

spot light (per-pixel), 572-574

stage states, 225

swizzling, 267-268

transformations, 275-277

write masks, 267-268

VertexApplication.h, 107

vertices

billboards, 354-355

bones. *See* skinning

color, 323-325

depth shader, 434-439

white, 179

coordinates

scaling, 208

setting, 206-207

data, remapping, 333

data structures, 97-98

defined, 96-97

edges (toon shaders), 470-471

FVFs, 97-99

lighting, 135

object space, 448-451

normals, scaling, 338-340

number, 172

overview, 112-113

performance, 98

pipeline, 45-46

processing, 74

rendering

2D, 664-666

performance, 143

primitives, 103-104

stream sources, 103-104

vertex shaders, 103-104

sine waves
  code, 345-350
  warping, 341-345
static buffers, 100
surfaces, 134-135
transparency
  x-ray shader, 439-442
  x-ray shader application, 442-445
vertex buffers. *See also* buffers
  buffer relationships, 324
  building, 106-112
  circles, 172
  curves, 172
  destroying, 101, 106-107
  filling, 106-107
  flags, 100, 102
  lighting, 170-171
  locking, 101-102, 111
  MemoryPool parameter, 100-101
  optimizing, 109
  overview, 112-113
  performance, 98, 105
  setting, 101-102
  static, 100
  vertex shaders. *See* vertex shaders
video. *See* DirectShow; streaming
  media
video cards, querying, 72
view frustums (projection
  transformations), 120-122

view transformations, 117
  building, 118-120
  cameras, 173
viewer (V), 36
viewports
  defined, 124-125
  mapping pixel data, 124-125
  transformations, 124-125
virtual camera view frustums,
  120-122
volumes
  shadow volume shader, 526-528
    application, 528-536
    troubleshooting, 536-538
  shadow volumes, 520-526

W

W buffering, 240
warping
  objects, 396
  vertices, 341-345
water, lighting, 485
Wave function, 349
waves, ocean effects, 351
weighting darkness (mipmaps), 471
whiteness, setting, 179
width, textures, 192
windows
  creating, 64
  defining, 59-60

devices, 75
handles, 64
painting, 66-67
Windows applications.
    See applications
WinMain function, 59-60, 62
wireframes. *See* Bezier patches
wobbling bubbles, 383
world matrices, inverse lighting, 451
world transformations, 117-120
wrapping textures, 220-221
write masks
  pixel shaders, 304
  vertex shaders, 267-268
writing functions, 17

X-Z

.X files, 56
  rendering, 141-143
  utilities, 141
Xbox, 5-6
x-ray shader
  application, 442-445
  vertex transparency, 439-442
XRayParams function, 443

Z bias (depth buffers), 241
ZeroMemory function, 89, 159, 163
zooming
  stencil buffers, 765-771
  transformations, 131

GAME DEVELOPMENT.
IT'S SERIOUS BUSINESS.

"Game programming is without a doubt the most intellectually challenging field of Computer Science in the world. However, we would be fooling ourselves if we said that we are 'serious' people! Writing (and reading) a game programming book should be an exciting adventure for both the author and the reader."

—André LaMothe,
Series Editor

Gamedev.net

The most comprehensive game development resource

The latest news in game development
The most active forums and chatrooms anywhere, with
insights and tips from experienced game developers
Links to thousands of additional game development resources
Thorough book and product reviews
Over 1000 game development articles!
Game design
Graphics
DirectX
OpenGL
AI
Art
Music
Physics
Source Code
Sound
Assembly
And More!

 Gamedev.net

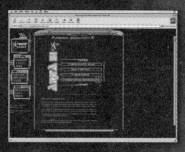